SECOND EDIT

A HIS
MODERN PSYCHOLOGY

C. JAMES GOODWIN
Wheeling Jesuit University

WILEY

JOHN WILEY & SONS, INC.

To Susan

Executive Editor   *Ryan Flahive*
Associate Editor   *Lili DeGrasse*
Editorial Assistant   *Deepa Chungi*
Media Editor   *Tom Kulesa*
Marketing Manager   *Kate Stewart*
Senior Production Editor   *Lari Bishop*
Senior Designer   *Kevin Murphy*
Illustration Editor   *Anna Melhorn*
Senior Photo Editor   *Lisa Gee*
Cover photograph   *Paul Hardy/Corbis Images*

This book was set in 10/12 Times by LCI Design, and was printed and bound by Malloy Lithographers. The cover was printed by Phoenix Color Corporation.

This book is printed on acid free paper. ∞

Library of Congress Cataloging-in-Publication Data

Goodwin, C. James.
    A history of modern psychology / C. James Goodwin.-- 2nd ed.
      p. cm.
    Includes bibliographical references.
    ISBN 0-471-41565-0
    1. Psychology—History—20th century. 2. Psychology—History—19th century. I. Title.

  BF105.G66 2004
  150'.9'04—dc22

                                                                2004041888

US ISBN 0-471-41565-0
WIE ISBN 0-471-65819-7

Printed in the United States of America

10   9   8   7   6   5   4   3   2   1

PREFACE

TO THE INSTRUCTOR

As you already know if you have taught the history and systems course, it can be a hard sell to students. They often come into the course with firm and long-standing negative preconceptions about studying history and prepared to agree that history is "just one d—d thing after another," as someone once said. And when they discover the last name of psychology's premier historian, E. G. Boring, they may nod their heads knowingly. This attitude is unfortunate, of course, because I can think of no more fascinating subject than the history of psychology. It is replete with extraordinary persons and events, and it yields insights into the basic questions still being asked in psychology today.

No one can be an informed psychologist without some knowledge of the discipline's history. Our task as instructors is to show students how valuable a knowledge of psychology's history can be, help them connect psychology's present with its rich past, and get them to understand how exciting the journey from past to present has been. I hope that my textbook will aid in this process.

The book is titled a history of *modern* psychology, reflecting the decision about where to begin the course that faces everyone who teaches it. Psychology has deep roots in Western philosophical thought; hence, a full understanding of important and recurring themes requires an understanding of this heritage. Texts, however, differ in the depth of coverage given to our philosophical ancestors, tending to fall into two groups. Some books invest considerable effort in exploring philosophical issues and provide in-depth coverage dating back to the ancient Greeks. This certainly is a legitimate strategy (indeed, a philosopher colleague of mine thinks that

nothing much of importance has happened since Plato and Aristotle), but not the one I have chosen to follow. Instead, my text belongs in the second grouping—that is, although not by any means ignoring philosophical roots, it devotes less space to them and more space to the recent history of psychology, especially that of the past 150 years. Like other "modern" histories, its treatment of philosophy will begin in the general vicinity of Descartes and the British empiricists.

The decision about a starting point is partly pragmatic—it has been my experience as a teacher of this course, which has to fit typically into a 15-week semester, that extensive treatment of philosophical thought between the time of the Greeks and Descartes makes it impossible to get very far into the twentieth century ("It's December and we've just started Watson!"). I always remind myself that the course is not just a history or a philosophy course, but part of the psychology curriculum, and that if I want students to make meaningful connections between my course and their other psychology classes, an important goal for me, it is necessary to get to the nineteenth and twentieth centuries as quickly as possible. The history course must teach students about the ideas and research of pioneer psychologists, especially those who worked within the past 100 years or so. Students have heard about some of these people in other courses (e.g., Hall in adolescent psychology, Watson in the learning course, Freud in personality, Binet in tests and measurements); the history course serves to build on that rudimentary knowledge and interconnect it.

A unique feature of this text is the *Original Source Excerpt.* I believe that students in the history and systems course should not just read accounts about psychology's pioneers; they should also be reading what the pioneers themselves wrote. The usual strategy for reaching this goal is to use a textbook and supplement it by putting copies of original source materials on reserve in the library or by using a supplementary book of readings. One problem with this approach is that even good students often find the readings difficult because authors in different historical eras have a variety of styles, use terms and phrasing no longer used, take certain contemporary but now forgotten theories and research for granted, and in general write for their peers rather than for today's students. Students often have a difficult time connecting readings with the narrative in their textbook and reading these original works critically; consequently, much valuable class time can be spent explaining what was meant by certain phrases, how an argument in a reading might be directed at some unnamed critic, and so on. I have tried to address the problem by including Original Source Excerpts in each chapter (except the opening and closing ones). These are reprintings of substantial portions of famous books or papers, interwoven with some of my own narrative. Hence, the student has the opportunity to read writings by such luminaries as William James, John Watson, and B. F. Skinner, while the interspersed narrative helps to explain what the material means and to fit it into the context of the rest of the chapter. In a sense, then, the book has a set of readings built into it.

The book includes several other pedagogical tools. Chapters begin with a Preview and a set of Chapter Objectives, which set the stage for what is to come, and end with a detailed Summary of the chapter's contents, a set of review questions, and a brief annotated list of articles and/or books in a For Further Reading section. Each chapter begins with a carefully selected quote that is also worked into the narrative at some point in the chapter. For each chapter I have also identified a year that corresponds to some especially important event in psychology's history, and have included a Key Date box that highlights other events occurring outside of psychology during that year. To further enable the student to make some links between psychology and the rest of the world, several timelines are included on front and back end papers of the book.

New to the Second Edition

The book has undergone considerable rewriting both for style and content, and 121 new references have been added. There have been several substantial changes and additions in the second edition, especially in the last third of the book. Specifically, I have taken the original Chapter 12, which dealt with early treatment of the mentally ill, Freud, and the early history of clinical psychology; and Chapter 13, which dealt with cognitive psychology, and created three chapters, mainly to elaborate on historical developments in psychology since the second World War. Chapter 12 has been shortened, with material on post-World War II clinical psychology moved to Chapter 13. Chapters 13 and 14 are organized with reference to the broad categories of science and practice that characterize modern psychology. Chapter 13 ("Psychology's Practitioners") concerns the professional practice of psychology and focuses on clinical and industrial psychology. Chapter 14 (Psychological Science in the Post-War Era) looks at developments in scientific psychology. The bulk of the material deals with the origins and evolution of modern cognitive psychology, but there is also extensive treatment of developments in neuropsychology, social psychology, personality psychology, and developmental psychology.

The second edition includes two new *Close-Up* boxes, one on Leta Hollingworth, a pioneer in gifted education who also did important research on alleged gender differences in ability; and one on the system for diagnosing mental illness created by Emil Kraepelin. I also made some changes in the *Original Source Excerpts*.

- The Broca excerpt on "Tan" has been expanded (Chapter 3).
- The Titchener excerpt has been replaced by Thorndike's puzzle box study (Chapter 7).
- The Watson and Rayner study has been replaced by Watson's so-called "behaviorist manifesto" (Chapter 10).
- The Skinner case history excerpt has been replaced with a selection from his *Science and Human Behavior* (Chapter 11).

- There is a new excerpt from *On Becoming a Person*, by Carl Rogers, in the new Chapter 13.

- There is a new excerpt from *Remembering,* by Sir Frederick Bartlett, in the new Chapter 14.

TO THE STUDENT

One of the primary themes of this book is that knowing the present requires knowing the past. You know something about psychology's present state by virtue of the other psychology courses you have taken, but you are probably not aware of the many interconnections that exist between the different areas of psychology you have encountered. One goal of a history course is to make those connections. For example, although I am sure that you know something about the nature-nurture issue, you probably are not knowledgeable about how our current understanding of it has been affected by the consequences of Darwinian theory, by the search for tests of mental ability, and by the behavior of rats in mazes. Presumably, this last sentence will have deeper meaning for you after you have finished the course than it does now.

You are about to meet some fascinating individuals who helped shape the psychology that you have been studying in other courses. While we tend to think of historical figures as being somehow above the rest of us, I have tried to show that these individuals were real human beings, often struggling with the kinds of problems that affect the rest of us. In the pages that follow, you will be meeting some people whose efforts led to some extraordinary accomplishments, but who also dealt with some of the same issues that are of concern to you. For example...

- Are you tired of school and ready to get out into the "real" world?
  Read about René Descartes (Chapter 2).

- Are you fed up with the way things are, wish you could change them, and willing to take on authority?
  Learn about John B. Watson (Chapter 10) or B. F. Skinner (Chapter 11).

- Are you faced with major decisions about your future and worried about taking a big risk?
  Refer to the discussion about E. B. Titchener (Chapter 7) or Wolfgang Köhler (Chapter 9).

- Are you fascinated by research and enjoy collecting and analyzing data?
  See Hermann Ebbinghaus (Chapter 4) or Ivan Pavlov (Chapter 10).

- Do you have a strong desire to help others?
  Read about Dorothea Dix (Chapter 12) or Carl Rogers (Chapter 13).

- Do you have a strong desire to achieve but face a stacked deck because of racism or sexism?
  See Francis Sumner (Chapter 6) or Mary Calkins (Chapter 6).

- Are you a slow starter, not doing well in school, and wondering if you have a future?
  Study the description of the life of Charles Darwin (Chapter 5) or Donald Hebb (Chapter 14).

- Are you concerned that health problems or a handicap will make it difficult for you to reach your goals?
  Read about Lewis Terman (Chapter 8) or Clark Hull (Chapter 11).

I hope that you will enjoy reading this book, that you will learn something about psychology's present by learning about its past, and that you will gain some insight into human behavior (including your own) in the process. At the end of the course, I hope that you will want to continue to learn more about psychology's fascinating history.

Tim Goodwin

ACKNOWLEDGMENTS

My graduate training was in the experimental psychology of memory and was typical in many ways: long hours in the lab, combined with joy whenever p was less than .05. What was a bit different for me, however, was the fact that my dissertation director, Darryl Bruce, had a great passion for psychology's history and it was infectious. While teaching me to be a good scientist, he was also convincing me of history's great truth—you cannot know the present without knowing the past. So to Darryl, who I try to see as often as I can for our almost-annual three-hour breakfasts at APA, I owe an enormous debt.

In Chapter 1, you will see a photo of John Popplestone and Marion White McPherson of the Archives of the History of American Psychology (AHAP) in Akron, Ohio. AHAP is about a 2-hour drive from my house, so I benefited from their hospitality and their eagerness to help aspiring historians on several occasions. John has now retired and Marion died in 2000. I think of them often. The new Director of AHAP, David Baker, has also been immensely helpful to me and has become an occasional golfing buddy. I would also like to thank Ludy Benjamin, Mike Sokal, Don Dewsbury, Laurel Furumoto, and Randall Wight for their support and encouragement as I struggled to become knowledgeable as a historian of psychology.

The editors and staff at John Wiley must be the best in the business; they made the entire production process a breeze (or, at least, much less onerous than I had any right to expect). Special thanks go to VP Anne Smith, who has been consistently supportive of the project; and associate editor Lili DeGrasse, whose enthusiasm, good cheer, and sharp mind have made this revision process considerably less burdensome than it otherwise would be.

Finally, thanks also goes to the stalwart reviewers for the text, who included:

Danny Benbassat, *Ohio Northern University*
L. Mark Carrier, *California State University Dominguez Hills*
John D. Hogan, *St. John's University*
Janet Kottke, *California State University San Bernardino*
Vicki Mack, *Clark Atlanta University*
Otto H. MacLin, *University of Northern Iowa*
John Northup, *Louisiana State University*
Brady J. Phelps, *South Dakota State University*
Harold R. Rodinsky, *DePaul University*
Bernard Whitley, *Ball State University*

CONTENTS

CHAPTER 1
INTRODUCING PSYCHOLOGY'S HISTORY   1

Psychology and Its History   **2**
Why Study History?   **3**
Why Study Psychology's History?   **6**
Key Issues in Psychology's History   **7**
  Old Versus New History   **7**
CLOSE-UP: *Edwin G. Boring (1886–1968)*   11
Historiography: Doing and Writing History   **15**
  Sources of Historical Data   **15**
  Problems with the Writing of History   **17**
  Approaching Historical Truth   **20**
Summary   **21**
Study Questions   **22**
For Further Reading   **22**

CHAPTER 2
THE PHILOSOPHICAL CONTEXT   24

A Long Past   **25**
Descartes and the Beginnings of Modern Philosophy and
    Science   **25**
  Descartes and the Rationalist Argument   **27**
  The Cartesian System: Rationalism, Nativism, and
    Mechanistic Interactionism   **28**
**ORIGINAL SOURCE EXCERPT: *Descartes on Mind-Body
    Interactionism*   29**
The British Empiricist Argument and the
    Associationists   **34**
  John Locke (1632–1704): The Origins of British
    Empiricism   **34**
  George Berkeley (1685–1753): Empiricism Applied to
    Vision   **38**
  British Associationism   **40**
CLOSE-UP: *Raising a Philosopher*   44
  John Stuart Mill (1806–1873): On the Verge of
    Psychological Science   **45**
Rationalist Responses to Empiricism   **49**
  Gottfried Wilhelm Leibniz (1646–1716)   **49**
  Immanuel Kant (1724–1804)   **50**

In Perspective   **50**
Summary   **51**
Study Questions   **52**
Questions from the Original Source Excerpt   **53**
For Further Reading   **53**

CHAPTER 3
THE NEUROPHYSIOLOGICAL CONTEXT   54

Heroic Science in the Age of Enlightenment   **55**
Sensory Physiology   **56**
  Reflex Action   **57**
  The Bell-Magendie Law   **57**
  The Specific Energies of Nerves   **59**
  Helmholtz: The Physiologist's Physiologist   **59**
Localization of Brain Function   **64**
  The Phrenology of Gall and Spurzheim   **64**
CLOSE-UP: *The Marketing of Phrenology*   67
  Flourens and the Method of Ablation   **68**
  The Clinical Method   **69**
**ORIGINAL SOURCE EXCERPT: *Broca Discovers the
    Speech Center*   70**
  Mapping the Brain: Electrical Stimulation   **73**
Early Twentieth-Century Studies of the Nervous System
    and Behavior   **75**
  Neuron Theory   **75**
  Sir Charles Sherrington: The Synapse   **76**
  Karl Lashley: Learning and the Cortex   **77**
Summary   **80**
Study Questions   **81**
Questions from the Original Source Excerpt   **82**
For Further Reading   **82**

CHAPTER 4
WUNDT AND GERMAN PSYCHOLOGY   83

An Education in Germany   **84**
On the Threshold of Experimental Psychology:
    Psychophysics   **85**
  Ernst Weber (1795–1878)   **85**

Gustav Fechner (1801–1889) **87**
Fechner's *Elements of Psychophysics* **89**
Wundt Establishes a New Psychology at Leipzig **90**
Wilhelm Wundt (1832–1920): Creating a New
Science **90**
Wundt's Conception of the New Psychology **92**
Inside Wundt's Laboratory **94**
CLOSE-UP: *An American in Leipzig* 97
Rewriting History: The New and Improved Wilhelm
Wundt **99**
The Wundtian Legacy **101**
The New Psychology Spreads **101**
Hermann Ebbinghaus (1850–1909): The Experimental
Study of Memory **101**
**ORIGINAL SOURCE EXCERPT: *Ebbinghaus on Memory
and Forgetting* 102**
G. E. Müller (1850–1934): The Experimentalist
Prototype **108**
Oswald Külpe (1862–1915): The Würzburg School **109**
Summary **111**
Study Questions **112**
Questions from the Original Source Excerpt **113**
For Further Reading **113**

CHAPTER 5
*DARWIN'S CENTURY:
EVOLUTIONARY THINKING* **114**

The Species Problem **115**
Charles Darwin (1809–1882) and the Theory of
Evolution **116**
The Shaping of a Naturalist **116**
The Voyage of the *Beagle* **117**
The Evolution of Darwin's Theory **120**
Darwin and Psychology's History **124**
The Origins of Comparative Psychology **125**
Darwin on the Evolution of Emotional Expressions **125**
**CLOSE-UP: *Douglas Spalding and the Experimental
Study of Instinct* 127**
George Romanes (1848–1894): The Anecdotal
Method **129**
Conwy Lloyd Morgan (1852–1936): The Principle of
Parsimony **130**
Comparative Psychology in America **132**
Studying Individual Differences **132**
Francis Galton (1822–1911): Jack of All Sciences **132**
**ORIGINAL SOURCE EXCERPT: *Galton on Measurement
and Association* 135**
Darwin's Century in Perspective **138**
Summary **139**

Study Questions **140**
Questions from the Original Source Excerpt **141**
For Further Reading **141**

CHAPTER 6
AMERICAN PIONEERS **142**

Psychology in Nineteenth-Century America **143**
Faculty Psychology **143**
The Modern University **145**
William James (1842–1910): America's First
Psychologist **148**
The Formative Years **149**
A Life at Harvard **150**
Creating American Psychology's Most Famous
Textbook **151**
**ORIGINAL SOURCE EXCERPT: *William James on
Emotion* 154**
James's Later Years **157**
Summing Up William James **159**
G. Stanley Hall (1844–1924): Professionalizing
Psychology **159**
Hall's Early Life and Education **160**
From Johns Hopkins to Clark **161**
Psychology at Clark **162**
CLOSE-UP: *Creating Maze Learning* 163
Mary Whiton Calkins (1863–1930): Challenging the
Male Monopoly **167**
Calkins's Life and Work **167**
Other Women Pioneers: Untold Lives **170**
In Perspective: The New Psychology at the
Millennium **172**
Summary **172**
Study Questions **174**
Questions from the Original Source Excerpt **174**
For Further Reading **174**

CHAPTER 7
STRUCTURALISM AND FUNCTIONALISM **176**

Titchener's Psychology: Structuralism **177**
From Oxford to Leipzig to Cornell **178**
Promoting Experimental Psychology at Cornell **179**
Titchener's Structuralist System **183**
CLOSE-UP: *The Introspective Attitude* 185
Evaluating Titchener's Contributions to
Psychology **187**
America's Psychology: Functionalism **188**
The Chicago Functionalists **189**
The Columbia Functionalists **194**

ORIGINAL SOURCE EXCERPT: *Thorndike on Puzzle Box Learning* **197**
Summary **206**
Study Questions **207**
Questions from the Original Source Excerpt **207**
For Further Reading **207**

CHAPTER 8
APPLYING THE NEW PSYCHOLOGY **209**

Pressures Toward Application **210**
The Mental Testing Movement **212**
    James McKeen Cattell (1860–1944): An American Galton **212**
    Alfred Binet (1857–1911): The Birth of Intelligence Testing **215**
    Henry H. Goddard (1866–1957): Binet's Test Comes to America **218**
    Lewis M. Terman (1877–1956): Institutionalizing IQ **223**
CLOSE-UP: *Leta Hollingworth: Advocating for Gifted Children and Debunking Myths About Women* **225**
    Robert M. Yerkes (1876–1956): The Army Testing Program **227**
    The Controversy Over Intelligence **233**
Applying Psychology to Business **234**
    Hugo Münsterberg (1863–1916): The Diversity of Applied Psychology **235**
ORIGINAL SOURCE EXCERPT: *Hugo Münsterberg and Employee Selection* **236**
    Other Leading Industrial Psychologists **242**
Summary **245**
Study Questions **246**
Questions from the Original Source Excerpt **246**
For Further Reading **247**

CHAPTER 9
GESTALT PSYCHOLOGY **248**

The Origins and Development of Gestalt Psychology **249**
    Max Wertheimer (1880–1943): Founding Gestalt Psychology **250**
    Koffka (1886–1941) and Köhler (1887–1967): The Co-Founders **252**
CLOSE-UP: *A Case of Espionage?* **253**
Gestalt Psychology and Perception **255**
    Principles of Perceptual Organization **255**
    Behavioral Versus Geographical Environments **257**
    Psychophysical Isomorphism **258**

The Gestalt Approach to Cognition and Learning **258**
ORIGINAL SOURCE EXCERPT: *Köhler on Insight in Apes* **258**
    Wertheimer on Productive Thinking **263**
    Other Gestalt Research on Cognition **264**
Kurt Lewin (1890–1947): Expanding the Gestalt Vision **265**
    Early Life and Career **266**
    Field Theory **267**
    The Zeigarnik Effect **268**
    Lewin as Developmental Psychologist **269**
    Lewin as Social Psychologist **271**
    Evaluating Lewin **273**
In Perspective: Gestalt Psychology in America **274**
Summary **275**
Study Questions **276**
Questions from the Original Source Excerpt **277**
For Further Reading **277**

CHAPTER 10
THE ORIGINS OF BEHAVIORISM **278**

Behaviorism's Antecedents **279**
Pavlov's Life and Work **280**
    The Development of a Physiologist **281**
    Working in Pavlov's Laboratory **282**
    Pavlov's Classical Conditioning Research **284**
    Conditioning and Extinction **284**
    Pavlov and the Soviets **287**
    Pavlov and the Americans **288**
CLOSE-UP: *Misportraying Pavlov's Apparatus* **288**
John B. Watson and the Founding of Behaviorism **290**
    The Young Functionalist at Chicago **290**
    Opportunity Knocks at Johns Hopkins **293**
ORIGINAL SOURCE EXCERPT: *Watson's Behaviorist Manifesto* **294**
    A New Life in Advertising **302**
    Popularizing Behaviorism **303**
    Evaluating Watsonian Behaviorism **304**
Summary **305**
Study Questions **306**
Questions from the Original Source Excerpt **306**
For Further Reading **307**

CHAPTER 11
THE EVOLUTION OF BEHAVIORISM **308**

Post-Watsonian Behaviorism **309**
    Logical Positivism and Operationism **310**
    Neobehaviorism **312**

Edward C. Tolman (1886–1959): A Purposive
Behaviorism **313**
Tolman's System **314**
Tolman's Research Program **317**
Evaluating Tolman **320**
Clark Hull (1884–1952): A Hypothetico-Deductive
System **321**
Hull's System **324**
Evaluating Hull **326**
B. F. Skinner (1904–1990): A Radical Behaviorism **328**
ORIGINAL SOURCE EXCERPT: *Skinner and Operant
Conditioning: An Experimental Analysis of
Behavior* **329**
Skinner and the Problem of Explanation **334**
A Technology of Behavior **335**
CLOSE-UP: *A Skinnerian Utopia* **337**
Evaluating Skinner **338**
Behaviorism in Perspective **339**
Summary **340**
Study Questions **341**
Questions from the Original Source Excerpt **342**
For Further Reading **342**

CHAPTER 12
MENTAL ILLNESS AND ITS TREATMENT **343**

Early Treatment of the Mentally Ill **344**
"Enlightened" Reform: Pinel, Tuke, and Rush **344**
Reforming Asylums: Dix and Beers **346**
CLOSE-UP: *Diagnosing Mental Illness* **348**
Mesmerism and Hypnosis **350**
Mesmerism and Animal Magnetism **350**
From Mesmerism to Hypnosis **351**
The Hypnotism Controversies **352**
Sigmund Freud (1856–1939): Founding
Psychoanalysis **354**
Early Life and Education **355**
Creating Psychoanalysis **358**
ORIGINAL SOURCE EXCERPT: *Freud's Lectures on
Psychoanalysis at Clark University* **360**
The Evolution of Psychoanalytic Theory **365**
Freud's Followers: Loyalty and Dissent **367**
Psychoanalysis in America **368**
Freud in Perspective **369**
Clinical Psychology in America **370**
Lightner Witmer (1867–1956): Creating Psychology's
First Clinic **371**
Clinical Psychology Prior to World War II **373**
Summary **374**
Study Questions **376**

Questions from the Original Source Excerpt **377**
For Further Reading **377**

CHAPTER 13
PSYCHOLOGY'S PRACTITIONERS **378**

Researchers and Practitioners **379**
The Emergence of Modern Clinical Psychology **380**
The Boulder Model **381**
The Eysenck Study: Problems for Traditional
Psychotherapy **382**
CLOSE-UP: *The Medical Strategy—Lobotomies,
Transorbital and Otherwise* **382**
Behavior Therapy **384**
The Humanistic Approach to Psychotherapy **385**
ORIGINAL SOURCE EXCERPT: *Rogers on Creating a
Therapeutic Environment* **388**
The Vail Conference and the Psy.D. Degree **392**
Psychology and the World of Business and Industry **394**
The Hawthorne Studies **395**
The Practice of Psychology in Perspective **397**
Summary **398**
Study Questions **399**
Questions from the Original Source Excerpt **400**
For Further Reading **400**

CHAPTER 14
*PSYCHOLOGICAL SCIENCE
IN THE POST-WAR ERA* **401**

Cognitive Psychology Arrives (Again) **402**
The Roots of Modern Cognitive Psychology **402**
Frederick C. Bartlett (1886–1969): Constructing
Memory **403**
ORIGINAL SOURCE EXCERPT: *Bartlett on Memory* **403**
A Convergence of Influences **409**
CLOSE-UP: *What Revolution?* **412**
Magical Numbers, Selective Filters, and TOTE
Units **414**
Neisser and the "Naming" of Cognitive
Psychology **416**
The Evolution of Cognitive Psychology **417**
Evaluating Cognitive Psychology **420**
Other Research Areas **421**
The Brain and Behavior **421**
Social Psychology **423**
Personality Psychology **426**
Developmental Psychology **429**
Research Psychology in Perspective **432**
Summary **432**

Study Questions **433**
Questions from the Original Source Excerpt **434**
For Further Reading **434**

CHAPTER 15
LINKING PSYCHOLOGY'S PAST AND PRESENT **435**

The Growth and Diversity of Psychology **436**
    Women in Psychology's History **436**
    Minorities in Psychology's History **439**
Trends in Contemporary Psychology **442**
The Future: Psychology or Psychologies? **443**
Summary **444**
Study Questions **445**
For Further Reading **445**

REFERENCES **447**

GLOSSARY **467**

PHOTO, TEXT, AND ILLUSTRATION CREDITS **479**

NAME INDEX **483**

SUBJECT INDEX **489**

SUMMARIES OF IMPORTANT FEATURES

Original Source Excerpts Summary

CHAPTER 2   *Descartes on Mind-Body Interactionism*

CHAPTER 3   *Broca Discovers the Speech Center*

CHAPTER 4   *Ebbinghaus on Memory and Forgetting*

CHAPTER 5   *Galton on Measurement and Association*

CHAPTER 6   *William James on Emotion*

CHAPTER 7   *Thorndike on Puzzle Box Learning*

CHAPTER 8   *Hugo Münsterberg and Employee Selection*

CHAPTER 9   *Köhler on Insight in Apes*

CHAPTER 10   *Watson's Behaviorist Manifesto*

CHAPTER 11   *Skinner and Operant Conditioning: An Experimental Analysis of Behavior*

CHAPTER 12   *Freud's Lectures on Psychoanalysis at Clark University*

CHAPTER 13   *Rogers on Creating a Therapeutic Environment*

CHAPTER 14   *Bartlett on Memory*

Key Date Boxes—Date Summary

CHAPTER 1   *1892 (APA founded)*

CHAPTER 2   *1843 (Mill's Logic)*

CHAPTER 3   *1861 (Broca's "Tan")*

CHAPTER 4   *1879 (Wundt's lab)*

CHAPTER 5   *1859 (Darwin's Origin)*

CHAPTER 6   *1890 (James's Principles)*

CHAPTER 7   *1906 (Angell's APA address)*

CHAPTER 8   *1917 (Army testing program)*

CHAPTER 9   *1929 (International Yale conference)*

CHAPTER 10   *1913 (Watson's manifesto)*

CHAPTER 11   *1953 (Skinner's Science and Human Behavior)*

CHAPTER 12   *1900 (Freud's dream book)*

CHAPTER 13   *1949 (Boulder conference)*

CHAPTER 14   *1932 (Barlett's memory book)*

CHAPTER *1*

INTRODUCING PSYCHOLOGY'S HISTORY

The seats on the train of progress all face backwards: you can see the past but only guess about the future. Yet a knowledge of history, although it can never be complete and fails miserably to foretell the future, has a huge capacity for adding significance to the understanding of the present.

—E. G. Boring, 1963

PREVIEW AND CHAPTER OBJECTIVES

This chapter opens by describing the evolution of psychology's interest in its past and the reasons why it is important to know and appreciate history. A contrast will be drawn between traditional histories of psychology, which emphasize the contributions of distinguished psychologists, the outcomes of famous experiments, and the debates among adherents of different "schools" of psychology, and a newer approach, which tries to situate events and people in the broader historical context. This chapter also considers the methods used by historians to conduct research in history and the problems they face when constructing a historical narrative from the accumulated data. After you finish this chapter, you should be able to:

■ Enumerate the events during the 1960s that led to a renewed interest in psychology's history

■ Explain the general reasons why it is important to understand history

■ Explain the specific reasons why it is important for students of psychology to understand psychology's history

■ Distinguish between "old" and "new" history, as Furumoto used the terms

■ Distinguish between a presentist and historicist view of history and articulate the dangers of presentist thinking

■ Distinguish between internal and external histories of psychology and the benefits of examining each

■ Explain the appeal of and the problems with a personalistic approach to history

■ Describe a naturalistic approach to history, the kind of evidence used to support it (e.g., multiples), and its limitations

■ Define historiography and describe the selection and interpretation problems faced by historians

■ Distinguish between primary and secondary sources of historical information and describe the kinds of primary source information typically found by historians in archives

▓ Explain how the process of doing history can produce some degree of confidence that truth has been attained

PSYCHOLOGY AND ITS HISTORY

One hundred is a nice round number and a one-hundredth anniversary is ample cause for celebration. In recent years, psychologists with a sense of history have celebrated often. The festivities began back in 1979, with the centennial of the founding of Wilhelm Wundt's laboratory at Leipzig, Germany. In 1992, the American Psychological Association (APA) created a yearlong series of events to commemorate the centennial of its founding in G. Stanley Hall's study at Clark University on July 8, 1892. During the centennial year, historical articles appeared in all of the APA's journals and a special issue of *American Psychologist* focused on history; several books dealing with APA's history were commissioned (e.g., Evans, Sexton, & Cadwallader, 1992); regional conventions had historical themes; and the annual convention, in Washington, D.C., that year, featured events ranging from the usual symposia and invited addresses on history to a fancy dress ball at Union Station featuring period (i.e., 1892) costumes and a huge APA birthday cake.

Interest in psychology's history has not been limited to centennial celebrations, of course. Histories of psychology were written soon after psychology itself appeared on the academic scene (e.g., Baldwin, 1913), and at least two of psychology's most famous books, E. G. Boring's *A History of Experimental Psychology* (1929; 1950) and Edna Heidbreder's *Seven Psychologies* (1933), are histories. It wasn't until the 1960s, however, that significant interest in the history of psychology as a specialized area of research began. During that decade, a number of individuals with training as psychologists and a keen interest in history banded together and did the sorts of things that mark the creation of a new specialized discipline—they formed organizations, they created a journal, and they established bases for the production of research.

Many people were involved, but the major impetus came from a clinical psychologist with a passion for history, Robert I. Watson (1909–1980). He began with a call to arms, an *American Psychologist* article entitled "The History of Psychology: A Neglected Area" (Watson, 1960). He then mobilized a group of like-minded psychologists within APA into a History of Psychology Group, the eventual outcome being the creation of a new APA division (#26) in 1965 (Hilgard, 1982). Not surprisingly, Watson was first president of the division. Also in 1965, (a) John Popplestone and Marion

---

KEY DATE *1892*

This year marked the founding of the American Psychological Association.

These events also occurred:

• The first automatic telephone switchboard was introduced

• Diesel patented his internal combustion engine

• "Gentleman Jim" Corbett defeated John L. Sullivan to win the heavyweight boxing title

• Tchaikovsky completed his *Nutcracker* ballet

• Toulouse-Lautrec painted *At the Moulin Rouge*

• Grover Cleveland was elected President of the United States

• These people were born:

　　Francisco Franco, Spanish dictator

　　Pearl S. Buck, American Nobel Prize-winning novelist

　　J. R. R. Tolkien, British philologist and author

• These people died:

　　Walt Whitman, American poet

　　Alfred Lord Tennyson, British poet

White McPherson (two more clinicians in love with history) established the archives of the History of American Psychology at the University of Akron, with Watson named to chair the Archive's Board of Advisors, and (b) the first issue of the *Journal of the History of the Behavioral Sciences* was published, edited by Watson. A few years later, as part of a reorganization of their graduate programs, the University of New Hampshire created the first doctoral program in the history of psychology. Guess who was named its first director? Finally, also under the leadership of Watson, Joseph Brozek, and Barbara Ross, the National Science Foundation sponsored a six-week summer institute on the UNH campus in 1968, which spawned Watson's final creation, the Cheiron Society, an "International Society for the History of the Behavioral and Social Sciences" (Brozek, Watson, & Ross, 1970). Within a decade, then, Watson was the prime mover in developing the history of psychology as a research specialty.

Over the past 35 years, interest in psychology's history has grown steadily. For example, membership in APA's division 26 in 2003 stood at just under 800, compared with the 234 who joined as charter members in 1965. The story is the same for Cheiron. Psychologists also recognize the importance of the history course to the psychology curriculum. At the most recent conference on the undergraduate curriculum, held at St. Mary's College in Maryland in 1991, one of the group's recommendations was for the curriculum to include a senior capstone course that integrated student experiences in other courses; the history and systems course was mentioned as a prime example of such a capstone (Lloyd & Brewer, 1992). In a recent survey of the "present status" of the history of psychology course, Fuchs & Viney (2002) worried that course content and textbooks did not always reflect recent scholarship in psychology's history, but found that virtually all psychology departments teach the course and that more than half require psychology majors to take it. On balance, they pronounced the history of psychology course to be "alive and well" (p. 12).

Despite the consensus among psychologists that studying the discipline's history is important, students majoring in psychology are often surprised to discover that a course in the history of psychology is offered in and perhaps required by their department. They check with their chemistry-major friends and find nothing comparable in that department. They examine the college catalog and discover that the closest course is one in the History of Science, but the history department teaches it, not one of the science departments. What's going on? Why is there a history of psychology course taught by a psychologist, but not a history of chemistry course taught by a chemist?

The rationale for a history of psychology course is important and it will be considered shortly. First, however, let us examine the more general question of why it is important to study the history of anything. Is it true that "history is more or less bunk," as Henry Ford put it, or is it more likely, in the words of Abraham Lincoln, that "we cannot escape history" (both quotes from Simonton, 1994, p. 3) and that to "neglect history does not mean to escape from its influence," as Robert Watson (1960, p. 255) declared in his call for psychologists to become more involved in the history of their discipline.

WHY STUDY HISTORY?

Every history course you have ever taken has preached to you that knowing history helps us to avoid the mistakes of the past and provides us with a guide to the future. There is a germ of truth to those old and well-worn platitudes, but both of these standard reasons are a bit simplistic. Concerning the "mistake" argument, rather than learning from the past, much of history appears to provide evidence that humans deliberately ignore the past. This possibility led the philosopher/historian G. W. F. Hegel to worry that the only true lesson of history is that people don't learn anything from history (Gilderhus, 2000). This overstates the case, of course. It is also true that when trying to convince others of some course of action, part of the argument usually involves references to the past. And if we seem to ignore the past more than we attend to it, it is also true that knowing the past only provides a very rough guide, for history never repeats itself—all events are tied into the historical context in which they occur, and no two are alike. History is also a less than reliable guide to the future, a fact that historians recognize, although the acknowledgement seldom prevents them from venturing forecasts. In his celebrated *What is history?*, for instance, the historian E. H. Carr wrote that "[g]ood historians, I suspect, whether they think about it or not, have the future in their bones. Besides the question why? The historian also asks the question: Whither?" (1961, pp. 142–143). This may be so, but it is worth noting that every paper I have ever read or listened to, for which the purpose was to predict the future, has begun with the same disclaimer. The writer or speaker always starts by going to great lengths to insure the audience that predictions about the future are notoriously inaccurate. As psychology's eminent historian, E. G. Boring, once wrote, "The past is not a crystal ball. It has more whence than whither to it. The seats on the train of progress all face backwards: you can see the past but only guess about the future" (1961, p. 5).

If knowing history is no guarantee that mistakes won't be repeated and if history is an imperfect (at best) means of forecasting the future, then what is left? *The present.* In the sentence immediately following the one I just quoted from Boring, he wrote: "Yet a knowledge of history, although it can never be complete and fails miserably to foretell the future, has a huge capacity for adding significance to the understanding of the present" (1961, p. 5). I believe the single most important reason to study history is that the present time we are living in cannot be understood without knowing something about the past—how the present came to be. Historian David McCullough (1992) expressed this idea eloquently in a commencement address when he drew an analogy between knowing history and knowing someone we love:

> Imagine a man who professes over and over his unending love for a woman but who knows nothing of where she was born or who her parents were or where she went to school or what her life had been like until *he* came along—and furthermore, doesn't care to learn. What would you think of such a person? Yet we appear to

have an unending supply of patriots who know nothing of the history of this country, nor are they interested. (p. 222, italics in the original)

Think of any current event and you will recognize that it is impossible to really understand that event without knowing some of the history leading to it. For example, consider some recent history within psychology. I am sure that you have heard about APA, the American Psychological Association. You might also know about or at least have heard of APS—the American Psychological Society. You might even know that the APS is a fairly recent creature—it was born in 1988. Perhaps you also recognize that the APS seems more focused on scientific research than the APA, although maybe you are not quite so sure about that, and you might be wondering why there are two organizations for psychologists. Knowing some history would help you understand this. Specifically, your understanding of why the APS exists and what its purpose is would be vastly enhanced if you knew of the long-standing tensions between research psychologists and psychologists whose prime interest is in the professional practice of psychology (e.g., psychotherapy). The problem traces to the very beginnings of the APA in the late nineteenth century and contributed to the formation of a separate group of "Experimentalists" in 1904 (the story of this remarkable group is elaborated in Chapter 7). Also, when the APA was reorganized after World War II, the divisional structure that exists today was designed in part to reconcile the conflicting goals of scientists and practitioners. The good will that accompanied the end of the war led those with different interests in psychology to unite, but the unity didn't last. Without knowing something of this history, you could never have a clear understanding of the APS, why it exists today, or why there is lingering tension between APS leaders and the APA governing structure.

Another aspect of the importance of the past for understanding the present is that knowing history helps us put present events in a better perspective. In the same commencement address quoted from earlier, David McCullough related the story of an encounter in Washington with a well-educated friend who had just visited the Vietnam Memorial and, like everyone who visits, was visibly moved by it. She asked if McCullough had visited the site and he said that he had; his first visit had been late on a day spent at the nearby Civil War battlefield of Antietam. McCullough was astounded to learn that his friend could not recall ever hearing of this battle, which included a day during which more American lives were lost than on any other day in history. McCullough pointed out that the Vietnam Memorial holds the names of about 57,000 Americans killed during 11 years, but at Antietam on September 17, 1862, there were 23,000 casualties—on one day. Knowing about Antietam in no way lessens the tragedy of the Vietnam War, and certainly every American should visit the wall, but an important perspective is gained by knowing about the battlefield just up the road. Knowledge of this kind adds an appreciation of the sacrifices of those from other times and yields an understanding of the idea that war and senseless death are not uniquely associated with just one period of recent history.

There is another way in which knowing history lends perspective to the present day. We sometimes believe that our current times are, as Dickens wrote, "the worst of times." We complain about the seemingly insurmountable problems that accompany life at the beginning of the twenty-first century. We long for the "good old days," a simpler time when nobody locked their doors and a good house could be ordered from a Sears kit (this is true). We think that there really used to be places like Disney World's Main Street, USA. But a knowledge of history is a good corrective here. Noted historian and former Librarian of Congress Daniel Boorstin, in an essay entitled "The Prison of the Present" (1971), describes this fallacy:

> We sputter against the Polluted Environment— as if it had come with the age of the automobile. We compare our air not with the odor of horse dung and the plague of flies and the smells of garbage and human excrement which filled the cities of the past, but with the honeysuckle perfumes of some nonexistent City Beautiful. We forget that even if the water in many cities today is not spring-pure, ... still for

> most of history the water of the cities (and of the countryside) was undrinkable. We reproach ourselves for the ills of disease and malnutrition, and forget that until recently, enteritis and measles and whooping cough, diphtheria and typhoid, were killing diseases of childhood, ... [and] polio was a summer monster. (pp. 47–48)

Knowing history won't give us easy answers to current problems, but it certainly can immunize us against the belief that these problems are many times worse than they used to be. In fact, knowing the past can provide a comforting connection with it, and being aware of how others have wrestled with similar problems can provide us with some present-day guidance. There is at least the potential for learning from the past.

Besides making it possible for us to understand the present better, studying history provides other benefits. For example, it forces an attitude adjustment: it keeps us humble. Sometimes an ignorance of the past can lead us to believe that the present is the culmination of centuries of progress and that modern-day accomplishments and thinking are more sophisticated and far surpass those of a crude and uninformed past. A knowledge of history, however, forces an understanding that each age has its own marvelous accomplishments and its own creative geniuses. Modern-day neuroscientists seem to make fascinating discoveries every day, but the importance of their discoveries and the quality of their scientific thinking does not outdo the elegance of Pierre Flourens's nineteenth-century investigations of the brain, which effectively disproved phrenology (see Chapter 3).

Finally, studying history ultimately means searching for answers to one of life's most fundamental yet perplexing questions: *What does it mean to be human?* That is, to study the history of World War II is to delve into the basic nature of prejudice, aggression, and violence. To study the American Revolution is to examine the human desire for freedom and self-determination. To study the history of Renaissance art is to study the human passion for aesthetic pleasure. And to the extent that history involves people behaving in various situations, studying history means studying and trying to understand human behavior. For this reason alone, psychologists should be inherently attracted to the subject.

WHY STUDY PSYCHOLOGY'S HISTORY?

The preceding rationale for studying history is by itself a sufficient justification for studying the history of psychology, but there are additional reasons why psychologists should be interested in their ancestry. First, compared with other sciences, psychology is still in its infancy, not much more than 100 years old. Much of the content of the other psychology courses you have taken traces back through at least half of those years, and many of the so-called classic studies that you learned about (e.g., Pavlov's conditioning studies) formed a major part of the first half of those years. Hence, modern psychology is closely tied to its past; being a literate psychologist necessarily requires knowing some history.

A second and related reason for an interest in psychology's history among psychologists is that the field is still grappling with many of the same topics that occupied it a century ago. Thus, an important issue today is the heritability of traits ranging from intelligence to shyness to schizophrenia. This nature-nurture issue, first popularized more than 130 years ago by Sir Francis Galton (see Chapter 5) and pondered by humans for centuries, reverberates through the history of psychology. Seeing the parallels between the arguments made now about the relative influence of heredity and environment, and comparing them with those made in earlier times, allows the psychologist a more informed understanding of the issue. Understanding something about the origins and early development of the IQ concept gives the modern psychologist a greater depth of understanding of the problems surrounding it.

Earlier, a question was raised about the presence of a history of psychology course and the absence of a history of chemistry course. While an understanding of current research and related issues is essential in psychology, the situation is somewhat different in chemistry. Although the history of alchemy makes for a fascinating story and can teach us a great deal about how science works and evolves, it doesn't inform today's students about the chemical properties of lead or of gold. Chemists, who tend to think (naively, as it happens) of their science as steadily progressing from the errors of the past to the truth of the present, aren't normally interested in cluttering their students' minds with "old" ideas. There is an element of truth to this model of science as advancing through history (nobody tries to reach the alchemist's goal of turning lead into gold anymore), but it is nonetheless unfortunate that many scientists don't see the value of studying the history of their discipline. At the very least, it would round out their education and teach them something about how scientific thinking has evolved. Indeed, there ought to be a history of chemistry course for chemistry students to take.

A third reason for the existence of the history of psychology course is that it can provide some unity for what has become a diverse and highly specialized field. Despite its youth, psychology in the early twenty-first century is notable for its lack of unity. Indeed, some observers (e.g., Koch, 1992) believe that a single field of psychology no longer exists, that a neuroscientist investigating the functioning of endorphins has virtually nothing in common with the industrial psychologist studying the effectiveness of various management styles. Yet all psychologists do have something in common—their history. For the student who has taken a seemingly disconnected variety of courses ranging from developmental to abnormal to social psychology, the history course can serve as a synthesizing experience. By the time you reach the final chapter of this text, where the issue of psychology's increased specialization will again be addressed, you will have learned enough to begin to understand the interconnectedness among the different areas of psychology.

Fourth, an understanding of psychology's history makes one a more critical thinker. Aware of the history of various treatments for psychological disorders, the discerning psychologist is better able to evaluate claims for a "revolutionary breakthrough" in psychotherapy. A close examination of this allegedly unique therapy might reveal similarities to earlier approaches. The historically literate psychologist will also be aware that on many other occasions, initial excitement over a flashy new therapy is tempered by a later failure to find any evidence that it works. Furthermore, knowing about the developmental course of various historical pseudoscientific approaches to psychotherapy, and understanding their common features, enables the psychologist to spot the presence of a new one.

Finally, the history of psychology course may be a history course but it is also a psychology course. Thus, one of its goals is to continue educating us about human behavior. Studying historical individuals as they helped develop the science of psychology can only increase our understanding of what makes people behave the way they do. For instance, our understanding of scientific creativity can be enhanced by studying the lives and works of historically creative individuals (Hermann Ebbinghaus is a good example; his work is featured in Chapter 4). Some insight into the psychology of controversy and the rigid, dogmatic adherence to one's beliefs can be gained by studying the behavior of scientists engaged in bitter debate with their peers (e.g., the Baldwin-Titchener controversy, described in Chapter 7). In general, if all human behavior reflects a complex interplay between individuals and the environments they inhabit, then studying the lives of historical characters being shaped by and in turn shaping their environments can only increase our understanding of the forces that affect human behavior.

KEY ISSUES IN PSYCHOLOGY'S HISTORY

A common misconception of history is that historians simply "find out what happened" and then write it down in chronological order. As you will learn in the next two sections of this chapter, the process is infinitely more complicated. When they are engaged in their craft, historians have to confront and take a stand on several important issues.

Old Versus New History

In 1980, the APA created the G. Stanley Hall Lecture Series. Prominent psychologists are invited to deliver these talks, which are designed to aid undergraduate instruction by informing teachers of the latest developments in the various subfields of psychology. In 1988, Laurel Furumoto, a psychologist/historian from Wellesley College, delivered the first of these lectures devoted to the teaching of psychology's history. The focus of her talk was on a distinction between what she referred to as "old" and "new" history.

The old history of psychology, according to Furumoto (1989), refers to an approach emphasizing the accomplishments of "great" philosophers and psychologists and concentrates on celebrating "classic studies" and "breakthrough discoveries." Within psychology, the preservation and retelling of these "great events" helped psychology secure an identity as a scientific discipline. The milestones, whether accurately described or not, are passed down from history text to history text as their authors rely heavily on secondary sources (e.g., earlier history texts). Furthermore, previous insights or achievements are valued only if they somehow "anticipated" some modern idea or research outcome. Old research that is of no current relevance is considered erroneous or quaint and is either discarded or held up as an example of "how far we've come." Thus, from the standpoint of old history, the purpose of the history of psychology is to emphasize and even to glorify present-day psychology, and to show how it emerged triumphant from the murky depths of its past.

According to Furumoto, old history tends to be presentist, internal, and personalistic. New history, on the other hand, is more historicist, external, and naturalistic. Let's examine these concepts in more detail.

Presentism Versus Historicism

Earlier, I argued that a major reason for studying history is to better understand what is happening in the present. This is indeed a valid argument. On the other hand, to interpret the past only in terms of present concepts and values is to be guilty of what George Stocking (1965) called **presentism**. In an editorial published in the opening volume of the *Journal of the History of the Behavioral Sciences*, Stocking contrasted presentism with an approach called **historicism**. As Stocking described it, the presentist interprets historical events only with reference to modern knowledge and values, whereas the historicist tries to understand the same event in terms of the knowledge and values in existence at the time of the event. Because the historicist tries to place historical events within the overall context of their times, this approach is sometimes called a contextual approach to history.

In absolute terms, presentist thinking is impossible to avoid. Our current thinking has been shaped by our experiences, and we cannot simply ignore those experiences. To illustrate, think of situations where you had to make the same basic decision at two different times. For example, suppose you just bought a computer to replace the one you acquired five years ago. In the present moment, you might say to yourself, "How could I have been so shortsighted back then, buying a computer with a hard drive that only had 100MB?" To say that is to forget the original context in which that first computer was bought, a time when a 100MB drive seemed as appropriately sized as a 10GB drive might seem now. Thus, it is easy to criticize the past when relying on knowledge of the present. It is also easy to think that because you have gone from a 100MB to a 10GB hard drive, you have somehow *progressed* as a decision maker. The larger hard drive might indeed make your life easier now (i.e., there has been some progress), but it doesn't mean that you are any better as a decision maker now than you were five years ago. The old decision might seem stupid now, but that's only because of what we now know; back then, it was precisely as reasonable a choice as the one made in the present. To understand the old decision requires us to avoid seeing it in the light of what we know now.

To demonstrate the point with reference to a more complex historical event than computer buying, consider some aspects of the history of intelligence testing. As you will learn in Chapter 8, in the years just prior to World War I, an American intelligence tester named Henry Goddard was invited to Ellis Island in New York to help in the screening of immigrants. Immigrants deemed "unfit" for some reason were returned to their country of origin. Goddard firmly believed that intelligence was an inherited trait and that it could be measured with a brand new technology—something created in France and just beginning to be called an IQ test. Goddard used a version of an IQ test that he had translated from the French version to identify "mentally defective" immigrants. He even convinced authorities that he could pick out defective immigrants simply by looking at them. His work contributed to the questionable deportation of untold numbers of people and his conclusion that large percentages of immigrants were "morons" (a term he invented to describe a sub-category of "feeblemindedness") contributed to the atmosphere that led Congress to pass restrictive immigration quotas in 1924. From today's standpoint, on the basis of an additional 75 years or so of research, we know about the problems with IQ testing and the need for caution when using and interpreting IQ tests. Hence, we find it difficult to believe that someone as intelligent as Goddard could have behaved with such obvious bias. But to truly understand Goddard's behavior, it is necessary to study it from the vantage point of the historical context in which it occurred instead of that of the present time. This means knowing about such things as (a) the powerful influence of Darwinian thinking on psychological testers of that day, which led easily to a belief that intelligence was a trait that had been naturally selected and enabled a physically weak species (humans) to adapt to their environment during the "struggle for existence" and was therefore inherited; (b) the nation's fears of being overrun with immigrants (large-scale immigration was a new phenomenon at that time); and (c) the assumption, not yet brought into question by such things as atomic bombs and aerosol cans, that any new technology (e.g., IQ tests) with the "scientific" seal of approval had to be good. The list could be continued but the point is clear. Goddard's work cannot be evaluated fairly by modern standards; it can only be understood in the context of its times. On the other hand, his work does have relevance for us in the present. Knowing about it can (a) help us better understand modern concerns about immigration; (b) inform us of the subtle influence of racism and other forms of bigotry, even in intelligent people; and (c) make us properly cautious about the alleged wonders of new technologies that arrive in our own day.

The Goddard episode illustrates how difficult it is for us to avoid a presentist orientation. After all, we are the products of our own personal histories, and it is perhaps impossible to ask us to think like a person who never experienced MTV, computers, World War II, or the events of 9/11/2001. Nonetheless, for the historian and the reader of history it is important to at least be aware of the dangers of a strictly presentist view of history, and to constantly seek to understand historical episodes on their own terms. One must recognize, as pointed out by historian Bernard Bailyn (Lathem, 1994), that "the past is not only distant, but different" (p. 53). He pointed out that the major obstacle in overcoming presentism (or "anachronism," as Bailyn referred to it) is the problem of "overcoming the knowledge of the outcome. This is one of the great impediments to a truly contextualized history" (p. 53). As to how one might go beyond our knowledge of outcomes and overcome presentist thinking, Bailyn had this suggestion:

> Somehow one has to recapture, and build into the story, contemporaries' ignorance of the future. ... One stresses the contingencies—looks for the accidents of the time and tries to avoid assigning the heroism or villainy that was unclear at the time but that was determined by later outcomes. And, if possible, one gives a sympathetic account of the losers. If one can, up to a certain point, work sympathetically with the losers, one can—in some small part at least—overcome the knowledge of the outcome. (pp. 53–54)

Let me close this section by giving you an example of presentist writing that I found while reading a biography of Sir Isaac Newton. One of Newton's strong avocations was alchemy, the quest for a means to create gold from other metals. Describing the alchemy interests of one of Newton's predecessors, Paracelsus (otherwise famous in the history of medicine), the author wrote that "[f]ollowing many an alchemist in a stereotypical fixation with finding the unattainable and achieving the impossible, he traveled Europe in search of the secrets of the ancients, squandering much of his talent and any money he earned along the way" (White, 1997, p. 120). This is a good example of writing from the standpoint of knowing the outcome (alchemy failed), while ignoring the importance of alchemy to the history of science and the historical context that made alchemy a respected endeavor for a time.

Internal Versus External History

Histories of psychology are often written by psychologists who wish to trace the development of theories of behavior that have been held by various psychologists, based on research completed by psychologists. This kind of approach is referred to as an **internal history**; what is written occurs entirely within ("internal to") the discipline of psychology. Such an approach has the value of providing detailed descriptions of the evolution of theory and research, but it ignores those influences outside of psychology that nonetheless have influenced the discipline. An **external history** focuses on those influences.

Internal histories are often referred to as histories of ideas. Typically, they are written by people trained in the specific discipline being analyzed, and they tend to be written by people with little or no expertise in history per se. They are inward-looking, focusing on the development of ideas to the exclusion of the larger world. On the other hand, external histories take the broader view: They examine societal, economic, institutional and extra-disciplinary influences. An exclusively internal history is narrow and loses the richness of historical context, whereas an excessively external history fails to convey an adequate understanding of the ideas and contributions of a discipline's key figures. A balance is needed.

The interplay between internal and external history is demonstrated nicely in the history of comparative psychology, the evolution-based study of animal behavior. It developed in the second half of the nineteenth century, primarily out of interest in demonstrating the continuity among species implied by Darwinian evolution. One interest of early comparative psychologists was in determining the extent to which other species showed evidence of consciousness. From the standpoint of internal history, students learn that comparative psychologists studying this question helped make the transition from psychology as the study of consciousness to psychology as the study of behavior. Why? Because studying animal behavior, even if the interest is in understanding "animal consciousness," requires developing procedures (e.g., maze learning) that involve the objective measurement of observable behaviors. John B. Watson, usually considered the founder of behaviorism as a school of thought (see Chapter 10), cut his research teeth in the world of comparative psychology, and saw how the methods for studying animals could be applied to the study of humans as well. Thus, there appears to be a logical progression from (a) being required to use behavioral methods if one is interested in studying animals, to (b) seeing that these methods could be used to study humans as well. In Watson's research, for example, there is a gradual shift from the study of animal behavior to the study of human behavior. In addition, other comparative psychologists of the time, especially Robert Yerkes, made a similar transformation from the study of animals to the study of humans.

There is some truth to this internal history of comparative psychology. Watson himself argued that his system of behaviorism first evolved out of his animal work. Nonetheless, a full understanding of the impact of comparative psychology requires knowing about some of the external factors that led researchers to shift from studying animals to studying humans. For example, consider the institutional context. In the early years of the twentieth century, experimental psychology was relatively new and psychologists normally resided within departments of philosophy. In the fight for an adequate slice of the budget pie, psychologists found it necessary to justify the costs of their laboratories. Senior members of the department, usually philosophers, could be difficult to convince. One approach was to demonstrate the usefulness of psychological knowledge in solving practical problems. For instance, sometimes it was argued that the fruits of psychological research would improve education. This problem of demonstrating utility was difficult enough for researchers studying humans in their laboratories; it was infinitely more arduous for comparative psychologists studying other species. Their arguments for the value of their research were even more difficult to sustain. In addition, they had a problem unique to their research interests—their laboratories were an assault on the olfactory senses. A combination of smell and no airconditioning relegated many laboratories to obscure corners of campuses (O'Donnell, 1985). For many, then, the desire to improve their institutional status was a major driving force in their change from animal to human psychology.

The experience of Robert Yerkes illustrates the problem for animal researchers. A brilliant comparative psychologist at Harvard University at the turn of the century, he found himself initially encouraged to pursue his animal work, primarily for political reasons. Harvard wished to maintain its exalted position in the academic world, and that meant competing successfully with young upstarts like Clark University, 30 miles to the west in Worcester. Clark had established an active program in comparative psychology, Harvard would not be outdone, and Yerkes would carry the torch. But he quickly discovered that his work was not valued very highly in a department that featured three of America's most famous philosophers: Josiah Royce, Charles S. Peirce, and William James. He was not promoted, he had difficulty securing laboratory space, and as the years passed, he was subtly told that his animal work was irrelevant. To be promoted, he would have to do more "on the human side." This he did, first by producing an undergraduate textbook that emphasized human experimental psychology and introspective methods, and later by embracing psychology's love affair with intelligence testing (O'Donnell, 1985). Thus, understanding the shift that some psychologists made from studying animals to studying humans requires knowing more than just the ideas that were debated within the discipline.

Personalistic Versus Naturalistic History

In addition to the presentist/historicist and internal/external distinction, one additional contrast needs to be drawn before returning to Furumoto's old versus new history. That distinction is between a personalistic history, one that sees the actions of individual historical characters as primary in bringing about history, and a naturalistic history, one that emphasizes the overall intellectual and cultural climate of a particular historical era—what Hegel called the **zeitgeist**.

According to a **personalistic history**, or what used to be called the "Great Man" theory, the important events in history result from the heroic (or evil) actions of individuals and without those individuals, history would be vastly different. This approach is often associated with the nineteenth-century historian and essayist Thomas Carlyle, whose "On Heroes, Hero Worship and the Heroic in History," written in 1840, is best remembered for this line: "The history of what man has accomplished in this world is at bottom the history of the great men who have worked here" (cited in Boring, 1963a, p. 6). According to this view, people like Newton, Darwin, and Freud changed the course of the history of science. Without them, the history would have been completely different. From this standpoint, the preferred method of writing history is biography, and as a consequence of this approach, what are sometimes called **eponyms** (Boring, 1963a) are created. That is, historical periods are identified with reference to the individuals whose actions are believed to be critical in shaping events. Thus, we read of Newtonian physics, Darwinian biology, and Freudian psychology.

The personalistic approach has intuitive appeal. Although psychology's most famous historian, Edwin G. Boring (featured in the Close-Up), favored a naturalistic model of history, arguing that "[h]istory is continuous and sleek," he recognized that great people "are the handles that you put on its smooth sides" (Boring, 1963b, p. 130). Boring argued that the persistence of a personalistic approach to history results from several factors, including a human need for heroes and the need of hard-working scientists for personal recognition (Who wants to eliminate the Nobel Prize?). More important, if history is continuous and sleek, then it is also immensely complex. In seeking to understand it, we try to reduce the complexity to understandable dimensions. More generally, a universal cognitive process, essential for achieving understanding, is to organize information into categories. Our recall of concepts like Freudian unconscious and Pavlovian conditioning is easier when the eponyms serve as retrieval cues.

CLOSE-UP:
Edwin G. Boring (1886–1968)

It is unfortunate that psychology's most famous historian has a name that students often associate with the general topic of history. In fact, E. G. Boring's writings are lively and elegant. In recent years, his version of psychology's history has been found to be flawed, but it is also true that historians of psychology owe a great debt to Boring's pioneering historical work.

While an engineering student at Cornell University, Boring first encountered psychology in the fall of 1905 by taking an elective course in elementary psychology, taught by the great E. B. Titchener (see Chapter 7). He described the lectures as "magic, so potent that even my roommates demanded, each lecture day, to be told what had been said" (Boring, 1961, p. 18). Yet Boring was not converted at that point and continued his engineering studies, earning a master's degree in 1908. After two marginally successful years as an engineer for a steel company and as a high school teacher, he returned to Cornell and earned a Ph.D. from Titchener in 1914. While at Cornell his research interests included (a) human maze learning, during which he met, fell in love with, and eventually married one of his research subjects, fellow doctoral student Lucy May (who died in 1996 at the age of 109); (b) nerve regeneration, studied firsthand and rather dramatically by severing a nerve in his arm and charting its recovery; (c) the learning processes of schizophrenics; and (d) his dissertation topic, visceral sensitivity. Boring studied this by learning to swallow a stomach tube to varying depths, then pouring different substances into the tube and noting the (often unpleasant) sensory effects (Jaynes, 1969). Nobody could ever accuse Boring of not being involved in his work!

After finishing his degree at Cornell and staying on briefly as an instructor, Boring served in World War I in the Army IQ testing program (see Chapter 8), taught briefly at Clark University, then chose Harvard over Stanford in 1922. He remained there for the rest of his career. At Harvard, Boring spent the next decade building up the laboratory and trying to convince the authorities that psychology should be a separate department, not a part of the philosophy department. This did not occur until 1934. It was during the 1920s that he wrote his famous *A History of Experimental Psychology* (1929), partly to further his political fight with the philosophers and administrators at Harvard, and partly to bolster basic research in experimental psychology at a time when the majority of American psychologists seemed to be interested in applied psychology.

In his years at Clark and Harvard, Boring's work habits, in imitation of Titchener, were legendary. In his words,

> ... my friends, my children, and my students know how I have talked about the eighty-hour week in the fifty-week year (the 4000-hour working year) and I have scorned those forty-hour academicians who take long summers off from work. I have no hobbies, except for a shop in my cellar. My vacations were never successful until I got a little study with a typewriter in it and could answer eight letters a day and write up the waiting papers. (Boring, 1961, p. 14)

Also in the tradition of Titchener, Boring taught the introductory course in psychology, believing that a student's first encounter with psychology should be from the master. He even became a pioneer in the video-course: 38 half-hour programs on Boston's educational TV channel WGBH in 1960 featured Boring demonstrating various phenomena, but mainly sitting "on the corner of a table and talk[ing] in a friendly, enthusiastic, paternal manner to the red lights on whatever camera was on the air" (Boring, 1961, p. 77; see Figure 1.1).

We have seen that the APA's Division 26, established in 1965, elected Robert Watson as its first president. According to Hilgard, this occurred after Boring refused to

FIGURE 1.1 Teaching to the masses: E.G. Boring on educational TV, from Boring (1961).

run for the office but agreed to be named "honorary president." Boring's increasing deafness kept him away from the division's inaugural meeting during the APA's 1966 convention, but he sent a written introduction to Watson's presidential address, describing himself as the "ghost of History Past, when the interest in the history of psychology had not yet become as vigorous as it is now" (Hilgard, 1982, p. 310). Clearly the current vigorousness of today's interest in psychology's history owes much to Boring's example.

The alternative to a personalistic history is a **naturalistic history**, an approach emphasizing the forces of history that act on individuals. The Russian novelist Leo Tolstoy was a famous advocate of this determinist approach. One of his goals in writing the massive *War and Peace* was to demonstrate that history is moved by forces beyond the control of individuals. For Tolstoy, so-called "Great Men" like Napoleon were in reality mere agents of historical causes larger than themselves. In Book IX in *War and Peace* he refers to kings and generals as history's slaves: "Every act of theirs, which appears to them an act of their own will, is in an historical sense involuntary and is related to the whole course of history and predestined from eternity" (Tolstoy, 1942, p. 671).

Among psychologists, Boring has most vigorously promoted a naturalistic view of history. Especially in his later years, he championed the zeitgeist concept, both in the second edition of his famous *A History of Experimental Psychology* (1950) and in numerous essays. For Boring, understanding history meant understanding the historical forces that influenced the men and women living in a particular era. While not denying Darwin's genius, for example, Boring would argue that the concept of evolution was common in the nineteenth century and extended beyond just biology (to geology, for instance). Without Darwin, someone else would have produced a theory of biological evolution. Indeed, Darwin's theory was for a brief time called the Darwin-Wallace theory of evolution, in recognition of Alfred Russell Wallace, a contemporary of Darwin's who independently developed virtually the identical theory (see Chapter 5 for this interesting story). A great scientist can and does influence events, but simply focusing on the person leaves unanswered the question of how that individual was affected by his or her contemporary environment.

In support of the zeitgeist concept, Boring pointed to two kinds of historical events. In the first, called a **multiple** by historian Robert Merton (1961), two or more individuals independently make the same discovery at about the same time. Darwin and Wallace codiscovering natural selection at a time when evolutionary thinking was "in the air" is an example. Darwin's grandfather, Erasmus Darwin, illustrates the second type of event, a discovery or a theory that is said to be "ahead of its time." Like his more famous grandson, Erasmus developed a theory of evolution, but did so in the eighteenth century, when belief in the immutability of species (i.e., each species is created in its finished form by God and it doesn't change over time) was even stronger than it was in the nineteenth century.

Relying on the zeitgeist as a way of explaining history can be problematic, however. For example, the uncritical observer might be tempted to reify (i.e., give a concrete and detached existence to an abstraction) the concept and consider it a controlling force that is independent of the historical persons who in fact give it meaning. That is, in answer to the question, "Why did event X occur instead of event Y at time Z?", one might be tempted to answer, "Because of the zeitgeist." But such an answer hardly explains the events in question. The concept of the zeitgeist invites one to examine the attitudes, values, and theories in existence at the time of some event to be explained, but it cannot exist by itself as some mysterious directing agent. As historian Dorothy Ross (1969) pointed out with reference to the history of educational psychology,

> It has been stated, for example, that neither James, Dewey, Hall, Thorndike, Cattell, Galton, nor Darwin were necessary to the rapid development of educational psychology in America, for that was the trend of the 'Zeitgeist.' But cer-

tainly we only know what the Zeitgeist in fact *was* by the way in which James, Hall, Cattell, Darwin and others behaved. If they had not thought and acted the way they did, neither would the 'Zeitgeist' they are said to embody. (p. 257, italics in the original)

Thus, a balanced view of history recognizes the complex interrelationships between people and the environments in which they act. The historical characters you are about to encounter were all products of the world in which they lived, but they also made decisions that helped form and transform the historical context that surrounded them. Wallace might have been inspired to write a paper proposing a theory of evolution that matched the essence of Darwin's, but it is no accident that recent years have seen at least three major biographies of Darwin and none of Wallace. It was Darwin who invested the years of research examining the intricacies of numerous species, and it was Darwin who followed up his initial writings with the monumental texts that brought evolution into its fullest development.

This Book's Point of View

This section of the chapter began by referring to Laurel Furumoto's distinction between old and new history; presentist, internal, and personalistic approaches typically go together and comprise what she refers to as the old history of psychology. It is a history that interprets events only from the standpoint of the present, concentrates on the development of ideas within a specific discipline, and views progress as reflecting the sequential accomplishments of important people. The new history of psychology, on the other hand, combines historicist, external, and naturalistic approaches. It tries to examine historical events on their own terms, with reference to the times in which they occurred, looks for the influence of extradisciplinary contextual forces, and looks beyond great men and women to examine the contextual factors that produced their ideas. Furumoto also points out that new history relies more on archival data and primary source materials than on secondary textbooks, and it is more critically analytical than ceremonial and celebratory.

For historians of psychology conducting research, Furumoto's description of the new history

of psychology provides a clear set of guidelines about how to proceed. The best historical research being published today is historicist, external, and naturalistic. For the author of a textbook and the teacher of the history of psychology course, however, the prescriptions about how to proceed are not as clear. As Dewsbury (1990) pointed out in a review of several history of psychology texts, it is important to distinguish between "scholarly research directed at colleagues and ... textbooks directed at introductory students" (p. 372). For the latter, the ideals of the new history need to be incorporated into the course, but they must be weighed against a need to inform students about content that is relevant to the psychology curriculum. This book presents a history of psychology that leans toward the values espoused by Furumoto, but it is important to remember that the course for which this text is designed is not just a history course, it is also a psychology course. Thus, while it is important to understand Pavlov's work within the historical climate of the early twentieth century in Russia, it is also important to understand the various classical conditioning phenomena that he investigated and how his work related to American behaviorism and conditioning research in more recent times. While it is important to understand the influence of the institutional context on the fate of comparative psychologists like Yerkes, it is also important for the psychology student to know about the animal research that Yerkes was able to complete. And although a purely personalistic history can degenerate into cute anecdotes and can overlook the complexities of historical events, it is also true that persons are interesting to study, and biographical information can increase the psychology student's understanding of human behavior.

In summary, this book will take a point of view that combines (a) presentist and historicist views, (b) internal and external histories, and (c) personalistic and naturalistic models. If each of the dichotomies can be conceived of as existing on a continuum, then this book will take the following stance:

presentist ....•... historicist
internal ....•......... external
personalistic ....•......... naturalistic

The only strong tendency will be to avoid presentist interpretations. On the other two dimensions, the book will blend (a) the various ideas, research, and theories that constitute psychology's internal history with the external historical context in which they developed, and (b) accounts of the persons who produced the history of psychology and the important features of the times in which they lived.

HISTORIOGRAPHY: DOING AND WRITING HISTORY

The simplest definition of **historiography** derives from the origins of the word itself: it is to write history. But the term goes far beyond the writing of historical narrative. Historiography also refers to theoretical issues like the ones just described and to the methods that historians use when doing historical research. Although the primary purpose of this book is to inform you about the history of psychology, a secondary goal is to give you some insight into the professional behavior of historians. That is, we will examine the kinds of data of interest to historians and the problems confronting historians as they do their work.

Sources of Historical Data

Traditionally, historians of psychology have often relied on secondary sources to write their histories, especially their textbook histories. A **secondary source** is a document that has been published and is typically an analysis or summary of some historical event or period. These sources include books, articles published in journals and magazines, encyclopedia entries, and the like. As Furumoto's new history of psychology replaces the old history, however, researchers are relying more on **primary sources** of information, usually found in archives. An **archive** is normally an area within a university library that holds unpublished information. This primary source information includes university records, correspondence, diaries, speeches, minutes of the professional organizations, and papers donated by individuals connected in some way with the university. In addition to these separate university archives, historians

of psychology often find primary source material at the Library of Congress archives in Washington, D.C., the British Museum Library in London, and the Archives of the History of American Psychology (AHAP) at the University of Akron, Akron, Ohio. In general, primary source materials are items written or created at or near the time of some historical event, while secondary sources are written at some time after a historical event and serve to summarize or analyze that event.

As mentioned previously, AHAP's 1965 founding by John Popplestone and Marion McPherson (Figure 1.2) was one of a series of events sparked by the efforts of Robert I. Watson to generate interest in psychology's history. AHAP holds the papers of more than 550 psychologists (e.g., Abraham Maslow) and organizations (e.g., APA's history division, #26), more than 700 pieces of original laboratory apparatus, several thousand psychological tests, and about 3000 photographs. By one estimate, stack-

FIGURE 1.2 Marion White McPherson and John Popplestone of the Archives of the History of American Psychology, University of Akron, from Cohen (1991).

ing the archive's materials vertically would produce the equivalent of two Washington Monuments (Cohen, 1991)!

What can you expect to find in a place like AHAP? Just about anything. Looking into the records of a professional organization, for instance, you would probably find lists of officers and correspondence between them, minutes of meetings, early drafts of position papers, and the like. When examining the papers of an individual psychologist, you might find (a) correspondence between that person and other psychologists, (b) personal diaries and/or calendars, (c) course lecture notes and course schedules, (d) laboratory protocols, drawings of apparatus, data summaries, and other laboratory-related information, (e) early draft manuscripts of writings that eventually became secondary sources, (f) photographs of people, places, and research equipment, and (g) minutes of professional meetings attended by the psychologist. There will also be some surprises. For instance, AHAP holds the papers of the experimental psychologist Walter Miles. They include the usual materials, but when the papers first arrived at the archives, they also included a brick that Miles took from the building site of a new lab. A more startling example was reported in *Civilization*, a magazine published by the Library of Congress. A researcher was studying a nineteenth-century Viennese physician (Carl Koller) who was experimenting with the use of cocaine as an anesthetic in eye surgery. One of the folders contained a small pharmacist's packet containing, you guessed it, white powder. Federal authorities were called in to remove the drug, but the envelope remains in the archive collection, labeled as follows: "Remainder of the 1st dose of cocaine, which I used in my first cocaine experiments in August 1884. Dr. Koller" ("A Stash in the Stacks," 1996, p. 15).

How does a researcher interested in psychology's history know which archives to contact or visit when starting a project? Because their holdings are so extensive, AHAP is a good place to start. Even if the archive is not the primary repository for the papers of the person being studied, AHAP might hold some correspondence from that person in the papers they do have. Another good starting place is

the university where the person in question worked. Third, bibliographic sources exist. The best known is *A Guide to Manuscript Collections in the History of Psychology and Selected Areas* (Sokal & Rafail, 1982). Suppose you are interested in the work of IQ researcher Henry Goddard, for instance. The guide briefly describes the contents of the Goddard papers, which happen to be held at AHAP. It also informs you of additional Goddard materials in the papers of Edgar Doll and Emily Stogdill at AHAP, and in the papers of developmental psychologist Arnold Gesell in the Library of Congress.

Historians also rely on their general knowledge to aid in their search. For example, some years ago I became interested in Edmund Clark Sanford (1859–1924), the first director of the psychology laboratory at Clark University (Goodwin, 1987). Naturally, Clark was the starting point for the search, and through contact with the archivist there and two visits, I accumulated some information, but not a great deal. Sanford didn't seem to save very much, or if he did, the information didn't find its way to Clark. Some of the university records were helpful, however, in determining such things as laboratory purchases, and the papers of psychologist/university president G. Stanley Hall yielded some additional data, including one exciting discovery—a series of photographs taken in the laboratory in 1892, several of which are to be found in later chapters of this book. Many of them showed (or simulated, most likely) experiments in progress, thus providing a glimpse of what it was like to be doing research in psychology then. By searching through secondary sources, I knew about other psychologists who were contemporaries of Sanford and I knew from his obituaries that Sanford was very close to E. B. Titchener of Cornell and Mary Calkins of Wellesley (Sanford died in 1924 on his way to give a talk at Wellesley). A visit to Wellesley and two visits to Cornell yielded more information. The Titchener papers were especially helpful—Titchener seemed to keep just about everything. I also wrote to about two dozen other archives that I guessed might be holding papers of Sanford's other professional peers, and hence some Sanford correspondence. Copies of a few pieces trickled in. At the same time, I was reading everything that Sanford published (not much, actually) and everything else that could shed some light on him and the world he inhabited.

Problems with the Writing of History

The journey from an archive visit to a published paper or book is long, often tedious, occasionally exhilarating, but never easy. Along the way, the historian must confront two major difficulties. First, there are problems associated with the collection of data. The historian must evaluate the validity of data and select a subset of these data for inclusion in the historical narrative. The second problem concerns writing history. Historians are human, so their interpretations of the data will reflect their beliefs, their theories about the nature of history, and potentially, their unexamined biases.

Data Selection Problems

Historians usually collect more information than will ever make its way into the historical narrative they write. Hence, they must make judgments about the adequacy and relevance of the data at hand and they must select a sample of the data while discarding the remainder. Sometimes, despite the large amount of data that might be collected during an archive visit, important pieces might be missing, further complicating the historian's life. For example, Titchener and Sanford wrote to each other frequently, but only Titchener saved his correspondence. The Titchener papers contain several hundred letters from Sanford to Titchener, but the Sanford papers include *none* from Titchener. In trying to piece together the Sanford-Titchener relationship, the historian gets only half the story.[1] Another example concerns Walter Miles, an experimental psychologist from Stanford, who once wrote an article on the early development of mazes (Miles, 1930) that included excerpts of letters he received from some of the early pioneers (e.g., Willard Small, who completed the first maze learning study with rats at Clark University). The Miles papers, in residence at AHAP, do not contain any of the cor-

respondence related to the maze history paper, however. This is surprising, considering the size of the Miles collection. It fills 128 boxes and the inventory alone runs to a numbing 756 pages (Goodwin, 1993).

Sometimes information that could aid a historian can be lost through what insurance adjusters would call an act of God. For example, after painstakingly tracking down descendants of Mary Whiton Calkins, the APA's first woman president, Laurel Furumoto discovered that many of Calkins's papers had been entrusted to her younger brother. Unfortunately, he put them in his cellar where they were destroyed by flooding that accompanied a devastating New England hurricane in 1938 (Furumoto, 1991).

Data might also be missing on purpose. In the last year of his life, John Watson, behaviorism's founder, burned all of his remaining notes, correspondence, and rough manuscripts. According to Watson's biographer, when "his secretary protested the loss to posterity and to history, Watson only replied: 'When you're dead, you're all dead'" (Buckley, 1989, p. 182). Similarly, on two separate occasions Sigmund Freud also destroyed his papers, partly to make it difficult for others to trace the sources of his ideas (Chapter 12 details one of these episodes).

In addition to missing data, some information might be restricted by the donor and inaccessible to the historian. Even someone with the status of E. G. Boring could be denied. In a letter to John Popplestone of AHAP, Boring wrote that even as a known historian and a faculty member at Harvard, he had been denied access to some papers at the Harvard archives. In his words,

> I trust the general atmosphere of the Archivists at Harvard. This is because I have been denied access to some things that are none of my business, graciously denied it because I am a Harvard professor. But, nevertheless, shut off from certain files of William James. (Popplestone, 1975, p. 21)

Beyond dealing with missing or incomplete information, the historian must make judgments about the adequacy of the available data. We know that eyewitness descriptions of everyday events can be quite wrong, that two witnesses can differ dra-

---

[1] More than half, actually. After about 1910, Titchener often made and kept carbon copies of the letters he sent.

matically in their accounts. If eyewitness unreliability can be demonstrated easily in modern psychology laboratories, then it is safe to say that the same lack of reliability exists for eyewitness accounts of historical events by psychologists. A good example of this was experienced by E. G. Boring. While preparing a history of Titchener's Experimentalists, a group of researchers who met each year to discuss their work (see Chapter 7), Boring launched a massive letter-writing campaign to colleagues who had been to meetings, asking for their first-hand descriptions. There were numerous discrepancies, including one amusing example from a colleague who recounted to Boring in great detail a dinner conversation with Harvard's Hugo Münsterberg at the 1917 meeting at Harvard. Boring wrote back gently reminding his friend that Münsterberg had died in 1916 (Goodwin, 2001). In general, any autobiographical description is subject to memory lapses.

Information found in someone's correspondence or diary can also be of questionable value. Was the letter writer providing insight into the personality of a colleague or merely passing on cruel and unsubstantiated gossip? When the diarist described the meeting as meaningless and a waste of time, would that same conclusion be drawn by others at the same meeting? Can letters and diaries be slanted by the writer's knowledge that historians might someday read his or her words? To what extent do the contents of letters and diaries reflect the personal prejudices of the writer? I think you can see the difficulty here.

Those who create the records that eventually occupy archives are human and therefore susceptible to the subtleties of human belief, preconception, and bias. Those who explore the archives and write the history are also human and subject to the same frailties. By virtue of their training, historians are certainly more disciplined than laypeople; nonetheless, when making decisions about what information to select for historical analyses and narratives, the historian is not a machine. E. G. Boring expressed the problem eloquently in the preface to his 1942 text on the history of research in sensation and perception.

Indeed, so much a matter of selection is the preparation of an historical text, that I am

sobered by the responsibility. The [history of psychology] text of 1929 has existed long enough for me to see how *the mood that determined the choice of an afternoon's exposition can fix the 'truth' of a certain matter upon graduate students for years to come.* With industry and patience one may avoid the falsification of facts, but those virtues are not enough to make one wise in choosing what to ignore. For that one also needs the wisdom and the integrity of objectivity, and who knows for sure whether he commands such? (Boring, 1942, p. viii, italics added)

As you will learn in a few paragraphs, this passage from Boring is ironic. One of the themes of modern historiography within psychology is that Boring distorted psychology's history and that his writings reflect a strong bias for a specific brand of psychology. It also appears that he was motivated at least partly by the political and institutional context that he occupied.

Interpretation Problems

Winston Churchill, who made history and also wrote it, is alleged to have said history would be kind to him because he was going to be the person writing it. Historians normally try to be more objective than this, while realizing that all historical narrative will necessarily reflect something about the writer. Decisions about selection and about writing history both involve interpreting the information at hand, and those interpretations are influenced by the individual characteristics of the historian and by the features of the historical context in which the historian is writing. That is, historians will be influenced by their preconceptions, by the amount of knowledge they already have, as well as by the theories they hold about the nature of history (e.g., personalistic versus naturalistic). In addition, even without their being aware of it, historians can be influenced in many ways by elements of the environment in which their histories are being written. For example, you will discover in Chapter 4 that the work of Wilhelm Wundt has been reevaluated recently (e.g., Blumenthal, 1975), and many of his ideas have been found to be similar to those of modern cognitive psychologists. This similarity, of course, could not have been noticed prior to the advent of modern cognitive psychology—Blumenthal was writing at the height of the so-called cognitive revolution in psychology. Thus, historical characters are not the only ones influenced by the historical context in which they live; historians are affected as well.

The history written by E. G. Boring is a case in point. You know from this chapter's Close-Up that Boring was a devoted student of E. B. Titchener, and in the 1920s he was a vigorous advocate for the development of a separate psychology department at Harvard that would emphasize "pure" laboratory research rather than application. Both of those facts played a role in the way he wrote history. First, his training as an experimental psychologist in Titchener's laboratory at Cornell surely affected his overall conception of psychology. More specifically, it influenced what Boring thought about Wilhelm Wundt, in whose laboratory Titchener earned a Ph.D. in 1892. In general, Boring believed that Titchener's brand of experimental psychology, called structuralism, was virtually identical to Wundt's psychology, and that Titchener had merely imported it to America. In fact, Wundt's system was quite different from Titchener's system (the details of Wundt's and Titchener's systems will become clear in Chapters 4 and 7, respectively), but because of Titchener's influence on Boring, combined with the fact that Titchener translated much of Wundt's work and that Boring was not conversant with some of Wundt's nonexperimental writings, the distinctions were lost. Thus, when writing his history, Boring's description of Wundt was filtered through Titchener's version and was consequently flawed. Because most psychologists trained in the period 1950 to 1980 learned their history by reading Boring's *A History of Experimental Psychology* (1929; 1950), the mythological identification of Wundt's and Titchener's systems became conventional wisdom.

A second distortion in Boring's history relates to his emphasis on basic experimental psychology to the exclusion of applied psychology. As O'Donnell (1979) has shown, Boring was disturbed by the growing status of applied psychology, especially mental testing. Believing basic laboratory research to be in jeopardy, he took several steps to restore its standing. One was writing the first edition of his history in 1929, which largely ignored the work of a substantial number of psychologists who were busily applying psychological principles to education, mental health, and the workplace. The reader of the 1929 history could be excused for believing that applied psychology barely existed.

A common misconception of history goes like this: The events occurred in the past; now that they have been described in a historical narrative, that's the end of it. As the E. G. Boring evidence shows, however, historical analyses are in continual need of revision in the light of new information and new ways of examining old information. In recent years, for instance, scholars (e.g., Leahey, 1981) have taken a fresh look at (a) the relationship between Wundt's and Titchener's ideas, and (b) the role of application in the development of psychology in America. As a result, newer histories describe the Wundt-Titchener differences more accurately and document the pervasive influence of applied psychology.

Comparing different editions of a history text can illustrate this reexamination process. For example, one popular undergraduate history text, clearly influenced by Boring in its early editions, also shows the impact of the recent scholarship on Wundt in its later editions. In the book's third edition (Schultz, 1981), Wundt is described in a chapter that has "structuralism" in its title. The following chapter, on Titchener, refers to Wundtian psychology being "transplanted" to America by Titchener and includes sentences like this: "A knowledge of Wundt's psychology provides a reasonably accurate picture of Titchener's system" (p. 87). Six years later, in the fourth edition, "structuralism" no longer appears in the title of the Wundt chapter, there is an explicit description of the problems with Boring's historical account, and the Titchener chapter opens by saying that the systems of Wundt and Titchener were "radically different," and that Titchener "altered Wundt's system dramatically while claiming to be a loyal follower" (Schultz & Schultz, 1987, p. 85).

The important lesson for the reader of history is to be alert to the dangers of assuming that if something is printed in black and white, it somehow must be true. Rather, it is important to read histories, including this one, with a healthy dose of skeptical awareness that other information might have been selected for inclusion in the narrative and that other ways of interpreting the historical record exist. This raises an interesting question: Can history uncover the truth?

Approaching Historical Truth

From the foregoing discussion, you might be tempted to accept a version of historical relativism in which five historians make five different claims for truth and there is no reasonable way to decide among them. Relativism among historians is a postmodern outgrowth of a reaction against traditional history, which held that the job of the historian is to search out the facts of "what really happened" and place them into a chronological narrative with enough style to attract readers. The outcome was a tendency to write history from the standpoint of "what really happened" to those who happened to be in positions of power and influence, while ignoring the rich variety of alternative perspectives. Thus, a traditional history of the American West, taught to American schoolchildren and grounded in a belief in the idea of manifest destiny, glorified the rugged pioneer who persevered in the face of daunting obstacles, including wild men who liked to shoot arrows. It is clear, though, that the very same history could be written from the standpoint of the Native American who valiantly defended the homeland against the invasion of wild men who liked to shoot guns.

The postmodern critique of the narrowness and arbitrariness of traditional history has had the meritorious effect of enriching our knowledge of it. Thus, we have come to recognize that history extends beyond the lives, deeds, and misdeeds of the stereotypical dead, white, European male; it must be more inclusive. On the other hand, an unfortunate consequence of this critique has been a relativism that, taken to extreme (an absolute relativism?), can lead to absurd claims like the one made occasionally that the Jewish Holocaust in World War II never really happened but was merely "constructed" out of a few isolated events (said to have explanations other than genocide) by historians sympathetic to the Jewish movement who wished to encourage the creation of the nation of Israel following the war. Those arguing for the "myth"

of the Holocaust claim that their version is as valid as any other. Yet this example makes it clear that some versions of history are indeed better (i.e., closer to truth) than others. How does one decide?

To reach the truth through historical analysis requires an objectivity that recognizes the limits of one historian's views but also has faith in the notion that meaningful historical narrative and analysis can emerge from the combined efforts of many scholars, according to historians Joyce Appleby, Lynn Hunt, and Margaret Jacob. In *Telling the Truth About History* (1994), they argue for a historiography in which truth about history emerges from a Darwinian-like struggle between competing ideas held by historians, that "knowledge-seeking involves a lively, contentious struggle among diverse groups of truth-seekers" (p. 254). Some measure of truth, then, evolves out of this struggle. Thus, just as individual variation within a species provides the basis for natural selection to operate, so do different versions of historical episodes exist, subject to competing critical analyses that determine which version adapts best to the scholarly environment. This does not mean that the goal is a single version of truth that is then "settled" and immune to change. Rather, historical truth continues to evolve as new information is discovered and brought to light and as old information is subjected to new interpretations. Also, evolving historical truth includes a variety of perspectives. Multiple eyewitnesses to an event might give different versions of it, but all agree that the event did indeed occur. From their combined information, a complex truth might emerge that would improve on a single description from one perspective. If one historian of the Civil War period "sees an event from a slave's point of view, that rendering does not obliterate the perspective of the slaveholder; it only complicates the task of interpretation" (p. 256).

Just as theories in science are temporary working truths that guide future research, their futures depending on the open and honest inquiry of scientists, so may historical truths be considered tentative yet valuable guides for further research by intellectually honest historians with open access to historical materials. And just as some theories in science are more durable than others, so are some historical truths: "all knowledge can be provisional, in theory, without eliminating the possibility of some truths prevailing for centuries, perhaps forever" (Appleby, Hunt, & Jacob, 1994, p. 284).

Presumably, on the basis of the hard work of many historians of psychology, some degree of truth about the discipline's history has emerged over the past 100 years, and I will try my best to describe it to you in the following chapters. Many disagreements among historians of psychology exist, but Appleby, Hunt, and Jacob (1994) would consider that to be a good thing, the basis for future historical truths to develop during psychology's next 100 years. Placing the word "A" in the title of this book, rather than "The," recognizes the fact that other histories exist now and more will exist in the future. Nonetheless, I believe that what you are about to read contains some truth about the discipline you have chosen to study. To the extent that some of the truth might be tentative, I hope it will motivate you to continue learning about psychology's history long after you have finished with this particular version of it.

SUMMARY

PSYCHOLOGY AND ITS HISTORY

- Recently, psychologists have celebrated several centennials, including the anniversary of the founding of Wilhelm Wundt's laboratory at Leipzig, Germany, in 1879, and the creation of the American Psychological Association in 1892.
- Interest in the history of psychology has grown steadily since the mid-1960s, primarily through the initiatives of Robert Watson. He helped establish professional organizations for historians of psychology (Division 26 of the APA, Cheiron), a journal (*Journal of the History of the Behavioral Sciences*), an archive at the University of Akron (Archives of the History of American Psychology), and a graduate program in the history of psychology at the University of New Hampshire.

WHY STUDY HISTORY?

- Knowing history helps us to avoid mistakes of the past and to predict the future, but its more important value is that it helps us understand the present day. Knowing history puts current events into a better perspective.
- Knowing history can immunize us against the belief that our current time has insurmountable problems, compared to the "good old days." Every age has its set of problems. Knowing history also reduces the tendency to think that modern-day accomplishments represent a culmination of the "progress" we have made from the inferior accomplishments of the past.

WHY STUDY PSYCHOLOGY'S HISTORY?

- Because psychology is a relatively young science, much of its history is recent and of relevance for understanding psychological concepts and theories. Also, many of the issues of concern to early psychologists (e.g., nature-nurture) are still important.
- The history of psychology course provides a synthesizing experience, tying together the loose threads that comprise the modern diversity of psychology.
- Knowing of historical examples of (a) supposed breakthroughs in psychological research or practice, or (b) new theories that were shown to be pseudoscientific, the student of history is better able to critically evaluate modern claims.
- Because the history of psychology course informs the student about historically important people behaving within their historical context, the course provides a further understanding of human behavior.

KEY ISSUES IN HISTORY

- The traditional approach to the history of psychology has been presentist, internal, and personalistic. Recently, historians have tended to be more historicist, external, and naturalistic.
- The presentist evaluates the past in terms of present knowledge and values, often passing judgment unfairly. The historicist tries to avoid imposing modern values on the past, and tries to understand the past from the standpoint of the knowledge and values present in the past.
- An internal history of psychology is a history of the ideas, research, and theories that have existed within the discipline of psychology. An external history emphasizes the historical context—institutional, economic, social, political—and how it influenced the history of psychology.
- A personalistic approach to history glorifies the major

historical figures and argues that history moves through the action of heroic individuals. A naturalistic approach emphasizes the zeitgeist, the mood or spirit of the times, as the prime moving force in history. The existence of multiples is consistent with a naturalistic view.

HISTORIOGRAPHY: DOING HISTORY

• Historiography refers to the process of doing research in history and writing historical narratives.

• Historical research often takes place in archives, which hold primary source information such as diaries, notes, original manuscripts, and correspondence. The major archive for historians is the Archives of the History of American Psychology, located at the University of Akron.

• Archival collections can be extensive, but they can also be incomplete, with important information missing for various reasons. The information that is available is subject to numerous sources of error (e.g., the biases of the diary writer).

• Historians are faced with two major problems: the selection of information for their historical narratives and interpretation of the information at hand. These decisions can reflect bias on the part of the historian, and they can reflect the historical context within which the historian is writing. Nonetheless, most historians believe that some degree of truth can be reached through the open exchange of information and by examining historical events through a variety of perspectives.

STUDY QUESTIONS

1. Describe the contributions of Robert Watson during the 1960s to the discipline of the history of psychology.

2. Explain why "understanding the present" is a more compelling reason for studying history than the traditional arguments about avoiding the mistakes of the past and predicting the future.

3. Explain why it is important for (a) any educated person to have an understanding of and appreciation for history and (b) any student of psychology to have an understanding of psychology's history.

4. What is the point made by Boorstin in his essay on "The Prison of the Present?"

5. Explain why psychology majors are more likely to be required to study the history of psychology than chemistry majors are likely to be required to study the history of chemistry.

6. Give an example of presentism and explain the dangers of presentist thinking.

7. Explain why a historicist approach to history is sometimes called a contextualized history.

8. Distinguish between internal and external histories. Use the example from comparative psychology to illustrate the point.

9. What is a personalistic history, how is it related to the concept of an eponym, and what are its limitations?

10. What is a naturalistic approach to history and what kinds of evidence are used to support this approach?

11. Distinguish between primary and secondary sources of information and describe some of the primary sources likely to be found in an archive.

12. Give three examples from psychology's history that illustrate the data selection problem that all historians face.

13. Use the example of Boring's famous text to illustrate the interpretation problems that face historians.

14. In their *Telling the Truth About History*, Appleby, Hunt, and Jacobs (1994) describe the process of arriving at truth in history in Darwinian terms. Explain what they mean, and explain why they would argue that while absolute truth might not be reachable, some historical accounts are "truer" than others?

FOR FURTHER READING

Appleby, J., Hunt, L., & Jacob, M. (1994). *Telling the truth about history*. New York: W. W. Norton.

Traces the rise of "intellectual absolutisms," such as the Enlightenment ideal of science and history as a purely objective chronicling of the facts, and their replacement with a postmodern relativism that questions the possibility of history ever achieving truth; proposes a "pragmatic" Darwinian approach to history that steers a middle course.

Boring, E. G. (1963a). Eponym as placebo. In Robert I. Watson & Donald T. Campbell (Eds.), *History, psy-*

chology, and science: Selected papers by Edwin G. Boring, Harvard University (pp. 5–25). New York: John Wiley & Sons.

A good example of Boring's erudition and his championing of the zeitgeist concept; argues that the effect of a "great man" theory is to create "eponyms" that give us an oversimplified and distorted view of history; given the complexity of history, eponyms serve as ways of classifying information.

Furumoto, L. (1989). The new history of psychology. In I. S. Cohen (Ed.), *The G. Stanley Hall lecture series.* Vol. 9 (pp. 9–34). Washington, DC: American Psychological Association.

An excellent introduction to historiographic issues, written for teachers, but of interest to students as well; includes an example of old and new history by comparing early and more recent articles written by Furumoto about Mary Whiton Calkins, APA's first female president.

Lathem, E. C. (1994). *Bernard Bailyn on the teaching and writing of history: Responses to a series of questions.* Hanover, NH: University Press of New England.

Wide-ranging question and answer session with a noted historian that covers such topics as historiography, the reasons to study history, presentism, and the teaching of history.

O'Donnell, J. M. (1979). The crisis of experimentalism in the 1920s: E. G. Boring and his uses of history. *American Psychologist, 34,* 289–295.

The best brief description of how Boring's concerns over applied psychology contributed to his efforts to reestablish the primacy of basic research through his behind-the-scenes APA activities and by constructing a history that emphasized experimental psychology.

CHAPTER 2

THE PHILOSOPHICAL CONTEXT

Psychology has a long past, yet its real history is short.
—Hermann Ebbinghaus, 1908

PREVIEW AND CHAPTER OBJECTIVES

This chapter introduces you to the major philosophical issues and concepts that have been and continue to be important for psychologists. A working knowledge of these ideas, along with an understanding of how they were dealt with by key philosophers, provides a necessary foundation for comprehending modern psychology. Although philosophers grapple with a wide range of problems, those especially relevant for psychology concern (a) whether mental and physical events are essentially the same or different and if the latter, how the two kinds of events relate to each other; (b) whether our knowledge of the world is derived primarily from our unique ability to reason or results from the cumulative effects of our sensory experiences; (c) the extent to which our heredity and our environment shape the way we are; (d) whether the things we think, feel, and do result from our own free choices or are the result of deterministic laws of nature; and (e) whether or not complex phenomena can be best understood by breaking them into their component parts. These issues will be explored through an examination of the ideas of several well-known philosophers, with special attention given to René Descartes, history's most famous rationalist and the father of modern philosophy; John Locke, the founder of British Empiricism; and John Stuart Mill, the nineteenth-century British empiricist/associationist. The Original Source Excerpt is from Descartes' writings on the mind-body problem. After you finish this chapter, you should be able to:

▨ Explain the meaning of the Ebbinghaus quote that opens the chapter

▨ Explain how the historical context shaped the ideas of Descartes (e.g., mechanism)

▨ Explain why Descartes is known as a rationalist and describe his arguments concerning the mind-body issue

▨ Explain why Descartes is considered a "father" of modern physiology (reflex model)

▨ Describe the essential features of Locke's ideas about how we develop our knowledge of the world and how he applied these ideas to education

▨ Distinguish between Locke and Berkeley on the question of primary and secondary qualities of matter

▨ Describe how Berkeley's system attempted to counter materialism

▨ Distinguish between Hume and Hartley on the question of the basic laws of association

▦ Distinguish between J. S. Mill and his father on the issue of atomism vs. holism

▦ Describe how Mill's rules for inductive logic provided an underpinning for modern conceptions of research in psychology

▦ Describe the alternative to Locke's white paper metaphor proposed by Leibniz

▦ Describe the mind-body solution proposed by Leibniz and how his ideas relate to the psychological concepts of the unconscious and thresholds

▦ Describe Kant's arguments about the origins of knowledge

A LONG PAST

Most psychology students know Hermann Ebbinghaus as the inventor of the "nonsense syllable" and as the first person to study human memory experimentally (he is featured in Chapter 4's excerpt). One cannot get through the memory chapter of an introductory psychology text, even today, without encountering the famous Ebbinghaus curve of forgetting, which seems to explain why students never seem to remember much the day after an exam. Among historians of psychology, Ebbinghaus is also known for the opening sentence of a brief introductory textbook that he wrote in 1908. It is the "long past, short history" quote that opened this chapter.

By referring to psychology's "long past," Ebbinghaus was reminding readers that basic questions about human nature and the causes of human behavior are not new. Rather, they have been asked in some form or another since humans first started asking questions. More specifically, Ebbinghaus was pointing out that psychologists must recognize their deep roots in philosophy; psychology's history cannot be understood adequately without knowing something of philosophy's history. All of the important issues that concern modern psychologists have been addressed by philosophers. In fact, you can notice the close association between psychology and philosophy the next time you go to the library—the place where you find the psychology books (BF...) is sandwiched between general philosophy, logic, and knowledge (B, BC, BD) on one side and aesthetics and ethics on the other side (BH, BL).

Does this close connection mean that psychology is just another name for philosophy? No. In the last half of the nineteenth century, a number of converging forces produced an attempt to study human behavior and mental processes through the application of scientific methods rather than through philosophical analysis, logical reasoning, and speculation—by working in the laboratory rather than in the armchair. Thus, what came to be called the "New Psychology" began to emerge as a separate discipline about 120 years ago, which led Ebbinghaus, just under 100 years ago, to proclaim that psychology's history as a new science had been quite brief.

A thorough analysis of the long past referred to by Ebbinghaus requires much more space than this chapter can offer. It would take us through ancient Greece, deep into the writings of Plato and Aristotle and others, through the great medieval church philosophers such as Thomas Aquinas, who united Christian faith with Aristotelian logic, and into the Renaissance. Instead, while we will reach into the Renaissance for some historical context, we will begin with the seventeenth century and the multitalented René Descartes, sometimes considered the father of modern philosophy, mathematics, physiology, and psychology.

DESCARTES AND THE BEGINNINGS OF MODERN PHILOSOPHY AND SCIENCE

Descartes appeared on the scene at the tail end of the Renaissance, thus benefiting from the changes that occurred during that dramatic historical era. The Renaissance lasted for approximately 200 years, during the fifteenth and sixteenth centuries. It derives its name from the rediscovery of ancient Greek and

Roman texts, especially those of Plato and Aristotle, which had been lost to the Western world for hundreds of years. The period was marked by tremendous advances in the arts, starting in northern Italy, but quickly spreading throughout Europe. It was the time of Leonardo Da Vinci (1452–1519), the prototypical "Renaissance Man," whose genius encompassed both art and science. His *Last Supper* and *Mona Lisa* are among the world's best-known paintings, and his scientific interests encompassed geology, astronomy, botany, anatomy, and the applied sciences of aeronautics, engineering, and weaponry. Another giant of the Renaissance was Michelangelo Buonarotti (1475–1564), who created artistic treasures ranging from a portrayal of the book of Genesis on the ceiling of the Sistine Chapel in the Vatican to the massive 17-foot-tall sculpture of David, now found in Michelangelo's home city of Florence.

In addition to rediscovering ancient texts and revolutionizing the arts, the Renaissance produced some notable advances in technology and science. In the 1450s, for instance, Johannes Gutenberg (c. 1394–1468) created a new form of the printing press, which enabled books to be created in larger numbers than ever thought possible, and at prices that brought literature, philosophy, and the Bible to more people than ever before. Also during this time, clockmakers improved upon simple medieval instruments to produce the elaborate mechanical displays mounted on the cathedrals and public buildings of Europe. On the hour at the Wells Cathedral in England, for instance, viewers would be treated to a performance that included lifelike figures of armored knights in combat, one of whom would unhorse the other as another uniformed character struck the hour with a hammer (Boorstin, 1983). Knowledge about the inner workings of the human body was advanced significantly in 1543, when the Belgian physician Andreas Vesalius established his reputation as the founder of modern anatomical studies with his *Fabric of the Human Body*, which featured incredibly detailed illustrations (Klein, 1970). In astronomy in the mid-1500s, the Polish amateur astronomer Nicolas Copernicus challenged the traditional **geocentric** view of the universe, which held that the earth ("geo") was at the center of the universe, and replaced it with a **heliocentric** theory, which argued that the sun ("helio") was at the center and the earth moved around it just like the other planets. Well aware of the religious controversy sure to result from the idea that "God's planet" was not in the center of the cosmos after all, Copernicus delayed publication until just before his death in 1543. The appearance of classic scientific works by Vesalius and Copernicus in the same year led one historian of science to declare 1543 as the year when modern science was born (Singer, 1957).

The Copernican model of the universe, which appeared near the end of the Renaissance, is the clearest example of one of its gradually evolving themes—a questioning of authority, especially the authority of the Church and the Church's official philosopher, Aristotle. The ancient geocentric model placed God's greatest creation, man, at the focal point of the universe. Copernicus questioned this notion. An even greater challenge soon arrived in the person of the renowned Italian scientist, Galileo Galilei (1564–1642), who supported Copernican theory with empirical observations aided by a telescope (20x power) that he constructed in 1609.[1] Galileo's observations of things never seen before, such as the moons of Jupiter, further eroded traditional authority. How could Aristotle's view of the universe be correct when he was not capable of seeing what now could be seen? Galileo, a devout Catholic (his daughter was a nun), would eventually be charged with heresy by the Church's Inquisition and forced to recant his claim of a heliocentric universe, but he did so with his fingers crossed. Even though his writings were placed on the Catholic Church's *Index of Prohibited Books* and remained there for nearly two hundred years, his works continued to be published and read widely (Sobel, 2000). By the end of the seventeenth century, the geocentric model was, as they say, history.

Another threat to the established order occurred in England, during the time of Galileo, in the person

---

[1] The inventor of the telescope is a matter of some dispute, but it was not Galileo—he improved existing technology. Credit for the telescope usually goes to Hans Lipperhey (d.1619), a lens maker from the Netherlands, primarily on the grounds of a letter that serves the function of a patent application, filed in September of 1608 (King, 1955).

of Sir Francis Bacon (1561–1626). Bacon was a strong advocate of an **inductive** approach to science. That is, he argued that the scientist must observe nature systematically and carefully as it presents itself, rather than follow the conclusions derived from a deductive analysis of Aristotle and other authorities. From many observations of individual cases, general statements about nature could be made. Bacon also believed that science should play an active role in controlling nature directly; indeed, for Bacon, a true understanding of nature only follows from the ability to create and recreate its effects at will (Smith, 1992). This, of course, is a plea for direct experimentation on nature to supplement careful observation. Bacon's insistence on acquiring knowledge through experience makes him an ancestor of British empiricism; his emphasis on induction and the control of nature made him a hero in the eyes of the twentieth-century behaviorist B. F. Skinner (Chapter 11), who adopted a Baconian value system.

Descartes and the Rationalist Argument

In the year that Galileo was observing the heavens with his telescope, René Descartes (1596–1650), a 13-year-old son of a prosperous French lawyer, was already in his third year of study at the College de la Flèche, which had recently opened and was being run by Jesuits, known for their skills as educators.[2] The education that Descartes received was in the **scholastic** tradition, which combined the received wisdom of Church authority with the careful use of reason. In particular, it relied on rational argument derived from the works of Aristotle to support the precepts of the Church. Descartes quickly established himself as a star pupil, so good that he was granted special privileges. He was given a rare private room and he was exempted from regular class attendance and routine assignments. The Jesuits also allowed him to stay in bed as long as he wished in the morning in order to conserve his apparently fragile health. Out of this Descartes developed a lifelong habit; his best ideas came while lying in bed while reflecting on whatever problem happened to be at hand.

Descartes left the college in 1614 at the age of 18, not entirely satisfied with his Jesuit education. Like modern-day students surprised to learn that their formal education fails to give them clear answers to life's significant questions, he was dismayed to discover of philosophy that "it has been studied for many centuries by the most outstanding minds without having produced anything which is not in dispute" (Descartes, 1637/1960, p. 8). Consequently, he resolved to find things out for himself, rather than relying on authority. Reflecting a sentiment familiar to all senior-level college students, he was ready to abandon the classroom and get out into the real world, "resolved to seek no other knowledge than that which I might find within myself, or perhaps in the great book of nature" (p. 8).

Because Descartes tried to keep his personal life private, the next few years are not well documented, but it appears that he spent some time sampling all that Paris had to offer (Vrooman, 1970). In 1619 he experienced what can only be called a conversion experience, in which a series of dreams effectively told him to get serious about making a meaningful contribution to knowledge. He spent the next 10 years living in and around Paris, learning as much as he could about as many different topics as possible, especially the sciences, firmly believing that he could produce a "unity of knowledge" that would be grounded in mathematics. Although it seems rather absurd in today's age of information overload to think that someone could aspire to unify all knowledge into a single system, such was not the case in the seventeenth century. A weakening of authority, combined with an increasing faith in science, created optimism that everything about the world could be known, perhaps in one's lifetime.

Descartes' time, the early seventeenth century, is known as an era of revolutionary developments in science. It was the time of Bacon, Galileo, and in the latter half of the century, the incomparable Sir Isaac Newton. It featured the telescope and the microscope of the Dutch lens maker Antonie van Leeuwenhoek,

---

[2] Descartes' birth date was March 31, 1596, a fact known only because it appeared below a portrait published after his death. During his lifetime, Descartes was very secretive about his private life, refusing to disclose his birthday out of fear that it would lead to speculation by astrologers (Vrooman, 1970).

tools which made it possible to observe things never seen before both in the heavens and in a drop of water (Boorstin, 1983). In medicine, for example, systematic observation by the British physician William Harvey refuted a widely held belief that the heart creates blood to be consumed by other parts of the body, and demonstrated (in 1628) instead that it acts as a mechanical pump that recirculates blood throughout the body.

During the early 1620s, Descartes resembled a scientist more than a philosopher, studying physics, optics, geometry, and physiology. For example, he combined his interests in optics and physiology by extracting the eye of an ox and examining the properties of the lens, thereby discovering the fact that retinal images are inverted (Vrooman, 1970). By 1633 he had written *The World*, designed to summarize his life's work to that point, demonstrating how the various disciplines could be united through the careful use of reason and based on a foundation of mathematics. The book attempted to describe the origins and the structure of the known universe, and it included topics such as geology, astronomy, and human physiology. The section on astronomy, centering on a strong defense of the Copernican/Galilean heliocentric model of the universe, was a problem, however. Descartes was ready to publish *The World* when he learned that the Church had condemned Galileo's work. Fearing a similar fate, and desiring to avoid notoriety and remain in the good graces of the Catholic Church, Descartes suppressed publication and the book did not appear until after he died. Portions of it, however, appeared in various forms in several treatises that Descartes published during his lifetime, including his *Discourse on Method*, to which we now turn.

The Cartesian System: Rationalism, Nativism, and Mechanistic Interactionism

Although skeptical of the merits of the scholasticism he encountered as a student, Descartes was always grateful to the Jesuits for teaching him to be precise and logical in his thinking. His belief that truth could emerge from the careful use of reason became his modus operandi and marks him as a **rationalist**. In his *Discourse on Method* (1637/1960), he explained

how he would accept as truth only that which could not be doubted. Thus, he rejected the evidence of the senses as being absolutely truthful, because the senses can deceive; he also questioned the plausible arguments of other philosophers, because equally plausible counterarguments existed. Yet he found that the one thing that he was unable to doubt was the fact that *he* was the one doing the doubting. As he put it in one of philosophy's most famous passages,

> I noticed that while I thus wished to think everything false, it was necessarily true that I who thought so was something. Since this truth, *'I think, therefore I am'* was so firm and so assured that all the most extravagant suppositions of the sceptics were unable to shake it, I judged that I could safely accept it as the first principle of the philosophy I was seeking. (Descartes, 1637/1960, p. 24, italics added)

For Descartes, then, the way to truth was through the human capacity to reason. In his *Discourse on Method*, he described the four basic rules he used to arrive at the truth of some matter. First, he would accept nothing as true unless "it presented itself so clearly and distinctly to my mind that there was no reason to doubt it" (Descartes, 1637/1960, p. 15). Second, he would take problems and analyze them, reducing them to their fundamental elements. Third, he would systematically work from the simplest of these elements to the more complex, and fourth, he would carefully review his conclusions to be certain of omitting nothing. Now to our twentieth-century way of thinking, these rules of method may not appear to be extraordinary. Descartes seems to be saying not much more than to think clearly, logically, and without bias, to reduce problems to sub problems, to work systematically from the simple to the complex, and to check your work. Yet to conclude that these rules are ordinary is to fall prey to the kind of presentist thinking discussed in Chapter 1. In the context of Descartes' times, when the power of authority was weakening but still considerable, his rules of method were truly revolutionary. In effect, he was casting off authority completely. The only way to get to the certainty of truth is to arrive at it oneself, relying on the clear use of one's own reasoning powers. An indication of how unsettling this notion was to the authorities is the fact that after Descartes' death, the Catholic Church put him in Galileo's company by adding his writings to their *Index*, the list of books to be avoided by right-thinking Catholics (Vrooman, 1970).

An implication of Cartesian rationalism was that the ability to reason is inborn or innate and that certain types of knowledge do not rely directly on sense experience, but derived from our native ability to reason. For example, although we come to know the properties of wax (e.g., heat melts it) on the basis of our experience with it, there are certain things about wax that we come to understand simply as a result of a logical analysis, using our native reasoning powers. Thus, Descartes would say that we could conclude, without doubt, that wax has the inherent property of "extension"—it exists in space and even though it may change form (e.g., through melting), it can never disappear. Because we can use our native reason to arrive at our knowledge of the concept of extension, Descartes considered this particular attribute to be an example of an **innate idea**. Similarly, he believed that we have other innate ideas that we can derive through the use of our reasoning ability. These included the ideas of God, the self, and some basic mathematical truths. On the other hand, many of our concepts result from our experiences in the world. These Descartes called **derived ideas**. Knowing that a wax candle of a certain size will burn for about 10 hours would be an example of such an idea. Descartes' position on innate ideas means that he can be considered a nativist as well as a rationalist. His innate versus derived ideas distinction foreshadows one of psychology's recurring issues, the relationship between nature and nurture.

Descartes was also history's best-known **dualist**, arguing for a clear separation between mind (or "soul") and body. They can be distinguished, according to Descartes, by the above-mentioned property of extension and by the additional property of movement—bodies take up space and move through it. Mind, on the other hand, possesses neither extension nor movement. The centerpiece of the unextended mind is the human ability to reason, while the body is in essence a machine. One implication of this dualism has come to be called the **Cartesian dichotomy**, which divides humans and animals. Descartes argued that animals were simple machines, incapable of reason and language, and therefore lacking a mind. Humans, on the other hand, combined a mechanical body with a mind that could reason. Thus, animals consist only of bodies, whereas humans combine both bodies and minds. In addition to the labels rationalist and nativist, then, Descartes can also be considered a **mechanist**, for his belief that the body operates like a complicated machine. He was also an **interactionist**, believing that the mind could have a direct influence on the body (a decision to improve our health causes us to exercise) and the body could have a direct influence on the mind (a pulled hamstring causes us to redesign our exercise plan).

Descartes' use of the machine metaphor when describing the properties of bodies was no accident. We have seen that in the Renaissance, clock-building technology had advanced to the point where mechanical yet lifelike figures would put on an hourly show on the cathedrals and public buildings of Europe. Similarly, the wealthy of Europe created gardens that included elaborate mechanical fountains and statues that moved through the action of water-driven hydraulic systems. The unwary visitor to one of these seventeenth-century Disney Worlds might step on a hidden plate, thereby activating a system that would result in a statue of Neptune rising from the water in an adjacent pond. A less whimsical example of the mechanistic zeitgeist that infused Descartes' times was Harvey's demonstration of the heart as a mechanical pump.

ORIGINAL SOURCE EXCERPT
Descartes on Mind-Body Interactionism

In the year before his death, Descartes published *The Passions of the Soul* (1649/1969), which established his status as a pioneer psychologist and physiologist. A portion of it is excerpted here. Primarily a treatise on human emotions, it included an attempt to explain what we now call the reflex, and it provided a physiological model for Descartes' position on the mind-body question. Descartes opened the book with a characteristic attack on the traditional, authority-based approach to the study of the emotions, arguing in his opening sentence that "[t]here is nothing in which the defective nature of the sciences which we have received from the ancients appears more clearly than in what they have written on the passions" (Descartes, 1649/1969, p. 331). He then introduced his mind-body distinction and began a discussion of the "bodily machine" which included a direct reference to Harvey, a description of the antagonistic action of the muscles, and an opening discussion of the nervous system:

> In order to render this more intelligible, I shall here explain in a few words the whole method in which the bodily machine is composed. There is no one who does not already know that there are in us a heart, a brain, a stomach, muscles, nerves, arteries, veins, and such things. ... Those who have acquired even the minimum of medical knowledge further know how the heart is composed. ... Likewise all those whom the authority of the ancients has not entirely blinded, and who have chosen to open their eyes for the purpose of investigating the opinion of Harvey regarding the circulation of blood, do not doubt that all the veins and arteries of the body are like streams by which the blood ceaselessly flows with great swiftness. ... We further know that all the movements of the members [e.g., arms and legs] depend on the muscles, and that these muscles are so mutually related one to another that when the one is contracted it draws toward itself the part of the body to which it is attached, which causes the opposite muscle to become elongated. ... We know finally that all these movements of the muscles, as also all the senses, depend on the nerves, which resemble ... little tubes, which all proceed from the brain, and thus contain like it a certain very subtle air or wind which is called the animal spirits. (pp. 333–334)

The **animal spirits** referred to by Descartes, a notion that traces to the ancient Greeks, were said to be derived from the "heat" of the blood and were the driving forces behind all movement. Descartes believed these spirits were tiny particles in constant motion and were found in the brain, the nerves, and the muscles.

> ... [F]or what I here name spirits are nothing but material bodies and their one peculiarity is that they are bodies of extreme minuteness and that they move very quickly like the particles of the flame which issues from a torch. Thus it is that they never remain at rest in any spot, and just as some of them enter into the cavities of the brain, others issue forth by the pores which are in [the brain], which pores conduct them into the nerves, and from there into the muscles, by means of which they move the body in all the different ways in which it can be moved. ...
>
> For the sole cause of all the movements of the members is that certain muscles contract, and that those opposite to them elongate ... and the sole cause of one muscle contracting rather than that set against it, is that there comes from the brain some additional amount of animal spirits, however little it may be, to it rather than to the other. Not that the spirits which proceed

immediately from the brain suffice in themselves to move the muscles, but they determine the other spirits which are already in these two muscles, all to issue very quickly from the one of them and to pass into the other. (p. 336)

Muscle movement results from the action of animal spirits, but what determines which muscles will move? Two things, according to Descartes. First, the mind can initiate the movement of animal spirits in the brain by activating the nerves controlling certain muscles rather than others. That is, the mind can influence the body (more on this shortly). Second, certain muscles can move automatically in response to the results of certain sensory events. That is, *reflexes* occur.[3]

Descartes explained the relationship between sensation and the automatic motor response by proposing the existence of thin wire-like "filaments" that existed within the nerves and extended to the brain. On the basis of his animal dissections and without the benefit of Leeuwenhoek's microscope, yet to be invented, Descartes believed the nerves to be hollow tubes (thus allowing for animal spirits to move through them) containing these thin filaments. Whenever our senses are stimulated, according to Descartes, these filaments move, causing certain "pores" in the brain to be opened. This in turn results in the flow of animal spirits that produces the reflex movement, as when we accidentally burn ourselves. Figure 2.1 shows a famous sketch by Descartes of this involuntary (i.e., reflexive) withdrawal of one's foot from a fire, taken from an earlier work called *Treatise on Man*, published in 1637. The fire touches the foot, causing a tug on the filaments within the nerve there. These filaments extend all the way to the brain where animal spirits are released into the nerve "tube." The spirits in turn are carried "partly to the

FIGURE 2.1 Descartes' illustration of reflex action, from Fearing (1930).

muscles which pull back the foot from the fire, partly to those which turn the eyes and the head in order to regard it, and partly to those which serve to advance the hands and to bend the whole body in order to shield itself" (Descartes, 1637, quoted in Fearing, 1930, p. 24).

In *The Passions of the Soul*, Descartes extended the reflex concept to include all of our automatic functioning (e.g., breathing, digesting) and drew an analogy to the mechanics of a clock:

In this way all the movement which we make without our will contributing thereto (as frequently happens when we breathe, walk, eat, and in fact perform all those actions which are common to us and to the brutes), only depend on the conformation of our members, and on the course which the spirits, excited by the heat of the heart, follow naturally in the brain, nerves, and muscles, just as the movements of a watch are produced simply by the strength of the springs and the form of the wheels. (pp. 339–340)

---

[3] Although Descartes was clearly describing reflex action, he did not invent or use the term "reflex." That distinction belongs to Thomas Willis (1621–1675), a British physiologist, who named the phenomenon "reflexion." Willis also coined the term "neurology" (Finger, 2000).

In addition to resulting in reflex action, sensations can also give rise to the movement of animal spirits in the brain that lead to deliberate decisions to act and the mind by itself can initiate action. That is, the mind can intervene between sensory stimulus and motor response. How to explain the nature of this interaction between mind and body was a problem, however. It is one thing to say that the mind can directly affect bodily movement and vice versa, but it is quite another thing to demonstrate just how this occurs. After careful analysis, Descartes

> ... clearly ascertained that the part of the body in which the soul exercises its functions immediately is in nowise the heart, nor the whole of the brain, but merely the most inward of all its parts, to wit, a certain very small gland which is situated in the middle of its substance and so suspended above the duct whereby the animal spirits in its anterior cavities have communication with those in the posterior, that the slightest movements which take place in it may alter very greatly the course of these spirits; and reciprocally that the smallest changes which occur in the course of the spirits may do much to change the movements of this gland. (pp. 345–346)

The structure in question is the **pineal gland**, and Descartes selected it as the locus for mind-body interaction because he believed it was strategically located in a place where the flow of the animal spirits could be controlled. In Figure 2.2, Descartes showed how the pineal gland's movement could send animal spirits off in different directions (represented by the straight lines). The pineal gland was also a brain structure that was not duplicated on both the left and right side of the brain. Because the mind (or soul) was considered to be unitary, Descartes reasoned, it must exert its effect through a structure that was also a single unit:

FIGURE 2.2 Descartes' illustration of the action of the pineal gland, from Finger (2000).

> The reason which persuades me that the soul cannot have any other seat in all the body than this gland wherein to exercise its functions immediately, is that I reflect that the other parts of our brain are all of them double, just as we have two eyes, two hands, two ears, and finally all the organs of our outside senses are double; and inasmuch as we have but one solitary and simple thought of one particular thing at one and the same moment, it must necessarily be the case that there must somewhere be a place where the two images which come to us by the two eyes, where the two other impressions which proceed from a single object by means of the double organs of the other senses, can unite before arriving at the soul, in order that they may not represent to it two objects instead of one. (p. 346)

It is worth noting that Descartes was not arguing that the pineal gland had its special function because it was a part of the brain found only in humans—he was well aware, on the basis of some of his own dissections, that other animals possessed the structure

(Finger, 2000). What he was arguing was that the gland had a function in humans that would not be found in animals—the locus for mind-body interaction.

Descartes was not asserting that the mind was *in* the pineal gland, only that the gland serves as the place where mind and body influence each other. Thus, sensations produce a stretching of the small filaments that open pores in the brain, thereby moving the animal spirits. These movements are felt by the pineal gland and result in the mental event of a "sensation." The animal spirits also continue their movement back down the nerve fibers into the muscles, producing movement. Movement can also be created by the direct action of the will. The decision to move causes the pineal gland to move, which in turn produces the movements of the spirits that eventually move the muscles.

Descartes used his model of the nervous system to explain other mental and emotional processes. For instance, he proposed that memory was the result of animal spirits moving more easily along pathways that have been made more accessible by experience:

> Thus when the soul desires to recollect something, this desire causes the [pineal] gland, by inclining successively to different sides, to thrust the spirits towards different parts of the brain until they come across that part where the traces left there by the object which we wish to recollect are found; for these traces are none other than the fact that the pores of the brain, by which the spirits have formerly followed their course because of the presence of this object, have by that means acquired a greater facility than the others in being once more opened by the animal spirits which come towards them in the same way. Thus the spirits in coming in contact with these pores, enter into them more easily than into the others, by which means they excite a special movement in the gland which represents the same object to the soul, and causes it to know that it is this which it desired to remember. (p. 350)

Of course, despite the noble effort, Descartes was wrong about the physiology. For example, the pineal gland, which secretes the hormone melatonin and remains little understood today (at least in mammals) is not a mind-body Grand Central Station. A more important problem, one pointed out almost immediately by critics in his own day, was that his proposal of the pineal gland as the point of mind-body interaction really did not explain *anything*, but merely pushed the problem back by one step. If it is unclear how the unextended mind can influence and be influenced by an extended body in general, it is just as unclear how the unextended mind can influence, and be influenced by, the movements of a small, extended piece of the brain (Cottingham, 1986). For psychology, the significance of Descartes' work is not that he made a serious yet flawed effort to solve the mind-body problem, but that in so doing, he created the concept of reflex action, with its explicit distinction between sensory stimulus and motor response, and he tried to explain psychological concepts (e.g., memory) by using a physiological model. He was the first physiological psychologist.

Shortly after publishing *The Passions of the Soul* in 1649, Descartes was persuaded by Queen Christina of Sweden to move to Stockholm in order to tutor her. She was hardly the stereotype of female royalty—it was said "she lacked virtually every feminine charm" (Vrooman, 1970, p. 212). Yet she had a keen mind, was fluent in five languages, and was determined to make Stockholm a center of learning in Europe. To that end she created a world-class library and began inviting scholars to her court, Descartes being among the first to be asked. He accepted with some misgivings and soon found himself conversing with and tutoring Christina for five hours a day, three days a week, beginning at 5 A.M., during a winter that was severe even by Swedish standards. For someone accustomed to lounging in bed until late morning while reflecting on the great issues of the day, the schedule was a killer. Sure enough, Descartes contracted pneumonia on February 1, 1650, and died 10 days later, just shy of his fifty-fourth birthday.

THE BRITISH EMPIRICIST ARGUMENT AND THE ASSOCIATIONISTS

Philosophy on the European continent has often been rationalist in spirit, especially after Descartes. In England, however, a different tradition arose at about the same time that Descartes' influence was spreading. This British tradition is strongly **empiricist**, based on the idea that our knowledge of the world is constructed from our experiences in it. Because this knowledge is woven together by the associations between our ideas, British empiricism is closely tied to the doctrines of **associationism**. Much of the history of British philosophy, from the seventeenth century on, has been concerned with the epistemological questions of how experience creates knowledge and how the rules of association work to organize that knowledge.

British empiricism has its roots in the inductive scientific thinking of Sir Francis Bacon and the social theories of Thomas Hobbes, a contemporary of Bacon and Descartes. We may conveniently begin with John Locke, however, usually considered the founder of this movement. We will then examine the work of other leading British empiricists and associationists, ending with the dominant British philosopher of the nineteenth century, John Stuart Mill.

John Locke (1632–1704): The Origins of British Empiricism

John Locke was a reasonable man who lived during unreasonable times. He spent most of his adult life in the rational academic environment of Oxford as a lec-

turer and tutor, but he interspersed the contemplative life of a philosopher with a political and diplomatic career. Also, he was trained in medicine, but he was primarily interested in the scientific aspects of it and he seldom practiced as a physician. In his lifetime, he witnessed (a) the English Civil War, which ousted the British monarchy in favor of a civilian Parliament; (b) the execution of one king and the overthrow of another (he might have been present at the former and had a hand in the latter); (c) several changes in England's official religion, each accompanied by varying degrees of persecution of those professing the "wrong" faith; (d) a fire that destroyed two-thirds of London (he could see the smoke from Oxford); and (e) a political alliance that led him to flee England for a time and settle in the safety of Holland (Jeffreys, 1967). Out of these experiences, he developed a liberal political philosophy based on tolerance of dissent and the right of the people to determine how they would lead both their worldly and their more spiritual lives, and in particular, how they would be governed. In his best-known political work, *Two Treatises on Government* (1690/1960), he elaborated the Hobbesian idea of a **social contract** between government and the people. The government would agree to govern wisely and protect the rights, welfare, and common good of its citizens; the citizens in turn would agree to support the government and participate in it. Citizens failing to do so could expect the government to act against them (e.g., throw them in jail for not paying taxes). On the other hand, governments failing their end of the bargain could expect to be overthrown by the people and replaced by a more just government. This concept should sound familiar. Thomas Jefferson modeled the Declaration of Independence on Locke's ideas.

Locke is important to psychology as a consequence of the concepts expressed in two of his books, *An Essay Concerning Human Understanding* (1690/1963) and *Some Thoughts Concerning Education* (1693/1963). The former explains Locke's views on how knowledge is acquired, how we as humans come to understand our world. The latter is based on a series of letters to a friend and shows how empiricist thinking can be applied to all aspects of a child's education.

Locke on Human Understanding

Like Descartes, Locke was much enamored of the science that was such a prominent feature of the seventeenth century. While a student at Oxford, he was drawn to the ideas of Sir Francis Bacon and he firmly rejected the same scholasticism that Descartes questioned. While studying medicine, Locke befriended other scientists, including Robert Boyle (1627–1692), one of modern chemistry's pioneers and a founder of the British Royal Society, established in 1662 to further the interests of science (Boorstin, 1983). Locke was also a contemporary of Sir Isaac Newton, whose *Principia Mathematica* was published just three years before Locke's *Essay*. What Bacon, Boyle, Newton, and others were doing for the physical sciences, transforming it from the Aristotelian-based "natural philosophy" into an experimental, empirically based group of disciplines, Locke was determined to do for **epistemology**, the study of human knowledge and its acquisition.

As Locke noted in the book's opening "epistle to the reader," the ideas in his *Essay* derived from discussions with friends at Oxford and evolved into a series of notes, "written by incoherent parcels; and, after long intervals of neglect, resumed again, as my humor or occasions permitted" (Locke, 1690/1963, p. xlvii). Twenty years after the originating discussions, it finally emerged in 1690 as *An Essay Concerning Human Understanding*.

Before describing how our ideas originate, Locke considered and rejected the existence of innate ideas. He was not entirely on the nurture side of the nature-nurture issue, however. He granted that we have innate "faculties" such as the ability to think, but he did not accept Descartes' contention that ideas derived from logical thinking (e.g., extension) could be considered innate ideas. He began by arguing that there is no need to propose innate ideas, because it can be shown that ideas originate from other sources, requiring only the use of our basic mental abilities ("faculties"). For instance, while our reasoning ability enables us to conclude that all physical objects have the property of extension, the conclusion is based on the fact that we have experienced lots of extended objects during our lifetimes. In the absence of such experiences, Locke believed that we would not arrive at the conclusion about extension being a property of all matter; indeed, it would not even occur to us to think about it.

Another argument for innate ideas was the belief that some ideas were universal, found in all people. If all cultures include the concept of the Deity, for example, it could be said that the concept of God does not require any specific experiences, but is innate. Locke would not buy it. Although he did not use this specific example, Locke's reply would be that a universal belief in God does not necessarily mean the idea of God is innate to us. Instead, it could be that because all people die (i.e., a common experience), they all worry about death and whether there is an afterlife, and proposing the idea of a supreme being is a natural and inevitable consequence of this line of thought.

A final argument for innate ideas is that some ideas seem to appear so early in life that they must be innate. Locke rejected this argument also, pointing out that even before children can use language, they are profiting from experience, by learning to recognize the difference between bitter and sweet for instance. Furthermore, in a tone similar to that taken later by American behaviorists in the twentieth century, Locke pointed out that we often overlook the fact that a child can have quite a few important experiences early in life. Thus, a two-year-old talking about God does not allow us to conclude that God is an innate idea. That child has probably been exposed to quite a bit of religion in two years.

Having rejected the concept of innate ideas, Locke turned to the question of how our minds develop ideas. In one of philosophy's most quoted passages, Locke declared that *all* of our knowledge about the world derives from our experiences in it:

> ... Let us then suppose the mind to be, as we say, white paper, void of all characters, without any ideas; how comes it to be furnished? Whence comes it by that vast store, which the busy and boundless fancy of man has painted on it with an almost endless variety? Whence has it all the materials of reason and knowledge? *To this I answer, in one word, from experience;* in that, all our knowledge is founded, and from that it ultimately derives itself. (Locke, 1690/1963, pp. 82–83, italics added)

The mind at birth, then, is an empty sheet of **white paper** (Locke was renaming an old Aristotelian metaphor of the mind as a blank slate or wax tablet), ready to be written upon by the experiences of one's lifetime. Furthermore, the ideas that result from our experience and compose the mind have two and only two sources, according to Locke. He believed that every idea we have, without exception, originated from the two processes of sensation and reflection. As he described it:

> First, our senses ... convey into the mind several distinct perceptions of things: ... and thus we come by those ideas we have, of yellow, white, heat, cold, soft, hard, bitter, sweet, and all those which we call sensible qualities. ... This great source of most of the ideas we have, depending wholly upon our senses, and derived by them to the understanding, I call SENSATION.
>
> ... Secondly, the other fountain, from which experience furnisheth the understanding with ideas, is the perception of the operations of our own mind within us, as it is employed about the ideas it has got; [these] operations ... are perception, thinking, doubting, believing, reasoning, knowing, willing, and all the different actings of our own minds; ... I call this REFLECTION, the ideas it affords being such only as the mind gets by reflecting on its own operations within itself. (Locke, 1690/1963, pp. 83–84)

Sensation, then, refers to all of the information taken in by our senses from the environment, and reflection refers to the mental activities involved in processing information from both the senses and from memory. Thus, our concept of green derives from all of our experiences with green objects and our further reflections about "greenness." The reflection process also can produce new ideas not encountered initially by our senses. For instance, even without encountering the Dr. Seuss story directly through sensation, we can conceive of "green eggs and ham" by combining, through the reflective processes of memory and imagination, our ideas of green, eggs, and ham.

In another part of the *Essay*, Locke made a distinction between simple and complex ideas. **Simple ideas** resulted from experiencing basic sensory qualities such as yellow, white, heat, and so on, and from making simple reflections such as "pleasant." A **complex idea** includes several other ideas, which can be a combination of simple and other complex ideas. The complex idea of a cold drink on a very hot day, for example, is composed of a number of simple ideas relating to color, temperature, shape, pleasantness, taste, and the additional complex idea of the good life. Complex ideas are compounds and can be ultimately reduced to simple ones, much as chemical compounds are composed of simple elements. This idea of the mind being an elaborate construction incorporating layers of ideas of varying complexity was a common feature of all British empiricist thinking, and reflects the influence of the other sciences, especially physics and chemistry. Just as water can be reduced to its elements and light can be broken down into the colors of the spectrum, so the mind could be analyzed into its fundamental units. The idea that complexity in nature can be understood by reducing objects to their most basic elements is sometimes referred to as **atomism**, and it is an assumption underlying many of the early systems of psychology, including E. B. Titchener's structuralism (Chapter 7) and John Watson's behaviorism (Chapter 10).

In the fourth edition of his *Essay*, Locke addressed the question of how simple ideas form compound ones, and in the process introduced the concept of **association** into the discussion. Just as gravity was the central concept of Newtonian physics, holding together the elements of the universe, so would association be the glue that held together one's experiences in life. But while Locke discussed the concept of association to some extent, it was for the other British philosophers we will meet shortly to develop it more fully. As will become evident, British empiricism and associationism went hand in hand.

A final distinction worth noting is between what Locke referred to as the primary and secondary qualities of matter. This was a distinction well known in the seventeenth century, first popularized by Galileo. **Primary qualities** were said to exist as an inherent property of an object. Extension, shape, and motion are examples. These were the features believed by Descartes to be innate ideas. To Locke, there was nothing innate about them; the concepts might indeed result from the mind's reflection, but the data for that reflection came from one's sensory experiences with a range of objects. **Secondary qualities**, on the other hand, are not inherent attributes of objects, but depend on perception. The color, smell, warmth, and taste of objects are examples. Thus, the redness of an object exists not in the object itself but in the perceptual experience of the observer. As it gets darker, the tomato in the garden does not change its shape, but its color changes, gradually fading from red to near black. In the next chapter, you will see how the concept of secondary qualities was a cornerstone of a famous nineteenth-century model of the nervous system, which proposed that the senses differed in terms of "specific energies." The primary/secondary distinction also raised questions that led naturally to a direct examination of how sensory systems actually work to create our "understandings." If "red" is not in the object but in the brain, how does it get there?

Locke's empiricist philosophy had several interesting implications. First, if our knowledge of the world is based on our experiences, and sensation is a major source of that experience, then defective senses should produce a distorted view of the world. This issue was posed to Locke in the form of a letter from William Molyneux, a friend in Dublin. Molyneux asked what would happen if a man blind from birth, whose experience of objects like cubes and spheres would be limited to the sense of touch, would recognize the objects if his sight was suddenly restored. Molyneux answered his own question in the negative, and Locke agreed. Once sight had been restored, the man would have to learn to distinguish cube from sphere all over again, by relating the information from the visual and the tactile senses. As early as the eighteenth century, congenital cataracts were being removed surgically, thus providing a direct test and strong support for this empiricist claim (Morgan, 1977).

Another implication of Locke's theory connects his psychology with his political theory and illustrates how the turbulent times in which he lived helped shape his ideas. If human understanding results from experience, then people living in different environments will necessarily have different sets of experiences. The result will be differences between people that range from food preferences to beliefs about the best way to live one's life to one's personal religious preferences. Locke did not believe in a total relativism—not all belief systems are of equal value, both intellectually and morally. But his commitment to the importance of the environment in shaping the mind, and the resulting differences between people, was tied closely to his political liberalism and in particular to his belief that individual differences, even differences in religious beliefs, should be tolerated. Having lived through several periods of extreme religious intolerance, Locke was aware of its destructive influence.

Locke on Education

A final implication of Locke's empiricist thinking concerned how to raise and educate children. If the mind is shaped by its experiences, then a deliberate program of education based on empiricist principles could be expected to produce the ideal person. Locke's contribution to the issue was *Some Thoughts Concerning Education* (1693/1963), a brief volume based on letters written to a friend who was seeking advice about the education of his son. Locke's advice was wide-ranging, and included the following:

1. Trained in medicine, Locke was a strong believer in the importance of physical health, and he began the book by advocating that a sound mind requires a sound body. His specific suggestions reflected his own strict Puritan upbringing, which fostered simplicity, individual initiative and effort, and the belief that good outcomes require some degree of suffering. Children should have hard rather than soft beds, for example; the former toughens the person, whereas "being buried every night in feathers, melts and dissolves the body, is often the cause of weakness, and the forerunner of an early grave" (Locke, 1693/1963, p. 22). Using an inoculation logic, he also suggested that children could develop resistance to disease by having their feet washed in cold water every day and by wearing leaky shoes.

2. Training must begin early, because young children are more malleable, and if they don't develop good habits early in life, they will develop bad ones. Locke believed that one of the greatest mistakes made by parents was that their child's "mind [had] not been made obedient to discipline, and pliant to reason, when at first it was most tender, most easy to be bowed" (Locke, 1693/1963, p. 27). Good habits also require practice. Children learn such habits by doing things repeatedly, not by learning rules, "which will be always slipping out of their memories" (p. 46).

3. Locke argued against the use of punishment, especially as children get older. The child who is beaten for not doing lessons soon comes to dislike learning (and tutors) completely. Furthermore, while punishment might reduce unruly behavior in a child, severe and repeated punishment carries the danger of "breaking the mind, and then, in place of a disorderly young fellow, you have a low-spirited moped creature" (Locke, 1693/1963, p. 38).

4. Concrete rewards are to be avoided also. Giving a child sweets for good performance produces a child only interested in obtaining sweets. On the other hand, Locke recommended the use of rewards and punishments in the form of parental approval and disapproval. "If you can once get into children a love of credit, and an apprehension of shame and disgrace, you have put into them the true principle, which will constantly work, and incline them to the right" (Locke, 1693/1963, p. 41).

Locke's views on education, and his empiricist philosophy in general, show a strong affinity with twentieth-century behaviorism, as will be clear when you read Chapters 10 and 11. Although Locke was concerned with mental life and the behaviorists focused on overt action, strong resemblances exist. Like the modern behaviorists, Locke believed that mental complexity could be understood by analysis into component parts, that the environment directly shaped the mind and behavior, and that you can tell a great deal about a person if you know something of the person's experiences in life. Empiricism and behaviorism also share an emphasis on the importance of association, but as mentioned earlier, it was for empiricists subsequent to Locke to develop associationist doctrine to its fullest. It is to Locke's intellectual descendants that we now turn.

George Berkeley (1685–1753): Empiricism Applied to Vision

As the seventeenth century drew to a close, it was clear to the intelligentsia that the century had been marked by a steady decline in the authority of the Church and scholasticism, accompanied by, and to a large extent precipitated by, enormous advances in science. From Bacon to Galileo to Harvey to Boyle to Newton, a zeitgeist evolved that envisioned the universe as a large machine, composed of material parts, and operating according to laws that could only be discovered by combining scientific methods with mathematical rigor. Although it was not until the nineteenth century that the "ism" called **materialism** would reach its full development, its roots were in the seventeenth century. Materialists are monists on the mind-body question, believing that the only reality is a physical reality, and that every event in the universe, including what we think of as mental events, involve measurable, material objects in motion in physical space. Materialism includes the above-mentioned atomism, the idea that complex entities can be understood by reducing them to their component parts. Materialism also poses a threat to the concept of free will by implying **determinism**, the belief that all events have prior causes. If we are not free to choose, then perhaps we cannot be held responsible for our actions.

Such a materialistic and scientific worldview does not necessarily rule out religion (e.g., Boyle thought that to do science was to discover God's will), but it threatens the concepts of free will and moral responsibility, and so some saw it as a danger. One thinker who was especially concerned about the materialistic implications of seventeenth-century science was George Berkeley, a bishop of the Anglican Church in Ireland.

Berkeley (pronounced "Bark'-lee") was a child prodigy who entered college at age 15 and completed his most important philosophical work before his thirtieth birthday. He was born in Ireland, educated at Dublin's Trinity College, and made a deacon in the Anglican Church in 1709 at age 24. He held several professorships and would eventually (1734) be named Bishop of Cloyne in Ireland. In his middle years, he became fascinated with the missionary possibilities in the New World. He believed that America was the great hope for civilization and reflected it in his poem entitled "Destiny of America," which contains the often-quoted line "Westward the course of empire takes its way." He lived for a time in Newport, Rhode Island, and tried unsuccessfully to establish a university in Bermuda. The city of Berkeley, California, about as westward as one can get in America, is named for him.

Berkeley is important for psychology because of two books that he published when he was in his mid-twenties: *An Essay Towards a New Theory of Vision* (1709) and *Treatise Concerning the Principles of Human Knowledge* (1710). Both are strongly empiricist and focus on an analysis of sensory processes. Legend has it that Berkeley's interest in sensation had its roots in a hanging that he witnessed while a student. Curious about the sensations accompanying being hung, he arranged to have *himself* hung from the rafters in the company of friends who were instructed to cut him down after a few minutes! Evidently, Berkeley lost consciousness and almost died from the incident, which contributed to his reputation for being a bit eccentric (Klein, 1970).[4]

Berkeley's work on vision was the first systematic example of how empiricist thinking could be applied to the study of perception. It was timely, written when advances in optics were producing new and improved telescopes, microscopes, and eyeglasses, while at the same time knowledge of the visual system was primitive. In his book, Berkeley tried to show that our perceptions of the distance, size, and locations of objects are judgments that depend entirely on *experience*. When judging distance, for example, Berkeley made use of what your general psychology book

referred to as the monocular (only one eye needed) cues of overlap, relative clarity and relative size:

> [T]he estimate we make of the distance of objects considerably remote is rather an act of judgment grounded on experience than of sens[ation]. For example, when I perceive a great number of intermediate objects, such as houses, fields, rivers, and the like, which I have experienced to take up considerable space, I thence form a judgment or conclusion that the object that I see beyond them is at a great distance. Again, when an object appears faint and small, which at a near distance I have experienced to make a vigorous and large appearance, I instantly conclude it to be far off. (Berkeley, 1709/1948, p. 171)

Berkeley also examined the question of judging depth for objects that are relatively close, and provided a clear description of phenomena today referred to as convergence, a binocular (two eyes needed) cue, and accommodation. In **convergence**, when objects move closer to us or farther away, "we alter the disposition of our eyes, by lessening or widening the interval between the pupils" (Berkeley, 1709/1948, p. 174). These eye movements are the result of muscle movements, which in turn create sensations that we come to associate with various distances. Similarly, objects are perceived clearly through **accommodation**, in which changes in the shape of the lens serve to keep objects focused on the retina. Closer objects produce a greater bulging of the lens than objects farther away. Again, these changes are accompanied by muscle action and sensations to be associated with different distances.

The basic principles of optics had been known for some time, and it had been common knowledge since Descartes that the retinal image was inverted, as shown in Figure 2.3, taken from Berkeley's book. The question was how we manage to see an upright world. Berkeley rejected as oversimplified the notion that our brain simply makes a correction and proposed instead that once again, the key lies in our experience with the world. Specifically, we learn to relate what we see with what we experience using our other senses, especially touch and the senses related to physical movement. We develop concepts

---

[4] The reputation was enhanced when Berkeley died. He believed that noticeable decay was the only sure sign of death, so he gave instructions that he not be buried until his body became offensive to the senses.

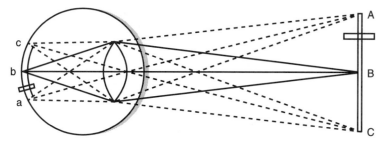

FIGURE 2.3 The inverted retinal image, from Berkeley (1709/1948).

of up and down through our sense of touch, according to Berkeley, by learning that "up" is farther away from the earth than "down." When we touch the top and the bottom of the cross in Figure 2.3, we learn to make the connection between the lower portion of the retinal image and the top of the cross and we come to "see" the top of the cross as being farther away from the earth (i.e., higher) than the bottom of the cross. Again, all depends on experience.

An important theme of Berkeley's theory of vision, clear from the opening sentence of the monocular cues quote, is that we do not see objects directly; rather we make judgments about them based on visual information and our experiences. The theme was carried into his other major work, *Treatise Concerning the Principles of Human Knowledge* (1710/1957), and provided the basis for Berkeley's attack on materialism. Just as we do not see "distance" directly, so it is the case that we do not see "material objects" directly. In both cases, they are "judged" on the basis of perception. Thus, we cannot be entirely certain of the reality of material objects; the only certainty is that we are perceiving. This position of Berkeley's is known as **subjective idealism** (sometimes "immaterialism"). It is in the empiricist tradition because experience is the source of all knowledge, but it destroys the distinction that Locke made between primary and secondary qualities of matter. For Berkeley, everything was a secondary quality. Just as color depends on the perceiving person, so does extension. The only thing that has reality for us is our own perception.

Does this mean that we can never be sure about the reality of the world? Does a tree falling in the forest only exist if we hear it? No. Reality truly exists, according to Berkeley, because objects,

including the tree in the forest, are *always* perceived by God, who Berkeley referred to as the **Permanent Perceiver**. We can be sure of the permanence of reality, but only through our faith in God. In this way, Berkeley sought to attack what he saw as a Godless materialism. Instead, faith in God becomes essential to our understanding of the world.

Berkeley was not successful in countering the trend toward materialism, as will be clear in the next chapter, and despite the complexity of his work on vision, he did not do experiments and thus cannot be considered an early experimental psychologist. By emphasizing the importance of perception in one's understanding of reality, however, and by directly attacking the question of how visual perception actually works, he furthered the cause of British empiricism, while at the same time turning the issue of *how knowledge is acquired* from a purely philosophical question to a more psychological one. As historian of psychology Daniel Robinson put it, Berkeley "rendered epistemology a branch of psychology, and the two have never been divorced since" (1981, p. 228). Once the problem of human knowledge became a psychological one, people began asking different questions. Rather than asking a philosophical question like "How much can be known about the nature of reality?" thinkers now began asking questions like "Just exactly how does visual perception work to enhance what we know?" This shift would eventually bring about a scientific psychology.

British Associationism

Like John Locke, Berkeley had little to say about how our sensory experiences and our reflections combine to produce the more complicated forms of our knowledge. That is, while both addressed the issue of association of ideas, neither carefully examined the phenomenon. Association would soon occupy center stage for British philosophers, however, and be seen as a force controlling the events of mental life. **Associationism** is the doctrine that the mind can be understood as a complex set of ideas, related to each other by the force of the associations between them. Things become associated in our minds by virtue of our experiences in the world; thus, associationism is grounded in empiricism. The British philosophers David Hume and David Hartley both made important contributions to the understanding of how association operated.

David Hume (1711–1776): The Rules of Association

Hume was born near Edinburgh, Scotland, around the time Berkeley was publishing the two books mentioned previously. He entered the University of Edinburgh at age 12, fell in love with literature and philosophy, but left after three years without finishing a degree. He tried the study of law, hated it, then decided on a business career and hated it as well. Determined to become a scholar, he retreated to the French countryside[5] for three years and wrote his first book, *A Treatise of Human Nature* (1739–1740/1969). Thus, like Berkeley, Hume published a major treatise while still in his twenties. Unfortunately, the book did not sell well, disappointing the ambitious Hume, who later said of the book: "It fell deadborn from the press, without reaching such distinction, as even to excite a murmur from the zealots" (quoted in Klein, 1970, p. 552). He later wrote shortened versions of the *Treatise* under different titles, but as a writer he was best known not for his philosophical works, but for a massive, five-volume history of England. Still highly regarded, it went beyond the usual military and political history and incorporated social and literary history into the narrative.

Never modest, Hume believed that his *Treatise* would do for philosophy what Newton had accomplished for physics. Indeed, the subtitle of the treatise is "Being an Attempt to Introduce the Experimental Method of Reasoning into Moral Subjects." By "experimental method," Hume did not mean the use of experiments as we understand the term today, but the careful and systematic observation of human thinking and behavior, mainly his own, accompanied by a logical analysis of the process in order to uncover basic laws of the mind.

In good British empiricist tradition, Hume built his system on the basic premise that all of our understanding is rooted in experience. To dissect human experience, Hume first tried to discover the mind's basic elements, analogous to the physicist's atoms. Upon reflection, Hume believed these elements were two in number: impressions and ideas. **Impressions** are basic sensations, the raw data of experience. We feel pleasure, we see red, we taste sweetness, and so on. **Ideas**, on the other hand, are "faint copies" of impressions. That is, while similar to impressions, and deriving from them, ideas are not as vivid. To support his contention that ideas derived from impressions, Hume noted that it is possible to reduce all of our ideas to impressions, even complex ideas that have never been experienced directly. Thus, even if we have never found a real four-leaf clover, we can have a complex idea of it by combining simple ideas (e.g., "four" and "clover" and "green") that can indeed be traced to impressions.

Note that Hume's analysis of impressions and ideas is mainstream British empiricism. If all ideas are faint copies of impressions, then all ideas derive from the impressions we experience in life. Hence, there are no innate ideas. Also, Hume included the Lockean distinction between simple and complex ideas. But how do impressions connect with ideas and how are complex ideas formed? How does one idea lead to another? In a word, from the process of association, the analysis of which Hume considered perhaps his major achievement.

Hume proposed three laws of association: resemblance, contiguity, and cause/effect. Sometimes an object reminds us of another because it is similar to or has a **resemblance** to it. Thus, a photo of Yosemite's Half Dome resembles the actual piece of granite, and brings to mind memories (ideas), perhaps of a visit to Yosemite Valley. **Contiguity** means experiencing

---

[5] He chose the quiet town of La Flèche, known for the Jesuit school that trained Descartes.

things together. Thus, because the purist eats lobster only in Maine, thinking of lobster brings to mind the Maine coast. Hume's third law of association concerned the relationship between **cause and effect**. If one event follows another with some regularity, we will develop an association between the two. Hume's example was a healed wound. The original wound "caused" us to experience pain; thus, when we now examine the old wound, we are reminded of the pain and the circumstances that produced it. But what determines causes and effects? Hume's answer made him a controversial figure in his day, but might have been his most important contribution to modern psychology.

Hume believed that we can never be absolutely certain about the causes of events. Rather, all we can know is that events occur together with some predictable regularity. To conclude that A causes B, he argued, it is necessary to know that (a) when A occurs, B occurs regularly, (b) A occurs before B does, and (c) B does not occur unless A does. Invoking empiricist thinking and aware of the basic problem of induction, Hume pointed out that we only know about these regularities because of our experience. Furthermore, because our experiences are limited, we can never be certain about the causes of events. Hume's conclusion that absolute certainty was unattainable labeled him a "skeptic," and brought him into conflict with sources of authority such as the church, which naturally took offense at the implication that the existence of God could be questioned.

It is important to note, however, that Hume did not deny the existence of reality, God, or the possibility of there being absolute causes of events. His point was that we could never arrive at them with certainty. From the practical standpoint of day-to-day living, what is important, Hume believed, is to be able to accumulate enough experience to make the best possible predictions. If events occurred together reliably in the past, we have every reason to expect that they will co-occur in the future. Thus, Hume was not denying causality; he was merely shifting it from a search for absolute causes to a search for greater-than-chance regularities. Modern psychologists searching for the "causes" of behavior are essentially following Hume's lead in this regard. They recognize that multiple factors contribute to all behaviors; the best one can hope

for is to identify the factors that predict behaviors with probabilities greater than chance.

David Hartley (1705–1757):
A Physiological Associationism
Hume certainly paid heed to the process of association, but the topic commanded an even greater share of David Hartley's attention. He broke little new ground and is not known as an original thinker, but his *Observations on Man, His Frame, His Duty, and His Expectations* (1749/1971) summarized the essentials of British empiricist thought with great clarity and added a forceful description of how association could be the guiding principle for a theory of how the human mind was structured and how it operated. Because the book also attempted to describe the neurological correlates of mental activity, it also marks an important step in the development of physiological psychology. Published exactly 100 years after Descartes' *The Passions of the Soul*, Hartley's *Observations* is a worthy successor.

Hartley was born in the north of England (in Yorkshire), educated at Cambridge, and headed for a career in imitation of his minister father when doctrinal problems intervened. He discovered that he was unable to believe in the idea of eternal damnation, one of the so-called Thirty-Nine articles of faith that had to be accepted by ministers of the Anglican Church. His next choice was medicine and he eventually earned his living as a successful practitioner. In his spare time, he founded British Associationism.

Hartley was a contemporary of Hume, but not influenced by him. He began preliminary drafts of his *Observations* in the early 1630s, prior to Hume's 1639 *Treatise*, and he seemed to be unaware of Hume's work (not surprising, considering the latter book's poor sales). Three years before producing the final *Observations*, Hartley published a version of the book as an appendix to a medical book on kidney and bladder stones. The appendix was written in Latin, under the tentative-sounding title of *Conjecturae*; apparently, Hartley wished to preview his ideas to a restricted group of scholars before going public with it (Webb, 1988).

Hartley made it clear in the book's opening sentence that he was a dualist on the mind-body question: "Man consists of two parts, body and mind" (Hartley, 1749/1971, p. i). Unlike Descartes' interactionism, however, Hartley took a stance known as **psychophysical parallelism**. That is, he considered psychological and physical (physiological) events separately, but operating in parallel, even structuring the book as a series of propositions that alternated between the mind and the body. The widely quoted propositions X and XI outline the core of his associationism, first on the mental side, then on the physical. Proposition 10 reads, in part:

> Any Sensations A, B, C, &c. by being associated with one another a sufficient Number of Times, get such Power over the corresponding Ideas a, b, c, &c. that any one of the Sensations A, when impressed alone, shall be able to excite in the Mind b, c, &c. the ideas of the rest.
>
> Sensations may be said to be associated together, when their Impressions are either made precisely at the same Instant of Time, or in the contiguous successive Instants. We may therefore distinguish Association into two sorts, the synchronous, and the successive. (Hartley, 1749/1971, p. 65)

For Hartley, then, the main law of association is **contiguity**, the experiencing of events together. If we repeatedly see Adam (A), Brent (B), and Charlie (C) together, with each sensory experience producing the corresponding ideas of them (A, B, and C), then in the future if we see Adam (A), the ideas of Brent (B) and Charlie (C) will occur to us. The chances of this happening relate to how often we have seen the three of them together. Thus, the strength of association relies on **repetition**. Furthermore, contiguity occurs either for events experienced simultaneously or in quick succession. Although Hartley used the terms synchronous and successive, these concepts are commonly referred to as **spatial contiguity** and **temporal contiguity**, respectively. Thinking of your house might lead you to think of your dog sitting by the front door (spatial), while your dog's drooling might be the result of it associating your smiling face with the immediate presentation of food (temporal).[6]

---

[6] As you can guess from the latter example, contiguity was an important concept for the Russian physiologist, Ivan Pavlov, whom you will encounter in Chapter 10.

There is no need to quote Hartley's Proposition 11 because it is identical to Proposition 10, except that the word "Vibrations" substitutes for "Sensations" and the phrase "miniature Vibrations" replaces "Ideas." This was Hartley's version of nervous system activity, taken from Sir Isaac Newton, who suggested that all matter could be conceptualized as vibrating particles in space. Hartley had the advantage over Descartes in knowing that the nerves were not hollow; hence, there was no space for animal spirits to be flowing back and forth. Rather, nerves were tightly packed fibers and he believed they conveyed sensory information by vibrating. In the brain, smaller nerves produced even smaller vibrations, which Hartley called "miniature vibrations" or miniatures. These correspond to ideas. Like Hume, who referred to ideas as "faint copies" of impressions, Hartley thought of ideas (miniature vibrations) as less "vigorous" than sensations (vibrations).

Hartley's model of the mind was a kind of building-block structure in which complex ideas were constructed from the individual component parts. He used the complex idea of a horse as an example, writing that "we could have no proper idea of the Horse, unless the particular Ideas of the Head, Neck, Body, Legs, and Tail, peculiar to this Animal, stuck to each other in the Fancy [i.e., occurred to us], from frequent joint Impression" (Hartley, 1749/1971, p. 71). These subparts can also be divisible into even simpler ideas (e.g., legs include hoofs, etc.). If we experience all these atomistic elements frequently enough, then seeing a part of a horse (e.g., a hoof) will make us think of the horse as a whole.

Hartley's analysis brings the issue of atomism versus "holism" into focus. Most of the British philosophers took an atomistic approach, with Hartley perhaps being the most explicit of the philosophers considered thus far. One problem with this approach is that it requires knowledge of the parts before one can know the whole. That is, complex ideas are built up from simpler ones. In his horse example, Hartley wrote of the parts "coalescing" into the whole animal. The whole is equal to the sum of its parts. **Holism**, on the other hand, argues for the primacy of the whole over its constituent elements, that the parts have no meaning without first knowing the whole. The psychologist G. F. Stout once used the example of a pyramid constructed of oval stones as an example (Klein, 1970). Each element of the pyramid may be perfectly round, but the whole figure has an overall triangular shape not found in any of its parts. The holistic approach would eventually find a voice within psychology through the work of the Gestalt psychologists (Chapter 9).

Hartley was clearly in the atomist camp and he had a direct influence on James Mill (1773–1836), another in the long line of British empiricists and associationists. The influence is clear from this often-quoted example provided by Mill in his *Analysis of the Phenomena of the Human Mind* (1829/1948):

> Brick is one complex idea, mortar is another complex idea; these ideas, with ideas of position and quantity, compose my idea of a wall. My idea of a plank is a complex idea, my idea of a rafter is a complex idea, my idea of a nail is a complex idea.

> These, united with the same ideas of position and quantity, compose my duplex idea of a floor. In the same manner, my complex idea of glass, wood, and others, compose my duplex idea of a window; and these duplex ideas, united together, compose my idea of a house. ... How many complex, or duplex ideas, are all united in the idea of furniture? How many more in the idea of merchandise? How many more in the idea called Every Thing? (p. 154)

Mill was an important character in British philosophy, and like Hume was also well-known as a historian; his *History of British India*, written in 1817, helped him to become financially secure. James Mill was not as important as his son, however, an outcome that Mill, Senior, deliberately set out to produce by systematically applying empiricist and associationist doctrine to the early education of Mill, Junior. Read the Close-Up for more on the deliberate shaping of a philosopher.

CLOSE-UP:
Raising a Philosopher

James Mill was not content simply to write about the importance of experience for developing the mind. When his son was born, he was determined to put empiricism into action by filling the empty white paper of his son's mind with as much information as possible. John Stuart Mill experienced (endured might be a better term) an unusual childhood and described it later in a brief yet remarkable autobiography (Mill, 1873/1989).

Mill, Junior, never went to school with other children, but by his twelfth birthday, he could match the intellectual accomplishments of any university graduate. Under his father's stern tutelage, he started learning Greek vocabulary at age three, Latin at age eight, and by the time he was 10 he had read most of the classic Greek and Roman texts, ranging from *Aesop's Fables* to Plato's *Dialogues* to the Greek histories of Herodotus (the "father" of history) to Aristotle's *Rhetoric*. He also devoured art and literature and mastered algebra and geometry. For fun he read books like *Robinson Crusoe*, the *Arabian Nights*, and Shakespeare's history plays. The latter might have reflected a minor rebellion against his father, who "never was a great admirer of Shakespeare, the English idolatry of whom he used to attack with some severity" (Mill, 1873/1989, p. 35).

Young Mill spent the better part of each day in his lessons. His father tutored him directly, but he was also expected to learn a great deal on his own. A typical routine was for Mill to read a portion of some book, take notes, then report on it to his father the following day, during prebreakfast walks through the countryside. Mill later wrote, "my earliest recollections of green fields and wild flowers [were] mingled [with] the account I gave him daily of what I had read the day before" (p. 29). During the walks, his father would also lecture to him on "civilization, government, morality, [and] mental cultivation, which he required me afterwards to restate to him in my own words" (p. 30). The education continued even when Mill, Senior, was doing his own work. Mill admired his father's ability to write while being constantly interrupted by the small boy at the other end of the table. The image painted by Mill is unintentionally humorous:

> What he was himself willing to undergo for the sake of my instruction, may be judged from the fact, that I went through the whole process of preparing my Greek lessons in the same room and at the same table at which he was writing: and as in those days Greek and English Lexicons were not [available], I was forced to have recourse to him for the meaning of every word which I did not know. This incessant interruption he, one of the most impatient of men, submitted to, and wrote under that interruption several volumes of his *History* [of India] and all else that he had to write during those years. (p. 28)

John Stuart Mill is often cited as an example of a brilliant child prodigy, one whose innate intellectual gifts enabled him to learn so much so soon. There is probably some truth in this, but Mill never believed it for a minute. Because he was not allowed to play with other children as he was growing up, he had no point of comparison except for his father. In fact, throughout his childhood he was under the impression, as he put it, that "I was rather backward in my studies, since I always found myself so, in comparison with what my father expected from me" (Mill, 1873/1989, p. 46). When he eventually realized how far advanced he was, he showed the empiricist spirit by crediting it to his experiences rather than to any innate ability. Indeed, he believed his "natural gifts [to be] rather below than above par" (p. 44) and that his advantages over others resulted from their inferior educations. In his self-effacing words, his accomplishments "could not be ascribed to any merit in me, but to the very unusual advantage which had fallen to my lot, of having a father who was able to teach me" (pp. 46–47).

John Stuart Mill (1806–1873): On the Verge of Psychological Science

Mill's adult life was no less extraordinary than his childhood. Following in his father's footsteps, he supported himself through what amounted to foreign service work with the British East India Company, starting as a clerk at age 17 and gradually rising through the ranks to an executive position; royalties from the sales of his books eventually assured him a comfortable living. In his later years, he was elected to Parliament's House of Commons and served there for three years. Very little else about his life was conventional. Raised by his father to be a "reasoning machine," he became a committed activist for political and social reform by age 15, but then suffered a severe "mental crisis" at age 20. While in a generally "dull state of nerves," he asked himself,

> "Suppose that all your objects in life were realized; that all the changes in institutions and opinions which you are looking forward to, could be completely effected at this very instant: would this be a great joy and happiness to you?" And an irrepressible self-consciousness distinctly answered, "No!" At this my heart sank within me: the whole foundation on which my life was constructed fell down. ... I seemed to have nothing to live for. (Mill, 1873/1989, p. 112)

After several lethargic years, Mill emerged from this depression, partly as a result of discovering Wordsworth. The beauty of the Lake poet's words awakened an emotional life in Mill for the first time, showing him there was more to life than cold rationality. His feelings were further developed when he met and fell madly in love with Harriet Taylor, a remarkable woman who combined great beauty with a keen intellect. Unfortunately for Mill, Taylor was married, happily it appears. Despite the impediment, a relationship between the two developed, with Mill even living with the Taylors for a brief time and tagging along on vacations. The alliance was evidently platonic, but it created a minor scandal nonetheless. They finally married in 1851, two years after John Taylor's death. Harriet contributed significantly to Mill's work while she lived, especially his most important political work, *On Liberty*, published in 1858. After she died unexpectedly in 1858, her daughter carried on the intellectual partnership with Mill. Helen Taylor contributed to Mill's classic feminist essay, *The Subjection of Women* (1869), which argued forcefully and well ahead of its time for equal treatment for women, including the vote. Helen was more of an activist than her mother, helping to create Britain's first women's suffrage organization and recruiting such well-known women as Florence Nightingale into the group (see Figure 2.4).

Mill's politics derived from and contributed to his psychology. As an empiricist, he believed that all knowledge came through experience and that under the proper circumstances, anyone could become knowledgeable. Thus, he favored government support for universal education and was appalled at the traditional English system that favored the landed gentry, an elite minority. At the same time, he was opposed to allowing everyone the vote. Rather, he endorsed a type of meritocracy, in which the vote would be given only to those men and women who had reached a certain level of education. In short, he aimed for a society that endeavored to fill everyone's blank slates to the maximum.

Mill's Psychology

Mill's views on psychology can be found scattered in several places, including his *System of Logic* (1843/1987), which will be examined shortly, in the extensive notes that he wrote for a republication of his father's *Analysis*, published in 1869, and in his *Examination of Sir William Hamilton's Philosophy* (1865). His attack on Hamilton is another illustration of the strong connection between Mill's reforming zeal and his psychological views, and places him

FIGURE 2.4 John Stuart Mill and stepdaughter Helen Taylor, from Mazlish (1975).

squarely on the nurture side of the nature-nurture issue. Mill identified Hamilton's rationalism with a belief in innate ideas and argued that the result produced an antireform philosophy. As he put it,

> I have long felt that the prevailing tendency to regard all the marked distinctions of human character as innate, and in the main indelible, and to ignore the irresistible proofs that by far the greater part of those differences, whether between individuals, races, or sexes, are ... produced by differences in circumstances, is one of the chief hindrances to the rational treatment of great social questions and one of the greatest stumbling blocks to human improvement. (Mill, 1873/1989, p. 203)

Mill subscribed to the basic tenets of British empiricism/associationism, but he extended the ideas of his father and others (especially Hartley) by using a chemical rather than a mechanical metaphor in his description of how complex ideas are built from simple ones. The earlier quote from James Mill ("Brick is one complex idea, mortar is another complex idea," etc.) portrays the mind as passively accumulating experiences in which the elements combine mechanically to form larger wholes. John Stuart Mill, however, believed the mind to be a more active force in synthesizing our experiences; he argued the holistic position that complex ideas are more than a passive combination of elements:

> When many impressions or ideas are operating in the mind together, there sometimes takes place a process of a similar kind to chemical combination. When impressions have been so often experienced in conjunction that each of them calls up readily and instantaneously the ideas of the whole group, those ideas sometimes melt and coalesce into one another, and appear not several ideas, but one. ... [So] it appears to me that the Complex Idea, formed by blending together of several simpler ones, should, when it really appears simple (that is, when the separate elements are not consciously distinguishable in it), be said to *result from*, or be *generated by*, the simple ideas, not to *consist* of them. (Mill, 1843/1987, p. 39–40, italics in the original)

A wall, then, derives from the simple ideas of our experiences, but goes beyond the basic combination of brick and mortar and has properties all its own, just as water has its own properties even though it results from the simple elements of hydrogen and oxygen. To use the phrase later popularized by Gestaltists, the whole is greater than the sum of its parts.

Mill's Logic

In 1843, Mill published *A System of Logic, Ratiocinative and Inductive, Being a Connected View of the Principles of Evidence, and the Methods of Scientific Investigation*. It included some of his beliefs about association and mental chemistry, and it included an argument for the creation of a scientific approach to the study of psychology (he called it *ethology*), on the grounds that while it might not reach the level of precision of physics, it could do as well as other disciplines that were considered scientific at the time (e.g., meteorology). The *Logic* also outlined a series of methods for applying inductive logic while trying to determine causality in science. He called them the methods of Agreement, Difference, and Concomitant Variation. Descriptions of these methods remain popular today—in my collection of some three dozen modern research methods texts, Mill is mentioned in many of them and his methods are described in some detail in half a dozen.

In the **Method of Agreement**, one looks for a common element in several instances of an event. For example, suppose a researcher suspects that a particular gene causes depression. Let X symbolize the proposed cause (the gene) and Y symbolize the effect (depression). To use the method of agreement, the researcher studies a sample of depressed people and looks to see if they all have gene X. If they do, then it can be said that X is sufficient for Y to occur: "if X, then Y." Does this mean that X caused Y? Not

KEY DATE *1843*

This year marked the publication of John Stuart Mill's *Logic*, which included the foundational rules for conducting empirical research.

These events also occurred:

- English physicist J. P. Joule determined the amount of work needed to produce a unit of heat
- The *SS Great Britain*, first propeller-driven ship to cross the Atlantic, was launched
- Congress granted S. F. B. Morse $30,000 to build first telegraph line (Washington-Baltimore)
- Charles Dickens published *Martin Chuzzlewit* and *A Christmas Carol*
- William Wordsworth was appointed English poet laureate
- Daniel Webster retired as U.S. Secretary of State
- These people were born:
    William McKinley, U.S. President
    Henry James, novelist and brother of psychologist William James
- These people died:
    John Trumbull, American painter
    Noah Webster, American lexicographer

necessarily, and the example illustrates the problem with induction. Every depressed person in the sample might have X, but it is possible that some yet undiscovered person is depressed but does not have gene X. Also, the coexistence of X and Y does not by itself mean that they are connected. It could be coincidental that the depressed people in the sample all have gene X. The method of agreement can both support some hypothesis and call it into question, but it cannot establish cause by itself.

Neither can the **Method of Difference**, in which one looks for evidence that the absence of an effect is always accompanied by the absence of a proposed cause: "if not X, then not Y." To stay with the depression example, this would mean examining nondepressed people and looking for gene X, hoping not to find it. If this outcome occurs, then one can say that gene X is necessary in order for depression to occur, because without X (the gene), nobody is Y (depressed). Again, there are problems. A sample of nondepressed people, none of whom have the gene, does not prove the case; there still could be some nondepressed people out there with gene X.

Combined, in what Mill called the **Joint Method**, the methods of agreement and difference have the potential for identifying cause, within the limits of induction (i.e., you will never study every case). Thus, if it could be determined that every person with gene X is also depressed, and that every person without gene X is not depressed, then it could be concluded that gene X is both sufficient and necessary for depression to occur (i.e., the gene causes depression). Of course, the conclusion about cause would be tentative, subject to potential disprove in the future sometime.

The logic of the methods of agreement and difference underlie the use of the modern-day experimental method in psychology, with the method of agreement corresponding to an experimental group and the method of difference corresponding to a control group (Rosnow & Rosenthal, 1993). Thus, a hypothetical experiment on the effect of gene (X) on depression (Y) would involve identifying two equal groups and implanting the gene in the experimental group but not in the control group. If everyone in the experimental group comes down with depression (if

X, then Y), and if nobody in the control group gets depressed (if not X, then not Y), then you have evidence that X causes Y (again, within the limits of the sample for your study). Of course, you would have a hard time finding volunteers for this study, an ethical limitation that Mill recognized and, along with a concern about precision of measurement and control, made him skeptical of psychology becoming as rigorously experimental as physics:

> ... Are the laws of the formation of character [i.e., personality] susceptible of a satisfactory investigation by the method of experimentation? Evidently not, because, even if we suppose unlimited power of varying the experiment (which is abstractly possible, but no one but [a] despot has that power ...), a still more essential condition is wanting—the power of performing any of the experiments with scientific accuracy. (Mill, 1843/1987, pp. 50–51)

Mill's third method, that of **Concomitant Variation**, is reminiscent of Hume and underlies today's correlational method. Using this approach, one looks to see if changes in X are associated with predictable changes in Y. The method is especially useful when either X or Y (or both) will be found in every person to some degree. For example, everyone gets at least some exercise and everyone is more or less healthy. Using the method of concomitant variation, a researcher could see if those who exercise a great deal are healthier than those who exercise infrequently.

Unlike any of the philosophers considered thus far, John Stuart Mill did not attempt to write anything like an essay on human understanding (Locke), a treatise on human knowledge (Berkeley) or human nature (Hume), a series of observations on man (Hartley) or an analysis of the mind (his father). That is, none of his books can be pointed to and labeled as "J. S. Mill's psychology." Because he saw himself above all as a political and economic philosopher, this is not too surprising. Yet Mill is as important for modern psychology as any of those philosophers who did write a "psychology." He brought British associationism to its zenith and he provided an analysis of scientific thinking that guides psychological research to this day. He was a key transition figure in the shift from the philosophy of the mind to the science of the mind.

RATIONALIST RESPONSES TO EMPIRICISM

Except for the section on Descartes, this chapter has focused on British empiricist and associationist philosophy. This makes sense, given a strong connection between this philosophical strategy and modern psychology, especially behavioral psychology. But other strong voices were heard during the times that have been described so far, and those voices also resonate with aspects of modern psychology. Two German philosophers make a notable contrast to British empiricism/associationism. Gottfried Leibniz was a contemporary of Locke and responded to Locke's *Essay Concerning Human Understanding* with his own *New Essays on Human Understanding*, published posthumously in 1765. Immanuel Kant lived during the same time as Hume and Hartley and wrote in response to them (especially Hume).

Gottfried Wilhelm Leibniz (1646–1716)

Leibniz had a remarkably wide range of interests, from politics to mathematics to engineering to alchemy to philosophy. As a mathematician, he is best known as the coinventor (with Newton) of calculus. His importance for psychology rests with his reply to Locke, his approach to the mind-body problem, and his "monadology." He was a great admirer of Locke, agreeing that experience is essential to the formation of knowledge. However, he disagreed with Locke's "mind = white paper" metaphor, proposing instead that the mind be seen as analogous to veined marble (Leibniz, 1765/1982). It's a beautiful metaphor for the nature-nurture issue. The sculptor can take a block of marble and shape it in many different ways, but the way the marble is veined limits the number of shapes that are possible. The veins in essence represent the innate properties of the marble, to be revealed by the artist's skill. Similarly, according to Leibniz, the mind has innate properties that help

determine the limits of and shape the effects of experience. The innate properties, such as reason, enable the individual to arrive at what Leibniz called "necessary truths," truths that are proven with reason and logic and not by direct experience. The fundamental principles of mathematics (e.g., three sides of a triangle will always add up to 180°) are examples of necessary truths. In response to the empiricist claim that there was nothing in the intellect that was not first in the senses, Leibniz replied, "except the intellect itself!" Like Descartes, Leibniz agreed that animals lacked the innate properties found in humans, and thus could be considered pure "empirics."

On the mind-body question, Leibniz could not accept the Cartesian notion of direct and mutual influence, because it led inevitably to a search for the manner of interaction and resulted in what Leibniz considered to be a fruitless hunt for things like pineal glands. Instead, he proposed a **psychophysical parallelism** solution to the mind-body problem, similar to that proposed by Hartley. Thus, he proposed that mind ("psycho") and body ("physical") work in parallel to each other, kept in a "pre-established harmony," as Leibniz put it, by the hand of God. He illustrated his parallelism with a metaphor of two clocks that are constructed to be in perfect harmony. Like mind and body, they operate independently of each other, but in agreement. By implication, parallelism legitimizes the separate study of mental (psychological) and physical (biological) events, thus providing a philosophical basis for "the eventual emergence of psychology as a separate science as distinct from physiology as a separate science" (Klein, 1970, p. 353).

The elements of both mental and physical reality were called **monads** by Leibniz. These were infinite in number and more like energy forces than individual material atoms. They were said to be arranged in a hierarchy, from rational to sentient to simple. Rational monads, according to Leibniz, form the essence of the human mind, sentient monads are found in all living beings that were not human, and simple monads make up physical reality. Rational monads account for consciousness, but Leibniz believed that awareness was not an all-or-nothing affair. Rather, he proposed a continuum of awareness, thus laying a foundation for two important developments in psychology. First, the continuum implies a level of unawareness, an idea similar to the concept of the unconscious, which was later to become the centerpiece of Freud's theories. Leibniz distinguished between what he called apperception, perception, and petites perceptions. **Apperception**, a term he coined, was the highest level of awareness, in which we focus our attention on some information and apprehend it fully. Perception is an awareness of something, but it is not as sharp as in apperception. **Petites perceptions** were below the level of awareness, but ultimately essential for enabling higher levels of perception to occur. To illustrate the latter, Leibniz used the example of an ocean wave or a waterfall. Petite perceptions are created by individual drops of water, which we never hear. Yet all of the drops, taken together, are necessary in order for us to perceive or apperceive the larger reality of the ocean wave.

The second implication of the proposal about different levels of awareness is that there must exist points on the continuum of consciousness where one goes from unawareness to awareness; these points can be called thresholds and as we will learn in the next chapter, identifying and measuring thresholds became an important feature of the earliest experiments in psychology.

Immanuel Kant (1724–1804)

In his role as a diplomat, Leibniz traveled throughout Europe. In contrast, Immanuel Kant evidently never ventured more than 40 miles from his home in the eastern German city of Königsberg. He was born there, went to school there, and eventually taught at the university there. Despite the apparent provincialism, Kant was a towering intellect in eighteenth-century German philosophy, doing for the rationalist view what Leibniz had done in the seventeenth century. Kant is best known to psychologists for three books published in his later years, *Critique of Pure Reason* (1781/1965), *Critique of Practical Reason* (1788/1959), and *Critique of Judgment* (1790/1952).

Kant agreed with the empiricists that our knowledge is built from experience, but like Leibniz, he argued that the more important question was how the

process occurs. That is, he wondered how experience itself was possible, and he concluded that it required the existence of some a priori (prior to experience) knowledge that helps shape the experiences we have. For instance, Kant pointed out that whenever we experience events in the world, we organize them with reference to space and time. Thus, we water the garden, which occupies space, and which takes X amount of time to complete. Our understanding of the concept "water the garden" is not possible without the a priori knowledge of space and time. The concepts of space and time, then, we know "intuitively," according to Kant; we don't have to "learn" about the concepts. To contrast Hume's view that we can never be certain of causality, Kant argued that the mind inevitably thinks in terms of cause and effect—everyone's experience of the world is that it operates according to causal laws (milk poured on earth always goes down). Like space and time, cause and effect were considered by Kant to be innate properties of the mind.

A final point about Kant is that he argued that psychology could never become a science like the physical sciences. He pointed out that compared with physical objects, mental phenomena could not be observed directly, nor could they be defined or measured with the precision of mathematics. As we shall learn, when German psychologists such as Wilhelm Wundt declared psychology a science in the nineteenth century, they had to specifically disavow their countryman's contentions about the feasibility of the endeavor.

IN PERSPECTIVE

This chapter only scratches the surface of psychology's "long past." Nonetheless, you should emerge from your reading of this material with a basic understanding of some of the philosophical underpinnings of modern psychology. Furthermore, you should be starting to develop a sense of the continuity of ideas in our discipline's history. Psychology did not just pop out of the ground in the late nineteenth century. Rather, psychology's founders were wrestling with the same issues that concerned the people highlighted in this chapter. They chose to attack the questions from a slightly different angle than the philosophers, that of direct experimentation, but they were trying to answer the same questions: How do we accumulate our knowledge of the world? How is the mind organized? How do the senses work? Is any of our knowledge built in to the system (i.e., innate)? The founders of nineteenth-century psychology also had an ever-increasing knowledge of how the brain and the rest of the nervous system worked and they were beginning to develop objective methods for studying the mind. You are about to encounter these developments in physiology and methods in Chapter 3.

Before closing this chapter, however, there is an important point to be made about presentism. From the standpoint of the early twenty-first century, knowing that psychology evolved into a large and successful scientific discipline, it is easy to look back at the early philosophers and wonder why they

failed to take what might appear to be an easy step— the one from careful observations and a close logical analysis of some mental phenomenon to the experimental investigation of it. That is, when we first read of people like Descartes and Locke and Mill, we tend to see them as gradually approaching but not quite reaching the "holy grail" of scientific psychology. It is a serious mistake, however, to think of these individuals as somehow falling short. In fact, they were clearly the best and the brightest of their day, going far beyond their peers in the brilliance of their insights. The proper way to view the philosophers in this chapter is to think of them as people living in the context of their times and grappling as best they could with the issues of their day. That these philosophers wrestled with the same questions that exist today is not an indication of steady progress upward from then to now, but of the universality of the issues. It is futile and patently unfair to criticize them for not seeing what others saw later.

SUMMARY

A LONG PAST

• The Ebbinghaus statement that psychology has a long past but a short history is a reminder that the issues of concern to psychologists have been addressed by serious thinkers for thousands of years, even though psychology as a self-defined discipline is just over 120 years old. The "new psychology" that emerged in the late nineteenth century differed from philosophy in that the questions about human behavior and mental life were taken into the laboratory for the first time.

DESCARTES AND THE BEGINNINGS OF MODERN PHILOSOPHY AND SCIENCE

• Descartes lived during the end of the Renaissance and during years of great advances in science and technology. It was a time when the authority of the Church and of Aristotle came to be questioned, by Galileo's support for the Copernican heliocentric model of the universe instead of the traditional geocentric model, for example. Descartes' life also overlapped that of Sir Francis Bacon, who argued for an inductive scientific strategy for understanding the universe.

• Descartes was a rationalist, believing that the way to true knowledge was through the systematic use of his reasoning abilities. Because he believed that some truths were universal and could be arrived at through reason and without the necessity of sensory experience, he was also a nativist. In addition, he was a dualist and an interactionist, believing that mind and body were distinct essences, but that they had direct influence on each other.

• To explain mind-body interactionism, Descartes developed a model of nervous system activity and was the first person to describe reflex action. His model of bodily action was a mechanistic one—the body was like a machine. According to the Cartesian dichotomy, animals are pure machines, but humans have a rational mind (soul) to complement their machinelike bodies.

THE BRITISH EMPIRICIST ARGUMENT AND THE ASSOCIATIONISTS

• The founder of British empiricism was John Locke, who rejected the nativist belief in innate ideas and argued that the mind was like a blank piece of paper, to be written on by our experiences. Ideas that result from our experiences have two sources: sensation and reflection. Locke used an atomistic model, assuming that complex ideas were built from the basic elements of simple ideas. Primary qualities (e.g., extension) exist independently of the perceiver, but secondary qualities (e.g., the perception of color) depend on perception. Locke's beliefs led him to recommend that parents take an active role in educating their children, that children be encouraged with praise rather than concrete rewards, and that punishment be avoided as an educational strategy.

- George Berkeley wrote a detailed analysis of visual perception based on empiricist arguments, in the process describing visual phenomena such as convergence, accommodation, and the effects of the inverted retinal image. He rejected Locke's primary/secondary qualities distinction, and to counter materialism, he proposed (subjective idealism) that we cannot be sure of the reality of objects except through our belief in God, the Permanent Perceiver.

- David Hume was an empiricist/associationist known for making a distinction between impressions, which result from sensation, and ideas, which he said were faint copies of impressions. He also identified the rules of association as resemblance, contiguity, and cause/effect. He believed that we cannot know causality absolutely, only that certain events occur together regularly.

- David Hartley is considered the founder of associationism because of his systematic attempt to summarize all that was known about it and his argument that the essence of association was contiguity (both spatial and temporal) and repetition. He developed a model of nervous system action based on the Newtonian concept of

vibrations, and his position on the mind-body issue was that of psychophysical parallelism.

- John Stuart Mill, a child prodigy, was the leading British philosopher of the nineteenth century. Compared with others (including his father, the empiricist philosopher James Mill) who described the mind in mechanical, atomistic, building-block terms, J. S. Mill used a more holistic chemical metaphor, arguing that complex ideas are greater than the sum of their individual simple ideas. Mill analyzed the logic of science, and described several methods for trying to arrive at inductive scientific truth: the method of agreement and the method of difference, which underlie today's experimental method, and the method of concomitant variation, similar to the modern correlational method.

RATIONALIST RESPONSES TO EMPIRICISM

- Gottfried Leibniz challenged Locke's white paper analogy and said the mind was more like veined marble, with the veins being analogous to the innate ideas and abilities that shape our experiences. He also challenged Descartes' interactionism, arguing a parallelist position and using the metaphor of two synchronous clocks to make his point. His monadology provided a basis for the concepts of the unconscious and sensory thresholds.

- Immanuel Kant recognized the importance of our experiences for developing our understanding of the world, but argued that experience itself was not possible without a basis in some a priori knowledge to provide the framework for our experiences. Kant believed that psychology could not achieve the status of a science.

STUDY QUESTIONS

1. What did Ebbinghaus mean when he said that psychology had a long past, but a short history?

2. How did a "mechanistic" zeitgeist influence Descartes' thinking?

3. Distinguish between a heliocentric and a geocentric model of the universe and explain why advocating the former earned Galileo a charge of heresy.

4. Explain what it means to advocate an inductive strategy for gaining knowledge of human behavior.

5. Explain why Descartes is considered (a) a rationalist, and (b) a nativist.

6. Describe Descartes' solution to the mind-body problem. What is meant by the "Cartesian dichotomy?"

7. Compare rationalist and empiricist explanations for how

we arrive at our knowledge of widely held concepts (e.g., God).

8. Compare Locke's white paper and Leibniz's veined model metaphors and relate them to fundamental epistemological questions.

9. Distinguish between primary and secondary qualities of matter and compare the views of Locke and Berkeley with regard to these qualities.

10. Define materialism and explain how Berkeley's subjective idealism attacked the concept.

11. Using Berkeley's examples, show how British empiricists applied their concepts to visual perception.

12. Distinguish between Hume's and Hartley's laws of association.

13. Describe J. S. Mill's mental chemistry and contrast it with his father's view.

14. Show how Mill's rules for inductive logic relate to modern conceptions of the experimental and correlational methods.

15. Show how Leibniz's monadology relates to the concepts of the unconscious and thresholds.

16. Describe Kant's rationalist response to empiricist thinking.

QUESTIONS FROM THE ORIGINAL SOURCE EXCERPT

1. What were animal spirits, how were they formed, and how do they relate to muscle action, according to Descartes?

2. According to Descartes, how does a reflex work? Use the example of the boy putting his foot in a fire.

3. In Descartes' model of the nervous system, how did mind and body interact, and why was the pineal gland chosen as the point of interaction? What was the essential flaw in the logic of identifying a part of the brain (pineal gland) as the point of mutual influence of mind and body?

4. How did Descartes account for memory with his model of the nervous system?

FOR FURTHER READING

Vrooman, J. R. (1970). *René Descartes: A biography*. New York: G. P. Putnam's Sons.

A relatively brief and very readable biography of Descartes, especially descriptive of the times in which Descartes lived; provides a good summary of Descartes' ideas, and how he developed them from his varied experiences.

Boorstin, D. J. (1983). *The discoverers*. New York: Vintage Books.

Includes substantial treatment of many of the scientists briefly mentioned in this chapter, including Vesalius, Galileo, Bacon, Boyle, Newton, and Harvey, written in a style that makes Boorstin one of the more popular modern historians.

Mill, J. S. (1989). *Autobiography*. London: Penguin Books. (Original work published 1873)

Fascinating account of Mill's childhood and relationship with his father, his mental crisis and how he overcame it, his relationship with Harriet Taylor, and the development of his ideas; can be occasionally confusing without some knowledge of British political history during Mill's time.

Sobel, D. (2000). *Galileo's daughter: A historical memoir of science, faith, and love*. New York: Penguin.

A lively account of Galileo's research and how it landed him in hot water with the Catholic Church; elegant description of the historical context of Galileo's (and therefore Descartes') time, with part of the story told through a remarkable set of letters between Galileo and his daughter, a cloistered nun.

CHAPTER 3

THE NEUROPHYSIOLOGICAL CONTEXT

The entire doctrine of [phrenology] is contained in two fundamental propositions, of which the first is, that understanding resides exclusively in the brain, and the second, that each particular faculty of the understanding is provided in the brain with an organ proper to itself.

Now, of these two propositions, there is certainly nothing new in the first one, and perhaps nothing true in the second one.

—Pierre Flourens, 1846

PREVIEW AND CHAPTER OBJECTIVES

Partitioning the philosophical antecedents to psychology and the neurophysiological background into two chapters implies the presence of two nonoverlapping paths that eventually merged to form the new psychology of the late nineteenth century. There is a grain of truth to this—the British empiricists did not spend their time cutting into spinal cords or stimulating nerves connected to frogs legs, and the scientists to be encountered in this chapter did not write long philosophical treatises on "human understanding." But the distinction between philosophical and physiological antecedents to psychology is artificial, brought about by the decisions made when structuring a textbook. In fact, developments in philosophy and in the natural sciences proceeded apace, especially in the eighteenth and nineteenth centuries. The physiologists and other natural scientists were deeply concerned with philosophical issues, especially the epistemological questions about human understanding and the problem of the relationship between mental and physical reality (the mind-body problem). In turn, philosophers were well aware of, and in some instances contributed to, developments in physiology (e.g., Berkeley's work on vision), and they proposed theories that led naturally to physiological research.

This chapter will focus on nineteenth- and early twentieth-century studies of the nature and functioning of the nervous system. In particular, we will examine research that explored (a) the physiology of basic sensory-motor processes and reflexes, (b) the issue of whether specific functions could be "localized" in different areas of the brain, and (c) the nature of the basic unit of the nervous system, the neuron. The chapter closes with a description of Karl Lashley's research on the role of the cortex in learning. Lashley was the twentieth century's first prominent physiological psychologist. The Original Source Excerpt is from Broca's famous case history of "Tan." This case helped establish the clinical method of identifying brain functions. After you finish this chapter, you should be able to:

■ Show how Enlightenment thinking contributed to the idea that psychology could become scientific

■ Describe and explain the importance of Whytt's research on reflex action

■ Describe and explain the importance of the Bell-Magendie law and the research that led to it

■ Describe the doctrine of the specific energies of nerves

■ Describe Helmholtz's research on nerve impulse speed and relate it to the vitalism-materialism issue

■ Describe the contributions of Helmholtz to vision, hearing, and to the problem of perception

■ Describe the essential tenets of phrenology, explain why it ultimately failed scientifically, and explain its popularity, especially in America

■ Describe the logic of the method of ablation and show how Flourens used it to dispute phrenology

■ Describe the clinical method and two different examples of how it shed light on brain function

■ Describe the method of electrical stimulation and the results it produced

■ Describe neuron theory and the research that led to the conclusion that synapses must exist

■ Describe Lashley's research on learning and the brain, his principles of mass action and equipotentiality, and the similarities with conclusions drawn by Flourens

HEROIC SCIENCE IN THE AGE OF ENLIGHTENMENT

As discussed in the last chapter, the years marking the end of the Renaissance were characterized by a gradual change from depending on authority as the source of truth to relying on scientific methodology and human reasoning powers. Bacon, Galileo, Harvey, and Descartes exemplified this shift in the beginning of the seventeenth century. Sir Isaac Newton solidified the change in the second half of the century. With the publication of his *Principia Mathematica* in 1687, serious thinkers began to take for granted the idea that objective truth could be gained through the methods of science and the unbiased use of reason. Because science and reason came to be seen as the only sure way to shed light on the darkness of ignorance, this period became known as the **Enlightenment** (Appleby, Hunt, & Jacob, 1994). Scientists like Newton became heroic figures, searching for "objective truth" about the universe by applying scientific methodology to its study. Newton's influence on the philosophers was mentioned in the last chapter—Newton's analysis of light into basic components and his theory of gravitation influenced the British empiricists, who tried to produce a similar analysis of the mind and thought of association as a force analogous to gravity.

Enlightenment thinking even spread into the political arena. America's founding fathers were passionate and knowledgeable about science, and Benjamin Franklin made substantial contributions to the theory of electricity, including the invention of the lightning rod. The Constitution itself borrowed from the Newtonian concept of equilibrium when developing the concept of a balance of powers among the executive, legislative, and judicial elements of government (Cohen, 1995).

The Enlightenment reached its height of influence in the second half of the eighteenth century, but its ideals remained strong throughout the nineteenth century, and well into the twentieth. By the early nineteenth century, the faith in science seemed to be paying dividends in the form of the kinds of technological innovations that eventually produced the Industrial Revolution. Thus, science seemed to lead inevitably to progress and scientists were viewed as being totally objective, simply looking for the truth without imposing their values in any way, and improving society through the inventions that derived from their science. It wasn't until such technological innovations as the poison gas that "efficiently" reduced the populations of concentration camps and the atom bomb that serious questions began to be raised about whether science could possibly be totally objective and value-free and whether scientific discoveries necessarily meant progress. Nonetheless, during the period when the idea of a scientific approach to psychology began to take shape in the minds of such philosophers as the British empiricists, the model of scientist as hero held sway. If scientific thinking and human reason could enlighten the world about physics and chemistry, why not biology? If biology, why not psychology?

In the middle of the nineteenth century, scientific psychology evolved out of the philosophical questions examined in Chapter 2 and research on the nervous system to be described in this chapter. Physiologists, trying to "shed light" on how the senses and the nervous system actually worked, developed methods and made discoveries that were directly relevant to the epistemological questions about the nature and origins of human knowledge being raised by philosophers such as John Stuart Mill. This dynamic convergence of philosophy and physiological science created an atmosphere out of which a "scientific" psychology was perhaps inevitable.

SENSORY PHYSIOLOGY

From the time of Descartes, scientists had been intrigued by the nature of nervous system activity. Most of the advances resulted from the medical community trying to deal with the problem of brain and nervous system damage, which was quite common in the context of two European wars in the middle of the eighteenth century and both the American and

French revolutions during the second half of that century. At a time long before the development of antiseptic surgical procedures and antibiotic drugs, the vast majority of those suffering head wounds died from infection. Many of those who lived, however, became case studies that increased our knowledge of the brain and nervous system.

One issue of interest was whether the brain was the center of consciousness and the controller of voluntary action. Decapitated soldiers who nonetheless showed arm and leg movements raised questions about how soon consciousness left the body after death and where consciousness was localized. The problem was directly investigated with reference to executions that used the invention of noted French physician Joseph Ignace Guillotin. The device, which now bears his name, was said to be a marvelous improvement over large hairy men with axes, who sometimes required several tries before completing their gruesome task of separating head from body. Although the guillotine was clean and quick and therefore considered humane, bodies continued to twitch for a brief time after execution. Eye movements and quivering facial muscles could also be seen. Did some level of awareness remain after a beheading? If so, then perhaps the instrument was not so humane after all. The problem was investigated in the early nineteenth century by Theodor Bischoff, who arranged to conduct tests on the decapitated head of a criminal immediately after execution. If consciousness remained, Bischoff reasoned, then the head should react predictably to having fingers thrust toward its eyes, having smelling salts placed under its nose, and having the word "Pardon!" spoken in its ear. Bischoff tried all of these tests, but the unfortunate head showed no reaction (Fearing, 1930). He concluded that consciousness ended with the moment of execution, thereby reinforcing the theory that consciousness resides in the brain, while at the same time reassuring investors in guillotines. The muscle twitches that occurred after death were therefore involuntary actions unrelated to consciousness. The question of why they occurred at all still remained, however, resulting in intensive research into the nature of basic reflex action and the role of the spinal cord in these movements.

Reflex Action

Prior to the nineteenth century, the most significant contribution to the study of reflexes was made by Robert Whytt (1714–1766) (pronounced "White") of Edinburgh, Scotland. The leading neurologist of his day, Whytt is known primarily by historians of psychology for his research into the physiology of the involuntary reflex, but he is also justly famous in the history of pediatric medicine for being the first person to adequately describe tuberculous meningitis (Radbill, 1972). With regard to reflexes, in 1751 Whytt published *The Vital and Other Involuntary Motions of Animals,*[1] the outcome of years of research on the role of the spinal cord in mediating reflex action. It was the first extensive treatment of reflexes to be based on experimental research (Fearing, 1930). Studying decapitated animals (mainly frogs) Whytt was able to show that leg muscles responded in predictable ways to physical stimulation. Pinching the leg of a headless frog produced a reliable muscle contraction. On the other hand, if the connection between the nerve in the leg and the spinal cord was severed, these "involuntary motions" failed to occur. Hence, Whytt demonstrated that the spinal cord played a defining role in reflexive behavior.

Whytt distinguished between voluntary and involuntary actions, the former under the control of the will, with the action originating in and requiring an intact brain, and the latter controlled through the spinal cord. In between voluntary and involuntary control, and serving to link them, was habit formation. Thus, actions that begin as voluntary, and under the deliberate control of the will, become similar to reflexes when they have been sufficiently practiced. As Whytt put it,

We not only acquire, through custom and habit, a faculty of performing certain motions with greater ease than we are wont to do them, but

[1] Whytt was a contemporary of David Hartley and published his book just two years after Hartley's *Observations of Man* appeared. You will recall that Hartley went beyond a philosophical treatment and attempted to explain the nervous system by appealing to "vibrations." Whytt does not seem to have been directly influenced by Hartley, but the fact that both men were concerned with the nervous system indicates the importance of the topic to intellectuals of the day.

also, in proportion as this facility is increased, we become less sensible of any share or concern the mind has in them. (cited in Fearing, 1930, p. 79)

Whytt also pointed out that a consequence of the formation of habits was that the mere idea of a stimulus was sometimes sufficient to bring about a response. In a passage that will make you think of Ivan Pavlov (Chapter 10), Whytt illustrated the point with two everyday examples of what would eventually come to be called conditioned reflexes: "Thus the sight, or even the recalled idea of grateful food, causes an uncommon flow of spittle into the mouth of a hungry person; and the seeing of a lemon cut produces the same effect in many people" (cited in Fearing, 1930, p. 80).

The existence of the kinds of reflexes documented by Whytt demands that a distinction be made between the sensory and motor components of a reaction, which in turn implies that some nerves may be for the purpose of conveying sensory information and others designed to pass messages along to the muscles, telling them to move. This distinction between sensory and motor nerves became established through the work of two scientists working at about the same time in different countries.

The Bell-Magendie Law

As you recall from Chapter 1, a "multiple" refers to a case in which two or more people make the same discovery during the same historical era, but do so independently of each other. E. G. Boring (1950) used the concept to support his idea that the zeitgeist helped to determine the activities and ways of thinking of scientists during a particular historical era. The Bell-Magendie law is sometimes used as an example of a multiple—two scientists, working in different laboratories (different countries in this case) at about the same time and neither aware of the other's research, arrive at similar results. The situation was not quite that simple in the case of Bell and Magendie, however, and during the years following their work, there was a nasty fight over priority. The judgment of history is that Magendie should have been credited with the discovery; his research was more systematic and he published it in the public forum of a journal. Bell's research, while occurring a few years earlier than Magendie's, was published in a private pamphlet with limited distribution, and was based more on inference from anatomy than actual experimentation (Sechzer, 1983). Furthermore, Magendie got it right; Bell didn't. That Bell's name became paired with Magendie's is more of a tribute to the public clamoring of the politically influential Bell and his equally vociferous friends than to the quality of his research.

François Magendie (1783–1855) grew up during the turbulent years of the French Revolution, the son of a surgeon who was a politically active "Republican" in the efforts to overthrow the French monarchy. Lacking much in the way of formal education, François used his father's influence to become an apprentice at a Paris hospital, where, at the tender age of 16, he was entrusted with the task of doing anatomical dissections (Grmek, 1972). After becoming a medical student and completing a degree in 1808, he quickly earned a reputation as a gifted scientist who distrusted theorizing in favor of inductively collecting "facts." This Baconian attitude he once described in this way: "I compare myself to a ragpicker: with my spiked stick in my hand and my basket on my back, I traverse the field of science and gather what I find" (cited in Grmek, 1972, p. 7).

In 1822, Magendie published a three-page article that summarized the results of a study on the posterior and anterior roots of the spinal cord. From his earlier dissections he knew that nerve fibers exited the spinal cord in pairs before joining together, with one type of fiber, the posterior root, closer to the surface of the skin, and the other (anterior root) closer to the interior of the body. Different structures suggest different functions, and Magendie's research aimed at identifying these functions.

Using a six-week-old dog as the subject, Magendie exposed its spinal cord and cut the posterior fibers (i.e., those closer to the surface) while leaving the spinal cord intact. He sutured up the wound and observed the animal after it recovered. As he described it,

> ... I did not know what would result from this operation. ... At first I believed the limb corresponding to the cut nerves to be completely paralyzed; it was insensitive to pricking and the hard-

est pressures and, further, it seemed immobile; but soon, to my very great surprise, I clearly saw it move, although sensibility remained completely absent. (Magendie, 1822/1965, p. 20)

Hence, the posterior roots controlled sensation. When destroyed, the animal could still move the limb, but had no sensation in it. Next, Magendie severed the anterior root in another animal, a task that required all of his considerable surgical skills. Because the anterior root lies below the posterior one, it is difficult to get to the former without damaging the latter. Nonetheless, Magendie worked out a successful procedure and managed to sever an anterior root cleanly (Bell, on the other hand, was never able to accomplish this). The results were clear: "there could be no doubt whatsoever; the limb was completely immobile and flaccid, although it retained an unequivocal sensibility" (Magendie, 1822/1965, p. 20). In summary, then, Magendie's finding, now known as the **Bell-Magendie law**, was that the posterior roots of the spinal cord controlled sensation, while anterior roots controlled motor responses. This was a major discovery, for it provided anatomical foundation for further study of the two sides of the reflex: sensation and movement. Furthermore, the distinction implied that nerves send messages in a single direction and there were different sensory and motor tracts within the spinal cord and perhaps different sensory and motor regions within the brain.

As for Sir Charles Bell (1774–1842), his *Idea of a New Anatomy of the Brain: Submitted for the Observation of His Friends* had been written 11 years prior to the publication of Magendie's work, but it had been sent privately to no more than 100 colleagues. Bell was a prominent English anatomist with influential friends, however, and together they launched a campaign against Magendie when the latter's work was published, accusing the Frenchman of everything from unnecessary replication of Bell's original finding to animal cruelty (ether had not been discovered when Magendie did his experiments, so the surgery must have been painful to the young dogs). Bell went as far as to alter the wording of some of his earlier work and republish it to make it appear that he had anticipated Magendie by a decade (Gallistel, 1981). Yet Magendie was unaware of Bell's work, which involved an analysis of anatomy of the spinal cord and an experiment on a "stunned rabbit." Bell deserves some credit for concluding that the posterior and anterior roots had different functions, but he mistakenly concluded that both roots had some sensory and motor function and they were differentiated primarily by virtue of their connections to the cerebellum (posterior roots) and the cerebrum (anterior roots) (Sechzer, 1983).

Magendie, personally affronted by the attacks from across the English Channel, recognized the value of Bell's research once he learned of it, but refused to concede priority for discovering the critical (and correct) distinction between sensory and motor functions. In particular, while acknowledging Bell's priority concerning the strategy of segregating the spinal roots and the discovery that the anterior root influenced "muscular contractility" more than the posterior root did, Magendie vigorously asserted that "as for having established that these roots have distinct properties, distinct functions, that the anterior ones control movement, and posterior ones sensation, *this discovery belongs to me*" (cited in Grmek, 1972, italics added).

The Specific Energies of Nerves

Another feature of Bell's 1811 pamphlet was his argument that different sensory nerves have different "qualities." Thus, "an impression made on two different nerves of sense, though with the same instrument, will produce two distinct sensations" (Bell, 1811/1965, p. 24). As an example, Bell pointed to the "papillae" on the tongue, some of which convey the sense of taste, others the sense of touch. When touching these latter papillae with a sharp steel pin, the resulting sensation is one of "sharpness." When touching one of the taste papillae with the same pin, however, the resulting sensation is one of a "metallic taste." Similarly, if two different types of stimuli affect a single type of nerve, then the sensation experienced will be determined by the type of sensory nerve stimulated. Thus, light waves stimulate the optic nerve to produce a visual sensation, but pressing on the side of the eyeball also results in the sensation of a flash of light and, according to Bell, cataract patients often reported seeing a "spark of fire" when the surgeon's needle pierced their eye.

This idea of Bell's eventually became known as the doctrine of the **specific energies of nerves**, and although Bell's 1811 paper once again had chronological priority, credit went elsewhere, this time to the leading German physiologist of the first half of the nineteenth century, Johannes Müller (1801–1858). Müller, whose frenetic pace of work alternated with several long periods of severe depression, was the first person ever named a professor of "physiology" at the University of Berlin, Germany's premier university. Müller elaborated on the specific energies doctrine and developed it more fully than Bell. In addition to making the point about different sensory qualities, Müller argued that in perception, we are not directly aware of the external world; rather we are only aware of the action of our nervous system, which conveys information of the world to us. Thus, our knowledge of the world is filtered through the physiology of the nervous system.

The doctrine of specific energies of nerves eventually became associated more with Müller than with Bell, mainly because Müller named it as such and presented it as a series of 10 related principles in his massive (eight books totaling more than 1600 pages) *Handbook of Human Physiology*, which first appeared in 1840. This was the authoritative physiology text of the mid-nineteenth century, and its stature guaranteed that Müller's name, not Bell's, would become attached to the doctrine (Boring, 1950).[2]

Helmholtz: The Physiologist's Physiologist

If Müller was the leading German physiologist of the first half of the nineteenth century, the honor for the second half goes to one of his followers, Hermann von Helmholtz (1821–1894). Shortly after he died, Helmholtz was eulogized by Carl Stumpf, another well-known German physiologist, as the person most responsible for building the "bridge between

---

[2] Müller believed that his status had declined after his famous *Handbook* was published and by the mid-1850s, he was convinced that his years as a productive scientist were over. This plunged him into his final depression, and few of his friends believed that his death in 1858 was anything but a deliberate overdose of morphine (Steudel, 1972).

physiology and psychology that thousands of workers today go back and forth upon" (cited in Turner, 1972). Helmholtz became *the* nineteenth-century authority on the sensory systems for vision and audition, developing theories still considered to be at least partly correct. He also provided a simple demonstration of nerve impulse speed that paved the way for one of psychology's most enduring methods, reaction time. And despite accomplishing more than any other nineteenth-century physiologist, his true love actually was physics, to which he also made original contributions!

Helmholtz was born in 1821 into a family of modest means (his father was a teacher) in Potsdam, Germany. He quickly emerged as an academic star at the local gymnasium (high school), where he developed his lifelong love for physics, but financial straits prevented him from attending a university. The government was offering full scholarships for students to attend the medical school in Berlin, however, and Helmholtz jumped at the opportunity, even though it meant committing himself to eight years of service in the army's medical corps (after completing five years of schooling). He left for Berlin in 1838, where he completed the five-year program in four years. While enrolled at the medical institute, he also studied informally at the University of Berlin with the great Johannes Müller. Helmholtz quickly moved into Müller's inner circle and developed lifelong friendships with three other students destined to become leaders in the world of German science: Ernst Brücke, Emil du Bois Reymond, and Karl Ludwig.

Although he was the leading physiologist of his day, Müller was already being challenged by his students in the 1840s, especially on the issue of **vitalism** versus **materialism.** Müller believed that in addition to the physical and chemical components that made up physiological systems, there also existed a "vital force," or a life force that could not be reduced further. It was an idea with deep roots and obvious theological connotations. Opposed to vitalism was a position that also had a long history but was becoming especially prominent in the nineteenth century—materialism (see Chapter 2, pp. 38–40). According to this view, the vital force was a myth: physical matter was the only reality and all

living organisms could be reduced to physical, mechanical, and chemical processes that would eventually be understood by applying scientific methods. The movement was naturally congenial to the advances in science that occurred during this time. Müller's students, joined by Helmholtz, were committed materialists with all the enthusiasm and confidence of youth (all were under 30), and all made important contributions to physiology that supported the materialist position.

After finishing his medical degree in 1842, Helmholtz began his stint as an army surgeon, while at the same time maintaining his Berlin connections. It was during this time that he made the first of his lasting contributions, one that simultaneously reflected his love of physics and his desire to support a materialist physiology. It was a paper on the mathematical basis for a law of **conservation of energy**, first read to a scientific society in Berlin in 1847, and then published privately after being rejected for publication by a leading journal (Warren, 1984). Helmholtz is today considered one of the originators of this important principle in physics, which states that the total energy within a system remains constant, even if changes occur within the system. For Helmholtz, the principle was an important weapon in the fight against vitalism. Thus, he argued that body heat and muscle force could be explained by chemical energy accumulated during the oxidation process that accompanied digestion—there was no need to propose a special life force that could create its own energy. He supported his argument by showing that muscle contractions generated measurable amounts of heat (Turner, 1972).

Measuring the Speed of Neural Impulses

After being released early from his army commitment, Helmholtz was hired by the University of Königsberg in 1849, where he stayed for six years.[3] It was during this time that he completed a series of

---

[3] Having well-connected friends never hurts. The position at Königsberg opened when Brücke, one of Helmholtz's Berlin friends, left a position there to take one at Vienna (where his prize student would be Sigmund Freud). The Königsberg job was first offered to du Bois Reymond, who turned it down but apparently recommended Helmholtz, who accepted (Turner, 1972).

studies that had important implications for the study of the reflex and that laid the groundwork for the reaction time methodology that would become a key feature of every laboratory of experimental psychology.

When Helmholtz began studying the problem of nerve impulse speed in the early 1850s, it was already known that the impulse had electrical properties. A theory of electricity had arisen in the eighteenth century, and several scientists, including Helmholtz's materialist friend du Bois Reymond, had demonstrated that nerves could conduct electricity in order to make muscles twitch. Authorities such as Müller believed that the nerve impulse might be instantaneous or at the very least that it occurred too rapidly to be measured, but a study by du Bois Reymond in 1850 suggested that the impulse was propagated along the nerve by an electrochemical process that would be slower than a pure electrical transmission. If so, then perhaps impulse speed could be measured. Helmholtz succeeded in doing so by isolating a motor nerve and a connected muscle from the leg of a frog. He then stimulated the nerve electrically at several different distances from the muscle and recorded the time from stimulus to response. Knowing distance and time, the calculation of rate was easy (rate = distance/time). It averaged about 90 feet per second (or just over 60 miles per hour), quite sluggish compared with estimates that placed it near the speed of light. Helmholtz also estimated impulse speed in sensory nerves by showing that human subjects took longer to respond to stimulation of their toe than their thigh.

For Helmholtz, the implications of the research were obvious. Here was more evidence that vitalism was wrong and materialism was right. Vitalists argued that the conscious decision to move an arm and the arm's movement were simultaneous, but Helmholtz had shown that the event took a measurable amount of time, a conclusion consistent with the idea that nervous action involved the movement of physical, material entities. For Helmholtz, this conclusion was enough: he was not interested in any further applications of the concept of reaction time. It would be for others to develop the idea into a technique for measuring the time of various mental activities. That story will be told in the next chapter.

Helmholtz on Vision and Audition

During the Königsberg years, Helmholtz also began investigating the physiology of vision and audition and invented a tool that made him famous among eye doctors: the **ophthalmoscope**, a device for directly examining the retina. His research on vision culminated in a massive three-volume *Handbook of Physiological Optics*, published over an 11-year period, from 1856 to 1867. During this same time he moved twice, first to Bonn and then to Heidelberg, where he spent 13 of the most productive years of his life (1858–1871).

Helmholtz is perhaps best remembered for elaborating a theory of color vision first proposed by the English scientist Thomas Young at the beginning of the nineteenth century. Sometimes considered another example of a multiple, it has come to be called either the Young-Helmholtz theory or as Helmholtz called it, the **trichromatic theory**. It is based on the facts of color-matching experiments. If you shine a red spotlight against a wall and then shine a green light so that it overlaps the red, the colors in the area of overlap will "mix" and be seen as a new color, yellow. Both Young and Helmholtz demonstrated that by mixing various combinations of three colors together, red, green, and blue, the resulting color could be made to match any other single color. On this basis, they concluded that the eye must contain three different kinds of color receptors, one for each of these so-called primary colors, red, green, and blue (or violet). Incoming light of a particular wavelength was said to stimulate these receptors to different degrees, resulting in the perception of a certain color. In Helmholtz's words,

> ... Suppose that the colors of the spectrum are plotted horizontally in Fig. [3.1] in their natural sequence, from red to violet, the three curves may be taken to indicate something like the degree of excitation of the three kinds of fibres, No. 1 for the red-sensitive fibres, No. 2 for the green-sensitive fibres, and No. 3 for the violet-sensitive fibres.
>
> Pure *red* light stimulates the red-sensitive fibres strongly and the two other kinds of fibres feebly; giving the sensation red.
>
> Pure *yellow* light stimulates the red-sensitive and green-sensitive fibres moderately and the violet-sensitive fibres feebly; giving the sensation yellow.

Pure *green* light stimulates the green-sensitive fibres strongly and the two other kinds much more feebly; giving the sensation green.

... When all the fibres are stimulated about equally, the sensation is that of *white* or pale hues. (Helmholtz, 1860/1965, p. 42, italics in the original)

Although Helmholtz's Figure 3.1 was hypothetical, it is quite similar to modern-day data plotted in what are called spectral sensitivity curves. Thus the trichromatic theory has held up over the years, at least in part. It failed to account for certain color phenomena that were better explained by other theories, however, most notably Ewald Hering's theory, which came to be called **opponent process theory**. Hering proposed that color-sensitive cells were designed to respond to opposing pairs of colors (i.e., red-green, yellow-blue, black-white). When seeing red, for instance, Hering proposed a chemical breakdown in the receptor for red-green, what he called a "catabolic" process. Seeing green resulted in an "anabolic" or building-up process. If both red and green were mixed together, Hering believed the two processes would cancel each other, resulting in the perception of a neutral gray color. One of the trichromatic theory's problems was its prediction that someone with severe red-green color blindness would not be able to see yellow properly either. Yellow, according to Helmholtz, relies on the stimulation of properly functioning red and green fibers, both of which would be defective for someone with red-green color blindness. Such persons do see yellow, however. Also, the phenomenon of color afterimages seemed to fit Hering's model better than the Helmholtz model. After staring at a red square for a minute or so, then shifting one's gaze to a white surface, an afterimage in the form of a green square appears briefly. Yellow and blue complement each other in a similar manner. Today, theories of color vision include elements of both theories. The Young-Helmholtz version applies well at the retinal level—there do seem to be three different kinds of cones, each maximally responsive to the three colors of trichromatic theory: red, green, and blue. As for the Hering theory, his notions of anabolic and catabolic processes within individual receptors have not held

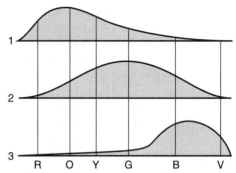

FIGURE 3.1 Relative sensitivity of the three color receptors proposed by Helmholtz, from his *Handbook of Physiological Optics*.

up, but there do seem to be opposing pairs of cells located in numerous sections of the visual pathway. For example, in the lateral geniculate nucleus, about midway between the retina and the visual cortex, there are cells that fire rapidly whenever red is presented to the retina, but are inhibited from firing when green is shown. In addition to these R+G- cells, the nucleus also holds a collection of R-G+, B+Y-, and B-Y+ cells (Goldstein, 1996).

Color vision was only a small portion of Helmholtz's work on the visual sense. His love of physics, for example, led him to examine the basic question of optics: How does light become focused on the retina? Thus, he provided a systematic analysis of how light rays are bent, both by the cornea and through the process of **accommodation**, in which the lens changes shape in order to alter the focus of objects at different distances. He also examined the perception of depth through the operation of **binocular vision**, and in the spirit of Bishop Berkeley, took a strong empiricist stance on the question of how we come to perceive objects in space.

Helmholtz would be justly famous even if he restricted his expertise to vision. In 1863, between the publication of volumes II and III of his *Optics*, however, he also published what quickly became the authoritative text on the sense of hearing, *The Theory of the Sensation of Tone as a Physiological Basis for the Theory of Music*. It is still in use today. In it Helmholtz presented his famous **resonance theory** of hearing, which proposed that different frequencies of sound were detected by receptors located in different places along the basilar membrane of the cochlea.

It is worth noting that both the trichromatic theory of color vision and the resonance theory of hearing were elaborations of Müller's doctrine of the specific energies of nerves. Whereas Müller proposed a single specific energy for each of the five basic senses, Helmholtz's theories amounted to proposing more than one specific energy for each sense: three for color vision and many for hearing.

Helmholtz and the Problem of Perception

As a physicist, Helmholtz was accustomed to look for precision in nature. Hence, he was perplexed by what could be called the **problem of perception**. On the one hand, it appears that the human sensory systems for seeing and for hearing are remarkably capable. On the other hand, the structures designed to deliver these senses seem to be terribly flawed. In vision, for example, Helmholtz noted that aberrations in the cornea often distorted light waves, that the fluids within the eye distorted the perceptions of shape, motion, and color, and worst of all, when light reached the retina, it had to pass through several layers of blood vessels and nerve fibers before reaching the receptors. Helmholtz once said that "... if an optician wanted to sell me an instrument which had all these defects, I should think myself quite justified in blaming his carelessness in the strongest terms, and giving him back his instrument" (cited in Warren, 1984, p. 257). Similar problems occurred with hearing.

Given such design flaws, Helmholtz asked, what accounts for the quality of our perception? The answer, he believed, could be found in the doctrine of the specific energies of nerves and in traditional empiricist philosophy. Thus, because our nervous system mediates between reality and the mind, we are only indirectly aware of the external world. As a result, the role of experience must be central to perception, he argued. The raw information processed by the sensory systems is meaningless in itself, then, but takes on meaning only when a particular combination of sensory events becomes associated with specific consequences. Consider, for example, the perception of objects located at different distances.

According to Helmholtz, we make what he called an **unconscious inference** about distance, based on our past experiences of various cues that are associated with distance. As a person gets closer to us, for example, the retinal image enlarges, but we perceive the person getting closer, not bigger. Helmholtz would say that because we know through experience that people don't grow or shrink as they approach or recede, we conclude logically (i.e., we infer unconsciously) that the person must be getting closer. All of this occurs quickly and without our awareness, hence the term "unconscious" inference.

Despite being sickly as a youth, Helmholtz was strong and energetic in his later years. His favorite hobby was mountain climbing, for example, and he could often be found hiking through the Alps (Wade, 1994). The experience gave him a metaphor that summed up his approach to science. The elegance of his final theorizing contrasted with the messy and unpredictable day-to-day process of doing research. To explain how he proceeded, he compared himself to

> ... an Alpine climber who, not knowing the way, ascends slowly and with toil, and is often compelled to retrace his steps because his progress is stopped; sometimes by reasoning, and sometimes by accident, he hits upon traces of a fresh path, which again leads him a little further; and finally, when he has reached the goal, he finds to his annoyance a royal road on which he might have ridden up if he had been clever enough to find the right starting-point at the outset. In my memoirs I have, of course, not given the reader an account of my wanderings, but I have described the beaten path on which he can now reach the summit without trouble. (cited in Warren, 1984, p. 256)

In 1871, at age 50, Helmholtz left Heidelberg for Berlin when he was offered a prestigious professorship in physics. Thus, in the last stage of his career he returned to his first love, physics. He traveled widely, even visiting the United States in 1893 to represent German science at the World's Fair in Chicago. On the return voyage he suffered a severe concussion and prolonged double vision from a fall down a flight of stairs. He died of a cerebral hemorrhage the following year.

LOCALIZATION OF BRAIN FUNCTION

In addition to the advances in knowledge about sensory physiology, nineteenth-century scientists also explored the nature of the brain, and argued over the problem of localization. Even a superficial visual inspection of the brain reveals some obvious structural differences. There are clearly two hemispheres, the cortex subdivides further into a number of ridges (convolutions), the cerebellum is separate from the cerebrum, and the lower brain areas, an extension of the spinal cord, have their own distinct shapes and features. It is only natural to suppose that there are functional differences corresponding to these structures, and this raises the question of **localization of function**. To what extent do the different locations in the brain correspond to different physiological and psychological attributes? That is, just how precise can localization be delineated? The answers range from very much to very little to it depends on the area of the brain being studied.

The Phrenology of Gall and Spurzheim

The phrenologists proposed the first major theory of localization and their answer to the question just raised was "very much." According to advocates of **phrenology**, human "faculties" could be identified and located in precisely defined areas of the brain. Phrenology began as a legitimate scientific attempt to study brain function, but it gradually degenerated into the nineteenth century's best example of pseudoscience. When portrayed in today's introductory psychology texts, it is usually caricatured as a bizarre scientific dead end in which charlatans read character by looking at the bumps on someone's head. Actually, the story is considerably more complicated and much that is characteristic of American psychology has its roots in the phrenological movement.

The origins of phrenology may be traced to the respected but eccentric Viennese physician and comparative anatomist Franz Josef Gall (1758–1828). Gall was born in Tiefenbronn, Germany, into an intensely devout Catholic family—his parents assumed that he would one day become a priest. Instead, his theory about the brain came to be considered antireligious, his

books were banned by the Church, the best that could be said about his personal life was that it was morally unconventional, and upon his death in 1828 he was denied a religious burial (Young, 1972). Gall decided on a career in medicine early in life, and he earned an M.D. in Vienna in 1785. There he developed a successful practice and became a skilled anatomist, although he was criticized for charging admission to those who wished to observe him in surgery and his theory about brain function became controversial. After his public lectures and surgical demonstrations were banned for allegedly promoting immorality and atheism, he took the show on the road and lectured throughout Europe before settling in Paris in 1807, where he remained until his death.

Gall secured a place in the history of medicine with his careful anatomical work. He identified the fibers connecting the two hemispheres and confirmed earlier speculation that some fibers crossed from one side of the brain to the opposite side of the spinal cord. Thus, Gall confirmed the concept of **contralateral function**, the notion that each side of the brain controls the opposite side of the body. Gall also compared the brain structures of different species and made a convincing argument that the mental abilities of different species correlated with the size and complexity of the brain, especially the cortex. He was also the first to argue that the brain's convolutions formed the same pattern within a given species; hence, the surface of the brain was not a random jumble of ridges and valleys but had a reliable structure. His anatomical research was impeccable—the great French physiologist Pierre Flourens, phrenology's harshest critic (below), nonetheless reported that when he saw Gall dissect a brain, it was like seeing the organ for the first time. Unlike most anatomists, including Flourens, who dissected brains by slicing off segments from the top down, Gall worked from the brain stem up, removing structures one by one and thereby tracing the interconnections between structures with a precision that was impossible when starting at the top (Temkin, 1947).

Despite these notable accomplishments, Gall is best known for originating phrenology, or what he called "cranioscopy." The theory is historically significant as the first serious theory of the localization of brain function, and Gall is justly credited with being among the first to argue that the brain was the organ of both the intellectual and the emotional components of the mind. Unfortunately, though, Gall identified the wrong functions and put them in the wrong places in the brain. In addition, his logic and his methods were flawed.

Gall began developing his ideas about localization very early in his life—as a youth, he thought he detected a relationship between the shape of a person's head and certain behavioral characteristics of that person. He noticed, for example, that schoolmates with protruding eyes seemed to have better memories than he did. This early experience began a lifelong pursuit of anecdotal evidence to support his theories. Thus, he claimed that the impulse to steal resulted from an overdevelopment of the faculty of "Property" (later called "Acquisitiveness"), located in the temporal lobe of the cortex about an inch above and in front of the ear. According to Gall,

> ... [w]hen these cerebral parts are very much developed, they produce a prominence on the head and skull. ... I have constantly found this prominence, in all inveterate thieves confined in prison, in all idiots with an irresistible propensity to steal, and in all those who, otherwise well endowed with intellect, take an inconceivable pleasure in stealing, and even feel incapable of resisting the passion which forces them to theft. (Gall, 1825/1965, p. 218)

Gall's beliefs eventually developed into the theory that his followers came to call phrenology, a term that derives from the Greek words for the study of ("-ology") the mind ("phrenos"). The term was coined by Johann Spurzheim (1776–1832), who collaborated with Gall for a time, but later broke with him. Spurzheim is the person most responsible for popularizing the theory, both in Europe and in America. As described in his *Outlines of Phrenology* (1832/1978) and elsewhere, phrenology's main principles reduced to five:

a. The brain is the organ of the mind.

b. The mind is composed of a large number (about three dozen) of abilities or attributes called "faculties"; some of these faculties are intellectual (cognitive) and some are affective (emotional).

c. Each faculty is associated with a specific brain location.

d. For a given faculty, some people have more than others, and those with more of a particular faculty will have more brain tissue in the corresponding location than those with less of that same faculty.

e. Because the skull corresponds roughly to the shape of the brain, the strength of various faculties can be inferred from the shape of the skull.

This last point came to be known as the **doctrine of the skull** and for the phrenologists it was the key to measurement. If the size and shape of various brain locations reflected the strength of faculties and if brain shape affected skull shape, then measuring the skull would yield a measurement of faculties. In short, everything of importance about people could be known by examining the shapes of their skulls. Figure 3.2 shows a typical phrenological skull with its faculties labeled.

In the first two decades of the nineteenth century, cranioscopy/phrenology was a legitimate attempt to identify the localized functions of the brain. By the

FIGURE 3.2 A phrenological skull, with faculties identified.

time Spurzheim produced his *Outlines of Phrenology*, in the year he died while on an American lecture tour (1832), thousands of skulls had been examined with an eye toward correlating skull shape with character. The *Outlines* includes detailed delineations of the faculties, with each description identifying the faculty's location in the brain and describing some of the supporting evidence for the faculty. On close examination, however, it is clear that there were serious weaknesses with the evidence. As indicated previously in connection with the faculty of Property (Acquisitiveness), the phrenologists relied heavily on **anecdotal evidence**. That is, they looked for specific case examples to support their theory. This approach is not necessarily flawed—gathering lots of data and then looking for generalizations is a standard inductive strategy. The problem, however, is that the phrenologists were not interested in examples that did not support their case. Thus, their theory failed an important criterion of an authentic scientific theory: it must be stated precisely enough to be capable of disproof. But the phrenologists would not do this. A thief with a small area of Acquisitiveness would either be ignored, described as a potential thief ("he will start stealing any day now"), or explained away by referring to combinations of other faculties that would be said to offset the lack of Acquisitiveness. For instance, the thief might be described as having large faculties of Imitation and Self-Esteem, causing him to maintain his self-image by copying his pickpocket older brother, despite his lack of "natural" Acquisitiveness. Perhaps the ultimate example of phrenological refusal to consider disproof was a comment attributed to a phrenologist upon learning that Descartes' skull was rather small in the areas related to some of the intellectual faculties. The phrenologist concluded that perhaps Descartes wasn't so smart after all (Fancher, 1990)!

This failure of phrenology as a theory did not seem to bother the phrenologists, but other scientists quickly recognized it as a fatal flaw, and phrenology was relegated to the status of pseudoscience by the mid-1830s. Unfortunately, it shared an important feature with other pseudosciences (e.g., handwriting analysis to measure personality)—the general public loved it. Phrenology became enormously popular throughout the rest of the nineteenth century. Gall and Spurzheim spread the faith throughout Europe and Spurzheim and others exported it to the United States.

It was in America that phrenology reached its zenith of popularity. The version that was imported by Spurzheim and spread by him and others fit in perfectly with the American culture of the "common man," especially during the middle and last half of the nineteenth century (Bakan, 1966). Although Gall believed the size of a person's faculties was an indication of native traits, Spurzheim argued that faculties could be affected by nurture. To Spurzheim, the brain was analogous to a muscle—its faculties could be exercised and strengthened through education and self-help. Thus, phrenology provided a seemingly scientific basis for the traditional American belief that anyone, regardless of heritage, could "pull oneself up by one's bootstraps" and accomplish virtually anything in life (e.g., go from a log cabin to the White House). The hopeful notion that children's brains and therefore their futures could be shaped by controlling their environments and improving their educations resonated with Americans. That same optimism would make behaviorism just as fashionable with the public in the 1920s. Phrenology also was consistent with the American idea that everyone is a unique person, possessing his or her own special talents. In phrenological terms, this translated into everyone having his or her own distinctive configuration of faculties, to be measured with proper phrenological tools. Thus, phrenology was an important early example of a major theme of research in psychology that continues today: the search for ways to identify and gauge individual differences (Bakan, 1966). And if individual differences could be identified and measured, then a person's strengths and weaknesses could be known and he or she could be counseled about careers, mate selection, and so on. A final reason for phrenology's appeal, then, was in its promise to deliver practical applications to improve daily living.

Phrenology's popularity with the masses was enhanced through the energetic marketing efforts of the New York firm of Fowler and Wells. Despite the fact that the scientific and more educated community rejected phrenology rather quickly, the public never seemed to tire of it. After all, it appeared to provide simple answers to life's difficult problems. Fowler and Wells published thousands of "improve-your-life-through phrenology" pamphlets, a phrenological journal, and paraphernalia ranging from busts with the faculties clearly marked on them to charts to simple tools for measuring head shapes. As you can see from the Close-Up, phrenology held the American public's interest into the early years of the twentieth century.

CLOSE-UP:
The Marketing of Phrenology

When Orson Fowler was a student at Amherst College in the early 1830s, he made pocket money by examining the heads of classmates for two cents per head (Joynt, 1973). Upon graduation, he joined with his brother Lorenzo and sister Charlotte in forming a museum of phrenology in New York City that featured a large collection of skulls, casts of heads, and other phrenological tools of the trade. Admission was free, but once the museumgoers were in the door, the Fowlers tempted them with a phrenological assessment that cost from one to three dollars. When Charlotte married a medical student named Samuel Wells, the firm of Fowler and Wells was born. Located at 753 Broadway, with branches in Boston and Philadelphia, it dominated the phrenology business from its inception in 1844 to the turn of the twentieth century.

Fowler and Wells, Inc., published a seemingly endless list of pamphlets designed to bring phrenological insights into every home. They also began the popular *Phrenological Journal*, trained and "certified" phrenologists, and during an era when the public lecture was a primary means of communication, maintained a list of accomplished public speakers ready to spread the phrenological faith. To give you some idea of the range of topics addressed by the firm, consider the following titles of pamphlets and books that could be ordered from Fowler and Wells, as advertised in the October 1881, issue of the *Phrenological Journal*:

> *The Indications of Character*, as Manifested in the General Shape of the Head and the Form of the Face. Illustrated. 15 cents.
> *Wedlock*; or, The Right Relations of the Sexes. A Scientific Treatise Disclosing the Laws of Conjugal Selection, Pre-natal Influences, and Showing Who Ought and Who Ought Not to Marry. $1.50; in fancy guilt, $2.00.
> *Amativeness*; or, Evils and Remedies of Excessive and Perverted Sexuality; Including Warning and Advice to the Married and Single. 25 cents.
> *Choice of Pursuits*; or, What To Do and Why. Describing Seventy-five Trades and Professions, and the Temperaments and Talents Required for Each. 508 pp. $1.75.

As for the journal itself, each issue contained brief phrenological sketches of well-known individuals, articles on other hot topics of the day (e.g., hypnotism, spiritualism) and short pieces covering just about anything (e.g., "Why Bees Work in Darkness"; "The Morality of Brakemen"). Although nothing quite like the *Phrenological Journal* exists today, the annual *Old Farmer's Almanac*, with its down-east commonsense wisdom, bears some similarity.

A typical phrenological article in the journal featured some well-known person and showed how a phrenological assessment could "explain" that person's character and behavior. For example, the September 1873, issue included a piece about a notorious triple murderer. Here's how he was described by a phrenologist who interviewed him:

I found his head to be 22 inches in circumference, 13.5 inches from Individuality to the occipital spine, and 14 inches from Destructiveness to Destructiveness, over the top of the head at Firmness. The animal portion of the brain predominates over all others. Destructiveness is the largest organ in his brain, the head swelling out enormously over the ears. The organ of Conscientiousness is, I think, the smallest I ever saw. ... All the spiritual organs are small and inactive, while Cautiousness and Secretiveness are both below the average.

The firm of Fowler and Wells had a long run, but interest in phrenology finally began to wane near the end of the nineteenth century, as the general public became more informed about the workings of the brain and as other approaches to measurement (e.g., IQ testing) began to be popularized. In 1911, the *Phrenological Journal* published its last issue.

Flourens and the Method of Ablation

Phrenology might have seemed like good science to Main Street America, but the real scientists were not fooled. As mentioned earlier, the scientific community rejected the Gall/Spurzheim theory well before the middle of the nineteenth century. Phrenology's worst enemy was the distinguished French physiologist and surgeon Pierre Flourens (1794–1867), who deliberately set out to show that the phrenologists were wrong. He reduced phrenology to two main points: the mind is centered in the brain, and the mind is composed of numerous faculties, each located in specific places in the brain. In his sharply worded *Examination of Phrenology*, first published in 1843, he sarcastically observed that "of these two propositions, there is certainly nothing new in the first one, and perhaps nothing true in the second one" (Flourens, 1846/1978, p. 18).

To falsify the phrenologists' claims, Flourens took an experimental approach to the problem of localization, using the method of **ablation**. Although he did not create the procedure, he raised it to such a level of refinement that it is now associated with his name. Rather than wait for natural experiments to occur, in the form of accidental brain damage, Flourens removed specific sections of the brain and observed the effects ("ablation" derives from the Latin words for "carry away" or "remove"). If the result of an ablation is an inability to see, then presumably the area of the removed portion has something to do with vision. Clearly, the method required animals as research subjects, and Flourens experi-

mented on numerous species, ranging from dogs to pigeons.

Flourens's attack on phrenology took the form of showing that specific areas of the brain that were alleged to serve function X in fact served function Y, and that the cerebral cortex operates as an integrated whole, rather than as a large collection of faculties located in specific places. One focus of his research was the cerebellum. To the phrenologists, this portion of the brain controlled sexual behavior and was the center of the faculty of "amativeness." Flourens had little trouble disproving this and demonstrating instead that the cerebellum is the center of motor coordination. Thus, pigeons deprived of the organ were unable to coordinate wing movements in order to fly, and dogs were unable to walk properly and would be observed staggering, falling down, and bumping into objects they could normally avoid. Also, the degree of abnormality in movement was directly proportional to the amount of cerebellum ablated.

As a result of removing varying amounts of the cerebral cortex, Flourens found a similar relationship between the amount removed and the seriousness of the ensuing problem. He could find no indication of distinct functions residing in specific areas of the cortex, however, so he concluded that it operated as a whole and served the general functions of perception, intelligence, and will. Thus, pigeons without a cortex or with most of it removed did seem to be able to perceive the world around them, but showed no indication of an ability to learn from their experiences, and did not seem to be able to do anything except to vegetate. The difference between a pigeon without a cerebellum and one without a cortex was that the first bird would attempt to fly but could not, while it would never occur to the second bird that flying was an option in life.

The general principles that the cortex acts as a whole and that the amount of disability is proportional to the extent of ablation were verified and extended by the discoveries of the great American physiological psychologist Karl Lashley, who referred to them as the principles of equipotentiality and mass action, respectively. (Lashley's work will be considered briefly at the end of the chapter.) Yet while Flourens was able to use these principles to attack phrenology in such a way that it never recovered, at least in the eyes of scientists, he overstated his case. He argued against any degree of localization in the cortex, a position soon to be shown inadequate by other brain scientists using methods other than ablation.

The Clinical Method

The results of ablation studies are not always easy to interpret, mainly because destroying one portion of a brain also influences connections to that portion, producing outcomes that are not always predictable or consistent. Also, ablation studies are sometimes impossible to do, as in the case of human subjects. It is one thing to systematically ablate portions of a person's brain for certain beneficial medical reasons (e.g., severing the corpus callosum to treat epilepsy), but destroying human brain tissue simply for the purpose of observing what happens is difficult to justify.[4] An alternative way to study human brain function is called the **clinical method**. This involves either (a) studying the behavioral and mental consequences of brain injury, events such as strokes, or illness, or (b) identifying people with some behavioral or mental disorder and examining their brains after death. The

person generally credited with developing the clinical method is Paul Broca, whom we will meet shortly, but there are numerous examples of famous clinical cases in the mid-nineteenth century. Perhaps the best known concerned a well-respected Vermont railroad worker, Phineas Gage.

The Remarkable Phineas Gage

While blasting rock in preparation for a new railway line near Cavendish, Vermont, in 1848, Gage survived an accident that seemed certain to be fatal. After pouring some gunpowder and a fuse into a hole drilled into rock that was about to be blasted away, Gage used a "tamping iron" to compress the powder. Momentarily distracted, he scraped the edge of the rock hard enough to create a spark that ignited the gunpowder. This converted the tamping iron into a missile that flew into the air and landed 30 meters away. Unfortunately for Gage, his head was in the flight path. The missile entered just below his left eye and exited from the top left of his forehead, taking a healthy portion of his left frontal cortex with it (see Figure 3.3). Miraculously, Gage only lost consciousness for a brief time, and once he arrived back in town, was able to walk (assisted) to a doctor's office. There he sat and conversed with friends (!)

FIGURE 3.3 Sketch of Gage's skull, showing position of tamping iron, from the original medical report by Harlow (1869).

---

[4] This fairly obvious ethical point was lost on Dr. Roberts Bartholow of Cincinnati in 1874, who inserted electrodes into the cortex of an unwitting immigrant domestic worker who had come to him for treatment of an ulcerous scalp wound that had exposed a portion of her brain. Mild stimulation produced some muscular contractions, but when the curious Bartholow inserted the electrodes deeper and increased the strength of the current, the unfortunate woman went into severe convulsions and soon died (Hothersall, 1995).

until the doctor arrived, about 30 minutes after the accident. Within two months he was sufficiently recovered to live independently,[5] but he was never able to work productively again and his personality changed dramatically. From a dependable, conscientious, respected community leader (he was foreman of the railroad crew), Gage degenerated into an obstinate, profane, irresponsible embarrassment to the community (MacMillan, 1986).

One of Gage's doctors, John Harlow, was amenable to phrenology and saw the case as providing support for the phrenologist's belief in cerebral localization. Harlow kept meticulous notes on the case and published accounts of it in 1848 and 1868, describing this case of frontal lobe damage as one in which

> ... [t]he equilibrium or balance ... between his intellectual faculties and animal propensities seems to have been destroyed. He is fitful, irreverent, indulging at times in the grossest profanity (which was not previously his custom), mani-

festing but little deference for his fellows, impatient of restraint or advice when it conflicts with his desires, at times pertinaciously obstinate, yet capricious and vacillating, devising many plans of future operation, which are no sooner arranged than they are abandoned. ... Previous to his injury, although untrained in the schools, he possessed a well-balanced mind, and was looked upon by those who knew him as a shrewd, smart businessman, very energetic and persistent in executing all his plans of operation. In this regard his mind was radically changed, so decidedly that his friends and acquaintances said he was "no longer Gage." (Harlow, 1868, cited in MacMillan, 1986, p. 85)

Thus, while Gage survived the injury, he was radically altered by it—the brain damage resulted in irreversible changes to his personality and behavior. Within 12 years (at age 37) he died, after experiencing a number of increasingly severe convulsions. The tamping iron and Gage's skull can be seen today at Harvard's Warren Anatomical Medical Museum.

ORIGINAL SOURCE EXCERPT
Broca Discovers the Speech Center

In the Gage case, it was possible for Harlow to trace events from the initial brain injury to the resulting psychological outcome. Another type of clinical case occurs when a patient manifests some specific mental or behavioral problem, but it cannot be correlated with brain damage until a post-mortem analysis. Such was the situation facing the French neurologist Paul Broca (1824–1880) in April of 1861, when confronted with a very unusual patient, known to history as "Tan," for reasons that will soon be apparent. This patient had been in the Bicêtre hospital in Paris for 21 years, and had been incapacitated and in bed for the seven years prior to 1861, when a severe case of gangrene brought him to Broca's attention. What follows is an excerpt from Broca's description of this remarkable case (Broca, 1861/1965), which eventually resulted in Broca's name being forever associated with a specific location on the cortex.

> On 11 April 1861 there was brought to the surgery of the general infirmary of the hospice at Bicêtre a man named Leborgne, fifty-one years old, suffering from a diffused gangrenous cellulitis of his whole right side, extending from the foot to the buttocks. When questioned the next day as to the origin of his disease, he replied only with the monosyllable *tan*, repeated twice in succession and accompanied by a gesture of his left hand. I tried to find out more

[5] That he survived at a time prior to the use of antibiotics to treat infection was nothing short of amazing, but his recovery was probably aided by the fact that the entry wound provided a natural drainage area that prevented him from developing the kind of abscess that would almost certainly be fatal (MacMillan, 1986).

about the antecedents of this man, who had been at Bicêtre for twenty-one years. I questioned his attendants, his comrades on the ward, and those of his relatives who came to see him, and here is the result of this inquiry.

Since youth he had been subject to epileptic attacks, yet he was able to become a maker of lasts,[6] a trade at which he worked until he was thirty years old. It was then that he lost his ability to speak and that is why he was admitted to the hospice at Bicêtre. It was not possible to discover whether his loss of speech came on slowly or rapidly or whether some other symptom accompanied the onset of his affliction.

When he arrived at Bicêtre he had already been unable to speak for two or three months. He was then quite healthy and intelligent and differed from a normal person only in his loss of articulate language. He came and went at the hospice, where he was known by the name of "Tan." He understood all that was said to him. His hearing was actually very good, but whenever one questioned him he always answered, "Tan, tan," accompanying his utterance with varied gestures by which he succeeded in expressing most of his ideas. If one did not understand his gestures, he was apt to get irate and added to his vocabulary a gross oath ["Sacré nom de Dieu!"]. ... Tan was considered an egoist, vindictive and objectionable, and his associates, who detested him, even accused him of stealing. These defects could have been due largely to his cerebral lesion. They were not pronounced enough to be considered pathological, and, although this patient was at Bicêtre, no one ever thought of transferring him to the insane ward. On the contrary, he was considered to be completely responsible for his acts.

Ten years after he lost his speech a new symptom appeared. The muscles of his right arm began to get weak, and in the end they became completely paralyzed. Tan continued to walk without difficulty, but the paralysis gradually extended to his right leg; after having dragged the leg for some time, he resigned himself to staying in bed. About four years had elapsed from the beginning of the paralysis of the arm to the time when paralysis of the leg was sufficiently advanced to make standing absolutely impossible. Before he was brought to the infirmary, Tan had been in bed for almost seven years. (pp. 224–225, italics in the original)

During the seven years in bed, Tan was more or less forgotten, and little information was available about him, except that his vision began to deteriorate. Because he remained continent, his linen was not changed regularly; thus, the gangrene that brought him to Broca's attention was not discovered until it had advanced considerably, infecting the whole leg. Broca reported that he hesitated examining Tan, because his general state "was so grave that it would have been cruel" (p. 225). Nonetheless, Broca proceeded, both with a physical exam that confirmed the paralysis of the right arm and leg, and with an examination of Tan's mental capacities:

Tan's hearing remained acute. He heard well the ticking of a watch, but his vision was weak. When he wanted to see the time, he had to take the watch

---

[6] A "last" is a wooden block in the shape of a foot, used in the making or repairing of shoes.

in his left hand and place it in a peculiar position about twenty centimeters from his right eye, which seemed better than his left.

The state of Tan's intelligence could not be exactly determined. Certainly he understood all that was said to him, but, since he could express his ideas or desires only by movements of his left hand, this moribund patient could not make himself understood as well as he understood others. His numerical responses, made by opening or closing his fingers, were best. Several times I asked him for how many days had he been ill. Sometimes he answered five, sometimes six days. How many years had he been at Bicêtre? He opened his hand four times and then added one finger. That made 21 years, the correct answer. The next day I repeated the question and received the same answer, but, when I tried to come back to the question a third time, Tan realized that I wanted to make an exercise out of the questioning. He became irate and uttered the oath, which only this one time did I hear from him. Two days in succession I showed him my watch ... [and] after having looked at the watch for a few seconds, he could each time indicate the time correctly. It cannot be doubted, therefore, that the man was intelligent, that he could think, that he had to a certain extent retained the memory of old habits. He could understand even quite complicated ideas. For instance, I asked him about the order in which his paralyses had developed. First he made a short horizontal gesture with his left index finger, meaning that he had understood; then he showed successively his tongue, his right arm, and his right leg. That was perfectly correct, for quite naturally he attributed his loss of language to paralysis of his tongue. (p. 226)

FIGURE 3.4 Tan's brain.

Broca guessed that Tan had a cerebral lesion that for the first 10 years of the illness remained confined to a fairly limited area in the left side of the brain, but then had spread. He did not have long to wait in order to confirm the diagnosis:

The patient died on 17 April [1861]. The autopsy was performed as soon as possible—that is, after 24 hours. The weather was warm but the cadaver showed no signs of putrefaction. The brain was shown a few hours later to the Société d'Anthropologie and was then put immediately into alcohol. It was so altered that great care was necessary to preserve it. It was only after two months and several changes of the fluid that it began to harden. Today it is in perfect condition and has been deposited in the Musée Depuytren. (p. 227)

Remarkably, Tan's brain still resides in the Musée Depuytren, with the damage to the left frontal cortex clearly visible (Figure 3.4). As Broca summed up the case,

Anatomical inspection shows us that the lesion was still progressing when the patient died. The lesion was therefore progressive, but it progressed very slowly, taking twenty-one years to destroy a quite limited part of the brain. Thus it is reasonable to believe that at the beginning there was a considerable time during which degeneration did not go past the limits of the organ where it started. We have seen that the original focus of the disease was situated in the frontal lobe and very likely in its third frontal convolution. Thus we are compelled to say, from the point of view of pathological anatomy, that there were two periods, one in which only one frontal convolution, probably the third one, was attacked, and another period in which the disease gradually spread toward other convolutions, to the insula, or to the extraventicular nucleus of the corpus striatum.

When we now examine the succession of symptoms, we also find two periods, the first of which lasted ten years, during which the faculty of speech was destroyed while all other functions of the brain remained intact, and a second period of eleven years, during which paralysis of movement, at first partial and then complete, successively involved the arm and the leg of the right side.

With this in mind it is impossible not to see that there was a correspondence between the anatomical and the symptomological periods. Everyone knows that the cerebral convolutions are not motor organs. Of all the organs attacked, the corpus striatum of the left hemisphere is the only one where one could look for the cause of the paralysis of the two right extremities. The second clinical period, in which the motility changed, corresponds to the second anatomical period, when the softening passed beyond the limit of the frontal lobe and invaded the insula and the corpus striatum.

It follows that the first period of ten years, clinically characterized only by the symptom of aphemia, must correspond to the period during which the lesion was still limited to the frontal lobe. (pp. 228–229)

Broca's term for Tan's disorder was soon replaced with "aphasia" when it was pointed out that the Greek origin of "aphemia" refers to reputation or fame, while the root translation of "aphasia" is "without speech" (Ryalls, 1984). The disorder is now referred to as expressive or **motor aphasia**, and it is characterized by an inability to articulate ideas verbally, even though the vocal apparatus is intact and general intelligence is normal. Over the next few years, Broca encountered several other aphasic patients like Tan, found the same general pattern of left frontal lobe damage, and concluded that the ability to produce speech was localized in the left frontal lobe. In his honor, the area is now known as Broca's area.

Broca's research challenged Flourens's conclusions about the degree of localization to be found in the cortex. Additional evidence for localized language function came from clinical studies by the German neurologist Carl Wernicke (1848–1905). He studied a group of 10 patients who could produce articulate speech, but the speech tended to be nonsensical; they also had difficulty comprehending the speech of others. He named the disorder **sensory aphasia**, to distinguish it from motor aphasia, and discovered consistent brain damage to an area of the left temporal lobe of the brain, several centimeters behind Broca's area.

Mapping the Brain: Electrical Stimulation

We have seen that in the nineteenth century, discoveries about the nature of electricity were being applied to research on sensory physiology, and the idea was evolving that neural activity was electrochemical. In that context, two young German physiologists, both lecturers at the University of Berlin, asked whether the surface of the cortex would respond to mild electrical current. Although listed as second author in their famous paper, the primary investigator was lifelong brain researcher Edward Hitzig (1838–1907); he was assisted by Eduard Fritsch (1838–1927), who soon left physiology for the study of anthropology. Hitzig had observed muscle movements when the exposed brain of a wounded soldier had been mechanically stimulated, but it was generally believed that touching the surface of the brain did not produce reliable effects. Using dogs as their subjects, Hitzig and Fritsch exposed the cortex and probed different surfaces. The stimulus was an electric current of "an intensity that just barely evoked a sensation of feeling on the tongue" (Fritsch & Hitzig, 1870/1965, p. 230). It was delivered across

two thin platinum wires that could be placed anywhere from 2 to 3 mm apart. Despite the relative crudeness of their procedures—the experiments were done in Fritsch's home—they contributed evidence of localization by identifying several motor centers in the front half of the brain. Stimulation of the areas marked in Figure 3.5 produced consistent movements in the right side of the dog's body, as follows:

Area 1:	neck
Areas 2 and 3:	anterior leg (extension and flexion, respectively)
Area 4:	posterior leg
Area 5:	face

The Fritsch and Hitzig research motivated a number of physiologists, who proceeded to map out motor areas in other species and with more precision. This activity became known as the "new" phrenology or "scientific phrenology": localization was the goal, but now the brain's functions would be identified scientifically, rather than through the selected anecdotes of Gall and Spurzheim. Just a few years after Fritsch and Hitzig published their work, for example, the Scottish neurologist David Ferrier (1843–1928) wrote *Functions of the Brain* (1876), which included the map of a monkey's brain shown in Figure 3.6.

FIGURE 3.5 Motor centers of a dog's brain, identified via electrical stimulation by Fritsch and Hitzig (1870/1965).

FIGURE 3.6 David Ferrier's map of the cortex of a monkey (from Boring, 1950).

Comparing this with Figure 3.5 makes it clear how rapidly brain science was advancing. Ferrier also extended the localization search beyond motor functions, identifying several sensory areas. Using both electrical stimulation and ablation, Ferrier was able to identify the occipital lobe as the primary sensory area for vision, and a portion of the temporal lobe as the center for hearing. It began to look like sensory nerves differed more in terms of their destinations in the cortex than in terms of "specific energies."

EARLY TWENTIETH-CENTURY STUDIES OF THE NERVOUS SYSTEM AND BEHAVIOR

As the nineteenth century drew to a close, knowledge of the nervous system in general and of the brain in particular was increasing at a rapid pace. In addition to research on sensory physiology and the localization of brain function, however, another line of research developed toward the end of the century and spilled over into the twentieth. This concerned the nature of the basic unit of the nervous system itself, the neuron. This is a long and complicated history in itself, but a few of the highlights can be sketched here.

Neuron Theory

The discovery of the neuron as the basic element of the nervous system did not occur until the second half of the nineteenth century, when several important developments occurred in histology (the study of the microscopic structure of plant and animal tissue). Microscopes became more powerful, for instance, and techniques for hardening the brain were perfected. Before it was discovered that the brain could be solidified by soaking it in alcohol, precise dissection was impossible. Once it was known how to harden the brain, however, its nerve pathways could be traced with some precision for the first time. For example, in 1857, Gratiolet was able to trace the optic nerve from the retina all the way to the back of the brain, where it radiated like a fan into the occipital cortex (Diamond, 1985).

It was also discovered that the brain could be immersed in paraffin, hardened, then cut into very thin slices, a procedure called sectioning. Furthermore, if these sections were stained with various dyes, identifiable structures could be observed in a microscope because the dyes would collect within these structures. When the Italian Camillo Golgi (1844–1926) began using what he called his "black stain," for instance, the result was the first picture of an intact nerve cell, complete with elaborately branching dendrites, intact cell body, and main axon. Golgi's discovery earned him a share of the 1906 Nobel Prize for medicine. He believed the nervous system to be composed of these neurons, but he also contended that the cells were physically connected to each other, a position that brought him into conflict with the other winner of the 1906 Nobel Prize for medicine.

Santiago Ramón y Cajal (1852–1934) (Figure 3.7) was a gifted Spanish neuroanatomist with a love of art, whose research laid the foundation for the modern theory of the neuron (Taylor, 1972). Ramón y Cajal's artistic side can be seen in his eloquent description of the neuron as the "aristocrat among the structures of the body, with its giant arms stretched out like the tentacles of an octopus to the provinces on the frontier of the outside world" (cited in Restak, 1984). Like Golgi, Ramón y Cajal believed the neuron to be the nervous system's basic unit. In contrast with Golgi, however, he argued that each neuron was a separate unit that was not physically connected with other units but merely in contact with them. Ironically, when he first proposed his neuron theory in 1889, he used Golgi's own staining techniques to make his case. Thus, the two winners of the 1906 Nobel Prize for medicine were strongly opposed over the nature of their discovery, the neuron. To complicate matters further, Golgi the Italian and Ramón y Cajal the Spaniard were both fiercely patriotic and convinced of the inferiority of each other's research. The 1906 Nobel Prize ceremony must have been interesting.

FIGURE 3.7 Santiago Ramón y Cajal (1852–1934)

Sir Charles Sherrington: The Synapse

Direct photographic evidence supporting Ramón y Cajal's neuron theory and refuting Golgi's would have to await the discovery of the electron microscope, but empirical evidence supporting the existence of gaps between neurons was provided by a British contemporary of both men, Sir Charles Sherrington (1857–1952).[7] It was Sherrington who coined the term **synapse** (from the Greek word meaning "to join together") for this proposed space between neurons. He did not observe its existence directly; rather he deduced it from a brilliant series

of studies on spinal reflexes. The research was presented as part of a prestigious series of lectures at Yale University in 1904, then published as *The Integrative Action of the Nervous System* in 1906, the same year that Golgi and Ramón y Cajal shared the Nobel Prize. Sherrington would eventually win a Nobel Prize of his own in 1932 (Swazey, 1972).

In the tradition of Robert Whytt, but with the advantages of improved technology, Sherrington examined reflex action in "spinal dogs," dogs with spinal cords surgically severed from their brains. As all dog owners know, stimulating a dog's side in the area of the rib cage will cause the dog's hind leg to produce a rapid and repetitive scratching reflex. The fact that Sherrington found these reflexes in spinal dogs replicated Whytt's basic finding about the role of the spinal cord in reflex action. Furthermore, the reflex was even more pronounced in spinal dogs than in intact dogs, which led Sherrington to conclude that the cortex has an inhibitory effect on reflex action.

Sherrington made several observations in his spinal dogs that led him to believe that synapses must exist. First, the reaction time of the reflexes he

---

[7] Obituary accounts of Sherrington describe him as a genial and mild-mannered man. He was said to be "[g]entle in criticism, whole hearted in admiration and appreciation of the work of others, embod[ying] the intellectual and physical serenity which appears so characteristic of the Victorian era" (Denny-Brown, 1952, p. 477). Yet this "serenity" did not keep him from his favorite sport during his youth—while a lecturer in physiology at St. Thomas's Hospital in London, he spent his Sunday mornings parachute jumping from the hospital's tower (Swazey, 1972).

observed was much slower than predicted from what was known of the speed of neural transmission. Thus, something must have been slowing down the impulse. A second line of evidence came from the phenomena of temporal and spatial summation. Sherrington discovered that a single stimulation at a certain point on the skin might fail to elicit a scratch reflex, but if the point was stimulated many times in succession (at a rate of about 18 per second), the reflex occurred (Sherrington, 1906). This is **temporal summation**—stimuli separated in time combine to produce a response. **Spatial summation** occurred when two or more adjacent points on the skin were stimulated at the same time. Again, responses only occurred to the combined stimulation. Sherrington concluded that summation must occur at the points where the endpoints of neurons met each other, the synapse. Each subthreshold stimulus caused some unspecified action at the end of neuron A that was by itself insufficient to fire neuron B, but the combined action of information coming many times from A (temporal) or from other locations (spatial) triggered the firing of B. In effect, Sherrington predicted the later discovery of neurotransmitters, chemicals that we now know cross the synapse to promote (or inhibit) neuron firing. After Golgi, Ramón y Cajal, and Sherrington, then, the neuron was established as the fundamental unit of the nervous system, interrelated with other neurons through synaptic activity.

Karl Lashley:
Learning and the Cortex

A brief consideration of the life and work of Karl Spencer Lashley (1890–1958) is a fitting way to end this chapter. Like the nineteenth-century physiologists, neurologists, and physicists encountered thus far, his training was not in psychology. Unlike anyone else in the chapter, however, he eventually came to think of himself primarily as a psychologist. Thus, Lashley provides a transition between the physiologists of the nineteenth century and the physiological psychologists of the twentieth. You will encounter him again in Chapter 10, as a research colleague of behaviorism's founder, John B. Watson; and yet again in Chapter 13, where his paper on "serial

order" attacked simplistic S-R (stimulus-response) models of behavior and helped set the stage for the shift from behaviorism to cognitive psychology.

Karl Lashley was born in rural West Virginia and earned a bachelor's degree in zoology from West Virginia University and a master's degree in bacteriology from the University of Pittsburgh, before enrolling in a doctoral program in zoology at Johns Hopkins University in 1911. There he completed his Ph.D. under the tutelage of noted zoologist H. S. Jennings. More important for psychology's history, Lashley also came under the influence of the behaviorist Watson and S. I. Franz, a psychologist at a psychiatric hospital (St. Elizabeth's) in Washington, D.C., who was interested in the effects of brain damage on behavior. With Watson, Lashley conducted field studies of animal behavior, laboratory experiments on the sensory abilities of various species, and research on the conditioning of salivary and motor responses, adapting the procedures of two Russian physiologists who were just beginning to be known to Americans: Vladimir Bekhterev and Ivan Pavlov. The conditioning research is especially noteworthy because it marked the point at which Lashley decided that his future would be not in biology but in the intersection between biology and psychology (Bruce, 1986). This decision was cemented when he completed postdoctoral research on the effects of brain injury on behavior with Franz. By 1920, he knew he would be an experimental psychologist specializing in how learning and memory affect the brain.

Lashley's distinguished academic career included stops at the Universities of Minnesota and Chicago, and at Harvard University. In 1942, he became director of the Yerkes Laboratories of Primate Biology in Florida, where his research on animal behavior bridged the laboratory-based comparative psychology favored by American scientists and the field-based, naturalistic approach of European ethologists (Bruce, 1991). He died of heart failure in 1958, while on holiday in France. Among psychologists, Lashley is best known for the research he completed in the 1920s while at Chicago, a series of experiments that was characterized at the time of his death as being "without equal in recent experimental psychology" (Hebb, 1959).

Equipotentiality and Mass Action

The year 1929 was an important one for Lashley. His peers elected him president of the American Psychological Association, recognizing the value of the research he had been engaged in during the decade of the 1920s. That research was summarized in *Brain Mechanisms and Intelligence*, which also appeared in 1929. Lashley defined the term intelligence in an animal learning context, using it to cover the behavior of rats learning to negotiate mazes and solve simple discrimination and puzzle box problems. He readily admitted that his choice of tests could be criticized: "They all deal with some aspect of the learning process, [but their] relation to the problem of intelligence is not yet clearly established" (Lashley, 1929, p. 14). Nonetheless, he argued that simple mechanical or reflexive explanations of learning, such as the ones proposed by Watson and Pavlov, were inadequate to capture the complexity of how animals went about solving the kinds of problems that enabled them to survive in their environments. Thus, he considered the tasks presented to his rats to be sufficiently intricate to bear at least some relation to the intelligent, adaptive behavior found in the animals' real-world environments.

Lashley's procedures were in the tradition of the great French physiologist Flourens—he observed the effects of brain ablations on behavior, systematically destroying different amounts of cortex and observing the effects on learning and retention. One of his procedures was maze learning and Figure 3.8 shows three of the four mazes he used. Maze I was a simple T-maze in which the animal had to make a single left-right choice. Maze II had three possible dead-ends, while Maze III had eight.[8] During training, each brain-damaged rat negotiated one of the mazes five times per day and learning was defined as 10 consecutive errorless runs through the maze. The relationship between the extent of cortical damage

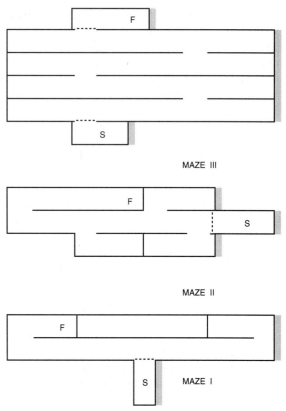

FIGURE 3.8 Mazes used by Lashley (1929) in his studies of equipotentiality and mass action (S = start box; F = food).

[8] Maze IV had the same design as Maze III, but with the pattern reversed. In addition, while Mazes I–III were alley mazes (i.e., they had walls), Maze IV was an elevated maze, which required the rat to run on the edges of boards (only 3/16 of an inch wide) that were placed vertically on a table.

and performance for each of these mazes can be seen in Lashley's graph, Figure 3.9. For simple mazes such as Maze I, performance was quite good even after large amounts of cortical destruction. With Maze II, the performance deteriorated slightly, but was still only marginally affected by the brain lesions. It is only with a more difficult problem, Maze III, that the rat's performance was dramatically affected by the extent of the damage. As the percent of destruction increased, performance declined precipitously. Hence, Lashley was reporting what amounted to an interaction between maze complexity and the degree of cortical lesioning. In simple tasks, the extent of destruction had little effect, while on difficult tasks, performance was directly related to the amount of destruction.

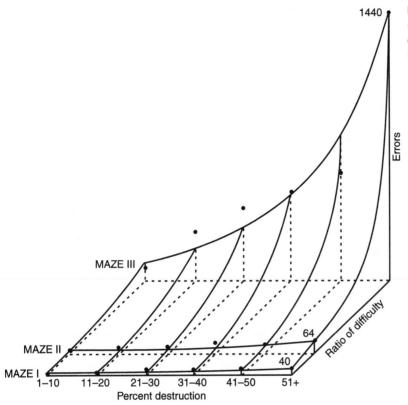

FIGURE 3.9 The effects of maze difficulty and degree of cortical destruction on maze learning, from Lashley (1929).

On the basis of the maze studies and similar experiments with his other procedures, Lashley reached two general conclusions very similar to the ones arrived at by Flourens nearly a century earlier. First was the principle that Lashley called **equipotentiality**, a term

> ... used to designate the apparent capacity of any intact part of a functional area to carry out, with or without reduction in efficiency, the functions which are lost by destruction of the whole. This capacity varies from one area to another and with the character of the functions involved. It probably holds only for the association areas and for functions more complex than simple sensitivity or motor coordination. (Lashley, 1929, p. 25)

Equipotentiality was a strong argument against cerebral localization of function, at least within the broad area of learning and in those cortical areas not

known to govern specific sensory-motor functions. It was supplemented, however, by the law of **mass action**:

> [E]quipotentiality is not absolute but is subject to a law of mass action whereby the efficiency of performance of an entire complex function may be reduced in proportion to the extent of brain injury within an area whose parts are not more specialized for one component of the function than for another. (Lashley, 1929, p. 25)

Thus, the process of learning does not seem to be localized in any specific area of the cortex, but learning efficiency is proportional to the amount of cortical destruction.

These principles of equipotentiality and mass action were Lashley's key findings, but he was also interested in the general process of maze learning. He was well aware of the maze research of his former colleague John Watson, for example, and disagreed with Watson's belief that maze learning involved the kinesthetic sense and the conditioning of a chain of specific motor responses (see Chapter 10). Lashley argued that Watson's model could not account for the strange behavior of those animals with lesions affecting their motor movements. They could still make it through the maze, even if their motor movements were considerably altered:

> One drags himself through with his forepaws; another falls at every step but gets through by a series of lunges; a third rolls over completely in making each turn, yet manages to avoid rolling into a cul-de-sac and makes an errorless run. ... If the customary sequence of movements employed in reaching the food is rendered impossible, another set, not previously used in the habit, and constituting an entirely different pattern, may be directly and efficiently substituted without any random activity. (Lashley, 1929, p. 136)

Lashley's conclusions about how the rat learned the maze were similar to those soon to be drawn by the neobehaviorist Edward Tolman (Chapter 11), who argued that rats developed an overall "cognitive map" of the maze and were thus aware of the general direction of the goal. When describing such maps, Tolman (1948, p. 203) referred specifically to Lashley's work for support. Although Lashley did not use the term "map," he clearly had the concept of directionality in mind when planning the following variation with Maze III. Removing the mesh cover normally on top of the maze, a few of his rats (5 out of 20 tested) climbed on top of the maze and went straight across the top of it to the point where the goal was located. Lashley noted that "the behavior of the 5 that followed the direct course to the food suggested that they were perfectly oriented with respect to its direction, although they had never before reached it save by the indirect path of the maze" (Lashley, 1929, p. 137).

Lashley's research on the relationship between brain and behavior was a natural culmination of the developments in nervous system physiology that occurred in the nineteenth century and a link to the physiological psychology of the twentieth century. We are now a bit ahead of the story, however, and must return to the nineteenth century to examine how psychology emerged as a "new science" in Germany (Chapter 4) and how it was influenced by the theory of evolution, the nineteenth century's most important intellectual event (Chapter 5). As you are beginning to discover, psychology in America has deep roots.

SUMMARY

HEROIC SCIENCE IN THE AGE OF ENLIGHTENMENT

• The Enlightenment was a period during the eighteenth and nineteenth centuries when great faith existed in the ability of science and human reason to produce true knowledge about the world. Scientists were heroes, considered to be objective and value free, with Newton being the prime exemplar. Science was thought to lead inevitably to progress through technological innovation. In this context, the belief that psychology could become scientific began to take hold.

SENSORY PHYSIOLOGY

• From the time of Descartes, scientists have been interested in the nature of the simple reflex. In the eighteenth century, Whytt completed the first systematic studies, showing conclusively that the spinal cord was necessary in order for reflexes to occur. Anticipating the concept of conditioning, Whytt also pointed out that the stimulus-response connections could develop through habit.

• When Magendie severed the posterior root of a dog's spinal cord, the affected area could move but was insensitive to stimulation. When the anterior root was severed, no movement occurred. Magendie concluded that the posterior root controlled sensation, while the anterior root controlled motor movements. Bell made similar observations, and the distinction is now known as the Bell-Magendie Law.

• According to Müller's doctrine of the specific energies of nerves, (a) we are directly aware of our nervous systems, not the world, and (b) each of the five basic sensory systems has nerve fibers designed for that specific sense.

• Helmholtz was opposed to vitalism and fought it through his doctrine of conservation of energy and by measuring the finite speed of the neural impulse. He was without peer as an expert on visual and auditory perception, known for the trichromatic theory of color vision, the resonance theory of audition, and his empiricist approach to perception, which emphasized unconscious inference.

LOCALIZATION OF BRAIN FUNCTION

• Phrenology, developed by Gall and promoted by Spurzheim, was the first serious theory of localization of brain function. Phrenologists believed that different parts of the brain served different faculties, that the portion of brain allocated to a faculty was proportional to the strength of the faculty, and that faculties and their strengths could be determined by measuring the skull.

• Because it relied too heavily on anecdotal evidence and faulty logic, phrenology lost scientific credibility quickly. It remained popular with the general public, however, being consistent with the American ideals of individuality and self-improvement.

• By developing the method of ablation, Flourens was able to falsify phrenological doctrine, while at the same time showing that the cortex operates as an integrated system.

• Evidence for localization came from clinical studies, in which those suffering from various forms of brain disease or damage were studied. The case of Phineas Gage illustrated the effects of severe frontal lobe damage on judgment and personality. Broca's study of "Tan," who suffered from motor aphasia, showed that the ability to produce articulate speech depended on a fairly circumscribed area of the left cortex.

• By developing the procedure of electrically stimulating the surface of the cortex, Fritsch and Hitzig in Germany and Ferrier in Great Britain began to map the functions of the surface of the brain with a "scientific phrenology."

EARLY TWENTIETH-CENTURY STUDIES OF THE NERVOUS SYSTEM AND BEHAVIOR

• The identification of neurons as the basic units of the nervous system was made by Golgi, who thought they were physically connected to each other, and Ramón y Cajal, who thought they were physically separate from each other.

• Ramón y Cajal's theory was verified by Sherrington, who is credited with discovering the synapse and demonstrating its existence in his research on reflexes and through the phenomena of temporal and spatial summation.

• Lashley's research on the brain and learning showed that maze learning was not localized in any particular area of the cortex. Rather, the cortex operated as a system and was characterized by equipotentiality and mass action.

STUDY QUESTIONS

1. What was the Enlightenment attitude toward science and how did this influence psychology's history?

2. Robert Whytt was able to demonstrate that the spinal cord, but not the brain, was necessary for reflexes to occur. What was the research that led him to this conclusion?

3. What is the Bell-Magendie Law? Explain why it should probably be the "Magendie Law."

4. What was the vitalism-materialism issue, and how did Helmholtz provide support for the latter?

5. How did Helmholtz measure the speed of neural impulses and what was the significance of this work?

6. Compare and integrate the color vision theories of Helmholtz and Hering.

7. According to Helmholtz, what is the "problem of perception?" Explain how his concept of unconscious inference was congenial to British Empiricist thinking.

8. Describe the five essential principles of phrenology and explain why it eventually failed as science. Be sure to consider the research of Flourens in your answer.

9. Explain why phrenology was highly popular in America. Why would the Spurzheim version be more popular with Americans than the Gall version?

10. Show how the two varieties of the clinical method for studying the brain are illustrated by (a) Phineas Gage and (b) Tan.

11. Describe the importance of the late nineteenth century research that came to be known as the "new phrenology."

12. What was neuron theory and what were the two versions proposed by the co-winners of the 1906 Nobel prize for medicine?

13. Describe the work of Sherrington that led the idea of the synapse.

14. Describe Lashley's research, his two principles, and relate the work to that of Flourens.

QUESTIONS FROM THE ORIGINAL SOURCE EXCERPT

1. Describe the verbal limitations of the patient who was analyzed by Broca. What was the sequence of disabilities that eventually brought this person to Broca's attention?

2. How did Broca establish the fact that Tan had relatively normal mental capacity?

3. What was Broca able to conclude on the basis of the post-mortem examination of Tan?

FOR FURTHER READING

Bakan, D. (1966). The influence of phrenology on American psychology. *Journal of the History of the Behavioral Sciences, 2,* 200–220.

A close analysis of the development of phrenology, its rejection by the scientific community, and its popularity with the American public; shows how phrenology fit in with the temperament of progressivism and was an early example of the approach to psychology that emphasizes individual differences.

Bruce, D. B. (1986). Lashley's shift from bacteriology to neuropsychology, 1910–1917, and the influence of Jennings, Watson, and Franz. *Journal of the History of the Behavioral Sciences, 22,* 27–44.

A description of Lashley's formative years and how his eventual self-identification as a physiological psychologist was affected by his doctoral studies with Jennings, his collaboration with Watson, and his postdoctoral work with Franz.

Finger, S. (2000). *Minds behind the brain: A history of the pioneers and their discoveries.* New York: Oxford University Press.

Using a biographical approach, Finger chronicles the life and work of the major pioneers in the study of the brain, starting with the ancient Egyptians, continuing with many of the scientists featured in this chapter (e.g., Gall, Broca, Ferrier), and going all the way into the twentieth century research on the split brain; includes more than 100 halftone photos and drawings.

MacMillan, M. B. (1986). A wonderful journey through skull and brain: The travels of Mr. Gage's tamping iron. *Brain and Cognition, 5,* 67–107.

Despite the odd title, a scholarly and detailed account of the case of Phineas Gage, including a description of his medical treatment by Harlow, and an analysis of how the case bears on the localization issue.

Ramón y Cajal, S. (1999). *Advice for a young investigator.* (Trans. N. Swanson & L. W. Swanson). Cambridge, MA: MIT Press.

A recent translation of a brief book by Ramón y Cajal that, in the guise of offering advice for budding scientists, reveals the author's depth of thinking on philosophy of science issues and his passion for science.

CHAPTER 4

WUNDT AND GERMAN PSYCHOLOGY

> The book which I here present to the public is an attempt to mark out a new domain of science.
>
> —Wilhelm Wundt, 1874

PREVIEW AND CHAPTER OBJECTIVES

Chapters 2 and 3 describe the context out of which modern psychology emerged in the nineteenth century. Philosophers, interested in the same fundamental questions about the human mind and behavior that occupy psychologists today, began to speculate about the need to examine these issues scientifically. At least one nineteenth-century British philosopher, John Stuart Mill, even proposed the development of a scientific psychology. Meanwhile, physiologists and physicians in Europe made great strides in furthering our understanding of the physiology of the nervous system and, in particular, of the brain. This chapter examines how this experimental physiology combined with philosophical inquiry to create a new experimental psychology in Germany in the late nineteenth century. The chapter opens with a brief discussion of some aspects of German education that made it attractive to American students, and then continues with a look at how Gustav Fechner's psychophysics provided a standardized set of methods for studying the mind. The creation of the "New Psychology" and its first laboratory by Leipzig's Wilhelm Wundt forms the focus of the middle of the chapter. The chapter ends with consideration of three other important German psychologists, Hermann Ebbinghaus, G. E. Müller, and Oswald Külpe. The Original Source Excerpt is from Ebbinghaus's famous book about his experiments on memory. After you finish this chapter, you should be able to:

- Describe the philosophy of education in Germany that facilitated the development of the sciences, including psychology
- Describe the early research in psychophysics completed by Weber
- Describe the methods of psychophysics developed by Fechner, and how his work related to the philosophical position of materialism
- Explain why Wundt is considered the founder of modern psychology, and not Fechner
- Describe Wundt's vision for his "New Psychology," distinguishing between his laboratory and his non-laboratory approaches to psychology
- Describe the kinds of research likely to be found in Wundt's laboratory at Leipzig
- Describe the logic of the complication experiment and explain why it was valued so highly at the time

- Compare the traditional description of Wundt and his work with more recent revisions, and explain why the discrepancies occurred
- Describe the methods developed by Ebbinghaus to study memory, his findings, and the importance of his research
- Describe the contributions to early experimental psychology made by G. E. Müller and contrast his approach to memory with that of Ebbinghaus
- Describe the contributions of Oswald Külpe and his students at Würzburg, especially their elaboration of the concept of introspection

AN EDUCATION IN GERMANY

American students have always looked to European universities as a way to further their educations. Even today, a semester abroad is a valued experience. In the nineteenth century, Germany was an especially attractive location for young scholars; it has been estimated that in the 100-year span beginning in 1820, at least 9,000 American students enrolled in one German university or another (Sahakian, 1975), usually to study medicine or one of the sciences. By the end of the century, they were going there to study psychology.

One reason for the popularity of German universities was mere quantity. Between the time of the 1815 Congress of Vienna and the unification of Germany under Bismarck in 1871, Germany did not exist as a "country," but was a loosely organized federation of 38 autonomous "principalities" (e.g., Bavaria, Hanover, Saxony) (Palmer, 1964). Each ministate wanted to keep up with its neighbors, of course, and one means of accomplishing this goal was to have its own university. Hence, universities proliferated throughout the federation of principalities, although many of them were little more than a building with some classrooms and a few professors. Several gained international stature, however, and drew students from all over Europe as well as from America.

Circumstances in nineteenth-century Germany were especially conducive to the development of a new and more scientific approach to psychology. Beginning in the middle of the century, and originating at the University of Berlin, German universities developed a distinctive philosophy of education known as

Wissenschaft. It was an approach that emphasized scholarly research combined with teaching and academic freedom for professors to pursue their research interests without fear of censure. Students were free to wander from one university to another, and earning a degree resulted more from the passing of special exams and the defense of a research thesis than from the completion of a specific curriculum.

For the professors who would create a new scientific psychology, many of whom you will meet in this chapter, the timing was perfect. The success of the physiologists (Chapter 3) reinforced the *Wissenschaft* emphasis on a research-based atmosphere and contributed directly to the growth of the new experimental approach to psychology in Germany, especially at Leipzig. As Blumenthal has pointed out, the methods being developed by the physiologists, "involving measurement, replicability, public data, and controlled tests" (1980, p. 29), which were being applied to the study of the nervous system, might just as well be applied to other aspects of human behavior. Gradually the term "physiological" in German came to mean "experimental." When Wilhelm Wundt referred to the new psychology as a "physiological psychology," he meant it in this broader sense of psychology being a discipline based on scientific methodology. He used the term "physiological" to refer to the fact that most of the methods in this new laboratory approach to psychology derived from the techniques first developed by the nineteenth century physiologists (Greenwood, 2003).

For the American student of the 1880s who desired to learn about this new field of study first-hand, several choices were available (e.g., Göttingen,

FIGURE 4.1 Map of Germany, showing locations of the universities relevant for psychology's history.

Heidelberg, Berlin: see map in Figure 4.1), but Wundt's laboratory was the best equipped and had the strongest reputation, so traveling to Leipzig became the most fashionable option. During Wundt's tenure, approximately three dozen Americans completed doctorates under his supervision and a number of others at least sampled the Leipzig environment (Benjamin, Durkin, Link, Vestal, & Accord, 1992). Before considering Wundt and his influence on the development of American psychology, however, some important preliminaries are in order.

ON THE THRESHOLD OF EXPERIMENTAL PSYCHOLOGY: PSYCHOPHYSICS

A strong case can be made that scientific research on psychological topics began as a natural extension of the physiological research being done in the nine-

teenth century. Later in this chapter you will encounter one example of this in the connection between Helmholtz's physiological studies of nerve impulse speed and the psychological method of reaction time. In this section, we examine an association between physiological research on sensory processes and the development of **psychophysics**, the study of the relationship between the perception of a stimulus event ("psycho") and the physical dimensions of the stimulus being perceived ("physics"). Psychophysics originated in the sensory research of Ernst Weber and became clearly defined with the enigmatic Gustav Fechner.

Ernst Weber (1795–1878)

Weber spent most of his academic career at the University of Leipzig, first as a student and then as a professor of anatomy and physiology from 1818 until his retirement in 1871. In the 1820s physiologists were beginning to learn a great deal about visual and auditory sensation, but little was known of the other senses. Weber set out to correct the imbalance by becoming the leading authority on the tactile senses (Dorn, 1972). He made two major contributions: mapping the relative sensitivity of various locations on the skin, and demonstrating a mathematical relationship between the psychological and the physical that would later be known as Weber's Law.

Two-Point Thresholds

To examine tactile sensitivity, Weber used a technique in which he touched the skin with a simple device resembling a two-point drawing compass. The distance between the points could be varied, and the blindfolded observer's task was to judge whether one or two points were being felt. For any specific area of the skin, there exists a **two-point threshold**—the point where the perception changes from "one" point to "two." For skin areas of great sensitivity, the thumb for instance, Weber found the threshold to be quite small. That is, the points didn't have to be very far apart before being noticed as two distinct points rather than one. On the other hand, for areas of less sensitivity, the upper arm for instance, the points would have to be placed farther apart before they

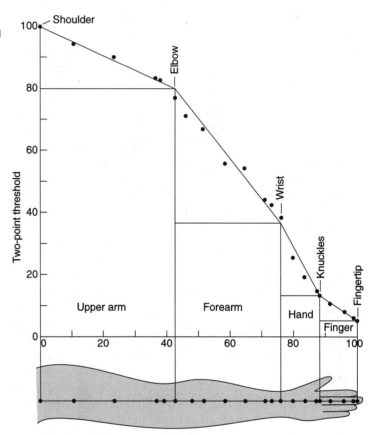

FIGURE 4.2 Two-point thresholds for various locations between shoulder and fingertip, from Boring (1942).

were perceived as being two separate ones. Figure 4.2 shows a series of two-point thresholds from shoulder to fingertip, taken from a later (1870) study by Vierordt (cited in Boring, 1942, p. 478).

Weber believed that the different two-point thresholds resulted from differences in the sizes of what he called "sensory circles," shown as hexagons on Weber's sketch in Figure 4.3 (Weber, 1852, shown in Boring, 1942, p. 476). These were areas of the skin that were sensed by the branching fibers of a single sensory nerve. If two points of a compass would both touch the skin within a single sensory circle, the perception would be of a single point, Weber thought. When the two points touched two different circles, two points would be felt. Skin areas of greater sensitivity had smaller circles. Thus, the set of four sensory circles on the left in Figure 4.3 might be from an area near the shoulder, while the

circles on the right might be closer to the fingertip. The sense of touch turns out to be more complicated than this, but Weber's model had the beneficial effect

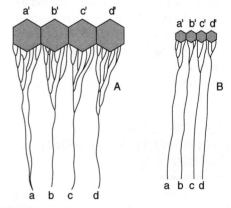

FIGURE 4.3 Weber's conception of sensory circles, from Boring (1942).

of generating considerable research on just how the tactile senses worked. Also, although he did not think of the research in these terms, Weber was measuring mental events (perceptions).

Weber's Law

Weber's second contribution derived from his interest in the "muscle sense," what we would today call kinesthesis. He wanted to know how important this sense was for making judgments about the comparative weights of objects (Heidbreder, 1933). Picture two tasks. In the first, your hand is resting on a table and first one then another weighted cylinder is placed in your palm. Your task is to judge which cylinder is heavier. In the second task, the two cylinders are on the table and this time you lift each one before making the same judgment. In performing such an experiment, Weber found that he and other observers could make finer discriminations when they lifted the weights, which brings the muscle sense into play. More important for the history of psychology, Weber also discovered that the ability to discriminate between two weights did not depend on the absolute difference between them in weight, but on a more complicated relationship. This relationship later became known as Weber's law.

In the weight-lifting experiments, Weber was dealing with thresholds again. For example, if observers cannot distinguish between 30 and 31 grams, and between 30 and 32 grams (they judge them to be the same weight), but *can* distinguish between 30 and 33 grams, then clearly some kind of threshold has been passed at 33 grams. Weber referred to the discrimination between 30 and 33 grams as a "just noticeable difference" or **jnd**. What he discovered was that the jnd depended not on the absolute size of the difference between the weights, but on the relationship between this jnd and the smaller of the two weights (called the "standard stimulus," or S). As the standard stimulus became heavier, a greater difference between the weights was necessary before the difference was noticed. That is, **Weber's law** was this: $jnd/S = k$. So observers would notice a difference between 30 and 33 grams, but not between 60 and 63 grams. If the standard stimulus is 60 grams instead of 30, no dif-ference can be detected until the second weight is at least 66 grams ($3/30 = 6/60$). Similarly, if S = 90 grams, the jnd will be 9 grams. Hence, the jnd was proportional to the size of S.

The importance of Weber's law is threefold. First, as with the two-point threshold research, Weber was subjecting mental events to measurement and mathematical formulation. This would eventually make psychophysics an essential element of Wilhelm Wundt's new psychology, which would claim to be a science. Science demands objective measurement and threshold research seemed to fit the bill nicely. Second, Weber showed that there is not a one-to-one relationship between changes in the physical world and the psychological experience of those changes. Increasing a weight by 3 grams does not always produce the same sensation. Sometimes differences will be perceived (if S = 30), sometimes not (if S = 60). Consequently, understanding how the mind organizes its experiences requires knowing more than just the physical dimensions of the stimuli to which we are exposed; it also requires an attempt to determine how the mind perceives those physical stimuli. Third, Weber's law showed that mental and physical events could be related mathematically. That insight would be developed more fully by another Leipzig scientist.

Gustav Fechner (1801–1889)

Weber's goal as a physiologist was to understand the nature of the tactile and muscle senses and to do so he used methods that would eventually be known as psychophysical. His younger Leipzig colleague Gustav Fechner had an even more ambitious goal, however. Fechner was obsessed with the idea of resolving the ageless mind-body problem in a way that would defeat materialism, and he thought that psychophysics was the way to do it. A case can be made for calling Fechner the first experimental psychologist, even though he was trained as a physician, made his reputation as a physicist, and when he was in the midst of his pioneering research in psychophysics, thought of himself as a philosopher.

Fechner was born in a Lutheran parsonage in southern Germany in 1801; he was a precocious child, familiar with Latin by age five. At age 16 he entered the University of Leipzig to study medicine, and his education included a dose of physiology with Weber. The M.D. was earned in 1822, but Fechner never practiced medicine. During the 1820s, his interests focused on math and physics, and during this time he lectured in these areas (without pay) and earned a living by translating physics and chemistry texts from French to German. He also made original research contributions in the new physics of electricity during this time.[1] His research was notable enough to earn him a position at Leipzig as professor of physics in 1834, the same year that Weber published his research on the sensation of touch.

Fechner's interests in science broadened in the 1830s to include the study of visual afterimages, the kind that occur after a bright light is flashed on and off. He discovered a relationship between the brightness of the light and the strength of the afterimage, which led him to consider the quality of afterimages resulting from a quick glance at the brightest of all lights: the sun. Quick glances become longer glances and even though Fechner wore filters to reduce the effects of staring at the sun, he severely damaged his eyesight. The problem was serious enough to force him to resign his professorship in 1839 and accept a disability pension from the university.

Long before the afterimage episode, Fechner suffered from headaches and an occasional inability to control his thoughts, but the blindness triggered a descent into neurosis that lasted several years (Balance & Bringmann, 1987). Fechner became an invalid, forced to spend long periods of time in total darkness and plagued by a variety of anxiety, depressive, and somatic symptoms. In his words,

My situation ... became even more depressing. Since I was accustomed to using my mind and had few skills in dealing with others merely on a social basis and was not good at anything other than working with pen and textbook, I suffered soon the tortures of deadly boredom. ... (cited in Balance & Bringmann, 1987, p. 39)

Fechner's ascent to normality began in 1842 and was complete by the mid-1840s. It was accomplished largely through his efforts at regaining control over his life, but was facilitated by a steady improvement in his vision. After recovering, he turned his attention to philosophical matters and in 1851 he was reappointed to the Leipzig faculty. It was during this period that he became immersed in the question of the relationship of mind to body and consumed with the idea of defeating materialism. As you recall from the last chapter, materialism, the belief that all events have causes that can be traced to physical and chemical changes, was favored by most of the younger physiologists of the day (e.g., Helmholtz).

Fechner referred to materialism as the *Nachtansicht*, or "Night View," and he hoped to replace it with a contrasting *Tagesansicht*, or "Day View." This Day View derived from an idealism movement then popular in German philosophy, which held that the universe as a whole had a form of consciousness to it that went beyond the individual consciousnesses of the organisms within it. Upon death, one's personal consciousness merged with this cosmic consciousness. For Fechner, this meant that while mind and body could be considered two aspects of the same fundamental reality, the mind was the primary and dominant feature of that reality. It was in searching for a way to conceptualize the exact mind-body relationship that he created psychophysics. He later claimed that he achieved the insight suddenly, upon waking on the morning of October 22, 1850.[2] It occurred to him that mind and body could be united harmoniously and with mathematical precision by measuring psychological sensa-

---

[1] Fechner's research on electricity reveals an interesting connection with his father, a Lutheran minister whose faith extended into the realm of science. The elder Fechner was aware of the famous electricity experiments of Benjamin Franklin, and of Franklin's invention of the lightning rod in 1787. Knowing that church steeples were favorite targets of lightning bolts, he prudently installed one of Franklin's devices on his church steeple. Members of the church felt that their pastor was not showing much faith in God's ability to protect the church, but Pastor Fechner commented that the laws of physics also had to be considered (Boring, 1950). Pastor Fechner died when his son was only five, but young Gustav apparently inherited his father's love of and respect for science.

[2] If you want to impress your professor, send him or her a "Happy Fechner Day" card on October 22. To this day, experimental psychologists, especially those who study sensation and perception, take some time out on that day to raise a glass in honor of Fechner's insight.

tions and the physical stimuli that produced the sensations. The insight triggered a decade of intense work, resulting in the publication in 1860 of the *Elements of Psychophysics*, often considered the first book of experimental psychology.

Fechner's *Elements of Psychophysics*

Fechner was aware of Weber's research on thresholds, but it was only after his great insight of 1850 that he realized its significance. The breakthrough for Fechner was the conviction that sensations could be subjected to exact measurement by assuming that jnds were subjectively equal in magnitude. Thus, weights of 30 and 33 grams are just noticeably different, as are weights of 60 and 66 grams. The differences in weight between the two pairs of stimuli are 3 and 6 grams, respectively. Psychologically, however, the difference between 30 and 33 feels the same as (i.e., is subjectively equal to) the difference between 60 and 66, according to Fechner. This assumption of subjective equality led Fechner to reformulate Weber's law as

$$S = k \log R$$

where *S* is the sensation, the perceived size of some stimulus in jnd units, *k* is a constant, and *R* is the physical measurement of the stimulus.

By assuming that jnds could be the unit of psychological measurement, Fechner was able to conceive of a scale that began at the point where sensation was first noticed. He called this point the **absolute threshold**. As stimulus intensity increases above this threshold, the person eventually experiences a just noticeable difference, then another, and so on. These jnds above the absolute threshold are **difference thresholds**. Consider the familiar example of a light with a dimmer switch. With the light completely off, there is of course no stimulation and no sensation of light. As the dimmer switch is slowly turned, there will continue to be zero sensation for a brief time, but soon we just barely notice the first glimmerings of light. This is the absolute threshold. If the dimmer switch continues to be turned, a point is reached where the light is now just noticeably brighter than a second ago. This is a difference threshold.

Fechner's assumption of equal jnds was challenged almost immediately, and his mathematical relationship was shown to be true only under limited circumstances. No matter. The enduring legacy of his *Elements of Psychophysics* was his systematization of the methods used to establish thresholds, which are still in use, both in the laboratory and in such applications as vision and hearing tests. These are known today as the methods of limits, constant stimuli, and adjustment.[3] Consider them in the context of a hearing test designed to establish absolute thresholds. In the **method of limits**, a stimulus is presented that is well above threshold, then gradually reduced in intensity until the subject reports that it can no longer be heard. This is called a descending trial, and it is followed by an ascending trial, in which the stimulus is first presented below threshold, then increased until the subject hears it for the first time. Descending and ascending trials are alternated a number of times, and the threshold is calculated as an average of all the trials. In the **method of constant stimuli**, sounds of varying intensities are presented in a random order and the subject's task is to indicate whether or not they are heard. This method solves a problem with the method of limits, which is a tendency to anticipate the place where the threshold lies. In the **method of adjustment**, the subject directly varies the intensity of the stimulus until it seems to be at threshold. While these examples involve absolute thresholds, all three methods can also be used in experiments on difference thresholds. Of the three techniques, a study using the method of adjustment takes the least amount of time, but is the least accurate; the method of constant stimuli is the most accurate, but takes the longest time (Goldstein, 1996). In an actual hearing test, the method of limits with descending trials is normally used, with "catch trials" inserted to prevent subjects from raising their hands ("I hear it") when there is in fact no stimulus presented.

Boring (1963b) has referred to Fechner as the "inadvertent founder of psychophysics." He believed that Fechner's main purpose was philosophical: to establish his Day View while defeating materialism

---

[3] Fechner referred to them as the methods of just noticeable differences, right and wrong cases, and average error, respectively.

(the Night View). Unfortunately for Fechner, that goal was not reached and the philosophical implications of his work were largely ignored. Fortunately for psychology, Fechner's efforts resulted in the creation of a program of research and a set of methods that enabled others to see what Fechner did not: that psychological phenomena could be subjected to scientific methodology. By inadvertently creating psychophysics in 1860, Fechner paved the way for another German physiologist, Wilhelm Wundt, to proclaim a "New Psychology" a few years later.

WUNDT ESTABLISHES A NEW PSYCHOLOGY AT LEIPZIG

The quote that opens this chapter comes from the preface of the epoch-making two-volume *Principles of Physiological Psychology*, published in 1873–1874 by the German most often described as the "founder" of experimental psychology, Wilhelm Wundt. To claim, as Wundt did, that one is making an "attempt to mark out a new domain of science" is the kind of statement that separates founders from their contemporaries. Clearly, Fechner's work on psychophysics entitles him to a claim as the first experimental psychologist. We've seen, however, that Fechner had other, more philosophical, purposes. Thus, as Boring (1950) has pointed out, founders are promoters; they might not be the first to accomplish something, but they are the first to proclaim loudly that their accomplishment breaks dramatically new ground. They might make some important scientific contribution, but their talent lies in their ability to propagandize. Wundt had that talent.

Wilhelm Wundt (1832–1920): Creating a New Science

Experimental psychology's founder had a childhood of modest accomplishment. Excessive daydreaming and marginal performance characterized his early school years, and it wasn't until his late teens that he became interested in the direction of his education. Despite a dismal academic record, family connections enabled him to begin medical studies at the University of Tübingen at the age of 19; after a year he switched to Heidelberg, where he finally began to show promise. By 1855, he had earned an M.D. (summa cum laude) from the University of Heidelberg and had finished first on a state board-certifying exam (Bringmann, Balance, & Evans, 1975).

The Heidelberg years also saw the blossoming of Wundt's interests in science. The famous chemist Robert Bunsen (yes, he invented the Bunsen burner) made a lasting impression: When Wundt eventually became a professor himself, he copied Bunsen's technique of illustrating points in class through the frequent use of visual displays and demonstrations. Bunsen also inspired Wundt's first independent research project, an examination of the effects of restricting salt input on the chemical composition of his urine. During these years, Wundt also completed some more sophisticated research, including a study of the roles played by several cranial nerves in breathing. This required an ablation method using live dogs and rabbits, a procedure that Wundt found troubling. He was bolstered by the support of his mother, who assisted in the surgery, which was completed in Wundt's home rather than at the university (Bringmann, Balance, & Evans, 1975). Wundt also conducted an experiment on the touch sensitivity of hysteric patients, using Weber's two-point threshold technique; this study served as his M.D. dissertation research.

Following completion of the M.D. in November of 1855, Wundt practiced medicine for a brief six months as a clinical assistant at Heidelberg's university hospital, but he was already beginning to think that a life of research was more appealing than a life of writing prescriptions and setting bones. He spent a semester in Berlin studying experimental physiology with the great Johannes Müller (Chapter 3), and then resolved to become a professor of physiology upon his return to Heidelberg. He was given a position of *Privatdozent* in February of 1857, which in the German system meant that he was entitled to offer courses, but that his entire salary depended on student fees. Wundt's first course attracted only four students and near the completion of the course he fell seriously ill, probably with tuberculosis (Bringmann, Bringmann, & Balance, 1980). After a year-long recovery, he applied for an opening as the assistant in the laboratory of the esteemed Hermann Helmholtz (Chapter 3), who had just begun his tenure at Heidelberg. Wundt got the job, a major boost for his career.

Wundt toiled as Helmholtz's assistant for six years, from 1858 to 1864, but he did much more with his time than just run the laboratory. He continued to offer courses as *Privatdozent* and he began publishing at a rate that is astounding by any standard.[4] In addition to technical papers and two brief texts based on his lectures, Wundt published two important books that marked him as an emerging experimental psychologist. *Contributions to a Theory of Sensory Perception* appeared in 1862, followed a year later by *Lectures on Human and Animal Psychology*. The first book is noteworthy because it marks the first time that Wundt called for an explicitly experimental approach to basic psychological questions. Thus, he was thinking about the possibility that psychology could be a science long before his famous pronouncement of 1873–1874. The second book repeated the call and described some of the early research in psychophysics and reaction time.

Wundt left Helmholtz's laboratory in 1864 but remained at Heidelberg for another decade. He set up his own private laboratory and earned a livable wage through teaching fees and book royalties. In 1871 his efforts were finally rewarded by the university, which appointed him to the rank of Extraordinary Professor (similar to the associate professor level in American universities). This meant that for the first time in his life, Wundt had full faculty status and a salary that was not tied to student enrollment. Nearing the age of 40, he was finally secure enough to marry his fiancée of many years. During this time he wrote the work best known to psychologists, his two-volume *Principles of Physiological Psychology* (1873–1874/1910), which included the chapter's opening quote in its Preface. The book, which eventually went through six editions, earned him a professorship in "inductive philosophy" at the University of Zurich (academic year 1874–1875). After just a year in Switzerland, Wundt was offered a

similar position at the more prestigious University of Leipzig, Germany's largest university at the time, and he accepted immediately. There he remained until his retirement in 1917. He died three years later.

We tend to associate Wundt only with Leipzig, but it is important to realize that when he arrived there in 1875, he was already in his mid-forties and had been an active scientist at Heidelberg for 17 years. He had already written three important books and numerous papers, more than most professors produce in a lifetime. Furthermore, he had announced that at least some aspects of psychology could be experimental, and he had set out a plan for establishing what quickly came to be called the New Psychology. Thus, he had accomplished what would be a life's work for many. Yet Wundt still had more than *40* highly productive years left in him during his time at Leipzig.

KEY DATE *1879*

This year marks the date normally associated with the establishment of Wundt's laboratory of experimental psychology in Leipzig.

These events also occurred:

- Electric light patented by Thomas Edison
- London established its first telephone exchange
- Ferdinand de Lesseps formed the Panama Canal Company
- The American novelist Henry James, brother of psychologist William James, published *Daisy Miller*
- In Utica, New York, Frank Woolworth opens the first of many of 5- and 10-cent Woolworth stores
- Mary Baker Eddy became pastor of the Church of Christ, Scientist, in Boston
- These people were born:

    Joseph Stalin, Soviet dictator

    Albert Einstein, German physicist

    Will Rogers, American humorist
- This person died:

    William Lloyd Garrison, American abolitionist

---

[4] By one estimate, Wundt published 53,735 pages during his professional years, an average of 2.2 pages per day (Boring, 1950, p. 345)!

FIGURE 4.4 An aging Wilhelm Wundt (center) in his laboratory at Leipzig.

During his years at Heidelberg, Wundt had accumulated a private collection of laboratory apparatus, both for his own research and for demonstrating various phenomena during his lectures (in the spirit of his old chemistry professor, Robert Bunsen). Upon arrival at Leipzig, he requested space to store the equipment. Although traditional accounts have it that the university gave him some space upon his arrival in 1875 and that the room eventually became his famous laboratory, careful archival research (Bringmann, Bringmann, & Ungerer, 1980) has shown that Leipzig delayed the assignment for a year, despite Wundt's repeated requests. Nonetheless, that the university granted the request at all is noteworthy, because space was quite limited at the time. This modest beginning, a room with approximately 400 square feet, eventually became experimental psychology's first laboratory and the model for dozens of imitators. Wundt used the lab for demonstrational purposes initially, but by 1879 he and his students were conducting original research in what he now called the *Psychologisches Institut*. The Institute quickly became a magnet, attracting curious students from all over Europe and from America. Additional rooms were added over the years, and in 1897 a new and more elaborate laboratory was built to Wundt's specifications. It was

destroyed by an Allied bombing raid in 1943. An inside look at the workings of Wundt's laboratory, a glimpse of which can be seen in Figure 4.4, will follow shortly; first, however, it is necessary to examine Wundt's vision for his New Psychology.

Wundt's Conception of the New Psychology

The "new domain of science" that Wundt attempted to "mark out" in his *Principles of Physiological Psychology* was a vision first outlined 12 years earlier in his 1862 book on perception (*Contributions to a Theory of Sensory Perception*). This new psychology called for the scientific examination of human conscious experience, using methods borrowed from experimental physiology and supplemented by new strategies. Please note that today, when we see a book with the label "physiological psychology," we are inclined to think the book will focus on the relationship between biology and behavior. Wundt, however, used the label physiological only to make reference to the fact that many of the methods for his new psychology (e.g., reaction time) had been developed in physiology laboratories (Greenwood, 2003). He could have just as easily called his book an "experimental psychology." Wundt's new psychology included two major programs: the examination of "immediate" conscious experience using the experimental methods of the laboratory and the study of higher mental processes, using nonlaboratory methods.

Studying Immediate Conscious Experience

To understand the contrast that Wundt drew between immediate experience and "mediate" experience, consider a simple example. If you look out the window at a thermometer and it reads 15°F, you are not experiencing the phenomenon of temperature directly. Rather, temperature is being *mediated* by a scientific instrument. On the other hand, if you then step outside without a coat, you have a direct experience of coldness. It is an immediate conscious experience. That is, there is no thermometer standing between you and the weather; you are encountering it firsthand. For Wundt, it was this immediate conscious experience that was to be the subject matter of his laboratory psychology.

Wundt recognized the problem with studying immediate consciousness. To examine mediate experience objectively is simple. Because the temperature reading is a public event, two or more observers can agree on it and it is a fairly straightforward matter to apply scientific methods. Various aspects of the environment can be manipulated systematically, and the resulting effects on temperature can be assessed with some precision. Describing immediate experience is more difficult, however. How can you be sure that your experience of coldness compares with mine? Here Wundt made a critical distinction between *self-observation* and *internal perception*. The distinction has been blurred over the years, according to Danziger (1980), with both terms being called **introspection**. Self-observation is the traditional philosophical attempt to analyze life's experiences through introspective reflection. This was unsystematic and because such observations by definition take place some time after the experienced event has occurred, they rely too heavily on faulty memory. Wundt rejected self-observation as nothing better than philosophical speculation. **Internal perception**, on the other hand, was like self-observation, but was a much narrower process of responding immediately to precisely controlled stimuli. The problem of memory was reduced by the immediacy of the response and by using observers

(Wundt and his students) trained to respond automatically and without bias. Such precision came with a price, however. Internal perception could only yield valid scientific data if its results could be replicated. For Wundt, this meant that laboratory research had to be limited to a narrow range of experiences. In practice, this amounted to basic sensory/perceptual/attentional ones. Such experiences could be controlled by means of sophisticated apparatus used to present stimuli to observers, who in turn would give simple responses to these stimuli. In Wundt's lab, these types of introspective responses were "largely limited to judgments of size, intensity, and duration of physical stimuli, supplemented at times by judgments of their simultaneity and succession" (Danziger, 1980, p. 247). These, of course, are the kinds of judgments made in psychophysics experiments, which comprised a significant portion of the research in Wundt's laboratory. As we will learn, Wundt's conception of introspection as internal perception differed sharply from the "systematic experimental introspection" used by two of his better-known students, Oswald Külpe (below) and Edward B. Titchener (Chapter 7).

Studying Higher Mental Processes

Although Wundt believed that laboratory investigation was necessarily limited to the immediate conscious experience of basic mental processes, he also had a broader aim for his psychology. He wished to examine other mental processes such as learning, thinking, language, and the effects of culture, but he believed that because these processes were so intertwined with an individual's personal history, cultural history, and the social environment, they could not be controlled sufficiently to be examined in the laboratory. Instead, they could only be studied through inductive observational techniques, cross-cultural comparisons, historical analysis, and case study.

These higher mental processes were a lifelong interest of Wundt's, first outlined in detail in his second major book (*Lectures on Human and Animal Psychology*, 1863). They fully occupied the last two decades of his life and during this time, he enhanced his reputation as a prodigious writer by publishing the massive 10-volume *Völkerpsychologie* ("volker" translates roughly as a combination of "cultural," "ethnic," "social," and/or "communal"). The books include detailed analyses of language and culture, and encompass topics that would today be considered under the headings of psycholinguistics, the psychology of religion and myth, social psychology, forensic psychology, and anthropology. Of the 10 volumes, there were three on myth and religion, two on language, two on society, and one each on culture and history, law, and art (Blumenthal, 1975).

Wundt, like other thinkers of his time, believed that an implication of evolutionary theory was that cultures could be arranged on a continuum, from "primitive" (e.g., Australian aboriginal) to "advanced" (German, presumably). By studying the social customs, myths, religions, and languages of cultures differing in their level of sophistication, Wundt thought that an understanding of the evolution of human mental processes could be attained (Farr, 1983). He was especially interested in language, and his descriptions give him a legitimate claim to the title of founder of modern psycholinguistics. Much of what he wrote about language was ignored at the time, only to be rediscovered in the 1950s and 1960s, when psycholinguistics became a key element in the rise of cognitive psychology (Blumenthal, 1975). For example, Wundt distinguished between the idea that was to be conveyed by a sentence, the actual structure of the sentence itself, and the manner in which the listener took the sentence structure and inferred the speaker's meaning from it. The relationship between the idea to be conveyed and the sentence structure is similar to the distinction later made by linguist Noam Chomsky between the deep and surface structures of a grammar, and Wundt's belief that the listener would not recall the actual sentence but the meaning of it is similar to later research on memory for the "gist" of communicated messages.

Inside Wundt's Laboratory

Once Wundt's students began producing original research at Leipzig, the need for a way to publicize the work became apparent. Wundt solved the problem in 1881 by creating the journal *Philosophische Studien* (*Philosophical Studies*). It was the first journal designed to report the results of experimental research in psychology and Wundt served as editor for its first two decades (1881–1903). The journal became a mouthpiece for the work done by Wundt and his students, so a look at its contents reveals the kind of research done at Leipzig during the last two decades of the nineteenth century. According to Boring (1950), who examined the 100 or so experimental studies published in the journal during this time, at least half of the research was in the area of sensation and perception. Of the remaining half, reaction time studies were the most popular, followed by studies on attention, feeling, and association.

Sensation and Perception

Most of the basic information about sensory systems encountered in today's courses in sensation/perception was known by the turn of the century and some of the research was carried out in Wundt's laboratory. As mentioned earlier, most of these "internal perception" studies were psychophysical in nature, examining such topics as the abilities to distinguish colors presented to different areas of the retina and tones presented in various combinations of pitch and loudness. In perception, Wundtians studied such topics as positive and negative afterimages, visual contrast, illusions, and the perception of size, depth, and motion (Boring, 1950).

Mental Chronometry

When Helmholtz measured the duration of a nerve impulse and found it to be more leisurely than expected (Chapter 3), he provided the impetus to a method that came to be known as **mental chronometry** in Wundt's lab. Today we call it reaction time. Wundt was aware of this research long before he arrived in Leipzig. He became Helmholtz's assistant at Heidelberg shortly after the nerve impulse studies had been carried out and he became very interested in the problem of measuring mental speed in the 1860s. The problem had also been around for a number of years in the form of a practical difficulty faced by astronomers. The creation of tables for calculating longitude required knowing the precise positions of various stars and planets at specific times of a lunar cycle (Sobel, 1995). Identifying these positions involved a complicated procedure that measured the time taken for a planet to make a "transit" from one side of the crosshair of a telescope lens to the other. Humans were making the judgments of course, and even though they were trained astronomers, their judgments of transit times tended to be different because of small differences in their reaction times. To solve the problem, an attempt was made to calibrate one astronomer against another by determining each one's **personal equation**. Thus, if astronomer A was regularly 0.12 second slower than astronomer B, their transit times could be made comparable through a personal equation: A = B + 0.12 second.

The individual who developed the reaction time procedure as it came to be used by the Wundtians was F. C. Donders (1818–1889), a Dutch physiologist. Donders reasoned that if nerve impulses take a measurable amount of time and if mental activity is composed of nerve impulses, then various mental events potentially could be determined with some precision. Assuming that mental events could be combined in an additive fashion, Donders developed the **subtractive method** in the late 1860s. First, he would measure the time taken for a simple reaction: holding down a telegraph key, then releasing it as soon as possible after perceiving a light, for example. The procedure would then be "complicated" by adding other mental tasks. For instance, the observer might be asked to respond only if a red light came on; if the light was another color, no response was to be made. This "discrimination reaction time" (DRT) was composed of everything involved in simple reaction time (SRT), *plus* the mental event of discriminating between the colors. Thus:

$$DRT = SRT + \text{discrimination time}$$
$$\text{discrimination time} = DRT - SRT$$

Similarly, "choice reaction time" (CRT) involved releasing one key if the light was one color and another key if the light was a second color. In addition to simple reaction time and the time taken to discriminate between the two colors, the observer also had to choose which key to release. Thus:

$$CRT = SRT + \text{discrimination time} + \text{choice time}$$
$$\text{choice time} = CRT - (SRT + \text{discrimination time})$$
$$\text{choice time} = CRT - DRT$$

For reasons that are apparent, this procedure was also called the **complication experiment**; studies using it flourished in Wundt's laboratory, especially in the 1880s. The procedure was eventually discarded, however, when it became clear that the additive assumptions underlying the method were overly simplistic. In the aforementioned procedures, for instance, certain more complicated reactions should always be longer than less complicated ones, but in actual experiments this outcome did not always occur. Wundt's student Oswald Külpe, to be discussed in more detail later in this chapter, pointed out that altering the procedure by adding discrimination and/or choice does not simply add elements; rather, it changed the entire experimental situation.

James McKeen Cattell (Chapter 8), perhaps the best known of the American students who studied with Wundt, was an enthusiastic advocate of the reaction time method (Garrett, 1951). He began his research while a student at Johns Hopkins in Baltimore, then continued it after arriving in Leipzig in 1883. An examination of one of his studies (Cattell, 1885/1948) nicely illustrates the logic of the reaction time method and the close attention to detail needed to carry out such research. In the article, Cattell described some research on simple, discrimination, and choice reaction times that were completed with his German colleague Gustav Berger. The research formed the basis for Berger's doctoral dissertation for Wundt on the effects of stimulus intensity on reaction time (Sokal, 1981).

In the first experiment, Cattell and Berger gave simple reaction times to lights that varied in intensity. The experimental setup probably looked something like the one in Figure 4.5 (photo taken at Clark University in 1892). As Cattell described it, "[t]he observer sat in the dark, and looked through a telescopic tube at the point where the light was to appear" (1885/1948, p. 323). Cattell and Berger each made 150 reactions for each of eight intensity levels, finding that reaction time generally decreased as the light brightened. They also found individual differences—Cattell was consistently faster.

In a similar manner, Cattell and Berger varied the intensity of an electrical shock to the left forearm, to examine its effect on the reaction time of the right

FIGURE 4.5 Reaction time experiment in progress at Clark University, 1892.

hand. Again, reaction time quickened with increased intensity, although at the highest intensity "the reaction was probably retarded, because the shock was painful" (p. 325). In his data summaries, Cattell described both the mean score and a measure of variability (the average deviation, an early forerunner of today's standard deviation). Also, note that there are just two observers in the study, Berger and Cattell. This was a common situation in early experimental psychology: Very few participants, each person contributing a great deal of data, and no clear distinction between what in later years would be called the *experimenter* and the *subject*. Furthermore, data from several participants would not be averaged together. Rather, all data from each subject would be reported, with additional subjects serving the purpose of replication.

After reporting the simple reaction times, Cattell described the logic of the complication experiment and, using three of the eight light intensities, reported results for simple RT ("reaction time"), discrimination RT ("reaction with perception time"), and choice RT ("reaction with perception and will time"). Thus, "perception time" means discrimination time and "will time" means choice time. Here is his description of the complication rationale and the data:

> The time is longer when it is necessary to distinguish the colours before the reaction is made.

We can determine this time, if instead of always reacting as quickly as possible, we react if it is red, but not at all if it is blue. We thus add to the simple reaction time. We can further let the subject lift his right hand if the light is red, his left hand if it is blue; we then have, besides the time necessary for the simple reaction and for distinguishing the colour, the time it takes to make a choice between two motions. The results of experiments made with three intensities of light (V, III, and I) are given in the table. [See Table 4.1] (Cattell, 1885/1948, p. 325)

As you can see, Cattell used the Donders system to arrive at his "perception" (i.e., discrimination) and "will" (i.e., choice) times. For example, with Cattell as the observer and the stimulus intensity at V:

$$\text{discrimination time} = \text{DRT} - \text{SRT}$$
$$= 274 - 189$$
$$= 85 \text{ (i.e., 0.85 sec)}$$

$$\text{choice time} = \text{CRT} - (\text{SRT} + \text{discrimination time})$$
$$= 356 - (189 + 85)$$
$$= 82 \text{ (i.e., 0.82 sec)}$$

Like Külpe, Cattell eventually became a critic of the complication experiment while continuing to see the usefulness of the reaction time method to test various hypotheses about mental processing. That is,

TABLE 4.1   The Results of a Complication Experiment

	B[erger]			C[attell]		
	V	**III**	**I**	**V**	**III**	**I**
Reaction Time	189	218	273	189	209	303
Reaction with Perception Time	238	293	373	274	328	417
Reaction with Perception and Will Time	287	320	393	356	388	495
Perception Time	49	75	100	85	119	114
Will Time	49	27	20	82	60	78

he eventually rejected the additive model while retaining the idea that reaction time could be used to compare mental activities that differed in complexity. This led him to study individual differences in reaction time and such phenomena as recognition times for different letters of the alphabet and reaction times for verbal associations (e.g., Cattell, 1886). Cattell also left a detailed account of day-to-day life in Wundt's laboratory, some of which is described in the Close-Up for this chapter.

CLOSE-UP:
An American in Leipzig

The most prominent of the three dozen or so American students who completed doctorates with Wundt was James McKeen Cattell (1860–1944). In 1886, he became the first American to earn a Leipzig Ph.D. in experimental psychology under Wundt's supervision (Benjamin, Durkin, Link, Vestal, & Accord, 1992). While at Leipzig, Cattell kept a detailed journal and corresponded frequently with his parents in America. These materials have been collected, organized, and annotated with great care by historian of science Michael Sokal, and published as *An Education in Psychology: James McKeen Cattell's Journal and Letters from Germany and England, 1880–1888 (1981)*. The book is a rich source of information about life in the early years of Wundt's laboratory at Leipzig.

Cattell first went to Leipzig as part of a European tour in 1881–1882. He then spent the 1882–1883 academic year at Johns Hopkins University in Baltimore, studying in the lab created by G. Stanley Hall (Chapter 6). He returned to Leipzig in the fall of 1883 and emerged with his doctorate three years later. Here are some of the observations he made about working in Wundt's laboratory, all taken from Sokal (1981).

Most of Cattell's research concerned the problem of reaction time. In a letter to his parents in 1884, he briefly described this research. Like others immersed in basic research that might seem trivial to outsiders, Cattell apparently felt a bit defensive and believed it necessary to convince his parents that his work was valuable:

Letter to Parents, 8 October 1884

In [my research] I determine the time required by simple mental processes—how long it takes us to see, hear or feel something—to understand, to will, to think. You may not consider this so very interesting or important. But if we wish to describe the world—which is the end of science—surely an accurate knowledge of our mind is more important than anything else. ... [I]f one thinks that knowledge for its own sake is worth the pursuit, then surely a knowledge of mind is best of all. Not only is the mind of man of infinitely more worth and importance than anything else, but on its nature the whole world depends.

As to my special work—it is surely ... in itself interesting to know how fast a man thinks—for on this, not on the number of years he lives depends the length of his life (p. 125)

Cattell's parents were apparently concerned that their son might overwork himself during his time at Leipzig. To reassure them, Cattell described a typical research day with his colleague, Gustav Berger. Only a portion of it required the kind of focused attention that would be fatiguing, Cattell reported:

Letter to Parents, 26 November 1884

Berger began work with me again this morning. I do not think I shall hurt myself in working, if I keep taking ... constant exercise. It is undoubtedly true that making experiments on one's self is trying, but I do not do this continuously. If I spend six hours a day at this work, perhaps two must be given to looking after apparatus, preparing things &c. This is very easy work indeed. Then in two of the other four hours the other man is the subject and my work is not especially difficult. So you see I only spend two hours in work that strains. It were a pity if at twenty-five I could not stand that. (p. 141)

Cattell's observation about the two hours set aside for the apparatus illustrates the difficulty of developing a new science. Most of the apparatus had to be either adopted from the physics or physiology lab or invented on the spot. Apparatus problems were a constant irritant, as Cattell made clear in this letter:

Letter to Parents, 5 January 1885

Berger turned up early this morning and we started work. By way of variety not one but both of the electric batteries were out of order. You have no idea how much one must fuss over apparatus. The trouble is not that one must know physics, but that he must be an original investigator in physics. For example Prof. Wundt thought that when a magnet was made by passing a current around a piece of soft iron, it was made instantaneously. I find with the current he used it takes over a tenth of a second. All the times he measured were that much too long. Now the time required for magnetism to be developed in soft iron has nothing on earth to do with psychology, yet if I had not spent a great deal of time on this subject all my work would have been wrong. Then it is hard to get apparatus made properly. ... All this, the getting the apparatus and running it, is very aggravating when one is in a hurry. (pp. 151–152)

Throughout his career, Cattell never hesitated to speak his mind and was not known either for modesty or tolerance. In the following comment, made near the end of his time at Leipzig, he made it clear what he thought of Wundt's laboratory.

Letter to Parents, 22 January 1885

I worked in Wundt's laboratory this afternoon probably for the last time. ... Wundt's laboratory has a reputation greater than it deserves—the work done

> is decidedly amateurish. Work has only been done in two departments—the relation of the internal stimulus to the sensation [i.e., psychophysics], and the time of mental process [i.e., reaction time]. The latter is my subject—I started working on it at Baltimore [at Johns Hopkins] before I had read a word written by Wundt—what I did there was decidedly original. I'm quite sure my work is worth more than all done by Wundt & his pupils in this department, and as I have said it is one of the two departments on which they have worked. Mind I do not consider my work of any special importance—I only consider Wundt's of still less. (p. 156)

Rewriting History: The New and Improved Wilhelm Wundt

In Chapter 1, you learned that histories are continually being rewritten in light of new information, new ways of interpreting information, and so on. Wundt's psychology is a perfect illustration. If you had taken a history of psychology course about 30 years ago, you would have learned this about Wundt:

- He founded the first "school" of psychology, called structuralism.

- The main goal of Wundt's school was to analyze the contents of the mind into its basic structural components or elements, using introspection of mental contents as the chief method.

- He was not really interested in cultural psychology; the 10-volume *Völkerpsychologie* was just a secondary hobby for an old man.

- Wundt's intellectual son was E. B. Titchener, who carried out Wundt's program and spread the Wundtian gospel of structuralism in America.

- His model of the mind was similar to that of the British empiricists; that is, he did not believe in the concept of the mind as an active agent, but as the result of passive associative experiences.

Today, the only time you read descriptions like this one will be in chapter sections pointing out that each of these points is either a serious distortion or just wrong. In the 1970s, historians began taking a closer look at Wundt (e.g., Blumenthal, 1975; Danziger, 1980; Leahey, 1979) and discovered that the traditional accounts were problematic. Since that time, histories have begun to include more accurate descriptions of Wundt's life and work. Three questions arise: How did the distortions occur, why were they discovered only recently, and what did Wundt really say?

The Source of the Problem

Part of the difficulty derives from the fact that Wundt wrote more in his lifetime than most people can read in theirs. Also, much of his work has not been translated from German. Hence, there is a tendency for non-German speakers to rely on what others have written about Wundt, rather than on what Wundt said himself. Most psychologists learned their history from E. G. Boring, Boring learned most of his from Titchener, and therein lies the root of the problem. As you will learn in Chapter 7, Titchener studied with Wundt for two years and earned a Leipzig Ph.D. in 1892. He then spent his academic career at Cornell, where he spread the gospel of structuralism— his school, not Wundt's. Titchener also translated several of Wundt's books and wrote a long obituary shortly after Wundt's death (Titchener, 1921). In essence, Titchener took a portion of Wundt's work and exaggerated its importance, while downplaying or ignoring other parts of Wundt's work. The distortions were reflected in the way he taught about Wundt and in his translations of Wundt's writings. There is no evidence of a deliberate attempt to distort. Titchener was simply emphasizing what was most congenial to his own way of thinking. For example, Titchener's lack of interest in nonexperimental psychology led him to shrug off Wundt's interest in cultural psychology, making the remarkable comment in his obituary that Wundt's 20-years-in-the-making, 10-volume *Völkerpsychologie* was little more than "a grateful occupation for his old age" (Titchener, 1921, p. 175) and that "the dominant idea of Wundt's life ... is the idea of an experimental psychology" (p. 175).

Boring was Titchener's best known student and psychology's most venerable historian (see Chapter 1's Close-Up). His *A History of Experimental Psychology*, written in 1929 and revised in 1950, was the book that informed several generations of psychologists and provided the model for other history texts, until recently. It was dedicated to Titchener and the chapter on Wundt contains many of the distortions perpetuated by Titchener. The *Völkerpsychologie*, for instance, is barely mentioned.

The Rediscovery of Wundt

There are two reasons why Wundt's ideas began to be reexamined in the 1970s. First, as you recall from Chapter 1, it was during the late 1960s and early 1970s that the history of psychology as a discipline gathered new momentum, under the leadership of people like Robert Watson. To some extent, new scholarship directed at Wundt's history reflects the increased interest in psychology's history. The second reason is more subtle and provides another reason why history is continually being rewritten. As you will learn in Chapter 14, during the decade of the 1960s, cognitive psychology happened. That is, psychologists became increasingly interested in the experimental study of mental processes, a topic that languished in America between 1930 and 1960, due to the influence of behaviorism. Some scholars versed in the new cognitive research, most notably Arthur Blumenthal and Thomas Leahey, saw connections between the cognitive psychology of the 1960s and Wundtian psychology. Indeed, some of the cognitive research methods essentially duplicated research completed at Leipzig, even though the modern researchers seemed unaware of it. Blumenthal and Leahey began examining Wundt's work in light of the new cognitive psychology, producing papers that showed the connections between the two (Blumenthal, 1975; Leahey, 1979). The broader lesson is that while not necessarily being

presentist, histories can be strongly influenced by the historical context within which they are written. One effect of modern cognitive psychology was to view Wundt in a new light. In the days of behaviorism's dominance, such a reexamination of Wundt would not have occurred.

The Real Wundt

The traditional but erroneous view of Wundt is that he was a structuralist. Now there is no question that one of Wundt's goals for his laboratory work was to identify the elements of immediate conscious experience. After all, he was originally trained in medicine and physiology and had a natural penchant for classification. Thus, his experimental papers include descriptions of the basic elements of consciousness, which he decided were sensations and feelings. Furthermore, each of these elements could be further categorized along certain dimensions. Sensations, for instance, were classified according to such dimensions as quality (e.g., different colors), intensity, and duration.

Analysis and classification, however, were only minor aspects of Wundt's system, and he was relatively uninterested in them. Rather, he was more concerned with the manner in which the mind actively organizes its experiences through an act of will. He labeled his system **voluntarism** to reflect the active nature of the mind. A central concept of his voluntaristic system was the phenomenon of **apperception**, a term borrowed from the German philosopher Leibniz (Chapter 2). To apperceive some event is to perceive it with full clarity and have it in the focus of one's attention. As you are reading this page, for example, your full attention and focus (let's hope) is on this sentence and its meaning. It is being apperceived. Other information is in the periphery of your attention; Wundt would say that it is being apprehended, but not apperceived.[5] Thus at any

---

[5] The apprehension/apperception difference was the key component of an important theory proposed by one of Wundt's more famous students, the psychiatrist Emil Kraepelin (1856–1926). Kraepelin devised a classification scheme for mental illness that produced the first clear description of what we call schizophrenia today. For more on Kraepelin, see the Close-Up in Chapter 12.

given time, there is information that is in the focus of attention, and other information in the margins. The former is said to be apperceived, the latter apprehended. Furthermore, apperception is a process that actively and vigorously organizes information into meaningful wholes. When we see the word "dog," we do not perceive three separate letters; we perceive a single concept that has meaning for us. Our visual sense might be initially processing meaningless lines and symbols, but our mind creates a meaningful whole. Wundt referred to the apperceptive process as a "creative synthesis."

Wundt's concept of apperception is a far cry from a more passive associationism. Yet Wundt did recognize that some elements of conscious experience do combine as passive associations. As the British associationists said, if you see John and Mary together often enough, you will soon come to think of one when you see the other. This happens automatically because of a passively formed association. On the other hand, apperception is occurring if, when you see John and Mary, you bring them into the focus of your attention and perceive them as a special couple, or perhaps as two people who seem completely ill suited for one another. That is, you are going beyond the information given and perceiving them clearly and distinctly.

The Wundtian Legacy

Because it was his intention to create a new way of conceptualizing psychology, Wundt is justifiably considered the first true psychologist of the modern era. Although it is difficult to identify a single Wundtian among the early American psychologists, he had a strong influence on the origins of American psychology. The Americans who studied with Wundt may not have returned as disciples, and Blumenthal (1980) has suggested that most came back with little more than a floor plan and an equipment list. Nonetheless, they emerged from Leipzig convinced that something new and exciting was in the air and they wanted to be a part of it. American psychology quickly established its own distinctive and non-Wundtian shape, but much of the motivation for it derived from Wundt's example.

THE NEW PSYCHOLOGY SPREADS

It should not be surprising to learn that Wundt did not hold a monopoly on the New Psychology. As you recall from the opening of the chapter, the *Wissenschaft* environment created an atmosphere conducive to the creation of an empirically based examination of psychological phenomena. Sure enough, several German contemporaries of Wundt were actively engaged in exploring this new approach to understanding the human mind. We will examine three of them: Hermann Ebbinghaus, G. E. Müller, and Oswald Külpe.

Hermann Ebbinghaus (1850–1909): The Experimental Study of Memory

One indirect effect of Fechner's *Elements of Psychophysics* is that it helped launch the experimental study of human memory. This occurred sometime in the mid-1870s when a young German philosopher named Hermann Ebbinghaus stumbled on an English translation of Fechner's book while browsing in a used bookstore in Paris. Fechner's demonstration that the mind could be subjected to scientific methods inspired Ebbinghaus, who was wrestling with the philosophical problem of the association of ideas at the time.

Not much is known about the formative years of Hermann Ebbinghaus. After finishing a normal gymnasium education, he studied at several universities and fought briefly for the German side in the Franco-Prussian War in the early 1870s. His academic interests shifted from history to philology (the historical study of language) to philosophy, and he eventually earned a doctorate in the latter from the University of Bonn in 1873. His dissertation topic was an analysis of "Hartmann's Philosophy of the Unconscious." During the mid-1870s he traveled in England and in France, discovered Fechner's *Elements* along the way, and evidently began to think about how to study the formation of associations.

As a philosopher, Ebbinghaus was thoroughly familiar with the British empiricists and their analysis of association processes. As you recall from Chapter 2, they considered association to be analogous to gravity as a force that attracted and bound together ideas. The

British philosophers all considered association to be an essential component of the mind's organizational structure, but they argued over the basic laws of association (e.g., is contiguity sufficient to explain associations or are other principles necessary?). For Ebbinghaus, Fechner's scientific approach to the mind apparently triggered a creative leap. If sensations could be measured, why not other mental processes? Why not association? Sometime during the late 1870s, Ebbinghaus became resolved to study the formation and retention of associations scientifically. By the middle of the next decade, he had produced *Memory: A Contribution to*

Experimental Psychology (1885/1964). This brief book (123 pages in a 1964 reprinting) inaugurated a research tradition that continues today and includes results that are still described in textbooks of general psychology. As Ernest Hilgard pointed out in an introduction to the 1964 reprinting, "[f]or the experimental study of learning and memory there is one source that is pre-eminent over all others: this small monograph by Ebbinghaus" (Hilgard, 1964, p. vii). Let us consider this remarkable achievement in more detail, through the following excerpt (page numbers from the 1964 reprinting of a 1913 English translation).

ORIGINAL SOURCE EXCERPT
Ebbinghaus on Memory and Forgetting

Ebbinghaus opened his book by considering the various forms of memory and the difficulty of studying the process experimentally. He pointed out that what little was known about memory was known through common sense and from anecdotes about "extreme and especially striking cases" (p. 4). As for more fundamental questions about the exact relationships between our experiences and our memories, however, "[t]hese and similar questions no one can answer" (p. 5).

For Ebbinghaus, the only way to understand memory was through the "method of natural science" (p. 7). In his opening description of this method, Ebbinghaus did not use the exact terms you might have learned in a research methods course, but you will recognize the following as a description of the essential components of the experimental method: manipulating an independent variable, holding extraneous factors constant, then measuring the outcome, the dependent variable:

> We all know of what this method consists: an attempt is made to keep constant the mass of conditions which have proven themselves causally connected with a certain result; one of these conditions is isolated from the rest and varied in a way that can be numerically described; then the accompanying change on the side of the effect is ascertained by measurement or computation. (p. 7)

Ebbinghaus recognized that keeping the "mass of conditions" under control was no easy task. In one of psychological science's more notable acts of creativity, he hit upon the idea of using materials that did not meaningfully relate to each other and were not especially meaningful in themselves. That is, he created **nonsense syllables**, three-letter units comprised of two consonants with a vowel in the middle:

> Out of the simple consonants of the alphabet and our eleven vowels and diphthongs all possible syllables of a certain sort were constructed, a vowel sound being placed between two consonants.
>
> These syllables, about 2,300 in number, were mixed together and then drawn out by chance and used to construct series of different lengths, several of which each time formed the material for a test.

... The syllables used each time were carefully laid aside till the whole number had been used, then they were mixed together and used again.

The aim of the tests carried on with these syllable series was, by means of repeated audible perusal of the separate series, to so impress them that immediately afterwards they could voluntarily just be reproduced. This aim was considered attained when, the initial syllable being given, a series could be recited at the first attempt, without hesitation, at a certain rate, and with the consciousness of being correct. (pp. 22–23)

Ebbinghaus realized that memorizing meaningful materials like poems or prose would be a problem; these materials would already carry with them innumerable meaningful associations that would affect how quickly they could be learned:

The nonsense material, just described, offers many advantages, in part because of this very lack of meaning. First of all, it is relatively simple and relatively homogeneous. In the case of the material nearest at hand, namely poetry or prose, the content is now narrative in style, now descriptive, or now reflective; it contains now a phrase that is pathetic, now one that is humorous; its metaphors are sometimes beautiful, sometimes harsh; its rhythm is sometimes smooth and sometimes rough. There is thus brought into play a multiplicity of influences which change without regularity and are therefore disturbing. Such are associations which dart here and there, different degrees of interest, lines of verse recalled because of their striking quality or their beauty, and the like. All this is avoided with our syllables. Among many thousand combinations there occur scarcely a few dozen that have a meaning and among these there are again only a few whose meaning was realized while they were being memorized. (p. 23)

Thus, Ebbinghaus recognized that some of the syllables would have meaning, but he was not overly concerned about it. Also, it is important to keep in mind that his main interest was in how associations *between* syllables were formed, not the relative meaningfulness of individual syllables. Individual syllables might have some meaning, but the chances were quite remote that two successive syllables would be meaningfully related to each other. Gundlach (1986) has pointed out that one of Ebbinghaus's phrases was translated as a "series of nonsense syllables"[6] when a better translation might have been "meaningless series of syllables." That Ebbinghaus chose **serial learning** as his task is a further indication of his intent to analyze the buildup of associations between elements of a fixed sequence. Serial learning, in which correct recall includes accurately reproducing a set of stimuli in the exact order of their presentation, is well suited for examining associations between a "meaningless series of syllables."

How Ebbinghaus actually hit upon the idea to use nonsense syllables is not clear, but Hilgard's (1964) analysis makes the most sense. Familiar with the mechanistic and atomistic assumptions of British empiricism/associationism, Ebbinghaus would have looked for the simplest possible unit that would still yield a large number of stimuli. Individual letters or numbers were too few, words too meaningful. Syllables of words

---

[6] The phrase appears at the bottom of page 23, in the context of a comparison with memorizing poetry.

comprise the simplest pronounceable unit in the language, so they would be a logical choice. The fact that Ebbinghaus called his stimuli nonsense "syllables" suggests that he was deliberately thinking of this reduction to a small functional unit.

Once he had created the materials, Ebbinghaus turned to other control problems and set up a standardized set of procedures:

> The following rules were made for the process of memorizing.
>
> 1. The separate series were always read through completely from beginning to end; they were not learned in separate parts which were then joined together; neither were especially difficult parts detached and repeated more frequently. There was a perfectly free interchange between the reading and the occasionally necessary tests of the capacity to reproduce by heart. For the latter there was an important rule to the effect that upon hesitation the rest of the series was to be read through to the end before beginning it again.
> 2. The reading and the recitation of the series took place at a constant rate, that of 150 strokes per minute. A clockwork metronome placed at some distance was at first used to regulate the rate; but very soon the ticking of a watch was substituted, that being much simpler and less disturbing to the attention. ...
> 3. During the process of learning, the purpose of reaching the desired goal as soon as possible was kept in mind as much as was feasible. Thus, to the limited degree to which conscious resolve is of influence here, the attempt was made to keep the attention concentrated on the tiresome task and its purpose. It goes without saying that care was taken to keep away all outer disturbances in order to make possible the attainment of this aim. The smaller distractions caused by carrying on the test in various surroundings were also avoided as far as that could be done.
> 4. There was no attempt to connect the nonsense syllables by the invention of special associations of the mnemotechnik type; learning was carried on solely by the influence of the mere repetitions upon the natural memory. As I do not possess the least practical knowledge of the mnemotechnical devices, the fulfillment of this condition offered no difficulty to me. (pp. 24–25)

This last point reveals an important feature of the study—Ebbinghaus was the *only* research participant. He completed the research during two yearlong periods: 1879–1880 and 1883–1884, with the second set of experiments serving primarily to replicate those of the first. Also, in order to become proficient at the task, he spent an unspecified "long time" (p. 33) practicing before he began the 1879–1880 studies. Thus, for more than two years, he devoted a significant portion of his time to memorizing lists of nonsense syllables (about an hour or two per day), by his own admission a "tiresome task." On just one set of experiments, the ones that produced his famous forgetting curve, Ebbinghaus memorized just over 1300 different lists. One attribute said to characterize famous scientists is a total immersion in their research. Ebbinghaus was certainly a case in point.

Ebbinghaus described the results of his research in several different chapters. First, he examined how quickly a series of syllables could be learned as a function of the number of syllables per list. "Quickly" meant the number of repetitions needed before the list could be produced without errors. He reported the results in a table (p. 47):

	Number of repetitions	
Number of syllables in a series	**necessary for first errorless reproduction (exclusive of it)**	**Probable Error**
7	1	
12	16.6	+/– 1.1
16	30.0	+/– 0.4
24	44.0	+/– 1.7
36	55.0	+/– 2.8

There are two things to note here. First, although it might not be surprising that it takes more repetitions to learn longer lists, this marks the first time that anyone had documented, with precision, the exact relationship between the length of material to be learned and the amount of effort required to learn it. Second, very little effort was needed when the list had just seven syllables.

> The question can be asked: What number of syllables can be correctly recited after only one reading? For me the number is usually seven. Indeed I have often succeeded in reproducing eight syllables, but this has happened only at the beginning of the tests and in a decided minority of the cases. In the case of six syllables on the other hand a mistake almost never occurs. (p. 47)

This result has recurred frequently in experimental psychology's history, and George Miller's (1956) systematic investigation of this "magic number seven" became a landmark paper in the rise of cognitive psychology (see Chapter 14). You probably recall learning about the number "7 plus or minus 2" in your general psychology course in the memory chapter under the heading "capacity of short-term memory."

After showing that it takes more repetitions to learn longer lists, Ebbinghaus wondered whether increasing the number of *original* repetitions would strengthen memory. Thus, he repeated lists of 16 syllables 8, 16, 24, 32, 42, 53, or 64 times, and discovered that the ease of relearning the list 24 hours later was directly proportional to the number of original repetitions. He apparently considered extending the number of repetitions beyond 64, but thought better of it:

> An increase of the readings used for the first learning beyond 64 repetitions proved impracticable. ... For with this number each test requires about 3/4 of an hour, and toward the end of this time exhaustion, headache, and other symptoms were often felt which would have complicated the conditions of the test if the number of repetitions had been increased. (p. 55)

Some aspects of the research were too intense even for the redoubtable Ebbinghaus.

The most famous of the studies completed by Ebbinghaus concerned the rate of forgetting for information that had already been learned. Here, Ebbinghaus relied on an ingenious measure of recall that he called the **savings method**, which enabled him to measure memory after the passage of time, even if nothing could be recalled after the interval. He described the logic of it early in the book:

> A poem is learned by heart and then not again repeated. We will suppose that after a half year it has been forgotten: no effort at recollection is able to call it back into consciousness. At best only isolated fragments return. Suppose that the poem is again learned by heart. It then becomes evident that, although to all appearances totally forgotten, it still in a certain sense exists and in a way to be effective. The second learning requires noticeably less time or a noticeably smaller number of repetitions than the first. (p. 8)

To examine the effects of time on memory, Ebbinghaus memorized lists of syllables, tried to relearn them after the passage of a fixed amount of time, and applied his savings method to assess the outcome.

> The investigations in question fell in the year 1879–1880 and comprised 163 double tests. Each double test consisted in learning eight series of 13 sylla-bles each ... and then in relearning them after a definite time. The learning was continued until two errorless recitations of the series in question were possible. The relearning was carried to the same point; it occurred at one of the following seven times—namely, after about one third of an hour, after one hour, after 9 hours, one day, two days, six days, or 31 days. (pp. 65–66)

Ebbinghaus recorded the total time for the original learning of the eight lists, which was typically about 20 minutes, and the time for relearning. Original learning minus relearning yielded a measure of savings, which was converted to a percentage by dividing by the time of original learning. Thus, if original learning took 20 minutes and relearning took 5 minutes, 15 minutes or 75% (15/20 × 100) of the original learning time was saved.

Ebbinghaus reported the results for each of the 163 separate experiments (i.e., "double tests") that he completed over the different retention intervals. The results of this study have made their way into almost every introductory psychology textbook of the twentieth century. They are normally shown in a graph like the one in Figure 4.6, although Ebbinghaus did not include a graph in his book (the results were presented as a table). The results are clear—forgetting was very rapid at first, then slowed in its rate. Thus, after just 20 minutes (0.33 hour), Ebbinghaus's memory held only about 60% of the learned material; 40% had been lost. After an hour, 55% was lost, and after just a day, about two-thirds was lost.

The forgetting curve is Ebbinghaus's best known result, but he also studied other memory phenomena. For example, he provided an early example of the advantages of distributed over massed practice by showing that:

> For the relearning of a 12-syllable series at a definite time, accordingly, 38 rep-etitions, distributed in a certain way over the three preceding days, had just as favorable an effect as 68 repetitions made on the day just previous. ... It makes the assumption probable that *with any considerable number of repetitions* a suitable distribution of them over a space of time is decidedly more advanta-geous than the massing of them at a single time. (p. 89, italics in the original)

A final example of the Ebbinghaus research program is his investigation of remote associations. When the sequence of syllables A, B, and C, is to be learned in order, direct

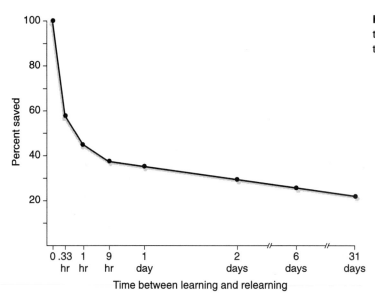

FIGURE 4.6 The Ebbinghaus forgetting curve, constructed from data in the excerpt.

associations are formed between A and B and between B and C, but are they also formed (remotely) between A and C? If so, then the association concept extends beyond the idea of two immediately contiguous events. Ebbinghaus devised a clever procedure to test for these potential remote associations. He first learned a list of 16 syllables in the usual serial order:

LIST A. 1 2 3 4 5 6 7 8 9 10 11 12 13 14 15 16

Next he would relearn the list in an order that skipped a syllable:

LIST B. 1 3 5 7 9 11 13 15 2 4 6 8 10 12 14 16

Similarly, for other lists he would relearn a list that skipped two syllables:

LIST C. 1 4 7 10 13 16 2 5 8 11 14 3 6 9 12 15

If remote associations had been forming during the original learning of syllables 1 through 16 (list A), then the relearning of lists B and C would be faster than learning a new list of 16 syllables, and this is exactly what Ebbinghaus found. Furthermore, there was a direct relationship between the ease of relearning and the degree of remoteness of the associations. As Ebbinghaus put it,

> ... the associative threads, which hold together a remembered series, are spun not merely between each member and its immediate successor, but beyond intervening members to every member which stands to it in any close temporal relation. The strength of the threads varies with the distance of the members, but even the weaker of them must be considered as relatively of considerable significance. (p. 94)

In Chapter 13, you will learn about the development of modern cognitive psychology. One of its recent trends is a tendency to criticize the narrowness and artificiality of the "Ebbinghaus tradition." For modern cognitive psychologists, the memorizer is actively processing information, not passively strengthening associations through mindless repetition. Also, there is more emphasis today on **ecological memory**: memory for more realistic everyday events rather than for abstract lists. One prominent contemporary researcher lamented the "terrible struggle our field has had just to overcome the nonsense syllable" (Kintsch, 1985, p. 461). The criticism has some merit, but for the historian it has somewhat of a presentist tone. Considering the Ebbinghaus memory research in the context of its time, a more apt evaluation of its importance comes from a retrospective review of *On Memory* by Roediger, written 100 years after its original publication:

> In sum, the corpus of Ebbinghaus's experimental results is large. Considering that he only began his research in the same year that Wundt founded his psychology lab and that he performed all experiments on himself and still produced such regular and compelling results, his achievement is nearly incredible. (Roediger, 1985, p. 522)

Other Contributions by Ebbinghaus

The memory research was Ebbinghaus's greatest accomplishment, but not his only one. He was also a pioneer in the field of mental testing, inventing a sentence completion test in 1895 that was similar in spirit to the intelligence test soon to be developed in France by Binet (see Chapter 8). Ebbinghaus held academic positions in the German universities at Berlin and Breslau, creating the psychology laboratories at each university, and at Halle, where he rebuilt an existing but inadequate lab. In 1890, he started the *Zeitschrift für Psychologie und Physiologie der Sinnesorgane* (*Journal of Psychology and Physiology of the Sense Organs*). While Wundt's *Philosophische Studien* was primarily a means for publishing the work completed in his Leipzig laboratory, Ebbinghaus's *Zeitschrift* filled its pages with research from laboratories throughout Germany. The journal's catholicity of interests and the prestige of its contributing authors (e.g., Helmholtz, G. E. Müller) led one historian to describe it as "the most important psychological organ in Germany" (Shakow, 1930, p. 509). Ebbinghaus also wrote two popular introductory psychology texts, including a brief version (just before his sudden death from pneumonia in 1909) that included the famous

opening sentence, quoted at the start of this book's Chapter 2: "Psychology has a long past, yet its real history is short" (Ebbinghaus, 1908, p. 3).

G. E. Müller (1850–1934): The Experimentalist Prototype

Although Wundt is rightly given credit as experimental psychology's founder, the psychology of the laboratory occupied only a small portion of his interest. This is a theme that will be repeated: Many of the early pioneers of laboratory psychology actually spent little time in the laboratory. An exception is G. E. Müller,[7] an experimenter's experimenter, who devoted 40 years of his professional life to the psychology laboratory at the University of Göttingen. From 1881 to his retirement in 1921, Müller's laboratory rivaled the other German facilities in terms of the quality of research produced. Studies completed in Müller's lab were known for their precision, experimental control, and meticulous attention to detail. That Müller is not well known today is primarily because little of his work was translated into English. Also, none of his research broke radically new ground; rather, it systematically replicated and extended the research of others. Thus, he made important contributions in extending Fechner's work in psychophysics,[8] Hering's work on color vision, and Ebbinghaus's work on memory. In this last area, Müller was a worthy successor to the venerable Ebbinghaus.

During the decade of the 1890s, Müller and his students replicated many of the Ebbinghaus findings, added several refinements, and reached different conclusions about the formation of associations. Whereas Ebbinghaus concluded that associations were formed automatically and mechanically as a result of stimulus

---

[7] No relation to Johannes Müller, the famous physiologist you met in Chapter 3. The name Müller is a very common one in Germany, a bit like their version of "Smith."

[8] According to Boring (1950), E. B. Titchener held up publication of the second volume of his famous laboratory manual (Chapter 7) until Müller had published a handbook of psychophysics in 1903. Titchener had to rewrite the psychophysics portions of his manual after Müller's book appeared, and the second volume of the lab manual was not published until 1905, four years after volume 1.

factors such as the number of repetitions and list length, and that the memorizer played a relatively *passive* role in the process, Müller believed that the individual forming the associations played a more *active* role. The conclusion resulted from a procedural modification—Müller added introspection to the process, and his observers reported that they engaged in a number of active strategies to learn the nonsense syllables. For example, they found themselves grouping nonsense syllables in clusters, organizing them by different degrees of meaning, and in general doing much more than just associating them by contiguity. This outcome foreshadows the modern view of memory, which assumes that the learner is actively involved in the memorizing process.

Müller and his students also made some discoveries that went beyond what Ebbinghaus had found. For example, with Alfons Pilzecker he discovered that if a second list is learned between the learning of list 1 and the subsequent attempt to relearn list 1, the second list interferes with the relearning. They named the phenomenon **retroactive inhibition**, thus initiating a long line of research that eventually produced the interference theory of forgetting. With another student, Adolph Jost, Müller discovered that if two associations have equal strength, further practice will strengthen the older of the associations more than the recent one. This phenomenon, later called **Jost's law**, was based on rather meager evidence, but was considered important as part of the explanation for the advantage of distributed practice over massed practice, another phenomenon studied in Müller's lab (Woodworth, 1938).

Another contribution of Müller to the experimental study of memory was the invention of the **memory drum**, which automated the presentation of stimulus materials. Müller and his assistant Friedrich Schumann cleverly altered a kymograph, a rotating drum normally used to record data (as shown in the reaction time photo of Figure 4.5). Stimuli were mounted on the drum, which revolved at a fixed speed, thereby displaying stimuli for measured amounts of time (Popplestone, 1987). Memory drums were standard laboratory equipment until recently, when computer presentation of stimuli became more efficient.

One final point is that although the University of Göttingen did not award advanced degrees to women, Müller welcomed several notable American women psychologists into his laboratory, including Christine Ladd-Franklin of Columbia (Chapter 6), Lillien Martin of Stanford, and Eleanor Gamble of Wellesley. As you will learn in Chapter 6, women faced numerous obstacles when trying to obtain graduate-level training. This was especially true in the United States, but it was also the case in Europe. Müller was well ahead of his time in recognizing that women were capable of high quality experimental research.

Oswald Külpe (1862–1915): The Würzburg School

After flirting with history and philosophy, Oswald Külpe became interested in psychology after taking a course from Wundt in the early 1880s. He then went to Berlin to study history and to Göttingen, where a year and a half in G. E. Müller's lab convinced him that psychology was to be his career. He eventually returned to Leipzig and earned a doctorate under Wundt's supervision in 1887, then remained with his mentor for another seven years, earning a living as a *Privatdozent* and as Wundt's assistant in the laboratory (he succeeded Cattell). It was during this time that he developed a lifelong friendship with E. B. Titchener (Chapter 7), who was at Leipzig during this time. In 1894, Külpe was called to Würzburg, where he created a laboratory sometimes considered second only to Wundt's and certainly a match for Müller's at Göttingen. It was at Würzburg that Külpe created a brand of experimental psychology distinctive enough to earn the label "Würzburg school." It investigated topics and produced outcomes that put Külpe at odds with both his mentor Wundt and his friend Titchener.

Wundt had declared higher mental processes (e.g., memory, thinking) off limits for laboratory research. He believed them to be too complex and too heavily influenced by one's language and culture to be controlled adequately. Instead, such topics needed to be investigated with nonlaboratory methods, while the lab was to be restricted to such topics as sensation/perception and mental chronometry. Yet

Ebbinghaus and Müller had managed to control conditions reasonably well in their studies of memory. It was up to Külpe, however, to challenge his former mentor directly by studying thought processes in the lab and by significantly elaborating upon the introspective procedure.

Külpe published little experimental research under his own name, but he exercised close but congenial supervision over his students. According to one of his American students, Robert Ogden, Külpe

> ... was intimately engaged in all that went on in his laboratory. It was a matter of principle to him to act as observer in the experimental work of his students. In the instance of my own study ... he came almost daily to the laboratory for what must have been weary hours of committing nonsense syllables to memory. His influence upon his students was never dominating. Instead, they were engaged together in a joint enterprise of scientific discovery. (Ogden, 1951, p. 9)

In order to study thought processes in the laboratory, Külpe found it necessary to expand the Wundtian concept of introspection. Recall that Wundt distinguished between "self-observation," in which someone experiences some event, then from memory describes the mental processes that occurred during the event, and "inner perception," a more controlled introspective procedure in which simple stimuli are presented many times (i.e., replicated) and responses are given immediately after stimulus presentation. For Wundt, only the latter procedure was appropriate in the laboratory. In Külpe's laboratory, however, introspection was more like Wundt's concept of self-observation. It came to be called **systematic experimental introspection**. Observers would experience more complicated events than in Wundt's laboratory, then give a full description of the mental processes involved. This created a potential memory problem, because as Woodworth (1938) later pointed out, the mental experience of a 10-second event might take 10 minutes to describe. To deal with the fact that giving an introspective account of a complicated event might be distorted by memory, Külpe and his students developed a procedure called **fractionation**, a separation of the task into its components, each of which could be introspected. For example, in

a study on word association by Watt (i.e., given a stimulus word, say the first word that comes to mind), the task was fractionated into "the preparation for the experiment, the appearance of the stimulus-word, the search for the reaction-word (if such search occurred), and finally the cropping up of the reaction-word" (Watt, 1904, cited in Sahakian, 1975, p. 162).

Külpe believed he was improving the introspective procedure, enabling it to be applied to higher mental processes, but Wundt rejected the Würzburg technique, calling it nothing but the unsystematic self-observation he had rejected years earlier. Thus, because he believed them to be built on unsound methods, Wundt dismissed the results of the Würzburg research. What were those results?

Mental Sets and Imageless Thoughts

The Würzburg research on thinking produced several surprising results. For example, in a study by Narziss Ach, observers were shown pairs of numbers after first being instructed that they would be performing some specific operation (e.g., add them, subtract them). Ach measured reaction time and also asked for detailed introspections. What he found was that reaction time was the same, regardless of the type of operation asked of subjects, and that observers reported no conscious awareness of the instructions themselves once the task had begun. In other words, after receiving the instructions, their mind was "prepared" to function in a specific way (e.g., adding), so that once the number pair was presented, the addition occurred automatically and without further thought. Thus, the instructions created what the Würzburgers called a determining tendency or **mental set**. This concept would eventually become important for the German gestalt psychologists (Chapter 9). The absence of a difference in reaction time was also significant, because Külpe used it to question the validity of the subtractive assumption underlying the mental chronography experiments that were such an important part of the Leipzig laboratory. Because instructions create a mental set, he argued, discrimination reaction time could not be equal to simple reaction time plus the mental event of discrimination. Rather, DRT results from a different kind of "set" than SRT.

A second important finding of the Würzburg lab, and a controversial one, concerned the phenomenon of **imageless thought**. According to Titchener (and Wundt), a close analysis of thought processes reveals that the essential element in all thinking is an image of some form. In a psychophysics weight-lifting experiment, for example, the standard description was that the observer would lift one weight and form a kinesthetic image of it, then lift the second weight and compare the sensation of it with the image of the first one in order to decide if the weights were the same or different. The judgment process was composed of sensory and image components from the two weights. In a weight-lifting study by Karl Marbe, however, no sensations or images occurred at the moment of judgment. Observers reported sensations and images while lifting the weights, but the judgment seemed to occur automatically and without images. That is, the judgment was an imageless thought. Furthermore, Marbe's observers reported other mental processes occurring just before the judgment and these didn't seem reducible to sensations and images either. These processes included things like hesitation, doubt, and vacillation; collectively they were referred to as **conscious attitudes**.

The potential existence of imageless thoughts, mental sets, and conscious attitudes posed an especially serious threat to Külpe's colleague E. B. Titchener, who believed that all mental content under analysis would be found to contain the basic elements of conscious experience. If some thoughts occur without images, however, then not all thinking can be reduced to the elements. This imageless thought controversy was never resolved; its most notable side effect, however, was to raise questions about the validity of introspection as a method and to help pave the way for a radical new movement in psychology that you will learn about in Chapters 10 and 11: behaviorism.

SUMMARY

AN EDUCATION IN GERMANY

- In the nineteenth century a large number of American students studied the sciences in Europe, especially in Germany. In the latter half of the century, many students went to Germany, in particular to Leipzig, to study a new approach to psychology that was developing there.

- The German educational system promoted a philosophy of *Wissenschaft*, which emphasized academic freedom and research. This created an environment conducive to new ideas, including the idea of a new psychology.

ON THE THRESHOLD OF EXPERIMENTAL PSYCHOLOGY: PSYCHOPHYSICS

- Psychophysics is the study of the relationship between physical stimuli and the psychological reaction to them. The first research in this tradition was completed by Ernst Weber, who investigated the relative sensitivity of various areas on the surface of the body using the two-point threshold. In experiments in which observers made comparisons between two weights, Weber discovered that the ability to distinguish between them depended on the relative rather than the absolute differences in their weights (Weber's Law).

- Gustav Fechner elaborated Weber's research and his *Elements of Psychophysics* is considered experimental psychology's first text. Although more interested in using his research to defeat materialism, Fechner is known for developing several important psychophysics methods in use today (limits, constant stimuli, adjustment) and for the precision of his work in measuring absolute and difference thresholds.

WUNDT ESTABLISHES A NEW PSYCHOLOGY AT LEIPZIG

- Wundt is generally known as the founder of experimental psychology. He explicitly set out to create a new psychology that emphasized the experimental methods borrowed from physiology, and he created the first laboratory of experimental psychology and the first journal devoted to describing the results of psychological research.

- Wundt's new science involved studying immediate conscious experience under controlled laboratory conditions. Because they could not be subjected to experimental control and replication, higher mental processes (e.g., language) had to be studied through nonlaboratory methods (e.g., observation).

- In Wundt's laboratory, most of the research concerned basic sensory and perceptual processes. The lab also produced a large number of "mental chronometry" studies, which attempted to measure the amount of time taken for various mental activities. James McKeen Cattell, an American student, and Wundt's first official lab assistant, completed a number of these studies, which utilized a subtraction procedure developed by F. C. Donders.

- Recent historical scholarship has uncovered serious distortions in the traditional accounts of Wundt's theories. Rather than being a structuralist, seeking to reduce consciousness to its basic elements, Wundt was more interested in the mind's ability to actively organize information. One of his main interests was the process of apperception, an active, meaningful, and attentive perception of some event. He called his system voluntarism to reflect the active nature of mental processing.

THE NEW PSYCHOLOGY SPREADS

- One of the most important programs of research carried out in psychology's history involved the study of memo-

ry by Hermann Ebbinghaus. To investigate the development of new associations between unassociated stimuli, he invented nonsense syllables. Ebbinghaus measured retention in terms of the amount of effort "saved" in relearning. His famous forgetting curve showed that forgetting occurs at a very rapid rate shortly after initial learning, then tapers off. He also documented the benefits of distributed practice and the effects of remote associations.

- G. E. Müller and his students significantly extended contemporary research on color vision, the psychophysics research of Fechner, and the memory research of Ebbinghaus. By adding introspection to the nonsense syllable experiments, he argued that memory was an active process, not the passive buildup of associative strength. He was the first to identify retroactive inhibition (i.e., forgetting results from interference from events occurring between initial learning and recall), and he invented the memory drum.

- Oswald Külpe and his students created the Würzburg school of psychology, which defied Wundt by studying thinking under laboratory conditions and liberalizing the method of introspection. In their research they found evidence for mental sets, imageless thought, and conscious attitudes.

STUDY QUESTIONS

1. Describe the *Wissenschaft* philosophy of education that developed in Germany in the nineteenth century. What were the implications for psychology?

2. Show how Fechner's three psychophysics methods could be used to determine a two-point threshold.

3. Describe Weber's Law and the concept of a jnd.

4. Boring describes Fechner as the "inadvertent" founder of psychophysics. Explain.

5. Wundt, rather than Fechner, is considered to be the founder of modern experimental psychology. Why?

6. Describe Wundt's contributions to psychology prior to his arrival at Leipzig.

7. Wundt's concept of psychology involved two major programs. Describe each.

8. Describe Wundt's version of introspection.

9. Describe how Wundt (and others) used reaction time to

measure the duration of various mental events. In what way was the method flawed?

10. Describe and criticize the traditional description of Wundt's "system." How did the misconceptions develop?

11. Explain why Wundt called his system voluntarism and show how the concept of apperception was important to him.

12. Describe how G. E. Müller's view of memory differed from that of Ebbinghaus. Why was Müller described as the "prototype" experimentalist?

13. Describe Külpe's version of introspection and how introspection would occur for a complex mental process.

14. How was mental set investigated in Külpe's lab and what were the implications of the findings for the complication experiment?

15. What was an imageless thought and how was it studied in Külpe's lab?

QUESTIONS FROM THE ORIGINAL SOURCE EXCERPT

1. What were nonsense syllabus, why did Ebbinghaus use them, and why was he unconcerned about the fact that some syllables might be more meaningful than others?

2. In terms of the overall goal for the research, what is the significance of the fact that Ebbinghaus used serial learning as his task?

3. What was the method of savings and why was it such a creative way to study memory?

4. Ebbinghaus recognized that maintaining control over conditions might be difficult with him being the only research participant. What methodological controls did he put into place?

5. Describe three of the findings from the Ebbinghaus research.

FOR FURTHER READING

Blumenthal, A. L. (1975). A reappraisal of Wilhelm Wundt. *American Psychologist, 30,* 1081–1086.

Probably the most frequently cited of the articles appearing in the 1970s that pointed out the errors in the traditional accounts of Wundt; draws comparisons between Wundt's research and theorizing and modern concepts from cognitive psychology.

Ebbinghaus, H. (1964). *Memory: A contribution to experimental psychology* (H. A. Ruger & C. A. Bussenius, Trans.). New York: Dover. (Original work published 1885)

A very readable, and brief (123 pages), account of the famous experiments by Ebbinghaus; the Dover republication includes a helpful foreword by Ernest Hilgard; a good retrospective review of the book can be found in Roediger (1985).

Leahey, T. H. (1981). The mistaken mirror: On Wundt's and Titchener's psychologies. *Journal of the History of the Behavioral Sciences, 17,* 273–282.

A clear description of Wundt's and Titchener's systems of psychology, highlighting their differences and drawing attention to the misconceptions that have developed over the years; shows how Wundt and Titchener had radically different philosophies of science (emphasis on causality for Wundt and on description for Titchener).

Sokal, M. M. (Ed.). (1981). *An education in psychology: James McKeen Cattell's journal and letters from Germany and England, 1880–1888.* Cambridge, MA: MIT Press.

A fascinating and highly detailed account of Cattell's years with Wundt at Leipzig, Hall at Johns Hopkins, and Galton in England. The entries are from letters written by Cattell, usually to his parents, and a diary/journal; the annotations by Sokal are highly detailed and as informative as Cattell's firsthand accounts.

Bringmann, W. G., & Tweney, R. D. (Eds.). (1980). *Wundt studies: A centennial collection.* Toronto: C. J. Hogrefe, Inc.

A collection of 21 articles about Wundt's life and work, ranging from biographical treatment to interpretation; main sections are the Heidelberg years, the Leipzig period, and impact and assessment.

CHAPTER 5

DARWIN'S CENTURY: EVOLUTIONARY THINKING

This preservation of favorable individual differences and variations, and the destruction of those which are injurious, I have called Natural Selection.
—Charles Darwin, 1859

PREVIEW AND CHAPTER OBJECTIVES

Chapter 4 documented the rise of scientific psychology in Germany in the nineteenth century. Preceding chapters examined the explosive growth of knowledge about the brain and nervous system in that same century, and the maturation of British empiricist and associationist thought during that time. As remarkable as these nineteenth-century developments were, they were overshadowed by the impact of one man's theory about the evolution of life itself. Biologists appropriately claim Charles Darwin as their most eminent historical figure, but his ideas also shaped the direction of psychology's history. This chapter examines Darwin's life and the development of his theory, and then considers the impact of his ideas on psychology's history. His argument for continuity among species challenged the Cartesian distinction between humans and animals and led to comparative psychology, the systematic study of animal behavior. His emphasis on the variability found within species led to the study of individual differences, most clearly manifested in the work of his cousin, Sir Francis Galton. This chapter's Original Source Excerpt is from Galton's research on a variety of topics relevant to psychology. In later chapters we will describe how Darwinian thinking resonated with the functionalist movement that has always been central to American psychology. After you finish this chapter, you should be able to:

- Describe the species problem and how the theological community responded to it
- Describe pre-Darwinian evolutionary concepts
- Trace the influence of Darwin's education and the *Beagle* voyage on his developing ideas about evolution
- Show the effects of Malthusian population ideas and the artificial selection principles of pigeon breeders on Darwin's thinking
- Describe the basic principles of Darwin's theory of evolution and why he delayed publishing for almost twenty years
- Explain how Darwin studied and interpreted the physical expressions of emotions
- Describe and critically analyze the comparative psychology of Romanes

- Explain the importance of Morgan's canon for the subsequent study of animal (and human) behavior
- Describe the work of Spalding and show how it connects with modern ethology
- Describe Galton's beliefs about the nature of intelligence, how he arrived at them, and how they led to his interests in eugenics
- Describe Galton's approach to mental testing
- Show how Darwin's ideas have influenced modern psychology

THE SPECIES PROBLEM

From the time that Newtonian physics burst on the scene in the late seventeenth century, intellectuals became increasingly convinced that the scientific approach was the way to all truth, that it would shed light on our ignorance of the laws of nature, and that it would lead to the inevitable improvement of life through technological advancement. Thus, as we discussed in Chapter 3, the eighteenth century became known as the era of Enlightenment, in which science became religion and scientists seemed heroic.

One manifestation of Enlightenment science was a questioning of the literal truth of the Bible's version of the origin of the earth's plants and animals. Global exploration was uncovering new species of plants and animals by the thousands. How did the earth come to be populated by such diversity? Why did some species seem to disappear, their existence known only from fossils? Why did some living animals seem to be structurally similar yet not quite the same as fossils? And for those accepting the literal truth of the Bible, how did all these species fit on the Ark? Collectively, these questions became known as the **species problem**, sometimes referred to as the "mystery of mysteries."

The problem created great stress within the academic community in Great Britain, where those in the intellectual elite were also leaders of the Anglican Church, the Church of England. One solution was to turn the problem into an argument for the supreme power of the deity. This **argument from design** is normally associated with the Reverend William Paley's 1802 *Natural Theology*, but it is also recognizable as one of the proofs for the existence of God suggested by the great medieval philosopher Thomas Aquinas

(Scott-Kakures, Castagnetto, Benson, Taschek, & Hurley, 1993). The argument held that the very existence of precision and complexity in nature required a supreme being to create and to manage it. Paley drew an analogy between the complex design of a watch, which necessitates a watchmaker to make it, and that of the infinitely more complicated human eye, which requires an "eyemaker" who is by definition infinitely superior to the humans using those eyes (Ruse, 1979). The argument from design enabled a minister/scientist to study the workings of nature while maintaining a belief in the Supreme Designer. There was no need to speculate about how species might develop; it was simpler to assume that God in His infinite wisdom had created each species and designed each to fit into its place in the world. Hence, the orderliness to be found in nature derived from explicit design, which in turn came from a mind greater than all of nature, and that mind belonged to God.

Despite the power of the theological version of the argument from design (it's still around today), numerous evolutionary ideas developed in the eighteenth and early nineteenth centuries. Two pre-Darwinian examples are worthy of note. First, Darwin was not even the first person in his family to propose an evolutionary solution to the species problem. A century earlier, his somewhat eccentric grandfather, Erasmus Darwin (1731–1802), a physician, had firmly rejected the biblical account of creation and proposed that all organic life evolved from a single living filament. Over time, new species developed from old ones, with later species being more "advanced" than earlier ones. The human species represented the culmination of evolution, but there was no reason to assume that humans would not continue to improve. In 1794, he produced *Zoonomia*, a rambling account of the medical knowledge of his era, spiced with his speculations on the origins and evolution of life.

The best-known pre-Darwinian theory of evolution belonged not to Darwin's grandfather, however, but to a leading French naturalist, Jean Baptiste de Lamarck (1744–1829). Like Erasmus Darwin, Lamarck believed that all the species on earth could be arranged on a linear scale with reference to their complexity, an idea sometimes referred to as the **chain of being** (Ruse, 1979). Furthermore, each species is constantly evolving into a species that is more complex, he believed, and new life at the bottom of the scale is continually being created from inorganic life. Thus, at any one point in time, a variety of species exists that can be classified in terms of how much they have evolved from the first spark of life. Lamarck also believed that an important mechanism of evolution was the idea that changes occurring during the lifetime of an organism could be passed on to offspring. For instance, if during the course of its life an animal developed the ability to use simple tools, that new ability would be inherited by the next generation. This concept became known as the **inheritance of acquired characteristics**. It was taken seriously throughout most of the nineteenth century before being discarded, and it was included as part of Darwin's original theory. But we are getting ahead of the story.

CHARLES DARWIN (1809–1882) AND THE THEORY OF EVOLUTION

There was little in the early life of Charles Robert Darwin to predict the greatness that would eventually come: he appeared to be just another aimless and spoiled child of wealthy parents. He was born and raised in the rural west of England, in Shrewsbury. His father, Robert, was a successful and affluent country doctor and his mother, Susannah Wedgwood, was heir to a fortune from the family that created the renowned Wedgwood china. Like most successful and ambitious men, Robert Darwin expected great things of his son, and was frustrated by the boy's indifferent performance in school and his apparent lack of purpose. By early adolescence, Darwin's wayward behavior drove his father to dis-

traction. "You care for nothing but shooting, dogs, and rat-catching, and you will be a disgrace to yourself and all your family," he exclaimed (quoted in Desmond & Moore, 1991, p. 20), in a scene easily imagined by parents of adolescents.

The Shaping of a Naturalist

Determined that his son would follow in his footsteps, Robert Darwin sent Charles to study medicine at Edinburgh, Scotland, one of Europe's best medical schools, and more prestigious at that time than either Oxford or Cambridge. The experiment failed, however. Darwin's academic performance did not improve and he was nauseated by the clinical procedures of the day. Anesthesia did not exist then, nor was the importance of a sterile environment widely recognized. Thus, surgery was a gruesome experience in which the main goal was to relieve the screaming patient by completing the procedure as soon as possible. For young Charles, medicine would not do. He left Edinburgh in 1827.

The next stop was Christ's College, Cambridge University, where Darwin studied for the clergy. The Cambridge that he encountered in the period 1828 to 1831 was not the fine academic university that we think of today. Rather, it was an institution under the firm control of the Church of England (the Anglican Church); its professors were Anglican priests who normally expected little scholarship on the part of their students, and its students (all male) tended to live up to those expectations.[1] Most students were there to prepare for the clergy, but they were primarily concerned with learning how to become proper gentlemen. Studying to be a clergyman in the Anglican Church was a common vocation for sons of wealthy Britishers, an activity described as a "safety net to stop second sons [from] becoming wastrels" (Desmond & Moore, 1991, p. 47). Honors programs for serious students did exist in the classics and in mathematics, but at a time when England was the most powerful nation on earth and was leading the Industrial Revolution, the university was strangely deficient in the study of science and

---

[1] The same could be said at this time of England's other famous university, Oxford.

technology (Ruse, 1979). Darwin never became a priest of the Anglican Church, of course. Nonetheless, he entertained the notion for several years, even after he had found his true vocation.[2]

Although he was not destined for the clergy, the Cambridge experience proved to be crucial for Darwin. He found his calling there. Young people who grow up in rural areas often seem to develop a love for the natural world, and Darwin was no exception. He might have been a mediocre student and an incipient failure in his father's eyes, but he also had the insatiable curiosity that marks the true scientist. From his earliest youth, he recalled being a collector of natural objects ranging from rocks to beetles to butterflies. It was at Cambridge that Darwin realized for the first time that his love of the natural world could become a life's work. Darwin's model and mentor was the Reverend John Henslow (1796–1871), a professor of botany at Cambridge. In the minister/scientist Henslow, Darwin saw his future: he could become a respectable Anglican clergyman, use his wealth to acquire a quiet rural parish, and devote most of his time to science. Darwin sat in on Henslow's classes and his fervor quickly caught the botanist's attention. Before long, Henslow began including Darwin in weekly meetings in his home, at which a small group of like-minded enthusiasts, including some of Cambridge's leading scientists, debated the scientific issues of the day (including evolution). Between 1828 and 1831, Darwin continued to be an average student in his formal preparation for the ministry, but he was in regular contact with some of the leading scientific minds of the day, and he was making a favorable impression on them (Ruse, 1979).

One of those scientific minds belonged to a noted geologist, the Reverend Adam Sedgwick (1785–1873). Sedgwick became a second mentor to Darwin, teaching him the basic tools of the geologic trade and sharpening his ability to make precise observations by taking him on a long geological field trip through the mountains of Wales in the summer

of 1831. Darwin eventually rejected Sedgwick's views about the earth's formation, but he profited immensely from the experience. Darwin began thinking of himself as a geologist.

After returning from the walk through northern Wales, opportunity knocked at Darwin's door. A voyage to South America was being planned, and the captain, 26-year-old Robert FitzRoy, was advertising for an on-board dinner companion, a "gentleman" whose intelligent conversation could relieve the long hours of boredom at sea. It would also help if this person had some training in science, for there would be many opportunities for collecting specimens of South America's fauna and flora. Henslow recommended Darwin, Darwin's father eventually approved of the scheme, and Darwin undertook the voyage of a lifetime aboard the *HMS Beagle*. It lasted five years and took him around the globe. In his autobiography, Darwin had this to say about the trip:

> The voyage of the *Beagle* has been by far the most important event in my life, and has determined my whole career. ... I have always felt that I owe to the voyage the first real training or education of my mind; I was led to attend closely to several branches of natural history, and thus my powers of observation were improved. ... (Darwin, 1892/1958, p. 28)

The Voyage of the *Beagle*

Darwin's home away from home for five years was a small (90 feet long and 24 feet wide) three-masted brig that carried just over 70 officers, marines, geographer/surveyors, and crew. Darwin shared a small cabin at the rear of the ship with two of the survey officers, sleeping in a hammock with his face two feet from the underside of the main deck, and contending with the surveyors for workspace on the small charting table during the day (Thomson, 1975). Some idea of the cramped living arrangements can be seen in Figure 5.1, a cross section of the ship.

The primary purpose of the *Beagle*'s voyage was to survey the southern coasts of South America, especially its port areas, thus allowing the powerful British merchant fleet to retain its edge in the competition for trade with developing South American

---

[2] In his autobiography, Darwin reported that later in his life, a German phrenological society requested a photograph of his head. He complied, the photo was carefully examined, and a member of the society proclaimed that Charles had "the bump of reverence developed enough for ten priests" (Darwin, 1892/1958, p. 18).

H. M. S. Beagle 1832

1 *Mr. Darwin's seat in Captain's Cabin*   2 *Mr. Darwin's seat in Poop Cabin*   3 *Mr. Darwin's drawers in Poop Cabin*
4 *Azimuth Compass*   5 *Captain's skylight*   6 *Gunroom skylight*

FIGURE 5.1 Cross section of the HMS *Beagle*.

countries; the ship would also circumnavigate the earth, using its 24 chronometers to check the precise longitude of various locations on the globe (Desmond & Moore, 1991). Once the *Beagle* reached South America, much of its time was spent going back and forth from one coastal region to another.[3] This enabled Darwin to spend months at a time ashore, exploring the continent, observing nature, and collecting. Long periods away from the ship were beneficial for another reason—Darwin suffered from a violent seasickness that lasted for the entire trip. When aboard ship, he was ill every day.

Darwin the Geologist

At the outset of the voyage, Darwin's prime interest was geology. The field trip with Sedgwick was still fresh in his mind, and just off the press and among his possessions was the first volume of a book destined to have the same effect on geology that his own book eventually would have on biology. Its simple title, *Principles of Geology*, belied its revolutionary nature. Its Scottish author, Charles Lyell (1797–1875), took issue with the prevailing theory of geological change, called **catastrophism**. Much

like the argument from design, catastrophism was an attempt to maintain the supremacy of God and the Bible while accounting for what scientists were discovering about nature. Catastrophists, including Darwin's geologist/mentor Sedgwick, argued that geological change occurred abruptly and dramatically as the result of major catastrophic events under the control of God. The flood in the Book of Genesis was the standard example. Lyell, on the other hand, argued that geological change occurred more slowly and involved forces that are constantly at work. These forces included such things as volcanic action, earthquakes, erosion, and the cumulative effects of weather. This view came to be called **uniformitarianism**, because of the assumption that uniform laws of nature operated to produce gradual geologic change. The Swiss Alps were not thrust up overnight in some cataclysmic upheaval; they only arose gradually, over vast amounts of time, Lyell believed.[4]

[3] The *Beagle* spent 57 months at sea. Forty-two of those months were spent in South American waters, 27 on the east coast, and 15 on the west coast (Browne, 1995).

[4] A modern form of catastrophism, minus the theological element, has gained adherents since the accumulation of evidence that comets or large meteors have occasionally struck the earth. It is estimated that one such meteor destroyed 95% of all marine species when it landed about 250 million years ago. More recently (a mere 65 million years ago), a huge meteor produced effects leading to the rapid extinction of about 70% of the earth's species, including the dinosaurs (Monastersky, 1997).

Lyell's revolutionary ideas about the origins and development of the earth's structures were never far from Darwin's thoughts. At the ship's very first landfall, in the volcanic Cape Verde islands (off the west coast of Africa), he came across some evidence to support Lyell's uniformitarian views. About 30 feet above sea level, the rocks contained a layer of compressed seashells and coral. The Atlantic could not have dropped that much during the island's lifetime, so the seabed must have risen, presumably because of volcanic activity. The geologic event seemed to be gradual rather than catastrophic, because Darwin observed that the shell/coral layer varied in height, suggesting the slow-moving effects of subsidence; the layer also included intact, rather than crushed, fossils. Darwin began to think the *Beagle* voyage might make his reputation as a Lyellian geologist. Indeed, while we now think of the trip as the event that gave Darwin the raw material for his theory of evolution of species, he also made important contributions to geology. For instance, he experienced, firsthand, the landscape-altering effects of an earthquake in Chile, and during the Pacific portion of the trip, he was able to demonstrate that coral reefs were built on the rims of slowly sinking volcanoes. Darwin's immersion in Lyellian geology convinced him that the earth had to be much older than previously thought. This idea would eventually be important to Darwin's evolutionary thinking, because the slow changes in species required vast amounts of time. The new geology seemed to supply an earth that was sufficiently ancient for evolution to do its work.

Darwin the Zoologist

With the *Beagle* in South American waters and completing its surveying work, Darwin collected specimens in earnest and kept encyclopedic notes on his geologic and zoological observations. By the end of the voyage he composed a 770-page diary sent home in installments, 1383 pages of notes on geology, and 368 more pages on zoology. He also wrote a specimen catalog that included 1529 species of animals that had been preserved in spirits and another 3907 labeled items that were either bones, fossils, skins, or dried specimens (Desmond & Moore, 1991).

For at least a year into the voyage, Darwin firmly believed that he would return to England and become the Anglican priest/amateur scientist that he so admired in Henslow. He also assumed that his work would have no important bearing on the biblical account of creation; he was initially a believer in the argument from design. Yet his zoological observations gradually led him to wonder about the species question. Why were some species similar to others, yet different in ways that suited them for survival in their own unique environments? Why did some species become extinct, their existence known only through their fossilized remains? Why did these fossils often seem to bear an uncanny resemblance to contemporary species living in the same geographical region? It began to occur to him that just as the earth evolved slowly, gradually, and according to uniform laws, perhaps the same was true of the organisms populating the earth.

The Galapagos Islands

On September 7, 1835, after spending more than three and a half years on its surveying mission, the *Beagle* left South America and headed across the Pacific. A week later, it made landfall at a remote series of about 20 volcanic islands owned by Ecuador, and located on the equator about 600 miles west of South America. They featured a variety of unusual species, including oversized, dinosaur-like lizards, and tortoises with shells up to five feet in diameter. The islands were named for the Spanish word for the giant tortoise, galápagos. They had little practical value, being used primarily as an Ecuadorian penal colony and as a stopping point for whaling vessels to replenish their stocks of food and water.[5] The lizards, tortoises, and numerous species of birds were oblivious to human presence, making it easy for crews to hunt them.

The Galapagos were to give Darwin his most obvious clues to evolution, although at the time of the visit and for some time thereafter, he had no inkling of the importance of what he encountered there. During the five weeks spent on the islands,

---

[5] While accumulating the experiences that would eventually yield *Moby Dick*, Herman Melville was aboard a whaling vessel that reached the Galapagos shortly after the *Beagle*'s visit. Of the islands, Melville wrote, "Little but reptile life is here found; the chief sound of life is a hiss" (cited in Moorehead, 1969, p. 187).

Darwin did some hiking and specimen collecting, but he was not as systematic as he had been in South America. Nor did he pay much attention to the claim, made by the vice governor of the penal colony, that it was possible to tell the home island of a tortoise merely by observing the design of its shell. He did notice differences from one island to another in the various bird populations, however, especially what he thought were mockingbirds, and it appeared that many of the species of birds and plants resembled those from the mainland, while having their own unique qualities. He later discovered that the shapes of the beaks of several species of finch provided an important clue to his theory, but while in the Galapagos he failed to notice these differences by mislabeling some of the finches as warblers, wrens, and "gross-beaks," and he was more intrigued by their coloration than their beaks (Sulloway, 1982). He even forgot to identify most of his finch specimens by their island of origin. These birds, now known as Darwin's finches, became an important source of data for naturalists who followed Darwin to the Galapagos,[6] and they still contribute to evolutionary theory. For example, modern research has shown that dramatic changes in the finch species can occur in just a few years, if climatic changes are sufficiently drastic (Weiner, 1994).

After leaving the Galapagos, the *Beagle* sailed west across the Pacific and made stops at Tahiti, New Zealand, Australia, and South Africa before finally returning to England in October of 1836. Upon his return, Darwin was a changed man. He now seriously doubted that life as an Anglican priest was for him; a full-time devotion to science seemed more in the cards. During the voyage, he routinely shipped crates of specimens home to Henslow, and they had made a strong impression on the scientific community during his absence. By the time he returned, he was already a celebrity among zoologists and geologists and viewed as a rising young star. Darwin's reputation even impressed his father, who rewarded his son with a generous allowance and a healthy

stock portfolio to enable him to continue his scientific work without having to seek gainful employment (Desmond & Moore, 1991).

The Evolution of Darwin's Theory

During the first few years after his return, Darwin set out to organize and classify his enormous collection of specimens, enlisting the help of other scientists and museum curators as much as possible. In 1837, he moved to London, and two years later he married his cousin, Emma Wedgwood. Their union was a long and happy one, even though Emma's strong religious beliefs eventually conflicted with her husband's gradual loss of faith. Emma was destined to become the family's source of strength, caring for the 10 children she would bear and for Darwin, who became ill soon after his return. Darwin was a partial invalid for the remainder of his life, suffering from a variety of chronic digestive, headache, and cardiac symptoms. For months at a time until his death in 1882, he spent a significant portion of the day either in bed or being violently ill. The Darwins remained in London for three years, but the unrelenting street noise, coal-generated smog, and stench from the polluted Thames seemed to contribute to Darwin's declining health, so in 1842 they bought a country house at Down, about 15 miles south of London. Down became their permanent home and Darwin's laboratory. Today Down House serves as the Darwin Museum.

Despite his illness, Darwin produced. Within 10 years of his return to England, he published a journal (Darwin, 1839), books on the geology of coral reefs, volcanic islands, and South America, and several technical reports that were read to various scientific societies in London (e.g., the Geological Society). During this time he also formulated his theory on the evolution of species and wrote a brief abstract of it in 1842. Two years later he elaborated the sketch into a 200-page document, instructing his wife to publish it in the event that his ailments proved fatal (Desmond & Moore, 1991).

Darwin's theory developed out of his reflections on the *Beagle* voyage. He was perplexed by the **species problem,** and while he rejected the biblical account that God had created each species separate-

---

[6] From 1905 to 1906, for instance, a project sponsored by the California Academy of Sciences collected 8691 finch specimens (Weiner, 1994).

ly, he maintained (initially, at least) his belief in God by allowing for the divine creation of a set of laws to guide evolution. But what were those laws? Hints came to Darwin from two sources. First, in 1838 he read an essay on population by political economist Thomas Malthus (1766–1834), who championed the idea that government welfare for the poor would only increase their number, thereby decreasing Britain's overall standard of living. Instead, Malthus argued, society must recognize that life is a constant "struggle for existence" and only those best suited for survival will do so. He pointed out that while food supplies grow at a relatively constant rate, population growth, if unchecked, occurs at a much more rapid rate. Eventually, the population will outgrow its resources and its members will begin to die until a level of stability is achieved. For Darwin, this idea provided a model to be applied to species changes. For any species, the time will come when unchecked population growth will result in food shortages, especially when growth combines with severe environmental changes such as a prolonged drought. Under such circumstances, *only those best suited to survive will do so.* If those characteristics enabling survival could be passed on to offspring, the next generation would be better suited for survival and would be different from previous generations. Over time, might these changes be sufficient to create a new species? Darwin began to think so.

Darwin's second clue came from his reflections on what he knew of breeding by farmers and hobbyists. For instance, pigeon breeders had been able to produce breeds of pigeons that hardly resembled each other. The breeders accomplished this by observing tiny variations that occurred naturally within a breed of pigeons, then developing those differences through generations of selective breeding. The results were such that if these pigeon varieties had been encountered in the wild, zoologists would have judged them to be different species! If such differences can be created artificially by pigeon breeders, could they not also be created naturally? Could there be a *natural* selection that was analogous to *artificial* selection? Darwin began to think so.

In the midst of these ruminations about population changes and selective breeding, Darwin learned from the famous ornithologist John Gould, who was classifying some of his *Beagle* specimens, that there was something very interesting about the birds from the Galapagos Islands. The birds that Darwin thought were finches, warblers, wrens, and "grossbeaks" were in fact different species of finch. Furthermore, Gould was "induced to regard them as constituting an entirely new group containing 14 species, and appearing to be strictly confined to the Galapagos islands" (Gould, cited in Weiner, 1994, p. 28). These finch species were distinguished by their size and by clear differences in the shapes of their beaks. Wondering about these differences, Darwin reexamined his sketchy notes on the islands of origin for the birds and supplemented the information by examining finch specimens that had been collected by Captain FitzRoy and others. He soon saw a distinct pattern—finches with specific beak shapes tended to cluster on islands that differed in terms of the sources of available food. For instance, finches living on islands with a large supply of certain types of hard shelled nuts and seeds had tough, blunted beaks, ideally suited for cracking open this food source. Other birds had thinner beaks, well designed to spear the insects that populated their islands.

Darwin concluded that at some time in the distant past, finches had arrived from the mainland as a single species and had dispersed throughout the islands. From generation to generation, the finches on each island produced offspring that varied slightly from each other, just as the domesticated pigeons did, and some of those variations had been beneficial, enabling certain finches to survive the kinds of periodic food shortages predicted by Malthus. Eventually, these variations produced new species. The theory was born.

Darwin's Delay

Much has been made of the fact that Darwin had outlined the essential features of his theory of evolution by the late 1830s, yet it took him another 20 years to publish the *Origin of Species* (Richards, 1983). Part of the reason was his health: he was often incapacitated for months at a time. A second reason for the delay was that he was concerned about the reactions of his peers. When the anonymously authored and highly speculative *Vestiges of Creation* appeared in 1844, the same year that Darwin was entrusting his 200-page manuscript to his wife's care, it was ridiculed by the British community of zoologists, geologists, and botanists (including Lyell, who was now a close friend of Darwin's). Some of the reaction was to the vagueness in the proposed mechanism for evolutionary change in *Vestiges*, and Darwin knew that his model was better, but much of the negative response was to the idea of evolution itself. In a letter to the botanist Joseph Hooker, a close friend to whom he was disclosing his theory, Darwin wrote that proposing a theory of evolution was like "confessing a murder" (Colp, 1986). If he published in 1844, he feared that his theory would be confused with *Vestiges* and condemned by association.

A third reason for Darwin's delay was his conservative scientific nature. He knew he had a good theory and some data to support it, but he also knew that he needed much more evidence before he would be willing to go public. Thus, he spent much of the intervening years carefully gathering evidence to flesh out the theory. For instance, in 1846 he began an intensive eight-year study of the evolutionary history of barnacles, eventually publishing the results in four volumes. He also joined a local pigeon fanciers club and did some of his own pigeon breeding. And at Down House, one could always find a dozen experiments going on at the same time. For example, to determine how seeds could be spread over large distances, he tested the idea that undigested seeds might be carried in the stomachs of birds. So he collected bird droppings, poking through them until he came across the occasional seed, which he planted. It is easy to imagine the satisfaction he felt when many of the seeds germinated and grew.

Darwin's 20-year delay would have been even longer if not for a letter he received on June 18, 1858. It was from a fellow naturalist with an interest in evolution, Alfred Russel Wallace (1823–1913), who was at the time on the other side of the world in Malaysia. Wallace asked Darwin's opinion on a brief paper that he enclosed with the letter—the paper outlined a theory of evolution that was remarkably similar to Darwin's. Darwin was shaken, writing to Lyell, "If Wallace had my MS. sketch written out in 1842, he could not have made a better short abstract!" (cited in Desmond & Moore, 1991, p. 467).

After seeking the advice of Hooker and Lyell, Darwin agreed to a joint presentation at the July 1, 1858, meeting of the Linnean Society. Thus it occurred that the first public disclosure of Darwin's theory of evolution came at a professional meeting of botanists. The secretary of the society read Wallace's paper and an abstract of Darwin's 1844 essay. Darwin did not attend the meeting; neither paper attracted much attention. The Wallace letter sent a clear message to Darwin, however. To estab-

KEY DATE *1859*

This year marked the publication of Darwin's revolutionary *Origin of Species*, perhaps the most important book published in the nineteenth century.

These events also occurred:

- America's first oil well was drilled in Titusville, Pennsylvania
- The steamroller was invented
- Abolitionist John Brown attacked the federal arsenal at Harper's Ferry in October; he was captured, tried, and hung
- German chemist Albert Niemann successfully isolated the drug cocaine from the leaves of the coca plant
- The French acrobat Charles Blondin crossed Niagara Falls on a tightrope
- Samuel Smiles published *Self-Help*, a manual on how to succeed in life
- Daniel Emmett composed "Dixie"
- These people were born:

    Arthur Conan Doyle, British creator of Sherlock Holmes

    Georges Seurat, French painter
- These people died:

    Washington Irving, American author (*The Legend of Sleepy Hollow*)

    Alexander von Humboldt, German astronomer, geologist, and explorer lish his legitimate priority, he needed to publish the complete theory, along with the supporting evidence that he had accumulated over the years. Despite continuing ill health and the death of one of his sons to scarlet fever, Darwin completed the work over the next 15 months and *On the Origin of Species by Means of Natural Selection or the Preservation of Favoured Races in the Struggle for Life* appeared in bookshops on November 22, 1859. The initial printing of 1250 copies sold out on the first day.

Elements of the Theory of Evolution

After a brief introduction, in which Darwin emphasized the importance of the *Beagle* voyage and gave credit to Wallace for his similar theory, the *Origin of Species* opens with two chapters establishing the fact that members of a given species vary from each other. In the first chapter, "Variation Under Domestication," Darwin showed how individual differences within a species could be accentuated through deliberate breeding—an artificial selection. This chapter prepared the way for him to argue later that just as there is deliberate selection by human breeders, there is also a "natural" selection by the conditions of normal existence. In Chapter 2, "Variation Under Nature," Darwin noted the universality of individual differences within species found in nature. He made the connection to Chapter 1 by pointing out that these differences "thus afford materials for natural selection to act on and accumulate, in the same manner as man accumulates individual differences in his domesticated products" (Darwin, 1859/1958, p. 59).

Because the science of genetics was yet to be born, Darwin had no concept of the phenomenon of genetic mutation, the primary means of creating individual differences within a species. Thus, he had to guess about the causes of variation. He believed that some variation was spontaneous and random, much like mutation, but he also allowed for the Lamarckian idea that characteristics acquired during one's lifetime could be passed on to offspring.

Darwin's third and fourth chapters, the "Struggle for Existence" and "Natural Selection," contain the core of the theory. Citing Malthus, Darwin first argued that in nature, species face an inevitable struggle to survive because they produce offspring at a rate that outpaces the food supply. If that is the case, then those individuals having a variation that puts them at a slight advantage in the struggle will be "selected" by nature; those without the advantage will die. Over several generations, the "adaptive" variation will become more common. In Darwin's words:

> ... Owing to this struggle [for life], variations, however slight and from whatever cause proceeding, if they be in any degree profitable to the individuals of a species, ... will tend to the preservation of such individuals, and will generally be inherited by the offspring. ... This preservation of favorable individual differences and variations, and the destruction of those which are injurious, I have called Natural Selection. (Darwin, 1859/1958, p. 74, p. 88)

Darwin's finches illustrate the manner in which life's **struggle for existence** and **natural selection** combine to alter species. Darwin believed that the original finches arrived as a single species from the mainland and settled in the various islands of the Galapagos. Because there is variation among members of a species in the wild, slight differences from one finch to another existed, including variations in the shapes of the birds' beaks. Suppose some of the birds happened to land on islands rich in certain types of seeds that are encased in hard shells. Those finches with slightly tougher and more blunted beaks would have an advantage in the hunt for these seeds. Finches with slightly thinner beaks would have a more difficult time getting at the seeds and would be more likely to die. Hence, the finches with the more "adaptive variation" would be "naturally selected" in the "struggle for existence." They would survive and pass on the advantage to their offspring. Over time, finches on that particular island would form a new species characterized by the specific beak shape. Similarly, on another island rich in insects, a species of finch with beaks thin enough to reach into small spaces would evolve.

Darwin believed that evolution by natural selection also explained extinction and the reason why modern species resemble fossils of extinct species found in the same geographical region. In South

America, for example, Darwin had uncovered fossilized bones of animals similar to modern llamas but two to three times as large. Over time, he argued, the larger species had encountered environmental events (e.g., droughts) that reduced the food supply and favored the survival of smaller variations that did not need to eat as much.

In the remaining 11 chapters of the *Origin*, Darwin wrote of the evidence, both zoological and geological, in support of his theory, and tried to answer the objections he knew would be forthcoming. He recognized that most people believed in the divine creation of every single species, but asked his readers to consider the evidence he had placed before them.

Dennett (1995) has pointed out that evolution by natural selection, Darwin's "dangerous idea," created for the first time a reasoned argument for a reversal of the sequence proposed by the well-entrenched theological argument from design. For the Reverend Paley and others, an all-knowing Divine Mind created the intricate designs found in an orderly and predictable natural world. The sequence was Mind→Design→Order. The blindly operating rules of natural selection, on the other hand, resulted in order, which in turn led to design, which could then produce a mind (hence the sequence Order→Design→Mind). Paley's watch and the watchmaker's mind, according to Dennett's scheme, would indeed be the result of design, but not necessarily design from above. Rather, it could be the outcome of what Dennett called the "Principle of the Accumulation of Design" (p. 68) resulting from the evolutionary process that produced visually oriented humans with the ability to build a watch.

After the Origin of Species

Reaction to Darwin's theory was not long in coming. Although he did not discuss humans in the *Origin*, the implications were clear and directly threatening to the Church of England. It might have been declining in power during the second half of the nineteenth century, but the Anglican Church was still capable of making its presence felt and Darwin was denounced from pulpits throughout England. To this day, evolution is a threat to the religious beliefs of some. The scientific community was a different matter, however. In his

autobiography, Darwin argued that while there was some initial resistance among some scientists (e.g., Lyell), general acceptance of the idea of evolution came quickly. While rejecting the idea that the success of his book demonstrated that the topic of evolution was "in the air," he did recognize the importance of Boring's zeitgeist: "What I believe was strictly true is that innumerable well-observed facts were stored in the minds of naturalists ready to take their proper places as soon as any theory which would receive them was sufficiently explained" (Darwin, 1892/1958, p. 45). By the end of the century, evolution had taken hold and the importance of Darwin's ideas eventually led some observers to refer to the entire century as "Darwin's Century" (Eiseley, 1958).

In the debates over evolution, Darwin himself stayed above the fray, preferring to have his case argued by others; he had work to do. He continued to collect evidence for his theory, publishing important works on topics ranging from orchids to earthworms. Although he avoided discussing human evolution in the *Origin of Species*, he addressed the topic head-on in *The Descent of Man, and Selection in Relation to Sex* (1871) and *Expressions of the Emotions in Man and Animals* (1872). In 1877, he published a pioneering article in child psychology in the British journal *Mind*, called a "Biographical Sketch of an Infant." It was based on extensive notes written years before on the physical and psychological development of his firstborn son, William (Figure 5.2).

Despite his ever-present illnesses, Darwin worked right up to the end of his life, which came on April 19, 1882. Although he wished to be buried quietly at Down, his cousin Francis Galton organized a successful campaign to have him interred among other British heroes at London's Westminster Abbey, just across the street from the Houses of Parliament. Today, the large rectangular stone marking Darwin's burial place can be found on the floor of the north side of the Abbey, just below the bust of Sir Isaac Newton.

Darwin and Psychology's History

Darwin's primary contribution to psychology was his theory of evolution, which promoted a way of thinking among American psychologists that eventu-

FIGURE 5.2 Charles Darwin and his firstborn son, William (the subject of Darwin's "Biographical Sketch of an Infant") in 1842, from Desmond and Moore (1991).

ally became known as **functionalism**. This school of thought will be examined in Chapters 7 and 8; for now it is enough to say that the functionalists were interested in studying human behaviors and mental processes in terms of how they served to adapt the individual to an ever-changing environment. Consciousness, for instance, was said to serve the adaptive function of enabling the individual to assess a problem situation and solve it quickly. Similarly, habits served to free the individual's limited consciousness to concentrate on unsolved problems.

Two specific aspects of the theory also had a direct impact on psychology's history. First, an obvious implication of the theory, which Darwin made explicit in *The Descent of Man* (1871), was that a continuity of mental processes existed between humans and other species. This led to an increased interest in **comparative psychology**, the systematic study of animal behavior. Second, the emphasis on individual variation led to the systematic study of **individual differences**, a research tradition that eventually led to the measurement of differences via

intelligence and personality tests. These developments need some elaboration.

THE ORIGINS OF COMPARATIVE PSYCHOLOGY

Studies of animal behavior preceded Darwin, but interest in comparative psychology accelerated in the wake of Darwin's argument for continuity among species. Darwin himself may be considered one of the earliest comparative psychologists, by virtue of his book on emotions. Originally intended as a chapter in *The Descent of Man* (1871), the topic of the origins of emotional expression took on a life of its own, and Darwin published it separately as *Expressions of the Emotions in Man and Animals* in 1872. As the first scientific attempt to study emotional expressions, the book is Darwin's most important direct contribution to psychology's history. It includes accounts of the circumstances producing the various types of emotional response, detailed descriptions of the precise manner in which these emotions are expressed by the facial musculature, and a theory of how the expressions might have evolved.

Darwin on the Evolution of Emotional Expressions

Darwin opened his book by arguing for an evolutionary approach to the study of emotional expressions, pointing out that for humans, things such as "the bristling of the hair under the influence of extreme terror ... can hardly be understood, except on the belief that man once existed in a much lower and animal-like condition" (Darwin, 1872, p. 12). He then described the problems encountered when studying emotions in normal adults. First, with the exception of the occasional extreme emotional reactions, most expressions are muted. Studying one's own emotions is not easy either, because the experience of a strong emotion is incompatible with a rational analysis of it. One cannot feel terror and dispassionately observe it in oneself at the same time. Investigating the forms and the causes of emotional expressions required a more creative strategy, and

(a) *(b)*

FIGURE 5.3 Expressing emotions, natural versus "galvanized" smiles, from Darwin (1872).

Darwin met the challenge by proposing several methods. For instance, he suggested studying children and the insane as a way to classify the precise patterns of emotional expression. Their expressions of such emotions as anger, joy, and fear, not restricted by normal adult inhibitions, would be more intense and their features more easily classified as a result. Another method was to use a technique called galvanization. As shown in Figure 5.3, electrodes touched the surface of the skin and stimulation produced recognizable muscle contractions. The idea was to establish exactly which muscles were involved in each emotional expression. Hence, Figure 5.3a shows an elderly man with a normal smile, whereas Figure 5.3b shows the result of stimulating the muscles to the sides of the mouth. Darwin used the example to show that laughter involves several sets of muscles.

Darwin also reasoned that if emotional expressions were the result of evolution, then the same basic expressions would be found around the world. By using a large network of correspondents, including many encountered on the *Beagle* voyage, Darwin conducted the first cross-cultural study of emotional expressions. Darwin asked his correspondents to examine the facial expressions displayed in cultures far and wide and answer questions like the following:

> Is astonishment expressed by the eyes and mouth being opened wide, and by the eyebrows being raised? ...
>
> When a man sneers or snarls at another, is the corner of the upper lip over the canine or

eye tooth raised on the side facing the man whom he addresses? ...

> Is contempt expressed by a slight protrusion of the lips and by turning up the nose, and with a slight expiration? ...
>
> Is the head nodded vertically in affirmation, and shaken laterally in negation? (Darwin, 1872, pp. 15–16)

Darwin's final method, studying the emotional expressions of animals, gave him clues for a theory about the origins of the various emotional expressions. His theory involved three basic principles. He devoted a chapter to each, and then filled the bulk of the 366-page book with chapters devoted to the detailed descriptions of the various categories of emotion.

Principle one, the principle of **serviceable associated habits**, was the most important one. Incorporating the Lamarckian idea of the inheritance of acquired characteristics, Darwin argued that some emotional expressions were initially serviceable, or useful. That is, they originated in bodily actions that served some adaptive function, helping the organism to survive the struggle for existence. Those actions then became associated with situations similar to the ones in which they originally occurred. These acquired expressions were then inherited. Consider the expression of contempt. In exaggerated form, it includes a pronounced intake of air through the nose, accompanied by a lifting and turning away of the head. According to Darwin, the characteristic expression of this emotion derived from a situation in which our evolutionary ancestors reacted to a physically offensive odor. Through habit and inheritance, the same reaction now occurs whenever a person is confronted with a person or situation judged to be offensive: "We seem thus to say to the despised person that he smells offensively, in nearly the same manner as we express to him by half-closing our eyelids, or turning away our faces, that he is not worth looking at" (p. 255). Similarly, the emotional expression of a sneer, directed at an object of dislike, and characterized by the slight lifting of the lip to show the canine teeth, was said by Darwin to derive from the preparations for fighting an enemy.

> ... We may readily believe from our affinity to the anthropomorphous apes that our male semi-

human progenitors possessed great canine teeth. ... We may further suspect ... that our semi-human progenitors uncovered their canine teeth when prepared for battle, as we still do when feeling ferocious, or when merely sneering at or defying some one, without any real intention of making an attack with our teeth. (pp. 251–252)

Darwin's second principle for explaining the form of emotional expression was based on the idea that emotions that are just the opposite of each other are expressed in bodily reactions that are similarly opposed. He called it the principle of **antithesis**. As examples, Darwin pointed to numerous animal expressions. When faced with a perceived threat, for instance, a dog will strike a pose designed to make it look bigger and more of a danger to a potential enemy (e.g., the hair on its back bristles). The opposite of this threat gesture, however, is a gesture of submission. While a stranger might elicit the dog's threat gesture, the dog's master would elicit the gesture of submission.

Darwin's third principle concerned what he called the **direct action of the nervous system**. In effect, these expressions are side effects of the physiological arousal that accompanies strongly felt emotions. As an example of direct action, Darwin mentioned the unusual case of a person experiencing

severe terror because he was about to be executed— his hair turned white almost immediately. As a more common example, Darwin cited the tendency to tremble, which could accompany any strong emotion and would therefore not be associated with any specific one.

A theme that runs through Darwin's book is the universality of emotional expression. His questionnaire results, which anticipate the findings of modern cross-cultural studies, showed that all over the world, basic emotions were expressed in the same manner. A smile means the same thing everywhere. If emotional expressions are universal, the implication is that they are instinctive and consequently, that human emotional behavior can only be understood by knowing its evolutionary past.

Along with Darwin's *Descent of Man*, the emotions book made it clear that humans shared traits with animals, that a continuity of mental and emotional processes existed. Almost immediately, other naturalists began exploring the dimensions of this continuum. Many people were involved, but the best known were two Britishers, George Romanes and Lloyd Morgan. Before reading about them, however, you should read the Close-Up, which describes the contributions of a third Brit, Douglas Spalding, normally ignored in histories of psychology, but worthy of special note.

CLOSE-UP:
Douglas Spalding and the Experimental Study of Instinct

An important but typically overlooked pioneer in the systematic study of animal behavior was Douglas Spalding. Had he lived a full life, he would almost certainly be known today as the founder of modern **ethology**, the study of instinctive animal behavior. Born in London of working class parents in 1840, he did not have the luxuries of inherited wealth and an Oxford/Cambridge education to support his scientific work. Instead, he earned his keep by repairing slate roofs and became educated through his own efforts. He did manage to complete a law degree in London in his early twenties, and it was during this time that he contracted the tuberculosis that would eventually kill him. While traveling for health reasons in southern Europe in the late 1860s, he met and came under the influence of the famous British philosopher John Stuart Mill (Chapter 2), who had by then retired to Avignon in the south of France. Mill recommended Spalding as a tutor for the two young sons of Lord and Lady Amberly, two ardent followers of Mill's liberal political philosophy. The younger son would become one of the best-known philosophers of the twentieth century, Bertrand Russell.

Spalding apparently began his animal research in the 1860s, influenced by the evolutionary fervor that swept through the intelligentsia of the day. Although he never wrote a book and his studies were scattered throughout several popular magazines of the day, his research was noteworthy enough to catch the attention of the famous American psychologist/philosopher William James (Chapter 6). In Volume II of his famous *Principles of Psychology*, James (1890/1950) described in detail "Mr. Spalding's wonderful article on instinct" (p. 396). He was referring to a piece that Spalding wrote for *Macmillan's Magazine* in 1873.

In the article, Spalding addressed the British empiricists' claim that such skills as depth and distance perception and sound localization were learned very early in life as the result of sensory experience. His results showed that experience was irrelevant—certain perceptual abilities, at least in animals, did not require experience, but were the result of instinct. Along the way, he anticipated the findings of the twentieth-century ethologists Konrad Lorenz and Niko Tinbergen, by demonstrating several phenomena that today would be called species specific.

Instinct. To determine whether sensory experience is necessary for depth perception in baby chicks, Spalding developed a clever procedure. In his words, "[t]aking eggs just when the little prisoners had begun to break their way out, I removed a piece of the shell, and before they had opened their eyes drew over their heads little hoods" (Spalding, 1873, reprinted in Haldane, 1954, p. 3). The hoods remained intact for several days, preventing the chicks from having any visual experiences. Other hatchlings had "gum paper" inserted into their ears to eliminate auditory experiences. When the hoods were removed, the chicks showed no ill effects. For example, after spending just a minute or two adjusting to light, they had no difficulty pecking accurately at the insects provided by Spalding. Those with plugged ears responded similarly—when the obstruction was removed, they immediately responded to the call from an unseen mother hen and ran in the proper direction. Spalding concluded that instinct played an important role in animal behavior and that the British empiricists had overstated the importance of sensory experience as a determiner of behavior.

Imprinting. A famous picture, found in virtually all general psychology texts, shows a fatherly Konrad Lorenz, the modern-day founder of ethology, walking through a field followed by a string of young goslings. Lorenz showed that the birds would follow the first object that they were able to detect moving, and he called the phenomenon **imprinting**. Although he did not label it, Spalding observed the same behavior:

> ... Chickens as soon as they are able to walk will follow any moving object. And, when guided by sight alone, they seem to have no more disposition to follow a hen than to follow a duck, or a human being.
>
> Unreflecting onlookers, when they saw chickens a day old running after me, and older ones following me miles and answering to my whistle, imagined that I must have some occult power over the creatures, whereas I simply allowed them to follow me from the first. (Spalding, 1873, reprinted in Haldane, 1954, p. 6)

Critical Periods. Spalding also described behavior illustrating the modern ethological concept of a **critical period**—certain behaviors must develop within a limited time frame, if they are to develop at all. For example, Spalding found that if chicks were prevented from hearing the call of the mother hen for 8–10 days, they would never recognize the mother. Also, while the chicks became attached to him when they were hooded for up to three days, those hooded for four days were afraid of him.

Spalding continued his animal studies when he began tutoring the children of Lord and Lady Amberly in 1873. The sprawling country house in England's Wye Valley was soon filled with a variety of species. The unconventional Lady Amberly, a strong advocate for women's equality, served as Spalding's research assistant; according to some accounts (e.g., Boakes, 1984), she also tutored the naive Spalding in the human instinct of love. It was during this time that Spalding studied the flight instinct, demonstrating that birds did not have to learn how to fly. After hatching, he placed swallows and other nesting birds in wire mesh enclosures that prevented them from using their wings. Once released, they nonetheless flew immediately.

Spalding's idyllic life with the Amberlys came to an abrupt end in 1874, when both Lady Amberly and a young daughter died of diphtheria. A dispirited Lord Amberly also died within two years, naming Spalding as guardian to his two sons. Amberly's parents successfully contested the will, however, and Spalding was on his own (Gray, 1962). He soon left England and his tuberculosis reappeared. He was 37 when he died in France in 1877.

George Romanes (1848–1894): The Anecdotal Method

Like Darwin, George Romanes was wealthy, stumbled through an adolescence of minimal accomplishment, appeared headed for the priesthood but didn't get there, and became devoted to science as a result of his experiences at Cambridge (Lesch, 1972). A skilled researcher in physiology, Romanes became caught up in the prevailing excitement over Darwinian evolutionary theory and decided to investigate the levels of mental ability that could be found in other species. Darwin apparently considered the younger man to be his protégé, often entertaining Romanes at Down House; he even turned over his notes on animal behavior to the young scholar (Desmond & Moore, 1991).

Romanes combined Darwin's data with information he had been collecting on his own and in 1882, shortly after Darwin's death, he published *Animal Intelligence*, a detailed catalog of animal behavior, from insects to primates. The book has earned Romanes the title of founder of comparative psychology, even though Flourens (Chapter 3) had introduced the term in 1864 (Jaynes, 1969), and several books similar to Romanes's effort appeared prior to his or appeared about the same time

(Johnston, 2003). Romanes gets credit because he made an effort to define the new field in a systematic fashion, doing so by drawing a parallel between comparative psychology and comparative anatomy. Romanes argued that just as the specialist in that latter discipline made comparisons among the physical features of various species, in order to examine the evolution of physical structure, so the comparative psychologist would examine differences among the psychological (i.e., mental) features of different species, in order to examine mental evolution.

Traditional accounts of Romanes's work focus on his overuse of uncritical stories about animal behavior supplied by others, the so-called **anecdotal method**, which has great potential for exaggerating the abilities of animals. And during this time of evolutionary zeitgeist, the popular press was full of accounts of what appeared to be remarkable accomplishments by animals. Thus, Romanes's work has sometimes been discredited. This is unfortunate, because Romanes was well aware of the problems with anecdotal evidence and took some care to include reliable reports of behavior in his book. For example, he tried to include accounts from observers known to be competent (e.g., Darwin), and he tried to accept unusual accounts of behavior only if they were independently reported by two or more persons. Nonetheless, Romanes himself recognized that the book, if considered by itself, might seem to be little more than a collection of unusual animal stories. He expected that his subsequent books, outlining a theory of mental evolution, would be more important, and that this initial "fact" book would come to be viewed as a preliminary step to the more systematic treatises (Boakes, 1984). Romanes indeed published his theory books, but they were largely ignored; his reputation, somewhat besmirched, rests on the fact book.

Romanes may have taken more precautions than are usually attributed to him, but *Animal Intelligence* does nonetheless rely mainly on stories told by others more than on direct observations. It also tends toward **anthropomorphism**, the attribution of human faculties to nonhuman entities. That is, Romanes rather uncritically sprinkled human characteristics among a vast array of species. For instance, he argued that ants are in the habit of keeping pets (p. 83), that spiders have a "fondness" for music (p. 205), that scorpions commit suicide when surrounded by fire (p. 222), that birds show sympathy and conjugal fidelity (pp. 271–273), and that beavers show "sagacity and forethought" when selecting sites for their lodges (p. 371) and have an intellectual appreciation for the architectural principles involved in dam building (p. 376).

Conwy Lloyd Morgan (1852–1936): The Principle of Parsimony

The problems with Romanes's first book on animal behavior, with its emphasis on anecdotes and its excessive anthropomorphism, were noted by another British naturalist, C. Lloyd Morgan. Son of a lawyer, Morgan attended the School of Mines at the Royal College of Science in London to be trained as a mining engineer. At the School of Mines, he came under the influence of the evolutionist Thomas Huxley, one of Darwin's most ardent defenders. This led Morgan to an interest in zoology and geology, and eventually to a lifetime position as a professor of these topics at University College, Bristol, starting in 1883. He published several books on the geology of the Bristol region, but he is best known for his work in compar-

ative psychology, reflected in books with titles like *Animal Life and Intelligence* (1890) and *An Introduction to Comparative Psychology* (1895). Just as Romanes was a protégé of Darwin, Morgan started as a follower and admirer of Romanes, but eventually went beyond his mentor.

Morgan is best known today for arguing that explanations for animal behavior should be in the simplest terms possible. This appeal for "parsimonious explanations" is still called **Lloyd Morgan's canon**. As he put it: "In no case may we interpret an action as the outcome of the exercise of a higher psychical faculty, if it can be interpreted as the outcome of the exercise of one which stands lower in the psychological scale" (Morgan, 1895/1903, p. 59). Two of Morgan's examples illustrate the point. First, before beginning his long tenure at Bristol, Morgan taught in South Africa for five years, where he had the opportunity to observe scorpion behavior firsthand. Thus, he had the opportunity to examine Romanes's anthropomorphic claim about scorpions committing suicide when surrounded by fire. Could there be a more parsimonious explanation of the fact that scorpions occasionally sting themselves to death? Morgan thought so, and in contrast to Romanes, who relied on reports from others, Morgan made his own direct observations. What he discovered was that scorpions regularly used their tails to remove foreign substances and other irritants (e.g., smoke) from the surface of their bodies. It was a simple reflex action, not a deliberate, calculated response arising out of "despair." Every once in a while, Morgan observed, the reflex action would be just a bit too vigorous, resulting in the demise of a scorpion. There was no need to propose a "higher psychical faculty" (a decision to commit suicide) when the behavior could be seen as the result of some factor "lower in the psychological scale" (a reflex action).

A second example used by Morgan is a famous one, often credited with opening the way to the objective study of animal behavior and an important landmark on the road to behaviorism. You will see in Chapter 7's Original Source Excerpt that Morgan's example influenced the choice of apparatus for the famous puzzle box research of Edward Thorndike. Romanes had credited cats and dogs with the mental ability to plan, based on the observation that some could open gates and consequently escape from yards. Morgan, however, believed that such behavior had a simpler explanation, and he used his fox terrier, Tony, as a case in point. As shown in the sketch in Figure 5.4, the dog could place his head through an opening in a gate and open the latch by lifting upward. The gate then swung open and Tony was free to leave the yard and "get out into the road, where there was often much to interest him; cats to be worried, other dogs with whom to establish a sniffing acquaintance, and so forth" (Morgan, 1895/1903, p. 292). To a naive observer, it might appear that the dog rationally "understood" the mechanics of the gate operation and the concept of lifting the latch as a planned means to a desired end. To Morgan, however, the behavior was simply the result of a three-week series of trial-and-error actions prompted by the dog's attempts to escape the yard for the romance of the road. He noted that before hitting on the correct solution, Tony had tried just about everything else, running back and forth along the fence, sticking his head between the bars at numerous locations, and eventually hitting upon the correct action by accident. After he had escaped one time, he soon abandoned the unsuccessful behaviors and learned to repeat the successful one.

Morgan's **law of parsimony** is sometimes used to highlight an important shift in how comparative psychologists thought about animal behavior and Darwin's notion of the continuity among species. It is often argued that prior to Morgan, naturalists were overly anthropomorphic and searched for evidence of higher mental processes in virtually all species. After Morgan, researchers looked for simpler processes to explain an animal's actions, gradually resulting in the behaviorist dictum that behaviors, even human ones, are best understood in terms of simple conditioning processes. That is, Morgan is often seen as a pivotal figure in the "progress" from cute animal stories to sophisticated experimental research and a mechanical conception of animal behavior. Such an interpretation overstates the case, however. Morgan can indeed be credited for arguing that an understanding of animal behavior must go beyond a collection of anecdotes and embrace more systematic observation-

FIGURE 5.4 Tony, Morgan's terrier, about to escape from the yard, adapted from Morgan (1895/1903).

al strategies. Yet to say that Morgan wished to rule out the existence of animal consciousness and intelligence is erroneous. As Morgan himself said, shortly after proclaiming the canon:

> ... To this, however, it should be added, lest the range of the principle be misunderstood, that the canon by no means excludes the interpretation of a particular activity in terms of the higher processes, if we already have some independent evidence of the occurrence of these higher processes in the animal under observation. (Morgan, 1895/1903, p. 59)

Thus, Morgan did not intend for the canon of parsimony to be a prohibition against the idea of higher mental processes in animals—he was merely urging methodological caution. According to Costall (1993), Morgan's true purpose was to broaden the range of criteria on which to base continuity among species. Rather than relying exclusively on a search for sophisticated rational reflection on the part of a variety of species, other types of mental processes, differing in degrees of complexity, could be included. Put in evolutionary terms, Morgan proposed that animals exhibited many levels of cognition, reaching a level of complexity just sufficient to enable them to survive their own unique struggle for existence. The point of the canon was to argue that there was no reason to suggest levels of mental capability beyond that needed to survive.

Comparative Psychology in America

Given Darwin's national origins, it is not surprising that comparative psychology developed a firm foothold in Great Britain in the mid to late nineteenth century, as reflected in the work of Romanes, Spalding, and Morgan. Interest in the topic developed quickly in America as well and you will learn about two prime examples in later chapters. First, an animal laboratory developed at Clark University in the mid-1890s, under the leadership of Linus Kline, Willard Small, and Edmund Sanford, the laboratory director. As you will discover in the Close-Up for Chapter 6, they can be credited with establishing one of psychology's more enduring methodologies— maze learning. Also, Kline wrote an article entitled "Suggestions Toward a Laboratory Course in Comparative Psychology" (1899) that influenced instruction in comparative psychology for years to come. The second example you will encounter in Chapter 7—Thorndike's work on puzzle box learning in several species, but primarily in cats. It is also worth noting that several American researchers developed interests in animal behavior and studied it in the British naturalist tradition. One, John Bascom, even wrote a textbook with "comparative psychology" in the title as early as 1878 (Johnston, 2003).

STUDYING INDIVIDUAL DIFFERENCES

A cornerstone of Darwin's theory, the raw material for natural selection, was the idea that individual members of a species varied from each other. For psychology, this fact led to the systematic study of **individual differences**, a research tradition that includes the creation of techniques to measure those differences. Today's intelligence and personality tests are just two outcomes of this tradition. The person most directly responsible for initiating the study of individual differences was Darwin's half-cousin, Francis Galton, whose obsession with measurement led one scientist to refer to him as the nineteenth century's "apostle of quantification" (Gould, 1981, p. 75).

Francis Galton (1822–1911): Jack of All Sciences

Like his more famous relative, Galton (Figure 5.5) was raised in affluence. Because he never found it necessary to earn a living, he was able to indulge an exceptionally wide range of interests. His insatiable curiosity, combined with a brilliant intellect that manifested itself at an early age,[7] resulted in a remarkably diverse list of accomplishments, only a small portion of which relates directly to psychology. For example, he became one of a number of famous British explorers of Africa during the Victorian era. From 1850 to 1852, he explored a little known territory in the south of Africa, mapping it accurately for the first time and displaying his devotion to the gods of precision in measurement. His exploits won him a gold medal from the Royal Geographical Society and he became a recognized public figure after publishing an account of his explorations and a highly successful (eight editions) travel guide for the inexperienced explorer. The latter included suggestions on everything from shelter to navigation to hunting to cooking, along with advice on dealing with native populations: "A frank, joking but determined manner joined with an air of showing more confidence in the good faith of the natives than you really feel, is the best" (Galton, 1855, cited in Forrest, 1974, p. 64).

[7] Galton resembled another child prodigy, John Stuart Mill, in this regard. Like Mill, Galton displayed adult-like abilities at a tender age. He could read and write English by age three, translate some Latin by age five, and quote from Shakespeare by his sixth birthday.

FIGURE 5.5 The ever curious Francis Galton.

In addition to geography and exploration, Galton made original contributions to several other fields. By gathering weather information from various locations at the same times during the day, for instance, he created the first systematic weather maps, and he was the first to observe the relationships between high and low pressure systems and how they influenced the weather. By measuring the patterns of swirls on the fingertips of hundreds of different people, he demonstrated that every person had a unique pattern. Scotland Yard eventually started using this "fingerprinting" technique for identification purposes. This procedure, of course, is an example of looking for individual differences. Indeed, Galton's work in fingerprinting was just a small piece of his overall strategy of quantifying differences between people over a range of variables. And this leads to Galton's importance for psychology.

The Nature of Intelligence

As a wealthy, upper-class, Victorian-era, British white male, living at a time when England was the most powerful nation on earth, Galton and his cohort group had little difficulty believing themselves to be superior to those from other classes, countries, races, or the other gender. Furthermore, more a product of his environment than he cared to admit, Galton shared the widespread assumption among his peers that this preeminence was no accident, but based on an inherent superiority in ability. When his cousin published on evolution in 1859, humans were not discussed, but Galton immediately saw the ramifications. If inherited individual variation, acted upon by natural selection, influenced the evolution of animal and plant species, it must have influenced humans as well. If human intelligence was a key trait enabling physically weak humans to survive the struggle for existence, then the more intelligent humans would naturally rise to the top of society. From this it was not hard for Galton to conclude that he and others of his class had achieved their lofty positions in society by virtue of their highly evolved and superior intellectual ability, rather than by the accident of being born to the right parents. He set out to collect evidence in support of his belief that intelligence was innate, producing *Hereditary Genius* in 1869.

To examine the question of whether intelligence was inherited, Galton relied on his proclivity for quantification and statistical analysis. First, by examining the contents of biographical dictionaries, which profiled people who had achieved eminence in some field, he estimated that the "rate of eminence" in Great Britain was about 1 person in 4000. He then looked at the family trees of these highly able people and discovered that talent tended to run in families. Of those noted in the dictionaries, about 10% had at least one relative who was also so noted, a rate much higher than could be expected by a one in four thousand probability for the general population. And talent within a family tended to be similar—lawyers related to lawyers, doctors related to doctors, and so on. Furthermore, if two relatives appeared in the dictionaries, they were four times more likely to be directly related (e.g., father-son) than related at a second level (e.g., uncle-nephew). Today, of course, we recognize that these patterns are just as likely to reflect environmental factors as genetic ones, but Galton was operating within the context of a social environment that was biased toward an assumption of inherited differences in ability and an intellectual environment that was dominated by the evolution discussion. For him, the signs all pointed to the same conclusion—intelligence was innate, the product of evolutionary forces.

Following *Hereditary Genius*, Galton continued his examination of talent by pioneering two methodological techniques in use today: surveys and twin studies. Although his cousin was using a similar technique to study emotional expressions at about the same time, Galton is credited with being the first person to use the **survey method**. Sometime in the early 1870s, he wrote a questionnaire and distributed it to 180 fellows of the Royal Society, the scientific elite of England. The survey asked its respondents to describe their personalities, physical attributes, family characteristics, and the details of their upbringing; it also asked them to describe the origins of their scientific interests and to indicate "How far do your scientific tastes appear innate" (cited in Forrest, 1974, p. 126). Galton received about 100 usable replies, and they formed the basis of his next book, which included a subtitle that popularized two words destined to become catchwords in the continuing debate over the origins of intelligence. The book was called *English Men of Science: Their Nature and Nurture* (Galton, 1874).[8] While granting that some of the replies demonstrated that the environment (nurture) helped to shape the scientists, Galton believed that his respondents overwhelmingly supported the idea that talent in science was inherited (nature). This he concluded from making the questionable assumption that scientific ability could be considered innate if a subject reported being interested in science very early in life and could not point to any particular set of circumstances bringing about such an interest. It just seemed to be there from the start. As one of his respondents put it: "As far back as I remember, I loved nature and desired to learn her secrets" (cited in Forrest, 1974, p. 126).

Galton's second methodological innovation, **twin studies**, was on firmer scientific ground. He sent questionnaires to twins known to him, asking them to supply names of other twins; he eventually surveyed 94 pairs about their physical and psychological attributes. As might be expected, he found support for his hereditarian beliefs—many similarities between pairs of twins, even in their later years, after they had been living in different environments. He reported the data anecdotally, and both his questionnaire wording and his interpretation of the results were affected by his preconceptions about intelligence, but the twin studies method itself has proven invaluable over the years as a way to evaluate the relative influences of nature and nurture.

The general conclusion that Galton reached on the basis of all these studies is clear from the opening sentence of *Hereditary Genius*: "I propose to show in this book that a man's natural abilities are derived by inheritance" (Galton, 1869/1891, p. 1). One implication of this statement, resulting from Galton's reading of Darwin's parallels between the artificial selection of the breeder and the natural selection of the wild, is spelled out in the book's second sentence. He wrote that just as it is possible "to obtain by careful selection a permanent breed of dogs or horses gifted with peculiar powers of running, ... so it would be quite practicable to produce a highly-gifted race of men by judicious marriages during several consecutive generations" (Galton, 1869/1891, p. 1). This suggestion eventually led Galton to coin the term **eugenics** to promote the idea that society should take active steps toward improving its genetic material. This would include encouraging certain people to reproduce, sometimes known as "positive" eugenics. These individuals presumably would be those with great talent, people like Galton (ironically, Galton and his wife were childless). On the other hand, he also advocated a "negative" eugenics, arguing that the poor (i.e., intellectually inferior, otherwise they would not be so poor, he believed) should be discouraged from having children and that immigration should be restricted. He founded a Eugenics Society in 1908, a journal a year later, and spent his remaining years promoting a eugenics-based society. Indeed, he came to think of eugenics as a new religion, as evidenced by this comment from his autobiography: "I take Eugenics very seriously, feeling that its principles ought to become

---

[8] Galton is sometimes credited with inventing the label "nature-nurture issue," by virtue of the subtitle to his 1874 book. He had numerous predecessors, however, including Shakespeare (Conley, 1984), who described the notorious Caliban in the *Tempest* (Act IV, Scene 1) in these terms:

A devil, a born devil, on whose nature
Nurture can never stick.

one of the dominant motives in a civilized nation, much as if they were one of its religious tenets" (Galton, 1908, p. 232). As will be seen in the chapter on mental testing (Chapter 8), Galton found a sympathetic audience for his eugenicist views, both in Great Britain and in the United States.

The Anthropometric Laboratory

In order to selectively breed for the intelligence that would keep Great Britain in its position as a world power, Galton knew that it would be necessary to have some means of identifying those best suited to improve the race. This meant developing ways to measure talent, a task close to Galton's quantitative heart. The measurement of ability was a natural outgrowth of his obsession with measuring all possible differences between people. His efforts reached their peak in the 1880s, when he established an Anthropometric Laboratory, initially as part of an international health fair held in South Kensington in 1884. It later moved to a nearby museum, where Galton collected data for another 10 years. Nearly 10,000 fair-goers were tested in 1884; about 17,000 were tested altogether (Forrest, 1974).

Each person entering the laboratory completed several tests, with many of the measuring instruments created by Galton. Some were simple physical measures: height, weight, arm span, and breathing capacity. Others tested basic sensory/motor capacities: reaction time, auditory and visual acuity, color naming, judgment of line lengths, how forcefully a target could be struck with the fist, and grip strength. After the lab moved from the health fair, head size was added as a measure. Although these might not appear to be valid measures of intelligence to us today,

Galton argued that superior mental capacity was related to neural efficiency and sensory ability: "The only information that reaches us concerning outward events appears to pass through the avenue of our senses; and the more perceptible our senses are of difference, the larger is the field upon which our judgment and intelligence can act" (Galton, 1883/1965, p. 421). Galton also argued that women were intellectually inferior to men, a widely held nineteenth-century prejudice, and traced the deficiency to their inadequate senses. He noted that professions requiring sharp senses, such as piano-tuners, wine tasters, and wool sorters, were all populated by men. Deeply immersed in his times, of course, he failed to consider the fact that women would never be given the chance to be employed in these trades.

Galton's measures never proved to be useful indexes of intelligence and they were soon replaced by tests like those devised in France at the turn of the century by Alfred Binet (Chapter 8). Galton's effort is noteworthy, however, as the first serious attempt to measure individual differences in human abilities. It is also important for the history of statistics—in his attempts to determine whether scores on his various measures were associated with each other, he invented the statistical concept of **correlation**. In an 1888 paper entitled "Co-relations and their Measurement, Chiefly from Anthropometric Data," Galton argued that the strength of association between any two measures could be stated mathematically. This idea was soon refined into the modern concept of the correlation coefficient by one of his followers, the mathematician Karl Pearson, whose name is associated with the most common expression of a correlation coefficient, Pearson's r.

ORIGINAL SOURCE EXCERPT
Galton on Measurement and Association

As a jack-of-all-sciences, Galton was unrelenting in the search for new phenomena to measure. The following excerpt, taken from a collection of Galton papers that were published together as *An Inquiry into Human Faculty and Its Development* (Galton, 1883), illustrate just a sample of his interests. First, one of his more famous inventions has come to be known as the Galton whistle. It was designed to measure auditory thresholds, and Galton's description of its use reveals something of his devotion to precision and his delight in making observations about behavior. His observation about age-related hearing

loss for high-frequency sounds ("shrill notes") is now a well-established auditory phenomenon ("presbycusis"). The page references in the excerpt are from a collection of
readings by Dennis (1948).

Whistles for Audibility of Shrill Notes

I contrived a small whistle for conveniently ascertaining the upper limits
of audible sound in different persons. ... I made a very small whistle from a
brass tube whose internal diameter was less than one tenth of an inch in
diameter. A plug was fitted into the lower end of the tube, which could be
pulled out or pushed in as much as desired, thereby causing the length of
the bore of the whistle to be varied at will. When the bore is long the note is
low; when short, it is high. The plug was graduated, so that the precise note
produced by the whistle could be determined by reading off the graduations
and referring to a table.

On testing different persons I found there was a remarkable falling off in
the power of hearing high notes as age advanced. The persons themselves
were quite unconscious of their deficiency so long as their sense of hearing
low notes remained unimpaired. It is an only too amusing experiment to test
a party of persons of various ages, including some rather elderly and self-
satisfied personages. They are indignant at being thought deficient in the
power of hearing, yet the experiment quickly shows that they are absolutely
deaf to shrill notes which the younger persons hear acutely, and they commonly betray much dislike to the discovery. Every one has his limit, and the
limit at which sounds become too shrill to be audible to any particular person can be rapidly determined by this little instrument. (p. 277)

Ever the creative scientist, Galton also arranged to attach his whistle to the end of a
hollow walking stick, enabling him to squeeze a bulb at the top of the stick to sound the
whistle. He took the contraption to the London zoo and used it to test the hearing of various species. He discovered that cats seemed to be especially capable of hearing his
"shrill" (high frequency) tones, which made evolutionary sense to him:

Cats, of course, have to deal with mice, and to find them out by their squeal-
ing. ... Cats are differentiated by natural selection until they have a power of
hearing all the high notes made by mice and other little creatures that they
have to catch. (p. 278)

As we have already seen, association was a mental process of great importance to
philosophers and scientists in the eighteenth and nineteenth centuries, and Galton was no
exception. He was aware of the long history of philosophical speculation about the
nature of association, of course, but he was unaware of the work that Hermann
Ebbinghaus (Chapter 4) was doing at about the same time (Ebbinghaus's *On Memory*
appeared two years after Galton's *Inquiry*). Galton's first concern was the difficulty in
studying the associations in one's own mind—the very act of closely attending to the
operation of the mind influences the sequence of ideas. Hence, the mind is not behaving
naturally while under the careful examination required to meet the demands of science.
He believed that he had succeeded in solving the problem:

... My method consists of allowing the mind to play freely for a brief period, until a couple or so of ideas have passed through it, and then, while the traces or echoes of those ideas are still lingering in the brain, to turn the attention on them with a sudden and complete awakening; to arrest, to scrutinize them, and to record their exact appearance. ...

I must add, that I found the experiments to be extremely trying and irksome, and that it required much resolution to go through with them, using the scrupulous care they demanded. Nevertheless the results well repaid the trouble.

... My first experiments were these. On several occasions, but notably on one when I felt myself unusually capable of the kind of effort required, I walked leisurely along Pall Mall, a distance of 450 yards, during which time I scrutinised with attention every successive object that caught my eyes, and I allowed my attention to rest on it until one or two thoughts had arisen through direct association with that object; then I took very brief mental note of them, and passed on to the next object. I never allowed my mind to ramble. The number of objects viewed was, I think, about 300, for I had subsequently repeated the same walk under similar conditions and endeavoured to estimate their number, with that result. It was impossible for me to recall, in other than the vaguest way, the numerous ideas that had passed through my mind; but of this, at least, I am sure, that samples of my whole life had passed before me, that many bygone incidents, which I never suspected to have formed part of my stock of thought, had been glanced at as objects too familiar to awaken the attention. I saw at once that the brain was vastly more active than I had previously believed it to be, and I was perfectly amazed at the unexpected width of the field of its everyday operations. (pp. 285–286)

Galton noticed in subsequent walks that many of his associations repeated themselves, which led him to temper his initial impression of the richness and diversity of mental life. He next set out to study the association process with more precision, in the process inventing the **word association test**, in which he thought of a stimulus word and recorded the first word that came to mind. He even attempted to measure the time it took to produce an association:

... I selected a list of suitable words, and wrote them on different small sheets of paper. Taking care to dismiss them from my thoughts when not engaged upon them, and allowing some days to elapse before I began to use them, I laid one of these sheets with all due precautions under a book, but not wholly covered by it, so that when I leaned forward I would see one of the words, being previously quite ignorant of what the word would be. Also I held a small chronograph, which I started by pressing a spring the moment the word caught my eye, and which stopped of itself the instant I released the spring; and this I did so soon as about a couple of ideas in direct association with the word had arisen in my mind. ... When the two ideas had occurred, I stopped the chronograph and wrote them down, and the time they occupied. I soon got into the way of doing all this in a very methodical and automatic manner, keeping the mind perfectly calm and neutral, but intent and, as it were, at full cock and on hair trigger, before displaying the word. ... The list of words that I finally secured was 75 in number, though I began with more. I went through them on four separate occasions, under very different circumstances, in England and abroad, and at intervals of about a month. In no case were the associations governed to any degree worth recording, by remembering what had occurred to me on previous occasions, for I found that the process itself had great influence in discharging the memory of what had just been engaged in, and I of course, took care between the experiments never to let my thoughts revert to the words. The results seem to me to be as trustworthy as any other statistical series that has been collected with equal care. (pp. 286–287)

Galton's word association tests confirmed the tendency for associations to repeat themselves in one's mind. For example, after going through his list of 75 words four times, he found that in about 25% of the cases, the word gave rise to exactly the same association on all four trials.

... This shows much less variety in the mental stock of ideas than I had expected, and makes us feel that the roadways of our minds are worn into very deep ruts. I conclude from the proved number of faint and barely conscious thoughts, and from the proved iteration of them, that the mind is perpetually travelling over familiar ways without our memory retaining any impression of its excursions. Its footsteps are so light and fleeting that it is only by such experiments as I have described that we can learn anything about them. (p. 288)

Galton concluded with the observation that we are only dimly aware of the course of our mental life, strongly hinting at the unconscious mind that would shortly become the focus of another famous nineteenth-century mind, Sigmund Freud (Chapter 12):

... Perhaps the strongest of the impressions left by these experiments regards the multifariousness of the work done by the mind in a state of half-consciousness, and the valid reason they afford for believing in the existence of still deeper strata of mental operations, sunk wholly below the level of consciousness. (p. 289)

It has been estimated that a mere 25% of Galton's research and writings were of direct concern to psychology (Forrest, 1974). Yet his contribution to the discipline is impressive: He pioneered the study of individual differences in human ability, introduced research methods and statistical tools still in use, and made some astute observations about human cognition. Galton's lifelong devotion to British science earned him a knighthood in 1909. Sir Francis Galton died two years later.

DARWIN'S CENTURY IN PERSPECTIVE

Although Darwin's major influence has been on the biological sciences, modern psychology cannot be properly understood without knowing about his theory and its implications. The study of individual differences derives from his observation about individual variation within a species, and comparative psychology has its origins in an attempt to evaluate the claim of an evolutionary continuity among species. As will be seen in Chapter 12, Darwin's theory also had a direct effect on Freud's thinking about the importance of sexual motivation in directing the course of human behavior. Finally, functionalism (to be encountered in varying degrees in Chapters 6, 7, and 8), which examined behaviors and mental processes in terms of their capacity for adapting the organism to the environment, also had its roots in evolutionary thinking. Darwin, in effect, naturalized the mind, causing it to be seen as the means by which the human animal survives in the struggle for existence.

In recent years, some psychologists have become even more explicit in looking toward evolution as a means to explain human behavior, and the result is a new subfield called **evolutionary psychology**. Advocates (e.g., Wright, 1994) argue that if evolutionary forces have been powerful enough to create the physical characteristics that make us human, then why not behavioral and mental characteristics as well? Evolutionary psychologists have paid special attention to social behaviors and to sexuality and gender differences in behavior. Their general strategy is to describe some behavior that occurred with some regularity, then look for an evolutionary explanation for it, and then develop testable predictions about behavior. They believe, for example, that much of the behavior that surrounds male-female relations reduces to an attempt to insure that one's genetic material makes it to the next generation. Many of their ideas have been controversial, especially among psychologists who tend to emphasize the importance of the environment in shaping human behavior. Yet their increasing presence in the discussion about the causes of human behavior is just another indication of the lasting power of Darwin's ideas.

SUMMARY

THE SPECIES PROBLEM

- During the Enlightenment, some scientists began questioning the biblical account of how species were created. The species problem concerned the question of how species originated, why there were so many, and how extinction could be explained. The argument from design enabled scientists to continue to examine nature scientifically while maintaining religious beliefs.

- An early theory of evolution that omitted reference to the deity was proposed by Charles Darwin's grandfather, Erasmus. A more important theory was proposed by the French naturalist, Lamarck. His theory included the concept of the inheritance of acquired characteristics.

CHARLES DARWIN (1809–1882) AND THE THEORY OF EVOLUTION

- After several false starts, Charles Darwin found a vocation in science while a student at Cambridge. He initially thought of himself as a geologist, but he was also greatly interested in zoology. Two important mentors were the botanist John Henslow and the geologist Adam Sedgwick.

- During a five-year voyage aboard the *Beagle*, Darwin collected evidence that led to important contributions to both geology and zoology. He made discoveries that supported Charles Lyell's uniformitarian model of geological change (the earth changes gradually according to known principles, rather than as a result of periodic geological catastrophes) and he collected data that would eventually provide evidence for his theory of evolution. Evidence from the Galapagos Islands (e.g., finches) was especially important.

- In developing his theory, Darwin was influenced by the views of Thomas Malthus, who pointed out that because populations tend to grow faster than food supplies, a struggle for existence occurs among members of those populations. He also observed that hobbyists and farmers were able to bring about dramatic changes in species by careful breeding.

- Darwin created the essence of his theory in the late 1830s, but did not publish for 20 years. He was slowed by ill health, a concern over how his theory would be received by the scientific community, and a scientific cautiousness that led him to accumulate as much evidence as possible to support his theory. He was motivated to publish in 1859 by the appearance of a similar theory by Alfred Russel Wallace.

- Darwin's theory proposes that individual members of

every species vary from each other, that some variations are more favorable in the struggle for existence than others, enabling the organism to adapt to the environment, and that nature "selects" (natural selection) those with the most favorable variations for survival.

THE ORIGINS OF COMPARATIVE PSYCHOLOGY

• An implication of Darwin's theory was that there existed a continuity between species. This led to the development of comparative psychology, the study of differences between and similarities among species on various traits (e.g., intelligence). Darwin was an early pioneer, who examined the evolutionary history of emotional expressions and demonstrated that human expressions had evolutionary roots.

• George Romanes is considered the founder of comparative psychology and he provided extensive descriptions of the behavior of many species. He relied on anecdotal observations and was too anthropomorphic in his interpretations of the behaviors he described. A more experimental approach was taken by Douglas Spalding, who demonstrated that certain behaviors were the result of instinct, not experience. C. Lloyd Morgan took issue with the excessive anthropomorphism shown by other comparative psychologists and argued for more parsimonious explanations. For example, some behaviors were

more parsimoniously explained as being examples of trial-and-error learning than rational thought.

STUDYING INDIVIDUAL DIFFERENCES

• Individual variation is a cornerstone of evolutionary theory, and Francis Galton was the first to carefully examine these individual differences in humans. He studied individual differences in visual imagery, studying it through the first systematic use of the survey method (questionnaire). He also invented the word association method to study the nature of associations.

• Galton believed that intelligence was an inherited ability; nurture played no significant role. As evidence, he pointed to the fact that certain abilities tended to run in families. He argued for a eugenics-based society—only those who are fit should be encouraged to reproduce. To identify those who were most fit, he set out to measure individual differences in ability. This resulted in the first widespread attempt to measure and classify human abilities. His measures relied heavily on basic sensory/motor processes and did not prove very useful.

DARWIN'S CENTURY IN PERSPECTIVE

• One modern indication of the power of Darwinian thinking is the development of evolutionary psychology, which aims to explain many social behaviors in evolutionary terms.

STUDY QUESTIONS

1. What was the species problem and did the argument from design propose to answer the problem?

2. Describe Lamarck's ideas about evolution.

3. What were the important events leading to Darwin's appointment to be on the *Beagle*, and why did he consider himself as much a geologist as a naturalist at this time?

4. Distinguish between catastrophist and uniformitarian views of geology and describe the evidence that Darwin collected relating to the issue.

5. Describe the example of Darwin's finches as a way of summarizing the essential features of his theory of evolution.

6. In developing his theory of evolution, what was the lesson that Darwin learned from Malthus?

7. In developing his theory of evolution, what was the lesson that Darwin learned from pigeon breeders?

8. Darwin had his theory worked out in the early 1840s. Why did he delay publication and why did he eventually publish in 1859?

9. Concerning the issue of whether his theory was in line with the zeitgeist, what were Darwin's thoughts?

10. Describe Darwin's contribution to comparative psychology. In particular, show how he applied evolutionary thinking to the concept of emotional expression.

11. Describe Spalding's research on instinct. How did his work demonstrate the phenomena that later came to be called imprinting and critical periods?

12. Describe and criticize the comparative psychology of Romanes. In what way has the criticism been unfair to him?

13. Describe Lloyd Morgan's canon and apply it to the example of Morgan's terrier. Explain the important misconception about Morgan's canon that has developed over the years.

14. According to Galton, why is one person more intelligent than another? What kinds of evidence did he use to support his claim?

15. What is the connection between Galton's beliefs about intelligence and (a) eugenics, and (b) mental testing?

16. Summarize the overall impact of Darwinian thinking on psychology.

QUESTIONS FROM THE ORIGINAL SOURCE EXCERPT

1. Describe Galton's psychophysics research on the audibility of tones. How does age affect hearing thresholds?

2. Describe how Galton used the questionnaire method to study the mental imagery of scientists and others. What did he find that surprised him?

3. Describe the two different methods that Galton used to study the nature of his own associations. What did he discover and conclude?

FOR FURTHER READING

Boakes, R. (1984). *From Darwin to behaviourism: Psychology and the minds of animals.* New York: Cambridge University Press.

Detailed yet highly readable treatment of the rise of comparative psychology from its evolutionary roots and its connection with behaviorism; notable for its collection of unique photos.

Desmond, A., & Moore, J. (1991). *Darwin: The life of a tormented evolutionist.* New York: W. W. Norton and Company.

One of several recent biographies of Darwin; as the subtitle suggests, the book deals extensively with Darwin's struggle to create and provide supporting evidence for his great theory; highly detailed account of the Beagle trip.

Ruse, M. (1979). *The Darwinian revolution: Science red in tooth and claw.* Chicago: University of Chicago Press.

Fits the development of Darwin's theory within the framework of nineteenth-century science and religion and within the historical context of Victorian England.

Weiner, J. (1994). *The beak of the finch.* New York: Vintage Books.

A scientific page-turner, and winner of a Pulitzer Prize; recounts the story of Darwin's finches and focuses on recent finch research, which provides direct evidence of evolutionary changes occurring in a relatively brief period of time.

CHAPTER 6

AMERICAN PIONEERS

> When ... we talk of "psychology as a natural science," we must not assume that that means a sort of psychology that stands at last on solid ground. ... This is no science, it is only the hope of a science.
>
> —William James, 1892

PREVIEW AND CHAPTER OBJECTIVES

Having considered the philosophical and scientific contexts out of which modern psychology evolved, its origins and early development in Germany, and the far-reaching importance of Darwin's ideas, we are ready to shift our focus to the development of psychology in the United States in the nineteenth century. The chapter opens with a discussion of the influence of faculty psychology in pre-Civil War America and a description of the development of higher education in America in the latter half of the nineteenth century. Considered in this section will be the limited possibilities for education available to women and to minority students during this era. The chapter then examines the life and work of America's first major psychologist: William James. Although he eventually thought of himself more as a philosopher than a psychologist, his *Principles of Psychology* is arguably the most important book written in psychology's brief history and his ideas influence the field to this day. The Original Source Excerpt is by James—a discussion of what came to be called the James-Lange theory of emotions. The chapter also examines the careers and contributions of several other members of the first generation of American psychologists, especially G. Stanley Hall and Mary Whiton Calkins. Hall exemplified the pioneering spirit said to characterize Americans: he spread the gospel of the New Psychology by founding laboratories, journals, and the American Psychological Association. He also encouraged and trained the first African American to earn a Ph.D. in psychology, Francis Sumner. Mary Calkins was the best known of a handful of pioneering women psychologists who made their presence felt despite daunting odds. After you finish this chapter, you should be able to:

- Explain what it was like to study psychology in America before the arrival of the new psychology and the writings of William James

- Describe the rise of the modern university and how the German model influenced education in America

- Enumerate the obstacles facing women and minority students who tried to obtain higher education and graduate education in the late nineteenth and early twentieth centuries

- Describe the formative influences on William James, especially the development of his pragmatic approach to philosophy

▨ Describe James's definition of psychology and his attitude about the new laboratory approach to psychology

▨ Provide a Jamesian description of consciousness and its attributes, and describe the functions of consciousness and of habit, according to James

▨ Describe the James-Lange theory of emotion, the evidence James used to support it, and the problems with the theory

▨ Explain why spiritualism was popular in late nineteenth century America and explain James's attitude about the investigation of spiritualism

▨ Describe the contributions of G. Stanley Hall to the professionalization of psychology in America

▨ Explain why Hall thought of himself as a genetic psychologist

▨ Describe the significance of the work of Francis Sumner and the obstacles that he faced

▨ Explain why Mary Calkins is considered an important pioneer in memory research and describe the difficulties she had in obtaining graduate education

▨ Describe the contributions of Margaret Washburn and Christine Ladd-Franklin to American psychology in its formative years

PSYCHOLOGY IN NINETEENTH-CENTURY AMERICA

E. G. Boring (1950) once described American psychology as the offspring of the new psychology created in Germany (i.e., Wundt) and of British biology (i.e., Darwin), and he asserted that American psychology did not really begin until William James appeared on the scene. Boring influenced a whole generation of psychologists, of course, and one consequence has been the neglect of pre-Jamesian psychology. Yet while William James was clearly a towering figure during the formative years of modern scientific psychology in the United States, he was not the first American thinker to write about psychological issues or to teach psychology in an American university (Fuchs, 2000). Prior to James, psychology was taught in courses called "moral philosophy" or "mental philosophy," and it was dominated by **faculty psychology**, which derived from a Scottish philosophical movement called Scottish Realism.

Faculty Psychology

As you recall from Chapter 2, empiricism and associationism, represented in the philosophies of Locke,

Berkeley, Hume, Hartley, and Mill, were the dominant intellectual forces in Great Britain during the eighteenth and nineteenth centuries. Empiricists argued that knowledge resulted from our experiences in the world, with the structure of our minds being organized through the laws of association. The Empiricists also addressed the concept of reality, with Locke distinguishing between primary and secondary qualities of matter, Berkeley arguing that only the secondary qualities were real, and Hume extending the argument to the verge of skepticism by contending that we cannot be absolutely certain about the reality of anything. Thus, when we look at a tree, Locke would say that its basic shape and mass ("extension") are primary qualities that have existence independent of our observations, but that color is a secondary quality, depending for its existence on the perceiving person. Berkeley would deny the distinction and say that all aspects of the tree rely on the subjective perception of the observer and we can only be sure of its existence by believing in God, the Permanent Perceiver. Hume would argue that we cannot even be 100% sure about the reality of our perception of the tree.

The Scottish Realist philosophers, most notably Thomas Reid (1710–1792) in the eighteenth century and Thomas Brown (1778–1820) in the nineteenth, took issue with the extreme Humean view of reality on the grounds that such an idea simply violates common sense. They believed that humans have an intuitive understanding that a real world truly exists—daily human life would have no foundation otherwise. They also rejected the implication that the mind is in essence nothing more than a collection of associated ideas based on experience. Instead, they argued that the mind has an independent existence in reality and is composed of various innate powers that they called *faculties*. Reid divided these faculties into two broad categories—intellectual and active (Evans, 1984). Intellectual faculties included such things as memory, abstraction, reasoning, and judgment, whereas active faculties concerned the emotions and the will. If the concept of faculty sounds familiar, it is because you encountered it in Chapter 3; Franz Josef Gall borrowed it when he developed the doctrine that eventually became known as phrenology. Reid identified more than 30 faculties; Gall and then Spurzheim tried to localize them in the brain. It is no coincidence that faculty psychology and phrenology were popular at the same time in America.

The Scottish influence in early American psychology arrived in the form of a wave of Scottish immigration in the eighteenth century. Many of the immigrants were educated—doctors, teachers, and ministers—and many played a role in the explosive growth of higher education in the United States in the years between the American Revolution and the Civil War. In the 140 years between the founding of Harvard in 1636 and the American Revolution of 1776, nine colleges had been created; by the start of the Civil War in 1861, 85 years later, students could choose from 182 colleges. Scottish Realism and faculty psychology dominated the curriculum of most of them.

American Psychology's First Textbook

Thomas Upham (1799–1872) of Bowdoin College in Maine is usually credited with authoring the first American psychology textbook when he organized his lecture notes and published them in 1827 as *Elements of Intellectual Philosophy*. The text even-

tually grew to three volumes and was given the broader title of *Elements of Mental Philosophy*. It quickly became the principal text in American colleges and universities for courses that today would be called introductory psychology (Evans, 1984). The book was organized along the lines of the Scottish faculty approach, although it included a healthy dose of associationism as well. It also included frequent references to the deity, and morality was a recurring theme. This is hardly surprising, given the fact that prior to the Civil War, most professors at American colleges (including Upham) were Protestant ministers. As will be seen shortly, the postwar rise of universities like Johns Hopkins, with its emphasis on the German model of research, created a need for a new type of textbook.

Upham subdivided Reid's "active" faculties, and his resulting book was organized into three main divisions: the intellect (cognition), the sensibilities (emotion), and the will (action). This "trilogy of mind" (Hilgard, 1980) was not unique to Upham, but represented a theme that can be traced back to the Greeks and ahead to the present day. For Upham, the mind that he described in his book was an active one, and the book had a distinctly functional tone to it, emphasizing the purposes and uses of the various faculties (Fuchs, 2000). Here is a sample of topics found under each of Upham's main divisions (cited in Evans, 1984, pp. 40–41):

Division I: The Intellect
– sensation, perception, consciousness, imagination
– concepts, abstraction, reasoning
– primary and secondary laws of association, memory
– disordered intellectual action: insanity later expanded by Upham in 1849 into abnormal psychology's first textbook: *Outlines of Disordered Mental Action)*

Division II: The Sensibilities
– instincts, appetites, propensities
– the malevolent affections (e.g., anger, jealousy, revenge)
– the benevolent affections (e.g., love, patriotism, pity)
– the moral sensibilities or conscience

Division III: The Will
– laws of the will
– freedom of the will implied in man's moral nature
– on the power of the will

Upham's text was a best seller on campuses well into the 1870s. By the end of the century, however, American psychology had changed dramatically, reflecting the mid-century influences identified by Boring: German psychology and British biology. The American system of higher education had also changed.

The Modern University

The impressive growth of colleges prior to the Civil War was nothing compared with the revolution in higher education that occurred between the war and the turn of the century. During this time, the modern university was created, the result of a complex interplay of forces. One factor was the emergence of the public high school and the heightened expectation that education was a key to a successful career. An increase in high school graduates in turn meant a greater number of students eligible to attend college, and attend they did. There were an estimated 67,000 students attending college in 1870, 157,000 in 1890, and 335,000 in 1910 (Hofstadter & Hardy, 1952). This expanding college student population produced a need for teachers who had degrees beyond the bachelor's level, thereby creating a demand for graduate education. The initial lack of it in the United States was one reason why students flocked to Germany in the late nineteenth century. There they encountered an approach to education that emphasized graduate training, independent research, and a variety of courses from which to choose—the *Wissenschaft* philosophy that you read about in Chapter 4. The decade of the 1880s was the high point for Americans studying in Germany. By the 1890s, several good American universities were available, and some of the second-level German universities were developing the reputation of being mere diploma mills (two semesters for a Ph.D. at the University of Halle, for example) (Veysey, 1965).

The American universities began to develop shortly after the end of the Civil War. One major catalyst was the Morrill Land Grant Act of 1862, which gave every state a minimum of 30,000 acres of federal land. If the state built a university on the land within five years, it could keep the land; otherwise it reverted to the government. This produced the great state universities, run by laypeople rather than clergy, and emphasizing science and practical applications (e.g., applying science to improve agriculture and mining). Also during this time, several of the Ivy League schools developed graduate training: Yale in 1860, Harvard in 1872, for instance. A third impetus was a consequence of the accumulation of great wealth by a handful of business tycoons in the second half of the nineteenth century. Several of them donated large amounts of money to found universities, motivated partly by a philanthropic desire to give something back to society, partly to blunt criticism of the exploitive manner in which they became wealthy, and partly to have their names associated with an enterprise that was universally valued. Four of the better-known schools created in this way were Johns Hopkins University (1876), Clark University (1887), Stanford University (1891), and the University of Chicago (1891). All but the last, which was created with Rockefeller money, was named for the major benefactor.

Johns Hopkins University in Baltimore became the prototype of the new university in America. It was explicitly modeled on the German example that emphasized research and the accumulation of new knowledge, and although it had a small undergraduate division from the start, its main focus was on graduate education. Endowed with $3.5 million by its founder, wealthy Baltimore merchant Johns (correct spelling) Hopkins, it quickly became the most important American university of the 1880s, the only legitimate competitor to the German universities (Hawkins, 1960). Its innovative president, Daniel Coit Gilman, attracted good students by creating the concept of the competitive "university fellowship," which included a $500 stipend plus free tuition, and encouraging the development of laboratory training and the seminar, to supplement the traditional lecture course. Gilman also recognized the growing need to train educators, and Johns Hopkins became a leader in this area—during the school's first 10 years, 56 of its doctoral graduates were employed as professors in 32 different colleges and universities (Ryan, 1939).

Education for Women and Minorities

The growth of opportunity for higher education that I just described was not equally available to all Americans; rather, it was mostly limited to middle- and upper-class white males. Women and minority group students faced significant barriers when trying to become educated.

Women in search of an education faced an entrenched set of beliefs referred to as the "women's sphere"—an integrated set of concepts that centered on the idea of woman as wife and mother. Nineteenth century women were socialized to believe that they were created for the purpose of perpetuating the family. This meant getting married, having and raising children, and being content with those roles. Women who wanted to pursue higher education or to have a career were discouraged from doing so. For one thing, it was believed that pursuing a degree beyond high school would have adverse medical consequences. One Harvard medical school professor urged women to abandon education after reaching puberty, because too much mental activity after that stage could retard the development of their reproductive organs, he warned (Scarborough & Furumoto, 1987). If education could reduce the chances of bearing children, then what would happen to the human species if too many women pursued higher education? And if undergraduate education could have such dangerous effects, education at the graduate level presumably would be much worse for a woman's health. As for pursuing a career, there was a zero-sum choice—it was considered to be out of the question for women to be both married and to have a career. It was one or the other. Furthermore, the unmarried woman, whether or not she had a career of some kind, had another family claim. She, not the brother(s) in the family, was the one expected to care for elderly parents.

In addition to the women's sphere, another impediment was the widespread belief that women were intellectually inferior to men. The belief had deep roots, even reflected in the biblical story of women's creation—built from a piece of a man (a rib). The belief was maintained in part by argument that women were intellectually incapacitated every month during menstruation—this handicap was referred to as the **periodic function**. Evolutionary theory provided additional fuel, producing what was called the **variability hypothesis**. You recall from Chapter 5 that one of the cornerstones of Darwin's theory was the idea that individual members of a species differed from each other, and this variability provided the material for natural selection to do its work. Nature "selected" those individuals whose variations had high survival value. It follows that the greater the degree of variability for a particular trait, the better off a species will be. According to the variability hypothesis, men had a greater degree of variability than women on a number of traits, including intelligence. Although this presumably meant a higher proportion of retarded men than women, it also meant that the brightest men would be more intelligent than the brightest women. One implication of the difference at the high end of intelligence was the belief that men were more suited for college and graduate education than women.

Despite these barriers to women's education, some opportunities arose in the second half of the nineteenth century. At the land grant universities, for instance, women were admitted, although they tended to be enrolled in programs of study that "suited" them—home economics, for instance. But they also began to be trained to meet the increasing need for teachers, both at land grant schools and at colleges created for the purpose of teacher training, the so-called "normal schools." Ivy league schools such as Harvard and Yale resisted efforts to have women enrolled, but attempted to achieve something of a compromise by creating women's schools affiliated with the men's school. At Harvard, for example, a "Harvard Annex" was created in 1879 and renamed Radcliffe College in 1894. The best opportunities for women to pursue a high quality college education came with the creation of a new educational phenomenon—elite colleges created for women only. One of the first, Vassar College, was created in 1865 with a gift from Matthew Vassar, a man with ideas well ahead of his time. He endowed the college, he wrote, because "[i]t occurred to [him] that women, having received from the Creator the same intellectual constitution as man, has the same right as man to intellectual culture and development" (quoted in Brubacher & Rudy, 1976, p. 66). Other women's colleges—Smith in 1871, Wellesley in 1875, and Bryn Mawr in 1885—soon followed, and by 1901, there were 119 of them in the United States (Brubaker & Rudy, 1976). As you will see shortly, these colleges produced the important women psychologists who will be highlighted in this chapter.

If educational opportunities for women were limited, they were even worse for minorities, especially African Americans in the wake of the Civil War. The slavery era had created a widespread belief among whites of the essential inferiority of blacks. This belief in the intellectual superiority of whites was so strong that it even colored the interpretation of research that might have suggested otherwise. For example, an early study by Bache (1895) comparing the reaction times of whites, blacks, and Native Americans found that whites had the slowest times. Ignoring the Galtonian idea that reaction time was assumed to be related to mental quickness and therefore to intelligence, the author concluded that the results provided evidence for the mental superiority of whites because it showed that whites, a "higher" human form, could be characterized as "reflective," while the swifter reactions of the more "primitive" blacks and Native Americans showed an immature and intellectually backward impulsiveness. Similarly, in a study comparing 500 white children with a like number of black children, Stetson (1897) found no differences in their ability to memorize poetry. Rather than drawing the reasonable conclusion that the groups were similar in this type of cognitive skill, however, Stetson decided that his study simply showed that memorization was useless as a test of intelligence. In short, strongly held prejudices rendered some scientists immune to data that might have called their beliefs into question.

One consequence of the prejudice against African Americans was inferior education and reduced opportunities for higher education. On the assumption that education would put ridiculous ideas like "freedom" into their heads, black slaves in the South were barred from formal education by "black codes" in the pre-Civil War years. After the war, conditions improved only marginally. Blacks were segregated into schools that were supposedly separate, but

equal, and higher education was limited mostly to whites. Colleges and universities designed for African Americans began to be created in the second half of the nineteenth century, however, mainly in the South. By 1940, there were more than 100 such schools. They focused on training teachers, who usually returned to their communities to teach in the segregated schools there (Guthrie, 1976).

Psychology, especially as it applied to education, was typically part of the curriculum in the black colleges, but few of these schools offered a concentration in psychology. A 1936 survey on psychology at black colleges by Herman Canady (1901–1970), a psychologist at West Virginia's black college (West Virginia State College at Institute, WV), found that only 14 of the 50 schools he surveyed had psychology departments. Of those 14, only four offered majors in psychology (data from Guthrie, 1976, p. 105). Very few laboratory courses were offered and, aside from introductory psychology, the most popular courses were educational, child, social, and adolescent psychology. Thus, few black students had the background necessary to pursue graduate degrees in psychology. Those who did faced further obstacles. They were denied admission to graduate programs in the South and although a handful of graduate programs in the North welcomed them (Clark University for instance), few could afford to travel that far from home.

For the African American who did manage to persevere and earn an advanced degree, the prospects for employment following graduate school were not bright. About the only opportunity for a black psychologist with an advanced degree was to return to a black college to teach, where conditions typically included a heavy teaching load, minimal salary, no benefits, and poor research facilities, if any (Guthrie, 1976). Nonetheless, many bright young African Americans took this path, significantly enhancing the educations of countless black college students.

The best known of these pioneers was Francis Sumner (1895–1954), shown in Figure 6.1 in his graduate student days. Sumner was born in Pine Bluff, Arkansas, but his family soon moved east, where he received his early education in New Jersey, Washington, D.C., and Virginia. During his high school years, he was taught at home by his father, who distrusted the quality of Virginia's segregated schools. In 1911, the 16-year-old Sumner was accepted "by examination" into Pennsylvania's Lincoln University, which had been founded in 1854 as the country's first black college. He earned a bachelor's degree in 1915, then a second bachelor's from Clark College in Massachusetts, the undergraduate counterpart of Clark University (both located in the same building on the Worcester campus). He then returned to Lincoln to teach psychology and German, while also completing the requirements for a master's degree. Sumner returned to Clark (University this time) in 1917 to study "race psychology" with G. Stanley Hall (discussed later in this chapter), financed by a university fellowship and strong moral support from Hall (Hicks & Ridley, 1979). Although Hall held stereotypical views about racial differences in intelligence, he welcomed "exceptionally talented" blacks at Clark. During Hall's years at Clark, three African American scholars earned master's degrees, and two, Sumner and Thomas Brown, earned doctorates (Guthrie, 1976). Sumner's doctorate came in 1920, and he was the first African American to complete a Ph.D. in psychology. His dissertation was a critical interpretation of Freudian and Adlerian psychoanalysis, which Hall praised by writing that Sumner had "shown unusual facility in mastering and even pointing out the limitations and defects of the great authorities in the field" (quoted in Guthrie, 1976, p. 182).

Like a handful of other black scholars, Sumner found his opportunities limited to teaching at black colleges, and he spent time at Wilberforce College in Ohio and West Virginia State College before finding his way to Howard University in Washington, D.C., in 1928. Sumner remained at Howard as psychology department chair until his untimely death from a heart attack while shoveling snow in the winter of 1954. At Howard he established the country's leading psychology department at a black institution, offering both bachelor's and master's degrees in psychology. An indication of Howard's importance, and by extension Sumner's influence, is that of the 300 African Americans who held doctorates in 1975, 60 had earned their bachelor's and/or master's degrees at Howard (Bayton, 1975).

FIGURE 6.1 Francis Sumner as a graduate student at Clark University.

The explosive growth of higher education at the end of the nineteenth century, accompanied by a willingness to experiment with new ideas, teaching methods, and the curriculum itself, made the new universities fertile ground for the creation of novel approaches to old problems. This was advantageous for psychology, which was of course undergoing a change from traditional faculty psychology to the new laboratory psychology. A major agent of this change was a troubled young man from a talented and wealthy Boston family.

WILLIAM JAMES (1842–1910): AMERICA'S FIRST PSYCHOLOGIST

William James did not establish a "school" of psychology, produced no meaningful experimental research, and did not leave behind a dedicated group of students to "carry on his work." Indeed, near the end of his life, he insisted on being referred to as a philosopher rather than as a psychologist. When delivering an invited address at Princeton in 1896, for instance, he was adamant about not being introduced as a psychologist (O'Donnell, 1985). In the quote that opens the chapter, taken from the closing pages of the briefer version of his monumental *Principles of Psychology*, he made it clear that in his opinion at least, psychology had a long way to go before it could claim the status of a science—it was "no science, ... only the hope of a science" (James, 1892/1961, p. 335). And when he was just finishing the briefer version of the *Principles*, he expressed his disenchantment with psychology in a letter to his Wellesley student and colleague Mary Whiton Calkins, writing that he was "sick of the association of ideas and all things connected with psychology. The result of too unending an application to ... the 'Briefer Course' of which the miserable proofs are not yet finished! ... Treadmill work seems preferable" (James, 1891).

On the other hand, it is quite clear that James was crucial to the development of modern psychology in the United States and that his role was recognized not just by historians but also by his contemporaries. When James McKeen Cattell asked psychologists to rank their peers for eminence in 1903, James was ranked first. In fact, he was ranked first on *every* return (Hothersall, 1995). His peers also elected him to the presidency of the American Psychological Association twice, in 1894 and again in 1904. Later, when second generation psychologists wrote chapters for the series *A History of Psychology in Autobiography*, at least a dozen explicitly mentioned James and/or his *Principles* as the main reason for their initial interest in psychology (King, 1992). Today, James's star continues to shine brightly. Several biographies have appeared (e.g., Croce, 1995; Lewis, 1991; Simon, 1998), and the early 1990s saw the publication of two edited books celebrating the centennial of the *Principles* (Donnelly, 1992; Johnson & Henley, 1990). In a 1991 poll of historians, he ranked second (behind Wundt) on a list of the most important contributors to psychology (Korn, Davis, & Davis, 1991). Who was this person who did not want to be called a psy-

chologist, yet is high on everyone's list of "most important psychologists of all time?"

The Formative Years

William James was raised in a very unusual family. His father, Henry James, Sr., had sufficient income from an inheritance to avoid working,[1] and he devoted himself to controlling the education and moral development of his five children, who were born within six years of each other in the 1840s. In addition to William, the oldest, there was Henry, Jr., the celebrated American novelist, two younger brothers, and a sister, Alice, the intellectual equal of her brothers, but unable to develop her creativity into a professional career because of prevailing nineteenth-century beliefs about the proper role for women (the women's sphere). Henry James, Sr., who had been raised by a domineering father who demanded strict obedience, was determined to raise his own children in a more liberal fashion, but he was controlling in his own way. On the surface it appeared that he indulged his children, allowing them to study whatever they wanted whenever they wanted to, taking them to Europe frequently to expand their horizons, and caring little about their formal education. However, Henry, Sr. insisted on being perceived as their prime educator, and some of the family's moving back and forth between America and Europe was motivated by Henry, Sr.'s desire to maintain control (Simon, 1998). His primary expectation was that his children learn foreign languages. Consistent with his liberal philosophy of learning, he believed that "[t]o learn a language was not to enforce particular points of view, but to gain access to another realm of culture and thought; to be fluent was to see the world from another perspective" (Croce, 1995, pp. 43–44). Thus, William did not attend school formally before the age of 10 and attended only sporadically through adolescence. He made three trips to Europe before the age of 21 though, spending at least a year there

---

[1] Henry's father (William's grandfather) lived the stereotypical American success story, an Irish immigrant who rose from store clerk to business tycoon, one of the wealthiest men of nineteenth-century America (Croce, 1995).

FIGURE 6.2 Self-portrait sketch of William James, completed in the early 1860s.

each time. By age 18, he knew the essentials of Latin, had a reading knowledge of German, and was fluent in French. He would later add Greek and Italian to the list.

As he neared the end of adolescence, however, one other fact characterized William James—he was utterly at a loss about what to do with his life. He had a strong interest in art and some talent for it (Figure 6.2 is a self-portrait drawn during this time of his life), but after some lessons in Paris and a brief stint under the tutelage of the American artist William Morris Hunt, he realized that he would not achieve greatness (Simon, 1998). Despite abandoning a career in art, however, James never lost interest in it, and at least one biographer (Bjork, 1983) has maintained that James remained an artist in temperament for the rest of his life. Also, historian David Leary (1992) has pointed to James's recurring use of artistic metaphors in the *Principles*. For instance, he used the metaphor of a sculptor creating one result from the number of possibilities in a piece of stone to make the point that individual minds create different reali-

ties out of the varying experiences of life: "Other sculptors, other statues from the same stone! Other minds, other worlds from the same monotonous and inexpressive chaos" (James, 1890/1950, v1, p. 289).

A Life at Harvard

In the fall of 1861, a 19-year-old William James enrolled in the Lawrence Scientific School of Harvard University, much to the delight of his father. Although his philosophy of child rearing prevented him from forcing careers on his children, Henry Sr. had always hoped that his oldest son would become a "scientist."[2] At the Lawrence school, William first studied chemistry with Charles W. Eliot, soon to be one of Harvard's most innovative presidents. He quickly learned to hate the subject, especially what he viewed as the tedium and obsession with detail that characterized laboratory work. It was an attitude that would later lead him to disparage much of the laboratory work of the new experimental psychology.

After abandoning chemistry, James sampled several of the other sciences at Lawrence. One of his biology professors there was the famed Swiss naturalist Louis Agassiz, a fervent believer in a close relationship between science and religion and in the use of science to confirm religious truths. Thus, he was a strong advocate of the argument by design (Chapter 5) and an anti-Darwinian who believed that all species were created separately by God. James, of course, was a student at Lawrence during the height of the debates about Darwin's theory, which had been published in 1859. Initially awed by Agassiz, James eventually became a firm Darwinian and realized that history would judge his professor to be on the wrong side of the argument over evolution. Agassiz also confirmed in young James his distaste for the minutiae of science. He accompanied Agassiz on a collecting expedition to the Amazon in 1865, enjoying it about as much as chemistry lab, and for similar reasons. As

[2] He was also pleased that his son was able to avoid the Civil War, which began that same year. Henry, Jr., the novelist, also avoided the war, but the two younger brothers both fought for the North and one was severely wounded in the attack on Fort Wagner, near Charleston, South Carolina (the battle was dramatized in the 1990 film *Glory*).

he wrote to his brother: "When I get home I'm going to study philosophy all my days" (quoted in Simon, 1998, p. 93). James also became ill during the voyage, beginning a long series of bouts with real and imagined illnesses that would plague him on and off for the remainder of his life (Lewis, 1991).

In 1864, James enrolled in the Harvard Medical School, completing his medical training in 1869, but not before taking yet another trip to Europe to (a) try to recover his health—he was afflicted with a bad back, severe headaches, and chronic gastritis after the Amazon trip, and (b) investigate the new experimental physiology that had been developing in Germany. In addition to health spas, his trip included stops at Heidelberg, where he met Helmholtz and learned of Wundt, and Berlin, where he attended lectures by the noted physiologist Emil du Bois Reymond. The experience was educational, but it also deepened a profound depression that had been lingering at the edges of his psyche for several years. He was completing a medical degree, but had no desire to actually practice medicine. He was trained in science, but hated the details. And as a reflective person, he was disturbed by the overwhelming determinism and materialism of the science that he was learning. If all life reduces to physical matter moving through space, then what happens to free will? If freedom of choice is an illusion, then what is the basis for personal responsibility and morality? James was driven to the point of despair, and he even contemplated suicide (Croce, 1995).

Salvation (temporary at least—he continued to suffer periodic bouts of depression throughout his life) came in the form of James's discovery of the French evolutionary philosopher Charles Renouvier. In an often-quoted diary entry from April 1870, James noted that his life had reached a crisis point when he encountered an essay by Renouvier and "saw no reason why his [Renouvier's] definition of free will—the sustaining of thought *because I choose to* when I might have other thoughts—need be the definition of an illusion. At any rate I will assume for the present ... that it is no illusion. My first act of free will shall be to believe in free will" (cited in Simon, 1998, p. 126, italics in the citation). The insight enabled James to continue studying physiology and psychology without being worn down by the implications. Free will

might be an illusion, but by choosing to believe in it, the concept became *useful* for him, enabling him to continue his scientific work without despair. This "pragmatic" approach to the concept of free will, in which the truth value of the idea was a consequence of its functional value or usefulness, would become a cornerstone of James's philosophical position of **pragmatism** and a reason why he is considered a forerunner of those American psychologists who came to be known as functionalists.

In 1873, James accepted an offer from Charles Eliot, his old chemistry professor and now president of Harvard, to teach a course in physiology. Two years later, he taught his first psychology course, a class on the relationship between physiology and psychology. By incorporating the latest research from Germany, it differed radically from the typical mental philosophy course based on faculty psychology, thus inaugurating a new approach to the teaching of psychology in America. It was so new that James would later say that the first psychology class he ever attended was also the first one he taught! To help students understand some of the research he was describing, he set up some apparatus in a small room, thus creating in 1875 what would gradually become Harvard's laboratory of experimental psychology.[3] James remained at Harvard until his retirement in 1907. He died three years later of heart disease, two days after a return from one final trip to Europe.

Creating American Psychology's Most Famous Textbook

In July of 1878, a 36-year-old William James married Alice Howe Gibbens, a 29-year-old teacher at Miss Sanger's School for Girls in Boston. Alice would become a stabilizing force in William's life, with a mind sharp enough to make her an intellectual colleague. Indeed, on their honeymoon in New York's Adirondacks, she helped him begin writing the *Principles of Psychology*, a book destined to become the classic among classics in psychology's history

---

[3] This event has led some to argue that James created psychology's first laboratory, beating Wundt by four years. The lab was no more than a demonstrational adjunct to his lectures, however Wundt's laboratory produced original research.

(Lewis, 1991). A month before the wedding, James had signed a contract with an aggressive young publisher named Henry Holt for a "manual" of psychology. Holt wanted the completed manuscript from James within a year, but reluctantly consented to James's proposal for two years. The book seemed to take on a life of its own, however, eventually requiring *twelve* years before it appeared in 1890. The book was encyclopedic, encompassing two volumes totaling nearly 1400 pages. It was an immediate best seller, in part because the academic public knew what was coming—James published numerous articles based on it during the 1880s, and Holt began advertising it in 1881 (King, 1992). Shortly after its publication, James agreed to write a smaller version (referred to earlier in the letter to Calkins), which appeared in 1892 as *Psychology: The Briefer Course*. Over the years, Harvard students learned to refer to the massive two-volume text as the "James" and the briefer version as the "Jimmy."

In the *Principle*'s opening sentence, James (1890/1950) defined psychology as "the Science of Mental Life, both of its phenomena and their conditions" (v1, p. 1). The phenomena of mental life included "such things as we call feelings, desires, cognitions, reasonings, decisions, and the like" (v1, p. 1). By "their conditions" he was referring to the physiological processes that accompany these phenomena, as well as the social, personal, and environmental circumstances in which they occur.

On Methodology

James was an eclectic, willing to include in his book the results of research using any methodological approach that could shed light on mental life. He was quite clear about what he believed to be the primary means of studying mental life, however: "Introspective Observation is what we have to rely on first and foremost and always" (James, 1890/1950, v1, p. 185). By **introspection** he meant careful self-observation, an examination and reflection on the states of consciousness that characterize one's mental life. He recognized the difficulties with the method—it was open to bias, one person's introspections could not be verified by a second person, and because it is impossible to experience a mental process and introspect to it at the same time, all introspection must rely on memory. Nonetheless, he believed that careful self-reflection was essential to gain insight into the workings of the human mind. One consequence of this belief was that the book was reviewed harshly by psychologists enamored of the new laboratory approach that had emerged from Leipzig. Thus, Wundt thought it was more like literature than science and G. Stanley Hall (discussed next), after writing that one's overall reaction to the book must be "gratitude and admiration" (Hall, 1890–1891, p. 578), criticized what he viewed as its "inconsistencies and incoherencies" (p. 589), and referred to James as an "*impressionist* in psychology" (p. 585, italics in the original).

KEY DATE *1890*

This year marked the publication of psychology's most famous textbook, The *Principles of Psychology* by William James.

These events also occurred:

- Rubber gloves were used in surgery for the first time, at Johns Hopkins Hospital, Baltimore
- The first entirely steel-framed skyscraper was built in Chicago by Louis Sullivan, mentor of Frank Lloyd Wright
- The Daughters of American Revolution was founded in Washington, D.C.
- Oscar Wilde wrote *The Picture of Dorian Gray*
- Japan held its first general election
- Idaho and Wyoming became states
- These people were born:

    Dwight David Eisenhower, American general and president

    Julius "Groucho" Marx, American comedic actor

    Agatha Christie, English mystery writer

- These people died:

    Vincent Van Gogh, Dutch painter

    Sitting Bull, Sioux chief on the winning side at the Battle of Little Big Horn

James did not ignore the new experimental methods. He gave a thorough description of reaction time methodology, for example, and he referred to the results of psychophysics research in numerous places. Nonetheless, his personal dislike of the tedium of laboratory work led him to declare that the German psychophysics and reaction time research "taxes patience to the utmost, and could hardly have arisen in a country whose natives could be *bored*" (James, 1890/1950, v1, p. 192, italics in the original). He later created a phrase that came to capsulize this laboratory approach, when he referred to it sarcastically as a **brass instrument psychology**.

In addition to introspective and experimental methods, James listed the "comparative method" as a third approach. This involved learning about mental life by comparing normal human consciousness with that of "bees and ants, ... savages, infants, madmen, idiots, the deaf and blind, criminals, and eccentrics" (James, 1890/1950, v1, p. 194), and included the use of data derived from the kinds of questionnaires pioneered by Darwin and Galton. While James recognized the value of this kind of information, he once again disliked the tediousness of the survey method, suspecting that the next generation of psychologists might rank these questionnaires "among the common pests of life" (p. 194).

Consciousness

The chapter on **consciousness** shows James at his most eloquent. It is a central chapter, one in which James made it clear that he vehemently opposed the analytic approach that presumed to understand consciousness by reducing it to its basic elements. That strategy characterized "structuralism," which you will learn about in the next chapter, but it also formed the basis for the reaction time and psychophysics research imported from Germany, and it was an integral part of most British empiricist/associationist thinking. James believed that trying to identify the individual elements of consciousness, and then seeing how they could be constructed to form "mind," was a meaningless, artificial exercise. In one of psychology's more frequently quoted passages, he argued that consciousness is not a set of interconnected units:

Consciousness, then, does not appear to itself chopped up in bits. Such words as "chain" or "train" do not describe it fitly as it presents itself in the first instance. It is nothing jointed; it flows. A "river" or a "stream" are the metaphors by which it is most naturally described. *In talking of it hereafter, let us call it the stream of thought, of consciousness, or of subjective life.* (James, 1890/1950, v1, p. 239, italics in the original)

The chapter in which this quote appears is titled "The Stream of Thought," and it is the first of several dealing with the nature of consciousness. Using an artistic metaphor, James told the reader that the chapter was introductory, with more detail to follow, describing it as being "like a painter's first charcoal sketch upon his canvas" (James, 1890/1950, v1, p. 225). His preliminary sketch included these additional attributes of consciousness:

- It is *personal*; all consciousness includes an element of self-consciousness; thoughts don't exist independently of the person having them ("Consciousness of Self" was elaborated in a complete chapter).

- It is *constantly changing*, as implied by the stream metaphor; no two states of consciousness are ever quite the same; once a state has disappeared, there will never be another one identical to it.

- It is *sensibly continuous*; our perception of consciousness is that it is one continuous stream of thoughts; the stream may be temporarily interrupted, as in sleep, but upon awaking, the sleeper immediately reenters the same stream.

- It is *selective*; out of the mass of sensory information available to it, it selects some for closer attention (James elaborated this in a chapter on "Attention").

- It is *active*, rather than a passive collection of associated elements; it is goal-directed and purposive.

Elaborating on this last attribute, James used an example that provides a compelling description of what has come to be known as the "tip-of-the-tongue phenomenon," investigated later by Brown & McNeill (1966):

Suppose we try to recall a forgotten name. The state of our consciousness is peculiar. There is a gap therein; but no mere gap. It is a gap that is intensely active. A sort of wraith of the name is in it, beckoning us in a given direction, making us at moments tingle with the sense of our closeness, and then letting us sink back without the longed-for term. If wrong names are proposed to us, this singularly definite gap acts immediately so as to negate them. They do not fit into its mold. (James, 1890/1950, v1, p. 251)

One final point about consciousness shows how James was affected by Darwinian thinking. In addition to describing the features of consciousness, he was interested in understanding the *function* of consciousness. How did it enable us to adapt to our environment? What was its survival value? For James, the answer was that consciousness served individuals by enabling them to adapt quickly to new environments, to learn new things, and to solve new problems that present themselves.

Habit

Habits also had an adaptive function, according to James. Because they occurred more or less automatically, they enabled the consciousness to focus attention on other, more important (i.e., survival-related) problems. On a broader scale, habits serve as:

> ... the enormous flywheel of society, its most precious conservative agent. ... It alone prevents the hardest and most repulsive walks of life from being deserted by those brought up to tread therein. It keeps the fisherman ... at sea through the winter; it holds the miner in his darkness, and nails the countryman to his log-cabin and his lonely farm through all the months of snow. ... It dooms us all to fight out the battle of life upon the lines of our nurture or our early choice. (James, 1890/1950, v1, p. 121)

In his typical pragmatic fashion, James also had some advice on forming good habits. The first was motivational, an admonition to "launch ourselves with as strong and decided an initiative as possible" (James, 1890/1950, v1, p. 123). For instance, he recommended making a public pledge about the habit to be developed. Second, we must not allow for any lapses to occur: "Never suffer an exception to occur till the new habit is securely rooted in your life" (p. 123). Third, he urged readers to arrange their lives to increase the opportunities to act on the new habit; mere good intentions are not sufficient.

ORIGINAL SOURCE EXCERPT
William James on Emotion

There are a number of quotations from the *Principles* in this part of the chapter, for the simple reason that James is so quotable. To get a closer look at his writing, however, and to see how he developed an argument, consider the following extended excerpt on emotion. It is taken not from the full *Principles*, but from the abridged version—*Psychology: The Briefer Course* (1892/1961). It describes one of the better known of James's ideas, which he acknowledged borrowing from a Dutch physiologist, Carl Lange. Today's students recognize it as the James-Lange theory of emotion, and it can be found in every introductory psychology text.

James began the chapter by distinguishing emotions from instincts. The former he referred to as tendencies to feel, while the latter were tendencies to act. He recognized that emotions had bodily "expression," however, so the distinction was not absolutely clear-cut. He then distinguished between the "coarser" emotions (e.g., anger, fear, joy, grief) from the "subtler" ones (e.g., aesthetic appreciation of art), but with his characteristic dislike of classification, refused to go any further in categorizing the emotions, writing that he would prefer to "read verbal descriptions of the shapes of rocks on a New

Hampshire farm" (James, 1892/1961, p. 242). Instead, James proposed to look for general principles, with a focus on the coarser emotions:

> The feeling, in the coarser emotions, results from the bodily expression. Our natural way of thinking about these coarser emotions is that the mental perception of some fact excites the mental affection called the emotion, and that this latter state of mind gives rise to the bodily expression. My theory, on the contrary, is that *the bodily changes follow directly the perception of the exciting fact, and that our feeling of the same changes as they occur IS the emotion.* Common-sense says, we lose our fortune, are sorry and weep, we meet a bear, are frightened and run; we are insulted by a rival, are angry and strike. The hypothesis here to be defended says that this order of sequence is incorrect, that the one mental state is not immediately induced by the other, that the bodily manifestations must first be interposed between, and that the more rational statement is that we feel sorry because we cry, angry because we strike, afraid because we tremble, and not that we cry, strike, or tremble because we are sorry, angry, or fearful, as the case may be. Without the bodily states following on the perception, the latter would be purely cognitive in form, pale, colorless, destitute of emotional warmth. We might then see the bear and judge it best to run, receive the insult and deem it right to strike, but we should not actually feel afraid or angry. (pp. 242–243, italics in the original)

This paragraph might seem vaguely familiar—portions of it are often quoted in introductory textbooks. After beginning with such a bold assertion, he spent the remainder of the chapter defending it. He began with some anecdotal examples, including an autobiographical one, which supported his case:

> To begin with, *particular perceptions certainly do produce wide-spread bodily effects by a sort of immediate physical influence, antecedent to the arousal of an emotion or emotional idea.* In listening to poetry, drama, or heroic narrative we are often surprised at the cutaneous shiver which like a sudden wave flows over us, and at the heartswelling and the lachrymal effusion that unexpectedly catch us at intervals. In hearing music the same is even more strikingly true. If we abruptly see a dark moving form in the woods, our heart stops beating, and we catch our breath instantly and before any particular idea of danger can arise. If our friend goes near to the edge of a precipice, we get the well-known feeling of "all-overishness," and we shrink back, although we positively *know* him to be safe, and have no distinct imagination of his fall. The writer well remembers his astonishment, when a boy of seven or eight, at fainting when he saw a horse bled. The blood was in a bucket, with a stick in it, and, if memory does not deceive him, he stirred it round and saw it drip from the stick with no feeling save that of childish curiosity. Suddenly the world grew black before his eyes, his ears began to buzz, and he knew no more. He had never heard of the sight of blood producing faintness or sickness, and he had so little repugnance to it, and so little apprehension of any other sort of danger from it, that even at that tender age, as he well remembers, he could not help wondering how the mere

physical presence of a pailful of crimson fluid could occasion in him such formidable bodily effects. (pp. 243–244, italics in the original)

James's argument was that the bodily changes that are the emotions are felt immediately, prior to the awareness of a cognitively recognizable emotion: Our heart pounds before we feel fearful. He also argued that we recognize different emotions because each one is associated with a unique pattern of bodily action:

... When worried by any slight trouble, one may find that the focus of one's bodily consciousness is the contraction, often quite inconsiderable, of the eyes and brows. When momentarily embarrassed, it is something in the pharynx that compels either a swallow, a clearing of the throat, or a slight cough; and so on for as many more instances as might be named. The various permutations of which these organic changes are susceptible make it abstractly possible that no shade of emotion should be without a bodily reverberation as unique, when taken in its totality, as is the mental mood itself. (p. 245)

Research on the physiology of the emotions was not sufficiently advanced for James to realize that the preceding idea was a fatal flaw for his theory. For James-Lange to work, each emotion must have its own unique pattern of bodily reaction, and be recognized as such. We now know that this is simply not the case. Rather, although there are some physiological differences between emotions, most strong emotions are accompanied by similar patterns of physiological arousal in the autonomic nervous system. There is no question, however, that the emotions are closely tied to bodily arousal. James drove the point home by asking the reader to imagine the opposite:

I now proceed to urge the vital point of my whole theory, which is this: *If we fancy some strong emotion, and then try to abstract from our consciousness of it all the feeling of its bodily symptoms, we find we have nothing left behind*, no "mind-stuff" out of which the emotion can be constituted, and that a cold and neutral state of intellectual perception is all that remains. ... Can one fancy the state of rage and picture no ebullition in the chest, no flushing of the face, no dilation of the nostrils, no clenching of the teeth, no impulse to vigorous action, but in their stead limp muscles, calm breathing, and a placid face? The present writer, for one, certainly cannot. The rage is as completely evaporated as the sensation of its so-called manifestations, and the only thing that can possibly be supposed to take its place is some cold-blooded and dispassionate judicial sentence, confined entirely to the intellectual realm, to the effect that a certain person or persons merit chastisement for their sins. In like manner of grief: what would it be without its tears, its sobs, its suffocation of the heart, its pang in the breast-bone? A feelingless cognition that certain circumstances are deplorable, and nothing more. Every passion in turn tells the same story. A disembodied human emotion is a sheer nonentity. (pp. 246–247, italics in the original)

As always, James was pragmatic. In the case of emotions, practical application was a natural consequence of another argument for his theory:

... If our theory be true, a necessary corollary of it ought to be this: that any voluntary and cold-blooded arousal of the so-called manifestations of a special emotion should give us the emotion itself. Now within the limits in which it can be verified, experience corroborates rather than disproves this inference. Everyone knows how panic is increased by flight, and how the giving way to the symptoms of grief or anger increases those passions themselves. Each fit of sobbing makes the sorrow more acute, and calls forth another fit stronger still, until at last repose only ensues with lassitude and with the apparent exhaustion of the machinery. In rage, it is notorious how we "work ourselves up" to a climax by repeated outbreaks of expression. Refuse to express a passion, and it dies. Count ten before venting your anger, and its occasion seems ridiculous. Whistling to keep up courage is no mere figure of speech. On the other hand, sit all day in a moping posture, sigh, and reply to everything with a dismal voice, and your melancholy lingers. There is no more valuable precept in moral education than this, as all who have experience know: if we wish to conquer undesirable emotional tendencies in ourselves, we must assiduously, and in the first instance cold-bloodedly, go through the *outward movements* of those contrary dispositions which we prefer to cultivate. The reward of persistency will infallibly come, in the fading out of the sullenness or depression, and the advent of real cheerfulness and kindliness in the stead. Smooth the brow, brighten the eye, contract the dorsal rather than the ventral aspect of the frame, and speak in a major key, pass the genial compliment, and your heart must be frigid indeed if it do not gradually thaw. (pp. 249–250, italics in the original)

The idea that forcing emotions to occur by deliberately producing specific bodily reactions, which might seem a bit far fetched, actually has been supported by some modern research on emotions. People whose facial muscles have been arranged to match certain emotions often experience those very emotions, at least to a degree (e.g., Izard, 1977).

James closed the chapter by considering the origins of emotions. Again showing his affinity for Darwinian thinking, his description is not very different from the one found in Darwin's book on emotional expressions (Darwin, 1872), which you read about in Chapter 5.

James's Later Years

After completing the *Principles* in 1890 and the abridged version two years later, James (Figure 6.3) began to turn away from psychology and toward philosophy. In 1892, he convinced the research psychologist Hugo Münsterberg (Chapter 8) to emigrate from Germany to America and run the psychology lab at Harvard, thereby separating James forever from the tedium of laboratory work. Although he continued to be involved in the American Psychological Association and was elected its president in 1894 and 1902, James also supported the formation of the American Philosophical Association

shortly after the turn of the century, and his publications after 1900 were mainly devoted to philosophy (e.g., *Pragmatism* in 1907) and religion (e.g., *Varieties of Religious Experience* in 1902).

Spiritualism

In addition to the shift from psychology to philosophy during his final two decades, James also became fascinated with spiritualism, a popular movement in the late nineteenth century. Spiritualists believed that consciousness survived death and that those who died could be contacted by certain people, called mediums. Mediums were also said to be able to predict the future and to know details of people's lives through telepathic means. The movement began at mid-century, but gained momentum after the Civil War—the war's appalling death toll dramatically increased the number of people desiring to contact deceased relatives and acquaintances. Furthermore, spiritualism was fueled by nineteenth-century technological advances such as the wireless telegraph. If living people could communicate over great distances via some mysterious invisible process, and if there was life after death, then why not a communication channel from the dead to the living (Coon, 1992)?

James became seriously interested in spiritualism in the 1880s, after discovering the Society for Psychical Research while on a trip to London (Benjamin, 1993). He helped establish a similar organization in the United States, and became a promoter of research into the phenomenon. He believed that psychologists, with their expertise in the powers of the mind, should be ideally suited for such investigations. And reflecting his pragmatic philosophy, in which the value of something is a consequence of its usefulness, he insisted on keeping an open mind about psychic phenomena—they might prove to be beneficial if they could be shown to be valid.

Starting in 1885, James began an extended study of Mrs. Leonore Piper, a popular Boston medium. Although most mediums, even in the nineteenth century, were easily shown to be frauds on careful investigation, James could find no trickery in Mrs. Piper's séances. In an article for the *Proceedings of the British Society for Psychical Research*, James wrote that he could not avoid concluding that in her séances, "knowledge appears which she has never gained by the ordinary waking use of her eyes and ears and wits. What the source of this knowledge may be, I know not, and have not the glimmer of an explanatory suggestion to make" (cited in Lewis, 1991, p. 494). On the other hand, James was somewhat skeptical about messages from the dead that were received by Mrs. Piper during séances. If the dead were truly communicating, surely they would have some rather important things to say—they might be expected to describe the afterlife for example. Instead, they tended to communicate inconsequential bits of information. In a letter to a col-

FIGURE 6.3 A healthy-looking William James in New York's Adirondack Mountains, taken in the 1890s when James was shifting his focus from psychology to philosophy, from Lewis (1991).

league, James questioned Mrs. Piper's ability to reach the dead, pointing to the "extreme triviality of most of the communications. What real spirit, at last able to revisit his wife on this earth, [wouldn't] find something better to say than that she had changed the place of his photograph?" (cited in Benjamin, 1993, p. 83). Furthermore, Mrs. Piper's spirit-control (the intermediary between her and the dead spirits) was supposed to be a French doctor. He was unable to respond when James asked questions in French, however (Murphy & Ballou, 1960).

James was not rewarded for open-mindedness by his peers in the medical and psychological communities. At a time when there was no formal licensure procedure for accrediting doctors, he was roundly criticized for opposing legislation to create such rules. His reason? The guidelines would prohibit mediums and "mental healers" from practicing without a license (Murphy & Ballou, 1960). The censure from psychologists was equally strong. At a time when psychology was trying to establish its identity as a legitimate scientific discipline, it was embarrassing for one of its stars to be regularly attending séances and publicly expressing faith in the veracity of a medium (Coon, 1992). In a letter to James published in his journal *Science*, for example, James McKeen Cattell wrote that the "Society for Psychical Research is doing much to injure psychology" (cited in Benjamin, 1993, p. 88); concerning James, Cattell pointed out that the psychological community "all acknowledge his leadership, but we cannot follow him into quagmires" (p. 88). Always independent, James was unmoved by the criticism, and in turn accused his critics of narrow and unscientific prejudgment. He continued to be fascinated by psychic phenomena for all of his remaining years.

Summing Up William James

In his lifetime, William James experienced the vast changes that characterized late nineteenth-century America. In his youth, America was an agricultural society, the western frontier was east of the Rocky Mountains, the possibility that Americans would kill each other in a Civil War was unthinkable, and higher education was limited mainly to the undergraduate college, which was aimed primarily at the training of ministers. In his last decade, America had entered the twentieth century an industrialized power, the western frontier had been declared closed, the trauma of the Civil War was becoming a memory, and higher education, which now included universities devoted to graduate studies, was producing professionals and Ph.D.'s in a variety of disciplines.

Psychology in America also changed significantly during this time, from mental philosophy to an independent discipline with aspirations to be a science. Despite his reservations about the new psychology, William James was a prime mover in bringing about its emergence. Trained in physiology, he

saw how advances in that field could make a new laboratory psychology possible. At heart an artist and philosopher, he could see the problems inherent in a purely scientific attack on the human mind. His monumental *Principles of Psychology* stands at the transition point, artfully blending physiology, philosophy, and the new laboratory psychology. James was the acknowledged leader of the first generation of American psychologists, but he was not alone.

G. STANLEY HALL (1844–1924): PROFESSIONALIZING PSYCHOLOGY

G. Stanley Hall (Figure 6.4) had none of William James's reluctance about psychology. Rather, he was a vigorous promoter of the new field, and more than any other American, responsible for its evolving identity as a distinct academic discipline. Like Wundt did in Germany, Hall professionalized psychology in the United States by founding laboratories and journals. In addition, he institutionalized psychology's professional status by creating the American Psychological Association. As a psychologist, Hall was a man of diverse interests, careening from one enthusiasm to another throughout his career, and aptly described by his biographer as a "prophet" for his zeal in promoting his ideas (Ross, 1972). He could be characterized as either creative and visionary or unsystematic and capricious. On the one hand, he pioneered the child study movement and the study of adolescence and aging, he demonstrated the importance of psychology to education, and he introduced Freud and psychoanalysis (Chapter 12) to America. On the other hand, a consequence of his catholicity of interests was a failure to contribute a substantial body of research knowledge to any one of them. He also alienated his peers, including James, and some questioned the value of his work. In a letter to Clark University librarian L. N. Wilson in 1906, for instance, this is what Cornell's E. B. Titchener (Chapter 7) thought of Hall's ability to prepare graduate students:

> ... you probably have no idea of the sort of contempt in which Hall's methods and the men trained solely by him are in general held in

psychology, whether here or on the continent. Whenever his questionary papers [i.e., research using questionnaires] get reviewed, they get slightly reviewed. ... He has made no impression on the men of scientific training. (Titchener, 1906)

You will discover in the next chapter that Titchener had a rather narrow concept of what scientific training should be like; the criticism might be overstated, but it was not far from the mark.

If there was a common thread and guiding principle to Hall's various interests, it was evolution. In his autobiography, Hall (1923, p. 357) wrote that "[a]s soon as I first heard it in my youth I think I must have been almost hypnotized by the word 'evolution,' which was music to my ear." Most of his work can be classified under the heading of **genetic psychology**, which could be defined as the study of the evolution and development of the human mind, and included comparative, abnormal, and especially developmental psychology.

Hall's Early Life and Education

Hall was born in the western Massachusetts town of Ashefield in 1844. His mother was a teacher and stern taskmaster and his father, who also had experience teaching, was mainly a farmer. The main benefit of being raised on a farm seemed to be the creation in Hall of a strong urge to leave it. He went to nearby Williams College and graduated (1867) with a strong interest in philosophy and history and a desire to imitate many of his peers by studying for an advanced degree in Europe. Cost was a problem, however, and the most reasonable postgraduate option for a young man interested in philosophy, and unable to cross the ocean, was to study for the clergy, so Hall enrolled in New York's Union Theological Seminary (Ross, 1972).

New York was somewhat daunting for the farm boy from rural Massachusetts, but Hall took advantage of the cultural, educational, artistic, and social opportunities available to him. After a year at Union, however, he was able to borrow enough money to finally go to Europe, and there he stayed until 1871, studying theology and philosophy, but also encountering scien-

FIGURE 6.4 G. Stanley Hall at Clark University, from Popplestone and McPherson (1994).

tific physiology. He then returned to New York and finished his education at Union. He was just going through the motions, however, and felt stifled by religious orthodoxy.[4] Ministry was out—Hall wanted to teach philosophy. After doing some private tutoring, he taught philosophy for four years at Antioch College in

---

[4] Hall (1923) probably embellished the story he told about how Union's president reacted to Hall's trial sermon, supposedly the culmination of one's theological development at Union. According to Hall (1923, p. 178), rather than critique the sermon, the president simply knelt on the floor and prayed for Hall's soul.

Ohio, where he encountered Wundt's *Principles of Physiological Psychology* and resolved to return to Germany to study this new laboratory psychology. First, however, he moved to Cambridge to study at Harvard, feeding himself by teaching English composition to Harvard sophomores. He met William James, took several courses with him, and completed a doctoral thesis on "the muscular perception of space" in 1878. It was primarily a philosophical piece, but it also included some experimental work in perception, conducted in the physiology laboratory of H. P. Bowditch. Harvard had just begun offering the doctorate in philosophy, and Hall was the first person to complete one. Because the topic was in the area that would eventually become known as experimental psychology, Hall's doctorate is sometimes considered to be the first one in psychology.

Doctorate in hand, Hall returned to Germany and found himself in Leipzig in 1879, the "official" year of the founding of Wundt's laboratory. He later claimed to be Wundt's first American student, but he actually had very little contact with Wundt, completed no publishable research, and was in fact preceded by at least one other American student (Benjamin, Durkin, Link, Vestal, & Accord, 1992). Hall was disappointed with his experience in Leipzig and was later critical of Wundt, writing to James that he considered Wundt's experiments "utterly unreliable and defective in method" (cited in Ross, 1972, p. 85). After Leipzig, Hall went to Berlin to study briefly with Helmholtz. While there, Hall became reacquainted with a young woman he knew from his days at Antioch, who was in Berlin to study art. They were married in Germany.

The Halls returned to Boston in the fall of 1880. Hall was 36 years old, highly educated, and devoted to his new bride. He was also poor and unemployed. Yet within 10 years, he would be a university president and one of the acknowledged leaders of psychology in America. His big break was an invitation from President Eliot of Harvard to give a series of lectures on education. Hall had already given considerable thought to how psychology might contribute to the educational reform that was occurring in the late nineteenth century. His lectures, given on Saturday mornings so that local teachers could

attend, were highly successful. The publicity caught the attention of President Gilman of Johns Hopkins, eventually leading to Hall's being asked to give a similar series of talks in Baltimore in January of 1882. Their success led to a job as part-time lecturer in philosophy. In 1884, Hall was hired as a professor at Hopkins at the generous (for the time) annual salary of $4,000 (Ross, 1972). His apparent expertise at using psychological principles to make recommendations about education was reflected in his title—Professor of Psychology and Pedagogy. At age 40, then, Hall had his first real job!

From Johns Hopkins to Clark

Hall did not stay long at Johns Hopkins, but while he was there, he significantly advanced the cause of psychology in America. In 1883, when still a part-time instructor, he created the first true research laboratory of experimental psychology in America and with the help of talented students such as James McKeen Cattell (Chapter 8), John Dewey (Chapter 7), and Edmund Sanford, he began to produce experimental research. In 1887, he founded the *American Journal of Psychology*, the first journal for the new psychology published in the United States. It served partly as a mechanism for publishing original research from Hall's lab and elsewhere, but it also included summaries and reviews of the psychological literature and sections devoted to "Notes and News" about psychology and psychologists. Journal finances were aided by a $500 donation from an advocate of spiritualism, who apparently thought the journal would be devoted to "psychic" research. This was an understandable confusion—the terms "psychic" and "psychological" were used interchangeably in those days. Hall did not correct the donor's misperception and took the money. Over the years, articles on spiritualism occasionally appeared in the journal, but only to ridicule the scientific basis for it. Hall, for example, argued that what passed for telepathy, clairvoyance, and the like, was nothing more than magic tricks and other forms of deception. Indeed, Hall became an accomplished magician and used his skills to demonstrate how easily people could be fooled by deception (Ross, 1972).

Hall's journal was a bold and risky venture, undertaken at a time when nobody could have predicted psychology's future. In an opening editorial, he made it clear that the purpose of the *American Journal of Psychology* would be "to record the psychological work of a scientific, as distinct from a speculative character [and to] record the progress of scientific psychology" (Hall, 1887, pp. 3–4). The opening number included research articles on "The Variations of the Normal Knee-Jerk," "Dermal Sensitiveness to Gradual Pressure Changes," "A Method for the Experimental Determination of the Horopter," and "The Psycho-Physic Law and Star Magnitudes."

In the late 1880s, an economic slowdown created financial difficulties for Johns Hopkins (Hawkins, 1960). Facing dwindling resources, Hall began to look for greener pastures and found them in Worcester, Massachusetts. Jonas Clark, a merchant made wealthy by selling mining supplies at inflated prices to prospectors during the California gold rush, had decided to buy respectability in his hometown by opening a college to educate its youth. Hall seemed the perfect choice for president—ambitious, knowledgeable about higher education, and with a record of accomplishment in his brief time at Johns Hopkins—and Clark hired him in April of 1888. Clark wished to create a school for the youth of Worcester, but Hall had a grander vision, and managed to convince Clark that the school should offer graduate education, in the mold of Johns Hopkins, and that the focus should be on science. An undergraduate division could be added later. Thus, when Clark University opened its doors in the fall of 1889, it offered graduate training in five areas: psychology, biology, chemistry, physics, and mathematics. There were 18 faculty members and 34 graduate students in the initial group and almost all of the instruction took place by means of directed research—the teaching load was just two lectures per week (Ross, 1972).

For three years, Clark University approached Hall's vision of a true university. Faculty produced cutting-edge research, students came from as far away as Japan to join the elite group of scholars, and Hall developed an international reputation as a visionary leader in education. All was not well, however. At the end of the first year, Hall suffered a personal tragedy when his wife and eight-year-old daughter died in an accident. In the second year, faculty began to hear about new opportunities and larger salaries being offered at another new university being created in Chicago with Rockefeller money. And throughout the three years, Hall was regularly in conflict with his faculty. Things came to a head in 1892, when a combination of financial problems (an economic depression), faculty unrest, and the lure of the University of Chicago almost closed the university. Approximately two-thirds of the faculty and students left Clark that year, leaving psychology as the only viable graduate department (Ross, 1972).

Psychology at Clark

Psychology survived after the fiasco of 1892 in part because Hall was deeply involved in the work of the department, and in part due to the loyalty of its two faculty members, Edmund Sanford and William Burnham. Both had been students of Hall at Johns Hopkins. In Clark's department of "psychology and pedagogy," Burnham was in charge of educational psychology and Sanford was in charge of the research laboratory. Hall was clearly the leader of the department, however, and dictated its general direction. He also directed the doctoral dissertations of most of the students, and his Monday evening seminars became legendary among Clark alumni. Held in the parlor of his home, they began at 7:30 and often lasted three hours. Students would make presentations, other students would contribute, and then Hall would have the final word:

> ... for a half-hour or longer, depending on the importance he attached to the theme, he presented from his armchair in the central archway a masterly critique of the research just reported and added to it new illumination from fresh angles that sometimes left the [students] gasping. ...
>
> After the intellectually provocative evening was ended, many of the graduate students set off for their boarding-places but found themselves so moved by the galvanism of their emotions that only a long walk near midnight and a warm bath before retiring could relax them enough to permit them to sleep. (Averill, 1982, p. 342)

(a)

(b)

FIGURE 6.5 The Clark Lab in 1892: (a) "brass instruments," including timing devices and reaction time apparatus; (b) a voice reaction time study (from the Clark University Archives).

During the early 1890s, the laboratory at Clark was a state-of-the-art facility, in part because when Hall left Johns Hopkins, he took most of the research equipment with him. As a result the Hopkins laboratory disappeared and did not reopen until 1903; the Clark lab, meanwhile, was off to a flying start. Hall was also generous with expenditures in the first two years, giving Sanford all he needed to equip a lab fully; the abundance of costly "brass instrument" technology is evident from Figure 6.5a. This photo is one of a series taken in 1892 for display at a psychology exhibit at the Columbian Exposition in Chicago the following year. Figure 6.5b provides an inside look at the experimental psychology of the day—it

illustrates an actual research project (voice reaction time) in action. Sanford gave students considerable leeway in the Clark laboratory; in addition, Hall was constantly suggesting ideas to students. Hence, although the research from Clark was unsystematic and scattered, it reflected the wide range of topics that interested American psychologists in the 1890s.

In the mid-1890s, as part of his deep interest in evolution, Hall began supporting research in comparative psychology. One consequence was the creation of the first studies using what would become a standard piece of laboratory equipment—the maze. For details on the origins of the venerable rats-in-mazes tradition, read this chapter's Close-Up.

CLOSE-UP:
Creating Maze Learning

Ask psychologists to name famous pieces of apparatus in experimental psychology and mazes will be at or near the top of the list. The maze reached its peak of popularity from about 1920 to 1950, especially in the research of neobehaviorists Edward Tolman and Clark Hull (Chapter 11), and the apparatus remains in use today as a tool to investigate spatial abilities and in psychopharmacological and neuropsychological research. Hundreds of maze studies have been completed over the years, and one might ask how it all started. Credit is sometimes given to the Darwinian Sir John Lubbock, who used crude Y-shaped mazes in the 1870s to study how ants followed scent trails, or to E. L. Thorndike (Chapter 7), who observed chicks escaping from simple mazes created by placing books on end (see Figure 7.6). The research that launched the systematic study of rats-in-mazes, however, was completed by Willard Small of Clark University at the turn of the century.

Small arrived in Worcester in 1897 as a 27-year-old graduate student and was soon doing animal research with another student, Linus Kline. Kline completed the first general study of the abilities of rats (Dewsbury, 1984) and one of his interests concerned the rat's "home-finding" capacities. He discussed the problem with the lab's director, Edmund Sanford, who gave him the idea for a maze study and suggested a specific maze design. As Kline later told the story:

> I ... described to [Sanford] runways which I had observed several years ago made by large feral rats to their nests under the porch of an old cabin on my father's farm in Virginia. These runways were from three to six inches below the surface of the ground and when exposed during excavation presented a veritable maze. Sanford at once suggested the possibility of using the pattern of the Hampton Court maze for purposes of constructing a "home-finding" apparatus. (Miles, 1930, p. 331)

One can only speculate about why the Hampton maze occurred to Sanford. That it was on his mind is clear from Kline's comment that "the readiness with which he directed my attention to the Hampton maze is presumptive evidence that he had thought of its use before" (Miles, 1930, p. 331). One possibility is that Sanford may have been in the Hampton Court maze himself just prior to the conversation with Kline. He was on sabbatical in the spring of 1898 and visited a number of laboratories in Europe (Goodwin, 1987). His last stop was in England and it is at least conceivable that he visited Hampton Court, which is just outside of London and is England's most famous hedge maze.

It is not clear why Small did the first maze study and not Kline. Kline reported that other work prevented him from pursuing the idea, and it was perhaps natural for his friend and laboratory coworker to take up the project. At any rate, in January of 1899, Small constructed three 6 × 8 foot mazes with wire mesh walls, using the Hampton Court design but adjusting it to a rectangular pattern, as shown in Figure 6.6. He then began his historic research on the manner in which rats learn mazes.

Sanford reported on Small's study at the December 1899 APA meeting, and Small published a highly detailed 33-page report in 1901. Modern accounts, perhaps inspired by

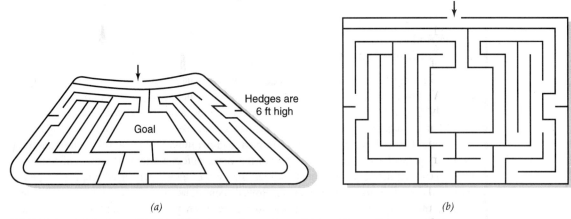

(a) *(b)*

FIGURE 6.6 (a) Design of England's Hampton Court maze; (b) Small's readjustment of the Hampton Court maze to a rectangular configuration.

Thorndike's rather caustic review of Small's earlier work (Thorndike, 1900), usually dismiss Small's description of the maze studies as a series of overly anthropomorphic comments about such things as the rat's alleged "disgust" over reaching a dead end. The criticism has some merit, but Small's report also gives a trial-and-error description of maze learning similar to other contemporary accounts by Thorndike and Lloyd Morgan (Chapter 5). Small also commented extensively on what he believed to be the mental processes involved, and he used blind rats to investigate the effects of sensory capacity on learning. These blind rats seemed to learn the maze as well as their sighted peers. Small concluded that "tactile motor sensations furnish the essential data for the recognition and discrimination involved in forming the special associations at critical points" (Small, 1901, p. 237).

Small's work is less important for its conclusions than for the fact that it initiated a flood of similar research. In the next few years, comparative psychologists used versions of the Hampton Court maze to study species ranging from rhesus monkeys (Kinnaman, 1902) to English sparrows (Porter, 1904). With the white rat, research followed up on Small's ideas about the influence of the various senses on learning. The most famous of these were the studies by Watson and Carr at the University of Chicago (Chapter 10), who concluded, like Small, that the kinesthetic sense was most critical. Subsequent research, and there were dozens of such studies completed by 1920, showed the process to be much more complicated, but it is worth noting that the animal maze literature began by investigating the sensory and mental processes involved in maze learning and by investigating how organisms adapted to their environment. These of course were topics clearly in tune with the psychology of the early 1900s, which was the psychology of mental life and which reflected the pervasiveness of evolutionary theory.

In his remaining years at Clark University, Hall left his stamp on psychology in several ways. First, he continued to professionalize psychology by creating its first formal organization, the American Psychological Association (APA). He and about a dozen other psychologists held an organizational meeting in his study in July of 1892, at which time 31 charter members were identified (Sokal, 1992). As you might expect, Hall was elected the association's first president. Eighteen of the charter members convened in December 1892, at the University of Pennsylvania, for the APA's first annual meeting. The organization grew rapidly: 74 members after four years and 127 by the turn of the century (Ross, 1972). It adopted a constitution in 1894, making clear its role in creating disciplinary identity for a "scientific" psychology. The purpose of the organization was to be "the advancement of Psychology as a science. Those are eligible for membership who are engaged in this work" (Cattell, 1895, p. 150). The APA also enhanced psychology's professional and scientific status by affiliating with older, more recognized associations, such as the American Association for the Advancement of Science (Camfield, 1973).

Hall and Developmental Psychology

In addition to activities connected with the journal and the APA, Hall contributed to American psychology by advancing his genetic psychology. He was a pioneer in developmental psychology, promoting the child study movement, writing the first textbook on adolescent psychology, and near the end of his career, writing a book on aging. He also continued to champion the importance of psychology for education, in part by establishing summer schools for the training of educators, but also by founding a second journal, *Pedagogical Seminary* (now the *Journal of Genetic Psychology*) in 1891.

Hall first became interested in child study while at Johns Hopkins, where he published the first in a series of studies about children using the results from questionnaires filled out by children, teachers, and parents (these were the "questionary" studies that Titchener disparaged in his letter to Wilson). His overall goal was identified in the title of his first research paper: "The Contents of Children's Minds" (Hall, 1883/1948). In this first survey, Hall accumulated data from more than 200 Boston children who were just beginning school. They were questioned by about 60 different teachers, who asked what they knew about a wide range of subjects. The level of knowledge was not high. For instance, 75.5% could not identify what season of the year it was, 87.5% didn't know what an island was, and 90.5% couldn't locate their ribs. Hall also discovered that children reared in the country did much better than those raised in the city. As a farm boy himself, Hall did not find this surprising:

> ... As our methods of teaching grow natural we realize that city life is unnatural, and that those who grow up without knowing the country are defrauded of that without which childhood can never be complete or normal. On the whole the material of the city is no doubt inferior in pedagogic value to country experience. A few days in the country at this age has raised the level of many a city child's intelligence more than a term or two of school training could do without it. It is there, too, that the foundations of a love of natural science are best laid. (Hall, 1883/1948, pp. 261–262)

In this quote can be seen the essence of Hall's philosophy of education. He ridiculed rote memorization and the rigid discipline of the classroom. Instead, he favored a more permissive approach that took for granted the child's "natural" curiosity about the world and encouraged what would be called "active learning" today—giving children problems to solve or activities to complete that would have some specific pedagogical value.

Hall was not only interested in children. Some of his questionnaire studies collected data from teenagers, and he reported the results, along with everything else then known about that age group, in his encyclopedic two-volume *Adolescence* (1904). It was the first book devoted to the study of teenagers, and Hall is the person most responsible for identifying adolescence as a distinct stage of development. The description of adolescence as a period of "storm

and stress" has its origins in Hall's book. The book also contains the most thorough description of Hall's use of the theory of **recapitulation**. The theory originated with the German evolutionary biologist Ernst Haeckel, who proposed that an organism's stages of development, from cell to a fully formed individual, can be seen as a recapitulation of the evolution of the species.[5] Thus, at one stage of development, the human fetus resembles a fish, reflecting that point in evolutionary history where the human species had aquatic ancestors. Hall extended the idea beyond embryonic development, arguing for example that children's play often reflected earlier stages of mental evolution. Recapitulation as a theory died shortly after the turn of the twentieth century, but it had the beneficial effect of spurring Hall's interest in all stages of development—testing recapitulation demands a close attention to development across the life span. For Hall, studying that development could shed light on the evolution of the race.

Toward the end of his life, Hall became interested in the middle and final stages of life, eventually writing about aging in *Senescence: The Last Half of Life* (1922). He once again relied on questionnaire data, asking the elderly their opinions about such topics as their fear of death and their ability to recognize the signs of aging. He also criticized the lack of retirement pension programs and recommended that the elderly organize politically, long before the advent of today's AARP.

Hall and Psychoanalysis

A significant portion of Hall's *Adolescence* concerned sexual behavior, including an entire 50-page chapter entitled "Adolescent Love." Hall also offered a course at Clark entitled "The Psychology of Sex" (Rosenzweig, 1992), and consistent with his ideas on education, he believed that the natural expression of sexual behavior should not be inhibited. This attitude raised eyebrows among his peers, leading one of them to wonder: "Is there no turning Hall away from this d——d sexual rut? I really think it is a bad thing morally and intellectually to harp so much on the

---

[5] Haeckel's theory had been highly visible and heavily debated during Hall's first visit to Germany in 1868 to 1871 (Ross, 1972).

sexual string, unless one is a neurologist" (letter from F. Angell to E. B. Titchener on March 19, 1990, cited in Ross, 1972, p. 385).

Hall's preoccupation with sex, combined with an interest in abnormal behavior, led him to become fascinated by Freud's theories. In 1909, to celebrate the university's twentieth anniversary, Hall organized the Clark Conference, a series of public lectures by prominent psychologists. The centerpiece was a series of talks given by none other than Freud himself.[6] Accompanied by his younger colleague Carl Jung, who lectured on his new word association technique, Freud made his first and only visit to America and delivered five lectures that were published in the *American Journal of Psychology* in 1910, then separately in book form (some of this lecture material is in the Chapter 12 Original Source Excerpt). A grateful Freud later said that the Clark Conference was an important point in the history of psychoanalysis, constituting the first international recognition of his theories.

Hall retired from the presidency of Clark in 1920, but remained active in his remaining four years of life. He published his book on aging in 1922 and an autobiography, *Life and Confessions of a Psychologist*, a year later (Hall, 1923). In 1924, he was elected to a second term as president of the APA, only the second person ever to be elected twice (William James was the other). He died before he could assume his duties, however.

MARY WHITON CALKINS (1863–1930): CHALLENGING THE MALE MONOPOLY

Professional women in the early twenty-first century often face discrimination in the workplace and find themselves unable to rise above the "glass ceiling." As frustrating as the problem is for modern women, it was many times worse 100 years ago. As described

earlier in the chapter, women were widely believed to be intellectually inferior to men in the 1890s, and they had little standing in society (they could not vote until 1920, for instance). Combining marriage and a career was virtually impossible—marriage was assumed to be their career. Even if they didn't marry, they were expected to care for other members of their family, especially parents as they aged. Although women began attending college in increasing numbers in the late nineteenth century, higher education for women was looked on with skepticism by a male-dominated society. It was even believed that an education could harm women—their weak constitutions could be permanently damaged by the cerebral demands of college. Hence, in the 1890s it was almost impossible for a woman to obtain a doctorate in psychology, a dilemma faced by Mary Whiton Calkins, one of the most important contributors to the new psychology in America.

Calkins's Life and Work

Mary Calkins grew up in Buffalo, New York, the oldest of five children in a close-knit family headed by a father who was a Congregationalist minister. He shared with William James's father a belief in the educational value of travel to Europe and in the importance of being multilingual. In fact, Mary's parents only spoke German in her presence during her first few years; by adulthood, Mary was fluent in English, German, and French (Furumoto, 1979). The Calkins family moved to the Boston area when Mary was 17 and soon after that she entered Smith College in western Massachusetts, one of the new women's colleges. She graduated in 1885, and then went to Europe with her family for 16 months, where among other things she added Greek to her list of language competencies. Upon her return, she took a position teaching Greek at Wellesley College. Calkins (Figure 6.7) remained at Wellesley for the rest of her career.

By the late 1880s, Wellesley's leaders decided that to keep up with trends in modern science, the college needed to offer the new laboratory approach to psychology. Calkins had expressed some interest in teaching philosophy and had impressed her supe-

---

[6] Hall originally hoped for an all-star cast of international psychologists, including not just Freud, but also Wundt and Ebbinghaus. Wundt declined to come, however, and while Ebbinghaus accepted the invitation, he died just before the conference began.

FIGURE 6.7 Mary Whiton Calkins as a young instructor at Wellesley College, from Scarborough and Furumoto (1987).

riors in her first few years as a teacher, so she was given the opportunity to develop a course in laboratory psychology. It was understood, however, that she would take a year off to learn about this new field. Thus began her frustrating search for graduate education in psychology.

Graduate Education for Females

Calkins quickly learned that opportunities for advanced training were quite limited for women. After considering Europe and a few American schools (e.g., Yale, Michigan), she attempted to become a student at Harvard—it had William James to offer and it was close to home. She also looked into Clark University, 30 miles to the west of Boston. At Harvard, she was grudgingly allowed to attend seminars with James and the philosopher Josiah Royce, both of whom supported her application vigorously, but Harvard officials made it clear that she was merely an unofficial "guest" of the university. It was the same story at Clark. Women were not allowed in officially, but Edmund Sanford welcomed her into his new laboratory. Calkins later credited

Sanford, who contributed time, advice, and apparatus, with being the true founder of the psychology laboratory at Wellesley (Calkins, 1930).

Calkins entered Harvard in the fall of 1890 and immediately encountered the educational opportunity of a lifetime. Calkins and four male students were enrolled in Philosophy 20a, Physiological Psychology, with William James, but the males, perhaps unnerved by the presence of a woman, dropped out within a few days. As Calkins (1930) later recalled, "... James and I were left ... quite literally at either side of a library fire. The *Principles of Psychology* was warm from the press; and my absorbed study of those brilliant, erudite, and provocative volumes, as interpreted by their writer, was my introduction to psychology" (p. 31).

After her year of study at Harvard and Clark, Calkins returned to Wellesley, but her appetite for the new psychology had been whetted, and she was soon looking into further training. In 1892, when William James recruited Hugo Münsterberg from Germany to run the Harvard lab, Calkins returned to Cambridge, once more as an unofficial guest. Again the timing was perfect for Calkins—Münsterberg's English was poor, but she was fluent in German. They became colleagues immediately. For the next two years, Calkins worked in Münsterberg's lab part-time while continuing to teach 10 miles away at Wellesley. In the academic year 1894 to 1895, she took a leave from the college to complete her studies.

Calkins's Research on Association

Münsterberg treated Calkins just like any other doctoral student. For her thesis, she completed a brilliant series of experimental studies on association, publishing the research in two parts (Calkins, 1894; Calkins 1896), then writing an extended account as a *Psychological Review Monograph* paper in 1896. Traditional philosophical and introspective accounts often described how the strength of associations could be influenced by such factors as frequency, recency, vividness, and primacy. In the spirit of Ebbinghaus, Calkins was determined to go beyond "ordinary self-observation" and examine these factors experimentally. She did not go into detail about how her procedures developed, but it is clear that she went through considerable trial and error, what today we would call "pilot studies," before arriving at her method. The procedure that evolved is an important one historically—although she did not use the name, she invented **paired-associate learning**, later to become a standard method in cognitive research. Her subjects first studied stimulus-response pairs comprised of sequentially presented color patches and numbers (each shown for four seconds), then tried to recall the number responses when shown the color stimuli. Calkins manipulated frequency by presenting the same color several times, once with one number, then either two or three times with a second number. Here's how she described series #89:

I. Medium gray, 29; blue, 82; violet, 61 (n); red, 23; violet, 12 (f); peacock, 79; violet, 12 (f); strawberry, 47; violet, 12 (f); light brown, 53; dark gray, 34; light green, 72.

II. Peacock, red, green, violet, medium gray, brown, strawberry, dark gray, blue. (Calkins, 1894, p. 478)

Thus, during presentation (I), violet was first paired with 61 (referred to by her as the "normal" pairing, or "n"), then three times ("f" = frequency) with the number 12. During recall (II), violet was the fourth color presented and the question was whether subjects would recall the number 61 or 12 (or both or neither). In like manner, Calkins studied recency by comparing the recall of two numbers paired with the same color, one pairing in the middle of the sequence and one at the very end. Vividness was examined by presenting a critical pair in some way that made it stand out from the other pairs, such as by altering the size of the numbers. Primacy was studied by looking at performance for the first pair in a series. In general, her results showed that recall was enhanced by each of the four factors: frequency, vividness, recency, and primacy. In subsequent trials in which she directly compared these factors by combining them within the same list, Calkins generally found that frequency was the most critical factor. She also ran some trials in which the colors and numbers were presented together on the same card. This enabled her to compare "simultaneous" associations with the earlier "successive" ones, thus examining the old British Empiricist distinction between simultaneous and successive forms of contiguity. She found no major differences.

Calkins did not mention the Ebbinghaus memory research, published in 1885 (and excerpted in Chapter 4), but she was clearly aware of it. She was fluent in German and very familiar with James's *Principles*, which includes a thorough description of the Ebbinghaus research in its chapter on "Memory." The Ebbinghaus influence is also apparent in Calkins's choice of materials when she altered her procedure to use auditory presentation. The stimuli in this case (and she used the term) were "nonsense syllables" instead of colors. Calkins found about the same outcome for both visual and auditory presentation, except that the recency findings were more striking with the latter.

Calkins (1896) summed up her overall results by emphasizing the importance of the frequency variable, but adding a caution that the laboratory results might not be completely "representative of ordinary trains of association" (p. 49). She even added a statement about the practical implications of her findings, referring to frequency as a "corrective influence. ... The prominence of frequency is of course of grave importance, for it means the possibility of exercising some control over the life of the imagination and of definitely combating harmful or troublesome associations" (p. 49). Calkins was thinking along the same lines as her teacher, William James, and her research can be seen as providing some empirical evidence for James's suggestions about how to firmly entrench a habit (discussed earlier).

Madigan and O'Hara (1992) closely examined Calkins's research on memory, including some studies completed after her dissertation research. They found clear indications that Calkins discovered a number of effects that would later be rediscovered half a century later, when psychologists once again became interested in studying cognitive psychology (Chapter 13). These included such immediate memory phenomena as the primacy, recency, and negative recency effects, the modality effect, and retroactive interference.

Although it was unofficial, Calkins completed a defense of her thesis and a Ph.D. examination in May of 1895. Münsterberg, James, and other examiners appealed to the Harvard authorities to grant her the Ph.D., with Münsterberg describing her as "superior ... to all candidates of the philosophical Ph.D. during the last years" and "surely one of the strongest professors of psychology in the country" (cited in Scarborough & Furumoto, 1987, pp. 44–45). Harvard refused though—after all, Calkins was a woman. Later, when Radcliffe College had been created as a Harvard-for-women, Calkins was offered a Radcliffe Ph.D. This time it was Calkins who refused. She would have a doctorate from the school where she earned it or none at all. Although she would earn several honorary degrees, Harvard never did change its mind, and Calkins was never awarded the Ph.D.

From Psychology to Philosophy

After completing her non-Ph.D. from Harvard, Calkins returned to Wellesley, continued building her lab with Sanford's help, and produced a string of research publications through the turn of the century. In 1898, she turned over the laboratory to Eleanor Gamble, a new Ph.D. from Cornell (one of the few institutions that admitted women doctoral students). From about 1900 on, her publications became less research-oriented as she developed her major theoretical contribution to psychology, **self psychology**. It was a system that clearly showed the influence of her first mentor, William James. Calkins argued that psychology could be the study of mental life, as James had said, but that the central fact of psychology must be that all consciousness contains an element of the self (Strunk, 1972).

At a time when strong disagreements were developing over the proper direction for the new psychology, Calkins saw her self psychology as a means of resolving disputes. For example, as will be clear from the next chapter, one conflict was between structural psychology, which emphasized analyzing consciousness into its basic elements, and functional psychology, which focused on how consciousness served to adapt the individual to the environment. When her peers elected her the fourteenth president of the APA in 1905, the first female so honored, Calkins (1906) delivered a presidential address called "A Reconciliation between Structural and Functional Psychology." In it she argued that both views could be accommodated within a system that recognized the self as the fundamental starting point. Thus, the structuralists could concentrate on discovering the elements that make up the self, while the functionalists could examine how the self relates to the environment.

Like James, Mary Calkins gradually shifted her interests over the years from psychology to philosophy. Shortly after her APA presidency, for instance, she wrote *The Persistent Problems of Philosophy* (1907), perhaps her most important work. In 1918, the American Philosophical Association elected her president of their organization, making her the first woman to be elected to the presidency of each of the APAs. Calkins retired from Wellesley in 1929 and died of cancer a year later.

Other Women Pioneers: Untold Lives

Calkins wasn't the only woman struggling against a male-oriented discipline at the turn of the century. In *Untold Lives: The First Generation of American Women Psychologists*, Elizabeth Scarborough and Laurel Furumoto (1987) have thoroughly documented the experiences of Calkins and several other pioneering women psychologists. Two of the better known were Christine Ladd-Franklin and Margaret Washburn.

Christine Ladd-Franklin (1847–1930)

Like Calkins, Ladd-Franklin was educated at one of the new women's colleges. She entered Vassar College in Poughkeepsie, New York, in 1866, a year after it had been founded. There she excelled in science and math and was inspired by the example of the astronomer Maria Mitchell, said to be the most eminent woman scientist in America at that time (Furumoto, 1992). She graduated in 1869, then taught in secondary schools for about 10 years before deciding to pursue a graduate education in math at Johns Hopkins. There she encountered the same roadblock that would later face Calkins—Hopkins did not admit women as official students. Nonetheless, she was allowed to attend classes and by 1882, she had completed all the requirements for a doctorate in math. It would be 1926, however, before Johns Hopkins officially awarded her the degree, which she accepted in person, at age 79 (Scarborough & Furumoto, 1987).

While at Johns Hopkins, Christine Ladd met, fell in love with, and married a faculty member in the math department, Fabian Franklin, and became Christine Ladd-Franklin. With her husband's active support, she was able to continue her interests in math and published several scholarly papers. In the mid-1880s she became interested in visual perception, a shift that led her to the new psychology. Her first publication, on binocular vision ("A Method for the Experimental Determination of the Horopter") appeared in 1887 in the very first issue of Hall's *American Journal of Psychology*. During her husband's 1891 to 1892 sabbatical, spent in Europe, she was able to conduct research on vision in the Göttingen lab of G. E. Müller. As you recall from Chapter 4, Müller's lab was one of the best in Germany. She also spent time in Helmholtz's lab in Berlin. It was during this time in Germany that she developed a theory of color vision that was grounded in evolutionary theory; it was an influential theory for several decades.

Of the three pioneer women considered here, Ladd-Franklin was the most outspoken about the lack of professional opportunities for women. For example, she directly challenged the "men only" rule of a group of psychologists known as the Experimentalists (see Chapter 7's Close-Up). Organized in 1904 by E. B. Titchener of Cornell, this select group met annually at various labs to discuss their current research. After being refused permission to attend in 1912, she wrote to Titchener that she was "shocked to know that you are still—at this year—excluding women from your meeting of experimental psychologists. It is such a very old-fashioned standpoint" (cited in Furumoto, 1988, p. 107). Two years later her persistence wore Titchener down somewhat and she presented her work on color vision at one of the Experimentalists' meetings. It was the only time a woman participated in a meeting during Titchener's lifetime.

Ladd-Franklin also vigorously campaigned for a faculty position at a research university, but never managed to obtain more than part-time lectureships, first at Johns Hopkins, then at Columbia when she and her husband moved to New York. She was seldom paid for her teaching. Nonetheless, she continued her work as a mathematician and expert on vision, never giving in to the prevailing belief that science was for men only.

Margaret Floy Washburn (1871–1939)

In addition to Ladd-Franklin, Vassar College also produced Margaret Washburn, then later reclaimed her. Washburn graduated from Vassar in 1890 with her interests divided between science and philosophy. She decided to pursue "the wonderful new science of experimental psychology" (Washburn, 1932, p. 338), because it seemed to combine her interests, so she applied for graduate studies at Columbia University, where she ran into the same problems faced by Calkins and Ladd-Franklin. She was welcomed as a serious student by James McKeen Cattell, but as usual, was only permitted to attend his classes unofficially. Cattell saw her potential and encouraged her to apply to Cornell, which accepted women graduate students. There she encountered none other than E. B. Titchener (Chapter 7), who had just finished his doctorate with Wundt at Leipzig. Women might have been excluded from Titchener's Experimentalists, but they were accepted into his laboratory, and Washburn was Titchener's first Ph.D. student. She became the first woman to earn a doctorate in psychology when she completed the degree in 1894, a study of the effects of visual imagery on tactile sensitivity. It was one of the few studies published in Wundt's journal (*Philosophische Studien*) that was not completed at the Leipzig laboratory.

After leaving Cornell, Washburn held several teaching positions, then was asked to return to her alma mater, Vassar. This she did in 1903, and there she spent her remaining professional career. Despite the heavy teaching load and inadequate research facilities that invariably accompany faculty life at small colleges, Washburn fashioned a remarkable career that included an APA presidency in 1921, co-editorship of the *American Journal of Psychology* for more than a decade, and election to the prestigious National Academy of Sciences in 1931. When the Experimentalists reorganized after Titchener's death in 1927, she was one of two women elected as a charter member of the new group, and she hosted a meeting of the refashioned "Society of Experimental Psychologists" at Vassar in 1931.

As a psychologist, Washburn published in the areas of perception, imagery, "social consciousness" (empathy and helping behavior), and developed a motor theory of consciousness, but she is best known for her work in comparative psychology. She contributed some original research (e.g., on the perception of color in fish) and summarized the field in her well-known text, *The Animal Mind*. First published in 1908, it went through four editions (1917, 1926, 1936) and became the standard textbook of its day (Dewsbury, 1992). It was notable for its exclusion of evidence based solely on anecdotal data; Washburn included only the results of experimental research. As implied by the title, its focus was on the cognitive processes of perception, attention, and consciousness, as exhibited by the behaviors of various species.

IN PERSPECTIVE: THE NEW PSYCHOLOGY AT THE MILLENNIUM

During the last 20 years of the nineteenth century, psychology in America changed dramatically. Prior to that time it had been dominated by traditional faculty psychology and taught as "moral" or "mental" philosophy. By the end of the century it was still being taught in philosophy departments for the most part, but it now reflected the influence of the new psychology of Germany and the revolutionary ideas of Charles Darwin. In the early 1880s there were no research laboratories of psychology in the United States, and most American psychologists wishing to study the new laboratory psychology had to travel to Germany. By 1890, laboratories had been established at nine American universities, and by the end of the century, there were at least 41 (Hilgard, 1987). Although in the early 1890s a German Ph.D. in psychology held higher status than one earned in the United States, this was no longer true by the end of the decade. The shift is reflected in the numbers: Between 1884 and 1892 the number of Americans earning Ph.D.s in America (n = 9) and Germany (n = 8), was about equal, but from 1893 to 1899, 63 American psychologists earned their doctorates in the United States, whereas only 10 earned theirs in Germany (O'Donnell, 1985).

Hall's Clark University was a leader in the production of Ph.D.s in psychology in the 1890s, but other young psychologists were being trained at several other up-and-coming universities. Foremost among them were Cornell, where students would find E. B. Titchener and a school of thought known as structuralism, and Columbia and Chicago, two leading centers of a uniquely American movement that became known as functionalism. The story of these "isms" will occupy the next chapter.

SUMMARY

PSYCHOLOGY IN NINETEENTH-CENTURY AMERICA

• Prior to the Civil War, psychology in America was taught as mental or moral philosophy. It was taught following the precepts of faculty psychology, which was based on Scottish Realistic philosophy. Faculties were separate subcategories of the mind, normally falling into three categories: cognitive, affective, and behavioral.

• Thomas Upham's *Elements of Intellectual (Mental) Philosophy* (1827) is considered to be the first textbook of psychology, and it was organized around the concepts of faculty psychology.

• The post-Civil War period was one of great expansion in higher education. The modern university (e.g., Johns Hopkins), based on the German model that emphasized graduate education and independent research, began during this time.

• Although educational opportunities multiplied for white males in the second half of the nineteenth century, they were limited for women and minorities. Higher education was believed to harm women and keep them from their preferred roles, but opportunities existed at newly founded women's colleges. Opportunities for minorities were limited by entrenched beliefs about their abilities. Nonetheless, some persevered, including Francis Sumner, the first African American to earn a Ph.D. (1920).

WILLIAM JAMES (1842–1910): AMERICA'S FIRST PSYCHOLOGIST

- Although he was trained in medicine and ultimately thought of himself as a philosopher, William James is considered America's first modern psychologist. He brought the new psychology to Harvard, and he wrote what is arguably the most important book in all of psychology's history, the *Principles of Psychology* (1890).

- Disturbed by nineteenth-century materialism and determinism, James decided to believe in free will because it was a useful belief for him to hold. Out of this emerged his general approach to philosophy, called pragmatism.

- In the *Principles*, James took issue with those who would analyze consciousness into its elements. Instead, he argued that it was more appropriately conceived of as analogous to a stream. Consciousness was personal, constantly changing, continuous, selective, and active, and it served individuals by enabling them to adapt quickly to new environments. Habit also had survival value, allowing individuals to avoid having to think about some activities so they could save their consciousness for more difficult and novel problems.

- According to the James-Lange theory of emotions, emotional responses were identified with the bodily reactions that accompanied the perception of some event. When trying to conceive of emotions without the physiological arousal, James argued, nothing remains. A problem with the theory is that it requires that a recognizably different pattern of arousal be associated with each different emotion.

- In his later years, James became interested in the possibility that there could be some validity to spiritualism. Despite criticism that he was harming the fragile scientific status of the new psychology, he believed that spiritualists and mediums should be investigated with an open mind.

G. STANLEY HALL (1844–1924): PROFESSIONALIZING PSYCHOLOGY

- Hall is best known for his efforts in professionalizing psychology. He founded the first psychology lab in America (at Johns Hopkins), America's first academic journal (the *American Journal of Psychology*), and the American Psychological Association.

- As the first president of Clark University, he copied the German ideal of graduate education that he first encountered at Johns Hopkins. For several years, Clark was a leader in graduate education in several scientific fields. After 1892, however, only psychology remained as a prominent field of study at Clark.

- Hall was interested in a wide range of topics, but they generally fell under the heading of genetic psychology, the study of the origins and development of consciousness and behavior. The importance of evolution was a consistent theme in Hall's work. At Clark, Hall encouraged research in developmental, abnormal, and comparative psychology. Under the direction of Edmund Sanford, Clark's laboratory produced important research throughout the 1890s, including the first studies of rats learning mazes.

- As a developmental psychologist, Hall pioneered the child study movement and is responsible for identifying adolescence as a distinct stage of development. He characterized adolescence as a time of "storm and stress." Later in life he wrote about the developmental changes associated with adulthood and aging. He believed in a theory of recapitulation—the development of the individual organism is a mirror of the evolution of the species.

- Hall's interests in development, sexuality, and abnormality led him to invite Freud to America for Clark's twentieth anniversary in 1909. It was Freud's only trip to America, and he believed that the invitation was the first sign that his ideas were developing an international reputation.

MARY WHITON CALKINS (1863–1930): CHALLENGING THE MALE MONOPOLY

- Mary Calkins was barred from being an official student at Harvard, but nonetheless completed an important experimental dissertation on association, during which she invented a memory procedure still in use, paired associate learning. In her thesis, Calkins investigated frequency, recency, vividness, and primacy as conditions that could strengthen associations, and found that frequency was the most important.

- In 1905, Calkins became the first woman elected president of the American Psychological Association; as her interests shifted to philosophy, she became (in 1918) the first woman elected president of the other APA, the American Philosophical Association.

- Calkins's major theoretical contribution was her self psychology, which was centered on the idea that all consciousness is personal. She used it as a way to reconcile competing theoretical schools of thought (e.g., structuralism and functionalism).

- Two other important women psychologists during this era were Christine Ladd-Franklin and Margaret Washburn. Both faced the exclusionary practices that made it difficult for women to become professional psychologists. Ladd-Franklin was a skilled mathematician and developed an evolutionary theory of color vision. Washburn was best known for her work in comparative psychology.

IN PERSPECTIVE:
THE NEW PSYCHOLOGY AT THE MILLENNIUM

• By the turn of the century, psychology in America had grown considerably and had shifted from faculty psychology to the new laboratory-based experimental psychology. Students also had numerous options for graduate study in America by 1900, and the number of students going to Germany quickly declined.

STUDY QUESTIONS

1. Describe the Scottish Realists' objection to British Empiricism and what they proposed instead.

2. Describe the three major divisions of American psychology's first textbook (by Upham).

3. Describe the German model of higher education and how it influenced universities in America.

4. Describe the barriers that made it difficult for women to obtain higher education and describe what opportunities were available to them.

5. Describe the barriers that made it difficult for African Americans to obtain higher education.

6. Describe the career and accomplishments of Francis Sumner.

7. Describe how William James overcame his concerns about materialism and developed a "pragmatic" philosophy.

8. What did James think of the "new psychology?" What did he propose as appropriate methodologies for psychology?

9. According to James, what is the best metaphor for consciousness? Explain.

10. According to James what are the attributes of consciousness and what are the functions of (a) consciousness and (b) habit?

11. Why was spiritualism popular in the late nineteenth century? What was James's opinion of the phenomenon?

12. What does it mean to say that G. Stanley Hall was a genetic psychologist?

13. Describe Hall's contributions to the professionalization of psychology in America.

14. Describe the importance of maze learning research in psychology's history and explain its origins.

15. Describe Hall's contributions to the study of human development, throughout the life span, but especially in adolescence.

16. Describe the difficulties encountered by Calkins when she tried to attain graduate training. What training was she able to accomplish?

17. How did Calkins study memory and association, and what did she conclude about the nature of the association process?

18. Describe the accomplishments of (a) Christine Ladd-Franklin and (b) Margaret Washburn.

QUESTIONS FROM THE ORIGINAL SOURCE EXCERPT

1. Briefly state the essence of the James-Lange theory of emotions. Use the example of meeting a bear in the woods to illustrate.

2. What were some of the examples used by James to support his theory (e.g., James used a personal example from his childhood)?

3. What was the fatal flaw in the James-Lange theory of emotion?

4. Describe how James used his theory to make some practical suggestions to improve one's life.

FOR FURTHER READING

Croce, P. J. (1995). *Science and religion in the era of William James: Eclipse of certainty, 1820–1880.* Chapel Hill: University of North Carolina Press.

Documents the early intellectual development of William James; shows how James was at the center of the debate about the relationship between science and religion and how the debate was affected by evolutionary thinking; first of a two-part biography.

Ross, D. (1972). *G. Stanley Hall: The psychologist as prophet.* Chicago: University of Chicago Press.

The definitive intellectual biography of American psychology's premier entrepreneur; also documents the development of psychology during Hall's time and sets it into its social and institutional context.

Scarborough, E., & Furumoto, L. (1987). *Untold lives: The first generation of American women psychologists.* New York: Columbia University Press.

Examines the lives, struggles, and contributions of several pioneering women psychologists, including detailed treatment of Mary Calkins, Milicent Shinn, Ethel Puffer, Margaret Washburn, and Christine Ladd-Franklin.

Special issue: The history of American psychology. (1992). *American Psychologist, 47(2),* 109–368.

Includes articles on the early years of the APA (Sokal), the founding of early laboratories (Capshew), spiritualism (Coon), William James (Leary), Mary Calkins's memory research (Madigan and O'Hara), Christine Ladd-Franklin (Furumoto), and G. Stanley Hall (Bringmann, Bringmann, and Early; Vande Kemp).

CHAPTER 7

STRUCTURALISM AND FUNCTIONALISM

The first object of the psychologist ... is to ascertain the nature and number of the mental elements. He takes up mental experience, bit by bit, dividing and subdividing, until the division can go no further. When that point is reached, he has found a conscious element.

—E. B. Titchener, 1896

PREVIEW AND CHAPTER OBJECTIVES

This chapter begins with the story of a remarkable Englishman who came to a remote new university in America in 1892 and fashioned a unique and powerful but ultimately sterile system of psychology. Cornell's E. B. Titchener was trained by Wundt at Leipzig but had his own ideas about the proper definition of a scientific psychology. Its main goal was to analyze the adult mind into its fundamental structural elements, using a precise form of introspection that required extensive training. For Titchener, psychology was a pure positivist science that was centered in the laboratory; he was not interested in applications. Titchener was an influential and commanding presence in academic psychology's early years in America, but most American psychologists rejected structuralism. Reflecting the influence of Darwin and traditional Yankee pragmatism, they were more interested in how the mind functioned than in its structure, and they knew that for psychology to succeed in America, it had to be applicable to everyday life. While Titchener believed that the structure of mind had to be clarified before its functions could be studied, most American psychologists disagreed and adopted what came to be called functionalism. Functional psychologists were scattered throughout the academic landscape, but two schools became closely associated with the movement—Chicago and Columbia. The second half of the chapter examines how functionalism "evolved" at these locations, through the efforts of James Angell, John Dewey, and Harvey Carr at Chicago, and James McKeen Cattell, E. L. Thorndike, and Robert Woodworth at Columbia. This chapter's Original Source Excerpt is from a famous series of studies of cats escaping from puzzle boxes, completed by Thorndike. After you finish this chapter, you should be able to:

▣ Distinguish between a structuralist and a functionalist approach to psychology

▣ Describe the general contents and the overall importance of Titchener's Manuals, and the content of a typical "drill course"

▣ Describe the impact of the Experimentalists and the effect of the group on opportunities for women in experimental psychology

▣ Articulate psychology's three main goals, as Titchener saw them

▣ Explain Titchener's version of introspection and explain how he believed the limitations of introspection could be overcome (three strategies)

- Describe the elements of human conscious experience, and their attributes, according to Titchener
- Show how the controversies over imageless thought and with Baldin pointed out the limitations of Titchenerian introspection as a methodology
- Evaluate the overall contributions of Titchener to experimental psychology
- Describe the link between evolutionary theory, social Darwinism, and functionalism
- Describe contributions to functionalist thought made by the Chicago functionalists Dewey, Angell, and Carr
- Describe Thorndike's puzzle box research and his conclusions about animal learning, and understand the significance of the research
- Describe Woodworth's dynamic psychology and reasons for proposing an S-O-R model for psychology
- Explain the importance of the Columbia bible for the training of psychologists

TITCHENER'S PSYCHOLOGY: STRUCTURALISM

In 1898, a paper appeared in the new journal *Psychological Review* entitled "The Postulates of a Structural Psychology." Its author, E. B. Titchener, was a young professor from Cornell University who had been in the United States for just six years, but already had a reputation as a talented laboratory psychologist with some clear and uncompromising ideas about the nature of the new psychology. In the article he named his approach a "structural" psychology, and he contrasted it with what he saw all around him at other American universities, which he labeled a "functional" psychology. Drawing an explicit parallel to biology, he wrote that **structuralism** is just like anatomy—the purpose is analysis. Just as the anatomist organizes knowledge about the body into component structures, so would a structural psychologist analyze the human mind and organize it into its elementary units. **Functionalism**, on the other hand, is like physiology. The physiologist examines how the various parts of the body operate and the functions they serve to help keep the individual alive; similarly, the functional psychologist studies how the mind serves to adapt the individual to the environment. Although not rejecting a functional approach outright, Titchener used the biology metaphor to argue that it was futile to study function before structure had been fully

understood. Anatomy provides the foundation for physiology, Titchener contended. Similarly, a thorough understanding of the structure of the human mind was a necessary prerequisite to the study of its function. As Titchener had written two years earlier in his first text, *An Outline of Psychology*, the psychologist's goal "is to ascertain the nature and number of the mental elements. He takes up mental experience, bit by bit, dividing and subdividing, until the division can go no further. When that point is reached, he has found a conscious element" (Titchener, 1896/1899, p. 16). Titchener's system was never widely popular in America, but after he died, his best-known student, psychologist/historian E. G. Boring (Chapter 1 Close-Up), could make the somewhat inflated but valid claim that

> ... The death of no other psychologist could so alter the psychological picture in America. Not only was he unique among American psychologists as a personality and in his scientific attitude, but he was a cardinal point in the national systematic orientation. The clear-cut opposition between behaviorism and its allies, on the one hand, and something else, on the other, remains clear only when the opposition is between behaviorism and Titchener, mental tests and Titchener, or applied psychology and Titchener. His death thus, in a sense, creates a classificatory chaos in American systematic psychology. (Boring, 1927/1961, p. 246)

From Oxford to Leipzig to Cornell

Such a position of prominence in American psychology was a long journey from relatively humble beginnings in southern England. Edward Bradford Titchener (1867–1927) was born in Chicester, an hour's drive southwest of London and a few miles from the English Channel. His early years were a bit unsettling—his father, only marginally capable in business, died when Titchener was 13 and the adolescent was raised mainly by his paternal grandfather. Titchener's grandfather, a lawyer and stereotypical British country "gentleman," gave Titchener the set of attitudes and values that he never lost. Even after residing in America for many years, Titchener never stopped living according to the strict code of behavior of a proper upper middle-class English gentleman (Leys & Evans, 1990).

Young Titchener was an industrious and talented student, good enough to win scholarships to attend Malvern, one of England's better "public" schools, and then Brasenose College of Oxford University.[1] Titchener remained at Oxford from 1885 to 1890, where he excelled in the classics and philosophy. He also became fascinated with evolutionary biology, Darwinism, and through the acquaintance of George Romanes, comparative psychology. Recognizing that his background in science was weak, he spent most of his final year at Oxford in the physiology laboratory of John Scott Burdon-Sanderson. In that setting, Titchener showed himself to be just the opposite of William James in at least one respect—he discovered that he loved the precisely detailed work of the laboratory. For the rest of his life, he judged the quality of his peers by their standing as "laboratory men," which accounts for his derogatory comments

about Hall (refer to Chapter 6, p. 159) and his paradoxically close friendship with John Watson (Chapter 10). Watson derided Titchener's structuralism and Titchener disliked everything about Watson's behaviorism, but Watson was a true laboratory scientist in Titchener's eyes and that was sufficient grounds for respect and friendship. After first meeting Watson, Titchener wrote to a colleague: "I think that he has a big career, and I like him very much personally" (cited in Larson & Sullivan, 1965, p. 340).

While at Oxford, Titchener learned of the new laboratory approach to "physiological" psychology that was developing at Leipzig. Fluent in German and enamored of Germanic culture, Titchener applied to and was accepted for study in Wundt's new laboratory, which was only 11 years old at the time. There he encountered a group of like-minded laboratory devotees, including Oswald Külpe (Chapter 4), who was Wundt's assistant at the time (i.e., in charge of the day-to-day operation of the lab), and several Americans. Titchener completed a doctorate with Wundt in just two years and returned to Oxford to teach a summer course in biology. He hoped to remain at Oxford or move to Cambridge, but neither school seemed interested in the new psychology—the British empiricist/associationist philosophical tradition had too strong a hold and when an attempt was made to create a psychophysics laboratory in 1877, the Cambridge Senate rejected the proposal on the grounds that such a laboratory "would insult religion by putting the human soul on a pair of scales" (quoted in Farr, 1983). Fate intervened on Titchener's behalf, however, in the form of an offer to cross the Atlantic and teach at Cornell University. Titchener was recommended to Cornell's president by Frank Angell, one of the American psychologists befriended by Titchener at Leipzig. Angell had created a small lab at Cornell on his return from Leipzig in 1891, but was now leaving for the just-created Stanford University in California. Angell recommended his British friend as his replacement, the offer was made, and Titchener accepted.

Cornell University, founded in 1868 in Ithaca, sits high on a hill overlooking the southern end of Lake Cayuga, in New York State's beautiful Finger

---

[1] In England, the term "public school" actually refers to a highly select and very expensive private high school. Malvern was not among the top tier of public schools like Eton, Harrow, or Rugby, but it had a solid academic reputation. Only a small percentage of British schoolchildren attend public schools, but the majority of students at England's prestigious universities, Oxford and Cambridge (sometimes referred to collectively as Oxbridge) come from the public schools. Oxbridge graduates thus represent a small elite group, mostly male, of the British upper middle class. Brasenose is one of several independent colleges that constitute Oxford University.

Lakes region. In 1892, it was in the middle of nowhere, barely accessible by the occasional train. Even today, residents refer to their town as "centrally isolated." If you can imagine finishing your education and deciding to take a job somewhere in a remote area of Australia, then you have some idea of what the decision must have been like for the young Britisher with his new doctorate. Yet he took the risk, arrived in 1892, and never left.[2] Over the years, "Titchenerian psychology," "structuralism," and "the Cornell school of psychology" became interchangeable terms.

Promoting Experimental Psychology at Cornell

Titchener (Figure 7.1) moved quickly upon his arrival at Cornell, expanding the laboratory, attracting students, and starting his research program—by the turn of the century, he and his students had published more than 60 research articles (Boring, 1927/1961). To ensure a forum for the research from the Cornell laboratory, he signed on with Hall in 1895 as editor of the *American Journal of Psychology*, enabling him to control one-third of the journal's pages (Hall and Sanford, the other editors, controlled the remaining two-thirds). In addition, Titchener spread the word about German psychology by translating books by Wundt and Külpe into English, and he began producing texts of his own. His *Outline of Psychology*, first published in 1896, went through several revisions and was rewritten and expanded as *A Textbook of Psychology* in 1909. It was the clearest overall statement of his structuralist system. He also wrote a simplified *Primer of Psychology* in 1896, later revising it as *A Beginner's Psychology*. By 1900, Titchener was firmly established as a major player on the American psychological scene. His status was confirmed when he published "the Manuals."

FIGURE 7.1 E. B. Titchener of Cornell, with ever-present cigar, from Popplestone and McPherson (1994).

The Manuals

In German laboratories, students learned laboratory procedures on their own, by participating in and running their own studies and by observing and questioning their more experienced peers, but American universities developed what came to be known as **drill courses**. Students in these courses did not produce original research but would repeat the classic studies, learn how to set up and work the "brass instruments," and in general become acclimated to the laboratory. As laboratory psychology expanded, these drill courses proliferated and even reached into the undergraduate level. Although some laboratory instructors were adequately trained, either in Germany or in one of the new American laboratories, many were not so knowledgeable about the new psychology. Thus, a need developed for a text that could explain how to train students in basic laboratory procedures. Edmund Sanford of Clark wrote the

---

[2] Titchener initially thought he would go to Cornell for a few years, and then return to Oxford when it came to its senses about laboratory psychology. Oxford didn't, and Titchener never returned to England, even to visit home. He later considered offers from Clark University and Harvard, but turned down both.

first one in the early 1890s, and it started the process of standardizing laboratory instruction in the drill course (Goodwin, 1987). Titchener recognized the value of his close friend's manual, but he also knew that it was just a beginning and that it had some weaknesses. For instance, Sanford's book was not always clear about how the instructor should proceed in the laboratory, seeming to take for granted more expertise than many instructors possessed. To remedy the problem, Titchener set to work on his own manuals and published them under the title of *Experimental Psychology: A Manual of Laboratory Practice*. They became his best-known work, serving for years as the guide into the complexities of laboratory investigation.

The Manuals, as they came to be known, were published in two volumes, in 1901 and 1905, each containing separate texts for students and instructors. Because of Titchener's concern that teachers might need to have procedures worked out step by step, the instructor manuals for both volumes were almost twice the length of the student manuals. The 1901 volume was subtitled "Qualitative Experiments" and it included experiments on basic sensory, perceptual, and affective processes. "Quantitative Experiments" filled the 1905 volume; these dealt mainly with psychophysics and reaction time procedures.

Students in drill courses worked in pairs, alternating between the roles of experimenter and **observer**, the latter being the person we would call the research participant today. Observers were so-called because while they were participating in the experiment, they would be observing their own mental processes and would give a description of these processes at the close of the experiment. This introspective procedure will be described more fully later in the chapter.

In the qualitative experiments, observers would experience some sensory, perceptual, or affective event, give an introspective account of it, and then answer some specific questions about it in their notebooks. For example, olfactory sensations were studied with the use of the double olfactometer sketched in Figure 7.2. The two thin glass tubes were bent at a 40° angle for insertion into the nostrils. Over their other ends were fitted slightly larger enclosed glass cylinders holding various odorous substances. These

FIGURE 7.2 Sketch of an olfactometer, from Titchener's manual of qualitative experiments.

cylinders could be moved back and forth over the narrow tubes to vary the intensity of the smell. Titchener cautioned that the middle partition must be made of an odorless wood—he suggested "cherry wood, well-aired and sunned" (Titchener, 1901, pt. 1, pp. 79–80). In a typical experiment, observers smelled pairs of substances (e.g., iodine, beeswax, various herbs) with differing degrees of intensity, described the experience introspectively, and responded in their notebooks to questions about "compensation" (did one smell overwhelm the other?) and "smell mixture" (did the smells mix to form a new odor?).

As is clear from the label, the quantitative experiments involved numerical data, such as stimulus intensities identified as just noticeably different in psychophysics experiments or times to respond in reaction time experiments. Figure 7.3 shows detailed sketches of two different ways of responding in a reaction time experiment. The most common device was an ordinary telegraph key (7.3a); it would be held down, and then released when the observer detected a stimulus. The right hand of the observer in Figure 4.5 (p. 96) is depressing this type of key. The second device (7.3b) is a lip key, to be used in voice reaction time experiments. It is probably the same one shown in the Clark photo in Chapter 6 (Figure 6.5b, p. 163). The right side of the key would be inserted into the closed mouth, and when observers opened their mouths to respond to a stimulus, the contacts separated from each other, breaking a circuit and stopping a clock.

(a)

(b)

FIGURE 7.3 Reaction time apparatus: (a) a telegraph key; (b) a lip key. From Titchener's manual of quantitative experiments.

TABLE 7.1 How to Fail in Laboratory Psychology

In the Instructor's Manual for the Qualitative Experiments (1901, pp. xxvii–xxviii), Titchener described a program on how to fail that he routinely gave to students at the start of the drill course. He obviously hoped for students to avoid each point and he told instructors that students wouldn't take offense at the list as long as it was presented "tactfully and good-naturedly." In Titchener's words, here are some ways to fail in lab:

- Do not accept any general explanation, under any circumstances. Cherish the belief that your mind is different, in its ways of working, from all other minds.
- Call upon the Instructor at the slightest provocation. If he is busy, stroll about the laboratory until he can attend to you. Do not hesitate to offer advice to other students, who are already at work.
- Tell the Instructor that the science is very young, and that what holds of one mind does not necessarily hold of another. Support your statement by anecdotes.
- Work as noisily as possible. Converse with your partner, in the pauses of the experiment, upon current politics or athletic records.
- Explain when you enter the laboratory, that you have long been interested in experimental psychology. ... Describe the telepathic experiences or accounts that aroused your interest.
- Make it a rule always to be a quarter of an hour late for the laboratory exercises. In this way you throw the drudgery of preliminary work upon your partner, while you can still take credit to yourself for the regularity of your class attendance.

Titchener's system of psychology faded rapidly after his death, but his encyclopedic manuals provided a lasting contribution to laboratory psychology. They remained in use well into the 1930s and trained several generations of experimental psychologists. Even today, they can provide excellent demonstrations of sensory and perceptual phenomena. One final aspect of their timelessness is illustrated in Table 7.1. Titchener's half-serious recommendations to students about "how to fail" the drill course might remind you of some of your student friends.

The Experimentalists

Titchener was one of the charter members of the American Psychological Association and although he was not at Hall's organizational meeting at Clark, he did attend the first annual meeting in the winter of 1892. He quickly became disillusioned with the organization, however, and resigned his membership (he rejoined the organization on two later occasions, only to resign twice more). Part of the problem was personal. Titchener felt like an outsider in an "American" Psychological Association, and the organization violated his strict code of proper behavior when it refused to censure an APA member accused by Titchener (with good cause) of plagiariz-

ing portions of his translation of one of Wundt's books. More important, the organization did not represent Titchener's vision of a true experimental psychology and the format of its meetings did not advance psychology, he believed. In 1895, in a note for the *American Journal of Psychology*, he complained that the presentations of research were "hardly possible to follow intelligently ... when method and results are thrown in lecture form and the lecture reduced to a compass of twenty minutes" (Titchener, 1895, p. 448). Instead, he suggested that "the meetings [be] allowed to take the form of a conversazione, the apparatus employed shown in their working, and the results made to speak for themselves in charts and diagrams arranged near the apparatus" (p. 448).

By 1904, Titchener was ready to correct the problem himself, and he proposed the creation of an informal "club" of experimental psychologists. He did not intend to rival the APA, but to provide a better means for researchers to present their work to peers. Thus was born a group that came to be known as the Experimentalists (Boring, 1967; Goodwin, 1985). They met for two or three days every spring, rotating from one laboratory to another. They discussed research in progress, tinkered with apparatus, and in general tried to keep the spirit of pure laboratory psychology alive. No formal papers were allowed and published descriptions of the meetings were discouraged. Titchener generally dominated the group; for instance, hosts would often check with him on whom to invite. Figure 7.4 shows a group photo taken at the 1916 meeting at Princeton.

Those invited to the spring meetings included laboratory directors and other researchers deemed satisfactory by Titchener. That is, they had to be committed to the laboratory, but it wasn't necessary that they be strict followers of Titchenerian structuralism. Also, to help ensure continuation of the ideal of a "pure" psychological science, talented graduate students often accompanied their mentors

to meetings. The group was small but influential beyond its size. Correspondence among its members frequently resulted in the placement of experimentalist colleagues or their students in good academic positions.

One other important feature of the group was gender—all the Experimentalists were men. Part of the reason was the pervasive sexism described in the previous chapter. In Titchener's mind, however, the prohibition followed from his code of gentlemanly conduct. His desire was to have something like an English club, where men could converse freely on any subject without being concerned about behaving "properly" in the presence of women. This meant being able to argue vociferously about some issue without either party taking offense; Titchener and other males of his time took it for granted that women would take such arguments personally (i.e., they would be too emotional). The club atmosphere also included smoking, and the social mores of the day usually excluded women from rooms where men smoked. These sentiments were summed up in a letter from Sanford to Titchener just before the group was formed. Probably thinking of Calkins, Washburn, and Ladd-Franklin (Chapter 6), he point-

FIGURE 7.4 Titchener's Experimentalists (many with cigars) at Princeton in 1916, from Popplestone and McPherson (1994).

ed out that several women "on scientific grounds have full right to be there and might feel hurt (in a general impersonal way) if women are not asked. On the other hand they would undoubtedly interfere with the smoking and to a certain extent with the general freedom of a purely masculine assembly" (cited in Furumoto, 1988, p. 104). Similarly, Lightner Witmer of the University of Pennsylvania (Chapter 12) wrote to Titchener that it would be impossible to have "an informal meeting of men and women. ... We want a small vigorous association where we can speak our minds with perfect freedom. ... I think that the presence of women ... adds greatly to this danger [of mistaking argument for attack], owing to the personal attitude which they usually take even in scientific discussions" (cited in Furumoto, 1988, p. 105).

In defense of the charge that Titchener was anti-female, it has been pointed out that about one-half of his graduate students were female, his first doctoral student was Margaret Washburn, and on at least one occasion he argued for the hiring of a particular woman psychologist at Cornell over the objections of the administration (Leys & Evans, 1990). On the other hand, part of the reason for there being women in Titchener's laboratory was institutional—Cornell for years was about the only place for a woman to go in order to be an "official" student. At any rate, the exclusion of women from Titchener's club created a barrier to advancement and contributed to their difficulty in securing major academic positions. Even after the group reorganized following Titchener's death and technically included women, few were ever nominated for membership (Furumoto, 1988).[3]

Titchener's Structuralist System

At the opening of the chapter, I pointed out that for Titchener, a prime goal for psychology was to analyze human consciousness into its basic elements or structural components. Hence, Titchener's psycholo-

gy was the science of the structure of the human mind, and a primary purpose of research was to determine this structure through experimental research. Analysis was not the sole purpose, however. Psychology must also understand the process of *synthesis*, how the mental elements combine and connect into more complex phenomena. In Titchener's words, the experimentalist "learns to formulate the laws of connection of the elementary mental processes. If sensations of tone occur together, they blend or fuse; if sensations of colour occur side by side, they enhance one another: and all this takes place in a perfectly regular way, so that we can write out laws of tonal fusion and laws of colour contrast" (Titchener, 1909, pp. 37–38). In addition to the goals of analysis and synthesis, both of which resulted in detailed descriptions of mental phenomena, Titchener argued that a third goal for psychology was explanation, by which he meant an understanding of how the nervous system produced the various sensory, perceptual, and cognitive phenomena that interested him. Very little of his research focused on this third goal.

To accomplish a thorough description of the analysis and synthesis of mental phenomena, Titchener developed a program of research that involved the kinds of qualitative and quantitative research described in the Manuals. To get a good idea of the topics that Titchener considered essential in an introductory course, examine Table 7.2, which summarizes the chapter organization for his *Text-book of Psychology*, a text you might have used had you taken Titchener's introductory psychology course in 1909. As you can see, the topics of sensation and perception dominated the book. There is very little about the nervous system in it, but a great deal concerning the descriptive goals of analysis and synthesis. Note that fully one-third of the book is devoted to describing basic sensory processes.

Titchener accompanied these research topics with a methodology that is often associated with his name—introspection. As you recall from Chapter 4, introspection was an important procedure in the Leipzig laboratory, but Wundt called it *internal perception* and limited it to simple verbal reports of the results of psychophysics ("this weight is heavier

---

[3] The noted physiological psychologist Donald Hebb resigned from the Society in 1953, mainly on the grounds that it seemed more like an exclusionary social club than a true honor society. His resignation letter included a handwritten note asking "Why no women? Charter admits them" (quoted in Glickman, 1996, p. 243).

TABLE 7.2 The Contents of Titchener's
Text-Book of Psychology

Chapter Heading	No. of Pages	Percent
Subject-Matter, Method and Problem of Psychology	43	8
Sensation, subdivided into:	179	33
vision		
audition		
smell		
taste		
cutaneous senses		
kinesthetic senses		
other organic sensations		
synaesthesia		
the intensity of sensation (psychophysics)		
Affection	39	7
Attention	38	7
Perception, subdivided into:	71	13
spatial perceptions		
temporal perceptions		
qualitative perceptions		
composite perceptions		
the psychology of perception		
Association	22	4
Memory and Imagination	31	6
Action	42	8
Emotion	33	6
Thought	43	8
Conclusion— The Status of Psychology	3	<1

conscious experience and reflect on it at the same time. To deal with the problem, he suggested three solutions. The first was to rely on memory, delaying the introspective "observation until the process to be described has run its course, and then to call it back and describe it from memory. Introspection thus becomes retrospection; introspective examination becomes post mortem examination" (Titchener, 1909, p. 22). Titchener's second suggestion for reducing the memory load was to break the experience into stages, using the fractionation method associated with Külpe's laboratory (Chapter 4). His third, and most important technique, was to acquire what he called the **introspective habit**:

> ... [T]he practiced observer gets into an introspective habit, has the introspective attitude ingrained in his system; so that it is possible for him, not only to take mental notes while the observation is in progress, without interfering with consciousness, but even to jot down written notes, as the histologist does while his eye is still held to the ocular of the microscope. (p. 23)

This is an important passage, for it is the main reason why Titchener insisted that his observers had to be highly trained. In effect, they were to become introspecting machines, behaving so automatically that problems of memory and any biasing influences would presumably disappear. Training was also important to avoid what Titchener referred to as the **stimulus error**. This was a tendency to report events by describing the stimuli presented rather than the conscious experiences resulting from those stimuli. For instance, when observing a tree, a proper introspective description would include statements about the sensory elements present: shapes, colors, textures, and movement, along with the affective dimensions of pleasantness/unpleasantness and any accompanying images that came to mind. To commit the stimulus error would be to report simply that you were observing a large "tree." The "introspective attitude" is difficult for us to grasp today, because this type of laboratory training no longer exists. This chapter's Close-Up should give you some insight into what the introspective habit was like, however.

than this other one") and other sensory studies. Wundt's student (and Titchener's friend) Oswald Külpe, however, elaborated the procedure into **systematic experimental introspection**, in which observers would give detailed reports of the conscious events occurring while completing some task (e.g., word association). It was this latter approach that was taken by Titchener and he developed it to a high level of sophistication.

Titchener was well aware of the fundamental problem of introspection—it is impossible to have a

CLOSE-UP:
The Introspective Attitude

The absence of Titchenerian introspection in contemporary psychology makes it difficult for us to grasp what an introspective description was really like. One way to find out is to read articles summarizing this kind of research, because they often include verbatim introspective accounts. For example, consider the following study on attention. It was the doctoral thesis of Karl Dallenbach, one of Titchener's students, and later a colleague on the Cornell faculty. Using procedures similar to those found in modern research on attention, Dallenbach (1913) was interested in what happens to consciousness when attention is overloaded. One of his methods was to have observers listen to two metronomes set at different speeds and try to count the number of beats occurring between coincident beats. At the same time, they were to complete some mental task, such as continually adding numbers, singing, or saying the alphabet backwards. Each "experiment" lasted 90 seconds. Here's how one observer reported the experience. Note the presence of all the basic Titchenerian elements described in the next section of the chapter—sensations, images, and affect.

> ... The sounds of the metronomes, as a series of discontinuous clicks, were clear in consciousness only four or five times during the experiment, and they were especially bothersome at first. They were accompanied by strain sensations and unpleasantness. The rest of the experiment my attention was on the adding, which was composed of auditory images of the numbers, sometimes on a dark grey scale which was directly ahead and about three feet in front of me. This was accompanied by kinaesthesis of eyes and strains in chest and arms. When these processes were clear in consciousness the sounds of the metronomes were very vague or obscure. (Dallenbach, 1913, p. 467)

Reading articles full of introspective accounts like this can be revealing, but they tend to be long, repetitive, and boring enough to make one understand why psychologists eventually abandoned the method. A more interesting way to gain insight into the introspective attitude is to read the letters that experimental psychologists wrote to each other during this era (Goodwin, 1991). Introspective thinking was so ingrained that their correspondence is liberally sprinkled with informal introspections relating to their experiences. After returning from a holiday in New Hampshire, for instance, Edmund Sanford wrote to Titchener about his fear of thunderstorms. He wrote that he had:

> ... observed enough this summer to find that I cannot find anything in it but organic and other sensations unpleasantly colored and, on the cognitive side, a cramp of apperception towards a small group of ideas related to the thing dreaded with certain resultants in instinctive act and thought. ... When the storm became imminent there would be cardiac and visceral symptoms to describe, etc. etc.—though when the thing was actually present these were as a general thing not so marked as in anticipation—i.e. as the storm approached. (Sanford, 1910)

A more dramatic example of how introspection was never far from the thoughts of turn-of-the-century psychologists comes from an 1893 letter from Lightner Witmer of the University of Pennsylvania to Hugo Münsterberg of Harvard. Witmer had been studying the psychology of pain firsthand in a rather unusual manner:

> ... I let a horse throw me from his back, allowing me to drop on my shoulder and head. I showed a beautiful case of loss of consciousness before the act ... I not only do not remember mounting and the horse running, but I forgot almost everything that happened ... [F]rom the time I got up in the morning till I regained complete consciousness, ... I can form no continuous series of events. My head was bad for a while but is all right now, but my arm has served the purpose of quite a number of experiments as it still continues quite painful at times. ... The psychological side of my afflictions will form the basis of at least three lectures next fall. (Witmer, 1893)

The Structural Elements of Conscious Experience

On the basis of his introspective analyses, Titchener identified three types of elementary mental processes: sensations, images, and affections. Sensations were the basic elements of the more complex process of perception, images were the elementary components of ideas, and affections (feelings) were the elements of our emotions. These basic elements could not be reduced further, but they did have various features or **attributes**. All sensations, for instance, had the attributes of quality, intensity, duration, and clearness. Quality is what distinguishes one sensation from another: red from green, cold from warm, a high-pitched tone from a low-pitched tone. Intensity refers to the strength of the stimulus, decibel level for example. Duration is self-evident—all sensations last for some measurable period of time. And clearness "is the attribute which gives a sensation its place in a consciousness: the clearer sensation is dominant, independent, outstanding, the less clear sensation is subordinate, undistinguished in the background of consciousness" (Titchener, 1909, p. 53). According to Titchener, attention essentially reduced to this attribute of sensory clearness.

Images have the same four attributes, according to Titchener, but compared with sensations, the qualities are "relatively pale, faded, washed out, misty"

(1909, p. 198).[4] In addition, he argued that the intensity and duration of images were "markedly less" (p. 198) than sensations. Affective states, the core of our emotional life, differ from sensations and images in two important ways. First, although there are literally thousands of different sensorial and imaginal qualities, Titchener believed that affects have only two fundamental qualities—pleasantness and unpleasantness. Second, affects have the attributes of quality, intensity, and duration, but they lack clearness. If we want to experience pleasure at a concert, for example, we must attend to the sensory elements (i.e., the music), not to the feeling of pleasure itself; if we focus on the feeling, the pleasure disappears. Titchener rejected the James-Lange theory of emotion, on the grounds that he believed that by equating emotions with bodily reaction, James was reducing affect to sensation (Heidbreder, 1933). For Titchener, on the other hand, pleasantness and unpleasantness could not be reduced to sensory qualities.

---

[4] Recall from Chapter 4 that Wundt identified two elements: sensations and affections. He believed, like Hume, that images were merely faint copies of sensations and ultimately reducible to them. Titchener was clearly thinking along similar lines, and even expressed some uncertainty about calling them separate elements, but nonetheless felt that sensations and images were sufficiently distinct to justify separate elementary status, at least at this stage of his thinking (Hindeland, 1971).

Titchener's structuralism continued to evolve over the years, and in the 1920s he moved away from an emphasis on elements and developed a more phenomenological model that described sensory processes in terms of dimensions. Thus, sensation shifted "from an observable entity to a classificatory term" (Evans, 1972, p. 172). Titchener also moved away from the idea that affect was a separate element after one of his students completed a dissertation that seemed to reduce the affective qualities of pleasantness and unpleasantness to the sensations of "bright pressure" and "dull pressure," respectively (Henle, 1974). Titchener was working on a major revision of his system along these lines, but his productivity dropped during the 1920s, possibly showing the early effects of the brain tumor that would kill him in 1927, and the final system was never completed. Some introductory chapters were published posthumously (1929) as *Systematic Psychology: Prolegomena*.

Evaluating Titchener's Contributions to Psychology

Psychology for Titchener was a pure laboratory science aimed at discovering the basic structure of human consciousness. Systematic experimental introspection was its prime method and because this form of introspection required extensive training, it was limited to highly motivated adult observers. Thus, according to Titchener, psychology was the science of the "generalized adult mind." Two immediate consequences of this rather limited definition of the field were that (a) Titchener was uninterested in individual differences between one mind and another and (b) he excluded from his definition of psychology all research using children, animals, and the insane—they could never introspect properly. Also, because the discipline was to retain the purity of the laboratory, Titchener omitted such applied concerns as industrial and educational psychology from his definition of the field. Although his vision of psychology was therefore extremely narrow, it also led directly to his major lasting contribution— the promotion of an experimental psychology that featured the tight controls found in the laboratory. Although his particular introspective methodology

has passed from the scene, his insistence on the value of basic laboratory research as the way to provide the foundation for psychological knowledge created a place for the laboratory in all colleges and universities with programs in psychology. As one historian put it, Titchener was "responsible for making psychology scientific—for setting psychology up in the laboratory and reaching his conclusions through experiment, under controlled conditions" (Hindeland, 1971, p. 28).

On the other hand, Titchener's psychology became as isolated from American psychology as Ithaca was from other centers of learning. Structuralism ultimately failed as a system, primarily because of the shortcomings of introspection as a method, but also because of Titchener's uncompromising insistence that his way was the only way. Despite Titchener's belief that highly trained observers gained the "introspective habit," thereby avoiding bias and allowing for replication of experiments to occur, it quickly became apparent that serious problems existed with the method. The difficulty is illustrated in several controversies that surrounded Titchener. One was the imageless thought problem, described in Chapter 4 (pp. 111). As you recall, introspectors in Külpe's lab at Würzburg discovered situations in which conscious thoughts occurred in the absence of images. In a psychophysics weight-judging study, for instance, images occurred at various points in the process, but not at the exact moment of judgment. The judgment itself seemed to be an "imageless" thought. This was a direct threat to Titchener's system, which held as dogma that images were the underlying elements of *all* ideas. To counter the assault, Titchener dismissed the Würzburg outcome as a failure of experimental control and found that in *his* laboratory, observers were indeed able to detect images at all stages of the weight-judging experiment. Because of the inherently subjective nature of introspection, however, there was no independent means of determining who was right. It began to appear that introspection could not produce objective data.

A second controversy, concerning reaction time, produced a similar outcome—data congenial to Titchener's view from the Cornell laboratory, but a different result elsewhere. This time a researcher at Princeton, James Mark Baldwin (1861–1934), had uncovered what he believed were individual differences in the simple reaction experiment. His sin, in Titchener's view, was to use naive (i.e., untrained) observers. Such individual differences didn't occur at Cornell, of course, where introspectors were "properly trained." The details of this controversy, including the name calling, can be found in an article by Krantz (1969), but for our purposes the controversy was another example of introspection's fundamental flaw.

Thus, psychologists began to suspect that the extensive training insisted on by Titchener produced bias rather than eliminated it—the training began to look like indoctrination. In the paper that launched behaviorism (Chapter 10's Original Source Excerpt), John Watson summarized introspection's objectivity problem:

> ... Take the case of sensation. A sensation is defined in terms of its attributes. One psychologist will state with readiness that the attributes of a visual sensation are *quality*, *extension*, *duration*, and *intensity*. Another will add *clearness*. Still another that of *order*. I doubt if any one psychologist can draw up a set of statements describing what he means by sensation which will be agreed to by three other psychologists of different training. ... I firmly believe that two hundred years from now, unless the introspective method is discarded, psychology will still be divided on the question as to whether auditory sensations have the quality of "extension," whether intensity is an attribute which can be applied to color, whether there is a difference in "texture" between image and sensation and upon many hundreds of others of like character. (Watson, 1913, p. 164, italics in the original)

The failure of introspection signaled the ultimate demise of structuralism, but the force of Titchener's personality provided one final contribution to psychology. As suggested by Boring's obituary at the start of this chapter, Titchener's death deprived American psychology of a focal point of opposition. Titchener, who lectured in his academic gown and said that the attire conferred on him the right to be dogmatic, insisted on the validity of introspective psychology and was a persistent and articulate critic of those who deviated from it. By so doing, he made it necessary for opponents to be intelligible about their own systems. If schools of thought in psychology gain momentum by virtue of their opposition to some established force, then Titchener's structuralism served the valuable purpose of giving movements such as functionalism and behaviorism a clear target.

AMERICA'S PSYCHOLOGY: FUNCTIONALISM

Titchener might not have been interested in applied psychology and individual differences, or in studying animals, children, or the insane, but practically every other psychologist in America was. Part of the reason for this derives from the historical context of late nineteenth-century America. During the final three decades of the century, following the Civil War, the United States entered a period of sustained growth. It was a time of reconstruction in the South, westward expansion, railroad building, technological innovation (e.g., telephone, typewriter), industrialization on a massive scale, and the amassing of great wealth by Gilded Age entrepreneurs with names like Rockefeller, Vanderbilt, Morgan, Carnegie, and Mellon. Of course, it was also a time when Native American populations were uprooted from their land and decimated, workers endured long hours and unsafe working conditions for pitiful wages, women and minorities were considered mentally inferior to white males, and an enormous gap developed between the very few rich and the very many poor. Nonetheless, most (white, male) Americans came to develop a concept of their national character that placed a high value on taking individual responsibility for success or failure, making something of oneself regardless of one's background, competing and winning in the marketplace, and always thinking of the usefulness or practical value of objects and ideas.

This emerging prototype of American pragmatic individuality was consistent with evolutionary thinking, although most Americans would have strongly denied that they were Darwinians. Nonetheless, Americans were attracted by the views of the British popularizer of evolution, Herbert Spencer (1820–1903), who promoted a brand of evolution congenial to Americans on the "winning" side of things. It was Spencer, not Darwin, who invented the phrase "survival of the fittest," but Spencer's idea of fitness was not the same as Darwin's.[5] Whereas any species attribute that furthered the cause of survival (e.g., camouflage) would constitute fitness for Darwin, Spencer's use of the term implied that survivors were winners of fierce battles for limited resources. As Spencer used the phrase, survival of the fittest blended with and contributed to the developing American character of the nineteenth century. Spencer's system has come to be known as **social Darwinism**.

Social Darwinists believed that evolutionary forces were natural and inevitable and that any attempt on the part of humans to alter these forces was misdirected and harmful. Evolution must be left unchecked, Spencer argued, an attitude that had direct implications for the social, political, and economic contexts of the time. It meant, for example, that government should not interfere with business practices—losers in business failed simply because they weren't "fit." Those who accumulated enormous wealth, on the other hand, should not in any way be regulated or penalized (e.g., taxed)—their wealth was simply a sign of their fitness. Government also should not provide services to the poor—their poverty was obviously the outcome of a lack of fitness. If supported by the government, their lack of fitness would spread as they produced similarly unfit children. Social Darwinists took the notion "if fit, therefore successful," and made the logically flawed reversal "if successful, therefore fit." Thus, evolutionary fitness became a means of rationalizing the huge gap between rich and poor and

of maintaining a belief in the superiority of the white male over all others (e.g., women, blacks, Native Americans). Most American psychologists, especially those interested in mental testing (see Chapter 8), were generally agreeable to social Darwinism.

The evolutionary thinking that psychologists found congenial led naturally to interests in studying individual differences, animal behavior, development, and abnormal behavior, and to the search for practical applications of psychological principles. This trend toward a more diverse psychology than Titchener's structuralism was clear from the work of James and Hall (Chapter 6), both of whom were influenced by Darwin and made important contributions before Titchener arrived from Leipzig. The movement came to be called **functionalism**, and while it was widespread enough to be called "America's psychology," it is normally associated with two schools, Chicago and Columbia. The remainder of the chapter will describe the work of several psychologists at these two schools. Chapter 8 will elaborate on the theme of application, a central component of functionalist thinking.

The Chicago Functionalists

In May of 1889, John D. Rockefeller, pockets bulging with Standard Oil profits, donated an initial $600,000 to establish a Baptist university, contingent on the Baptists contributing an additional $400,000 (Ryan, 1939). It would be located in Chicago, a city already developing the reputation that would lead the poet Carl Sandburg to call it the "City of the Big Shoulders." Nearly destroyed by the famous fire of 1871 that burned 1688 acres, consumed buildings valued at $192 million, and bankrupted 64 different insurance companies (Cashman, 1993), Chicago was one of America's fastest growing cities in the late 1800s. Its hundreds of acres of cattle and hog pens, slaughterhouses, and packinghouses made it the center of the beef and pork industry, and its location made it a natural hub for railroads and a key location for industries (e.g., lumber, steel, agriculture) relying on transportation via rail and Great Lakes steamers. The new university was a bold enterprise, far removed from the East Coast academic community, with its success entrusted to President William Rainey Harper, a biblical scholar who had

[5] Another important difference between the men was that Darwin was scientifically conservative, unwilling to speculate in the absence of a large database. As discussed in Chapter 5, this unwillingness to go far beyond the data was one reason for his delay in publishing the *Origin of Species*. Spencer, on the other hand, did not hesitate to speculate far beyond available evidence. It was once said of Spencer that his "idea of a tragedy was a deduction killed by a fact" (cited in Boakes, 1984, p. 10).

earned a doctorate from Yale at age 18. Harper's main challenge was to hire a quality faculty, a task made easier by the troubles at Clark University. As you recall from the previous chapter, Harper filled a number of his faculty positions with disgruntled Clark University faculty and graduate students when financial problems and Hall's capriciousness as president led them to look for greener pastures.

The University of Chicago opened in 1892 and quickly became a leader in higher education, despite its remoteness from the East. It included separate colleges of liberal arts, practical arts, literature, and science, as well as a graduate school and a school of divinity. It began with a large staff of 120 faculty, and within three years they were teaching 534 graduate students, more than Johns Hopkins and Clark combined (Ryan, 1939).

Two years after the opening, Harper hired a young instructor from the University of Michigan to chair the philosophy department at Chicago. Although he would become better known for his philosophical writings on democracy and his innovative approach to education, John Dewey also wrote a paper that is often considered the official starting point for functionalism in America.

John Dewey (1859–1952): The Reflex Arc

John Dewey was born in Burlington, a small city in western Vermont that borders on Lake Champlain. There he was raised in a setting that shaped in him the traditional Yankee values of hard work, respect for others, thrift, simplicity, and a love of democracy. After completing high school at age 15, Dewey enrolled in the nearby University of Vermont, whose eight faculty members taught just a few dozen students; along with 16 peers, Dewey graduated in 1879 (Barone, 1996). While at Vermont, he studied the traditional curriculum of the classics and humanities, but he also sampled evolutionary thinking by studying the new sciences of geology and zoology.

After graduating, Dewey taught high school for several years, and then decided to continue his education. Johns Hopkins was the rising star in academia, and Dewey enrolled there to study philosophy in 1882. The new psychology was included in the Hopkins philosophy curriculum, so Dewey's schedule included work in G. Stanley Hall's brand new laboratory. After earning his doctorate in philosophy in 1884, Dewey's next stop was Michigan. There he taught both philosophy and psychology, working his notes into a text, *Psychology*, in 1886. The book was used on numerous campuses for several years and was the standard text at Michigan for a decade (Raphelson, 1973), but met its demise upon the 1890 publication of William James's instant classic. Dewey himself readily acknowledged *The Principles of Psychology* to be superior to his own effort.

As mentioned earlier, Harper hired Dewey to direct Chicago's philosophy program in 1894. His new department included traditional philosophy, laboratory psychology, and another area of great interest to Dewey—pedagogy. During his 10 years at Chicago, Dewey established the university as a center of functionalism, partly through recruiting colleagues sympathetic to the movement, but mainly through an article published in 1896 entitled "The Reflex Arc Concept in Psychology." In it, he took issue with the traditional manner of thinking about reflexes. Dating from Bell and Magendie's separation of the reflex into separate sensory and motor pathways (Chapter 3), physiologists thought of the **reflex arc** in terms of three separate elementary components: the stimulus producing sensation, central processing producing an idea, and the act or motor response. Dewey believed that dividing the reflex into these "elements" was artificial, however, resulting in a reflex concept that was "not a comprehensive, or organic unity, but a patchwork of disjointed parts" (Dewey, 1896/1948, p. 356). Instead, Dewey proposed a model of the reflex that substituted a functional for a structural analysis.

The reflex, Dewey argued, is best conceived of as an integrated, coordinated whole that serves the function of adapting the organism to its environment. Also, it is more like a continuous circuit than an "arc," the latter implying distinct starting and ending points. Consider a child reaching for a candle flame, to use Dewey's example. Those using the reflex arc model would analyze the event into a series of stimulus-response elements—seeing the flame, reaching for it, feeling the heat, and withdrawing (S-R-S-R). For Dewey, though, such an analysis oversimplified a complex action. Reaching for something after seeing it, for example, can only make sense in the larger context of the child's learning history: "seeing and grasping have been so often bound together to reinforce each other, to help each other out, that each may be considered practically a subordinate member of a bigger coordination" (p. 356). The second part of the event, being seared by the flame and withdrawing the hand, is also part of the larger coordination that produces a learning event; the flame now takes on new meaning for the child. From that point on, seeing a burning candle is "no longer mere seeing; it is the seeing-of-a-light-that-means-pain-when-contact-occurs" (p. 357). Hence, the child has adapted to the environment as a result of experience. Furthermore, the sight of a burning candle now has a specific meaning that differs from the same sight viewed by a different child with different experiences. As will be seen in Chapter 9, the notion that actions result not from a specific stimulus but from a stimulus-as-perceived was central to the German gestalt psychologists. Dewey argued forcefully that psychologists studying human action should not be concerned with microscopic analysis into elements, but with how the act functions to promote the organism's well-being in the struggle to adapt to its ever changing world. That is, Dewey was proposing a change in emphasis about behavior, a shift in thinking from an emphasis on "what?" to a focus on "what for?"

America at the turn of the century was just entering the Progressive Era, a time of sweeping reform and the beginning of a reaction against social Darwinism. It was during this time that business monopolies were being attacked and their leaders were as likely to be called robber barons as heroes of the struggle for existence. Labor unions made significant gains on behalf of workers, the federal government enacted regulations to protect ordinary Americans from a variety of abuses (for instance, child labor, unsanitary conditions in food production industries), and social reformers set out to improve the welfare of those who used to be written off as "unfit." John Dewey fit perfectly into this context, making significant contributions to educational reform and launching the movement that came to be known as **progressive education**.

Dewey had been a schoolteacher for a brief time after graduating from college. He developed a strong dislike for the conventional approach to education, which emphasized rote learning, drill and practice, and strict discipline. Such an atmosphere made the classroom a place to avoid rather than a place to learn. Yet education was the key to an effective democracy, Dewey believed, because it offered everyone an equal opportunity to advance. At a time when public education was growing by leaps and bounds,[6] educational reform was essential. Dewey responded by creating a "Laboratory School" at Chicago in 1896 to study how children learned best in the classroom, and by writing *The School and Society* (1899), which established his reputation as a leading philosopher of education. He also implored psychologists to use their new knowledge of the mind to improve education, using his presidential address to the American Psychological Association in 1899 as a forum (Dewey, 1900). According to Dewey, children learn by interacting with their environment—they learn by doing. Consequently, the school must create an atmosphere that encourages children to explore on their own, to think critically and creatively, and to be actively involved in learning.

Dewey left Chicago for Columbia University in 1904, turning over departmental leadership to James Angell. At Columbia, he made no further contributions to psychology, but he continued to agitate for educational and social reform within the context of his democratic philosophy. He was a strong supporter of teachers' unions, helped found the American Association of University Professors, became a member of the American Civil Liberties Union, and actively campaigned for women's suffrage (Hilgard, 1987). He remained a committed activist for liberal causes well into his eighth decade.

James R. Angell (1869–1949): The Province of Functional Psychology

Like Dewey, James Rowland Angell was born in Burlington, Vermont, the son of the president of the University of Vermont. When his father took the

---

[6] Attending school was compulsory in just six states in 1871, but was virtually universal by 1900. Between 1890 and 1910, the number of students in public schools increased by a factor of four (Cashman, 1993).

same job at the University of Michigan in 1871, the Angells moved to the Midwest and James was raised in the academic environment of Ann Arbor. He went to school at his father's university, studying philosophy, the classics, and learning about natural science via courses in botany. His introduction to psychology came in a course with Dewey, using the professor's new textbook. Angell graduated from Michigan in 1890, and then stayed another year to earn a master's degree in philosophy. During this last year his courses included a seminar with Dewey that used James's new *Principles of Psychology* as the text. As he later recalled, the text "unquestionably affected my thinking for the next 20 years more profoundly than any other" (cited in Raphelson, 1973, p. 120). To experience William James firsthand, Angell went to Cambridge and spent a year under James's tutelage, during which time he attempted some unsuccessful research into psychic phenomena. He then decided to earn a German doctorate. By this time doctoral training in America was as good as if not superior to training in Germany, but there was still a high prestige value to a doctorate from the Continent. That Angell was aware of this status benefit is clear—his cousin Frank, with Leipzig credentials paving the way, had just been lured from Cornell to Stanford by an outstanding offer of $3,000 annually (O'Donnell, 1985).

Angell intended to follow his cousin to Leipzig, but Wundt's laboratory was full, so he studied briefly with Ebbinghaus in Berlin before settling into the University at Halle. There he completed the work for his doctorate, but never finished the final version of it (he was asked to improve the German) after receiving an offer to teach at the University of Minnesota. The salary and the stability of real employment enabled him to marry the woman he had known since his Michigan days, and for the 24-year-old Angell, love and a new job were sufficient to offset the loss of what seemed to be a mere piece of paper. Thus, although he would go on to direct the doctoral projects of several prominent American psychologists, he never quite finished his own.

After a year at Minnesota, Dewey hired the young instructor to be in charge of the psychology portion of the philosophy curriculum and the Angells moved to Chicago in 1894. When Dewey moved on

to Columbia a decade later, psychology became its own department, separate from philosophy, and Angell was made department chair. He moved further toward administration and away from psychology by being named Dean of the Faculty in 1911. He eventually followed in his father's footsteps and became a university president, leading Yale University for most of the 1920s and 1930s before retiring in 1937.

Angell's importance for psychology derives from his work in the period from 1894 to 1911. During this time he contributed valuable research in areas such as reaction time, imagery, and sound

KEY DATE *1906*

This year marked the publication date of James Angell's APA presidential address ("The Province of Functional Psychology") that brought functional psychology into clear focus.

These events also happened:

- The first U.S. Pure Food and Drugs Act was passed, after Upton Sinclair's description of the Chicago stockyards and slaughterhouses in *The Jungle*
- China and Britain agreed to a reduction in the production of opium
- The San Francisco earthquake killed 700 and produced $400 million in property loss
- Teddy Roosevelt visited the Panama Canal, the first trip outside the United States by a president in office
- U.S. troops occupied Cuba, remaining for three years
- The first running of the French Grand Prix motor race occurred
- These people were born:
    Greta Garbo, Swedish film actress
    Dmitri Shostakovich, Russian composer
    Gracie Allen, comedic actor and wife of George Burns
- These people died:
    Henrik Ibsen, Norwegian playwright
    Paul Cezanne, French artist

localization,[7] and he built one of the top two or three departments in the country. He also became the most visible spokesperson for functionalism by writing a popular introductory textbook (Angell, 1904) and by delivering a memorable address after being elected to the presidency of the American Psychological Association in 1906 (Angell, 1907/1948). Dewey's reflex arc paper might have been the foundation paper for functionalist thinking, but it was not a "Here is what functionalism means" type of paper. Angell's was—he called it "The Province of Functional Psychology." In part, it was a response to Titchener's 1898 paper, "The Postulates of a Structural Psychology."

Angell opened the paper with the modest disclaimer that functional psychology was not a dogmatic "school" of psychology,[8] but rather "little more than a point of view, a program, an ambition" (Angell, 1907/1948, p. 439). He then drew a sharp contrast between functional and structural psychologies. Whereas a structuralist is interested in mental contents, the "what?" of conscious experience, Angell stated, the functional psychologist wants to study mental operations, the "how?" and "why?" of consciousness. If the structuralist was asking *what is consciousness?* the functionalist was asking *what is consciousness for?* Furthermore, with a dig at what he considered to be the highly artificial nature of the results from Titchenerian-style research, Angell argued that a minute analysis of some hypothetical "moment of consciousness" fails to capture the importance of consciousness for everyday life:

> ... If you adopt as your material for psychological analysis the isolated "moment of consciousness," it is very easy to become so absorbed in determining its constitution as to be rendered somewhat oblivi-

ous to its artificial character. The most essential quarrel which the functionalist has with structuralism ... arises from this fact and touches the feasibility and worth of the effort to get at mental process as it is under the conditions of actual experience rather than as it appears to a merely post-mortem [introspective] analysis. (p. 441)

Angell then explicitly rejected the analogy between psychology and biology that Titchener had used to argue for the primacy of a structuralist approach. As you recall, Titchener had likened structuralism to anatomy and argued that just as anatomy provides the basis for physiology, so must structuralism precede functionalism. But Angell would have none of it. Anatomy involves material objects that can be manipulated, observed, and measured with some precision, but mental contents are "evanescent" and "fleeting." We can attempt to isolate them, but they are fundamentally different from the materials being studied by anatomists. With the analogy between anatomy and structuralism shown to be faulty, Angell believed the supposed primacy of structuralism over functionalism to be meaningless.

Angell's functionalist approach to consciousness had the same evolutionary flavor found in James. Like James, Angell described the function of consciousness to be in allowing the individual to solve problems and therefore to adapt to novel situations. Near the close of his article, he pointed out the connections between functionalist thinking and the interests of American psychologists. If the psychologist is interested in the functions of consciousness, then it is important to understand how those functions develop, both ontogenetically and phylogenetically. Therefore, the psychologist has legitimate interests in developmental and comparative psychology. Similarly, an interest in failures to adapt leads naturally to the study of abnormal psychology, an interest in how some individuals adapt better than others leads one to study individual differences and develop mental tests to measure those differences, and an interest in how the individual learns to adapt and can be best trained to do so leads to the study of educational psychology and of learning in general. In short, all of the topics valued by American psychologists could be gathered under the umbrella of functionalism. Furthermore, studying these diverse areas

---

[7] Sound localization depends in part on sound waves reaching our ears at slightly different times. Angell, who was deaf in one ear, served as his own observer in a study on how localization was accomplished monaurally (Hunter, 1949).

[8] Traditionally, histories of psychology have been organized around the concept of "schools of psychology," a term referring to a major conceptual framework that includes statements about psychology's definition, its preferred methods, and its important concepts. Thus, structuralism, functionalism, behaviorism, gestalt psychology, and psychoanalysis are normally considered to be the predominant schools of psychology.

requires a liberal attitude about appropriate methods. Angell had no quarrel with introspection, but he believed that it had to be defined more broadly than Titchener would allow and that it must be supplemented with more direct observational methods.

In his productive years at Chicago, Angell mentored several individuals destined to become key figures in psychology's story. One was John Watson, normally considered the founder of behaviorism as a school of psychology (Chapter 10); another was Harvey Carr, Angell's successor as department head.

Harvey Carr (1873–1954): The Maturing of Functionalism

Carr was almost 30 when he landed in Chicago in 1902. The son of Indiana farmers, Carr's college education had been interrupted by financial problems and ill health, but he managed to complete both a bachelor's and a master's degree in psychology at the University of Colorado just prior to his arrival in Angell's department. At Colorado, he learned of the new psychology and its laboratory procedures from Arthur Allin, who had studied with Hall and Sanford at Clark. While at Chicago, he developed lifelong interests in two diverse topics, the perception of space and maze learning. His doctoral dissertation in 1905 was on the former topic and eventually led to a book (Carr, 1935). Most of his research publications concerned maze learning, however. Following Small's lead (refer to the Close-Up in Chapter 6) Carr investigated the sensory basis for maze learning, and two of his studies with John Watson are featured in Chapter 10. He was also interested in the general problem of maze standardization. In the early years of maze learning

research, results often failed to replicate because the mazes used from one study to the next varied considerably. Carr improved the situation substantially by inventing a type of maze that came to be called the "Carr maze" (Warner & Warden, 1927). Two examples are shown in Figure 7.5. As you can see, although each maze has a different solution, the number of choices per maze is held constant, as is the length of each pathway and cul de sac. Also, the mazes were constructed so that patterns could be changed quickly.

After earning his doctorate in 1905, Carr taught elsewhere for several years, then returned to Chicago in 1908. With Watson leaving for Johns Hopkins that year, Angell hired Carr to run the psychology laboratory. Carr remained at Chicago until his retirement in 1938, chairing the department for the second half of his years there. He contributed to the evolution of Chicago functionalism through his effect on students and by the publication of a popular textbook in the mid-1920s—*Psychology: A Study of Mental Activity* (Carr, 1925). In his years at Chicago, Carr had a hand in the doctoral work of no fewer than 131 students and he directed 53 dissertations, 18 in comparative psychology, 6 in space perception, and 29 in learning (Pillsbury, 1955). The 1925 text can be considered a statement of the "mature" functionalism, with the understanding that functionalism always remained more of an attitude than a systematic theoretical position.

The Columbia Functionalists

Because functionalism was more of a state of mind than a rigorous system, it existed well beyond Chicago. Indeed, elements of functional thinking

FIGURE 7.5 Designs for two typical Carr mazes.

could be found throughout the academic landscape, with the possible exception of Cornell. Even there, however, Titchenerian orthodoxy occasionally relaxed. For instance, E. G. Boring once ran a human maze learning study that featured blindfolded humans navigating an outdoor maze, their pathways marked by trails of flour leaking from sacks attached to their backs; Boring reported that the only significant outcome of the study was that he became infatuated with one of the maze-runners, later marrying her (Jaynes, 1969). Beyond Chicago, however, functionalism at the turn of the century was associated with Columbia University in New York. In its formative years, James McKeen Cattell headed the psychology program. You met him in the Chapter 4 discussion of reaction time, and you will learn more extensively of his work in the next chapter. While at Columbia from 1891 to 1917, Cattell created a vibrant graduate department, possibly the best in the country. Under his tutelage, dozens of historically important psychologists earned their doctoral stripes, and Cattell personally directed more than 50 dissertations (Jonçich, 1968). Two of his better-known students were Edward Thorndike and Robert Woodworth.

Edward L. Thorndike (1874–1949): Connectionism

Thorndike spent practically his entire professional career making major contributions to educational psychology and psychological testing, but he is most often remembered among psychologists for studying how cats learned to escape from crudely constructed puzzle boxes. For this reason he is considered a pioneer in comparative psychology, an example of what Lloyd Morgan had in mind as the proper way to do animal research. He also appears occasionally in chapters on behaviorism as a precursor to the conditioning work of Pavlov and Watson. In a certain sense, then, he was a transition figure from the early comparative psychologists to the later behaviorists. More important, he was a leader of the functionalist movement, interested in studying how individuals adapted to their environments and how this knowledge could be applied to improve the human condition.

Thorndike's early life was somewhat nomadic; his father was a Methodist minister who moved his

family from one New England town to another as he was reassigned to different congregations every two or three years. Always the new kid in town, young Thorndike became terribly shy, but he also developed self-reliance, and under the stern eye of his puritanical and demanding mother, he became an excellent student. He gained easy acceptance to the Methodist-run Wesleyan University in Connecticut, graduating with honors in 1895. While there, he found his vocation by discovering James's *Principles of Psychology*, which electrified him as it had James Angell and countless others of their generation. Thorndike (1936) later described the book as more stimulating "than any book that I had read before, and possibly more so than any book read since" (p. 263). As Angell had done four years earlier, Thorndike entered Harvard's graduate program to experience James directly.

It is not clear exactly how Thorndike's interests in animal behavior developed, but a seminar taken with James used Wundt's *Lectures on Human and Animal Psychology* (which had just been translated by Titchener), and he might have attended public lectures given by the visiting C. Lloyd Morgan, Britain's premier comparative psychologist (Chapter 5). Like every educated person of his day, he was thoroughly familiar with evolutionary thinking; his knowledge of contemporary comparative psychology and its problems are evident from his half-hearted explanation for his choice of research topic: "My first research was in animal psychology, not because I knew animals or cared much for them, but because I thought I could do better than had been done" (cited in Jonçich, 1968, p. 89).

Thorndike first studied instinct and intelligence in baby chicks by asking them to escape from simple mazes formed by placing books on end. Figure 7.6 shows three of the patterns he used. Chicks would be placed in the maze at location A, then observed to see if they could find the exit. Thorndike reported that they initially jumped at the walls, made a lot of noise, and were just as likely to go more deeply into the maze than to escape from it. After several trials, however, they eliminated the useless behaviors and learned their way out. Incidentally, some of this research was completed in the cellar of the William

FIGURE 7.6 Configurations of three mazes that Thorndike created by placing books vertically on a table.

James household. Thorndike's landlord had evicted the animals, perhaps as a consequence of their noisy attempts to escape the mazes, and James had taken them in after being unable to secure space for them on campus. Thorndike believed that the "nuisance to Mrs. James was ... somewhat mitigated by the entertainment to the two youngest children" (Thorndike, 1936, p. 264).

For reasons that were partly financial and partly the consequence of a romantic relationship that seemed to be going nowhere (with the woman who would become his wife, as it turned out; see Figure 7.7), Thorndike applied for and received a fellowship to Columbia. Cattell was impressed with the young comparative psychologist and Thorndike was award-

ed $700 a year in aid, more than the average annual income for most families at that time (Jonçich, 1968). At Columbia, he expanded his animal research to several different species, but his most famous work was done with cats in puzzle boxes, published as "Animal Intelligence: An Experimental Study of the Associative Processes in Animals" in 1898. It is a classic series of studies, worthy of closer examination. The following excerpt is from a book that Thorndike wrote in 1911, *Animal Intelligence: Experimental studies* (2000); it included the 1898 monograph, plus some additional chapters written between then and 1911. The page numbers in the excerpt are from a 2000 reprinting of the book.

FIGURE 7.7 Edward L. Thorndike during the time of his puzzle box studies, with his eventual spouse, Elizabeth Moulton, from Jonçich (1968).

ORIGINAL SOURCE EXCERPT
Thorndike on Puzzle Box Learning

As is evident from his explanation for undertaking the study of animal behavior, Thorndike was a strong critic of most of his contemporary comparative psychologists, especially when they relied on nonrepresentative anecdotal data to support claims of higher mental powers for a variety of animals. He thought he could do better, and the most important aspect of the puzzle box studies was the methodological rigor that Thorndike brought to the project (Galef, 1998). In an early section of his 1898 dissertation, Thorndike dealt directly with the issue of methodology, making it clear that his approach would break the mold, and serving notice that he was not impressed with the state of comparative psychology in his day. He was sometimes accused of displaying the arrogance of youthful exuberance, and you will see some justification for the charge in this opening passage:

Although no work done in this field [comparative psychology] is enough like the present investigation to require an account of its results, the *method* hitherto in use invites comparisons by its contrast and, as I believe, by its faults. In the first place, most of the books do not give us a psychology, but rather a *eulogy*, of animals. They have all been about animal *intelligence*, never about animal *stupidity*. Though a writer derides the notion that animals have reason, he hastens to add that they have marvelous capacity of forming associations, and is likely to refer to the fact that human beings only rarely reason anything out, that their trains of ideas are ruled mostly by association, as if, in this matter, animals were on a par with humans. The history of books on animals' minds thus furnishes an illustration of the well-nigh universal tendency in humans to find the marvelous wherever it can. ...

In the second place, the facts have generally been derived from anecdotes. Now quite apart from such pedantry as insists that a man's word about a scientific fact is worthless unless he is a trained scientist, there are really in this field special objections to the acceptance of the testimony about animals' intelligent acts which one gets from anecdotes. ... Besides commonly misstating what facts [these anecdotes] report, they report only such facts as show the animal at his best. Dogs get lost hundreds of times and no one ever notices it or sends an account of it to scientific magazines. But let one find his way from Brooklyn to Yonkers and the fact immediately becomes a circulating anecdote. Thousands of cats on thousands of occasions sit helplessly yowling, and no one takes thought of it or writes to his friend, the professor; but let one cat claw at the knob of a door supposedly as a signal to be let out, and straightway this cat becomes the representative of the cat-mind in all the books. ...

Finally, in all cases, whether of direct observation or reports by good observers or bad, there have been three other defects. Only a single case is studied, so the results are not necessarily true of the type; the observation is not repeated, nor are the conditions perfectly regulated; the previous history of the animal in question is not known. Such observations may tell us, if the observer is perfectly reliable, that a certain thing takes place; but they cannot assure us that it will take place universally among the animals of that species, or universally with the same animal. Nor can the influence of previous experience be estimated. (pp. 22–25, italics in the original)

Disdaining the anecdotal strategy and the tendency to report only the "marvelous," Thorndike instead developed more systematic procedures to test claims for animal intelligence, deliberately aiming to correct the three defects just mentioned—he would study more than a single case, he would repeat the experiments, and he would control the learning history of the animals he studied.

... After considerable preliminary observation of animals' behavior under various conditions, I chose for my general method one which, simple as it is, possesses several other marked advantages besides those accompanying experiment of any sort. It was merely to put animals when hungry in inclosures from which they could escape by some simple act, such as pulling at a loop of cord, pressing a lever, or stepping on a platform. ... The animal was put in the inclosure, food was left outside in sight, and his actions observed. Besides recording his general behavior, special notice was taken of how he succeeded in doing the necessary act (in case he did succeed), and a record was kept of the time that he was in the box before performing the successful pull, clawing, or bite. This was repeated until the animal had formed a perfect association between the sense-impression of the interior of that box and the impulse leading to the successful movement. (p. 26)

Thorndike's strategy was clear and logical, and from the elegance of his plan, you might think that the puzzle boxes would be models of mechanical sophistication. Not quite. Thorndike was the exception to the rule that the early experimentalists were talented and creative apparatus builders. His books-on-end mazes for chicks hinted at a certain lack of mechanical aptitude, and his puzzle boxes confirmed the handicap.[9] Thorndike included a sketch of one of the 15 boxes he built, one that suggests a neat, clean design. Historian John Burnham (1972) discovered photographs of the actual boxes used, however, and describing them as crude might be an understatement. Figure 7.8 shows two of the photos, boxes A (7.8.a) and D (7.8.b), and Thorndike's sketch (7.8.c), which was Box K. Here are Thorndike's descriptions of these three boxes:

A. A string attached to the bolt which held the door ran up over a pulley on the front edge of the box, and was tied to a wire loop (2 1/2 inches in diameter) hanging 6 inches above the floor in front center of box. Clawing or biting at it, or rubbing against it even, if in a certain way, opened the door. We may call this box A '*O at front.*' ...

D. The door was in the extreme right of the front. A string fastened to the bolt which held it ran up over a pulley on the top edge and back to the top edge of the back side of the box ... and was there firmly fastened. The top of the box was of wire screening and arched over the string. ... A slight pull on the string anywhere opened the door. This box was 20x16, but a space 7x16 was partitioned off at the left by a wire screen. D may be called '*String.*'

---

[9] Also, Thorndike never learned how to use a typewriter or how to drive a car, and his son could never recall seeing his father "fix" anything (Thorndike, 1991).

(a)

(b)

(c)

FIGURE 7.8 Three of Thorndike's puzzle boxes: (a) A (required a wire pull), (b) D (with extra chamber for imitation study), and (c) K (complex, requiring three responses, sketched by Thorndike) (from Burnham, 1972).

> K was a box arranged so that three separate acts were required to open the door, which was held by two bolts at the top and two bars outside. One of the bolts was connected with a platform in the back center so that depressing the platform raised the bolt. The other was raised by a string which ran up over a pulley in the front, across the box 1 inch above the bars, over a pulley near the corner of the box, and down to the floor, where it was fastened. Pulling on this string ... would raise the bolt. If both bolts were raised and *either* bar was pushed up or down far enough to be out of the way, the cat could escape. K, or '*Triple*,' as it may be called, is the box reproduced in [the sketch]. (pp. 31–34, italics in the original)

Despite appearances, there was a systematic method to the apparent chaos in the box construction. Box K ("triple"), for instance, was designed to combine responses that had been the only ones necessary in each of three other boxes. This box was used with cats that had learned each of the individual responses, to see if they could combine the information and escape quickly. Box D, with its extra compartment, was used for Thorndike's experiments on imitation.

Thorndike used thirteen different cats in his puzzle boxes. It is not clear from his description exactly how many cats were tested in each of the boxes, but it appears that each cat was tested in at least several of the boxes. How did they behave?

> ... When put into the box the cat would show evident signs of discomfort and of an impulse to escape from confinement. It tries to squeeze through any opening; it claws and bites at the bars or wire; it thrusts its paws out through any opening and claws at everything it reaches. ... It does not pay very much attention to the food outside, but seems simply to strive to escape its confinement. The vigor with which it struggles is extraordinary. For eight or ten minutes it will claw and bite and squeeze incessantly. ... The cat that is clawing all over the box in her impulsive struggle will probably claw the string or loop or button so as to open the door. And *gradually all the other nonsuccessful impulses will be stamped out and the particular impulse leading to the successful act will be stamped in by the resulting pleasure*, until, after many trials, the cat will, when put in the box, immediately claw the button or loop in a definite way. (pp. 35–36, italics added)

Thorndike's explanation for this behavior, which also applied to his chicks-in-mazes experiments and a small series of studies with dogs in puzzle boxes, was the same as that given by Morgan to explain the behavior of terriers opening gates to escape from yards—**trial-and-error learning** (Thorndike preferred the phrase "trial and accidental success"). Because he believed that the cat learned to make *connections* between stimuli in the boxes and successful escape responses during this trial and error learning, Thorndike's learning model is sometimes called **connectionism**. When first placed in the puzzle box, the cat exhibits behavior that is a random sequence of acts—clawing, biting, pushing, screeching, and so on. Eventually, the animal hits upon the correct response (e.g., claws a loop), but its first solution is accidental. Nonetheless, that behavior has been successful, and such behaviors tend to be repeated, "stamped in" by their pleasurable consequences (escape), as Thorndike put it. On subsequent trials, the failed behaviors are gradually eliminated and the successful one occurs earlier and earlier in the sequence. Before long, the animal is in and out of the box in a few seconds. Figure 7.9 charts the gradually improving, if erratic, progress of one of Thorndike's cats.

Thorndike completely rejected the idea that cats are capable of more complex reasoning or able to benefit from imitation when escaping from the boxes. For instance, in Box K (Figure 7.8.c), which combined three responses that had been learned earlier, the cats showed no evidence of combining what they had learned into a more complex sequence of behaviors. Also, Thorndike almost derisively included a long quote from Romanes that attempted to argue for a cat's aptitude for inference based on imitation. After observing humans open latched doors, according to Romanes, the cat "must reason, by the 'logic of feelings'—'If a hand can do it, why not a paw?'" (quoted in Thorndike, 2000, p. 69). Thorndike rejected the idea in favor of his more parsimonious trial and error explanation. He also tested for imitation directly—box D (Figure 7.8.b) had two chambers separated by wire mesh. One side had an escape mechanism and the other did not. Thorndike would

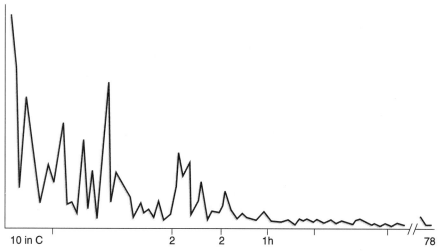

FIGURE 7.9 Performance of cat #10 in puzzle box C. On the X axis, the unlabeled vertical dash meant a day, "2" meant two days, "1 h" meant an hour, and "78" meant 78 hours (from Thorndike, 1911).

put two cats in the box, one on either side of the wire partition, and recorded instances when the "observer" cat was watching the other cat escape successfully. There was no evidence of observational learning—when put to the test, the observer cats behaved exactly like other, naive cats, prompting Thorndike to conclude, "No one, I am sure, who had seen them, would have claimed that their conduct was at all influenced by what they had seen" (p. 89). Finally, Thorndike even tried holding onto his cats' paws and moving them through the correct actions. Even this "direct instruction" had no effect on learning.

In his 1898 dissertation, Thorndike did not propose general principles of learning, but he did in the 1911 monograph that I have been using for this excerpt. He postulated two principles, a **Law of Effect** and a **Law of Exercise**. Also, to account for the fact that every situation encountered in life is somewhat unique, Thorndike applied the results of some research on transfer that he completed with Woodworth (discussed later). He proposed that if a new situation, S_1, had some elements in common with an old situation, S_2, then the response to S_2 would transfer to some degree to S_1. For example, he found that some of his cats, having learned to escape from one box, and then put into a box with a similar but not identical escape mechanism, would learn more quickly than a cat without such an experience. Here are the two laws in Thorndike's words:

> The Law of Effect is that: *Of several responses made to the same situation, those which are accompanied or closely followed by satisfaction to the animal will, other things being equal, be more firmly connected with the situation, so that, when it recurs, they will be more likely to recur; those which are accompanied or closely followed by discomfort to the animal will, other things being equal, have their connections with that situation weakened, so that, when it recurs, they will be less likely to recur. The greater the satisfaction or discomfort, the greater the strengthening or weakening of the bond.*

> The Law of Exercise is that: *Any response to a situation will, other things being equal, be more strongly connected with the situation in proportion to the number of times it has been connected with that situation and to the average vigor and duration of the connections.* (p. 244, italics in the original)

As will be seen in Chapter 11, Thorndike's Law of Effect bears a close resemblance to B. F. Skinner's concept of operant conditioning, and Skinner recognized his debt to Thorndike, referring to the Columbia psychologist's work as "[o]ne of the first serious attempts to study changes brought about by the consequences of behavior" (Skinner, 1953, p. 59).

In 1911, Thorndike was confident that his two laws could account for most learning. By the early 1930s, however, after years of studying human learning, he modified both laws. For the Law of Effect, he concluded that the first half was more strongly supported than the second half—rewards are more effective than punishments in producing learning. As for the Law of Exercise, he reached the conclusion that it had limited value. Practice might make perfect for some types of learning (e.g., motor skills), but repetition was often less effective for higher forms of learning (e.g., comprehending textbook material).

The Thorndike-Mills Controversy

Thorndike was excited about his dissertation research and willing to take on critics, writing to his future wife that his (1898) "thesis is a beauty ... I've got some theories which knock the old authorities into a grease spot" (cited in Jonçich, 1968, p. 146). One authority who was not amused by Thorndike's youthful exuberance was Wesley Mills, a comparative psychologist who criticized Thorndike's research at the 1898 meeting of the American Psychological Association and followed it up with an article in *Psychological Review*. Mills started by criticizing Thorndike's lack of respect for his "elders," noting that "Dr. Thorndike has not been hampered in his researches by any of that respect for workers of the past ... which usually causes men to pause before differing radically from them, not to say gleefully consigning them to the psychological flames" (Mills, 1899, p. 263). More important, Mills rejected the study's conclusions entirely because of the *artificiality* of the environment created by Thorndike. Cats placed in small enclosures, Mills argued, cannot be expected to act naturally. Thus, nothing about their normal behavior can be determined from their behavior in highly artificial, abnormal surroundings. Mills concluded that one might as well "enclose a living man in a coffin, lower him,

against his will, into the earth, and attempt to deduce normal psychology from his conduct" (p. 266).

Far from being chastened, Thorndike (1899) offered a point-by-point rebuttal. He admitted to being unimpressed with animal research based on uncritical observation and anecdote and made no apology for it. He denied Mill's claim that his cats must have been in a panic, pointing out caustically that if Mills had acted like a genuine scientist and bothered to repeat the puzzle box studies, he would have discovered that little if any panic occurred. Furthermore, those cats that did show a higher "fury of activity" (p. 412) did not differ in learning speed from their more sanguine peers. As for the charge of "unnaturalness," Thorndike simply asked what Mills could mean by natural. Animals constantly face new situations; who is to say one is more "natural" than another? To drive home the point, Thorndike turned around an example that Mills had used, of the effects "of certain mental functions on the conduct of a kitten in gaining a certain resting place (in a bookcase, if I remember rightly), in spite of mechanical obstacles interposed. The situation here coped with is as 'unnatural' as that in ... my experiments" (p. 414).

The Mills-Thorndike exchange is a good illustration of a difference of opinion about the appropriateness of laboratory methods that continues to this day. On the one hand are those who argue that understanding animal behavior requires the precision afforded by a controlled laboratory environment. In such a setting, the effects of various influences on behavior can be studied systematically. As will be seen, this approach was taken by the majority of American animal researchers who came to be known as behaviorists (e.g., Skinner). In contrast, other psychologists have followed Mills and argued that animal behavior can only be understood if it is studied outside of the artificial confines of the laboratory. Most twentieth-century European researchers took this route, producing a field known as **ethology**—the study of animal behavior in its "natural" surroundings. The best known of these scientists are Konrad Lorenz, Karl von Frisch, and Niko Tinbergen, who shared the 1973 Nobel prize in biology for their work on instinctive animal behavior. Lorenz is familiar to most students from a photo of him being followed by ducklings. Although you know from the Chapter 5 Close-Up that Spalding also studied this phenomenon, Lorenz is normally credited with the discovery of *imprinting*.

After earning his doctorate, Thorndike taught for a year at Case Western Reserve in Cleveland, then returned to Columbia's Teachers College, where he remained for the rest of his professional career. There he extended his research on learning to humans and became a leading educational psychologist. He also developed a series of aptitude tests for schoolchildren, thereby contributing to the psychological testing movement as well. Honors came his way in the form of an APA presidency in 1912 and election to the National Academy of Sciences in 1917. He was a prolific writer, averaging about a dozen articles a year. He also wrote numerous textbooks, including a three-volume *Educational Psychology* in 1913, which made his name "practically synonymous with the field of educational psychology for many years to come" (Goodenough, 1950, p. 295). Most of his texts were compilations of lecture notes, and as Titchener pointed out in a scathing review of an introductory text by Thorndike, publishing "lecture courses as soon as the lectures have been delivered ... must inevitably show marks of hasty preparation and of immaturity

of judgment" (Titchener, 1905). The criticism didn't slow Thorndike down for a minute, however, and by the 1920s his royalty earnings far exceeded his Columbia salary. In 1924, for instance, his royalty income of $68,000 was five times his faculty salary (Jonçich, 1968).[10] Thorndike retired from Columbia in 1940 and died nine years later.

Robert S. Woodworth (1869–1962): A Dynamic Psychology

Woodworth, named Robert Sessions after an ancestor who participated in the Boston Tea Party, was born in the small western Massachusetts town of Belchertown. Like Thorndike, he was the son of a minister; his mother was an educator, a graduate of Mt. Holyoke College and the founder of the Lake Erie Female Seminary in Ohio (Poffenberger, 1962). Considering a career in the ministry himself, Woodworth attended Amherst College, but emerged with an interest in teaching. After a few years of teaching high school science and math, he discovered (who else?) William James and *The Principles* and decided to pursue a career in either philosophy or psychology. Like Angell and Thorndike, Woodworth wanted to experience the master directly, so off he went to Harvard in the fall of 1895. Woodworth stayed in Cambridge for three academic years, earning a second bachelor's degree, a master's degree, and serving as assistant in physiology at the Harvard Medical School. During this time he developed two lifelong friendships, one with the noted physiologist Walter B. Cannon, whose work with Bard would eventually yield a theory of emotion to rival the James-Lange theory, and a second with Thorndike. This latter friendship contributed to Woodworth's next stop after Harvard—Cattell offered him a fellowship to Columbia, partly the result of being pestered to do so by Thorndike (Jonçich, 1968).

Woodworth completed his doctorate at Columbia in 1899 and was immediately appointed instructor in physiology there. After spending a productive year in England in the laboratory of the esteemed physiolo-

---

[10] To put Thorndike's royalty income in perspective, $68,000 in 1924 is equal to approximately $170,000 today (see www.westegg.com/inflation for an inflation calculator).

gist Charles Sherrington (Chapter 3, pp. 76–77), he accepted Cattell's invitation in 1903 to join the psychology department, where he remained until his retirement in 1939 at age 70. Retirement barely slowed him down, however, for he continued to teach part-time until he was 89 and to write until he was 91.

Woodworth was a modest man who once wrote this to a friend: "I rate my achievement very low, believing that I am one of the sort whose name will soon be forgotten, though of service during his lifetime" (cited in Poffenberger, 1962, p. 687). It was true that he did not contribute much in the way of original research and he did not create a school of thought that produced "Woodworthians," but he was quite wrong about his influence. He is remembered for (a) his research with Thorndike on transfer of training, (b) his "dynamic" psychology, with its emphasis on drives and organismic variables, and (c) his impact on students, both directly and through textbook writing, especially "The Columbia Bible." This latter achievement, by itself, was sufficient to insure his lasting importance to twentieth-century experimental psychology.

The research on **transfer** derived from a fundamental problem in higher education—the validity of claims made on behalf of the doctrine of "formal discipline." Rooted in faculty psychology, it was the mid-nineteenth century belief that the curriculum for higher education should be designed to "exercise" and strengthen the intellectual faculties. This was to be accomplished through the study of such disciplines as Latin, Greek, and classical literature. Once the faculties were "in shape," the skills that had been developed were assumed to transfer to other disciplines to be learned later. The doctrine came under fire near the end of the century, when several schools copied Harvard's radical concept of an "elective" curriculum, which enabled students to avoid Latin and Greek if they wished. The debate generated much rhetoric, but little evidence accumulated for or against the idea that learning topic A (e.g., Greek) made it easier to learn topic B (e.g., zoology). Thorndike and Woodworth, in a series of coauthored publications (e.g., 1901), set out to find direct evidence for transfer of training. Their subjects practiced one simple task, and then tried other tasks that varied in the degree of resemblance to the original task. After estimating the areas

of rectangles, for instance, they estimated the areas of triangles (high resemblance) or the weight of objects (low). Briefly, what they found was that the amount of transfer occurring was directly proportional to the number of elements shared by the tasks. Although their tasks were quite different from curricular topics, Thorndike and Woodworth generalized their results to the issue of formal discipline, concluding that the doctrine had little merit. Because subjects like Greek bore minimal relationship to subjects like zoology, Thorndike and Woodworth predicted very little benefit to zoologists from studying Greek (except for some word origin information). As mentioned earlier, Thorndike also used the transfer concept to explain how cats that escaped from one box would find it easier to escape from a new box, assuming the two boxes shared some components.

Woodworth is often described as an "eclectic" when it came to theorizing, willing to incorporate the features of various diverse systems. In his popular introductory text, for example, he defined psychology as the study of both mental processes and behavior, thus blending the new behaviorism with the traditional psychology of consciousness. This definition continues to be found in virtually all general psychology texts. Woodworth also believed that psychologists should use a variety of methods, ranging from introspection to mental testing to the objective observation of behavior. He disliked those who would define psychology narrowly, naming both Titchener (structuralism) and Watson (behaviorism) as examples, and he revealed his basic philosophy by ending his popular history of psychology, *Contemporary Schools of Psychology*, with a chapter called "The Middle of the Road" (Woodworth, 1931, pp. 205–219). He was especially critical of a simple mechanistic, stimulus-response psychology, arguing for what he referred to as an **S-O-R model.** That is, he insisted that psychologists must understand not just the stimulus and response, but also the organism (O) that stands in between. This includes studying what motivates or drives the organism. In his *Dynamic Psychology* (1918) and *Dynamics of Behavior* (1958), Woodworth established the importance of studying motivational factors influencing behavior. In the process he introduced the term **drive** to psychology.

Like his best friend Thorndike, Woodworth became wealthy by writing textbooks. His *Psychology*, with editions appearing in 1921, 1929, 1934, and 1940, introduced thousands of students to the field for over two decades. More important for research psychologists, his *Experimental Psychology* shaped the very definition of the term "experiment." When the book made its initial appearance in 1938, it was already so well known that no psychologist was perplexed when the publisher announced "The Bible is out" (Estes, 1981). As early as 1909, Woodworth had been distributing mimeographed handouts for his course in experimental methods, and by 1920 these had grown into a 285-page handout called "A Textbook in Experimental Psychology" (Winston, 1990). Columbia students who became professors used the materials in their own classes. By 1938, the eagerly anticipated volume finally appeared and was an immediate success, selling more than 44,000 copies by 1954, when it was revised and a coauthor added (Woodworth & Schlosberg, 1954). Historian Andrew Winston (1990) estimated that between 1938 and 1959, more than 100,000 psychology majors learned about research in psychology from Woodworth.

Woodworth's 1938 text was encyclopedic, with more than 823 pages of text and another 36 pages of references. After an introductory chapter, it was organized into 29 different research topics, including such diverse topics as memory, transfer of training, maze learning, reaction time, hearing, the perception of color, and thinking. Students using the text learned about the procedures related to each content area, as well as virtually everything there was to know in 1938 about each topic. They also learned some distinctions that were to have important ramifications for future psychologists.

Prior to Woodworth, the term "experiment" had been used broadly as a label for procedures ranging from the introspection of a mental event to a mental test to an observation under controlled circumstances. Woodworth, however, narrowed the definition and contrasted experimental research with what he referred to as correlational research. The defining feature of the experimental method was to be the manipulation of a factor that was the main focus of study, what Woodworth called an **independent variable**, and this variable would have its effects on some measure of behavior, or as he called it, the **dependent variable**. Woodworth did not invent the terms, but he was the first to use them in this manner. While the experimental method manipulates independent variables, Woodworth wrote, the correlational method "measures two or more characteristics of the same individuals [and] computes the correlation of these characteristics. This method ... has no 'independent variable' but treats all the measured variables alike" (Woodworth, 1938, p. 3). Furthermore, Woodworth originated the argument, now found in the opening chapter of every introductory text but not widely accepted during his time, that the experimental method was the only technique allowing causal conclusions; no causation could be inferred from correlations. Although Woodworth argued that correlational research should have the same overall status as experimental research, he omitted correlational findings from the remainder of the text. The reader could be excused for thinking that the experimental approach was superior. Indeed, the consequences of Woodworth's distinction were sufficient to become the focus of a cautionary APA presidential address in 1957. In "The Two Disciplines of Scientific Psychology," Lee Cronbach argued for reestablishing the status of correlational research.

Woodworth is a prime example of the reason why functionalism was less of a school of psychology than a set of attitudes about psychology. He would be surprised to find himself in a chapter on "functionalism"—like most of his peers, he considered himself simply a psychologist. The same can said for the other psychologists featured in this chapter and for those functionalists who extended their research interests into the areas of applied psychology. Their work occupies the next chapter.

SUMMARY

TITCHENER'S PSYCHOLOGY: STRUCTURALISM

- E. B. Titchener earned a Ph.D. with Wundt at Leipzig, then came to Cornell University, where he established an approach to psychology called structuralism. Its main goals were to analyze human conscious experience into its elemental units, then show how these units could be synthesized into mental processes.

- Titchener promoted an experimental/laboratory approach to psychology by writing a series of highly detailed training manuals that introduced students and instructors to the particulars of precise laboratory work and by forming a close-knit group of fellow male researchers called the Experimentalists, who met annually to share the details of their ongoing research.

- The main goals for a structuralist psychology, according to Titchener, were to achieve a complete analysis of the "generalized adult mind," show how elements could be combined into more complex phenomena (synthesis), and provide an explanation of mental processes by understanding the workings of the brain and nervous system.

- Titchener identified introspection as psychology's primary method and believed that introspections could yield valid data only if introspectors were highly trained and capable of the introspective habit. Training was also needed to avoid the stimulus error, a tendency to describe a meaningful stimulus instead of the direct conscious experience of the stimulus.

- The main elements of conscious experience, according to Titchener, are sensations, images, and affects. Sensations and images have the attributes of quality, intensity, duration, and clearness, but images aren't as clear as sensations. Affects have but two qualities—pleasantness and unpleasantness—and they lack clarity.

- Titchener's primary contribution was to promote laboratory psychology, but his system omitted major topics of interest to most American psychologists, and his method of introspection was shown to be fundamentally flawed because of its lack of objectivity.

AMERICA'S PSYCHOLOGY: FUNCTIONALISM

- Most American psychologists, influenced by evolutionary theory and a generally pragmatic attitude, were interested more in the functions of consciousness than in its structure. Functionalism was widespread, but mainly associated with the University of Chicago and Columbia University.

- The origins of functionalism are often traced to a paper on the reflex arc by John Dewey of Chicago. Dewey argued against the analytic strategy of reducing the reflex to its elements and argued instead that the reflex needed to be seen in its broader context as a coordinated system that served to adapt the organism to its environment. Dewey was known primarily for his progressive views on education, believing that students should be active learners, and for his philosophical writings on democracy.

- The earliest clear statement of the functionalist philosophy came from the 1906 APA presidential address of James Angell, who succeeded Dewey at Chicago. Angell explicitly compared structuralism and functionalism, pointing out that structuralists were more likely to ask the question "What is consciousness?" whereas functionalists were more concerned with the question "What is consciousness for?" This led them to study topics ranging from developmental to abnormal psychology and led them to be interested in individual differences and how psychology could be used to solve everyday problems.

- Harvey Carr was Angell's successor at Chicago, bringing functionalism to its maturity there. He was known for his maze learning research and for developing Chicago into one of the country's best graduate programs.

- Functionalism at Columbia was led by James McKeen Cattell and associated with two of his students, Edward Thorndike and Robert Woodworth. Thorndike became a leading educational psychologist, but in his early years he was known for his studies of cats in puzzle boxes. He was highly critical of contemporary comparative psychology, which relied on anecdotal evidence and was anthropomorphic. He studied trial-and-error learning systematically and proposed that learning occurred through the creation of connections between situations and responses that were successful in those situations (Law of Effect) and that connections were strengthened with repetition (Law of Exercise). His debate with Mills reflected a fundamental disagreement between those advocating laboratory methods and those who preferred to study animals in their daily environments.

- Woodworth is remembered for his research with Thorndike on transfer, which called traditional educational practices into question; his dynamic psychology, which replaced an S-R model with an S-O-R framework and emphasized motivational influences on behavior; and his textbook writing, especially on methodology. His "Columbia bible" institutionalized the distinctions between experimental and correlational research and between independent and dependent variables in experimental research.

STUDY QUESTIONS

1. In his 1898 paper on structural psychology, what was the argument that Titchener made for studying structure prior to function?

2. Distinguish between German and American (drill course) methods for training students how to be experimental psychologists.

3. Describe the contents of Titchener's Manuals, distinguish between the qualitative and quantitative manuals, and explain the significance of the work.

4. What were the Experimentalists, why were they formed, what did they do, and why did they exclude women?

5. According to Titchener, what were psychology's three main goals?

6. Describe Titchener's version of introspection and explain why it was so important for introspectors to be highly trained. Be sure to work the concept of the stimulus error into your answer.

7. What did Titchener conclude were the elements of human conscious experience? And what were the attributes of those elements?

8. Why did Titchener exclude the study of children, animals, and the insane from his definition of psychology?

9. Describe the imageless thought controversy and show how it was a good illustration of the problems with introspection.

10. What was the Baldwin-Titchener argument and what was its significance for the methodological issue of introspection?

11. Show how the school of functionalism is related to evolutionary thinking.

12. Describe the main points of Dewey's reflex arc article and the significance of the article.

13. Use Angell's APA presidential address of 1906 to provide a comparison of structuralist and functionalist ways of thinking about psychology.

14. What was a "Carr maze" and what was the importance of this apparatus?

15. What was the substance of the Thorndike-Mills controversy and what was its significance?

16. How did Thorndike and Woodworth study transfer, what did they conclude, and what were the implications of their research for the educational philosophy of the day?

17. What was the importance of Woodworth inserting an "O" between the "S" and the "R," when describing behavior?

18. What was the significance of Woodworth's "Columbia bible," and what distinctions did he make in the book that continue to be in use today?

QUESTIONS FROM THE ORIGINAL SOURCE EXCERPT

1. Summarize the criticisms made by Thorndike of comparative psychology in his day.

2. Describe the methodological innovations in Thorndike's puzzle box studies.

3. How did Thorndike describe the process by which cats escaped from his puzzle boxes? How did this illustrate the laws of effect and exercise?

4. Explain how Thorndike ruled out the idea that cats could learn the escape through reasoning and imitation.

FOR FURTHER READING

Furumoto, L. (1988). Shared knowledge: The Experimentalists, 1904–1929. In J. G. Morawski (Ed.), *The rise of experimentation in American psychology* (pp. 94–113). New Haven, CT: Yale University Press.

Examines the origins and development of Titchener's Experimentalists, with a focus on the consequences for female psychologists, who were excluded from the group during Titchener's lifetime, and only marginally included after his death.

Dewsbury, D. A. (ED.) (1998). History of psychology: Commemorating E. L. Thorndike. *American Psychologist, 53,* 1121–1152.

Edited by comparative psychologist and historian Don Dewsbury, includes a reprinting of a portion of Thorndike's 1898 paper, along with papers on Thorndike's life, his influence on comparative psychology, and his influence on educational psychology.

Heidbreder, E. (1933). *Seven psychologies.* New York: AppletonCenturyCrofts.

A well-known early history of psychology that gives an especially strong description of the functionalism found at Columbia, written by a woman with firsthand experience as a student of Woodworth's.

Krantz, D. L. (1969). The Baldwin-Titchener controversy. In D. L. Krantz (Ed.), *Schools of psychology: A symposium* (pp. 1–19). New York: AppletonCenturyCrofts.

Details one of several controversies involving Titchener; technically concerning an issue in reaction time research, the controversy was actually over the adequacy of Titchener's introspective procedures and the basic question of how psychology should proceed—structurally (Titchener) or functionally (Baldwin).

Winston, A. S. (1990). Robert Sessions Woodworth and the "Columbia Bible": How the psychological experiment was redefined. *American Journal of Psychology, 103,* 391–401.

Documents the development and impact of Woodworth's text in experimental psychology, emphasizing how the impact of his distinction between experimental and correlational research consigned the latter to second-class status in psychology.

CHAPTER 8

APPLYING THE NEW PSYCHOLOGY

Unless our laboratory results are to give us artificialities, mere scientific curiosities, they must be subjected to interpretation by gradual approximation to the conditions of life.
—John Dewey, 1900

PREVIEW AND CHAPTER OBJECTIVES

In the discussion of historiography in Chapter 1, I pointed out that E. G. Boring's famous text, *A History of Experimental Psychology*, was written in part as a way for him to return laboratory research to what he saw as its rightful place at the forefront of American psychology. Boring's concern about the threat to "pure science" was justified—American psychologists in the 1920s seemed to be obsessed with finding new ways to apply psychological principles to everyday life. Actually, interest in application existed from the earliest days of psychology in America, and this chapter will explore both the roots and the development of applied psychology. Its origins lie deeply embedded in the American character and in the economic and institutional contexts of the late nineteenth and early twentieth centuries.

This chapter will examine several examples of applied psychology, starting with the mental testing movement. We will learn how Galton's approach was replaced by the strategy of Alfred Binet of France, how Binet's methods were brought to America, and how a hereditarian view of mental ability colored interpretations of intelligence. The major American mental testers discussed will be James McKeen Cattell, who brought the Galton tradition to America where it quickly failed; Henry Goddard, who brought Binet's test to America where it quickly succeeded; Lewis Terman, developer of the Stanford-Binet IQ test and chief architect of psychology's longest-running experiment; and Robert Yerkes, a comparative psychologist at heart, whose development of the Army testing program was a major reason for Boring's fear that the spread of applied psychology was a direct threat to "pure" experimental psychology.

A second major application of psychology took place in the area of business or industrial psychology. This part of the chapter will feature the work of Hugo Münsterberg, who earned his doctorate with Wundt and came to America to run the Harvard laboratory, but quickly developed applied interests. Münsterberg made contributions to several applied areas, but is best known for his text on industrial psychology. The Original Source Excerpt for this chapter is taken from Münsterberg's industrial psychology text. The chapter concludes with brief descriptions of the work of several other industrial psychologists. Clinical psychology, another important area of application, is considered in Chapters 12 and 13. After you finish this chapter, you should be able to:

■ Understand the reasons why it was important for early American psychologists to show that their "new psychology" had practical applications

- ▓ Describe Cattell's approach to mental testing and, after the Wissler study, why it declined
- ▓ Contrast Binet's individual psychology with a more "general" psychology
- ▓ Describe the origins, the content, and the original purpose of the Binet-Simon scales
- ▓ Describe how Binet's beliefs about mental testing and intelligence differed from most American psychologists who were interested in mental testing
- ▓ Describe Goddard's classification scheme for the different levels of feeblemindedness
- ▓ Describe and critically analyze the Kallikak study
- ▓ Describe and critically analyze Goddard's work at Ellis Island
- ▓ Explain the differences between the original Binet-Simon scale and Terman's revision, the Stanford-Binet
- ▓ Explain how Terman's model of democracy led him to investigate gifted children and describe the findings of his research
- ▓ Describe the contributions of Leta Hollingworth to (a) gifted education and (b) the understanding of gender differences in ability
- ▓ Describe the origins of the Army testing program, distinguish between Alpha and Beta, and explain why the program was so controversial
- ▓ Describe the wide range of contributions made by Hugo Münsterberg to applied psychology
- ▓ Distinguish between the two general strategies used by Münsterberg to improve the employee selection process
- ▓ Describe the contributions to applied psychology of Walter Van Dyke Bingham, Lillian Gilbreth, and Harry Hollingworth

PRESSURES TOWARD APPLICATION

In 1895, Yale psychologist E. W. Scripture published *Thinking, Feeling, Doing*, a book that was intended to explain the new experimental psychology to the general public. He wrote in the preface that he hoped his effort would "be taken as evidence of the attitude of the science in its desire to serve humanity" (Scripture, 1895, p. iii). Perhaps to hold the reader's interest, he included 209 photos and drawings in the 295 pages of text. Most of the book described the basic laboratory procedures in vogue at the time—psychophysics, reaction time, basic sensory processes, and so on. What was unusual, however, was Scripture's attempt to convince the reader that basic

laboratory techniques could improve everyday life. For example, after describing laboratory research in reaction time, Scripture pointed out that the method could be used to study the "psychological elements involved in sports, gymnastics, and all sorts of athletic work" (p. 57). He then proceeded to illustrate the point by adapting the reaction procedures to measure the reaction times involved in such activities as fencing, as you can see in Figure 8.1. He used a similar approach for other standard laboratory methods, as is evident from these captions describing some of the photos found in the book:

Recording a Sportsman's Unsteadiness

Everyone is Somewhat Deaf. Finding the Threshold of Intensity

FIGURE 8.1 Photo from Scripture's *Thinking, Feeling, Doing* (1895) designed to show how reaction time methodology can improve the performance of fencers.

Taking an Orchestra Leader's Record [of rhythmic action] with the Electric Baton

That Scripture believed it necessary to convince the public of psychology's usefulness is just one example of the pressures for application felt by all of the early American psychologists. These pressures were recognized explicitly by John Dewey, in his APA presidential address (1900), when he warned of the dangers inherent in emphasizing pure laboratory research. It could "give us artificialities, mere scientific curiosities [unless] subjected to interpretation by gradual approximation to the conditions of life" (p. 119).

The need for application was partly the consequence of traditional American pragmatism, combined with the progressive drive for reform that infused the late nineteenth and early twentieth centuries. In an age of dramatic technological change, Americans were becoming accustomed to the idea that science should be used to improve their lives. In the last few decades of the century they had witnessed the arrival of such inventions as telephones, the telegraph, typewriters, electric lights (and chairs), skyscrapers, barbed wire, and the kinetoscope (for showing moving pictures). Railroads had expanded so dramatically that by 1900, virtually everyone in America lived within hearing distance of a train. The 35,000 miles of track that existed at the close of the Civil War had expanded to 193,000 miles by 1903 (Cashman, 1993). In the eyes of the public at that time, technology meant progress and progress meant a better life. For psychology to gain public support, it needed to produce useful results.

In addition to the general expectation that science ought to be practical, psychologists at the turn of the century faced institutional pressures for application. Most psychologists still taught within larger departments of philosophy, for instance, and while the philosophers needed little more than an adequate library budget and space for a decent office with a comfortable armchair, the psychologists among them needed significantly greater funds for equipment and physical space for their laboratories. To justify such costs, psychologists felt pressured to show that their new science could be helpful to society.

The pressure for application created strong internal conflicts for many laboratory psychologists. Most had been trained for basic research, conditioned to value the pursuit of knowledge for its own sake. They were also aware of the dangers inherent in promising more than they could hope to deliver. Yet reality forced them to adjust their activities toward application. For one thing, while laboratories proliferated in the decades before and after 1900, those with doctorates in laboratory psychology grew at an even faster rate. Historian John O'Donnell (1985) pointed out that in 1894 the number of psychology Ph.D.'s just about matched the number of available American laboratories, thus providing adequate employment opportunities for psychological scientists. By 1900, however, the number of Ph.D.'s outnumbered labs by three to one (90 to 33 by O'Donnell's count). Thus, not everyone was going to find the ideal job—directing the psychology laboratory at a college or university. Developing expertise as an applied psychologist enhanced one's résumé and put bread on the table.

Some psychologists embraced the idea of using their laboratory training for applied ends, but others were torn by the belief that by engaging in applied work, they were somehow "selling out" their "pure laboratory" principles. For many, the selling was literal because low academic salaries forced them to supplement their income. Taking on extra courses and teaching in the summer were shortcuts to burnout, however, and only minimally useful in easing the financial burden. Hence, many psychologists adjusted their priorities and engaged in the more remunerative activities associated with applied psychology. The experience of Harry Hollingworth illustrates the dilemma. Although he became known as a leading applied psychologist, near the end of his life he wrote that he became one only to earn a living. His "real interest, now and always, has been in the purely theoretical and descriptive problems of my science, and the books, among the twenty I have written, of which I am the proudest, are the ... ones which nobody reads" (cited in Poffenberger, 1957, p. 138).

Applied psychologists contributed their expertise to the areas of education, business, medicine, and the law. One activity common to all of these areas is mental testing. Because psychological testing, especially intelligence testing, is a controversial issue even today, the early history of this movement is worth examining in some detail.

FIGURE 8.2 James McKeen Cattell as an intense young professor at Columbia, from Popplestone and McPherson (1994).

THE MENTAL TESTING MOVEMENT

Mental testing has its origins in the attempts by Galton to measure individual differences. As you recall from Chapter 5, one of his goals was to create measures that could identify those best able to further his eugenic vision. He believed that intelligence was inherited and that it was important to encourage procreation among the able and discourage it among those less capable of strengthening Britain's "racial stock." Galton's attitudes were generally shared by American psychologists and later caused controversy that continues to the present day. The strongest American supporter of Galton in the nineteenth century was Cattell.

James McKeen Cattell (1860–1944): An American Galton

You met James McKeen Cattell briefly in Chapter 4. His research on reaction time in Wundt's laboratory was representative of the technique of estimating the

duration of mental events by adding "complications" to the simple reaction time procedure. Cattell earned his doctorate from Wundt, although as you recall from the Chapter 4 Close-Up, he did not hold a high opinion of Wundt's research operation. Instead, Cattell was enthused by Galton's work in mental testing and the study of individual differences, and he imported the Britisher's ideas to America.

Cattell (Figure 8.2) was raised in an academic environment similar to James Angell's—both had college presidents for fathers. Cattell's father presided over Lafayette College in Easton, Pennsylvania, just across the Delaware River from New Jersey. Young Cattell was schooled at home, and then sent to Lafayette at age 16. There he found the type of education mentioned at the outset of Chapter 6—an emphasis on shaping students to reflect Protestant values (Presbyterian in this case) and a curriculum based in Scottish Realist philosophy, with its focus on strengthening the productive and moral **faculties**. Cattell breezed through, graduating with honors in 1880. One lasting impact of this education resulted from courses taught by Francis Marsh, a well-known philologist (i.e., he studied the nature and history of language). Marsh was a dyed-in-the-wool Baconian inductivist, believing in the importance of collecting data exhaustively, with the assumption that once enough data were at hand, significant patterns and conclusions would become clear (Sokal, 1987). Cattell embraced this strategy, which prepared him to be awed by another Baconian, Francis Galton.

After graduating from Lafayette, Cattell traveled in Europe for a time, and then spent a year (1882–1883) with Hall at Johns Hopkins, where he began the reaction time research that he would continue at Leipzig. In one of his studies, he measured the times taken to identify different letters, which led him to make the practical suggestion that the shapes of those letters taking the longest time to recognize should be altered to improve their legibility. Using himself as the only subject, Cattell also studied the effects of various drugs on behavior and consciousness, later writing that the amounts of caffeine, morphine, hashish, and opium he ingested were "perhaps the largest doses ever taken without suicidal intent" (cited in Sokal, 1971, p. 623).

Cattell planned to stay in Baltimore and perhaps complete a doctorate with Hall, but after a year his fellowship was not renewed; instead, it was given to another promising student, John Dewey (Chapter 7). Cattell then returned to Europe, entered studies with Wundt, and completed his doctorate in 1886. While at Leipzig, he continued his reaction time research, improving technical aspects of the method while completing important studies on mental chronometry and, in keeping with his Baconian principles, contributing extensive data on the effects of such factors as attention, practice, and fatigue on reaction time (Sokal, 1987).

After completing the doctorate, Cattell went to England and briefly studied medicine at Cambridge, but the significant outcome of his time spent there was his exposure to the anthropometric testing being done at this time by Galton. Cattell never studied formally with Galton, but the two met, and for some time after they exchanged correspondence. Cattell later wrote that Galton was the greatest man he had ever known. The two shared the fundamental inductive belief that the more one could measure, the more one would know.

Cattell returned to America in 1889, after being appointed professor of psychology at the University of Pennsylvania. The title was unusual at a time when most psychologists were still considered professors of philosophy, and indicative of the changes that were starting to occur within departments of philosophy. He quickly established a laboratory and set out to continue his reaction time studies and to bring the Galtonian testing approach to America. In an 1890 article in the British journal *Mind*, he summarized the results of testing Penn students on 10 different tests (Cattell, 1890/1948). Some were borrowed from Galton, but Cattell eliminated the strictly physical measurements (e.g., height, weight, length of arm span), which led him to call his article "Mental Tests and Measurements." With this article, Cattell coined the term **mental test**.

The article's opening sentence revealed Cattell's inductivism: "Psychology cannot attain the certainty and exactness of the physical sciences, unless it rests on a foundation of experiment and measurement" (Cattell, 1890/1948, p. 347). He did not propose any specific purpose for the tests, merely indicating in vague terms that people might "find their tests interesting" (p. 347) and that the results might somehow be "useful in regard to training, mode of life or indication of disease" (p. 347). The 10 tests, which Cattell estimated to take an hour, are summarized briefly in Table 8.1.

Cattell spent just two years at Penn before accepting (at a still youthful age of 31) an offer to head the psychology program at Columbia, where he remained until being fired in 1917. At Columbia, his testing plans became even more ambitious as he expanded the number of tests beyond the original 10 and reinstated some of the physical measurements. Within a few years he was lobbying the authorities for permission to test every incoming Columbia freshman, suggesting that the results could be useful "to determine the condition and progress of students, the relative value of different courses of study, etc." (cited in Sokal, 1987, p. 32). Initially, he was not thinking of using the tests to predict the success of

Table 8.1   Cattell's Mental Tests

In his article on mental tests, Cattell (1890) described these procedures.

1. *Dynamometer pressure.* This was a measure of grip strength, which Cattell believed to be more than just a physical measure; mental effort and concentration were involved.
2. *Rate of movement.* How quickly one's hand could move across a 50 cm interval was determined; Cattell believed that mental effort and concentration also contributed to this measure.
3. *Sensation-areas.* Two-point thresholds on the back of the closed right hand were measured.
4. *Pressure causing pain.* The narrow (5 mm in radius) tip of hard rubber was pressed into the forehead until pain was reported.
5. *Least noticeable difference in weight.* This was a traditional psychophysics procedure involving the lifting of small boxes that differed slightly in weight.
6. *Reaction time for sound.* For Cattell, this was the most reliable variety of reaction time.
7. *Time for naming colors.* Ten colored papers were pasted adjacent to each other, to be named as quickly as possible.
8. *Bisection of a 50 cm line.* A movable line had to be adjusted until it was at a perceived midpoint.
9. *Judgment of 10 sec time.* After an experimenter tapped a pencil twice, with 10 sec between, those being tested had to repeat the task
10. *Number of letters repeated on once hearing.* This was an early version of a short-term memory test, to determine how many letters could be repeated verbatim.

Columbia students. Instead, he was keeping to his Baconian program of accumulating as much information on individual differences as possible, and then seeing what could be concluded from them. He assumed that the results would eventually reveal relationships between different measures and provide some overall indication of mental capacity.

For the remaining years of the 1890s, Cattell and his students accumulated masses of data, but the project collapsed shortly after the turn of the century. Cattell, who was mathematically inept, had learned of Galton's correlational procedures. He asked one of his graduate students, Clark Wissler, to apply the new technique to the testing results, hoping to reveal strong mathematical relationships between the measures and to relate them to academic performance. Wissler completed the correlations and the outcome was devastating for Cattell—the tests were unrelated to each other and unconnected with anything academic. A student's performance in any one class (including gym!) correlated more highly with academic performance than did any of Cattell's tests (Wissler, 1901/1965). Table 8.2 shows some of these correlations. As you will learn shortly, Wissler's research appeared at the time when Alfred Binet was pioneering a different approach to mental testing in France. Almost immediately, the Binet approach succeeded and the Galton/Cattell strategy passed quietly from the scene.

After the mental testing debacle, Cattell turned his attention away from research and toward another of his interests, the professionalizing of psychology. A charter member of the American Psychological Association, he was an active participant and in 1895, its fourth president. In 1894, he helped to launch what would become one of psychology's more prestigious journals, *Psychological Review*, and a year later he took over the editorship of the financially ailing journal *Science* and rejuvenated it. By 1910, he had made it into the most important scientific journal published in America (Sokal, 1981b).

After the turn of the century, Cattell devoted most of his time to editorial and departmental administrative work. Always outspoken, he continually irritated the Columbia administration by arguing for greater faculty participation in academic decision making and for increased academic freedom (i.e., a faculty member's right to investigate and teach about controversial topics). In 1917, he finally pushed the administration over the edge by publicly protesting the government's policy of quickly sending conscientious objectors into combat in World War I. Columbia's president accused him of treason and fired him. Cattell sued for libel and won a large settlement, but his academic career was effectively over. He continued his editorial work, however, and returned to applied psychology by founding the Psychological Corporation in 1921. Designed to be

Table 8.2   Sample Results of Wissler's Study on Mental Testing

Correlations among various mental tests
(those tests in Table 8.1 plus some additional ones):

	No. of Cases	Correlation
Reaction time and color naming	118	+.15
Reaction time and association	153	+.08
Marking A's and color naming	159	+.21
Rate of movement and color naming	97	+.19

Correlations between mental tests and "college standing":

	No. of Cases	Correlation
Reaction time	227	−.02
Marking A's	242	−.09
Association	160	+.08
Naming colors	112	+.02
Logical memory	86	+.19

Correlations between performance scores for different school subjects:

	No. of Cases	Correlation
Latin and math	228	+.58
Math and rhetoric	222	+.51
German and math	115	+.52
Latin and Greek	121	+.75
Gymnasium and average grade	119	+.53

Source: Wissler (1901/1965, pp. 443–445).

an organization of psychologist-consultants, it began at a time when American psychologists had high expectations for the applicability of their knowledge. Cattell proved to be a poor administrator, however, and although the Psychological Corporation exists today as a profitable subsidiary of a major publishing house, it barely survived the 1920s under Cattell's flawed leadership (Sokal, 1981a).

Alfred Binet (1857–1911): The Birth of Intelligence Testing

The Cattell/Galton strategy for assessing individual differences relied on an assortment of physical measurements and the results of simple sensory and

perceptual tasks. A completely different approach, which focused on more complex mental phenomena and used children rather than college students or adults as subjects, developed in Europe. One advocate was Hermann Ebbinghaus, the famous memory researcher (Chapter 4), who developed a completion test in the mid-1890s as a way to assess the effects of mental fatigue in schoolchildren. He was responding to a practical problem—it seemed to the authorities in the German city of Breslau that the five-hour uninterrupted morning school session (8:00 to 1:00) was producing "fatigue and nervous irritability" (Ebbinghaus, 1897/1965, p. 433). City leaders appointed a commission to study the problem, and its first task was to determine the precise degree to which this five-hour school day affected children. Some research in the Galtonian tradition used two-point thresholds as a measure, finding that changes in the thresholds occurred during the course of the school day. Ebbinghaus was unimpressed with the method, however, questioning the connection between skin sensitivity and school performance: "Are children who show a deterioration [in sensitivity] also to be regarded as mentally exhausted in other respects, or have they merely become incapable of performing that fixed, relatively insignificant task to which they are not accustomed?" (p. 435). If the goal was to assess mental fatigue, he argued, then the measures ought to be of cognitive activities, not sensory ones. On the assumption that an important aspect of intellectual ability involves taking incomplete information and forming it into a comprehensible whole, Ebbinghaus came up with the idea of giving students incomplete prose passages. That is, they were shown sentences that had syllables missing from words and in some cases whole words missing from sentences. Their job was to fill in the gaps to make the sentences complete and meaningful. Ebbinghaus was able to show that his completion tests distinguished between strong and weak students, but he did not find any consistent differences in performance over the five-hour school day, which remained intact.

Ebbinghaus did not develop his testing program further, but his basic strategy was the one taken by another European, Alfred Binet of France. Like Ebbinghaus, Binet was responding to an educational dilemma. We have already seen that public education increased dramatically in the United States toward the end of the century. The phenomenon was not limited to America, however—the same thing was occurring in Europe. Compulsory education, however, meant that some children would be in school even though their lack of mental ability made it impossible for them to succeed in normal classes. By the turn of the century, school officials in Paris were faced with the problem of how to identify these children so they could be placed in what we would call special education classes today. In 1904, a commission was formed to study the problem; it included Binet, one of France's leading psychologists.

Binet's status among his peers was not always so high. In the mid-1880s, he published some dubious research on hypnosis, claiming that hysteric symptoms displayed in that state could be transferred from one side of the body to another by reversing the polarity of a magnet held next to the patient. More sober researchers demonstrated that the effects were entirely the result of suggestion, and an embarrassed Binet was forced to retract his claim in print. He gradually resurrected his reputation, however, after becoming an unpaid research assistant at the recently created Laboratory of Physiological Psychology at the Sorbonne in Paris in 1891. He was successful enough to be named director of the laboratory in just three years, a position he held until his premature death in 1911 at the age of 54.

Even before starting his work at the Sorbonne, Binet had begun making careful observations of his two young daughters (Figure 8.3). The work shaped his belief in the value of conducting detailed case studies, and it contributed to his lifelong interest in studying and measuring individual differences. Binet was aware of Galton's work and used some of Galton's sensory tests on his daughters. He was surprised to discover that there didn't seem to be much difference between his daughters' scores and the scores reported for adults. Adults appeared to be superior only on tasks that involved mental processing that went beyond sensory capacity. For example, compared with adults, his daughters did quite poorly on color naming, a task requiring memory and language, but very well on color matching, a purely perceptual task. These and other similar results led Binet to conclude that Galton's sensory measures were inadequate to assess mental ability.[1] He made the key insight that differences between the intellects of children and adults could only be determined by examining the more complex higher mental processes (Fancher, 1985).

During his years at the Sorbonne, Binet developed a program of research that focused on the study

---

[1] Cattell, during the time he was deeply immersed in his Galtonian program of testing at Columbia in the 1890s, knew all about Binet's work but rejected the new tests of "higher" mental processes as poorly defined and not capable of sufficient quantification (Sokal, 1987).

FIGURE 8.3 Alfred Binet, with his wife and the two daughters whose development he studied, from Popplestone and McPherson (1994).

of individual differences. In an important paper coauthored with his assistant Victor Henri, he contrasted his **individual psychology** with a more general psychology. The latter is concerned with the discovery of general laws that apply to some degree to everyone (e.g., repetition strengthens memory), while individual psychology "studies the properties of psychic processes that vary from individual to individual—it has to determine the various properties and then study how much and in what ways they vary with the individuals" (Binet & Henri, 1895/1965, p. 428). Studying these differences required being able to measure them, of course, and that problem led Binet directly to his attempts to develop tests of mental processes. By 1904, when Paris school officials needed a way to identify students with low ability for special classes, Binet already had some definite ideas about what kinds of tests to use.

The term retarded did not exist as a category of mental disability in Binet's time. Instead, children with limited capacity were divided into three overlapping and poorly defined categories. *Idiots* were severely handicapped and not capable of caring for themselves; *imbeciles* were somewhat more capable but still not able to be independent; the third level included children capable of learning, but not in normal school classes. These were the children to be identified for special education, and Binet labeled

them *débiles* (translation: weak ones). He was appalled at existing diagnostic criteria and determined to develop a more reliable way of differentiating these "weak" children from the normal school population. He drew on a dozen years of his research into individual psychology, and the result was the first intelligence test.

The Binet-Simon Scales

Along with his research assistant Theodore Simon, Binet published the first version of his test in 1905. They revised it three years later and again in 1911, just before Binet's death. They did not begin with a preconceived definition of intelligence, from which they derived the tests to be used. Rather, they developed the test empirically by identifying two groups of students, one normal and one clearly impaired, and giving them a long series of tests that appeared to be conceptually related to intelligence, looking for tests that differentiated between the groups. They eventually produced a series of 30 tests of increasing difficulty for their original 1905 test. By the 1908 revision, the number of tests grew to 58, and Binet and Simon incorporated age levels between 3 and 13. Table 8.3 lists some of the tests at different ages (note the contrast with Cattell's tests in Table 8.1).

Adding age levels was Binet's way of solving the diagnosis problem. He believed that subnormal

Table 8.3   A Sample of Binet & Simon's Tests of Mental Levels

The 1908 revision of the Binet-Simon scale contained 58 different tests, arranged within 11 different age levels (313). Here are some of the tests.

Three Years

show eyes, nose, mouth
repeat 6-syllable sentence
name objects in picture

Five Years

copy a square
compare 2 boxes, different wts.
repeat 10-syllable sentence

Seven Years

copy written sentence
repeat five digits
indicate omissions in drawings

Nine Years

name days of week
retain 6 memories after reading
arrange five weights in order

Eleven Years

criticize absurd sentences*
place 3 given words in a sentence
give abstract definitions

Thirteen Years

differentiate word meanings
solve reversed triangle problem
solve paper cutting problem

* For example: The body of an unfortunate girl was found, cut into 18 pieces. It is thought that she killed herself.
Source: Dennis (1948).

children could be defined in terms of how far behind they were in years. Thus, a normal 5-year-old could solve the tasks at the 5-year level, but a subnormal 5-year-old might only be able to score at the 4-year level. Binet called the level at which a child scored the **mental level**, a term later mistranslated as "mental age." He believed that children scoring at a mental level two years behind their actual age, a group he estimated to include 7% of the population, should be considered débiles and placed in special classes (Fancher, 1985). In general, Binet defined intelligence in functional terms as "the faculty of adapting oneself. To judge well, to understand well, to reason well—these are the essential wellsprings of intelligence" (Binet & Simon, 1905, cited in Fancher, 1985, p. 74).

In light of how the concept of IQ evolved over the years, it is instructive to note Binet's attitudes about intelligence and its measurement. First, he believed that intelligence was multifaceted, composed of a variety of skills. Thus, while he reduced the outcome of the tests to a single unit, mental level, he did so reluctantly. Had he lived, he would have been disturbed at the way in which the concept of IQ came to connote a unitary concept of intelligence. Second, he believed that within broad limits, mental levels could increase with training, and he developed a set of mental orthopedics to help children improve their intelligence levels. Binet was scornful of the prevailing opinion of his day, derived from evolutionary thinking, that intelligence was a fixed and unchangeable trait. Third, Binet believed that his scale was useful only within the narrow educational context of identifying weak students. He would have been surprised at how quickly the tool became much more widely used, as we are about to see.

Henry H. Goddard (1866–1957): Binet's Test Comes to America

Henry Goddard (Figure 8.4) was a product of Hall's genetic psychology at Clark University, earning a doctorate there in 1899. After teaching for a few years at West Chester Teacher's College in Pennsylvania, he accepted an invitation from the Vineland Training School for the Feeble-Minded in southern New Jersey to develop a research program there. His initial efforts reflected his training—he set up a laboratory in imitation of the one he knew at Clark and began testing the children using standard

FIGURE 8.4 Henry Goddard, atop one of the pyramids of Egypt, from Popplestone and McPherson (1994).

existing classification system, based on Binet's mental level concept, which was now being called **mental age**. Idiots would now be defined as those scoring at mental ages 1 to 2, and imbeciles would be those with mental ages between 3 and 7. As for the third category, Binet's débile, Goddard proposed a new name. These children had sometimes been called feebleminded, but that term was also used to describe the entire spectrum of mental retardation. Yet it was important to have a clear category for these children, Goddard argued, "in order to make the public understand that there is a special group of children that requires special help" (Goddard, 1910, p. 395). Goddard proposed using the term **moron**, from the Greek word moronia, which means "foolish." These would be people with mental ages between 8 and 12.[2] Goddard's creation of the term and his promotion of its use helped to legitimize psychology as a professional discipline. Morons were believed to be responsible for many of society's ills, but to the average person they appeared to be normal, Goddard argued. To identify them, therefore, society needed the help of highly trained experts. Psychologists such as Goddard made it clear that they were the ones best prepared for the role.

Over the next few years, Goddard became a leading advocate of the Binet-Simon tests, and many others were soon using it to identify and classify those with limited mental capacity. Vineland distributed about 20,000 copies of his translated Binet-Simon test between 1910 and 1914 (Watson & Evans, 1991). Goddard's ultimate goals, however, were very different from Binet's. Unlike Binet, Goddard was a strong believer in the widely held notion that intelligence was inherited and represented a fixed quantity. Well aware of the recent rediscovery of Mendel's work on genetics, Goddard came to believe that most feeblemindedness was caused by a single recessive gene. To support his hereditarian case, he published the results of a seemingly conclusive study of the family roots of one of the Vineland children.

laboratory tasks similar to the ones being used by Cattell. Goddard quickly learned that he was in a new environment and that using basic sensory tasks was easier said than done, however. His notes contain entries such as this: "A boy frightened at an insignificant thing so that it took six men to hold him could not squeeze a pound on the Dynamometer tho he clearly understood what was wanted" (quoted in Popplestone & McPherson, 1984, p. 242).

In search of better methods, Goddard discovered Binet's work while on a European tour of institutions for the feebleminded in 1908. He was unimpressed with the Binet-Simon tests at first, but brought the scale back with him anyway, translated it into English, and began administering it to the Vineland children. When the Binet-Simon results matched the expectations based on other observations of the children, Goddard became a convert. At a 1910 meeting of the American Association of the Feeble-Minded, he reported the results of testing 400 Vineland children and proposed a refinement of the

---

[2] These terms—idiot, imbecile, and moron—did not carry the derogatory connotation they do today. They were meant to be clinical terms used for diagnostic purposes, not names to be tossed around derisively in schoolyards.

The Kallikaks

Goddard made his case that feeblemindedness had a genetic basis in a 117-page book published in 1912 called *The Kallikak Family: A Study in the Heredity of Feeblemindedness*. In it he described an extensive genealogical study of one of his wards at Vineland. "Deborah Kallikak" was 22 at the time and had lived at Vineland for 14 years. She had been referred to Vineland when she was eight, supposedly because she "did not get along well at school and might possibly be feebleminded" (Goddard, 1912, p. 1). In reality, the refusal of her mother's third husband to provide support for several of the woman's younger children, including Deborah, contributed to the placement. At Vineland, Deborah was tested periodically with the Binet-Simon scales, never achieving a mental age greater than 9 years. Goddard considered her to be an illustration of the person ideally suited for Vineland. Although she had learned to sew, cook, and do quite competent woodworking, she could barely read or do math. If Deborah were to leave the safe and controlled environment of Vineland, Goddard believed,

> ... she would at once become a prey to the designs of evil men or women and would lead a life that would be vicious, immoral, and criminal, though because of her mentality she herself would not be responsible. There is nothing that she might not be led into, because she has no power of control, and all her instincts and appetites are in the direction that would lead to vice. (p. 12)

How could one account for such an individual? For Goddard the answer was simple: "'Heredity'— bad stock. We must recognize that the human family shows varying stocks or strains that are as marked and breed as true as anything in plant or animal life" (Goddard, 1912, p. 12).

Goddard routinely sent workers into the field to gather information about the backgrounds of those referred to Vineland. In Deborah's case, it soon became clear that many relatives lived close by and that the family was "notorious for the number of defectives and delinquents it had produced" (Goddard, 1912, p. 16). Goddard's diligent assistants were able to trace six generations and "an appalling

amount of defectiveness was everywhere found" (p. 16). On the other hand, field workers occasionally found themselves among relatives who were highly educated and living in comfortable environments. Further digging yielded a tale of a family that had branched in two decidedly different directions.

It seemed that a distant relative, a soldier in the Revolutionary War, behaved like soldiers sometimes do and had a brief affair with a young "feebleminded" girl that he met in a tavern. The result was a feebleminded son, Deborah's great-great grandfather, and the start of a long line of mental deficiency, the "bad" Kallikaks. Meanwhile, the soldier, unaware of the havoc he had created by sowing his wild oats, settled down, married "a respectable girl of good family" (p. 29), and began producing the "good" Kallikaks. Because the unfortunate girl at the tavern gave her young son the father's name, both sides of the family bore the same surname.

Upon examining the Kallikaks, Goddard uncovered a stark contrast in the fates of those representing the two sides of the family. On Deborah's side, Goddard's field workers identified 480 descendants and on the basis of historical records, family histories, and some direct testing of living relatives, classified 189 of them: 143 were found to be feebleminded, while only 46 were normal. On the other hand, the descendants of the soldier and his respectable bride tended to be pillars of the community: doctors, lawyers, educators, and so on. Of 496 descendants, only 3 were found to be "somewhat degenerate, but ... not [mentally] defective. Two of these were alcoholic, and the other sexually loose" (p. 29).

Despite the apparent thoroughness of the Kallikak study, it was seriously flawed. The most obvious problem was Goddard's failure to recognize that the environment had any significant effect on the fates of the two sides of the family. Nutritional and health care differences alone could have accounted for the large differences between the groups in infant mortality: 82 (bad side) versus just 15 (good side). Rather than a case study of the genetics of feeblemindedness, then, the Kallikak study could just as easily represent a case study of the differential effects of poverty and privilege. Goddard himself was of course highly intelligent; his inability to believe that the environment was important in the Kallikak family histories says more about the powerful influence of the contemporary historical context than it does about his individual shortcomings. Indeed, the strong belief that intelligence level was a consequence of heredity, taken for granted by most turn-of-the-century psychologists, even led Goddard to argue that the environments of the two groups were about the same.

Goddard's bias also affected the way he interpreted his data. Much of the information about family members was secondhand and sketchy, with ambiguous events interpreted according to whether the person was on one side of the family or the other. Also, Goddard forgot some basic rules of logic. For example, a feebleminded person might be led into a life of crime or vice, but the reverse does not necessarily follow, for there are lots of other reasons to become a criminal (e.g., poverty). Yet any Kallikak from the "bad" side with questionable morals was automatically classified as a moron by Goddard and his assistants. At the very beginning of the story, Goddard merely assumed that the girl in the tavern was feebleminded, apparently on the questionable grounds that she was working in a tavern and let herself be seduced by a soldier! In short, the Kallikak study, rather than being good science, is a classic illustration of how preconception can influence the collection and interpretation of data.

The name Kallikak was a pseudonym, of course, constructed by Goddard to protect Deborah's identity. He chose the name from two Greek words— Kalos, meaning "good," and Kakos, meaning "bad." He thought the name nicely captured the two sides of the unfortunate Deborah's family.

Goddard's conviction about the cause of mental defectiveness led him to an obvious solution to the problem—eliminate the gene. Hence, Goddard became a confirmed eugenicist, arguing that the mentally defective should be prevented from breeding. If this social engineering could be accomplished, then feeblemindedness could be eliminated in just a few generations. Goddard's primary recommendation was that states build more institutions like Vineland, so that idiots, imbeciles, and morons could be properly diagnosed, removed from society, and prevented from having children by being carefully

monitored. He also supported other prominent psychologists, including Thorndike, Yerkes, and Terman, in recommending the sterilization of the mentally unfit, pointing out that "[t]he operation itself is almost as simple in males as having a tooth pulled. In females it is not much more serious" (Goddard, 1912, p. 108). Sterilization was a relatively new procedure, however, so Goddard advised caution until its long-term effects were better known.

Thus, Goddard had a plan for dealing with feeblemindedness in America. But what about the importation of mental deficiency? In the early years of the new century, there was growing concern about an apparent threat to the American gene pool—rampant immigration. Goddard thought he had a solution to this problem also.

Goddard and the Immigrants

The United States has always been a nation of immigrants, but a regular feature of American political life is that immigrants who have lived in America for a few generations often seek to restrict new immigration. This was true at the turn of the century when the number of immigrants increased dramatically, and these "new" immigrants seemed to be decidedly inferior to "old" immigrants. Throughout most of the nineteenth century, the majority of immigrants came from western and northern Europe. For instance, 788,992 hopeful men, women, and children arrived in 1882; of these 87% were from Germany, Great Britain, and Scandinavia, whereas a mere 13% were from southern and eastern European countries such as Italy, Poland, and Russia. By 1907, however, when the total number of arrivals grew to 1,285,349, the proportions had reversed—just over 80% now came from southern and eastern Europe (data from Cashman, 1993). With this shift came increased fears among those whose ancestors had arrived from northern Europe about the "quality" of the new immigrants. The old immigrants, generally Anglo-Saxon, Protestant, and at least moderately well-educated, contrasted strongly with the new immigrants, who were generally poor and uneducated, had larger families, were more culturally diverse, and were more likely to be Catholic or Jewish. Most Americans simply disagreed with the sentiments of the poet Emma Lazarus, who wrote that the Statue of

Liberty, unveiled in 1886, symbolized a welcome to "your tired, your poor, your huddled masses yearning to breathe free."

New York was the main entry point for European immigrants and to handle the growing numbers of huddled masses, the federal government in 1892 built a large immigration station on Ellis Island, a mile southwest of Manhattan and within sight of the Statue of Liberty. Immigrants arriving there, as many as 10,000 a day in the early 1900s, had to go through a series of evaluations before being allowed to enter the country.[3] Most immigrants passed through the Ellis Island inspections in a few hours, but about 20% were held for more detailed evaluations, and 1% to 2% were not allowed into the country (Schlereth, 1991). To be admitted, immigrants had to show that they were free from contagious diseases and mental illness, physically capable of working, not completely destitute, and not mentally defective. This latter criterion was difficult to measure, however, and Ellis Island examiners were concerned that "high-grade" defectives were slipping through the system.

It was in this context that Goddard, anxious to demonstrate the diagnostic usefulness of the Binet tests, appeared on the scene. He first visited Ellis Island in 1911, and then returned with two research assistants in 1912. With one of his assistants picking out immigrants who "looked" defective and a second administering some of the Binet tests, Goddard contended that his team could quickly identify mental defectives with about 90% accuracy. In one instance, Goddard's workers selected a young boy suspected of being defective and gave him the test with the aid of an interpreter. The boy scored an 8 on the Binet-Simon scale. Goddard reported that the "interpreter said 'I could not have done that when I came to this country,' and seemed to think the test unfair. We convinced him that the boy was defective" (Goddard, 1913, p. 105). Clearly, because of his naive faith in the technology of testing, Goddard failed to consid-

er that the immigrants were undoubtedly intimidated and confused by the entire Ellis Island experience and that they probably failed to understand why they were being asked to complete these odd tests.

Some physicians working at Ellis Island objected that the Binet tests, being highly verbal, were inadequate for detecting feeblemindedness (Richardson, 2003). Nonetheless, officials at Ellis Island were impressed enough to invite Goddard to expand his operation. In 1913, two female assistants spent two and a half months at Ellis Island. Through interpreters, they tested 165 Russian, Hungarian, Jewish, and Italian immigrants on the Binet-Simon and several other tests. Goddard found that a disturbingly large proportion, about 80%, scored at a mental level of 12 or below (i.e., morons). Even after readjusting the scores to take cultural factors into account, he estimated that about 40% of the sample was feebleminded and concluded that "one can hardly escape the conviction that the intelligence of the average 'third class' immigrant is low, perhaps of moron grade" (Goddard, 1917, p. 243).

As a result of Goddard's work, mental testing became a part of the screening process at Ellis Island, perhaps contributing to an increase in the percentage of deportations over the next few years. In 1913, for example, 555 people were deported on the grounds of being "feebleminded," triple the number deported in each of the previous five years (Richardson, 2003). No accurate estimate exists, but it is safe to say that during the second decade of the twentieth century, a few thousand hopeful immigrants, yearning to breathe free, were nonetheless sent back to Europe because they performed poorly on the Binet-Simon scales.

As for Goddard, he only remained at Vineland for a few more years. In 1918, the state of Ohio hired him to direct their Bureau of Juvenile Research, which had just been established to deal with the problem of juvenile delinquency. Four years later he became professor of abnormal and clinical psychology at the Ohio State University where he remained until his retirement in 1938. While there, he broadened his interests by studying children at the other end of the spectrum from those at Vineland—the so-called gifted students. These later experiences led him to write a remarkable

---

[3] When ships carrying immigrants arrived in New York harbor, only those passengers traveling in "steerage" (i.e., poor) were transported to Ellis Island for examination. Immigrants traveling first or second class were given a brief examination in their cabins on board ship and then allowed to enter the city (Richardson, 2003).

paper in 1928, in which he reversed many of his earlier views. He decided that a mental age of 12 did not necessarily mean feeblemindedness, that many of those diagnosed as morons could function in society and did not need to be institutionalized, and that the danger of them producing feebleminded offspring had been overstated. He considered the problem of the moron to be primarily one of education and argued that "when we get an education that is entirely right there will be no morons who cannot manage themselves and their affairs and compete in the struggle for existence" (Goddard, 1928, p. 224). By the end of his career, then, Goddard had moved closer to Binet's original vision for educating those of marginal ability.

Lewis M. Terman (1877–1956): Institutionalizing IQ

Like Goddard, Lewis Terman was a product of Hall's psychology program at Clark University. He arrived there in 1903, just after finishing a master's degree at Indiana University, not far from his boyhood home on a large farm in the Hoosier State. Indiana was rather like a midwestern branch of Clark University—its philosophy department featured three psychologists, William Bryan, Ernest Lindley, and John Bergström, who were all Clark graduates. In their classes, young Terman "became fired with the ambition to become a professor of psychology and to contribute something myself to the science" (Terman, 1932, p. 310). Lindley was especially influential and in a seminar with him, Terman wrote extensive papers on "degeneracy" and "great men." The projects brought him in contact with the writings of Binet and Galton, and began to foreshadow his life's work (Minton, 1988). At Clark, his interests in intelligence and its testing only deepened, and his doctoral dissertation compared the mental and physical abilities of 14 preadolescent boys, "seven bright and seven dull" (Terman, 1906, p. 314). The former group outperformed the latter on all of the mental tests, which included Binet-like procedures such as problem solving, language, and memory, whereas the dull group did better on some motor coordination tasks. Perhaps influenced by his strong attraction to Galton's ideas, Terman believed that his study supported "the relatively greater importance of

endowment over training, as a determinant of an individual's intellectual rank" (p. 372). Terman never wavered in his belief that heredity was the prime determiner of intelligence.

Terman suffered from periodic bouts with tuberculosis, both before and during his Clark years, which led him to search for warm-climate employment after completing his doctorate in 1905. He spent a year as a school superintendent in San Bernardino, California, then landed an academic position, teaching child psychology and pedagogy at Los Angeles State Normal School (which later became UCLA). The big break came in 1910, when he was asked to move north to Palo Alto and join the faculty at Stanford University. The opening was sudden and unexpected—Terman replaced his former Indiana teacher, John Bergström, who went to Stanford in 1908, but died two years later at age 42 (Capshew & Hearst, 1980). Within 12 years, Terman was chairing the psychology department, which he built into one of the premier departments in the country. Terman, three of his faculty recruits, and four of the doctoral students there during his tenure became APA presidents (Hilgard, 1957). He was much admired as a teacher, especially for the stimulating Monday evening seminars held at his home, recreating the atmosphere he had experienced as a student in Hall's famous Monday seminars. Terman retired from Stanford in 1941, but remained professionally active until his death in 1956, just a few weeks before his eightieth birthday. His legacy to psychology includes (a) developing one of the world's best-known IQ tests and (b) conducting the longest-running psychology research project of all time.

The Stanford-Binet IQ Test

We have seen that Goddard translated the Binet-Simon scales into English and first introduced them to America. Terman, however, went far beyond translation, accomplishing a revision and the first standardization of the test. On the basis of some research with local schoolchildren, he determined that some of the Binet tests were too easy for young children and too hard for older children. For instance, average 5-year-olds often tested at a mental age greater than 5, while average 10-year-olds tested at a mental age less than 10. Terman added some new tests, including some of the ones created for his dissertation, revised others, and eliminated a few. Between 1910 and 1914, he standardized his test, using about 2300 participants, mostly children and adolescents from middle-class environments, but also about 400 adults. He eventually arrived at a series of 90 test items, compared with 54 in Binet's final (1911) version. Along with a complete set of norms that resulted from his standardization effort, Terman published in 1916 what he called the Stanford Revision of the Binet-Simon test. It became known as the Stanford-Binet, and it quickly dominated the market and earned Terman a healthy income in royalties. Terman completely revised and restandardized it again in 1937. In a more recent version, it remains perhaps the best known individual test of intelligence.

The 1916 Stanford-Binet included a concept that Binet would have found disturbing—IQ. Terman borrowed it from a leader of the testing movement in Germany, William Stern. Stern had pointed out that an average 5-year-old should score at a mental level of 5, while a very bright 5-year-old might achieve a mental level of 6 or higher, and a slow 5-year-old could score lower than 5. He suggested that mental ability be summarized in a "mental quotient" that represented the relationship between mental age and chronological age, found by dividing the former by the latter. For Terman, the idea meshed nicely with his norming procedures and with his growing belief that intelligence was a unitary trait. He changed Stern's "mental quotient" to **intelligence quotient** or IQ, multiplied the ratio by 100 to lose the decimal point, and built it into the revision. With the 1916 Stanford-Binet, then, the IQ was born. Three 5-year-olds with mental ages of 4, 5, and 6 would have IQs of 80, 100, and 120, respectively. The message was clear—mental capacity could be represented in a single number.

Terman Studies the Gifted

Binet's original purpose in developing his test was to identify children in need of special training. Terman went beyond this vision, however, and believed that his IQ test could identify special children at both ends of the continuum. His long-standing interest in students at the upper end of the scale led him to design his best-known research, a study of giftedness. His original intent was to identify a group of talented children, then follow up on their lives at some later time to see if their promise had been fulfilled. Instead, the project took on a life of its own, continuing long after Terman himself died. It became psychology's longest-running longitudinal study.

In formulating his plans for the study, Terman was motivated by his hereditarian ideas about intelligence and his strong belief that America should be a **meritocracy**. That is, he believed its leaders should be those shown to be capable of leading. IQ testing, he suggested, would be a good way to identify such people. With the possible exception of one's morals, he once wrote, "nothing about an individual [was] as important as his IQ" (quoted in Minton, 1988, p. 99). Terman's vision of a true democracy meant equal opportunity, but only for those with the ability to profit from their opportunities. Those with low IQs, which Terman referred to as "democracy's ballast" (p. 99), could also reach fulfillment in life if properly identified, trained, and placed in jobs suitable for them. Thus, large-scale IQ testing could produce a classification system that would result in different types of education for different levels of ability. Terman believed this system would "go far toward insuring that every pupil, whether mentally superior, average, or inferior, shall have a chance to make the most of whatever abilities nature has given to him" (quoted in Minton, 1987, p. 102).

With this ideal meritocracy in mind, Terman set out to identify gifted children in 1921. His aim was to select the top 1% of all California schoolchildren, but because of logistical and financial problems, his team of field workers concentrated on just a few large and medium-sized urban areas. Teachers were asked to identify the three smartest children and the youngest child in their classes. These children were then tested with a group intelligence test and a brief version of the Stanford-Binet. Those scoring highest were given the full Stanford-Binet.

The outcome was a group of 1470 children, 824 boys and 646 girls. Most were in elementary school, but the group included 444 from junior or senior high school (sample size data from Minton, 1988, pp. 114–115). The average IQ was 151 for the younger children and 143 for the high schoolers. Interestingly enough, the student most likely to be chosen for the study was not one of the three smartest identified by teachers in a particular class, but the youngest. The sampling procedures appeared to be reasonable, but the resulting sample was not representative. Students tended to be middle- to upper-class, Protestant, and white, and their fathers tended to hold professional rather than working-class occupations. Jewish children were also over-represented, while nonwhites and the poor were underrepresented (Cravens, 1992). The bias occurred in a number of subtle ways, from teacher selections to the reluctance of field workers to go to some schools in urban areas. For example, one of Terman's workers omitted 14 Los Angeles schools that had been set aside by authorities "to handle children who had been found guilty of minor offenses" (Minton, 1988, p. 114).

Having selected a sample, Terman's team compiled considerable information for each child, the result being the 600-page *Genetic Studies of Genius: Mental and Physical Traits of a Thousand Gifted Children* (Terman, 1925). Terman retested the group in the late 1920s and conducted major follow-ups 25 (Terman & Oden, 1947) and 35 years (Terman & Oden, 1959) after the original testing. After Terman died, Robert Sears, a member of the gifted group and by then a distinguished research psychologist himself, took over the project. He produced five additional follow-ups between 1960 and 1986 and was preparing *The Later Maturity of the Gifted* when he died in 1989 (Cronbach, Hastorf, Hilgard, & Maccoby, 1990).

The traditional view of gifted children is that while they are intellectually superior, they are physically weak, socially inferior, and they burn out at a young age, never quite fulfilling their childhood promise. Terman's research questioned all aspects of this stereotype, however. In follow-up after follow-up, his group appeared to be not just smarter than others but more successful, productive, well adjusted, and physically healthy. Most entered professional life, but this was less likely to occur for the females in the group. Although more likely to be in a career than their nongifted peers, the women of Terman's group tended to be frustrated by the lack of opportunities for women in America at mid-century (Minton, 1988).

One final aspect of the study worth noting is Terman's devotion to the group and the corresponding loyalty of those who came to call themselves "Termites." A typical problem in longitudinal research is **attrition**—as time goes by, subjects drop out of the study for a variety of reasons. Attrition was not a problem for Terman, however. Of those subjects who were alive for the follow-up studies done after 10, 25, and 35 years, the percentages of those participating were 92, 98, and 93, respectively (Minton, 1988). Terman corresponded regularly with hundreds of his Termites and cared very much about the progress of their lives. This is not too surprising, of course, for in Terman's mind, these were the meritorious people holding the key to America's future.

Terman is often credited with being the pioneer in the study of gifted children, and with reason. But there were others interested in the topic, Goddard for instance, and a woman whose work on the gifted preceded Terman's. She might not have studied them as systematically as Terman did, but a strong case can be made that Leta Hollingworth was the first advocate for specialized education for gifted children. This chapter's Close-Up examines her work on behalf of gifted children and also describes her research that debunked the idea that women were intellectually inferior to men.

CLOSE-UP:
Leta Hollingworth:
Advocating for Gifted Children and Debunking Myths About Women

At the end of this chapter, you will learn about the applied psychology of Harry Hollingworth. He was just half of one of psychology's dynamic duos, however, and his wife Leta (Figure 8.5) made contributions at least as important as her husband's. At a time when women faced the obstacles you learned about in Chapter 6, Leta Hollingworth (1886–1939) managed to earn a doctorate from Columbia, become the "mother of gifted education," in her biographer's words, and directly attack the belief that men were superior to women intellectually.

Like her husband, Leta Stetter Hollingworth was a native Nebraskan, born and raised in rugged frontier conditions and taught in the proverbial (and in this case literal) one room schoolhouse. She graduated from the University of Nebraska in 1906, and then taught for two years before marrying Harry and following him to New York, where he was in his second year of graduate studies at Columbia. She immediately encountered one of the gender biases described in Chapter 6—the non-zero-sum marriage vs. career choice. Her plan was to teach in the New York City school system, thereby supporting Harry in grad school. What she discovered was a Board of Education policy prohibiting married women from being teachers (Hollingworth, 1990). Instead, she started taking graduate courses and enrolled full time after Harry finished his doctorate. She earned a Ph.D. from Columbia's Teachers College in 1916, under Thorndike's direction, and was immediately hired there as an instructor.

FIGURE 8.5 Leta Hollingworth, debunker of the variability hypothesis, and early promoter of special educational opportunities for gifted children.

In the spring semester of the academic year 1918–1919, Hollingworth began offering a new course, Education 254, which was designed to examine "fortunate variants, the generally and specifically gifted" (quoted in Klein, 2002, p. 120). It is believed to be the first course ever designed to study gifted children, and it marked the official beginning of Hollingworth's devotion to this population. The work culminated with her widely cited *Gifted Children: Their Nature and Nurture* (1926), the first textbook of gifted education. Although the primary means of treating gifted children at that time was acceleration in grade, Hollingworth argued that such a path could damage children who would not spend much of their time with age-related peers. Instead, she advocated for a full immersion enrichment approach. Gifted children, she argued, should be placed in classes with their peers, and given a curriculum that included the normal curricular topics, plus a level of enrichment that went far beyond what was taught to non-gifted children.

Gifted education was her life's passion, but Hollingworth was also a determined feminist, and active in several groups advocating for, among other things, the right of women to vote (which came in 1920). In 1912, for instance, she was a founding member of the "Heterodoxy Club," a group of women who met weekly to discuss women's issues. Hollingworth's feminist beliefs were informed by data. In particular, two of her early studies directly challenged two widely held beliefs, both described earlier in Chapter 6 (p. 146). These were sex differences resulting from the **variability hypothesis**, the evolution-based idea that women showed less variation in traits than men and were therefore less suited for highly intellectual tasks, and the differences due to **periodic function**, the notion that women were intellectually incapacitated during menstruation (Poffenberger, 1940).

Leta published several studies refuting both beliefs, and summarized her work in a chapter ("The Vocational Aptitudes of Women") she wrote for Harry's *Vocational Psychology: Its Problems and Methods* (1916). Concerning the variability hypothesis, Hollingworth discovered that the belief rested on no empirical data whatsoever. One study, which showed no differences among adult men and women in variability in physical traits, had been criticized on the grounds that young children should have been investigated in order to get at "inherent or original differences in variability" (Hollingworth, 1916, p. 230). This prompted Leta and a pediatrician friend, Helen Montague, to study 2,000 newborns (1,000 of each sex). Collecting a variety of physical measurements, they found that the boys were slightly larger than the girls, but that the amount of *variability* in physical size was the same for both boys and girls (Montague & Hollingworth, 1914).

As for periodic function, it was the subject of Hollingworth's dissertation. Prevailing opinion was that men and women were inherently unequal, because while men were capable "of sustained and regular hard labor, [a woman], for one quarter of each month, during the best years of life, is more or less sick and unfit for hard work" (Maudsley, quoted in Klein, 2002, p. 91). This apparently irritated Hollingworth's social conscience, prompting her to reply,

> It is positively stated that women are on this account [i.e., periodic function] unfitted to pursue professional and commercial life; yet it is not proposed that cooks, scrub women, mothers, nursemaids, housekeepers, or dancers should be periodically relieved from their labors and responsibilities. (Hollingworth, 1916, p. 235)

In her dissertation, Hollingworth carefully studied 23 women and compared their performance with a group of men. On tests for "speed and accuracy of perception, controlled association, steadiness, speed of voluntary movement, fatigability, and rate of learning" (Hollingworth, 1916, p. 236), she found no gender differences, and for the women, no differences traceable to periodic function.

Hollingworth recognized that at the time she wrote her chapter on women in her husband's book, little actual research had been done on gender differences. As she put it,

> All we can say is that up to the present time experimental psychology has disclosed no sex differences in mental traits which would imply a division of labor on psychological grounds. ... So far as is ... known, women are as competent intellectually as men are, to undertake any and all human vocations. (Hollingworth, 1916, p. 244)

Leta Hollingworth's research on gifted education and on gender would have been even more substantial had she not become desperately ill with abdominal cancer during the last ten years of her brief, 53-year life.

Robert M. Yerkes (1876–1956): The Army Testing Program

You met Robert Yerkes briefly in Chapter 1, as an example of how an institutional context could influence the careers of early psychologists. As you recall, Yerkes began his academic career as a promising comparative psychologist at Harvard, his love of animals tracing from his childhood on a farm (Carmichael, 1957). But Harvard's interest in comparative psychology was never great—research in the topic was expensive, the laboratory smelled, and it didn't seem especially relevant or useful (Reed, 1987). Thus, Yerkes was pressured to produce more on the "human side" if he expected to advance through the ranks. Although comparative psychology remained his first love, he compromised by writing a mainstream introductory textbook that centered on the study of consciousness and even included introspective exercises at the end of each chapter (Yerkes, 1911). He further broadened his credentials by working part-time in the Psychopathic Department of Boston State Hospital from 1913 to 1917, where he first became familiar with intelligence testing by administering Binet tests to patients and improving the scoring system. Harvard still did not promote him, however, even though his reputation among peers was sufficient to get him elected to the presidency of the American Psychological Association in 1917. In that same year, perhaps tired of waiting for Harvard to promote him, he accepted an offer to chair the psychology department at the University of Minnesota. Fate intervened, however, and Yerkes never made it to the upper Midwest.

In April of 1917, while Yerkes was cohosting a meeting of Titchener's Experimentalists at Harvard, the United States declared war on Germany and entered World War I. The group held an impromptu meeting to discuss how psychology might help the war effort and as APA president, Yerkes naturally took the lead. He later said that he had no real desire to take on the Army project, but did so out of a sense of duty (Dewsbury, 1996). Nonetheless, he quickly demonstrated superb organizational and persuasive skills, convincing the Army that psychological testing could aid the war effort.

By August of 1917, the Army had commissioned Yerkes as a major and placed him in charge of an elite group of psychologists (including Terman and Boring) charged with preparing mental tests. Their task was daunting. For one thing, the sheer number of people to be examined meant that traditional Binet-style testing, with examiners giving tests one at a time, had to be replaced by group testing procedures. Second, although part of the goal was in the Binet tradition of identifying those who

were unfit, in this case for Army service rather than for normal schooling, Yerkes also had more ambitious plans. He hoped to create tests that would enable the Army to identify those with special skills so they could be placed where they could best serve the cause. For instance, he hoped to be able to select the best candidates for officer training. The tests were pilot tested at four Army camps in October and by the end of December, 1917, the Surgeon General

KEY DATE *1917*

This year marked the origins of the Army testing program during World War I that gave great impetus to applied psychology in the United States.

These events also occurred:

- A 100-in. reflecting telescope was installed at Mount Wilson, California

- Four women were arrested for picketing the White House on behalf of women's suffrage, and sentenced to six months in jail

- The actor Charlie Chaplin's annual salary reached $1 million

- The Allies executed dancer Mata Hari as a German spy

- Revolution in Russia brought Bolsheviks to power, eventually resulting in the Union of Soviet Socialist Republics (U.S.S.R.)

- Literacy requirements for U.S. citizenship were passed, over President Wilson's veto

- In World War I, German forces withdrew on the Western Front, a February revolution occurred in Russia, and Pershing arrived in Paris to lead American troops

- These persons were born:

    John Fitzgerald Kennedy, U.S. President

    I. M. Pei, Chinese-American architect

    Andrew Wyeth, American artist

- These people died:

    William F. ("Buffalo Bill") Cody, American cowboy and entrepreneur

    Auguste Rodin, French sculptor

decreed that psychological testing would be extended to all new recruits. The program was in full swing in early 1918 and by the time the war ended in November of that year, Yerkes and his team had tested 1,726,966 soldiers (Yoakum & Yerkes, 1920).

Army Alpha and Army Beta

Because nearly 30% of recruits could not "read and understand newspapers and write letters home" (Yoakum & Yerkes, 1920, p. 12), Yerkes developed two versions of his test. Recruits literate enough to read and follow written directions were given the **Army Alpha** test, while **Army Beta** was created for those with reduced literacy. Each took just under an hour to administer. Any soldier failing Alpha was to be given Beta, and those failing Beta were supposed to be tested individually. Logistical problems and time pressures usually eliminated both levels of retesting, however. Army Alpha comprised eight different tests, whereas Army Beta had seven (see Table 8.4). Soldiers given Army Alpha were told at the outset that the purpose of the test was to "see how well you can remember, think, and carry out what you are told to do. We are not looking for crazy people. The aim is to help find out what you are best fitted to do in the Army" (Yoakum & Yerkes, 1920, p. 53). By contrast, those taking Army Beta were simply told to follow instructions and "ask no questions" (p. 82); they were not told why they were taking the exam.

To get an idea of what confronted soldiers, consider the first test in Army Alpha: the directions or commands test. Soldiers had the score sheet in Figure 8.6 in front of them and were told that in the Army it was important to be able to follow orders. The test would determine how well they could do so. For each of the 12 items, they were ordered to make specific marks on the page and given just a few seconds to do so. Here are three of the commands:

> 4. Attention! Look at 4. When I say "go" make a figure 1 in the space which is in the circle but not in the triangle or square, and also make a figure 2 in the space which is in the triangle and circle, but not in the square.—Go! (Allow not over 10 seconds)
>
> 7. Attention! Look at 7. When I say "go" *cross out* the letter just before C and also draw a line *under* the second letter before H—Go! (Allow not over 10 seconds)
>
> 11. Attention! Look at 11. When I say "go" draw a line through every even number that is not in a square, and also through every odd number that is in a square with a letter.—Go! (Allow not over 25 seconds) (Yoakum & Yerkes, 1920, pp. 55–56)

Three of the Army Beta tests can be found in Figure 8.7. In the maze test, recruits had to draw a line to negotiate the maze accurately—the dashed lines are the correct answers. In test 4, digit-symbol, the symbols paired with each number had to be written into the blank spaces. In test 6, recruits were instructed to draw in the missing elements of each picture. They had two minutes to complete as many mazes and digit-symbols as they could, and three minutes to do the picture completion test.

Despite the fact that close to two million soldiers were given the tests, the war ended before they could be used effectively by the Army. Indeed, most historians conclude that the Army derived little if any benefit from the enterprise (e.g., Kevles, 1968). During the war, many within the military welcomed the tests as more efficient than traditional methods for placing soldiers. Yet others stubbornly refused to use the test results, some local commanders didn't cooperate with the examiners giving the tests, and testing conditions were often so poor as to render the results meaningless. At one point the Secretary of

Table 8.4 Subtests for Army Alpha and Army Beta

Army Alpha Subtests	Army Beta Subtests
Commands Test	Maze Test
Arithmetic Problems	Cube Analysis
Practical Judgment	X-O series
Synonym-Antonym	Digit-Symbol
Disarranged Sentences	Number Checking
Number Series Completion	Pictorial Completion
Analogies	Geometrical Construction
Information	

FORM 5 GROUP EXAMINATION ALPHA GROUP NO. ....

Name .... Rank .... Age ....
Company .... Regiment.................... Arm .... Division ....
In what country or state born? .... Years in U.S.?......... Race ....
Occupation .... Weekly Wages ....
Schooling: Grades, 1.2.3.4.5.6.7.8: High or Prep. School, Year 1.2.3.4: College, Year 1.2.3.4.

TEST 1

1. ◯ ◯ ◯ ◯ ◯

2. ① ② ③ ④ ⑤ ⑥ ⑦ ⑧ ⑨

3. (square and triangle overlapping)

4. (triangle, square, and circle overlapping)

5. ◯ ◯ ◯ *Yes No*

6. ◯ ◯ ◯ ◯ ◯

7. **A B C D E F G H I J K L M N O P**

8. ◯ ◯ ◯ *MILITARY GUN CAMP*

9. **34-79-56-87-68-25-82-47-27-31-64-93-71-41-52-99**

10. (rectangle divided into sections)

11. 7F △4 ③ △5A ⑧ 2 △6 ⑨B 3

12. **1 2 3 4 5 6 7 8 9**

FIGURE 8.6 Test on following orders, a part of Army Alpha, from Yoakum and Yerkes (1920).

Test 1

1.

2.

3.

4.

5.

(a)

FIGURE 8.7 Subtests of Army Beta included (a) mazes, (b) digit-symbol, and (c) picture completion, from Yoakum and Yerkes (1920).

Test 4

1	2	3	4	5	6	7	8	9
−	И	⊐	L	∪	O	∧	✕	=

1.

3	1	2	1	3	2	1	4	2	3	5	2	9	1	4

2.

6	3	1	5	4	2	7	6	3	8	7	2	9	5	4

3.

6	3	7	2	8	1	9	5	8	4	7	3	6	9	5

4.

1	9	2	8	3	7	4	6	5	9	4	8	5	7	6

5.

9	3	8	6	4	1	5	7	2	6	2	4	8	1	3

6.

4	9	5	1	7	5	2	6	9	3	7	8	4	1	8

(b)

Test 6

(c)

War polled camp commanders about the value of the testing program and most of the 100 responses were negative (Gould, 1981). That the Army discontinued the testing shortly after the war ended suggests that its top brass were less than impressed with the program's utility. On the other hand, the testing program laid the groundwork for a scientific approach to Army personnel work and a number of younger officers saw its potential benefits. And the program certainly gave psychology a boost. As one historian put it, "[w]hile testing may not have made a significant contribution to the war, the war had made a significant contribution to testing and as a by-product to psychology in general" (Minton, 1988, p. 74).

Yerkes believed the project showed that mental testing could be applied on a large scale, and after the war he spared no effort to propagandize the benefits of testing. Other psychologists soon joined in. Terman, for instance, claimed that testing had "brought psychology down from the clouds and ... transformed the 'science of trivialities' into the 'science of human engineering'" (Terman, 1924, p. 106). Yerkes and Terman joined with other prominent psychologists (e.g., Thorndike) to create the "National Intelligence Tests" in 1920. The advertisement reproduced in Figure 8.8 shows how the alleged success of the Army testing program was used explicitly to promote group testing in schools.

The 1920s soon became known as "the heyday of the testing movement" (Goodenough, 1949, quoted in Dennis, 1948, p. 23), as mental testing spread into schools, business, and industry. Universities began using test scores to screen applicants, and informal tests of character, personality, and ability began appearing in popular magazines. A writer in Harper's magazine, referring to the mental test as "this bright little device," noted wryly that "[i]n practically every walk of life ... [it was] being introduced as a means of finding out what people don't know, and for what particular business they are specially unfitted" (quoted in Dennis, 1948, pp. 23–24). The glow soon faded, though, as the proponents and detractors of testing launched an acrimonious debate about the nature of intelligence and IQ that remains with us today. Before proceeding with the controversies over testing, however, let us close the book on Robert Yerkes.

FIGURE 8.8 Advertisement for National Intelligence Tests for schoolchildren, based on the Army tests, from Gould (1981).

After the war, Yerkes turned down the prewar offer from Minnesota, and remained in Washington as an administrator in the National Research Council, which had just been organized to promote science in America. In 1924, he returned to academia when his good friend, fellow "Harvard man," and now university president, James Angell, recruited him for the newly created Institute of Psychology at Yale. There he returned to his first love, the study of animal behavior, and began a campaign to create a research center to study primate behavior. The eventual result was the Anthropoid Experiment Station of Yale University, which opened in 1930 in Orange Park, Florida, near Jacksonville. When Yerkes retired in 1941, the center was renamed the Yerkes

Laboratories of Primate Biology. It moved to Atlanta in 1965, and today the Yerkes Primate Center is perhaps the leading center of primate research in the world (Dewsbury, 1996).

The Controversy Over Intelligence

As leaders of the mental testing movement, Goddard, Terman, and Yerkes shared the beliefs that (a) mental capacity was primarily the result of genetic inheritance, (b) environment had little if any effect on this overall ability, (c) intelligence might be composed of a variety of skills, but underlying all of them was a single, unitary capability,[4] and (d) this capability was what intelligence tests measured. In the 1920s, the tests were at the forefront of the previously mentioned "heyday" of mental testing. By the middle of the decade, however, mental testing was under assault from several directions and Anne Anastasi, author of the best-known modern textbook on testing, would later write that "[t]he testing boom of the 1920s probably did more to retard than to advance the progress of testing" (Anastasi, 1992, p. 17). What happened?

An early sign of trouble was in Yerkes's 1921 report summarizing the Army testing program. Buried in the 890-page mass of data was this statement: "It appears that the intelligence of the principal sample of the white draft, when transmuted from Alpha and Beta exams into terms of mental age, is about 13 years" (Yerkes, 1921, p. 785). Combining the widely held belief that the mental age of an average adult should be 16 and the Goddard scale of deficiency that considered those scoring between 8 and 12 to be morons, this was disturbing news indeed. If the Army testing program was valid and the sample representative (at 1.7 million it was certainly big enough), then it appeared that the United States was becoming a nation of morons. Even though critics later pointed out that problems like the abysmal test-

ing conditions and the failure to implement the retesting scheme made the results virtually impossible to interpret, the report reinforced existing biases and created alarm. Could the fears of the eugenicists be coming true? Could all those years of unrestricted immigration and the failure to control the breeding of feebleminded people be reducing the overall intelligence of America? To add fuel to the fire, Yerkes observed in the *Atlantic Monthly* that on the basis of the Army tests, no more than 10% of Americans "are intellectually capable of meeting the requirements for a bachelor's degree" (quoted in Degler, 1991, p. 168).

Yerkes also presented data on intelligence as a function of national origin and found higher scores for native-born Americans. And in support of prevailing fears about the new immigrants, he reported that for soldiers of northern European origin, mental age was higher than for those with roots in southern or eastern Europe. The average mental age for this latter group was about 11. Carl Brigham, who participated in the Army project, highlighted the immigrant findings in his *A Study of American Intelligence* (1923), and warned that continued mass immigration from southern and eastern Europe, combined with the tendency of these groups to have large families, would threaten the national IQ. In a theme that would echo ominously in Germany in the 1930s, Brigham suggested that the fair-haired Nordic races were inherently superior to others.

All of this was happening at a time when the general political climate was characterized by an increasing **nativism**, a defensive nationalism that viewed all outsiders with suspicion and alarm. It was exacerbated in the 1920s by several factors. Immigration, which had declined during the war years, was surging again. The new immigrants, already disliked, seemed increasingly unwilling to join into the mythical American melting pot. They retained their own communities and language, and a large proportion had no intention of remaining in America—their goal was to make a sufficient amount of money to return home. In addition, with the 1917 Bolshevik revolution in Russia creating headlines, the 1920s witnessed the first genuine "Red Scare," and Americans often viewed immigrants from Russia as subversives rather than

[4] In this regard, most Americans agreed with the British psychologist/statistician Charles Spearman, who argued that although separate intellectual skills might exist, underlying all of them was a unitary intellectual ability, which he called "g," for "general" intelligence.

refugees from the harsh new Soviet regime. Thus, it came as no surprise when Congress passed the National Origins Act of 1924, which established immigration quotas with reference to 1890 data (i.e., before the shift from old to new immigration patterns). The American psychologists who led the mental testing movement have sometimes been portrayed as leading the charge for restrictive immigration, but they reflected the context of their times as much as they contributed to it.

While fears about immigration were widespread, not everyone was willing to accept the beliefs about IQ held by Goddard, Terman, Yerkes, and others (e.g., Thorndike). Although the popular press cranked out articles about the dangers of immigration that suggested unity among social scientists, there was in fact considerable disagreement within the professional community (Satariano, 1979). Noted anthropologist Franz Boas, for instance, was a strong critic of the hereditarian view, arguing instead for the effect of culture on mental abilities (Degler, 1991). Within psychology, behaviorism (Chapters 10 and 11), with its emphasis on the powerful effects of conditioning, was beginning to have a moderating effect, shifting opinion from nature to nurture. Furthermore, numerous psychologists (e.g., Freeman, 1922) urged caution when interpreting the Army data, pointed out that mental testing was still in its infancy and that the effects of upbringing on IQ scores could not be ignored when interpreting IQ data. In general, before behaviorism began shifting psychologists toward the nurture side of the issue, psychologists and biologists tended toward hereditarian explanations of mental capacity, whereas anthropologists and sociologists leaned toward an environmental emphasis (Hilgard, 1987).

The most visible debate about intelligence and IQ testing in the 1920s resulted from a series of six articles in the *New Republic*, by its founder, the noted columnist Walter Lippmann, and replies in the same magazine from Terman. Neither Lippmann nor Terman minced words. Conceding that the tests might have some value in placing students or selecting employees, Lippmann ridiculed the notion that the tests were measuring innate general "intelligence," arguing that "[w]e cannot measure intelligence when we have never defined it, and we cannot speak of its hereditary basis after it has been indistinguishably fused with a thousand educational and environmental influences from the time of conception to school age" (Lippmann, 1922a, p. 10). Also, Lippmann was outraged at the possibility that testing could forever doom a child who happened not to perform very well for one 50-minute segment of his or her life. With the implications of Terman's meritocracy firmly in mind, he wrote that the result could be "an intellectual caste system in which the task of education had given way to the doctrine of predestination and infant damnation" (1922b, p. 298). Terman, who Lippmann mentioned by name when likening testing to other "fads" such as phrenology and palm reading, responded in an article that did not really answer Lippmann, but merely dismissed him as a rank amateur who should mind his own business and let the professionals deal with these complex issues. It was not one of Terman's better moments, part of a basic problem he experienced with being criticized (especially by non-scientists), and he later regretted writing the article (Minton, 1988). Indeed, although Terman is known as one of the most vocal proponents of the hereditarian view of intelligence, near the end of his life he had some second thoughts. In an autobiographical chapter for the series *A History of Psychology in Autobiography*, Terman wrote that differences in IQ could never be completely accounted for by environmental factors—heredity was the key. However, in Terman's personal copy of the volume, this section of his essay is circled and he wrote in the margin "I am less sure of this now (1951)! And still less sure in 1955!—L. M. T." (quoted in Hilgard, 1957, p. 478). Questions about the relative influence of nature and nurture on intelligence, whether the IQ is a useful measure of intelligence, and the very nature of intelligence, continue to be debated today.

APPLYING PSYCHOLOGY TO BUSINESS

Its major impact was on education, but testing also came to be used frequently in business settings. Psychology applied to business went far beyond mere testing, however. As early as 1895, in *Thinking, Feeling, Doing*, Scripture pointed out that advertisers could benefit from what psychologists knew about attention and memory. Shortly after the turn of the century, Walter Dill Scott (1869–1955), who had been trained in traditional experimental psychology by Wundt at Leipzig, launched a distinguished career in applied psychology by writing *The Theory and Practice of Advertising* (1903). In it he argued that consumers were not rational decision makers and could be influenced by suggestion and appeals to emotion. Scott also wrote *Human Efficiency in Business* (1910), in which he applied psychological principles to suggest ways of increasing productivity. During this same time, Hugo Münsterberg, a young German psychologist, also a product of Wundt's laboratory and now at Harvard, was beginning to be involved in what he called "economic psychology." Although he became one of the most reviled public figures in America at the time of his death, he was psychology's most visible applied psychologist in the first decade and a half of the new century.

Hugo Münsterberg (1863–1916): The Diversity of Applied Psychology

As one of Germany's rising stars in the new experimental psychology, Hugo Münsterberg (Figure 8.9) attracted the attention of William James at a time when America's premier psychologist was shifting his interests from psychology to philosophy and desiring to distance himself from the laboratory. Young Münsterberg had earned both a Ph.D. with Wundt at Leipzig and an M.D. from Heidelberg, and he had established a productive laboratory of experimental psychology at Freiburg in the late 1880s. James was greatly impressed with Münsterberg's research, citing it frequently in his *Principles of Psychology*. With promises of a well-equipped laboratory and minimal teaching demands, James lured Münsterberg to Harvard in the same year that Titchener arrived at Cornell, 1892. Münsterberg stayed for three years while on leave from Freiburg, then returned home to Germany hoping to secure a professorship there. This was not forthcoming, however, and he came back to Harvard for good in 1897. There his career was noth-

FIGURE 8.9   Hugo Münsterberg

ing short of remarkable, although until recently his work has largely been ignored (Moskowitz, 1977). It included presidencies of both APAs (Psychological and Philosophical), a major position at Harvard as chair of the Philosophy Department from 1899 on, and status as a friend of the rich and famous.

Although he could barely understand English when he arrived in Cambridge and it took him two years before he could lecture adequately in it, Münsterberg managed to write more than two dozen books between his arrival in America and his death in 1916. He also became a well-known public figure by writing extensively in popular magazines (e.g., *Harper's*, *Atlantic Monthly*) on such topics as hypnosis, gambling, lie detection, democracy, coeducation, and communicating with the dead (Benjamin, 2000). And he was a controversial figure: one of his goals was to explain the American temperament and personality to a German audience, and to an American audience, all the good qualities of Germans. His motives might have been pure, a simple desire to enhance intercultural understanding, and for a time his reputation as an ambassador of goodwill even earned him dinner at the White House with Teddy Roosevelt (Moskowitz, 1977). As World War I approached, however, his defense of German culture, and his attacks on what he saw as anti-German propaganda, changed public opinion about him. He was editorially condemned, hated by the general public, and accused of being a spy (Landy, 1992). After an editorial in the *London Times* labeled Harvard a center for pro-German agitation, Münsterberg became an outcast even among his colleagues and his sanity was questioned by former Harvard president Eliot (Spillman & Spillman, 1993). The effects of this vilification can only be guessed at, but the resulting stress probably contributed to the cerebral hemorrhage that killed the 53-year-old Münsterberg in the midst of a lecture at Radcliffe on December 16, 1916.[5]

During his productive years at Harvard, Münsterberg contributed substantially to the growth of experimental psychology in America. His research interests were eclectic, and his students found him willing to direct research on a wide range of topics. He welcomed anyone with an interest in research, even students, like Mary Calkins (Chapter 6, pp. 167–170), whose gender prevented them from being there officially. Shortly after his arrival, he lobbied successfully for the construction of a new building to house a state-of-the-art 24-room laboratory. It included facilities for both human and animal research, with Robert Yerkes placed in charge of the latter. By the turn of the century, however, Münsterberg was spending less time in the laboratory and more in developing his interests in applied psychology. One of his many interests was in forensic psychology, which examines how psychology applies to legal issues. His celebrated and best-selling *On the Witness Stand* (1908) included detailed descriptions of the reasons why eyewitness testimony often fails, many of which have been confirmed by modern research. He also warned against the use of hypnosis in the courtroom as a means of determining guilt or innocence, and in his final chapter on "The Prevention of Crime," he argued against the prevailing hereditarian view of human behavior and promoted the idea that the "prevention of crime is more important than the treatment of crime" (p. 233). For Münsterberg, criminals were made, not born.

In addition to writing about the law, Münsterberg contributed to abnormal psychology, taking an approach to the treatment of insanity that was based on suggestion. In essence, his strategy was to assume that if he suggested to patients how they should behave and think, the power of his authority would lead them to obey and be cured. In his *Psychotherapy* (1909), he was also critical of the newly popular Freudianism, with its belief in the importance of the unconscious. Münsterberg, often ahead of his times but behind them in this case, wrote that the subconscious mind had little if any impact on behavior. He did recognize the importance of Freud's emphasis on the early childhood determinants of later pathology, however.

It was in the area of industrial psychology, or "economic" psychology as he called it, that Münsterberg had his greatest impact as an applied psychologist. The following excerpt details just a few of the highlights of his best-known book.

ORIGINAL SOURCE EXCERPT
Hugo Münsterberg and Employee Selection

As he did with most of his books, Münsterberg compiled his industrial psychology text from a set of lectures. He published it in German in 1912, then in English a year later as *Psychology and Industrial Efficiency* (Münsterberg, 1913). The wide range of topics can be seen in the Table of Contents, found in Table 8.5.

---

[5] After Münsterberg's passing, psychology went into a decline at Harvard. Titchener was offered Münsterberg's position but declined and Cattell sought the job but was rejected. Harvard brought the British psychologist William McDougall to America, but he quickly became isolated and left. The department only began to recover when E. G. Boring was induced to leave Clark and come to Cambridge in 1922 (Hilgard, 1987).

Table 8.5   Table of Contents for Münsterberg's *Psychology and Industrial Efficiency*

I.	Applied Psychology
II.	The Demands of Practical Life
III.	Means and Ends

The Best Possible Man

IV.	Vocation and Fitness
V.	Scientific Vocational Guidance
VI.	Scientific Management
VII.	The Methods of Experimental Psychology
VIII.	Experiments in the Interest of Electric Railway Service
IX.	Experiments in the Interest of Ship Service
X.	Experiments in the Interest of Telephone Service
XI.	Contributions from Men of Affairs
XII.	Individuals and Groups

The Best Possible Work

XIII.	Learning and Training
XIV.	The Adjustment of Technical to Psychological Conditions
XV.	The Economy of Movement
XVI.	Experiments on the Problem of Monotony
XVII.	Attention and Fatigue
XVIII.	Physical and Social Influences on the Working Power

The Best Possible Effect

XIX.	The Satisfaction of Economic Demands
XX.	Experiments on the Effects of Advertisements
XXI.	The Effect of Display
XXII.	Experiments with Reference to Illegal Imitation
XXIII.	Buying and Selling
XXIV.	The Future Development of Economic Psychology

Münsterberg opened Chapter 1 with a rationale for the book and an overall description of its contents:

> Our aim is to sketch the outline of a new science which is intermediate between the modern laboratory psychology and the problems of economics: the psychological experiment is systematically to be placed at the service of commerce and industry. ... What is most needed today at the beginning of the new movement are clear, concrete illustrations which demonstrate the possibilities of the new method. In the following pages, accordingly, it will be my aim to analyze the results of experiments which have actually been carried out, experiments belonging to many different spheres of economic life. (pp. 3–4)

As the Table of Contents shows, after some introductory chapters, Münsterberg divided his book into three broad topics: the "Best Possible Man," the "Best Possible Work," and the "Best Possible Effect." In the first section, his concern was how psychological methods could be used to select workers. He argued for the importance of efficient selection of human resources by drawing an interesting parallel to the threats then existing to natural resources (which would soon lead to the creation of National Parks such as Yellowstone and Yosemite). Just as the country was beginning to recognize "how the richness of the forests and the mines and the rivers had been recklessly squandered without any thought of the future" (p. 38), so too were economists coming to believe that "no waste of valuable possessions is so reckless as that which results from the distribution of living force by chance methods instead of examining carefully how work and workmen can fit one another" (p. 38). Münsterberg's final two sections of the book concerned (a) ways to improve worker productivity and (b) how to advertise and sell products.

To show how psychology could contribute to the process of fitting work and workers together, Münsterberg described three specific examples in Chapters 8 through 10. The first involved the hiring of driver/operators ("motormen") for the electric railways that provided the primary means of public transportation found in cities in those days, but now requires a trip to San Francisco to experience anything comparable. The job was not easy, for the motorman had to stay on schedule while watching out for the carriages, motorcars, and pedestrians that filled the typical city street, often crossing in front of the rail car. Mishaps were not uncommon—Münsterberg wrote that railway companies reported "up to fifty thousand accident indemnity cases a year" (p. 64)! Some operators had better records than others, and Münsterberg was asked to identify the attributes of the competent ones. If he could, then the initial selection process would be improved. Münsterberg believed there were two different ways to proceed, either by simulating, as a whole, the essential processes involved in successful work, or breaking the work down into subprocesses and developing tests for each:

> ... One way is to take the mental process which is demanded by the industrial work as an undivided whole. In this case we have to construct experimental conditions under which this total activity can be performed in a gradual, measurable way. The psychical part of the vocational work thus becomes schematized and is simply rendered experimentally on a reduced scale. The other way is to resolve the mental process into its components and to test every single elementary function in its isolated form. In this latter case the examination has the advantage of having at its disposal all the familiar methods of experimental psychology, while in the first case for every special vocational situation perfectly new experimental tests must be devised. (p. 59)

With regard to the "motormen," Münsterberg considered using the second, more analytic approach. Competent workers might be expected to have faster reaction times, for instance. He quickly discovered a ceiling effect: no differences in reaction time could be found between good and bad drivers. As Münsterberg put it, "the slow individuals do not remain in the service at all" (p. 65). Having rejecting the piecemeal approach, Münsterberg turned to his other method—simulation. After observing several motormen, he identified what he thought to be the critical process in a rather complex job:

> ... I found this to be a particular complicated act of attention by which the manifoldness of objects, the pedestrians, the carriages, and the automobiles, are continuously observed with reference to the rapidity and direction in the quickly changing panorama of the street. Moving figures come from the right and

from the left toward and across the track, and are embedded in a stream of men and vehicles which move parallel to the track. In the face of such manifoldness there are men whose impulses are almost inhibited and who instinctively desire to wait for the movement of the nearest objects; they would evidently be unfit for the service, as they would drive the electric car too slowly. There are others who, even with the car at high speed, can adjust themselves for a time to the complex moving situation, but whose attention soon lapses, and while they are fixating a rather distant carriage, may overlook a pedestrian who carelessly crosses the track immediately in front of the car. In short, we have a great variety of mental types of this characteristic unified activity, which may be understood as a particular combination of attention and imagination. (p. 66)

But how could this "combination of attention and imagination" be simulated in the laboratory? He ruled out using what he called "miniature situations," in which individuals would have to maneuver tiny models of electric cars on models of streets. Instead, he argued that a task should be created that catches the essence of the mental processes being evaluated:

... The essential point for the psychological experiment is not the external similarity of the apparatus, but exclusively the inner similarity of the mental attitude. The more the external mechanism with which or on which the action is carried out becomes schematized, the more the action itself will appear in its true character.

In the method of my experiments with the motormen, accordingly, I had to satisfy only two demands. The method of examination promised to be valuable if, first, it showed good results with reliable motormen and bad results with unreliable ones; and, secondly, if it vividly aroused in all the motormen the feeling that the mental function which they were going through during the experiment had the greatest possible similarity with their experience on the front platform of the electric car. (pp. 68–69)

After several false starts, Münsterberg created a clever simulation, one that at least met his second demand—his participants indeed reported that the task was similar to what they encountered "on the front platform." He created cards 4.5 inches wide and 13 inches long, divided into half-inch squares. Two parallel lines ran down the middle, representing tracks, and the 26 squares between the tracks were labeled with the letters of the alphabet. In the squares to either side of the "tracks" were a random array of numbers representing people, horses, and automobiles, moving at different speeds, and moving either parallel to or perpendicular to the electric trolleys. Münsterberg rigged an apparatus so that the card was covered except for an area the width of the card and 2.5 inches long. By turning a crank, the motormen would successively expose various portions of the card and would be asked to identify objects that could end up being on the track, and therefore be dangerous.

Münsterberg tested each individual on 12 different cards, then combined time and errors into a weighted measure when describing the results. Unfortunately, his description of the outcome is incomplete. For example, the reader never learns how many men were tested, only that the company supplied "a number of the best motormen in its service," others "who had only just escaped dismissal," and a third group "neither especially good nor especially bad" (p. 74). Despite identifying these main groups, however, Münsterberg failed to report exactly how the groups differed on the simulation. Despite his claims for success, it appears that group differences might not have occurred, perhaps due to what researchers today would call a subject selection confound. That is, the reliable workers had also been with the company longer and were significantly older than the other workers. The fact that Münsterberg went out of his way to point out that older workers might be slower to pick up the simulation procedure suggests that these men did not do as well as he originally expected:

> We must consider ... that those men whom the company naturally selects as models are men who have had twenty to thirty years of service without accidents, but consequently they are rather old men, who no longer have the elasticity of youth and are naturally less able to think themselves into an artificial situation like that of such an experiment. It is therefore not surprising, but only to be expected, that such older, model men, while doing fair work in the test, are yet not seldom surpassed by bright, quick, young motormen who are twenty years younger, even though they are not yet ideal motormen. (p. 75)

Despite the apparent lack of differentiation between the groups, Münsterberg proclaimed the simulation a success and made a series of recommendations about what score should be obtained before a potential motorman could be considered competent. Although he recognized that the "experiments could be improved in many directions" (p. 81), he concluded that

> ... an experimental investigation of this kind which demands from each individual hardly 10 minutes would be sufficient to exclude perhaps one fourth of those who are nowadays accepted into the service as motormen. (p. 81)

Münsterberg had better luck with his experiments on telephone operators. These underpaid and overworked women handled up to 300 calls per hour, which sometimes resulted in "fatigue and finally to a nervous breakdown of the employees and to confusion in the service" (pp. 98–99). The Bell Telephone Company spent a lot of time and money on training, so they were looking for a way to screen those most likely to have difficulty. Enter Münsterberg.

After observing operators for a time, Münsterberg was impressed with the complexity of their task:

> The user of the telephone is little inclined to consider how many actions have to be carried out ... before the connection is made and finally broken again. From the moment when the speaker takes off the receiver to the cutting off of the connection, fourteen separate psychophysical processes are necessary in the typical case. (p. 97)

Instead of developing a simulation task, as he did with the motormen, Münsterberg used his second strategy of breaking down a complex task into its elements and testing each component separately.

> After carefully observing the service in the central office for a while, I came to the conviction that it would not be appropriate here to reproduce the activity at the switchboard in the experiment, but that it would be more desirable

to resolve that whole function into its elements and to undertake the experimental test of a whole series of elementary mental dispositions. Every one of these mental acts can then be examined according to well-known laboratory methods without giving to the experiments any direct relation to the characteristic telephone operation as such. I carried on the first series of experiments with about thirty young women who a short time before had entered into the telephone training school ... I examined them with reference to eight different psychophysical functions. (p. 100)

The young women who participated in the study were tested in a group setting for "memory, attention, intelligence, exactitude, and rapidity" (p. 101). To give you the flavor of these tests, consider the first two:

The memory examination consisted of reading to the whole class at first two numbers of 4 digits, then two of 5 digits, then two of 6 digits, and so on up to figures of 12 digits, and demanding that they be written down as soon as a signal was given. The experiments on attention ... made use of a method the principle of which has frequently been applied in the experimental psychology of individual differences and which I adjusted to our special needs. The requirement is to cross out a particular letter in a connected text. Every one of the thirty women in the classroom received the same first page of a newspaper of that morning. ... As soon as the signal was given, each one of girls had to cross out with a pencil every 'a' in the text for six minutes. After a certain time, a bell signal was given and each of them then had to begin a new column. In this way we could find out, first, how many letters were correctly crossed out in those six minutes, secondly, how many letters were overlooked, and thirdly, how the recognition and the oversight were distributed in the various parts of the text. (pp. 101–102)

After the group tests, the women were tested individually on word association, card sorting, and accuracy in touching a pencil to crosses drawn on a page (i.e., similar to hitting the correct hole in the switchboard). After three months on the job, Münsterberg examined the work performance of the women he had tested. Once again, he failed to describe the results in any detail, but a sly move on the part of Bell Telephone, inserting some veterans into what Münsterberg had thought was a class of 30 novices, provided some unexpected validation:

These three months had been sufficient to secure at least a certain discrimination between the best, the average, and the unfit. ... First, the skeptical telephone company had mixed with the class a number of women who had been in the service for a long while and had even been selected as teachers in the telephone school. I did not know, in figuring out the results, which of the participants ... these particularly gifted outsiders were. ... The results showed ... that these women who had proved most able in practical service stood at the top of our list. (pp. 108–109)

The "motorman" and telephone operator selection examples are the best known of the studies reported in Münsterberg's pioneering book, but there are dozens more, examining such topics as the effects of monotony and fatigue on productivity, whether magazines should place ads together in one section or spread them throughout the magazine, and the effects of the size of ads on memory for products. He closed the book by recommending the creation of a "government bureau for applied psychology" (p. 306) and by painting a rosy picture of the "splendid betterments" (p. 308) resulting from the study of economic psychology:

> We must not forget that the increase of industrial efficiency by future psychological adaptation and by improvement of the psychophysical conditions is not only in the interest of the employers, but still more of the employees; their working time can be reduced, their wages increased, their level of life raised. And above all, still more important than the naked commercial profit on both sides, is the cultural gain which will come to the total economic life of the nation, as soon as every one can be brought to the place where his best energies may be unfolded and his greatest personal satisfaction secured. The economic experimental psychology offers no more inspiring idea that this adjustment of work and psyche by which mental dissatisfaction in the work ... may be replaced in our social community by overflowing joy and perfect inner harmony. (pp. 308–309)

Other Leading Industrial Psychologists

Münsterberg was far from alone in his involvement with business and industry. The commercial world provided fruitful opportunities for many psychologists needing to supplement meager academic incomes. This part of the chapter began by mentioning one of them, Walter Dill Scott. Other prominent industrial psychologists included Walter Van Dyke Bingham, Lillian Gilbreth, and Harry Hollingworth.

Walter Van Dyke Bingham (1880–1952)

Bingham's career found him in direct contact with many of the psychologists who are or soon will be familiar to you. He was a graduate student at functionalist Chicago from 1905 to 1908, where he completed a dissertation on the perception of tones under James Angell and worked as John Watson's student assistant. In 1907, he traveled briefly in Europe, where he met the gestaltists Köhler and Koffka, then spent some time at Harvard getting to know James and Münsterberg while acquiring a minor in philosophy. His shift to applied psychology began to occur after he went to Columbia in 1908 to start his academic career. There he encountered Cattell and Thorndike, who sparked his interests in mental testing and educational psychology, respectively. After two years he moved to Dartmouth College, where he remained until 1915. For the next nine years, he presided over a unique academic enterprise, the Division of Applied Psychology at the Carnegie Institute of Technology, a school founded 10 years earlier and now known as Carnegie Mellon University.

It was in Pittsburgh that Bingham established his reputation for applying psychological principles to business. With the aid of generous funding from local business executives (e.g., Westinghouse, Heinz), he established units within his division specifically oriented to business psychology. One example was the Bureau of Salesmanship Research, directed by Walter Dill Scott. On temporary leave from Northwestern University, Scott is believed to be the first person ever given the title of Professor of Applied Psychology (Landy, 1993). The bureau produced a useful guide for personnel directors called *Aids in the Selection of Salesmen*, which included a standardized application form, a set of questions for interviewers, and recommendations for tests to be given to applicants (Bingham, 1952). The sales bureau soon spawned a related enterprise, the Research Bureau for Retail

Training. It was also generously underwritten, this time by department store magnate Edgar Kaufmann. The bureau "prepared employment tests, training manuals, merchandise manuals, and specific procedures for correcting defects of sales personality and of supervision" (Bingham, 1952, pp. 15–16). A third Bingham innovation was the School of Life Insurance Salesmanship, which trained a legion of sales reps to convince people that they were underinsured.

In addition to his work at Carnegie from 1915 to 1924, Bingham was also a key player in establishing the credibility of the Psychological Corporation. He replaced Cattell in 1926 when the temperamental founder was ousted as president of the corporation by its board (Sokal, 1981a). He also served with Yerkes in World War I, helping with the Army testing program, and he played a similar but even larger role in World War II. Given the title of Chief Psychologist by the War Department, he chaired a committee that produced the Army General Classification Test (AGCT), which was eventually given to 10 million soldiers (Hilgard, 1987). From the mid-1920s through the end of World War II, Bingham consistently promoted industrial psychology, making him the discipline's most visible advocate.

Lillian Moller Gilbreth (1878–1972)

The career of Lillian Gilbreth (Figure 8.10) can be divided into two segments by the early death of her husband, Frank. Prior to this unfortunate event, she was able to combine the roles of mother and professional in ways seldom seen before or since. Frank Gilbreth, a former bricklayer without the benefit of a college education, was a pioneer in the new field of time-and-motion study. By carefully observing bricklayers, for instance, he identified wasteful motions and recommended more efficient ones, thereby increasing worker productivity. Lillian collaborated with this work, contributing equally to their successful consulting business, Gilbreth, Inc. In the process, she completed the requirements for a doctorate at Berkeley by writing a dissertation called "The Psychology of Management," but was not given the degree because she could not meet residency requirements. After the Gilbreths moved to Rhode Island, she finished a second doctorate at

FIGURE 8.10   Lillian Gilbreth, mother of 12 and pioneer in ergonomics and industrial psychology.

Brown University, with a dissertation on how worker efficiency principles could be applied to the teaching profession. Her Ph.D., awarded in 1915, is the first ever granted in industrial psychology (Perloff & Naman, 1996). During this time she also published her initial dissertation in book form, after reluctantly bowing to pressure from her publisher to disguise her gender by having the book attributed to "L. M. Gilbreth." Together, the Gilbreths published books on ways to eliminate fatigue (1916) and on the uses of time-and-motion study (1917).

These achievements, remarkable by any measure, approach the incredible when one realizes that during the 20 years of their marriage, Frank and Lillian Gilbreth raised *12* children, six boys and six girls. You might be familiar with this part of the story from the book or the movie *Cheaper by the Dozen*, written by two of the children (Gilbreth & Carey, 1949). It is a marvelous tale about living in a large family run by principles of worker efficiency (e.g., "shave" a few seconds off the morning's whisker removal by using two blades, one in each hand).

Their family also became the focus of a paper written by one of Terman's students in 1923 called "IQ Farming." With both parents and all the children testing in the "gifted" range, the Gilbreths were the prototypical example of the kind of family destined to lead Terman's meritocracy (Minton, 1988).

After her husband's fatal heart attack in 1924, Lillian Gilbreth's accomplishments increased, even though she was now raising a dozen children on her own, while continuing to run the consulting business and teaching part-time at Purdue and MIT. She became a pioneer in the field of **ergonomics**, the study of how systems and products can be made most efficient for human use. Her ideas included the redesign of household tasks, based on her own ample experiences. For instance, she became largely responsible for modern kitchen design: pop-up trash cans and side-door shelves for refrigerators are among her innovations (Perloff & Naman, 1996). She was also a major force in helping people with physical handicaps become productive citizens—she considered this her most important work. When she died in 1972 at age 94, Gilbreth had added 16 honorary doctorates to her two earned ones.

Harry Hollingworth (1880–1956)

You met Hollingworth earlier in the chapter, as the psychologist who confessed to being involved with applied psychology only to put food on the table. Regardless of his motives, however, he is justly recognized as a leader in the field of industrial psychology. As an undergraduate at the University of Nebraska, Hollingworth encountered the new psychology in a laboratory course taken with T. L. Bolton, who had recently finished his doctorate with Hall at Clark University. He left Nebraska in 1907 to pursue graduate studies at Columbia, where he studied with Cattell, Thorndike, and Woodworth. After a year, he married fellow Nebraskan Leta Stetter, who you met in this chapter's Close-Up.

Hollingworth finished his doctorate in 1908, then took a position as instructor at nearby Barnard College. The increasingly frustrated young couple barely managed on Harry's $1,000 annual salary. Salvation came in the form of an offer from the Coca-Cola Company, which hired both Hollingworths in 1911 to conduct research on the effects of caffeine. The company had been charged by the government with adding an element to its formula, caffeine, which had what were believed to be unhealthy stimulant properties. The Hollingworths completed an elaborate series of studies, using sophisticated double-blind procedures, and Harry was able to testify in court that the amount of caffeine in the cola had no discernible adverse effects, except that relatively large amounts taken late in the evening could interfere with sleep (Benjamin, Rogers, & Rosenbaum, 1991).

The Coca-Cola project provided enough money for Leta to complete her own doctorate at Columbia's Teachers College and launched Harry onto the path of applied psychology. He became inundated with consulting opportunities from businesses ranging from railroads that wanted to know what color to paint their cars, to city planners who wanted to know how to improve the legibility of traffic signs, to chewing gum manufacturers who wanted some evidence that gum chewing provides useful relaxation (Benjamin, 1996). While he took advantage of many of these requests, he did so reluctantly, seeing himself first as a "psychologist," and only secondarily as an applied psychologist, writing that "[i]t has been my sad fate to have established early in my career a reputation for interests that with me were only superficial" (quoted in Benjamin, 1996, p. 134).

Despite his desire to be known as more than an applied psychologist, Hollingworth's other research has been generally forgotten. His doctoral dissertation on motor accuracy in reaching, however, emphasized the importance of the overall context within which the reaching behavior occurred. The gestalt psychologist Kurt Koffka once told him that the study had been a "cornerstone" of the gestalt movement, our next topic.

SUMMARY

PRESSURES TOWARD APPLICATION

- From the time when the new psychology first appeared in America, in the late nineteenth century, psychologists have been concerned with how psychological knowledge could be put to good use. The concern over application was partly a natural consequence of traditional American pragmatism, and the belief that scientific progress should result in beneficial technology.

- Psychologists also experienced institutional pressures to justify their existence within departments of philosophy and their needs for fully equipped laboratories.

THE MENTAL TESTING MOVEMENT

- Galton's approach to mental testing, which emphasized physical and basic sensory measures, was imported to America by James McKeen Cattell, who created the term "mental test" and developed an elaborate testing program at Columbia. The program failed when the measurements could not be correlated with academic performance, however. Cattell played an important role in the professionalization of psychology in America, primarily through his editorial work.

- Modern intelligence testing, with its emphasis on measuring cognitive rather than sensory processes, originated with the Ebbinghaus completion tests and the creation of the Binet-Simon test. Binet's goal was to identify students who were academically weak (débiles), so that special programs could be developed for them. The test was scored in terms of mental level (later called mental age) and children in need were considered to be those scoring two mental levels below their actual age. Binet's approach to psychology, which he called individual psychology, was to emphasize the study of individual differences rather than the search for general laws.

- The Binet tests came to America when they were translated by Henry Goddard of Vineland Training School. Goddard used the tests to classify degrees of feeble-mindedness in terms of mental age and created the term "moron" to identify those with mental ages between 8 and 12. He believed that mental deficiency was inherited, and supported his case with the methodologically flawed Kallikak study, which traced the lineage of one of the Vineland children. Goddard also used the tests to help officials at the Ellis Island immigration center try to identify those who were mentally unfit. His results added to the perception that immigrants from southern and

eastern Europe were mentally inferior to those from northern and western Europe.

- Lewis Terman institutionalized intelligence testing by revising and standardizing the Binet tests, thereby creating the Stanford-Binet, one of the best-known tests of intelligence. The test was scored in terms of William Stern's concept of IQ, a ratio of mental age to chronological age. To support his belief in a meritocracy, Terman conducted an extended study of gifted children, finding that they broke the stereotype that such children are intellectually superior but socially and physically inferior. Leta Hollingworth was another pioneer in the area of gifted education, and she also completed research questioning both the variability hypothesis and the alleged adverse effects of menstruation on women's mental abilities.

- Robert Yerkes, a comparative psychologist at heart, became involved in mental testing in World War I by organizing the Army testing program. He and his team developed two group intelligence tests, one for literate soldiers (Army Alpha) and one for illiterates (Army Beta). The program was minimally useful to the Army, but launched intelligence testing as big business and made testing a popular enterprise in the 1920s. After the war, Yerkes's report on the program, which suggested that the typical American soldier scored barely higher than moron level, generated much controversy over mental testing, IQ, and the question of how much intelligence resulted from nature and nurture.

APPLYING PSYCHOLOGY TO BUSINESS

- The first psychologists to apply psychological principles to business were Walter Dill Scott, who wrote books on advertising and how to improve business practices, and Hugo Münsterberg, who came from Germany to run the laboratory at Harvard, but soon developed interests in several applied areas, including forensic psychology, educational psychology, psychotherapy, and industrial ("economic") psychology.

- Münsterberg's *Psychology and Industrial Efficiency* included several examples of how psychological principles could be used to select employees. He recommended two approaches to measurement: simulations of critical features of the worker's task, as in driving an electric railcar, and analysis into component skills, as in being a telephone operator. The book also included research-based advice on improving the workplace and on how to market products.

• Other pioneering industrial psychologists include Walter Van Dyke Bingham, whose Division of Applied Psychology at the Carnegie Institute developed programs for training people in sales and retailing, Lillian Moller Gilbreth, an efficiency expert and one of the first to study ergonomics, and Harry Hollingworth, a reluctant applied psychologist, but an effective one who applied sophisticated experimental design to applied problems such as the effects of caffeine on performance.

STUDY QUESTIONS

1. What was the significance of Scripture's *Thinking, Feeling, Doing*, which included numerous examples of how laboratory methods had a wider use?

2. Why was it important for advocates of the "new psychology" to show that their work had applications?

3. Explain how Galton influenced Cattell's approach to mental testing and describe any five of Cattell's original mental tests.

4. Describe the Wissler study and explain its significance for the Galton/Cattell approach to mental testing.

5. When testing for fatigue in schoolchildren, what was the approach taken by Ebbinghaus? Explain.

6. Binet's approach to psychology has been referred to as "individual" psychology. Explain and contrast his approach with an alternative strategy.

7. What was Binet's idea about the reason for developing mental tests, and what did he conclude about the placement of schoolchildren?

8. Had Binet learned of the subsequent history of IQ testing after his death, he might have turned over in his grave. Explain.

9. According to Goddard, define the term "moron," and explain why Goddard thought it was critically important to study and be able to identify this type of person.

10. Describe and criticize the Kallikak study. Explain why it is an example of how preconceived bias can influence empirical research.

11. Describe and criticize Goddard's work at Ellis Island.

12. Describe the origins of the term "intelligence quotient."

13. Describe Terman's contribution to the measurement of intelligence.

14. Explain how the concept of a meritocracy led Terman to complete psychology's longest longitudinal study.

15. According to Leta Hollingworth, what was the best strategy for educating gifted children?

16. Describe the research completed by Leta Hollingworth that raised questions about gender differences in intellect.

17. Describe the Army testing program. Why were the results so controversial?

18. Aside from his work in industrial psychology, what other contributions did Münsterberg make to applied psychology?

19. Describe the contributions to applied psychology made by Walter Bingham and Lillian Gilbreth.

20. Using the Coca-Cola study as an example, describe how research psychologists brought special expertise to the area of applied psychology.

QUESTIONS FROM THE ORIGINAL SOURCE EXCERPT

1. Describe the strategy used by Münsterberg to assess the skills of the "motormen" of the electric railway.

2. Describe the strategy used by Münsterberg to assess the skills of the telephone operators.

3. In the study of telephone operators, an unexpected validation procedure occurred. Explain.

4. Münsterberg's industrial psychology text is divided into three main parts. What are they and what are the general contents of each part?

FOR FURTHER READING

Fancher, R. E. (1985). *The intelligence men: Makers of the IQ controversy.* New York: W. W. Norton.

An excellent history of the testing movement, with detailed descriptions of the work of Galton, Cattell, Binet, Goddard, Terman, and Yerkes; brings the controversy up to date by examining modern descendants of the hereditarian side of the issue—Burt, Eysenck, and Jensen—and the debate over the alleged fabrication of twin study data by Burt.

Gould, S. J. (1978). *The mismeasure of man.* New York: W. W. Norton.

A highly readable but presentist history of how intelligence has been conceptualized and measured over the years, and used as a means of perpetuating stereotypical beliefs about various groups; includes an excellent layman's overview of factor analysis, the statistical tool used to examine whether intelligence is unitary or multifaceted.

Sokal, M. M. (Ed.). (1987). *Psychological testing and American society.* New Brunswick, NJ: Rutgers University Press.

A collection of essays written by leading experts on the history of testing; includes chapters about Cattell, Goddard, Yerkes, Terman, and the origins of the multiple-choice testing format.

Benjamin, L. T., Jr., Rogers, A. M., & Rosenbaum, A. (1991). Coca Cola, caffeine, and mental deficiency: Harry Hollingworth and the Chattanooga trial. *Journal of the History of the Behavioral Sciences, 27,* 42–55.

A description of Hollingworth's research of the effects of caffeine, set nicely into its historical context; shows how Hollingworth was reluctantly drawn into the project, how he tried to protect his scientific integrity while doing the research, and how his experiments, still cited today, were models of experimental design.

CHAPTER 9

GESTALT PSYCHOLOGY

> There are wholes, the behaviour of which is not determined by that of their individual elements, but where the part-processes are themselves determined by the intrinsic nature of the whole.
>
> —Max Wertheimer, 1924

PREVIEW AND CHAPTER OBJECTIVES

Advocates of a new way of thinking often find that they must speak loudly in order to be heard. Such was the case for those who became known as gestalt psychologists. With missionary zeal, these German psychologists promoted an approach to psychology that objected deeply to the prevailing analytical strategy that characterized certain aspects of other German psychologies, Titchenerian structuralism, American behaviorism, and any theory derived from associationist principles. The gestaltists argued that understanding mind and behavior could not be achieved by trying to identify the basic sensory elements of conscious experience, or by reducing complex behavior to elementary stimulus-response units. Rather, their emphasis was on wholes, and before long their movement came to be identified with this catch phrase: the whole of an experience is more than and different from the sum of its parts. The first section of this chapter highlights the work of three Germans who established the gestalt movement: Max Wertheimer, normally considered the founder by virtue of his elegant yet simple demonstrations of apparent motion; Kurt Koffka, who first introduced gestalt concepts to an American audience and extended gestalt ideas into developmental psychology; and Wolfgang Köhler, whose research on learning and problem solving in apes challenged behaviorism. The chapter's Original Source Excerpt is from Köhler's problem-solving studies.

All three gestalt pioneers left Germany and came to the United States, two of them (Wertheimer and Köhler) as a consequence of Adolph Hitler's dismantling of German science in the 1930s. The gestalt psychology that arrived in America was sometimes associated only with perception, but the gestaltists also made important contributions to the psychology of thinking and problem solving, and their ideas influenced the later development of cognitive psychology.

The final portion of the chapter describes the life and work of Kurt Lewin. He was for a time associated with the gestaltists in Germany, and like Wertheimer and Köhler, he came to the United States to escape the Nazi menace. Lewin went beyond gestalt psychology, however, and developed a complex theory of human behavior that led him to make important contributions to developmental, social, and industrial/organizational psychology. Impatient with abstract laboratory studies, he developed "action research," aimed at making a direct impact on people's lives and solving social problems. After you finish this chapter, you should be able to:

- See the connection between gestalt psychology and the atomism-wholism issue raised in Chapter 2
- Describe the immediate antecedents to gestalt psychology, in the ideas of Mach and von Ehrenfels
- Describe Wertheimer's apparent motion study, show how he ruled out traditional explanations, and explain the significance of the study
- Summarize Koffka's contributions to gestalt psychology
- Describe and apply the gestalt perceptual organizing principles
- Distinguish between geographical and behavioral environments, and the implications for understanding behavior
- Describe Köhler's research on problem solving in apes and contrast it with the approach taken by Thorndike
- Describe Wertheimer's ideas about productive thinking and the general gestalt approach to thinking and problem solving
- Describe the essentials of Lewin's field theory
- Explain the Zeigarnik effect and show how it fits into Lewin's theory
- Describe the contributions made by Lewin to developmental psychology and social psychology
- Describe the overall impact of gestalt psychology on American psychology and explain why it did not become a dominant system

THE ORIGINS AND DEVELOPMENT OF GESTALT PSYCHOLOGY

The starting date for gestalt psychology is normally thought to be somewhere between 1910 and 1912, the years when German psychologist Max Wertheimer looked at a common perceptual phenomenon from a new angle. Like all intellectual movements, however, this one had roots. The gestaltists were influenced indirectly by the German philosophical tradition of Kant, with its emphasis on how a priori perceptual and cognitive categories shape our experiences (see Chapter 2), and by the late nineteenth-century phenomenology of Edmund Husserl, which stressed the importance of relying on direct descriptions of our experiences over the artificial introspective accounts that attempted dissection when trying to understand the nature of these experiences. The gestaltists were also influenced by con-

temporary physics, especially the work of Max Planck, an important pioneer of field theory, which emphasized how overall fields of force determined the nature of the relationships among components of the field. A magnetic field, for instance, represents a force that produces an overall pattern of interrelations among elements that cannot be understood by analyzing each of the elements within the total field.

Three direct influences on the creation of gestalt psychology were the physicist Ernst Mach (1838–1916), and the philosopher/psychologists Christian von Ehrenfels (1859–1932) and Carl Stumpf (1848–1936). In a book on sensation written in 1886, Mach argued that certain "space-forms" resisted analysis into more basic elements. For example, a square has the essential spatial feature of "squareness" that cannot be further reduced. The four lines that compose it can change in size, but the relationship among the four lines must stay the same for squareness to occur. The overall relationship is what counts when identifying squares, not the individual components. The Austrian von Ehrenfels, in an 1890 paper called "On Gestalt Qualities," came to a similar conclusion. There are certain qualities of experience, he contended, that go beyond individual sensory elements and persist even if the elements are altered. A talented musician, von Ehrenfels used melody as an example. By playing a song in a different key or with a different instrument, the physical properties of every single note (element) might change, yet the melody itself does not change—it has a **form-quality** ("Gestaltqualität") that is different from the sum of the individual notes. Stumpf, like von Ehrenfels a talented musician, was a noted experimentalist who contributed important work on the auditory perception of tones. He also engaged in a spirited debate with Wundt over who was best qualified to be an "observer" in experiments about judging musical tones. At issue was an auditory phenomenon with a distinct gestalt theme. When listening to two pure tones simultaneously, the experience is of a unique third tone that does not seem to be a combination of its two components. Wundt believed that suitably trained laboratory workers would be capable of analyzing the phenomenon into its elements, but Stumpf contended that skilled musicians were better observers and that the phenomenon resisted analysis. If a laboratory analysis contradicted the phenomenal experience of a trained musician, Stumpf argued, then the analysis was in error. While not denying the importance of laboratory work, Stumpf and his followers urged the primacy of direct experience over an abstract reduction to elements (Ash, 1985). As will be seen, two of the original three gestaltists took their doctorates with Stumpf, and the third studied with him for a time.

Max Wertheimer (1880–1943): Founding Gestalt Psychology

Max Wertheimer (Figure 9.1) was born in Prague and initially studied law at its university, before his broad interests led him to switch to philosophy. He took courses with von Ehrenfels, where he undoubtedly learned of his teacher's concept of

FIGURE 9.1   Max Wertheimer, gestalt psychology's founder.

Gestaltqualität, then studied in Berlin for three semesters, where he encountered Stumpf, and Würzburg, where he completed a doctorate with Oswald Külpe (Chapter 4) in 1904. His dissertation derived from an earlier interest in criminal law and used a word association technique to discern characteristic patterns of thinking (Newman, 1944). The next few years following 1904 are not well documented, but family wealth apparently made it possible for Wertheimer to indulge his varied interests in philosophy and psychology.

Somewhere around 1910, Wertheimer became fascinated by the perceptual problem of **apparent motion**. The phenomenon was well known at the time and the basis for the newly created motion picture industry. It can be illustrated with a simple example. In a darkened room, two adjacent small circles are flashed on and off in sequence. If the interval between the flashing of the two lights is just right (about 60 msec), the perception is not of two lights, but of a single light that moves back and forth. Thus, two separate sensory events occur, but the perception is that of a single continuous event.[1] In the space between the lights, the circle is perceived even though there is no sensory basis for this perception. How could this occur?

Traditional explanations for apparent motion centered on sensory-motor events or higher cognitive inferences. The first idea was that as the circles flashed alternately, the person would shift the eyes from left to right, over and over. Sensory stimulation resulting from the eye movements was said to produce the perceptual "fusion" that was experienced as movement. The second explanation, in the spirit of Helmholtz, was that the individual made an unconscious logical inference that if a light was in position A then in position B, it must have moved there. The perception, held to be illusory, was the result of this "reasonable" inference.

With the cooperation of Friedrich Schumann, laboratory director at the University of Frankfurt (and coinventor, with G. E. Müller, of the memory drum), Wertheimer was able to acquire laboratory space and equipment to develop his ideas about apparent motion into a program of research. He was aided by two young psychologists then working in Schumann's lab, Wolfgang Köhler and Kurt Koffka (Figure 9.2), who served as participants in the experiments (as did Koffka's wife). The outcome was a 1912 paper, "Experimental Studies on the Perception of Movement," often considered the founding event of gestalt psychology. In the research, Wertheimer and his colleagues demonstrated the phenomenon under a variety of conditions and raised serious questions about prevailing explanations. In one of their studies, for example, three lights in a straight line, A, B, and C, were used. If lights A and C were flashed on and off simultaneously, then B was flashed after 60 msec, the perception was that two lights (A and C) had moved at the same time to the center point.

FIGURE 9.2 Kurt Koffka (left) and Wolfgang Köhler at 9th International Congress of Psychology, held at Yale University, 1929, from Popplestone and McPherson (1994).

This demonstration eliminated the eye movement explanation, because the eyes cannot move in two directions at the same time. The inference explanation was rejected on the grounds that the movement perception occurred too quickly to involve such a complicated sequence of mental events and that the perception of motion was real, not illusory. Instead, Wertheimer argued that the phenomenon must stand on its own as a valid example of an immediately given phenomenological experience that does not require any reference to constituent parts. Indeed, because perception occurred in areas devoid of any sensory information (i.e., the space between the flashing lights), analysis into sensory elements could not possibly explain the phenomenon. Wertheimer referred to the perceived motion as the **phi phenomenon**; he disliked the term "apparent" motion because it implied that the motion was not really perceived (Henle, 1980). As he later concluded, we perceive whole, meaningful figures, not elements that somehow combine to form wholes. Not only is the

---

[1] If the interval between the flashing of the lights is too short, about 30 msec or less, the perception is that both lights are on at the same time and neither is moving. If the interval is above 200 msec, two separate flashing lights will be seen. The precise timing also depends on the intensity of the lights and the distance between them (Goldstein, 1996).

whole different from the sum of its parts, but "the part-processes are themselves determined by the intrinsic nature of the whole" (Wertheimer, 1924/1967, p. 2). The assault on atomism had begun.

Wertheimer lectured and continued doing research at Frankfurt until 1916, then went to Berlin, where he became a central figure at the Berlin Psychological Institute until 1929.[2] In that year Schumann retired from Frankfurt, and Wertheimer returned there to chair the department. He probably would have remained at Frankfurt until his own retirement, but world events intervened with the rise of Nazi Germany. After Hitler came to power in 1933, academic freedom in German universities quickly disappeared and Jewish professors, including such luminaries as Wertheimer's close friend, Albert Einstein, began to be dismissed from their positions. In response to the argument that Germany would be losing an invaluable resource, Hitler is said to have replied: "If the dismissal of Jewish scientists means the annihilation of contemporary German science, then we shall do without science for a few years!" (quoted in Henle, 1986, p. 226). At least with regard to psychology, Hitler was correct. The effects of his leadership effectively destroyed psychology in Germany for a generation.

Shortly after Hitler came to power, Wertheimer, who was Jewish and could see the writing on the wall, gathered up his wife and three children and emigrated to the United States, settling in New York.[3] There he joined a number of other German refugee-scientists at the recently created New School for Social Research. For the remaining 10 years of his life, he continued to work on perception and expanded an earlier interest in problem solving. The outcome was *Productive Thinking* (1945/1982) published posthumously, which will be described later in the section on the gestalt approach to cognition and learning.

[2] For a sense of the geography, refer again to the map of Germany in Chapter 4 (Figure 4.1).

[3] One of the children, Michael Wertheimer, is currently a professor of psychology at the University of Colorado. He is a prominent historian of psychology, nationally recognized as a master teacher by the APA, and a leader in Psi Chi, psychology's national honor society for students.

Koffka (1886–1941) and Köhler (1887–1967): The Co-Founders

Kurt Koffka was born in Berlin and, except for a year spent at the University of Edinburgh in Scotland, educated there as well. He earned a Ph.D. from Carl Stumpf at the University of Berlin in 1908. Under Stumpf, Koffka developed research in the perceptual topics of color contrast and auditory rhythm that would prepare the way for his acceptance of gestalt psychology (Harrower-Erickson, 1942).

After completing his doctorate, Koffka studied physiology, then went to Würzburg for several years where he worked in Külpe's laboratory. Starting in 1910 he spent three semesters in Schumann's lab at Frankfurt, and it was during this time that he encountered Wertheimer, participated in the famous apparent motion studies along with Köhler, and became a convert to gestaltist thinking. As he later wrote, the three young researchers "were thrown into the closest contact which resulted in lasting collaboration" (quoted in Harrower-Erickson, 1942, p. 279). Koffka left Frankfurt in 1911 to begin his first professorial job at the University of Giessen. He remained there until 1924, producing a modest but steady flow of experimental papers on such topics as sound localization and memory. During World War I, he studied the cognitive consequences of severe brain injury in soldiers. In 1921, he extended gestalt ideas into the realm of developmental psychology by writing *The Growth of the Mind*.

Of the three early gestaltists, Koffka was primarily responsible for introducing the movement to America. He accomplished this first by writing an article in 1922 for the *Psychological Bulletin* called "Perception: An Introduction to Gestalt-Theorie" (Koffka, 1922). It was an unfortunate choice of a title, however. Although the gestaltists thought of their movement as a new theory applicable to all psychology, the article implied that gestalt psychology was merely a new approach to the study of perception. This "misperception" lingers today—in modern introductory texts, discussion of gestalt psychology occurs mainly in the perception chapter.

Koffka also spread the gestalt word in person starting in 1924, in a 30-campus lecture tour, in an invited address to the annual meeting of the APA in 1925, and in a pair of visiting professor appointments at Cornell and Wisconsin (Sokal, 1984). In 1927, he accepted a full-time academic position at Smith College in western Massachusetts, a private liberal arts college for women, where he remained until his death in 1941. At Smith, the absence of a graduate program effectively curtailed Koffka's research productivity, but he influenced the careers of several talented women psychologists, including Eleanor Gibson, who later invented the visual cliff as a means of studying the development of depth perception in infants. In 1935, Koffka wrote his most important book, *Principles of Gestalt Psychology*. It established his reputation as gestalt psychology's major theorist, but also contributed to a growing impression among Americans that the gestaltists were more interested in theory than data. At a time when most American psychologists were firmly in the positivist camp, this tendency was seen as a weakness. Koffka's arguments in his highly abstract book were also somewhat difficult to follow. The works of his more erudite gestalt colleague, Köhler, were more widely read.

Wolfgang Köhler was just a year younger than Koffka and 7 years younger than Wertheimer, but he outlived his peers by 25 years and 23 years, respectively. This longevity, combined with his deliberate promotion of gestalt ideas, made him the best-known gestaltist of the three originators, especially in America. In 1958, he became the only one of them to be elected president of the APA. His early career was not unlike Koffka's—he earned a doctorate from Stumpf in 1909. He then became Schumann's assistant at Frankfurt, just in time for the arrival of Wertheimer and Koffka and their fateful collaboration (Asch, 1968).

In 1913, an intriguing opportunity came Köhler's way in the form of an invitation to direct the research at a primate colony that the Prussian Academy of Sciences had created at Tenerife, largest of the Canary Islands, which lie off the northwest coast of Africa. He accepted, arriving just before the outbreak of World War I, which effectively marooned him on the island with his family and his small colony of apes. As this chapter's Close-Up relates, though, research might not have been his only activity during these years—some think he could have been a German spy. Regardless of the espionage claims, the Tenerife years made Köhler's reputation as a scientist. There he produced his most famous research, the studies of problem solving in apes. This research will be examined in more detail later in this chapter when you will encounter an excerpt from Köhler's book-length account of his studies—*The Mentality of Apes* (1917/1926).

CLOSE-UP:
A Case of Espionage?

Wolfgang Köhler's research on the Canary Island of Tenerife during World War I established his scientific reputation. The insight studies are widely cited, even today, and not just in history texts. But was research into the mental capabilities of apes Köhler's only interest during these years? No, according to psychologist Ronald Ley. During a visit to the island in 1975, in an attempt to locate the original site of Köhler's Research Station, he happened to meet 87-year-old Manuel González y García, who was none other than the animal handler and caretaker during Köhler's years on Tenerife! Despite the passage of years, González y García's memory of the work done at the Research Station and of the behavior of the apes appeared to be intact. For instance, his recollections of the apes weren't all fond. He remembered that Köhler's most famous ape, Sultan, almost bit off a finger, and he showed Ley the scars from encounters with other apes in the colony. Concerning Köhler, he revealed that the German scientist seemed to enjoy working with the animals, but that he never went into the animal enclosures alone; he made most of his observations from outside the cages. And one other thing—Köhler was a German spy.

Naturally, the espionage claim astounded the initially skeptical Ley, who eventually wrote *A Whisper of Espionage: Wolfgang Köhler and the Apes of Tenerife* (Ley, 1990), a scientific detective story that describes his search for information to verify the assertion by González y García. It took him from Tenerife to archival collections throughout Europe to the homes of Köhler's wife and son. Ley failed to find direct evidence that Köhler was a spy, but he was able to piece together some circumstantial evidence suggesting that Köhler might have contributed to the German war effort. Located close to allied shipping lanes, the mountainous Canary Islands had strategic importance. Observers could easily spot allied shipping and convey information about it to German U-boats. Throughout the war, the British, who had numerous ships sunk in the area, made repeated claims to Spain that German spies on the island were doing just that. The islands were owned by Spain, supposedly a neutral country. Nonetheless, the British claimed that German scientists on the island had the means (wireless telegraph) to conduct espionage. According to Ley, Köhler, who kept a wireless radio at the Research Station, was one of those scientists.

Ley's espionage claim is intriguing, but it has been criticized. According to Pastore (1990), the radio might simply have been for general communication with the mainland, Köhler's research and writing output would not have left much time for active spying, and the whole story might be nothing more than a rumor that eventually turned into a "fact" in an old man's mind. Köhler himself referred to such a rumor in some of his correspondence: "certain Englishmen ... take us for German spies, and are even so kind as to spread the rumors that the animals are just a pretext" (quoted in Pastore, 1990, p. 369). On the other hand, it would not be unusual for any young patriotic scientist, given the opportunity, to pass along information that might be of use to the homeland.

Ley's claim might be debatable, but his research uncovered interesting details about Köhler's years on Tenerife, including the role played by his first wife Thekla. While raising two young children, she managed to contribute substantially to the research. She was apparently more at ease with the apes than Köhler, and according to her daughter, "the one who pressed to continue the work during times when things were going poorly" (quoted in Ley, 1990, p. 226). A talented artist, she drew the profile sketch of one of the apes that appeared as the frontispiece for *The Mentality of Apes* (Figure 9.3), and she filmed the research. Her photos, including the famous picture of Sultan that appears in this chapter (Figure 9.7), appear in the book. Köhler recognized her value, writing to German authorities that Thekla was capable of running the Research Station herself, and indicating that he wished her to be a coauthor of the book that summarized the research. He apparently changed his mind on the latter point, however. Thekla's initials below the sketch in the frontispiece are the only tangible sign of her contribution to the book.

FIGURE 9.3 Sketch of one of Köhler's apes, drawn by his first wife Thekla, and appearing as the frontispiece to *The Mentality of Apes* (Köhler, 1917/1926).

Köhler returned to a war-ravaged Germany in 1920 and was initially unable to find full-time employment. In 1922, however, his status as a rising star in academia was confirmed when he was named to succeed the venerable Stumpf, his former mentor, as Director of the Psychological Institute at the University of Berlin. Wertheimer was also there, as was a young Kurt Lewin (discussed later in the chapter). Along with a talented group of students, the gestaltists created a "golden age" for their movement that lasted for about a decade (Henle, 1986). They produced important research, founded the journal *Psychologische Forschung* (*Psychological Research*) to promote their work, and sent their students throughout Germany to expand their base of operations. It all ended with the Nazis, however.

Of the three founding gestaltists, Köhler was the last to leave Germany when he emigrated in 1935. Because he was not Jewish, he did not face the kind of threat encountered by Wertheimer (and Lewin), but he was nonetheless appalled by the Nazi destruction of academia and he spoke out publicly about it. In April of 1933, for instance, he wrote the last anti-Nazi article to be published during the Hitler years, denouncing the dismissal of Jewish professors. In the article, he argued that "only the quality of a human being should determine his worth, that intellectual achievement, character, and obvious contributions to German culture retain their significance whether a person is Jewish or not" (quoted in Henle, 1986, p. 228). Although Köhler was not arrested for writing the article (somewhat to his surprise), his situation deteriorated steadily. He was forced to open his lectures with a Nazi salute (which he did with notable sarcasm), Nazi sympathizers began to "monitor" his lectures, and on one occasion troops appeared outside his classroom and students had their identification papers examined. By early 1935, after refusing to sign a loyalty oath to Hitler, Köhler had had enough. He resigned his beloved directorship and accepted a position at Swarthmore College in eastern Pennsylvania, where he remained until his retirement in 1958. He died nine years later. In addition to his ape book, he wrote *Gestalt Psychology* in 1929. It was shorter, easier to read, and more popular than Koffka's gestalt book. It is notable for its

assault on American behaviorism. Just as the structuralists and associationists had faltered by trying to analyze consciousness into its elements, Köhler argued, so would behaviorism fail because of its similar atomistic strategy of reducing behavior to artificial stimulus-response units.

GESTALT PSYCHOLOGY AND PERCEPTION

Wertheimer launched gestalt psychology with his research on a perceptual phenomenon, apparent motion, and the study of perception became an important part of the gestalt program. Much of their effort went into describing the basic rules determining how phenomena become organized into whole, meaningful figures. These **gestalt organizing principles**, first articulated by Wertheimer (1923/1967), are now familiar fixtures in the perception chapters of general psychology texts. Here are some of the more important ones.

Principles of Perceptual Organization

One of our most basic perceptual tendencies is to separate whole figures from their backgrounds. It provides the foundation for all object perception (Goldstein, 1996). This **figure-ground** segregation was first described in detail in 1915 by Edgar Rubin, a Danish psychologist who studied with G. E. Müller at Göttingen and was also known for establishing the phenomenon of "paradoxical warmth" (Prentice, 1951). Rubin was not a gestalt psychologist, but the gestaltists used his figure-ground phenomenon to support their cause. According to Rubin's phenomenological description, figures have several distinct features that enable them to be isolated from backgrounds. The border seems to "belong" to the figure, for example, while the ground seems to extend behind the figure, and this perceptual impression is a powerful one, even though we "know" otherwise. Also, the figure is more memorable than the ground and seems to have a substance that is lacking in the ground (Rubin, 1915/1958). In Figure 9.4a, for instance, observers usually perceive the segments

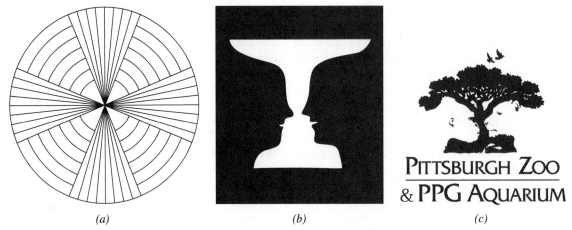

(a)   *(b)*   *(c)*

FIGURE 9.4 Reversible figure-ground illustrations (a and b), from Rubin (1915/1958), and (c) a modern application of a figure-ground reversal.

with the straight, radiating lines as a figure against a background of fully concentric circles. The result is an overall perception of a type of cross. With effort, it is possible to reverse the figure-ground relations in Figure 9.4a, making a cross with each arm composed of arcs. This reversal is more easily accomplished in Figure 9.4b, the most famous portion of Rubin's 1915 paper. By changing the focus of attention, the figure can either be a vase or two faces in profile. Note that only one of these perceptions can occur at a time. When the vase is the figure, the black area cannot be perceived as anything but an unformed background. When the faces are figures, the reverse happens. If you stare at Figure 9.4b, you will find your perception switching rapidly from one "whole" to another. One creative modern application of a figure-ground reversal is to be found in the logo for the Pittsburgh Zoo & PPG Aquarium (Figure 9.4c).

Three other gestalt organizing principles are illustrated in Figure 9.5, taken from Wertheimer's 1923 paper on "Laws of Organization in Perceptual Forms" (Wertheimer, 1923/1967). In Figure 9.5a, the first two dots, a and b, seem to belong together, as do the next two and the final two. They are organized by the principle of **proximity**. Wertheimer (1923/1967, p. 72) demonstrated the power of this simple principle by challenging readers to perceive the dots as a/bc/de/f rather than ab/cd/ef, a task he considered

impossible. If proximity is held constant, then stimuli might be organized according to **similarity**, as shown

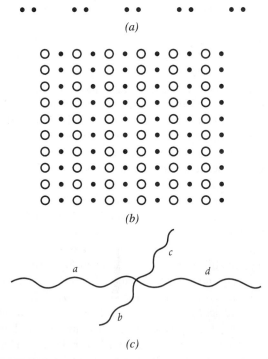

FIGURE 9.5 Gestalt perceptual organizing principles of (a) proximity, (b) similarity, and (c) good continuation, from Wertheimer (1923/1967).

in Figure 9.5b, and we are compelled to perceive alternating vertical columns of open and closed dots. The third principle, **good continuation** is a tendency to organize our perceptions in smoothly flowing directions. Thus, we perceive Figure 9.5c as two wavy lines a-d and b-c. It is difficult to perceive the figure as two lines that sharply change direction, a-b or c-d.

All of the organizing principles have in common what is sometimes called the law of simplicity or what the gestaltists called **Prägnanz** (rough translation: "good figure"). It refers to the basic tendency for our perceptions to mirror reality as closely as possible. When the situation is ambiguous, the organizational principles work to provide the most reasonable guess about the nature of what is being perceived. Thus, even though Figure 9.6 could have been created in several different ways, we tend to perceive the figure as being composed of a rectangle and a triangle, the simplest and most likely hypothesis. Similarly, when we encounter incomplete figures, we often construct a "good figure" by filling in the gaps, a phenomenon called **closure**. You might recognize the law of Prägnanz as the perceptual equivalent of Lloyd Morgan's Canon of Parsimony.

One final point about these organizing principles is that psychologists have often referred to them when making the claim that the gestaltists were nativists with regard to perception. On the contrary, they argued that the organizing principles had nothing to do with the nature-nurture issue. Rather, these principles were considered to be inherent in the nature of objects in the world; our perceptual systems are designed to make the best guess about what is out there. As Wertheimer (1923/1967) put it, "one recognizes a resultant 'good Gestalt' simply by its own 'inner necessity'" (p. 83).

Behavioral Versus Geographic Environments

The organizing principles might be designed to help us perceive the world as it is, but that is not to say that our perceptions mirror physical reality. The gestaltists, most notably Koffka in his *Principles of Gestalt Psychology* (1935) made an important distinction between the world as it is, what he called the **geographical environment**, and the world as we perceive it, the **behavioral environment**. It is the latter perception that determines how we act. Koffka used an old German folktale to drive home the point. It concerned a weary traveler in the dead of winter who reached an inn after riding on horseback for hours over what seemed to be an open snow-covered plain. When he arrived, the innkeeper asked from which direction he had come. The rider pointed to the plain and the innkeeper, "in a tone of awe and wonder, said: 'Do you know that you have ridden across the Lake of Constance?' At which the rider dropped stone dead" (p. 28). Apparently, realizing that the behavioral environment ("this seems to be a wide open plain") does not match the geographical environment ("a frozen lake that could easily crack under the weight of a horse—I could have drowned!") can be rather stressful.

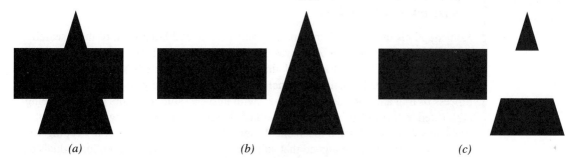

(a)   *(b)*   *(c)*

FIGURE 9.6 The gestalt principle of Pragnänz. The figure on the left could have been created in several ways. We tend to perceive it as being composed of a rectangle and a triangle, the simpler of the two possibilities shown on the right.

This distinction between physical reality and reality as perceived led Koffka to a point that would soon be elaborated by Kurt Lewin, with his concept of "life space" (discussed later in the chapter). If the behavioral and geographic environments differ, then two people in the same geographic environment might perceive it differently. Thus, the descriptions of a walk in the woods by a geologist and a botanist will vary considerably.

Psychophysical Isomorphism

The gestaltists did not limit themselves to phenomenological descriptions of perceptual events; they also theorized about the relationship between perception and underlying brain processes. Their position on this ancient mind-body problem was a version of psychophysical parallelism that Köhler (1929/1947) called **isomorphism**: "in a given case the organization of experience and the underlying physiological facts have the same structure" (p. 300). That is, for a given experience, the underlying brain processes mirror the experience in some fashion. This does not mean that brain processes duplicate experience—Köhler was not suggesting that when we experience a circle that a circular set of neurons in our brain fires. Rather, there is a functional isomorphism between the two. A geographical metaphor illustrates the point: The actual terrain over a 20-square mile-area looks nothing like the map of the area and represents a different kind of experience altogether, but the map is structurally isomorphic to the terrain. Similarly, the gestaltists believed that brain activity was isomorphic to phenomenological experience.

The gestaltists' model of brain function was speculative (and attacked by American physiological psychologists such as Lashley), but it was consistent with their orientation. It suggested that the brain operated as a field of force and that cortical activities were interrelated in complex ways and parallel with experience.

THE GESTALT APPROACH TO COGNITION AND LEARNING

Although the title of Koffka's 1922 landmark article in *Psychological Bulletin* gave the impression that gestalt psychology was concerned only with perception, such was not the case. Rather, the gestalists conceived of their system as a general psychology, and they made specific contributions to the study of thinking, problem solving, and learning. The two best-known examples are Köhler's research on problem solving in apes and Wertheimer's posthumous book on *Productive Thinking* (1945/1982). A portion of Köhler's *The Mentality of Apes* (1917/1926) is excerpted here. The book was first published in German in 1917, then translated into English and expanded slightly in 1924. The excerpt is from a 1926 printing.

ORIGINAL SOURCE EXCERPT
Köhler on Insight in Apes

Köhler and his family lived on Tenerife from 1913 to 1920, but most of the research reported in *The Mentality of Apes* was completed within the first full year on the island. Early in the book, Köhler took dead aim at Thorndike's puzzle box experiments. As you recall from Chapter 7, Thorndike concluded that learning and problem solving was a process of trial and "accidental success," with unsuccessful behaviors gradually being eliminated in favor of behaviors that worked. Köhler, however, strongly disagreed that problem solving was such a mechanical, step-by-step process. Instead, in keeping with his gestalt orientation, he argued that solutions to problems occur when individuals can view the entire problem field and rearrange the elements of the problem into a new configuration. Solutions have a perceptual quality to them, then, and they occur quickly, once the components have been reconfigured. Köhler used the term **insight** to label such a process. The main procedural problem with Thorndike's research, according to Köhler, was that the animals could never perceive the entire field. Hence, they were unable to see how the components of the apparatus related to each other in an overall configuration.[4] Thorndike's studies, Köhler wrote,

> ... were designed as intelligence tests of the same type as our own, ... and ought, therefore, to have conformed to the same general conditions, and above all, to have been arranged so as to be completely *visible* to the animals. For if essential portions of the experimental apparatus cannot be seen by the animals, how can they use their intellectual faculties in tackling the situation? It is somewhat astonishing to find that (in Thorndike's experiments) cats and dogs were frequently placed in cages containing the *extreme end* only of one or the other mechanism, or allowing a view of ropes or other parts of the mechanism, but from which a survey over the *whole* arrangement was not possible. (p. 23, italics in the original)

Köhler was determined not to make the same "mistake" in his research. His animals would have the entire field in front of them, and all of the elements needed to solve the problems would be in full view. Furthermore, his problems would take advantage of the animals' natural hand-eye coordination and not force them to behave in ways unnatural to them. That is, Köhler was keenly aware of what we would today refer to as the biological constraints on behavior:

> ... [T]he response of the chimpanzee ... will always be limited and determined by his own very pronounced natural proclivities. For I must most emphatically state, after a full acquaintance with chimpanzees, that it may perhaps be possible ... by beating or such means, to compel them to an action, to a habit, an omission, or a method of procedure which is not spontaneous and the natural anthropoidal response to the particular conditions; but so to *weld* an alien nature into his own that the chimpanzee will continue to exhibit it when not under pressure, appears to me difficult in the extreme, and probably impossible. I should have the highest admiration for a pedagogic talent which could achieve such a result. It is a continuous source of wonder, and often enough of vexation, to observe how every attempt to re-mould his biological heritage "runs off" an otherwise clever and ductile animal of this species "like water from a duck's back." (p. 70, italics in the original)

The Mentality of Apes includes descriptions of dozens of experiments on problem solving. One of the most famous occurs in a chapter called "The Making of Implements" and concerned a problem in which bananas lying outside a cage were to be retrieved. Two hollow bamboo sticks with different diameters were available, each too short to reach the food. Köhler wondered if one of his smartest chimpanzees, Sultan, could solve the problem by joining the sticks. Traditional accounts of this famous experiment portray a thoughtful animal that carefully examined the elements of the situation and suddenly

---

[4] Köhler criticized maze learning studies for the same reason, complaining that "American animal psychology makes animals (or people) seek their way out of mazes, over the whole of which there is no general survey from any point inside" (p. 18).

hit upon the insight that solved the problem. Actually, the animal tried several other strategies first, each doomed to failure, and he even failed to take the hint when the essence of the solution was shown to him directly!

> ... Beyond the bars lies the objective, just so far away that the animal cannot reach it with either rod. ... Nevertheless, he takes great pains to try to reach it with one stick or the other, even pushing his right shoulder through the bars. When everything proves futile, Sultan commits a "bad error," or, more clearly, a great stupidity, such as he made sometimes on other occasions. He pulls a box from the back of the room toward the bars; true, he pushes it away again at once as it is useless, or rather, actually in the way. (pp. 130–131)

Sultan's "bad error," dragging a box over to the bars of the cage, was probably the result of an earlier experiment, in which a banana was suspended from the ceiling of the cage and could be reached by dragging a box under it, climbing on the box, and jumping. Sultan had solved this problem quickly (pp. 40–41). After recognizing that the box would not work in this new situation, Sultan tried a different strategy:

> ... Immediately afterwards, he does something which, although practically useless, must be counted among the "good errors": he pushes one of the sticks out as far as it will go, then takes the second, and with it pokes the first one cautiously towards the objective, pushing it carefully from the nearer end and thus slowly urging it towards the fruit. This does not always succeed, but if he has got pretty close in this way, he takes even greater precaution; he pushes very gently, watches the movements of the stick that is lying on the ground, and actually touches the objective with its tip. Thus, all of a sudden, for the first time, the contact "animal-objective" has been established, and Sultan visibly feels (we humans can sympathize) a certain satisfaction in having even so much power over the fruit that he can touch and slightly move it by pushing the stick. ... But although, in trying to steer it cautiously, he puts the stick in his hand exactly to the cut (i.e., the opening) of the stick on the ground, and although one might think that doing so would suggest the possibility of pushing one stick into the other, there is no indication whatever of such a practically valuable solution. Finally, the observer gives the animal some help by putting one finger into the opening of one stick under the animal's nose (without pointing to the other stick at all). This has no effect; Sultan, as before, pushes one stick with the other towards the objective, and as this pseudo-solution does not satisfy him any longer, he abandons his efforts altogether, and does not even pick up the sticks when they are both again thrown through the bars to him. The experiment has lasted over an hour, and is stopped for the present, as it seems hopeless, carried out like this. As we intend to take it up again after a while, Sultan is left in possession of his sticks; the keeper is left there to watch him. (pp. 131–132)

When Sultan did manage to solve the double-stick problem, Köhler was not there to see it. Instead, he had to rely on the description given by the animal's keeper (presumably the same Manuel González y García mentioned in the Close-Up). In a footnote, Köhler vouched for the keeper's honesty. There was "no suspicion that the keeper quickly 'trained the animal'; the man would never dare it" (p. 132). The keeper's description is one of psychology's most quoted passages:

> Keeper's report: "Sultan first of all squats indifferently on the box, which has been left standing a little back from the railings; then he gets up, picks up the two sticks, sits down again on the box and plays carelessly with them. While doing this, it happens that he finds himself holding one rod in either hand in such a way that they lie in a straight line; he pushes the thinner one a little way into the opening of the thicker, jumps up and is already on the run towards the railings, to which he has up to now half turned his back, and begins to draw a banana towards him with the double stick." (p. 132)

Sultan's famous solution was captured about a month later on film and appears in Köhler's book; it is reproduced in Figure 9.7. Despite the drama of the keeper's report, the suddenness of the solution is less impressive in the context of what preceded it. In addition, the solution was far from ideal—the sticks kept falling apart. Nonetheless, Sultan persevered, using the double-stick solution to drag everything within reach into his cage. That the solution depends on the perceptual aspects of the situation is clear from the following. Even after solving the problem many times, Sultan hesitated when he saw the sticks in certain configurations:

> Sometimes, however, he experiences a difficulty, where one would least expect it. Holding both tubes in his hand and wanting to proceed as usual to connect them, he hesitates for a few minutes and seems strangely uncertain; this is when the tubes lie in his hand in certain positions, namely almost parallel, or else across each other in the shape of a very narrow "X." This difficulty has now almost disappeared, but at first it occurred frequently. (pp. 135–136)

In addition to the double-stick problem and the problem of using a single box to reach bananas, Köhler's chimps also retrieved suspended fruit by stacking several boxes. They

FIGURE 9.7 Köhler's ape Sultan, solving the two-stick problem, from Köhler (1917/1926).

learned the task gradually, as Köhler raised the fruit higher and higher. They first learned to use a single box, then two, then three. Hence, the procedure was similar to one later called "shaping" by behaviorists. In one experiment, Sultan was once again center stage:

> The objective hangs still higher up; Sultan has fasted all the forenoon and, therefore, goes at his task with great zeal. He lays the heavy box flat underneath the objective, puts the second one upright upon it, and, standing on the top, tries to seize the objective. As he does not reach it, he looks down and round about, and his glance is caught by the third box, which may have seemed useless to him at first, because of its smallness. He climbs down very carefully, seizes the box, climbs up with it, and completes the construction. (p. 142)

Köhler declined (p. 194) to develop a new theory of intelligence to explain his findings, but he spent the bulk of a chapter refuting the "theory of chance," his phrase for the approach taken by Thorndike and other American psychologists wedded to a strategy based on associationist and reductionist principles. In so doing, he described several attributes of what he considered to be insightful behavior. For example, in the early stages, the problem solver systematically surveys the field:

> We can ... distinguish sharply between the kind of conduct which from the very beginning arises out of a consideration of the characteristics of a situation, and one that does not. Only in the former case do we speak of insight, and only that behaviour of animals definitely appears to us intelligent which takes account from the beginning of the lie of the land, and proceeds to deal with it in a smooth, continuous course. Hence follows this characteristic: *to set up as a criterion of insight, the appearance of a complete solution with reference to the whole lay-out of the field.* (p. 198, italics in the original)

Another feature of insightful problem solving is that it is goal-directed. Contrary to Thorndike's "chance" theory, which had the animal behaving randomly at first, Köhler believed that animals behaved quite differently, unless placed in a situation (e.g., Thorndike's puzzle boxes) in which the inability to survey the field made it impossible for the animal to see the objective clearly:

> ... It is certainly not a characteristic of the chimpanzee, when he is brought into an experimental situation, to make any chance movements. ... As long as his efforts are directed to the objective, all distinguishable stages of his behavior (as with human beings in similar situations), tend to appear as complete attempts at solutions, *none* of which appears as the product of accidentally arrayed parts. This is true, most of all, of the solution which is finally successful. Certainly, it often follows upon a period of perplexity or quiet (often a period of survey), but in real and convincing cases, the solution never appears in a disorder of blind impulses. It is one continuous, smooth action, which can be resolved into its parts *only by the imagination* of the onlooker. (pp. 199–200, italics in the original)

According to Köhler, then, when placed in a problem situation, the animal first surveys the whole field with reference to some clear objective. Eventually, the animal will insightfully reorganize the problem elements in the field into a new configuration which quickly solves the problem. The necessary condition for insight is that all aspects of the problem must be within the animal's field of view.

Köhler's explanation did not go unchallenged by American psychologists, who questioned the methodological sophistication of Köhler's demonstrations and pointed out that a careful reading of the descriptions finds ample evidence of trial-and-error learning. Some attempts to replicate the research produced ambiguous results and suggested that the more prior experience the animal had with similar problems, the more likely a "quick" (i.e., insightful) solution would appear (Windholz & Lamal, 1985). On the other hand, Köhler's research introduced a new way of thinking into the debate about learning and problem solving and extended animal methodology beyond puzzle boxes and mazes.

Wertheimer on Productive Thinking

Köhler was not the only gestaltist studying cognition. Max Wertheimer had a long-standing interest in thinking and problem solving that culminated in *Productive Thinking* (1945/1982), which he sent to the publisher just before his death in 1943. Its topics ranged from how children learn arithmetic to how Einstein developed his theory of relativity. A good example of his use of gestalt principles can be found in his description of how to teach children about geometry. Wertheimer deplored the traditional approach to teaching math, which relied heavily on asking students to memorize rules and formulas without giving them true insight into the concepts behind the symbols.

Early in the book, Wertheimer described his visit to a class in which the teacher was explaining how to find the area of parallelograms. Using the example in Figure 9.8a, the teacher explained the rules:

> "I drop one perpendicular line from the upper left corner and another perpendicular from the upper right corner."
>
> "I extend the baseline to the right."
>
> "I label the two new points e and f."
> (Wertheimer, 1945/1982, p. 14)

Because students had already memorized the rule for finding the area of rectangles, they could now determine the area of the parallelogram by multiplying its base (e-f) by its height (d-e). The teacher then gave the students several more problems, which they solved by going through the same steps. More problems were assigned for homework.

The next day, Wertheimer again visited the class, and with the teacher's permission, gave students a slightly different parallelogram—the one in Figure 9.8b. Most students could not find its area. Some

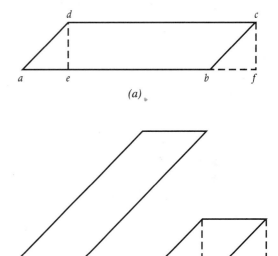

FIGURE 9.8 The area of a parallelogram: (a) diagram used to teach by formula; (b) problem presented by Wertheimer that caused difficulty for students taught by formula; (c) one solution attempt from students taught by formula, from Wertheimer (1945/1982).

gave up immediately—"Teacher, we haven't had that yet" (Wertheimer, 1945/1982, p. 15)—while others tried applying the rules they had been taught, producing drawings like Figure 9.8c, but being unsure of how to proceed from that point. A minority rotated the parallelogram 45°, then applied their rules successfully. The teacher was not amused, claiming that Wertheimer had given his students "a queer figure. Naturally they are unable to deal with it" (p. 16).

Wertheimer believed that children would be more productive thinkers if they truly understood the concept of area. He suggested that teachers start with simple concrete examples. For instance, students could easily grasp the idea that two equivalent square fields would produce the same amount of some crop. Next, rectangular surfaces could be understood as combinations of square fields. With that knowledge, students could be shown that any parallelogram could be transformed into a rectangle by chopping off one end and attaching it to the other. He demonstrated that children with such an insightful understanding had no trouble (a) solving area problems like those in Figure 9.9a, which he called "A-Figures," and (b) recognizing instantly that the procedure would fail for the problems in the "B-Figures." For students who memorized the traditional base by height routine for parallelograms, however, none of the problems in Figure 9.9 seemed to be solvable.

For Wertheimer, then, productive thinking in the classroom went far beyond the memorization of sets of rules and formulas for "correct" solutions. True understanding involved a complete restructuring of the problem in order to gain insight into its solution. By moving a portion of the parallelogram from one end to the other, children accomplished this "restructuring" and thereby created a "good gestalt," a simpler figure (rectangle) from which their understanding of squares and rectangles could be used to calculate area.

Other Gestalt Research on Cognition

As mentioned earlier, while at Berlin in the 1920s, the gestaltists attracted a talented group of students. Among them were Hedwig Von Restorff and George Katona, who made important contributions to the study of memory, and Karl Duncker, whose studies

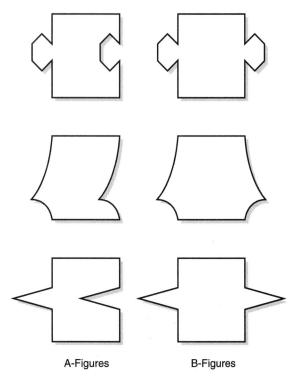

A-Figures   B-Figures

FIGURE 9.9   Sketches used by Wertheimer to illustrate productive thinking. Students with productive knowledge of area solve A-Figures and recognize the problem with B-Figures. For students who have learned area by rote, both types of figures seem unsolvable, from Wertheimer (1945/1982).

of problem solving and insight are routinely found in general psychology texts today. All three ran afoul of the Nazi regime, and while Von Restorff remained in Germany after her dismissal from Berlin and died sometime before the end of World War II (Henle, 1980), Katona and Duncker joined the emigration of scholars to the United States.

Hedwig Von Restorff (1901–unknown) discovered that if people learned lists with a three-digit number embedded in a series of nonsense syllables, the number would almost always be recalled better than the syllables. In good gestaltist fashion, she interpreted the result as an illustration of the figure-ground relationship—the number provided a sharp figure against the background of nonsense syllables (Baddeley,

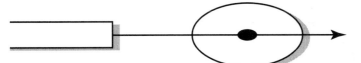

FIGURE 9.10 Diagram used by Duncker to induce functional fixedness in the tumor problem, from Duncker (1945).

1990). Today, her result is called the **Von Restorff effect**. Anytime a stimulus in an information array stands out in some fashion, it will be recalled more easily than the remaining information. George Katona (1901–1981) had a long and distinguished career. His contribution to memory research came in the form of his 1940 book, *Organizing and Memorizing*, in which he applied gestalt organizational principles to the memory process. Like Wertheimer, he considered rote learning to be useless. Instead, he argued that memory would be enhanced if the information could be organized in meaningful patterns. The importance of organization in memory would be rediscovered by cognitive psychologists in the 1960s, most of whom were unaware of Katona's pioneering efforts.

Karl Duncker (1903–1940) was a student of Köhler's who followed his mentor to Swarthmore College during the Nazi years. Although he died young (suicide), he managed to produce a major work on thinking, extending his teacher's ideas about insight into the area of human problem-solving behavior. His innovative *Psychology of Productive Thought* appeared in German in 1935 and was translated into English and reprinted in *Psychological Monographs* 10 years later (Duncker, 1935/1945). It has been called by Hilgard (1987) "the most careful and analytical account of insight ever published" (p. 233). Duncker studied the cognitive processes of college students by asking them to think out loud while they were trying to solve problems. He then analyzed the written transcripts of their protocols, searching for patterns of thinking and typical problem-solving strategies. He discovered, for instance, that students often solved problems creatively if they were able to imagine uses for objects that differed from typical uses. Duncker's famous candle problem illustrates the point. Subjects must mount a candle vertically on a wall so that it won't scorch the wall. They are given several objects, including a box of tacks. The correct solution involves seeing the box not as serving its nor-

mal function as a container, but as a platform on which to mount the candle. Subjects who failed to solve the problem were said by Duncker to show **functional fixedness**, an inability to think beyond the typical function of an object. Similarly, in his "tumor" problem, he asked subjects to figure out how to destroy an inoperative stomach tumor using radiation. The difficulty was that radiation of sufficient intensity to destroy the tumor would also destroy surrounding tissue. The solution was to expose the tumor to several rays from different directions that would focus on the tumor. Each individual ray would be relatively weak, leaving healthy tissue intact, but when the rays combined at the point of the tumor, they would be strong enough to kill it. Duncker found that when he showed students the diagram in Figure 9.10, only 9% solved the problem. On the other hand, 37% arrived at the solution when the diagram was not shown (Mayer, 1992). Duncker concluded that the diagram induced functional fixedness by making subjects think about using a single direction for the radiation.

KURT LEWIN (1890–1947): EXPANDING THE GESTALT VISION

Kurt Lewin[5] was a contemporary of gestalt psychology's "big three," Wertheimer, Koffka, and Köhler, and although he did not consider himself a gestalt psychologist per se, he recognized his debt to "these outstanding personalities. ... The fundamental ideas of gestalt theory are the foundation of all our investigations in the field of the will, of affect, and of the personality"

[5] The correct German pronunciation of Lewin is "La-Veen" but he began pronouncing it "Loo-in" after arriving in America. Apparently, his children's peers and schoolmates used the latter Americanized pronunciation and Lewin decided to save his children the aggravation of continually "explaining to their friends why the family name was spelled 'Lewin' but pronounced 'Laveen'" (Marrow, 1969, p. 177).

(quoted in Marrow, 1969, p. 76). Like the gestaltists, Lewin built his theory around concepts taken from field theory, and he borrowed freely from gestalt perceptual and cognitive ideas. While the gestaltists tended to focus on perception, learning, cognition, and their neurological correlates, however, Lewin was more interested in motivation, emotion, personality and its development, and the influence of social forces on human action. Researchers investigating those topics today, especially developmental and social psychologists, all claim Lewin as a pioneer in their fields.

Early Life and Career

Lewin was born on September 9, 1890, in the small Prussian village of Mogilno, now a part of Poland. The son of a merchant, he was raised in an environment that combined the relative comfort of middle-class status with a pervasive and state-approved anti-Semitism. Being on the receiving end of sanctioned discrimination created in Lewin a strong sense of social justice that characterized his career. The Lewins moved to Berlin in 1905, where Kurt's intellectual potential blossomed. As a university student, Lewin spent a semester each at Freiburg and Munich, studying medicine and biology but unsure of a vocation. At some point he decided to emulate his professors and be one himself, and he returned to Berlin, completing a doctorate on association with this chapter's most recognizable mentor—Carl Stumpf. That Lewin thought highly of his teacher is clear from an obituary that he later wrote, in which he placed Stumpf and G. E. Müller (Chapter 4) at "the highest rank ... within the pyramid of psychologists participating in research" in Germany (Lewin, 1937, p. 189). Stumpf earned Lewin's high regard despite the fact that they had little personal contact. During the years spent on his doctoral research, for example, Lewin did not recall discussing his thesis with Stumpf until he defended it! Lewin generously characterized this aloofness as an indication of Stumpf's willingness to give his students considerable leeway in their own work. Lewin greatly admired Stumpf, but he was just the opposite in this regard, always taking a very active role in directing his students' research (Marrow, 1969).

Lewin finished his dissertation at a momentous time—the outbreak of World War I. As a loyal citizen, he enlisted in the Army in 1914, and spent the next several years trying to survive the brutal trench warfare that decimated a generation of young European men. He entered as a lowly private, left as an officer, was wounded once, and earned Germany's Iron Cross. While on furlough to recover from his wounds in 1917, he reflected on his experiences and wrote "The War Landscape," an article containing the seeds of many of his later concepts. In a distinction similar to the one made later by Koffka between geographical and behavioral environments, Lewin pointed out that the same objects in the environment can be phenomenologically different, as a function of whether they are part of the war landscape or the peace landscape. A narrow path in the woods, for example, which might produce enjoyment and relaxation under peaceful circumstances, becomes potentially deadly in the war landscape because it can provide cover for the enemy. That is, the same physical environment can be perceived in two completely different ways.

Lewin returned to Berlin's Psychological Institute at the end of the war (1918), became an instructor in 1921, and remained there until 1933. During these years, he developed his ideas and his research program, attracted many talented graduate students, and began establishing an international reputation. He also befriended his Berlin colleagues Wertheimer and Köhler during these years, and he got to know Koffka. As his biographer wrote, although "he was never a completely orthodox Gestaltist, he did become a vital force in the new movement and contributed to it his own special insights" (Marrow, 1969, p. 13).

Lewin remained in Berlin until 1933, when his status as war hero was not sufficient to overcome the liabilities of his Jewish heritage.[6] He was already well-known in the United States, after giving a stirring invited address at the 1929 International Congress at Yale and spending a six-month leave as visiting pro-

---

[6] While in America, and with the Nazi menace becoming more evident, Lewin tried desperately to arrange for his mother's emigration, first to the United States, then to Cuba, but was unsuccessful. Sometime in 1943 she perished in one of the Nazi death camps (Marrow, 1969).

fessor in Terman's department at Stanford. Cornell's Robert Ogden, an early convert to the gestalt vision and as responsible as anyone for bringing the gestaltists to America (Freeman, 1977), arranged for Lewin to spend two academic years in Ithaca. In 1935, he and his family moved from New York to Iowa, where Lewin joined the Child Welfare Research Station, a research institute connected to the University of Iowa, but separate from the psychology department. The institute was created in 1917 to study the development of normal children and train child development researchers (Ash, 1992). Lewin remained there for nine years, then moved back east to Boston in 1944 after successfully lobbying for funding to create a Research Center for Group Dynamics, to be housed at the Massachusetts Institute of Technology. His work there had just begun when he died suddenly of a heart attack in February of 1947.

Field Theory

Lewin contributed more empirical research than the three gestalt founders combined, but like them he was first and foremost a theory builder—in response to the criticism that theories are sometimes far removed from useful applications, he once said that "[t]here is nothing as practical as a good theory" (quoted in Marrow, 1969, p. 128). Lewin called his theory a **field theory** because he believed that understanding a person's behavior required knowing about all the forces acting on a person at a given moment. Lewin named the particular field within which the person operates the **life space**. It is the pivotal concept in his theory, and he defined it as a psychological field that includes the "totality of facts which determine the behavior (B) of an individual at a certain moment. ... [It] includes the person (P) and the environment (E)" (Lewin, 1936, p. 216). Person factors include such things as personality variables, needs, goals, and beliefs, while environmental factors include things external to the person that directly affect him or her. Furthermore, it is not simply the physical environment, but the environment as perceived by the individual that influences behavior. Thus, all behavior is a joint function of the characteristics of the person behaving and the features of the psychological envi-

ronment in which the person is behaving. Or as Lewin summarized it in a now-famous formula:

$$B = f(P, E)$$

Lewin symbolized the life space concept by borrowing from **topology**, a nonquantitative spatial geometry. He represented life space with various ovals, which contained symbols of features influencing the individual. Two examples of these, which his students came to call "Lewin's eggs," are drawn in Figure 9.11. Figure 9.11a is a simple representation of the basic formula. Life space includes everything within the oval (i.e., the person, P, and the environment, E). Outside the oval, which Lewin referred to as the **foreign hull**, could be found all the events, circumstances, and stimuli that were having no effect on a person at a particular moment.

A major difference between the original gestaltists and Lewin was the latter's emphasis on motivational constructs and goal-directed behavior. He believed that the person is a complex energy system, in which individual actions can be predicted with reference to the amount of tension in the system, which in

(a)

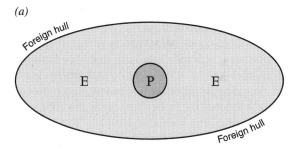

Life space = everything within oval

(b)

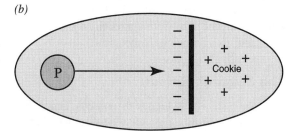

FIGURE 9.11 Two examples of Lewin's "eggs": (a) basic life space; (b) a child desiring an out-of-reach cookie.

turn is the consequence of the predominant needs being felt, the strengths of those needs, and the various obstacles in the life space. When all needs are satisfied, the individual is said to be in a state of **equilibrium**. The creation of a need produces disequilibrium, and a person is therefore motivated to satisfy the need in order to return to a steady state. Consider Figure 9.11b as an illustration. It represents a situation in which a hungry child desires a cookie, which resides in an out-of-reach jar. The desire has created a tension in the life space. The cookie is the desired object, or in Lewin's terms, it has a positive **valence** (symbolized by the plus signs). The arrow pointing from the child (P) is a **vector**—these arrows symbolize a push that is directed toward a specific desired goal, an approach tendency, or away from a goal to be avoided, an avoidance tendency. The arrow's length is proportional to the strength of the need. The vertical bar is a barrier (the cookie jar), which has a negative valence.

Lewin used his topological system to analyze conflicts, one of his best-known contributions. He described three common situations in which a conflict between needs occurs. In Lewin's scheme, a conflict exists whenever there are at least two vectors that are exerting pressure in different directions. In an **approach-approach** conflict, there are two desirable goals of equal strength from which to choose. For instance, a diner might have to decide between steak and lobster. Two equally undesirable goals characterize **avoidance-avoidance** conflicts, as when a student might be faced with the choice of studying one of two disliked topics. Third, in an **approach-avoidance** conflict, the person experiences simultaneous approach and avoidance tendencies with reference to a single goal. Thus, our decision about whether to order the hot fudge sundae will be influenced by both approach (it's good) and avoidance (it's fattening) tendencies.

The Zeigarnik Effect

Lewin's system was highly theoretical, and it has been criticized for being merely descriptive. That is, the diagrams might be able to describe virtually any event, but they are said to be of little use in predicting behavior (Frank, 1978). Lewin and his students

did conduct considerable research, however, and their studies produced results consistent with the theory (of course, many of the outcomes could have alternative, non-Lewinian explanations). One example is a series of studies completed by one of Lewin's first students, the Russian psychologist Bluma Zeigarnik (1927/1967).

Ideas for research often come from everyday observation, and that appears to have been the case for Zeigarnik's research. In Berlin, Lewin gathered a team of active graduate students around him. From about 1924 on, his group typically consisted of 12 to 15 doctoral candidates (Marrow, 1969). Because the German university system did not prescribe a rigid set of course requirements, a major element of doctoral education was a continuous small-group seminar, characterized by discussions of work in progress, what research to do next, and so on. Lewin's group often met informally for hours at a time at a café across the street from the Institute, keeping their table by occasionally ordering refills on coffee and pieces of cake. In that setting, Lewin was impressed by a waiter who seemed to be able to keep track of what each student had ordered, without writing it down. Soon after the bill was settled, however, the waiter had no memory of it. To Lewin the explanation was simple. As long as the bill was unpaid and the students remained at the café, the waiter's life space had a tension to it. Once the bill was paid, the tension resolved and closure had been achieved.

Zeigarnik's study tested Lewin's interpretation directly. In her main experiment, she individually tested 164 teachers, students, and children by giving them between 18 and 22 simple tasks, each requiring a few minutes to finish. They included such things as constructing a cardboard box, making a clay figure, completing puzzles, and performing arithmetic and other mental tasks. Each subject was allowed to complete half of the tasks, but was interrupted and not allowed to finish the other half. To ensure that the interruption was clearly felt to be a disruption, Zeigarnik "always chose a time when the subject was most engrossed in his work" (1927/1967, p. 303). What she found was that the interrupted tasks were 1.9 times as likely to be recalled as the uninterrupted ones. In Lewinian terms, the enhanced memory was the result of the unrelieved tension of the incomplete task. This phenomenon, that memory is better for incomplete rather than complete tasks, is today called the **Zeigarnik effect**.

Lewin as Developmental Psychologist

Lewin arrived in New York in the fall of 1933, at a time when the United States was in the depths of its worst economic crisis, the Great Depression. His

KEY DATE 1929

This year marked the convening of the Ninth International Congress of Psychology at Yale University, which included important talks by Köhler and Lewin that helped advance the gestalt cause.

These events also occurred:

- The term "apartheid" was used for the first time
- The German Graf Zeppelin airship circled the globe in 20 days
- The U.S. stock market crashed on October 28 ("Black Friday"), signaling the start of the Great Depression
- Kodak introduced 16mm color movie film
- Herbert Hoover was inaugurated as thirty-first U.S. president
- Six notorious Chicago gangsters were machine-gunned by a rival gang in the "St. Valentine's Day Massacre"
- These people were born:

  Martin Luther King, Jr., American civil rights leader

  Arnold Palmer, American golfer

  Jacqueline Bouvier Kennedy Onassis
- These people died:

  Thorstein Verblen, American social scientist

  Katherine Lee Bates, American author and composer (wrote "America the Beautiful")

  Wyatt Earp, legendary figure of the American West

position at Cornell, made possible through limited grant funds from a committee to help displaced European scholars, was not in the psychology department but in the School of Home Economics, and it was not a faculty appointment. This might not seem very impressive, in light of Lewin's growing international status, but it must be seen in light of the academic job market in the 1930s. One effect of the Depression was that few families could afford college and with low enrollments, few colleges could afford new faculty. As a result, finding an academic position was virtually impossible. The depth of the problem was revealed in an APA survey which found that in 1932, there were 32 positions available for 100 new psychology Ph.D.'s; the prospects looked even worse in 1933—46 jobs and 146 newly minted Ph.D.'s competing for them (Napoli, 1981). In this context, Lewin's appointment is perhaps an indication of his elevated stature rather than a puzzling loss of status.

When Lewin arrived in the United States, he was perceived by American psychologists as a developmental psychologist whose approach contrasted sharply with (a) the developing behaviorist movement and (b) an increasing tendency to study groups of children and take statistical averages of their behavior (Ash, 1992). In contrast, Lewin believed that the behaviorists overemphasized the environment at the expense of personality factors. That is, in contrast to his balanced $B = f$ (P,E), the behaviorists had too much E and not enough P. Methodologically, Lewin criticized the strategy of trying to identify some mythical average child; he preferred nonstatistical in-depth case studies of individual children.

The impression of Lewin as a developmentalist was based on his much-discussed presentation at the Yale International Congress in 1929 and a chapter on developmental psychology that he wrote for the first edition of the *Handbook of Child Psychology* (Lewin, 1931). In the latter, he introduced his $B = f$ (P,E) formulation to the American audience. His Yale talk was highlighted by a film that he showed of an 18-month-old girl trying to sit on a rock. She apparently thought that she would miss the target if she took her eyes off the stone, so she circled the rock several times trying to figure out how to sit on it accurately without removing her eyes from it. She finally devised the solution of putting her head between her knees and slowly backing up to the stone before sitting. In that way she could watch the stone while depositing herself on it. In his talk, Lewin described this simple event in terms of field forces, vectors, and valances, and tied it to other research on reaching goals by making detours. Older children solve detour problems, according to Lewin, because they perceive the problem as a whole and recognize that the first step, a movement away from a goal (to get around the detour), is part of the overall structure of the solution. Thus, a solution can be achieved even if the initial vector points away from a goal. An older child would solve the rock-sitting problem as a detour problem, by recognizing that taking one's eyes off the goal, while seeming to be a step away from the goal, could be organized as part of the solution. The 18-month-old could not make that detour step, however, and was forced to rely on maintaining a simple goal-directed vector by not letting the rock out of sight. The difference between the younger and older child, according to Lewin, was that the older child had a greater degree of **differentiation**. For this older child, this means that the life space has become more complex over time. Thus, development proceeds from less to greater differentiation.

Lewin's two years at Cornell were busy ones. In addition to acclimating himself to an environment vastly different from Berlin and polishing his weak skills in English, Lewin plunged into a research program on how social pressure affected the eating habits of children, and with the help of translators, published a collection of essays on personality theory (Lewin, 1935) and a book on his topological theory (Lewin, 1936). He also organized a loose confederation of former and current students and colleagues into the "Topology Group." It first met in 1933 as a reunion of sorts, hosted by Koffka at Smith College. Its success produced its replication, and except for a few years during the World War II era, it met annually until 1965. In a manner reminiscent of Titchener's meetings of experimental psychologists, the sessions were marked by informality, camaraderie, and discussions of work in progress. Unlike Titchener's group, though, women were welcome.

It was not until he moved to Iowa, however, and developed a research team at the Iowa Child Welfare

Station, that Lewin was able to recreate the environment that reminded him of Berlin. Just as in the old days, his research group combined seminars with informal sessions. Lewin even found a substitute for the Berlin café where his observation of a waiter's memory inspired Zeigarnik's research. In Iowa City, Lewin and his students congregated at the Round Window Restaurant, where they dubbed their group the "Hot-Air Club" (Marrow, 1969).

Lewin's research on children continued at Iowa and yielded one of his best-known studies—"Frustration and Regression: An Experiment with Young Children" (Barker, Dembo, & Lewin, 1941). Roger Barker came to Iowa from Stanford, where he had been a student during Lewin's brief time there as visiting professor. Tamara Dembo was one of Lewin's most loyal students, with him at Berlin, Cornell, and Iowa. The experiment evolved from some earlier research by Dembo in which children in detour problems sometimes became frustrated at not being able to reach the goal and gave up trying. Barker, Dembo, and Lewin decided to study the problem more systematically, the goal being to determine the effects of frustration on the quality of play for children just under four years of age.

Each of the 30 children in the study first encountered a "free play" period in a room where they could play with some simple play materials, while the experimenter took notes on their behavior. After a half-hour, a partition was raised revealing a much richer play environment which included a large doll house and "toy lake" complete with real water and boats. Each child spent up to 15 minutes in this enriched environment, then was led back to the front of the room and a wire mesh partition was lowered and secured with a padlock. The child then spent a second 30-minute session with the same toys found in the original free play session. Unlike the first session, however, they could now see what they were missing! In Lewinian terms, the toys on the other side of the room had a much higher valence than the ones now available to them; the barrier had a negative valence and was producing tension. And the behavior of the children reflected their frustration. They spent some of their time trying to get around the barrier or out of the room entirely. Failing that, their play deteriorated significantly from that of the original free play situation. They became more destructive in their play, easily distracted by what they could see across the room, and more emotionally upset. Under high frustration, then, their behavior regressed to less constructive patterns than shown just a few minutes earlier.[7] Although increased age produces differentiation, Lewin pointed out that under stress, a temporary shift in the opposite direction, what he called **dedifferentiation**, could occur. The Barker, Dembo, and Lewin study has become a classic in the developmental psychology literature, and it still shows up in most modern developmental psychology textbooks.

Lewin as Social Psychologist

Lewin's American colleagues might have identified him as a developmental psychologist, but his self-identity was much broader, as reflected in his general theory and research on such topics as prejudice, group influence, and leadership. These latter studies are the reason why he is considered one of the pioneers of modern social psychology. The leadership research, still frequently cited, grew out of his reflections on the state of the world in the mid-1930s. Mindful of the contrast between the democracy of his new home and the increasingly dictatorial environment of his old one, Lewin became interested in the consequences of different leadership styles. Along with Ronald Lippitt and Ralph White, he completed several experiments on the problem (Lewin, Lippitt, & White, 1939; Lippitt & White, 1943).

The basic procedure in the leadership research was to create different environments for five-person groups of 10-year-old boys who were given various craft-making projects (e.g., making masks) to complete. The main experiment contrasted three different leadership styles—authoritarian, democratic, and laissez-faire. Table 9.1, taken from Lippitt and White (1943), describes the three approaches. Each group of boys experienced all three styles, and their behavior was dramatically influenced by how they were guided. When led by an autocratic leader, the boys quickly became submissive, failed to take any initiative, did not produce high-quality products, and showed no real interest in the tasks. They also tended to be aggressive when the leader was out of the room, and they often made fun of disliked group members, a form of scapegoating. Those in the laissez-faire group did not fare much better. Because they were in an "unstructured field," they spent a great deal of time unsuccessfully trying to decide what to do. The lack of adult direction often led to confusion, frustration, and hostility. Under this form of leadership, nothing was accomplished. On the other hand, under a more democratic leader, the group became cohesive, task-oriented and motivated, and they produced more high-quality products. One disturbing finding was that when the boys switched from a democratic to an authoritarian environment, they quickly and with minimal protest succumbed to the tyranny. As Lewin later described it, "[t]here have been few experiences for me as impressive as seeing the expression on children's faces during the first day under an autocratic leader. The group that had formerly been friendly, open, cooperative, and full of life, became within a short half-hour a rather apathetic-looking gathering without initiative" (quoted in Marrow, 1969, p. 127). On the other hand, and equally troubling, those shifting from authoritarian to democratic settings had a difficult time overcoming the effects of being told what to do.

The broader implications of the leadership studies were obvious to Lewin. Although he recognized the problem of generalizing beyond the experimental setting, he saw the results as a strong endorsement of the democratic form of government and an indictment of anything short of it. They also reinforced his belief that scientists needed to be "in the arena" rather than confined to the rarified atmosphere of their laboratories. To that end, he became the prototype of the scientist-activist. He became a committed Zionist, vigorously advocating the creation of an independent Jewish state in Palestine, as

---

[7] Although the experiment occurred long before the APA adopted an ethics code, Lewin was sensitive to the emotional states of his young subjects. After they finished the final 30 minutes of observation, the barrier was again raised, and the children were allowed to play with the high-valence toys for as long as they wished.

Table 9.1 **Leadership Styles Compared by Lewin's Research Group**

Authoritarian	Democratic	Laissez-faire
1. All determination of policy by the leader.	1. All policies a matter of group discussion and decision, encouraged and assisted by the leader.	1. Complete freedom for group or individual decision, with a minimum of leader participation.
2. Techniques and activity steps dictated by the authority, one at a time, so that future steps were always uncertain to a large degree.	2. Activity perspective gained during discussion period. General steps to group goal sketched, and where...advice was needed, the leader suggested...alternative procedures from which choice could be made.	2. Various materials supplied by the leader, who made it clear that he would supply information when asked. He took no other part in work discussion.
3. The leader...dictated the particular work task and work companion of each member.	3. The members were free to work with whomever they chose, and the division of tasks was left up to the group.	3. Complete nonparticipation of the leader.
4. The dominator tended to be too "personal" in his praise and criticism of each member; remained aloof from active group participation except when demonstrating.	4. The leader was "objective" or "fact-minded" in his praise and criticism and tried to be a regular group member in spirit without doing too much of the work.	4. Infrequent spontaneous comments on member activities unless questioned and no attempt to appraise or regulate the course of events.

Source: Lippitt & White (1943, p. 487).

a place for Jews to establish their own democratic system.[8] He also lobbied (unsuccessfully) for the creation of a psychological research institute at Hebrew University in Jerusalem. Third, Lewin became an early leader in the APA-affiliated Society for the Psychological Study of Social Issues (SPSSI), founded in 1936 and concerned with applying psychological knowledge to the solution of social problems. Activism pervaded his work and much of his research was designed specifically to solve some real-world problems (Heims, 1978). He called this work "action research."

Action Research

The leadership research is just one example of a constant theme in Lewin's work—using science as a means of bringing about productive social change. Psychology must do more than simply explain behavior, Lewin argued; it must "be equally con-

cerned with discovering how people can change their ways so that they learn to behave better" (quoted in Marrow, 1969, p. 158). During his Iowa years, which extended into the World War II era, he was involved in several studies designed to solve immediate real-world problems, several of which involved group processes. During World War II, for instance, in a project with anthropologist Margaret Mead, Lewin looked at the effects of group processes on convincing people to include more visceral meats (e.g., liver, kidney) in their diets. Such a change would help the war effort; by expanding the range of foods eaten, shortages in more preferred foods could be avoided. Lewin and Mead found that people were more likely to change following group discussions than after hearing lectures on nutrition.

Much of Lewin's group research occurred in work settings, and for this reason he is an important historical figure for industrial psychologists. For example, in a series of studies designed to increase worker productivity in an industrial setting, Lewin showed that letting workers set production goals after

[8] The state of Israel was created in 1948, a year after Lewin's death.

meeting in groups had the twofold effect of improving morale and increasing worker output. Group processes could also be used effectively to train managers and to overcome male prejudice against women workers.

To further his mission of using science to promote social change, Lewin in the late 1930s began planning for the creation of a research institute devoted to action research that would be affiliated with a university, yet autonomous. He began the search for funds, recognizing the dangers involved— donors might expect tangible results sooner than science typically provided them. Nonetheless, Lewin was determined, writing that he was "ready to go to any lengths to find a productive solution. Social action is part of the changing social world. Security, I realize, will have to be established every day anew. But I am ready to take the risk" (quoted in Marrow, 1969, pp. 163–164).

Lewin's aggressive pursuit of private funding paid off, and in late 1944, he founded the Research Center for Group Dynamics, to be affiliated with the Massachusetts Institute of Technology (MIT) in Cambridge. There he quickly assembled an enthusiastic research team, most of them from the Iowa Hot-Air Club, and set out to study group processes and social action. At the same time, he accepted an invitation from the American Jewish Congress to organize a second action research initiative, the Commission on Community Interrelations (CCI), to be centered in New York City. Under Lewin's leadership, the CCI sponsored research on discrimination and prejudice, attempting to answer questions such as these (cited in Marrow, 1969, pp. 175–176):

> Which procedures in giving jobs to minority members serve to increase, and which to decrease, group tension?
>
> Under what circumstances and to what degree is the building of self-respect among minority members a prerequisite for improvement?
>
> What problems develop in a community with the arrival of minority group members?
>
> Which methods of dealing with these problems resolve them most readily?

For the remaining two years of his life, Lewin immersed himself in the work of his two parallel projects, the MIT center for group dynamics and the CCI. The resulting studies, investigating such topics as interracial housing and in-group loyalty, combined with his other work on leadership and group dynamics, provide the foundation for modern experimental social psychology. The graduate students and colleagues who conducted the studies, such as Leon Festinger, Harold Kelley, Morton Deutsch, and Fritz Heider, are among the recognized leaders of the field. Even today, their names figure prominently in the author indexes of social psychology textbooks.

Evaluating Lewin

When asked to describe Lewin's appeal for students, Jerome Frank, who studied with Lewin in Berlin, summed up his mentor's overall personality with a single word—"zest." He went on to describe Lewin as "a little man with an apparently inexhaustible supply of energy and a ruddy complexion that suggested vigorous health. Although he must often have been seated in my presence, in my memories he is almost always in motion" (Frank, 1978, p. 223). Other students had similar recollections of Lewin's passion for his work, their memories usually including images of Lewin filling the blackboard with his graphic representations of life space, "the air ... heavy with chalk dust" (Marrow, 1969, p. 137).

Lewin's topological theory, along with his egg-shaped illustrations of it, has disappeared from modern psychology, yet the research it generated makes him one of the leading psychologists of the twentieth century. During his years in the United States, Lewin never landed a full-time academic position in the psychology department of a major university, yet he was able to surround himself with enthusiastic students who turned his ideas into experimental reality and perpetuated his unique blend of basic and applied research long after his premature death in 1947. Ralph White, a Lewin student and one of the authors of the famous study of leadership styles, acknowledged in a symposium in 1976 that field theory in its strictest sense was a thing of the past—few psychologists refer to "valences" or "vectors" anymore, and "one doesn't often see diagrams consisting of goals, paths, barriers, and little arrows, all within an elliptically-shaped outline" (White, 1978,

p. 245). On the other hand, White argued that Lewin's influence could still be clearly felt:

> ... It is alive in the form of paying continual attention to the patterns of motivation and cognition that directly determine behavior. ... It is alive in the form of a selective but fairly widespread use of Lewin's more specific theories and concepts, such as the approach-avoidance conflict and the differentiation of the cognitive field. It is alive in the very frequent quoting of Lewin's famous formula: B = f (P,E). In other words, much of the substance of his field theory, though not usually in his words, is still very much alive. (pp. 245–246)

IN PERSPECTIVE: GESTALT PSYCHOLOGY IN AMERICA

During the 1920s, gestalt psychology flourished in Germany, especially at Berlin, but as seen in the biographical sketches of its leaders, it also made its first inroads into American psychology in that same decade. In Germany, the gestaltists established themselves by opposing what they believed to be the wrong way to study human experience. It was fruitless to attempt an analysis of experience into elementary units, they argued, because the whole of an experience had properties not evident in a description of component parts. When they came to America, the gestaltists perceived in behaviorism another form of the same elementist foe, and much of their writing was directed at the perceived shortcomings of this American psychology that seemed interested in analyzing behavior into S-R units. Gestalt psychology failed to become a major force in American psychology, but its influence was felt and is still being felt in many ways. Modern cognitive psychology, for example, which investigates such topics as the "organization" of information in memory, owes much to gestalt thinking.

Gestalt psychology's failure to become America's mainstream psychology stems in part from the historical circumstances of its early leaders. Its three originators found themselves in small schools without graduate programs to give birth to gestalt heirs, and of the four men highlighted in the chapter, three died in their early or mid-50s. More fundamentally, however, the gestaltists were simply unable to convert most American psychologists to their message. While a number of psychologists found the gestalt approach an appealing *addition* to the mix of competing viewpoints in psychology, few were convinced that *all* of psychology could be organized under the gestalt banner, and many were caught up in the new wave of behaviorism, the topic of the next two chapters. And pragmatic American psychologists, more comfortable with the concrete than the abstract, also viewed the gestalt movement as being long on theory and philosophy and short on data and science. Furthermore, American psychologists were put off by the gestaltists' missionary zeal. Köhler, for example, recalled this about a conversation he once had with Karl Lashley (Chapter 3), who was generally supportive of the gestalt position: "Once when we discussed the main tenets of gestalt psychology, he suddenly smiled and said, 'Excellent work—but don't you have religion up your sleeve?'" (Köhler, 1967/1969, p. 79).

Most American psychologists, reflecting a functional attitude receptive to any approach that helped explain human actions, tended to be more eclectic than would be acceptable to the gestaltists (Ash, 1985). Thus, when describing the new German movement in his *Schools of Contemporary Psychology*, first published in 1931, Robert Woodworth (Chapter 7) applauded their "great vitality" while at the same time gently chastising them for oversimplifying the ideas of their opponents. Specifically referring to Thorndike's trial-and-error learning and its law of effect, Pavlov's conditioned reflex research, and Köhler's insight studies, Woodworth argued that some truth could be found in all three and that "supporters of each interpretation could make out a plausible case for explaining all the facts in their own way" (Woodworth, 1931, p. 124). He closed the chapter by referring to gestalt psychology as "a strong and valuable addition to the varieties of psychology" (p. 125), and helped to perpetuate the idea that the movement was concerned mostly with perceptual phenomena by applauding them for emphasizing "the importance of the topic that has usually been called perception, neglected by the behaviorists and handled very meagerly by the [structuralists]" (p. 125).

In the final analysis, Wertheimer, Koffka, Köhler, and Lewin added considerable "insight" into our knowledge of the human experience and provid-

ed an important caution to those building psychological theories on the foundation of associationist principles. The tradition of understanding complexity through analysis was a strong one, however, as will be seen in the next two chapters.

SUMMARY

THE ORIGINS AND DEVELOPMENT OF GESTALT PSYCHOLOGY

- The gestalt movement had it roots in the philosophical traditions of Kant and Husserl and in nineteenth-century developments in physics, in particular the work of Max Planck, a pioneer of field physics. Force fields can only be understood in terms of the overall patterns of relationships among objects in the field.

- The physicist Ernst Mach argued that some of our sensory experiences are of forms (e.g., squareness) that cannot be further reduced. Similarly, Christian von Ehrenfels used the example of a melody that changes key to illustrate the concept of form-qualities. A melody played in a new key retains its form-quality even though all the individual elements are different. The prominent philosopher/psychologist Carl Stumpf directed the dissertations of three of the four men featured in the chapter, and briefly taught the fourth.

- Gestalt psychology was founded in the period from 1910 to 1912 when Max Wertheimer, with the help of Kurt Koffka and Wolfgang Köhler, completed research on apparent motion, which Wertheimer called the phi phenomenon. By flashing separated lights at certain intervals, the observer perceives one light in motion, and the whole experience cannot be analyzed into its component parts. Wertheimer concluded that the whole is different from and determines the nature of its parts.

- When the Nazi party came to power in the early 1930s, posing a direct threat to Jewish scientists, Wertheimer emigrated from Germany to America and spent his remaining years at the New School for Social Research in New York.

- Kurt Koffka, one of Wertheimer's observers in the apparent motion study, earned his doctorate under Stumpf. He is known for introducing the gestalt movement to America, both through his publications and visits. He was the first gestaltist to move to the United States permanently, accepting a position at Smith College in 1927.

He was gestalt's major theorist, and he extended gestalt ideas into the area of developmental psychology.

- Wolfgang Köhler also earned a doctorate with Stumpf, and he also aided Wertheimer in the apparent motion study. From 1913 to 1920 he studied primate behavior at a German research station in the Canary Islands, where he completed research on insightful problem solving. He moved to the United States permanently in 1935, where he became gestalt's most influential spokesperson.

GESTALT PSYCHOLOGY AND PERCEPTION

- Wertheimer described a number of basic principles that determine how our perceptions are organized. These gestalt organizing principles included figure-ground, grouping by proximity and similarity, and good continuation. Our perceptions are governed by Pragnänz, a tendency to organize perceptions into the simplest meaningful whole. We often construct such good figures by filling in gaps, a phenomenon called closure.

- Koffka made an important distinction between the world as it exists in reality, the geographical environment, and the world as perceived by the individual, the behavioral environment. Our behavior is most clearly influenced by the latter.

- Köhler's principle of isomorphism stated that phenomenal reality and the underlying physical reality of the nervous system were functionally equivalent to each other.

THE GESTALT APPROACH TO COGNITION AND LEARNING

- Köhler's *Mentality of Apes* summarized his research on problem solving in animals. He criticized Thorndike's mechanical trial-and-error explanation of animal learning and argued instead that animals could show insight and solve problems quickly if they were able to perceive all elements of the problem situation. Köhler's apes were able to solve problems by stacking boxes to retrieve fruit suspended from a ceiling and by building crude instruments to retrieve other fruit. Sultan, for example, joined two sticks to reach beyond his cage for fruit.

- Wertheimer's *Productive Thinking* described how thinking could be inhibited by an educational system that relied on rote learning and rule memorization. Alternatively, the productive thinker had a true understanding of relationships and could solve novel problems. He used the example of figuring the area of a parallelogram as one illustration of the weakness of rule memorization and the advantage of his more insightful productive thinking approach.

- Other gestaltists who worked on cognition included Hedwig Von Restorff, who showed that memory would be improved for information that stood out from the background (Von Restorff effect), George Katona, who studied the effects of organization on memory, and Karl Duncker, who investigated factors that inhibit insightful problem solving, such as functional fixedness, a tendency to think only of the normal uses for objects.

KURT LEWIN (1890–1947): EXPANDING THE GESTALT VISION

- Like Koffka and Köhler, Lewin earned a doctorate in Stumpf's laboratory, then joined Köhler and Wertheimer at Berlin during the 1920s. He emigrated from Nazi Germany in 1933, and spent his remaining years at Cornell, the Child Welfare Research Station at Iowa, and the Research Center for Group Dynamics at MIT, which he founded shortly before his death.

- Lewin's field theory is centered on the concept of the life space, which includes all of the factors influencing a person's actions in a given moment. These factors include those within the person (P) and those in the environment (E). Thus, $B = f(P,E)$. Lewin borrowed from topology to represent various life spaces symbolically. He emphasized the importance of motivation and the goal-directedness of behavior.

- Lewin used his system to describe various conflict systems (e.g., approach-avoidance). One of his students,

Bluma Zeigarnik, showed that unresolved tension in the system could have behavioral consequences. The Zeigarnik effect states that memory will be greater for uncompleted than completed tasks.

- As a developmental psychologist, Lewin argued for the study of individual cases over the "average child," and he considered development to be a process of increased differentiation. He studied the effects of frustration by giving children the opportunity to play with attractive toys, then removing the toys. The frustration resulted in the deterioration (regression) of their behavior.

- Lewin is often considered a founder of modern social psychology. His most famous work in this area involved studying the consequences of different types of leadership styles. Adolescent boys were more effective when led by a democratic leader, than by either an autocratic or a laissez-faire leader.

- Much of Lewin's research has been called "action research" because of its social relevance. A committed activist, Lewin always believed that his research should contribute to the improvement of society. Examples of his action research include studies of prejudice and its reduction, in-group loyalty, and the effectiveness of group processes. Interest in the dynamics of group action led to the development of Training-groups (T-Groups), designed to improve in-group communication and leadership skills.

IN PERSPECTIVE: GESTALT PSYCHOLOGY IN AMERICA

- Gestalt psychology was a vigorous movement that continually criticized psychologies that were based on the idea of understanding behavior and mental processes through analysis into constituent parts. In America, they were regular critics of behaviorism.

- American psychologists tended to be more eclectic than the gestaltists liked, willing to learn from gestalt principles but not willing to commit themselves entirely to gestalt psychology. Americans were also critical of the gestaltists' tendency to rely more on theory than research and application.

STUDY QUESTIONS

1. What did von Ehrenfels mean by a form-quality? Give an example.

2. Describe Wertheimer's apparent motion study and show how the phenomenon illustrates the essence of gestalt psy-

chology. Explain Wertheimer's arguments against (a) an eye movement explanation and (b) the Helmholtz unconscious inference explanation.

3. For psychologists in America, gestalt psychology is

sometimes assumed to involve only perception. What is the origin of this misperception and to what other areas did the gestaltists contribute?

4. What are the arguments for and against the idea that Köhler was a German spy in World War I?

5. What is figure-ground perception and what are some of the characteristics of figures and grounds?

6. Describe any three gestalt organizing principles and show how they can all be seen as variants of Prägnanz.

7. Use the Lake of Constance story, or Lewin's "war landscape" story, to illustrate the distinction between geographical and behavioral environments.

8. Use the concept of a map to illustrate how the gestaltists used the principle of isomorphism.

9. Use the area of a parallelogram example to illustrate Wertheimer's ideas about thinking and problem solving.

10. What is the von Restorff effect and how does it relate to figure-ground?

11. What is functional fixedness and how does it relate to insight?

12. In Lewin's field theory, use the example of a child desiring an out-of-reach cookie to illustrate his concepts of life space, foreign hull, valence, vector, and equilibrium.

13. Describe the three varieties of conflict examined by Lewin.

14. How did Zeigarnik investigate the effect named for her? How does the phenomenon relate to the Lewinian concept of equilibrium?

15. Describe Lewin's famous frustration and regression study and what he concluded from it.

16. Describe Lewin's famous leadership study and what he concluded from it.

17. Describe any three examples of Lewin's action research.

18. Consider the impact of gestalt psychology on American psychology. Why was it not greater than the gestaltists hoped?

QUESTIONS FROM THE ORIGINAL SOURCE EXCERPT

1. Explain Köhler's criticism of Thorndike's puzzle box research.

2. Describe the problem solving attempts of Sultan prior to his successful solution.

3. In gestalt terms, what was Köhler's explanation for Sultan's success in the two stick problem?

FOR FURTHER READING

Henle, M. (1986). One man against the Nazis—Wolfgang Köhler. In M. Henle (Ed.), *1879 and all that: Essays in the theory and history of psychology* (pp. 225–237). New York: Columbia University Press.

A sobering portrayal of the effect of Nazi policies on German science, as seen through the particular experiences of a courageous Wolfgang Köhler; includes an excerpt from the protest letter sent by Köhler, as well as other correspondence concerning the matter.

Ley, R. (1990). *A whisper of espionage.* Garden Park, NY: Avery Publishing Group.

An intriguing and readable account of Ley's search for information about Köhler's alleged espionage activities while on the island of Tenerife; a circumstantial case is built, but Ley found no smoking gun; includes an interesting account of Köhler's life on Tenerife.

Marrow, A. J. (1969). *The practical theorist: The life and work of Kurt Lewin.* New York: Basic Books.

A flattering and uncritical biography of Lewin; provides solid information on the events in Lewin's life and provides good descriptions of his research and theories; weak as a historical account, however (overly internal and personalistic).

Sokal, M. M. (1984). The Gestalt psychologists in behaviorist America. *American Historical Review, 89,* 1240–1263.

A detailed account of the arrival of gestalt thinking and the gestalt psychologists in America during the 1920s and 1930s; excellent treatment of the contemporary historical context and the shifting opinions of American psychologists about the quality of the gestalt movement.

CHAPTER 10

THE ORIGINS OF BEHAVIORISM

In a system of psychology completely worked out, given the response the stimuli can be predicted; given the stimuli the response can be predicted.

—John B. Watson, 1913

PREVIEW AND CHAPTER OBJECTIVES

In the first two decades of the new century, psychologists in America became increasingly immersed in the kinds of applications described in Chapter 8. In addition, a new force arrived on the scene—behaviorism. The behaviorists set out to alter the direction of psychology in America and, to a large extent, they succeeded. The founder of behaviorism as a school of thought in American psychology was John Broadus Watson (1878–1958). Like Wundt, Watson has been awarded the title of "founder" by historians, not because he was an originator, but because he was a self-conscious promoter. For Watson, the thing to promote was a program with the seemingly impossible goal outlined in the quote that opens this chapter, taken from his 1913 "Behaviorist Manifesto." You will read more of this remarkable paper in this Chapter's Original Source Excerpt.

This chapter will document the trends toward increased objectivity that led to the eventual acceptance of behaviorism by most American psychologists. Then it will chronicle the life and work of the renowned Russian physiologist Ivan Pavlov, whose conditioning research provided an approach to learning that some American behaviorists adopted. Third, the chapter will look at Watson's life and work in some detail. Trained by the Chicago functionalists, he quickly rose to the top of his profession as head of the psychology department at Johns Hopkins University, only to be forced out of academia at the height of his career. The chapter will examine his Behaviorist Manifesto and the reaction to it, his ideas about learning, and his research, including the (in)famous Little Albert experiment. Most of Watson's middle adult years were spent in the world of advertising, where he became a living example of applied psychology. After you finish this chapter, you should be able to:

▨ Describe the similarities between British empiricism and twentieth century behaviorism

▨ Describe the trends toward increased objectivity that preceded the behaviorist movement

▨ Describe the work that earned Pavlov the Nobel Prize in physiology in 1904

▨ Describe the organization and operation of research in Pavlov's laboratory

▨ Describe the basic conditioning phenomena studied by Pavlov

▨ Explain how Pavlov produced what he called experimental neurosis

- Describe Pavlov's relationship with the Soviets and why the Soviets valued his work
- Describe Pavlov's influence on American psychologists
- Describe Watson's research on animal behavior, from mazes to natural environments, and explain the significance of the work
- Explain Watson's analysis of contemporary structural and functional psychology, and what he proposed instead, in his "behaviorist manifesto"
- Describe Watson's research on basic emotions
- Describe and critically analyze Watson and Rayner's demonstration of conditioned fear
- Show how Watson brought his behaviorist ideas and scientific training to the world of advertising
- Describe Watson's attempt to popularize the science of behavior

BEHAVIORISM'S ANTECEDENTS

American behaviorists often trace their roots to John B. Watson and in particular to his so-called **Behaviorist Manifesto**, a paper he tried out in a talk at Columbia University in February 1913, and soon published (Watson, 1913). Yet history seldom turns dramatically on such events—they are usually individual chapters of a more complex narrative. Long before Watson saw the inside of the psychology laboratory at the University of Chicago, forces were at work paving the way for behaviorist thinking to become accepted as the norm by American psychologists. Furthermore, the psychological world did not convert to behaviorism just because of Watson's "revolutionary" pronouncements. Rather, Watson contributed a strong voice to the growing dissatisfaction with introspective psychology. Few psychologists, however, were immediately converted to Watsonian behaviorism (Samelson, 1981). Indeed, it was not until Watson was far removed from the scene that behaviorism became the central force in American experimental psychology.

Behaviorism has a clear affinity with several of the philosophical movements described in Chapters 2 and 3. For example, the behaviorist's belief in the importance of the environment in shaping behavior resonates with the British empiricist/associationist dictum that experience is the all-important determiner of one's mind and character. There are also parallels between the behaviorist's stimulus-response connections and the concept of association. In Chapter 3, you learned about the influence of nineteenth-century mechanistic and materialist thinking on physiologists; these philosophies are also congenial to behaviorist thinking. During the nineteenth century **positivism** also emerged, normally associated with the French philosopher Auguste Comte (1798–1857), and eventually taken as an article of faith by behaviorists. Comte argued that we could only be certain of knowledge that results from publicly observable events. *Positive* knowledge was said to be the result of *objective* observations using the systematic methods of science, to be made by unbiased (i.e., machinelike) observers. Truth, then, amounted to agreement among observers. Metaphysical speculation about the fundamental nature of events (including behavioral ones) in the universe was considered to be a worthless exercise, according to the positivists, because such speculations could never be verified objectively. Positivists also valued "practical" knowledge, believing that an intimate connection existed between understanding nature and controlling it. Indeed, Comte argued that the ability to control nature was evidence that it was understood—creating an effective steam engine, for instance, demonstrated an understanding of a number of principles of physics. Comte's faith in science even led him to recommend the deliberate redesign of society. This theme of controlling nature, virtually identical to arguments made 200 years earlier by Sir Francis Bacon (Chapter 2), later became a centerpiece of behaviorist thinking, evident in such works as Skinner's *Walden Two* (1948), a description of an ideal community based on principles of behavioral control (see Chapter 11). John Watson's prescriptions about child rearing, which you will encounter near the end of this chapter, also fall under the heading of using science to exert control over nature.

At the start of the twentieth century, psychologists were beginning to turn toward increased objectivity in their measures of psychological phenomena. One important influence was the rapid acceptance of evolutionary thinking among scientists and the resulting growth of animal psychology, as documented in Chapter 5. Animals cannot introspect, of course, so studying the relationship between human and animal consciousness required the creation of objective, behavioral measures. Most nineteenth-century descriptions of animal behavior were unduly anthropomorphic, but as we have seen, Morgan established the principle that parsimonious explanations for animal behaviors were to be favored over unnecessarily complex ones. Explaining a dog's ability to open a gate in terms of trial and error learning, rather than by means of intelligence and planning, moved comparative psychology from anecdotes to objective descriptions of stimuli and responses. Thorndike's puzzle box research in the late 1890s (Chapter 7) is perhaps the clearest manifestation in America of this movement toward increased objectivity in animal psychology. In Czarist Russia at the same time, however, an even greater level of precision could be found in the laboratory of Nobel Laureate Ivan Pavlov. American psychologists did not immediately realize the value of Pavlov's research for their own growing desire for objectivity, but his approach to research eventually became a model for many American behaviorists to emulate.

As the new century unfolded, the trend toward greater objectivity led a number of American psychologists to become disillusioned with the state of experimental psychology, especially its reliance on introspective procedures. The imageless thought controversy, described in Chapters 4 and 7, is a good illustration of this developing uneasiness. It came as no surprise to some American psychologists that an observer at Würzburg would experience imageless thoughts, while another at Cornell would fail to find them. Because introspective data were ultimately subjective, no independent way of evaluating each claim existed. In an address delivered at the 1904 World's Fair in St. Louis and later published in *Popular Science Monthly*, James McKeen Cattell declared that psychology should not be limited to the study of conscious experience and that introspection need not be the dominant method used by psychologists. In fact, "the rather widespread notion that there is no psychology apart from introspection is refuted by the brute argument of accomplished fact" (Cattell, 1904, cited in Woodworth, 1931, p. 48). In his own research, according to Cattell, introspection played a minimal role. And reflecting the positivist thinking just described, he said that he saw "no reason why the application of systematized knowledge to the *control of human nature* may not in the course of the present century accomplish results commensurate with the nineteenth century applications of physical science to the material world" (Cattell, 1904, cited in Woodworth, 1931, p. 49, italics added).

In the same year that Cattell addressed the St. Louis World's Fair, another event marked a milestone in a career that was shifting from a fascination with the digestive system to a passion for discovering how the brain works. The event was the awarding of a Nobel Prize for physiology to the Russian scientist Ivan Petrovich Pavlov.

PAVLOV'S LIFE AND WORK

Pavlov earned the Nobel Prize for his long years of painstaking and ingenious investigations of the physiology of digestion. In particular, he was known for inventing or perfecting a number of surgical techniques that facilitated this research. Yet when the 54-year-old scientist delivered his acceptance address in

December of 1904 at the Nobel awards ceremony in Stockholm, Sweden, he did not have much to say about the work that won him the prize. Rather, in an address entitled "The First Sure Steps Along the Path of a New Investigation" (Babkin, 1949), Pavlov described the research that had interested him for the past several years and would occupy the rest of his life. This research is familiar to you, of course, and probably brings to mind images of dogs salivating. Pavlov's conditioning research eventually provided an important model for American behavioral scientists, despite the fact that Pavlov himself always insisted that he was a physiologist, not a psychologist, and he had little regard for those who called themselves psychologists. He once pointed out that while the study of reflexes had been dominated historically by those taking a psychological (by which he meant introspective) approach, his more objective strategy offered the hope of these investigations of the reflex "being liberated from such evil influences" (Pavlov, 1906, p. 618).

The Development of a Physiologist

Ivan Petrovich Pavlov (1849–1936) was born into relative poverty in the small farming village of Ryazan in west central Russia in 1849. His father was a priest and his mother was the daughter of a priest, but despite their resulting social status, both parents had to work as peasant farmers to feed their large family. Ivan was the firstborn of 11 children, six of whom died in childhood. His early schooling was geared toward following in his father's clerical footsteps, but while studying at the Ryazan Ecclesiastical Seminary, an interest in science blossomed from his discovery of (a) Darwin's *Origin of Species* and (b) *Reflexes of the Brain*, published in 1863 by Russia's leading nineteenth-century physiologist, Ivan Sechenov (1829–1905). Sechenov argued that all cortical processes involved complex relationships between excitatory and inhibitory processes in the nervous system and that "psychical" (psychological) events could be reduced to and explained by reflex action in the cortex. It was a model very much in tune with the mechanistic and materialistic climate of nineteenth-century science, and it was influenced by Sechenov's direct contact with some of Europe's leading physiologists. In turn, these ideas eventually became the cornerstone of Pavlov's model of nervous system functioning.

Pavlov left the seminary and enrolled as a student of physiology at the University of St. Petersburg in 1870, thereby trading a simple rural life for the glamour of Russia's most important city.[1] St. Petersburg, located in northwest Russia near the Gulf of Finland, was the cultural, political, and intellectual center of Russia in the late nineteenth century. It was also Russia's capital city until it was replaced by Moscow in 1918, following the Soviet Revolution. In this high-powered setting, Pavlov completed a degree in medicine in 1883 and became a research physiologist. After additional years of study, several low-level research positions, and financial hardship, he was named the first director of the physiology division of St. Petersburg's Institute of Experimental Medicine in 1891. It was during the 1890s that he systematically investigated the physiology of the digestive system; this was the research that led to the Nobel Prize in 1904.

Pavlov studied digestion by isolating various parts of the digestive system and extracting digestive fluids. The quantities of the various fluids secreted were measured as a function of the type of substance fed to the animal. The research was noted for its precision and for the development of several surgical techniques to isolate and collect digestive secretions in dogs that were otherwise functioning normally. The best known was the so-called Pavlov pouch. It was created by segregating a small section of stomach (about one-tenth of it) and redesigning it as a miniature stomach. It was situated so that food could not enter when it reached the stomach from the esophagus. A small tube or fistula led from the pouch to the exterior, thereby providing a means to collect the fluids secreted by the mini-stomach. Uncontaminated by food, these fluids could be measured with precision (Gray, 1979).

---

[1] After Lenin's death in 1924, the Soviets renamed the city Leningrad; in 1991, following the collapse of the Soviet Union, it was rechristened St. Petersburg.

In addition to investigating gastric secretions, Pavlov also studied salivary responses, relating them to the type of substance placed in the dog's mouth. He measured salivation with another fistula, this time a small tube directly connected to a salivary duct. Inevitably, as all dog owners know, the dogs would begin to salivate before food would reach their mouths. One of Pavlov's students, S. G. Vul'fson, studied the phenomenon systematically, in a study comparing salivation to moist vs. dry foods. The main finding was that dogs salivated more to dry foods (less saliva needed for moist foods), but a secondary finding was that after a number of trials, the dogs salivated before the food arrived (Windholz, 1997). The outcome presented Pavlov with a dilemma. On the one hand, these "psychic" secretions were a nuisance, reducing the accuracy of Pavlov's attempts to measure an exact amount of saliva in response to a specific amount of a certain type of food. On the other hand, the animal's behavior was predictable, and these and other "psychic" secretions (e.g., the flow of gastric juices before food reached the stomach) intrigued Pavlov, suggesting an objective way to study those "reflexes of the brain" that Pavlov had read about in Sechenov's book. Whereas a less creative scientist might have tried to control the secretions to focus on the problem at hand, the basic physiology of digestion, Pavlov chose to examine this new phenomenon directly. After the turn of the century it became his life's work.

Working in Pavlov's Laboratory

In a biography of Pavlov, Babkin (1949) sketched a fascinating account of life within Pavlov's laboratory. As a student of Pavlov at the turn of the century, Babkin was present during the early years of the research on conditioning. The Institute of Experimental Medicine was about a dozen years old and although it was prestigious within Russia, it was not very impressive to the international visitor in those early years: Babkin described Pavlov's original laboratory as "small and dirty" and as a "mere hovel" (p. 68). Although its budget was fairly large by Russian standards, Pavlov found it necessary to raise additional money through the sale of gastric juices

taken from the dogs during "sham feeding" experiments. Dogs would eat normally, but a fistula connected to the esophagus redirected the food to a collection tube. The dog would eat and swallow, but the food never made it to the stomach, which nonetheless secreted gastric fluids in anticipation of the food's arrival. Another tube in the stomach collected the juices. Pavlov marketed the vile-tasting fluid as an elixir for those suffering from various digestive ailments, especially those resulting from "an insufficient flow of [their] own gastric juice" (p. 69).

Despite the difficult conditions, Pavlov managed to institutionalize demanding controls in the laboratory and gradually created a world-class research environment. He was especially rigorous in creating an antiseptic environment for his surgical procedures. That, combined with Pavlov's skill as a surgeon, produced an environment that dramatically reduced infection and ensured the survival of virtually all of the animals in Pavlov's care. He also developed a systematic method to train the dozens of research assistants who passed through his laboratory. Most of the assistants, who were already qualified as physicians, were looking to add a doctorate in physiology to their medical degree (Todes, 1997). Whenever a new worker would enter the lab, Pavlov would assign this person a problem that had already been investigated. Thus, the student would learn experimental procedures without being under pressure to produce new findings, while also providing an ongoing program of **replication**. Once the earlier research had been replicated successfully, the worker would be given a new problem to investigate. A failure to replicate would trigger additional research (by yet a third worker) to clear up the contradiction. Replication, of course, is a cornerstone of sound scientific research; results that cannot be repeated are of no value.

Beginning in 1910 (but not fully equipped until 1925), the Institute built a special laboratory for Pavlov's conditioning research. Later known as the Tower of Silence, it featured extensive soundproofing techniques to ensure that the dogs would respond only to the stimulus being studied at the time and not to any extraneous stimuli. As Figure 10.1 shows, there were eight experimental chambers, four on

Sand

Straw

Box for
animals

Straw

FIGURE 10.1 Cross-section and floor plan of Pavlov's laboratory at St. Petersburg, from
Pavlov (1928).

each of two floors that were separated by an inter-
mediate floor. Each research chamber was fully insulated and separated from other chambers by a corri-
dor. To further reduce noise and vibration, the building itself was supported by beams immersed in sand
and surrounded by a sand- and straw-filled moat!
Experimenters were separated from the dogs by the
double wall that is evident in Figure 10.2.

FIGURE 10.2 Apparatus
arrangement in Pavlov's
laboratory, around 1915, from
Pavlov (1928).

Pavlov's Classical Conditioning Research

In the spring of 1924, Pavlov organized a series of lectures that summarized about 25 years of his work on conditioning. He gave the lectures at the Military Medical Academy in St. Petersburg and then rewrote them for publication. They were translated into English by G. V. Anrep, a British researcher and another former student of Pavlov's, and published as *Conditioned Reflexes: An Investigation of the Physiological Activity of the Cerebral Cortex* by the British Royal Society in 1927 (Pavlov, 1927/1960).

In his opening lecture, Pavlov acknowledged his debt to Sechenov and Darwin, credited the American psychologist Thorndike with doing the first systematic work on the relationship between "visual and tactile stimuli on the one hand and the locomotor apparatus on the other" (p. 6), then described the start of his own inquiries and his recognition that the problem had to be attacked from a purely physiological rather than a psychological standpoint. Pavlov believed that restricting the investigation to specific external stimuli and measurable physiological responses was the only scientifically defensible strategy to use. The "psychological approach," on the other hand, implied a dualism of mental and physical processes that Pavlov was not willing to accept. He often referred to an episode from the early years of his laboratory when one of his students, Anton Snarskii, investigated the effects of severing the facial nerves on the development of a conditioned response. Despite opposition from Pavlov (or so Pavlov later claimed), Snarskii interpreted his results in mentalistic terms and referred to such processes as "visual association" and "recognition" (Windholz, 1986). Pavlov believed such an approach to be unnecessarily speculative.[2]

After a detailed description of basic reflex action, Pavlov concluded his opening lecture by referring to the accidental demonstrations of salivary conditioning that launched him into his 25 years of research. First describing how salivation occurs automatically if either food or some objectionable substance is placed into the dog's mouth, to begin the process of digesting the food or to wash out the offending stimulus, Pavlov then pointed out that a similar reflex can occur "when these substances are placed at a distance from the dog and the receptor organs affected are only those of smell and sight; ... further, the secretion may be provoked even by the sight of the person who brought the vessel, or by the sound of his footsteps" (Pavlov, 1927/1960, p. 13).

In his second lecture, Pavlov began by describing some of the technical details of his procedures and the measures taken to control experimental conditions. He explained that the dog presented with food shows both secretory (i.e., salivary) reflexes and motor reflexes. It drools, but it also turns its head, moves its mouth, and so on. That Pavlov decided to study the secretory reflex and ignore the motor reflexes is another indication of his concern over precise measurement and a desire to avoid anthropomorphic speculation about what the animal might be "trying" to do.

Conditioning and Extinction

Having set the stage, Pavlov described the basic procedure for the acquisition of a conditioned response. The essence of the technique is to pair a stimulus known to produce a particular response (i.e., salivation) with a neutral stimulus, such as a tone or a metronome. During acquisition, then, the starting point is an already existing reflex. For Pavlov, this

---

[2] Pavlov often told the Snarskii story, using it as an illustration of the failure of a purely "psychological approach." Todes (1997) examined the original episode carefully, however, and discovered that Pavlov's memory became altered over the years. At the time of the Snarskii research (1901), Pavlov was actually the one thinking in more subjective terms, whereas Snarskii was proposing a more mechanistic and associationistic model. As the

years went by, Pavlov apparently felt the need to distance himself from his earlier psychological theorizing. Reorganizing memory to make it consistent with his later beliefs, Pavlov convinced himself that he had been the objective one and Snarskii had been subjective, when the reverse was closer to the truth. The interesting historiographic point here is that you cannot always rely on the accuracy of autobiographical accounts.

reflex was the **unconditioned reflex** (UCR) of salivating when food (the **unconditioned stimulus**, or UCS) was presented to the animal. Conditioning involved presenting a neutral stimulus, then the UCS. This neutral stimulus Pavlov called a **conditional stimulus** (later translated as conditioned stimulus), or CS, because the resulting reflex depended on (was "conditional" on) the CS-UCS pairing. This resulting reflex was called a **conditioned reflex**, or CR.

After describing acquisition, Pavlov showed how a CR could undergo **extinction** if the metronome (the CS) was sounded without being accompanied by food (the UCS). Pavlov let the metronome run for 30-second intervals every two minutes, recording the amount of saliva secreted and what he called the "latent period"—the amount of time between the starting of the metronome and the beginning of salivation. As Pavlov described it, the "weakening of the reflex to a conditional stimulus which is repeated a certain number of times without reinforcement may appropriately be termed experimental extinction of conditioned reflexes" (Pavlov, 1927/1960, pp. 48–49). An indication of Pavlov's concern for precision can be seen from his results, which he presented as follows (p. 49):

Latent period in seconds	Secretion of saliva in drops during 30 seconds
3	10
7	7
5	8
4	5
5	7
9	4
13	3

With successive extinction periods, then, it took longer (i.e., greater latency) for the animal to begin salivating, and there was a steady decline in the amount of salivation.

Generalization and Differentiation

Pavlov's subsequent lectures describe his procedures for demonstrating a wide range of conditioning phenomena, including many of the ones you learned about in your introductory psychology course. Two of the most familiar are generalization and discrimination (the latter referred to as differentiation by Pavlov). **Generalization** is in evidence when a response conditioned to stimulus A also occurs, to some degree at least, in response to stimuli that are similar to stimulus A. So if the CS of a 60 cps tone produces eight drops of saliva, the animal will also respond to a 70 cps tone, perhaps with six drops. A generalization gradient also exists—the amount of saliva secreted is proportional to the similarity of the CS and the tested stimulus. **Differentiation** results from pairing the 60 cps tone with food, while presenting the 70 cps tone without the food. Eventually, the dog salivates only to the 60 cps tone.

Pavlov also went to great lengths to incorporate Sechenov's constructs of cortical excitation and inhibition into his descriptions. For example, excitatory processes were said to be involved in acquisition and generalization, whereas inhibitory cortical processes contributed to extinction and differentiation. In general, Pavlov was not interested in the conditioning phenomena per se, but only in terms of the light they shed on how the brain operated.

Experimental Neurosis

One interesting outgrowth of Pavlov's research on generalization and differentiation was his discovery of how a breakdown in differentiation could produce **experimental neurosis** or "pathological disturbances," as he put it in the title of his Lecture 17. He first projected a circle onto a screen in front of the dog's face, pairing its presentation with food. Soon, the circle became a normal CS for the CR of salivation. After creating this conditioned reflex, Pavlov then trained the dog to make an easy differentiation between the circle and an ellipse that had a 4:3 ratio between its two axes (the August 4 data). The shape of the ellipse was then changed until it reached a 9:8 ratio; that is, the ellipse was made to look more and more like the circle. The dog showed the ability to discriminate at first, but it then deteriorated, and eventually its behavior reached the point where it even had some difficulty distinguishing an easy 2:1 ellipse from the circle. Here are the results as

Pavlov's presented them (Pavlov, 1927/1960, p. 292, key trials in boldface):

Time	Conditioned stimulus applied during 30 seconds	Salivary secretion in drops during 30 seconds
Experiment of 4th August, 1914		
4.10 pm	Circle	4
4.22 pm	Circle	6
4.37 pm	**4:3 ellipse**	**0**
4.55 pm	Circle	4
Experiment of 2nd September, 1914		
1.10 pm	Circle	2
1.27 pm	Circle	8
2.06 pm	Circle	10
2.16 pm	**9:8 ellipse**	**1**
2.30 pm	Circle	6
2.48 pm	Circle	8
Experiment of 17th September, 1914		
3.20 pm	Circle	4
3.31 pm	Circle	7
3.54 pm	**9:8 ellipse**	**8**
4.09 pm	Circle	9
Experiment of 25th September, 1914		
2.17 pm	Circle	9
2.47 pm	**2:1 ellipse**	**3**
3.08 pm	Circle	8
3.22 pm	Circle	8
3.46 pm	**2:1 ellipse**	**3**

In the experiments on August 4, then, the animal had no difficulty differentiating between the circle and the 4:3 ellipse. In experiment 2, the animal showed an apparent ability to discriminate between the circle and the 9:8 ellipse, but the performance deteriorated dramatically in experiment 3 (September 17), and even spilled over into experiment 4, when the animal could not even successfully avoid salivating to a 2:1 ellipse. For Pavlov, then, neurotic behavior meant a breakdown in the ability to make normal differentiations. The neurosis also manifested itself in other ways. As Pavlov described it,

... At the same time the whole behavior of the animal underwent an abrupt change. The hitherto quiet dog began to squeal in its stand, kept wriggling about, tore off with its teeth the apparatus for mechanical stimulation of the skin, and bit through the tubes connecting the animal's room with the observer, a behavior which never happened before. On being taken into the experimental room the dog now barked violently, which was also contrary to its usual custom; in short it presented all the symptoms of an acute neurosis. (Pavlov, 1927/1960, p. 291)

During the course of his research on experimental neurosis, Pavlov noticed that although all the dogs were adversely affected, they displayed individual differences in how they displayed their pathology. Furthermore, these variations seemed to reflect overall differences in the temperaments of the dogs. Thus, some dogs were generally more excitable than others—they tended to respond to the experimental neurosis procedure like the dog just described. Others, however, who were ordinarily of a more placid temperament, reacted to the procedure by becoming even more withdrawn. As he did with all of his results, Pavlov interpreted these outcomes in terms of excitatory and inhibitory cortical processes. He believed that the individual differences in temperament related to whether excitatory or inhibitory processes were more dominant in them. Hence, he concluded that the first category of dog had a relatively higher proportion of excitatory than inhibitory processes, whereas the reverse was true for the second type of dog.

A Program of Research

Pavlov's research over the years is a classic example of how experiments never occur in isolation, but are embedded within an ongoing systematic program of research. The outcome of one study has interest in itself, but it also raises new questions and leads invariably to the next study. For instance, the acquisition research led naturally to the question of the precise timing of the CS and UCS, and Pavlov and his students completed dozens of studies that carefully varied the timing and the sequencing of the CS-UCS interval. Similarly, research developed over the years on such topics as (a) higher order conditioning, which involved pairing a new CS with an already conditioned one, (b) the durability of extinction, in which it was found that if a dog was returned to the laboratory several days after extinction, the CR would occur to some degree (i.e., spontaneous recovery occurred), and (c) the effectiveness of various types of conditional stimuli, in terms of how quickly conditioning could be established.[3] Indeed, the sheer size and relentless productivity of Pavlov's lab made it easy to overlook other experimental demonstrations of the same type of conditioning that occurred at the time of or before Pavlov's initial studies. Both the American psychologist E. B. Twitmyer and the Viennese physiologist Alois Kreidl produced classical conditioning in their labs (Logan, 2002). However, neither Twitmyer, who studied the knee jerk reflex, nor Kreidel, who was studying sensory capacity in fish, developed anything like the research program that Pavlov did.

Pavlov and the Soviets

Pavlov was the prototype of the scientist whose life was his work, a philosophy reflected in an article he wrote near the end of his life for a Soviet youth organization. He told them that scientists must be systematic, modest, and passionate about their work, and that "science demands of a man his whole life. And even if you could have two lives, they would not be sufficient. Science calls for tremendous effort and great passion" (cited in Babkin, 1949, p. 110). While in the laboratory, and from September through May he was there seven days a week, Pavlov was totally absorbed in the research at hand, and expected everyone else to share his passion. Thus, he was occasionally a stern taskmaster and was known for his frequent but short-lived outbursts of temper when mistakes were made. Nonetheless, his workers were intensely devoted to him, knowing that his anger passed quickly and was not directed at them personally.

One famous story about Pavlov provides an indication of his single-minded devotion to his work.

Although the story might be more mythical than real, it clearly illustrates Pavlov's priorities. Pavlov is said to have admonished a worker for being 10 minutes late during the height of the 1917 Russian Revolution. When the worker told of bloody skirmishes in the streets of St. Petersburg, causing him to take a more circuitous route to the laboratory, Pavlov was not impressed. After all, he had made his customary three-mile walk to the lab, arriving safely and promptly at nine o'clock. Pavlov made it clear to the worker that a mere revolution was not to interfere with the important work of the laboratory. The assistant was told to leave home earlier during the next revolution (Babkin, 1949).

Of course, the revolution of 1917 had a profound effect on everything in Russia, including Pavlov's work. Pavlov was initially hostile to the winners of the Soviet Revolution, Lenin's Bolsheviks, once saying publicly that if "that which the Bolsheviks are doing with Russia is an experiment, for such an experiment I should regret giving even a frog" (cited in Babkin, 1949, p. 161). He also protested directly to Stalin in the late 1920s about a policy to admit only communist professors to the Russian Academy of Science, telling the Russian leader: "On account of what you are doing I am ashamed to be called a Russian" (cited in Gantt, 1973). Pavlov's ambivalent attitude was not hard to understand: the Soviets had confiscated his Nobel Prize money and when he requested permission to emigrate in 1923, they refused. Yet by the end of his life, Pavlov had adjusted to the reality of the Soviet Union, and on one public occasion in the 1930s, even proposed a toast to "the great social experimenters." According to Babkin, Pavlov's change of heart came about primarily because of the developing threat of the Nazis in Germany, who came to power in 1933. Fiercely patriotic, Pavlov recalled the huge Russian losses at the hands of Germany in World War I and feared (accurately) that the Nazis would bring more suffering to his beloved homeland. In that context, the Soviets appeared to be the lesser of two evils.

Pavlov's accommodation to the reality of the Soviet state also was aided by the strong backing the government gave to his work. As early as 1921, when Russia was immersed in civil war and condi-

---

[3] Ironically, although most students think that Pavlov's typical CS was a bell, Pavlov reported that "the violent ringing of a bell" was seldom effective as a CS, because the dog tended to be startled by it (Pavlov, 1906, p. 616).

tions were generally chaotic, the Soviets saw to it that Pavlov's research continued with full support. For example, it was officially decreed that a special committee be formed "to create as soon as possible the most favorable conditions for safeguarding the scientific work of Academician Pavlov and his collaborators" (cited in Babkin, 1949, p. 165). These conditions included extra rations and a guarantee to fully equip Pavlov's laboratory.

It is easy to see why the Soviets were so enamored of Pavlov. A major theme of his research was that behavior could be changed by controlling the environment—actions could be "conditioned." That, of course, was exactly what the Soviets hoped to do on a broad scale. The essence of their "great social experiment" was to bring about changes in behavior to accomplish the Marxist-Leninist ideal whereby each should produce according to one's abilities and receive according to one's needs. Thus, although Pavlov had no interests beyond understanding the physiology of the brain, his research had great propaganda value for the Soviets. This tolerance by the Soviets is shown in a brief notice in *Time* magazine, which the American psychologist Walter Miles cut out and pasted into his diary in late 1929. It said that Pavlov had

> refused an official celebration of his 80th birthday. ... Said he: "I deplore the destruction of cultural values by illiterate Communists." Mindful that upon his research rests the behavioristic

> "Science of Marxism", ... the Soviet tolerates his slaps gently and without reproach, babies him. Birthday gifts from the Soviet to him include $50,000 endowment of his laboratory and an assurance that traffic would be diverted from the street near it so as not to disturb the conditioned reflexes of some six score dogs, kept there for experimental purposes. (Miles, 1929)

After Pavlov's death from pneumonia in 1936, the Soviets treated him like a war hero. A monument to him was erected in St. Petersburg (at that time renamed Leningrad), the Medical Institute was renamed the Pavlov Institute, his wife was given a generous pension, and his brain was preserved.

Pavlov and the Americans

Western scientists knew about Pavlov because of the Nobel Prize, but the impact of his conditioning research was slow in being felt. Most American psychologists were introduced to Pavlov through an article published in *Psychological Bulletin* in 1909 by Robert Yerkes, whose interests at that time were mainly in comparative psychology (see Chapters 1 and 8), and Sergius Morgulis, a Russian student. One feature of the article was a series of apparatus sketches that eventually resulted in mistaken portrayals of Pavlov's apparatus that continue to this day. See the Close-Up for this story.

CLOSE-UP:
Misportraying Pavlov's Apparatus

You probably recognize the sketch in Figure 10.3a. It shows up in one form or another in most general psychology texts, probably including the one you used, and it is usually identified as Pavlov's conditioning apparatus. It wasn't. Rather, it was devised by a German physiologist, G. F. Nicolai, who worked for a brief time in Pavlov's laboratory (Goodwin, 1991). He wished to improve on how the saliva was recorded in the early years in Pavlov's lab, when the drops of saliva were simply counted as they fell into the graduated cylinder portrayed in Figure 10.3b. The early apparatus was cumbersome, a problem recognized by Pavlov, who eventually developed the more sophisticated apparatus shown in Figure 10.2. How did the mistaken attribution of Nicolai's apparatus occur?

The article by Yerkes and Morgulis (1909), which introduced Pavlov's research to American psychologists, included both the sketches in Figure 10.3. Neither was labeled, but the text of the article described Figure 10.3b as showing a dog prepared for condi-

(a)   *(b)*

FIGURE 10.3 (a) Conditioning setup developed by German physiologist Nicolai, but usually attributed to Pavlov; (b) Early device used by Pavlov for recording salivary responses (both from Nicolai, 1907).

tioning research in Pavlov's lab, whereas Figure 10.3a was described as showing "the modification of experimental technique *which has been devised by Nicolai in Berlin*" (p. 259, italics added).

The distinction between Nicolai's and Pavlov's procedures was recognized by John Watson, who reproduced and correctly labeled both drawings in his well-known comparative psychology text of 1914. The first erroneous attribution seems to have been in a popular introductory textbook by Walter Hunter (1919); it included only Figure 10.3a, referred to it as Pavlov's apparatus, and cited the Yerkes and Morgulis article. From this point on, the sketch of Nicolai's experimental setup became the standard depiction of Pavlov's apparatus, partly because it is consistent with Pavlov's eventual separation of dog and experimenter into two separate rooms, but also because it is simply a more interesting sketch than Figure 10.3b.

The perpetuation of this error over the years provides an important lesson for any textbook writer: beware of relying too heavily on secondary sources. Many subsequent writers probably included the wrong drawing simply because it had become so widely used in other texts. Seeing the same drawing over and over, it is easy to assume it must be accurate.

Despite the detailed descriptions in the Yerkes and Morgulis (1909) article, Pavlov's research had little immediate impact on American psychologists. The work was of interest to those studying animal behavior, but at a time when American psychology was still the study of human conscious experience, salivating dogs did not seem especially pertinent. Most introductory psychology textbooks prior to

1920 either failed to mention Pavlov at all (including a 1911 text by Yerkes) or mentioned his work just briefly (Goodwin, 1991). Even John Watson, whose proclamation of behaviorism you will read about shortly, did not see the immediate relevance of Pavlov's work for his model of learning. Instead, he was initially more influenced by the conditioning work of another Russian physiologist and rival of Pavlov's, Vladimir Bekhterev (Skinner, 1981). Bekhterev investigated motor rather than salivary conditioning, in which muscle movements were conditioned to various stimuli. This lent itself more readily to Watson's interests in overt behavior.

Pavlov's major impact on American psychology began in the 1920s, when much of his work was translated into English for the first time. Pavlov also visited the United States twice, once in 1923 for a conference and lecture series at Rockefeller Institute in New York, and again in 1929 for the Ninth International Congress of Psychology at Yale University. There he delivered one of the major addresses (Duncan, 1980), an impassioned description (in Russian) of his research on conditioning to a large audience of American and international psychologists. As one observer noted, "the audience was spellbound, and the following standing ovation brought little smiles and bows of appreciation from the Guest of Honor of the Congress" (Withington, cited in Duncan, 1980).

American psychologists, especially behaviorists, eventually understood the importance of Pavlov's research for their own theories of learning. A passage from Ernest Hilgard's well-known *Theories of Learning* (1948) shows that Pavlov's importance was taken for granted by the late 1940s. Hilgard pointed out that research on "conditioned salivary responses in dogs was carried out systematically by Pavlov over many years, and he discovered most of the relationships which later studies have more fully explored. The translations of his terms have become common in the literature of learning" (Hilgard, 1948, p. 55).

Finally, Pavlov had a direct impact on the career choice of a young B. F. Skinner (Chapter 11), whose decision to pursue behavioral research was strongly influenced by reading a translation of Pavlov's

Conditioned Reflexes (1927/1960). Skinner once wrote that a guiding principle in his scientific life was Pavlov's simple dictum that if you "control your conditions ... you will see order" (Skinner, 1956, p. 223). Skinner was also excited by the writings of an American psychologist who shared with Pavlov a passion for systematic research grounded in measurable behavior. This person was John B. Watson, usually considered to be the founder of the American school of thought that came to be known as behaviorism.

JOHN B. WATSON AND THE FOUNDING OF BEHAVIORISM

Near the beginning of the chapter it was mentioned that at the start of the twentieth century, a number of American psychologists were arguing that psychology should adopt a more "objective" methodology than introspection. One example was the 1904 address by Cattell to an audience at the World's Fair in St. Louis. Also at St. Louis and probably in the audience for Cattell's address was John B. Watson, a young psychologist with a brand new Ph.D. from the University of Chicago. The developing trends toward objectivity in psychology were beginning to crystallize in the thinking and writing of this young man, and he would shortly become the mouthpiece for the movement that came to be called behaviorism.

The Young Functionalist at Chicago

Watson was born in 1878 in a rural area just outside of Greenville, South Carolina, into a family that would earn the label "dysfunctional" today. His father was a marginally successful farmer whose interests included consuming large amounts of alcohol, brawling, and committing adultery. He frequently left home for extended periods of time. Watson's mother was fiercely religious, enough so to name her son after a well-known fundamentalist Baptist preacher, John Broadus, and to insist that her son aspire to the ministry. Growing up in this environment, Watson understandably developed behavior problems of his own; by mid-adolescence he was a known troublemaker and had been arrested at least twice. Nonetheless, he was known to be an intelligent young man when he entered Furman University in Greenville at the age of 16. He graduated with a master's degree in 1900.

Watson's mother died during his final year at Furman, releasing him from any obligation to pursue the ministry. Instead, influenced by one of his professors at Furman, he applied to and was accepted at the University of Chicago. Eight years old in 1900, the university was established with Rockefeller oil money, and was presided over by William Rainey Harper. As you recall from Chapter 7's discussion of functionalism, Harper envisioned a "practical" university that would produce leaders for an emerging class in America—the professional elite, experts who would manage society's improvement and industry's productivity. Watson's initial intention was to study philosophy and psychology, which coexisted in the philosophy department at Chicago. He quickly discovered that neither philosophy nor introspective psychology appealed to him (he had no talent for introspection), but he was comfortable with the general precepts of a functionalist psychology. He was especially attracted to comparative psychology—not a surprise considering his rural background and familiarity with animals. Many years later, Watson's son rather painfully recalled that his father "preferred the company of animals to people most of the time" (Hannush, 1987, p. 150).

Watson's interests in animal behavior began to shape his beliefs about psychology in general. When reflecting on his Chicago years, he later wrote that he was always uncomfortable with introspective methods and human subjects but that with animals, he was "at home. ... More and more the thought presented itself: Can't I find out by watching their behavior everything that the other students are finding out by using [human subjects]?" (Watson, 1936, p. 279). This belief was reinforced by Watson's contacts with Jacques Loeb and Henry Donaldson. Loeb was a German physiologist who studied **tropisms**, movements of plants or animals that are forced automatically by some aspect of the environment. For example, a flower that always faces the sun is said to be showing a positive heliotropism (helio = sun). Loeb was an uncompromising materialist and mechanist who believed that all organic life could be understood as a series of automatic responses to stimuli. Donaldson was a neurologist specializing in the nervous system of white rats.

Watson's doctoral dissertation, co-directed by Donaldson and James Angell, was a study of the relationship between cortical development and learning in young white rats. It was an important study because at the time many leading physiologists believed that rats were incapable of true "associative learning" because their brains contained few if any "medullated" fibers.[4] Through a painstaking series of studies that showcased his talents as a careful scientist, Watson demonstrated that rats showed minimal learning ability for approximately the first three weeks of their lives, but that their ability to form associations improved dramatically in their fourth week. Furthermore, during this same time, the number of medullated fibers increased significantly. Thus, Watson concluded that associations could be formed in young white rats and that these associations were correlated with cortical development. Watson borrowed $350 from Donaldson and had his results published as *Animal Education: An Experimental Study of the Psychical Development of the White Rat, Correlated with the Growth of its Nervous System* (Watson, 1903). It earned him the doctorate and an offer to remain at Chicago as an instructor. Watson accepted.

The Watson/Carr Maze Studies

Watson remained on the faculty at Chicago from 1903 to 1908. During that time he began to build a reputation as a good teacher and a careful scientist. His most important research during this time involved studying rats in mazes; it was completed with Harvey Carr, then a graduate student at Chicago, later an important leader in the functionalist movement, and eventually chair of Chicago's psychology department (Chapter 7).

The goal of the Watson/Carr studies (Carr & Watson, 1908; Watson, 1907) was to determine which senses were needed for a rat to learn a maze. Watson was intrigued by the maze studies done at Clark by Willard Small (see the Close-Up in Chapter 6), but

---

[4] Today such fibers would be called "myelinated axons."

believed that Small had not been very systematic when trying to identify the factors contributing to the rat's ability to learn a maze. For example, Small's willingness to let the rats live in the maze at night made it impossible to evaluate how the learning occurred. Watson and Carr remedied that problem and others, producing a methodologically brilliant series of studies that established (at least for a time) the importance of the kinesthetic sense for maze learning.

In their first study (Watson, 1907), Watson and Carr systematically eliminated the ability of the animals to use their senses when solving a version of the Hampton Court maze. Displaying skillful surgical techniques, Watson removed the eyes from some rats, the middle ears from others, and the olfactory bulbs from a third group. Deprived of their various senses, the rats nonetheless learned the maze with ease. Watson and Carr also found that learning ability was not markedly hindered by removing the rats' whiskers, or by anesthetizing the rats' feet. By a process of elimination (literally!), they concluded that the only important factors in the formation of learned associations were "the kinesthetic impressions coupled with certain other intra-organic impressions" (Watson, 1907, p. 84). That is, the animals were learning to associate sequences of muscle movements with the various turns in the maze. In essence, they learned to take 10 steps, then turn right for another five steps, then turn left, and so on.

Having ruled out one sense after another, Watson and Carr set out to provide direct evidence of their remaining hypothesis about the kinesthetic sense. In their second study (Carr & Watson, 1908), they hit on the clever idea of shortening or lengthening the mazes that their rats had already learned. Figure 10.4 shows the maze they used, in its full-

FIGURE 10.4 Maze used by Watson and Carr to test their kinesthetic model of maze learning; shaded piece could be removed to produce a shorter version of the maze, from Carr and Watson (1908).

length version, with the piece that could be removed shaded. The effects were dramatic—rats initially trained in the full-length maze literally ran into the walls of the shortened maze. For example, according to Watson's lab notes, one rat "ran into [the wall] with all her strength. Was badly staggered and did not recover normal conduct until she had gone 9 feet" (Carr & Watson, 1908, p. 39). Similarly, rats trained in the shortened maze and tested in the long version often started to turn at the point where the correct turn used to be.

The Watson/Carr studies are models of scientific research, arriving at an empirical conclusion by first eliminating one alternative hypothesis after another, then producing a direct demonstration of the viability of the remaining (kinesthetic) hypothesis. They also provide a good illustration of how scientists can be naive about how their research will be accepted in the public eye. Watson might have thought he was simply pursuing an important question about learning, but in the public eye he became a target for antivivisectionists[5] and was portrayed in the *New York Times* on December 30, 1906, as a butcher of helpless white rats, chopping out bits and pieces of them in order to satisfy what seemed to be some idle scientific curiosity.

Opportunity Knocks at Johns Hopkins

By 1908, Watson was known among his professional colleagues as an up-and-coming star in the world of experimental psychology (see Figure 10.5). He was also beginning to feel unappreciated at Chicago, where he still held the low academic rank of instructor after five years. Thus, when offered a full professor position, control of a laboratory, and more than double his salary from Johns Hopkins University, he could hardly refuse. Furthermore, within a year of his arrival in Baltimore, the head of the psychology department, James Mark Baldwin, was fired for moral reasons (arrested in a police raid on a house of

FIGURE 10.5 John B. Watson in 1908, at age 30.

prostitution, he claimed he was doing research). Barely into his third decade, then, Watson found himself in charge of psychology at Johns Hopkins University. Over the next 12 years, before he also would be fired for moral reasons, he would (a) cement his reputation as a leading researcher in the world of animal psychology, (b) proclaim behaviorism, and (c) develop a program of research in developmental psychology, with an emphasis on the study of emotional development.

Watson and Animal Behavior

Once settled into his new position at Johns Hopkins, Watson launched a wide-ranging program of research in animal behavior. Like his dissertation and the maze studies with Carr at Chicago, some of the research was of the basic laboratory variety and included work in animal psychophysics. For example, he studied the visual abilities of several species by training them to make choices between pairs of slightly different stimuli (e.g., Watson, 1909), and by using the motor conditioning procedures of Pavlov's Russian colleague Bekhterev (Watson, 1916). The logic of Watson's psychophysics research was simple—if an animal could be trained or conditioned to

---

[5] Like today's animal rights activists, antivivisectionists protested the use of animals for research purposes; their influence on early comparative psychology has been documented by Dewsbury (1990).

respond correctly to one stimulus (e.g., light red) while not responding to another (e.g., a darker shade of red), then the animal must be able to perceive the difference between the two. Although Watson made much of this research in his 1915 APA presidential address, it appears that the results were not always clear and that the research was abandoned after little more than a year (Rilling, 2000).

Outside of the laboratory, Watson continued a series of naturalistic studies begun while he was still at the University of Chicago. He spent several summers on a small island near the Florida keys (Bird Key, one of the Dry Tortugas) observing the behavior of several species of terns. In contrast with Watson's later writings, which downplayed the importance of the instinctive control of behavior, especially human behavior, this research reads like an early version of the kind of ethological research later associated with names like Konrad Lorenz and Niko Tinbergen, emphasizing the importance of instinctive behavior for species survival (Dewsbury, 1994). He carefully documented the mating behaviors of the terns on Bird Key, their nest building and territoriality, and their behavior relating to the care of offspring, before and after their hatching (Todd & Morris, 1986). He also observed that recently hatched birds would often persistently follow him around the island. This of course is the same behavior studied by Spalding (see the Close-Up in Chapter 5) and later called imprinting by Lorenz.

KEY DATE 1913

This year marked the publication of Watson's behaviorist manifesto, "Psychology as the Behaviorist Views It."

These events also occurred:

- Niels Bohr formulated his theory of atomic structure
- Albert Schweitzer opened his hospital in the French Congo
- Henry Ford pioneered new assembly line procedures in his car factory
- Grand Central Station opened in New York
- Federal income tax was introduced via the 16th Amendment to the Constitution
- Mahatma Ghandi, leader of Indian passive resistance movement, was arrested
- These people were born:

  Richard Nixon and Gerald Ford, U.S. presidents

  Albert Camus, French author and philosopher

  Rosa Parks, pioneer in American civil rights movement

- These people died:

  Harriet Tubman, American abolitionist and reformer

  J. Pierpont Morgan, wealthy American industrialist

ORIGINAL SOURCE EXCERPT
Watson's Behaviorist Manifesto

In 1913, Watson accepted an invitation from Cattell to speak at Columbia University. By then he believed he had sufficient stature to proclaim what he had believed for at least 10 years—that it was time for the field to move away from an introspective psychology that studied consciousness and toward a psychology of behavior. His Columbia lectures, published with the provocative title "Psychology as the Behaviorist Views It" (Watson, 1913), have come to be called the Behaviorist Manifesto. What did Watson proclaim? The opening paragraph set the tone:

> Psychology as the behaviorist views it is a purely objective experimental branch of natural science. Its theoretical goal is the prediction and control of behavior. Introspection forms no essential part of its methods, nor is the scientific value of its data dependent upon the readiness with which they lend

themselves to interpretation in terms of consciousness. The behaviorist, in his efforts to get a unitary scheme of animal response, recognizes no dividing line between man and brute. ... (p. 158)

This is one of psychology's most quoted passages. In five sentences, Watson (a) firmly assigned psychology to the natural sciences, (b) articulated a clear set of goals for a scientific psychology, (c) completely rejected the introspection-based research of the majority of his peers, and (d) fully accepted an evolutionary model of behavior. The remainder of the paper essentially elaborated on these points. He began by facing the introspective establishment, describing in several paragraphs the difficulties inherent in defining psychology as the study of consciousness. He then focused specifically on the problem of the subjectivity of the introspective method as championed by Titchener's structuralist strategy (Chapter 7), again not failing to mince words:

I do not wish unduly to criticize psychology. It has failed signally, I believe, during the fifty-odd years of its existence as an experimental discipline to make its place in the world as an undisputed natural science. Psychology, as it is generally thought of, has something esoteric in its methods. If you fail to reproduce my findings, it is not due to some fault in your apparatus or in the control of your stimulus, but it is due to the fact that your introspection is untrained. ... If you can't observe 3–9 states of clearness in attention, your introspection is poor. If, on the other hand, a feeling seems reasonably clear to you, your introspection is again faulty. You are seeing too much. Feelings are never clear.

The time seems to have come when psychology must discard all reference to consciousness; when it need no longer delude itself into thinking that it is making mental states the object of observation. ... I firmly believe that two hundred years from now, unless the introspective method is discarded, psychology will still be divided on the question as to whether auditory sensations have the quality of 'extension', whether intensity is an attribute which can be applied to color, whether there is a difference in 'texture' between image and sensation and upon many hundreds of others of like character. (pp. 163–164)

Having disposed of structuralism and introspection, Watson was not done. Because they also were unwilling to reject introspection as method and because they also investigated consciousness (from the standpoint of its adaptive value rather than to identify its contents, however), functionalist psychologists were also targets for Watson's criticism. One might think that Watson might have been more sympathetic to an approach that was so deeply rooted in evolutionary thinking, and perhaps would have been more respectful of his own intellectual roots, but not so:

My psychological quarrel is not with the systematic and structural psychologist alone. The last fifteen years have seen the growth of what is called functional psychology. This type of psychology decries the use of elements in the static sense of the structuralists. It throws emphasis upon the biological significance of conscious processes instead of upon the analysis of conscious states into introspectively isolable elements. I have done my best to understand the difference between functional psychology and structural psychology. Instead of clarity, confusion grows upon me. The terms sensation, perception, affection, emotion, volition are used as much by the functionalist as by the structuralist. ... Surely if these concepts are elusive when looked at from a content standpoint, they are still more deceptive when viewed from the angle of function, and especially so when function is obtained by the introspection method. ... I was greatly surprised some time ago when I opened Pillsbury's [a student of Titchener] book and saw psychology defined as the 'science of behavior'. A still more recent text states that psychology is the 'science of mental behavior'. When I saw these promising statements I thought, now surely we will have texts based upon different lines. After a few pages the science of behavior is dropped and one finds the conventional treatment of sensation, perception, imagery, etc., along with certain shifts in emphasis and additional facts which serve to give the author's personal imprint. (pp. 165–166)

Having rejected structuralist and functional approaches to psychology, Watson shifted his argument to his behaviorist alternative. A key statement is his admittedly simplistic assertion that the fundamental goal of his behaviorism is to be able to specify stimulus-response connections (what follows includes the quote you read at the very beginning of the chapter).

This leads me to the point where I should like to make the argument constructive. I believe we can write a psychology, define it as Pillsbury, and never go back upon our definition: never use the terms consciousness, mental states, mind, content, introspectively verifiable, imagery, and the like. ... It can be done in terms of stimulus and response, in terms of habit formation, habit integrations and the like. Furthermore, I believe that it is really worthwhile to make this attempt now.

 The psychology which I should attempt to build up would take as a starting point, first, the observable fact that organisms, man and animal alike, do adjust themselves to their environment by means of hereditary and habit equipments. These adjustments may be very adequate or they may be so inadequate that the organism barely maintains its existence; secondly, that certain stimuli lead the organisms to make the responses. *In a system of psychology completely worked out, given the response the stimuli can be predicted; given the stimuli the response can be predicted.* Such a set of statements is crass and raw in the extreme, as all such generalizations must be. Yet they are hardly more raw and less realizable than the ones which appear in the psychology texts of the day. (pp. 166–167, italics added)

It is worth noting that Watson believed that all human behavior could be understood in stimulus-response terms, even such mental activities as thinking. According to Watson, thinking was in essence nothing more than **subvocal speech**, and the subject of this thinking would be determined by the immediate stimulus situation and by habits that he referred to as "laryngeal habits." He later even suggested (Watson, 1926) that some evidence in support of his position was the observation that our thinking tended to suffer when we had a sore throat!

In the latter half of the manifesto, Watson emphasized a point that ultimately made behaviorism attractive to psychologists and to the American public at large. Unlike introspective psychology, he argued, behaviorism had the potential to deliver direct applications that would positively affect people's lives. Note that Watson makes a clear distinction between applications and the applied research that makes the applications possible. Applications are important, but the research underlying those applications is no less important.

> What gives me hope that the behaviorist's position is a defensible one is the fact that those branches of psychology which have already partially withdrawn from the parent, experimental psychology, and which are consequently less dependent upon introspection are today in a most flourishing condition. Experimental pedagogy, the psychology of drugs, the psychology of advertising, legal psychology, the psychology of tests, and psychopathology are all vigorous growths. These are sometimes wrongly called 'practical' or 'applied' psychology. Surely there was never a worse misnomer. In the future there may grow up vocational bureaus which really apply psychology. At present these fields are truly scientific and are in search of broad generalizations which will lead to the control of human behavior. For example, we find out by experimentation whether a series of stanzas may be acquired more readily if the whole is learned at once, or whether it is more advantageous to learn each stanza separately and then pass to the succeeding. We do not attempt to apply our findings. The application of this principle is purely voluntary on the part of the teacher. In the psychology of drugs we may show the effect upon behavior of certain doses of caffeine. We may reach the conclusion that caffeine has a good effect upon the speed and accuracy of work. But these are general principles. We leave it to the individual as to whether the results of our tests shall be applied or not. Again, in legal testimony, we test the effects of recency upon the reliability of a witness's report. We test the accuracy of the report with respect to moving objects, stationary objects, color, etc. It depends upon the judicial machinery of the country to decide whether these facts are ever to be applied. For a 'pure' psychologist to say that he is not interested in the questions raised in these divisions of science because they relate indirectly to the application of psychology shows, in the first place, that he fails to understand the scientific aim in such problems, and secondly, that he is not interested in a psychology which concerns itself with human life. (pp. 168–170)

After describing examples of how behavioral procedures could be used to study such cognitive processes as sensation (conditioning different responses to slightly distinguishable stimuli—animal psychophysics) and memory (the recall of nonsense syllables is a behavioral act), Watson wrapped up his argument:

> In concluding, I suppose I must confess to a deep bias on these questions. I have devoted nearly twelve years to experimentation on animals. It is natural that such a one should drift into a theoretical position which is in harmony with his experimental work. ... Certainly the position I advocate is weak enough at present and can be attacked from many standpoints. Yet when all

> this is admitted I still feel that the considerations which I have urged should have a wide influence upon the type of psychology which is to be developed in the future. What we need to do is to start work upon psychology, making *behavior*, not *consciousness*, the objective point of our attack. Certainly there are enough problems in the control of behavior to keep us all working many lifetimes without ever allowing us time to think of consciousness. ... Once launched in the undertaking, we will find ourselves in a short time as far divorced from an introspective psychology as the psychology of the present time is divorced from faculty psychology. (pp. 175–176, italics in the original)

Watson's behaviorist manifesto was a powerful statement, sometimes seen as the starting point for a behaviorist "revolution" in psychology and as the vehicle that catapulted Watson to the presidency of the APA in 1915. Yet Samelson (1981) has shown that the immediate effect of the manifesto was that most psychologists ignored it or saw it as just one more instance of a growing number of assaults on introspection. Only two psychologists—Titchener (1914) and Calkins (1913)—responded in print to it, and both were highly critical.[6] As for Watson's APA presidency, it was more likely the outcome of his already-existing status among his peers, earned by virtue of a decade of research, his friendships with influential APA members, his position as chair at Johns Hopkins, and his editorship of *Psychological Review*. Also, his nomination for the APA presidency occurred before the manifesto had been delivered (Samelson, 1981). On the other hand, while the manifesto might not have been a revolutionary event, it certainly energized Watson. For the remainder of the decade, he vigorously advocated behaviorism, and eventually elaborated the manifesto into a book-length treatise—*Psychology From the Standpoint of a Behaviorist* (1919). According to historian James Todd (1994), it was this book and Watson's promotional efforts in the 1920s, more than the earlier manifesto, that were responsible for the increased influence of behaviorism among American psychologists as the 1920s drew to a close.

Studying Emotional Development

In the manifesto and elsewhere, Watson made some large claims about the ability of behaviorism to deliver applications that would improve the quality of life. Yet at the time of the manifesto, Watson's own research had been limited largely to animals. Thus, when an opportunity arose to study infants, Watson saw this as a major chance to apply behaviorism in a way that would convince skeptics and,

more important, secure Watson's position as a leader in the application of psychological principles to improve society. Furthermore, Watson was feeling some of the same pressure felt by other comparative psychologists who were finding it increasingly difficult to maintain institutional support for their basic research in animal behavior. University administrators were becoming reluctant to supply budgetary support for research that seemed esoteric, of little practical value, and required facilities with strong, unpleasant odors (Buckley, 1989).

The opportunity came to Watson in the form of an invitation from Adolf Meyer, a well-known psychiatrist, to set up a human laboratory in Meyer's clinic at the Johns Hopkins Medical School. The new lab was adjacent to the medical school's obstetrical ward, thereby providing Watson with a supply

---

[6] Despite the obvious contrast between the psychologies of Titchener and Watson, they maintained a mutual respect for each other—both were "laboratory men." They corresponded with some regularity, and when Watson hosted a meeting of Titchener's Experimentalists in 1910, Titchener was Watson's houseguest. When Watson was fired from Johns Hopkins in 1920, Titchener was one of the few psychologists who lent public support to his colleague (Larson & Sullivan, 1965).

(a)   *(b)*

FIGURE 10.6 According to Watson, the reflex of fear could be elicited either by (a) a loud noise or (b) loss of support. Rage (c) resulted from having one's movements hampered. From Watson's (1928) book on child rearing.

(c)

of infants for his research. The result was a series of studies investigating reflexes, basic emotional responses, and conditioned emotional responses.

The work on basic emotions was coauthored with J. J. B. Morgan. They set out to identify the fundamental human emotional responses and the stimuli that produced these responses. They identified three: fear, rage, and love. According to Watson and Morgan (1917), the fear response, defined behaviorally as "a sudden catching of the breath, clutching randomly with the hands, ... blinking of the eye lids, puckering of the lips, then crying" (p. 166), occurred in response to either of two classes of stimuli: sudden loud noises (producing by banging a steel bar with a hammer, right behind the baby's head) and loss of support (produced by dropping the infant or pulling out the infant's blanket just as the infant is falling asleep). The second emotion, rage, resulted from hindering the infant's movements: "If the face or head is held crying results, quickly followed by screaming. The body stiffens and fairly well coordinated slashing or striking movements of the hands and arms result" (pp. 166–167). The third emotion, love, defined as smiling, gurgling, or cooing, resulted from gently stroking the infant's skin or gently rocking or patting the child. Watson made films of some of his infant research, and Figure 10.6 shows still pictures from those films that illustrate the stimuli producing fear and rage.

The Zenith and the Nadir of a Career: Little Albert

From the infant research, then, Watson concluded that only a few stimuli would elicit the three instinctive emotions of fear, rage, and love. Why do older children show these emotional responses to a much wider range of stimuli? For Watson, the answer was simple: conditioning. His attempt to demonstrate this directly resulted in what has come to be called the Little Albert study. It was published as "Conditioned Emotional Reactions" in the *Journal of Experimental Psychology* in 1920 and it was coauthored by Watson and Rosalie Rayner, a graduate student at Johns Hopkins. As will be seen shortly, she was to play a pivotal role in another important event for Watson in 1920—his forced resignation from Johns Hopkins.

Watson and Rayner (1920) opened the article by stating their belief that emotional reactions develop through conditioning but that "direct experimental evidence in support of such a view has been lacking" (p. 1). Hence, the goal of their study was to provide just such evidence, using an 11-month-old infant given the pseudonym of Albert B. Albert was chosen for the study because "[h]e was on the whole stolid and unemotional. ... We felt that we could do him relatively little harm" (pp. 1–2). Before the experiment began, Albert (then nine months old) was put through a series of tests—the same ones used in

Watson's earlier infant research with Morgan. Albert showed no fear when presented "with a white rat, a rabbit, a dog, a monkey, with masks with and without hair, cotton wool, burning newspapers, etc." (p. 2). Unlike other infants, Albert did not show a fear response to the stimulus of a loss of support. Like the others, however, he was afraid of a loud, unexpected noise, so Watson decided to use that stimulus to produce the fear. Watson and Rayner's first session only lasted two trials:

> 1. White rat suddenly taken from the basket and presented to Albert. He began to reach for rat with left hand. Just as his hand touched the animal the bar was struck immediately behind his head. The infant jumped violently and fell forward, burying his face in the mattress. He did not cry, however.
>
> 2. Just as the right hand touched the rat the bar was again struck. Again the infant jumped violently, fell forward and began to whimper.
>
> In order not to disturb the child too seriously no further tests were given for one week. (Watson & Rayner, 1920, p. 4)

One week later, Albert experienced, in succession, the rat, three trials of the rat combined with the loud noise, the rat alone, two more "joint stimulations," and the rat alone again. On this last trial, this happened:

> Rat alone. *The instant the rat was shown the baby began to cry. Almost instantly he turned sharply to the left, fell over on one side, raised himself on all fours and began to crawl away so rapidly that he was caught with difficulty before reaching the edge of the table.* (p. 5, italics in the original)

Modern textbook accounts of the Albert study often describe it as a human example of classical conditioning, labeling the loud noise an unconditioned stimulus (UCS) and the fear of the noise an unconditioned response (UCR). The rat is the conditioned stimulus (CS) that comes to produce the conditioned response (CR) of fear through the pairing of CS and UCS, just as pairing a tone (CS) with food (UCS) yields salivation to the tone in the standard Pavlovian procedure. A close reading of Watson and

Rayner's lab notes, however, suggests that an operant punishment procedure might have occurred instead, at least on the first two trials. The baby's behavior of reaching for the rat resulted in the immediate consequence of the loud noise. Whether the same sequence of events occurred on other trials that are simply labeled "joint stimulation" is not clear. It is clear that Albert was affected by the procedures and became afraid of the rat, but the ambiguity over precisely what happened is one reason why the study has been criticized (Harris, 1979).

After conditioning (by whatever procedure) Albert to fear the rat, Watson and Rayner's second goal was to see if the response would "transfer" to other stimuli (or "generalize," as Pavlov would say). Five days after the famous trials just described, Albert was returned to the lab and tested first with blocks and the rat. He played with the former and continued to be afraid of the latter. After showing that the conditioned response still existed, Watson and Rayner presented other stimuli, alternating them with occasions for the child to play with his blocks. Albert showed some degree of fear of a rabbit, a dog, and a fur coat. Also, in a trial that suggests Albert's primary fear might have been of the experimenter, Watson "put his head down to see if Albert would play with his hair. Albert was completely negative. Two other observers did the same thing. He began immediately to play with their hair" (Watson & Rayner, p. 7).

Believing that transfer had been demonstrated, Watson and Rayner moved to a third research question: Would the response be retained for a significant period of time? The retention interval was limited to a month by a practical consideration—Albert was about to be removed from the hospital (no details provided by Watson and Rayner). During the interval, Albert was tested in other ways (e.g., in some research on handedness), and at the end of the month, he was once again shown the rat and some of the other stimuli used for generalization. He again showed fear responses.

In the final section of their paper, Watson and Rayner addressed the question of how Albert's fear might have been alleviated, if additional time had been available. Although they gave the impression that they wished they could have had more time with

Albert, it is clear that they knew of his forthcoming departure a month ahead of time and chose to test the persistence of the fear rather than to attempt its reversal. Nonetheless, they did make several suggestions about how the fear might be "unlearned."

Although Watson and Rayner made no attempt to alleviate Albert's fear, Watson later redeemed himself to some extent by supervising the research of Mary Cover Jones (Figure 10.7). Watson was by then out of academia and working in advertising (discussed later in the chapter), but his research with children inspired Jones, a young Columbia graduate student and friend of Rosalie Rayner. Working with several children who feared various objects, Jones tried a number of methods (1924a), most of them unsuccessful. For example, fears were not reduced (a) simply through the passage of time, (b) through the method of verbal appeal (i.e., trying to convince the child that the fear was groundless), or (c) by having peers ridicule the child. What did work, however, was a method suggested in the Watson and Rayner paper. In a study that is often cited as a pioneering example of the behavior therapy technique of **systematic desensitization**, Jones (1924b) reduced a young boy's fear of rabbits by placing the animal at some distance from the boy while he was eating, then gradually moving the rabbit closer. The pleasurable responses associated with eating apparently replaced the fear response associated with the rabbit.

The Little Albert study can be found in the chapters on learning in virtually all modern introductory psychology texts. The study is often thought of as a "classic," displaying the power of behavioral principles to condition our emotions. If learning is a change in behavior brought about by experience, then clearly the study illustrated learning of some kind. Albert was certainly affected by his encounter with Watson and Rayner. Yet the study had some serious flaws. First, there is some question about whether the initial procedure actually produced a strong fear of animals in Albert (Harris, 1979). Films of Albert show him a bit hesitant about the animals even before testing began, and after testing, while he appears to be concerned about the animals, he does not seem to be in a panic. Second, during the start of generalization testing ("transfer"), his reactions were often so weak that

FIGURE 10.7 Mary Cover Jones of Columbia, during the time of her studies on the unlearning of fears.

they needed to be "freshened up" with additional pairings of the animals with the loud noise. These additional pairings constituted further learning trials, thus rendering the generalization test meaningless. Third, even if one concedes that the child developed a fear, just what he was afraid of is not clear. As mentioned earlier, it is conceivable that Albert became afraid, not of the animals, but of Watson himself. One gets an impression of some relatively rough treatment of infants on the part of Watson when viewing the films. Fourth, it is inappropriate to draw a general conclusion about fear conditioning on the basis of a study using a single baby. Research limited to individual subjects is acceptable, and represents an important tradition in psychological research, but confidence in the generality of results only comes with continued replication of the basic finding. Several attempts to produce conditioned emotional responses in the 1920s and 1930s produced ambiguous results, however. For instance, English (1929) failed to condition a 14 month old to fear a wooden duck, primarily because the child did not react adversely to the loud noise. Also, Valentine (1930) failed to condition a child to fear opera glasses, but apparently succeeded with a caterpillar. Similarly, Bregman (1934) failed to condition fear to biologically neutral stimuli, including a curtain and some wooden blocks. Both the Valentine and Bregman studies were seriously flawed methodologically, however, making it difficult to determine if replication occurred or not (Todd, 1994).

In summary, then, the Little Albert study cannot be considered a conclusive demonstration of the widespread applicability of conditioning principles. Why has it become so well known? One reason is political. For behaviorism to become recognized as an important force in American scientific psychology, it needed examples of the power of conditioning. It was one thing for Watson to proclaim behaviorism, but proof of its viability was needed. The Little Albert study seemed to fit the bill, and in subsequent descriptions of it by Watson and others sympathetic to behaviorism, the methodological weaknesses were ignored and it eventually achieved the status of an unambiguous case of "conditioning in action" (Prytula, Oster, & Davis, 1977). A second reason for the study's popularity, related to the first, is that it has a certain dramatic appeal and applicability to one of life's important tasks: how we raise our children. If their lives can be affected so strikingly by the experiences they encounter, then managing the child's environment becomes an important way to shape the child's future.

Thus, the Little Albert study served the important function of legitimizing the new behavioral approach that within a decade would become a dominant force in American psychology. Watson was not destined to be a major player during that decade of the 1920s, however. The year the Little Albert study was published, 1920, was also the year that Watson was fired from Johns Hopkins.

A New Life in Advertising

While a young bachelor instructor at the University of Chicago, Watson fell in love with Mary Ickes, a student in his introductory psychology class; he eventually married her. As an established experimental psychologist at Johns Hopkins, he had a sim-

ilar experience with two major differences. This time the student was a graduate student (Rosalie Rayner) rather than an undergraduate; more important, this time Watson was already married—to the same woman who had been that undergraduate some 17 years earlier. The details of this unhappy situation can be found elsewhere (e.g., Buckley, 1989). It is enough to say that Watson's love for Rayner led to (a) his highly publicized divorce from Mary Ickes Watson, which featured the publication of love letters written by Watson to Rosalie and discovered by Mary, (b) his forced resignation from Johns Hopkins, and (c) his marriage to Rosalie.

The dismissal from Johns Hopkins was a devastating blow to Watson. Furthermore, the attendant publicity ruined any chance that he would secure another academic position. Instead, through the intercession of a friend, he entered the business world by joining the J. Walter Thompson advertising agency in New York City. After an apprenticeship, during which Watson (Figure 10.8) served in all departments of the agency, he rose to the position of vice-president within four years (Buckley, 1989).

As an advertising executive, Watson had the opportunity to put into practice some of his claims about the applicability of behaviorism. For instance, he developed a number of advertising campaigns around themes derived from his research on the three basic emotions of fear, rage, and love. To sell a product to a consumer, Watson suggested, one must "tell him something that will tie [him] up with fear, something that will stir up a mild rage, that will call out an affectionate or love response, or strike at a deep psychological or habit need" (cited in Buckley, 1989, p. 137). For example, an ad campaign for Johnson & Johnson baby powder sent a clear message designed to scare young parents into buying the product: if they failed to use baby powder, they risked exposing their children to serious infection. Watson also relied heavily on the use of testimonials by well-known personalities and experts to sell products. The baby powder campaign used testimony by doctors, for example.

Watson brought to his new career the same passion for scientific method that characterized his life in academia. In an autobiographical statement, for

Popularizing Behaviorism

Watson began communicating with the general public early in his academic career, by publishing articles in popular magazines (e.g., *Harper's Monthly*) with titles like "The New Science of Animal Behavior" (1910), but this activity blossomed in the 1920s, with additional magazine articles, radio broadcasts, and two books: *Behaviorism* (1924/1930) and *Psychological Care of Infant and Child* (1928). The former became the most widely known statement of Watson's ideas. Although Columbia's Robert Woodworth (1931) aptly described it as "certainly not one of [Watson's] most scientific books from the psychologist's point of view" (p. 91), the *New York Times* said that it would begin "a new epoch in the intellectual history of man" (cited in Buckley, 1989, p. 173). It was the book that interested a young B. F. Skinner in behaviorist thinking. The book included one of Watson's most famous quotations, a reflection of his belief in the importance of the environment in shaping our lives:

> Our conclusion, then, is that we have no real evidence of the inheritance of traits. I would feel perfectly confident in the ultimately favorable outcome of careful upbringing of a healthy, well-formed baby born on a long line of crooks, murderers and thieves, and prostitutes. ...
>
> I should like to go one step further now and say "Give me a dozen healthy infants, well-formed, and my own specified world to bring them up in and I'll guarantee to take any one at random and train him to become any type of specialist I might select—doctor, lawyer, artist, merchant-chief and, yes, even beggar-man and thief, regardless of his talents, penchants, tendencies, abilities, vocations, and race of his ancestors." (Watson, 1924/1930, pp. 103–104)

Watson admitted that he was going beyond the data in making his "dozen infants" claim and he was probably overstating the case to contrast his views with those psychologists, including most of the mental testers (see Chapter 8), who were promoting the role of inherited traits in individual behavior. Although Watson always recognized the interaction of nature and nurture in the production of behavior, his "dozen infants" quote has become a regular fea-

FIGURE 10.8 John B. Watson as an advertising executive.

example, he claimed that "it can be just as thrilling to watch the growth of a sales curve of a new product as to watch the learning curve of animals or man" (Watson, 1936, p. 280). Indeed, his major contribution to consumer psychology was not the introduction of new advertising techniques—historian Deborah Coon has shown that he merely adopted strategies in use at the time and pioneered by Walter Dill Scott (Chapter 8). Rather, his more lasting impact was in the application of scientific thinking to the areas of marketing (e.g., using demographic data to target certain consumers) and in the development of training programs and productivity evaluations for sales personnel (Coon, 1994).

Advertising did not occupy all of Watson's time during the 1920s, however. He lectured on behaviorism in New York at the New School for Social Research, joined the board of directors of Cattell's Psychological Corporation, and renewed his work on infants by supervising research financed through a grant from the Laura Spelman Rockefeller Memorial Fund (Buckley, 1989). The Fund provided $15,000 to Columbia University to continue the research begun at Johns Hopkins, and the experiments funded by the grant included the famous study mentioned earlier by Mary Cover Jones that successfully eliminated a learned fear in a young boy. Watson also continued writing about behaviorism during the 1920s, securing his reputation as behaviorism's popular voice.

ture of introductory textbooks in psychology, and Watson is routinely but inaccurately portrayed as someone who completely denied the significance of the nature side of the nature-nurture dichotomy (Todd, 1994).

Watson's reputation as an extreme environmentalist was enhanced by many of the recommendations in his *Psychological Care of Infant and Child* (1928), written "with the assistance of Rosalie Rayner Watson" (frontispiece). The book contains Watson's strongest statements about how the technology of behavior could be brought to bear on that most important of tasks, the raising of children. He dedicated it to "the first mother who brings up a happy child" and began by stating the urgency of the task: Healthy babies can overcome the short-term effects of physiological deprivation, but "once a child's character has been spoiled by bad handling which can be done in a few days, who can say that the damage is ever repaired?" (p. 3).

In a chapter entitled "The Dangers of Too Much Mother Love," Watson warned against being overly affectionate with children. The result would be "invalidism"—a failure of the child to become responsible, independent, and ultimately successful in life. He warned that there were "serious rocks ahead for the over-kissed child" (p. 71). What to do instead?

> There is a sensible way of treating children. Treat them as though they were young adults. Dress them, bathe them with care and circumspection. Let your behavior always be objective and kindly firm. Never hug or kiss them, never let them sit in your lap. If you must, kiss them once on the forehead when they say goodnight. Shake hands with them in the morning. Give them a pat on the head if they have made an extraordinarily good job of a difficult task. Try it out. In a week's time you will find how easy it is to be perfectly objective with your child and at the same time kindly. You will be utterly ashamed of the mawkish, sentimental way you have been handling it. (Watson, 1928, pp. 81–82)

Watson (1936) later said that he regretted writing the child-rearing book, that it was not sufficiently supported by data. Yet it stands as a perfect exam-

ple of the faith that he had in the ability of behaviorism to affect daily living. More broadly, it illustrates the positivist belief that understanding and control go hand in hand.

Evaluating Watsonian Behaviorism

In a certain sense, Watsonian behaviorism was a magnificent failure. The grand scheme of being able to predict all responses, given the stimulus, was never realized. Most of Watson's proclamations went far beyond the available empirical evidence—the data never caught up with the excessive claims. What, then, was the impact of Watson's system?

Watson's lasting importance for psychology derives from his propagandizing on behalf of his strong beliefs. As mentioned previously, behaviorism certainly did not take hold immediately. Indeed, the initial reaction in academia was decidedly mixed. But Watson's forceful and repeated arguments started a process that by the mid-1930s brought behaviorism to the center of American experimental psychology. Thus, he deserves the title "founder" of behaviorism.

Second, by attacking introspective psychology directly and exposing its Achilles' heel, its lack of objectivity, Watson contributed to the gradual shift from psychology as the study of immediate conscious experience to psychology as the study of behavior. By making observable and measurable behavior the dependent variable, rather than an introspective report, Watson ultimately helped place the field of psychology on firmer scientific ground.

Third, Watson's popularity with the general public suggests that his ideas struck a responsive chord with Americans. His belief that the environment could be arranged to shape someone's future development was consistent with the American ideal that through proper child rearing and education, people could aspire to any goal. As we have seen before (Chapter 3), this optimistic attitude helped maintain the popularity of phrenology long after the scientists had given up on it. It was an especially appealing message in the 1920s, a time of prosperity in America and a time when average Americans were optimistic about their futures and had no comprehension that the Great Depression of the 1930s was just around the corner. Watson himself was a living example of this attitude, a poor farm boy who rose to the top of his profession twice—once in psychology and once in the business world. This message was much more inviting for average Americans than the one they were receiving from the mental testers. As you recall from Chapter 8, the advocates of mental testing were agitating for a meritocracy based on an IQ that was assumed to be largely innate.

Finally, Watson's behaviorism effectively bridged the gap between basic and applied psychology. Laboratory work in areas like conditioning and maze learning gradually became scientifically rigorous, thereby fulfilling the promise of a scientific psychology. At the same time, the possibilities for application, repeatedly stressed by Watson, also bore fruit as behaviorist ideas eventually influenced child rearing, education, industry, and even psychotherapy.

And what of Watson himself? His productivity as an advertising executive and as a popularizer of psychology declined precipitously in 1935 with the sudden death of Rosalie, the great love of his life. In that same year, he left J. Walter Thompson for a similar position with the William Esty Company and retired 10 years later. In his remaining years he became increasingly reclusive. In 1957, a year before his death, the American Psychological Association honored Watson at their annual convention and although he traveled to the meeting in New York from his home in Connecticut, he backed out at the last moment and did not attend the ceremony, sending his son in his place. According to his biographer, "Watson was afraid that in that moment his emotions would overwhelm him, that the apostle of behavior control would break down and weep" (Buckley, 1989, p. 182).

SUMMARY

MOVING TOWARD GREATER OBJECTIVITY

- Prior to Watson, many psychologists were becoming concerned about the objectivity of their measures. One influence was evolutionary theory, which led to the study of animal behavior. Studying animals meant developing behavioral measures, and American psychologists did just that (e.g., Thorndike's puzzle box studies).

- The philosophies of empiricism and associationism, which both emphasize the importance of experience, provided a foundation for behavioral thinking. Positivism, which argued that the only valid knowledge is obtained through inductive, systematic observations, also contributed.

- Many psychologists became interested in more objective measures of psychological phenomena because they were becoming increasingly critical of introspection.

PAVLOV'S LIFE AND WORK

- Pavlov thought of himself more as a physiologist than psychologist, and his 1904 Nobel prize was for research on the physiology of digestion. He was especially known for developing surgical procedures (e.g., the Pavlov pouch) that allowed the digestive processes of live, intact animals to be studied.

- Pavlov's work on conditioning developed out of the digestion research, when he decided to investigate why his dogs would often salivate before food reached their mouths. He systematically examined a large number of conditioning phenomena, including acquisition, extinction, generalization, differentiation, and experimental neurosis (a breakdown in the ability to differentiate stimuli). He interpreted these phenomena in terms of the reciprocal brain processes of excitation and inhibition.

- Although initially hostile to the Soviet government, Pavlov eventually accommodated himself to the government when the threat from Nazi Germany developed. The Soviets saw Pavlovian conditioning as a foundation for shaping the modern communist citizen; consequently, Pavlov's research was heavily subsidized by the government.

- Pavlov's work was generally known to American psychologists from the early years of the twentieth century, but not widely known and appreciated until his research was translated into English in the 1920s.

JOHN B. WATSON AND THE FOUNDING OF BEHAVIORISM

- Watson was trained at the functionalist University of Chicago, where he developed a distaste for introspection and a love of animal research. His dissertation on the relationship between cortical development and the learning abilities of rats was followed by several important studies on how rats learned mazes by relying on their kinesthetic sense.

- After teaching at Chicago for several years following his doctorate, Watson moved to Johns Hopkins in 1908, where he stayed until 1920. In his behaviorist manifesto (1913), he proclaimed that introspective psychology should be replaced by a psychology that specified the relationships between stimuli and responses. In his APA presidential address (1915), he showed how behaviors could be conditioned using procedures similar to Pavlov's.

- In his final years at Johns Hopkins, Watson studied newborns and young children, especially their emotional development. He argued that fear, rage, and love were the three fundamental emotions, each resulting from specific stimuli. More elaborate emotional responses resulted from conditioning.

- Watson attempted to demonstrate the conditioning of emotional responses in the famous Little Albert experiment. By pairing a loud noise with a white rat, Watson and Rayner created a fear of the latter. The fear generalized to similar stimuli (e.g., rabbits) and lasted at least a month. Later, Mary Cover Jones demonstrated that fears could be unlearned.

- Watson spent his final professional years as an advertising executive, applying behavioral principles to marketing. During this time, he also became a popularizer of behaviorist philosophy, especially in the area of child rearing.

STUDY QUESTIONS

1. What are the similarities between John Locke's empiricist ideas and John Watson's behaviorist ideas?

2. What was positivism and what was its significance for American psychology?

3. What was the influence of comparative psychology on the development of behaviorist thinking?

4. While being trained for the ministry, what influenced Pavlov to switch to science?

5. Describe the research that won Pavlov the Nobel Prize.

6. Describe the operation and organization of Pavlov's lab.

7. What is the important point about history made in footnote 2?

8. How did Pavlov demonstrate the basic phenomena of conditioning, extinction, generalization, differentiation?

9. What did Pavlov mean by experimental neurosis and how did he demonstrate its existence?

10. Explain why Pavlov's ideas were valued by the Soviets and explain why Pavlov initially disliked the Soviets, but later made an accommodation.

11. How were Pavlov's ideas made known to American psychologists and what was Pavlov's influence on American psychology?

12. What is the important point about historiography made in the chapter's Close-Up?

13. Describe the factors that turned Watson into a behaviorist while at Chicago.

14. Describe the Watson/Carr maze studies from the standpoint of (a) methodology and (b) ethics.

15. On the Dry Tortugas, what did Watson learn about the behavior of birds?

16. Describe how Watson determined that three fundamental emotions existed. What were the emotions, and what stimuli elicited them?

17. Describe and critically analyze the Little Albert study.

18. Watson and Rayner didn't even try to remove Albert's fear, but Jones showed that fear could be removed. How did she do it?

19. Describe how Watson influenced the world of advertising with his (a) general scientific attitude and (b) behaviorist ideas.

20. Describe a Watsonian approach to parenting.

QUESTIONS FROM THE ORIGINAL SOURCE EXCERPT

1. What was the nature of Watson's criticism of structuralist psychology?

2. In addition to attacking structuralism, Watson also criticized functionalism. Why?

3. According to Watson, what should psychology's goals be?

4. What did Watson have to say about application in his manifesto?

FOR FURTHER READING

Babkin, B. P. (1949). *Pavlov: A biography.* Chicago: University of Chicago Press.

Provides a unique glimpse into Pavlov's life and his research, through the eyes of a former student. It is especially effective in portraying life inside Pavlov's laboratory during the early years of the twentieth century.

Buckley, K. W. (1989). *Mechanical man: John Broadus Watson and the beginnings of behaviorism.* New York: The Guilford Press.

The only existing scholarly biography of Watson; a thorough and critical analysis of how his ideas were shaped, and how they in turn influenced American psychological thought. A good example of a biography that fits its central character into the social, cultural, and institutional context of the times.

Harris, B. (1979). Whatever happened to Little Albert? *American Psychologist, 34*, 151–160.

A critical examination of how the Little Albert study became a "classic study" of the application of conditioning principles, despite the fact that the study was seriously flawed and that replication efforts were not successful. Textbook descriptions of the experiment are often inaccurate, mainly because writers rely on secondary sources rather than on the original article.

O'Donnell, J. M. (1985). *The origins of behaviorism: American psychology, 1870–1920.* New York: New York University Press.

Scholarly yet highly readable description and analysis of American psychology's formative years, and the factors leading to the development of behaviorism; excellent example of an external, historicist, contextual history.

CHAPTER 11

THE EVOLUTION OF BEHAVIORISM

> I believe that everything important in psychology ... can be investigated in essence through the continued experimental and theoretical analysis of the determiners of rat behavior at a choice-point in a maze.
>
> —Edward Chace Tolman, 1938

PREVIEW AND CHAPTER OBJECTIVES

This chapter continues to describe the evolution of behaviorist thinking by focusing on the work of three research psychologists who have come to be known as "neobehaviorists"—Edward Tolman, Clark Hull, and B. F. Skinner. But first it opens by examining the fate of Watsonian behaviorism and describes several trends (e.g., operationism) that prepared the way for American experimental psychologists to accept the behaviorism that became dominant in the discipline in the 1930s through the 1950s, at least in the United States. You will also learn, however, that not all American psychologists were behaviorists during this time, and that behaviorism was largely an American phenomenon.

The learning theories to be considered here differed from each other substantially—concerning the definition and role of reinforcement in learning, for instance. All were grounded in research using animals as subjects, however, and all focused their research efforts on discovering the essential laws of conditioning. Although not discounting the importance of biological factors, the neobehaviorists, in the tradition of the British empiricists, believed that understanding human action largely meant discovering how life's experiences (i.e., conditioning history) shaped the individual. This chapter's Original Source Excerpt highlights B. F. Skinner's ideas about a form of learning he called operant conditioning. After you finish this chapter, you should be able to:

- Distinguish between the myth of the behaviorist revolution and what really happened between Watson's 1913 manifesto and behaviorism's rise in the 1930s
- Describe how the relationship between logical positivism and operationism paved the way for the theorizing of the neobehaviorists Tolman and Hull
- Explain the importance of using operational definitions in psychology
- Describe the beliefs held in common by the neobehaviorists
- Describe the major features of Tolman's theory of learning
- Describe and explain the significance of Tolman's research on latent learning, place learning, and cognitive maps
- Describe Hull's contributions to psychology prior to the development of his learning theory

- Describe the major features of Hull's hypothetico-deductive theory of learning, especially postulate 4
- Describe how Skinner's approach to psychology differed from that of Tolman and Hull
- Describe the essential components of an experimental analysis of behavior, according to Skinner
- Explain the influence of Sir Francis Bacon on Skinner's ideas
- Describe examples of Skinner's attempts to apply his operant principles to real life concerns
- Evaluate the effect of neobehaviorism on the history of psychology

POST-WATSONIAN BEHAVIORISM

Traditional accounts of psychology's history often refer to Watsonian behaviorism as revolutionary. The myth goes something like this: Before Watson, there was the darkness of introspective psychology. Because of its intensely subjective nature, introspectionism prevented psychology from being a truly objective science. Then along came Watson and his 1913 "behaviorist manifesto." Except for a few narrow-minded holdouts, psychologists everywhere saw the light, and psychology dramatically changed from the quasi-science of consciousness to the true science of behavior. After Watson, behaviorism quickly became the dominant way of thinking among experimental psychologists. This might be a dramatic plot, but it is not what happened. The actual story is infinitely more complex and considerably at odds with the legend.

As mentioned in the previous chapter, Watson's behaviorism did not catch on immediately, and the initial response to his 1913 manifesto was more likely to have been indifference or criticism than support (Samelson, 1981). Most American psychologists simply went about their business: if they were interested in imageless thoughts, they continued to study them by combining cognitive tasks with introspection; if they were interested in the functioning of the visual system, they continued to study phenomena like afterimages and illusions; if they were interested in comparative psychology, they continued to study animal behavior. And after World War I, of course, many psychologists became involved in the mental testing movement (Chapter 8). Indeed, more can be

learned about the nature of psychology in 1920s America by examining the growth of mental testing than by studying the development of behaviorist thought (Samelson, 1985). Furthermore, nonbehavioral approaches to psychology did not simply disappear after Watson's manifesto and during the 1920s. At least a dozen varieties of psychology were examined in Murchison's *Psychologies of 1925* (1926) and *Psychologies of 1930* (1930), and gestalt psychology (Chapter 9) attracted as much attention as behaviorism. As late as 1931, Robert Woodworth's widely read *Contemporary Schools of Psychology* preceded the chapter on behaviorism with one on introspective psychology, and included chapters on gestalt psychology, Freudian psychoanalysis, and "hormic" (i.e., focused on instincts) psychology. Woodworth correctly predicted that after 50 years, historians would assign much significance to the behaviorist movement, but he was "puzzled to guess exactly where [the historians] will find its significance to lie" (p. 89). He granted that behaviorism had an appeal to some of the younger psychologists, but he also pointed out that advocating objective methods was not unique to Watson, and that despite his arguments, introspective studies were still being carried out.

Beginning in the decade of the 1930s, however, behaviorism did begin to take hold in American experimental psychology. Watson certainly played a role, especially with his consistent proselytizing on behalf of behaviorism, even after leaving academia. During the 1920s, his child-rearing advice and his *Behaviorism* (1924/1930), while "not one of his most scientific books from the psychologist's point of view" (Woodworth, 1931, p. 91), made great claims about shaping future generations during a decade of great optimism in America. In the Roaring 20s, the United States had emerged from World War I as a world power and it was not until the end of the decade that its confidence was shaken by the stock market crash that brought on the Great Depression. The traditionally conservative *New York Times* said Watson's book "marks an epoch in the intellectual history of man" (cited in Woodworth, 1931, p. 92). Woodworth believed that behaviorism's significance would lie primarily in its appeal to those who believed that science could be used to improve the common good. To some extent, then, the development of behaviorism as a force in American psychology derived from an optimistic public's belief that a way had been found to raise their children efficiently, to improve their marriages and their businesses, and in general to help them lead more productive lives.

Public enthusiasm for behaviorism cannot account for the whole story of its rise to power, however. Other events in the 1920s played an equally important role in bringing behaviorism to the forefront of American psychology. First, as pointed out in the preceding chapter, a substantial amount of Pavlov's research was translated into English for the first time. Americans knew about Pavlov, but before the 1920s, they had little idea about the scope of his work, its precision, and its implications. If American psychologists were looking for a model of a systematic research program focusing on overt, measurable behavior, this was it. As discussed in the previous chapter, by the time of the International Congress at Yale in 1929, Pavlov was widely recognized by American psychologists as a major figure. Another event that paved the way for behaviorism was the publication of a book by a Harvard physicist. In *The Logic of Modern Physics* (1927), Percy Bridgman introduced American psychologists to operationism. Along with its close relation, logical positivism, operationism provided the intellectual foundation for neobehaviorism.

Logical Positivism and Operationism

Operationism appeared at about the same time a small group of philosophers, mathematicians, and scientists began meeting Thursday evenings in a Viennese coffee house to discuss the logic and philosophy of science. Known as the Vienna Circle, they promoted a version of positivist thinking that came to be known as **logical positivism** (Gillies, 1993). Since the nineteenth century, positivists had taken a strictly empiricist stance, maintaining that certain knowledge about natural phenomena could only result from the public observation of measurable events. This philosophy suited Watson just fine, because it was consistent with his belief that psychology must be the study of observable behavior rather than subjective introspections. The difficulty was that even by focusing on observables, it is difficult if not impossible to avoid discussing unobservable concepts when developing a theory. For example, if you believe that human behavior can be motivated by the need to reduce a strong drive such as hunger, you are forced to address the question of just what is meant by hunger and how does it function to motivate us to behave. Yet hunger is an unobservable event, seemingly limited to an introspective description ("my stomach just feels empty and I feel a bit light-headed"). The logical positivists, dealing with this problem in the context of physics—such forces as magnetism or gravity also are not observed directly—resolved the issue to their satisfaction by distinguishing between observable and theoretical events, but insisting that the two be closely tied to each other. Specifically, they admitted the use of abstract, nonobservable concepts into a scientific theory, as long as these concepts were closely tied to some observable event(s). Thus magnetism could be proposed as a theoretical force having specific properties if certain objects (e.g., metal filings) behaved in a predictable fashion and could be observed and measured objectively. Similarly, hunger could be used in a theory of motivation if it could be tied to observable behaviors. Operationism provided the link.

The essential idea of **operationism** was that scientific concepts were to be defined, not in absolute terms, but with reference to the operations used to measure them. The concept of length, for instance, would be defined by agreed-upon procedures. As Bridgman put it, in his *The Logic of Modern Physics* (1927), the "concept of length is ... fixed when the operations by which length is measured are fixed;

that is, the concept of length involves as much as and nothing more than a set of operations" (p. 5). Bridgman also discussed what he called "pseudo-problems," questions that might be interesting, but were unanswerable by means of scientific observations. Whether or not time has a beginning or an end is an example.

A Harvard colleague of Bridgman's, experimental psychologist S. S. Stevens, was the most vocal promoter of operationism within psychology. Stevens was a doctoral student of E. G. Boring in the early 1930s and became the best-known twentieth-century researcher in psychophysics. He also developed the classification scheme for measurement scales (nominal, ordinal, interval, ratio) recognized by all those who have survived a statistics course. His 1935 paper, "The Operational Definition of Concepts," was the first of several attempts to convince psychologists of the wisdom of adopting an operational strategy. For Stevens, operationism provided an answer to the problem confronted by the logical positivists—how to define scientific concepts that could not be observed directly. By using operational definitions, that is, definitions involving precise descriptions of procedures for measurement and for specifying the variables in an experiment, psychologists could study such seemingly invisible concepts as hunger, anxiety, aggression, and memory while remaining faithful to the dictates of a positivist philosophy. Researchers could now define a motivational state like hunger or a perceptual quality like loudness in terms of the set of operations that were assumed to bring them about. Thus, hunger could be defined as the outcome of a certain number of hours without food, perceived loudness could be defined as a series of discriminations of quantitatively different tones made by research participants, and so on.

Stevens also saw the relevance of Bridgman's pseudo-problems for experimental psychology. One of Bridgman's examples was the problem of whether person A's sensation of blue is the same as person B's sensation of blue. That can never be known for certain; all that can be done is to determine if similar discriminations are made by person A and B to a series of visual stimuli of known wavelengths. Thus, one outcome of operational thinking was to raise

additional questions about the validity of introspective observations and to argue that they should be replaced with behavioral observations (i.e., discriminations between stimuli).

Operational definitions continue to be widely used among psychological scientists today, but a rigid operationism did not last long in psychology. One of operationism's implications is that the meaning of a concept does not go beyond the operations used to measure it. Thus, hunger is nothing more than 24 hours without food. The problem was that researchers often disagreed on the "best" operational definition of a term. The idea that one definition could be better than another necessarily meant that researchers believed that the meaning of terms like hunger went beyond a mere set of operations. To complicate matters further, many of psychology's concepts resisted simple operational definitions. For instance, researchers studying aggression have created operational definitions ranging from the delivery of shocks from one subject to another to horn honking among drivers at intersections. Is aggression being studied in both cases? Do widely different measures of a phenomenon measure the same thing? A strict operationist would have to argue that different operations measure different phenomena. Consequently, either all researchers would have to agree on a single definition of aggression, or all would have to agree that they are investigating different phenomena when using different measures.

Hilgard (1987) argued that the essence of operationism was simply to force experimental psychologists to define their terms more precisely. The chief advantage is **replication**. If terms are defined clearly enough, other researchers can repeat a particular study. Successful replications produce increased confidence in some research outcome; unsuccessful replications generate additional research to clear up the inconsistency. Furthermore, if researchers using slightly different operational definitions of terms nonetheless produce the same outcome (e.g., frustration tends to be accompanied by aggression), the generality of the outcome is increased. The phrase **converging operations** refers to this idea that our understanding of some psychological phenomenon is enhanced when several studies, each using different operational definitions, "converge" on the same basic conclusion. According to Hilgard, metaphysical arguments over the "real" meaning of phenomena in the world could be left to philosophers. Thus, he contended that psychologists mostly ignored the debate over the merits of operationism and its philosophical cousin, logical positivism (Hilgard, 1987, p. 779). For them, the necessity of precisely defined measures came to be taken for granted. To this day, operational definitions are a standard feature of any text in research methodology.

Neobehaviorism

Public enthusiasm for the promise of behaviorism, a recognition of the importance of Pavlov's long series of conditioning studies, and the general acceptance of operationism and logical positivism, along with the emergence of several hard-working and highly creative experimental psychologists, converged in the late 1920s and early 1930s to produce a movement in psychology called **neobehaviorism**. This movement became the dominant one in American experimental psychology, lasting roughly from 1930 to 1960. It was not a unified school of thought by any means; large differences existed between the three examples of neobehaviorism that you are about to study. Nonetheless, there was a certain consensus among the neobehaviorists.

First, all neobehaviorists took for granted the evolutionary assumption of continuity among species. Laws of behavior that apply to one species should apply, at least to a degree that can be calibrated, to other species as well. Consequently, phenomena relevant for human behavior could be examined by using nonhuman subjects in research. For experimental psychology, the result was a dramatic increase in the use of animal subjects for basic research on learning/conditioning during the period 1930–1960. Although said partly tongue-in-cheek during his APA presidential address, Edward Tolman's comment—"I believe that everything important in psychology ... can be investigated in essence through the continued experimental and theoretical analysis of the determiners of rat behavior at a choice-point in a maze" (Tolman, 1938, p. 34)—

FIGURE 11.1 Tolman's bookplate.

reflected the neobehaviorist faith in the lessons to be learned by studying animal behavior. Tolman (1932) even dedicated his most important book to "M.N.A." (Mus Norvegicus Albinus—the white rat), and his bookplate further reflected his research focus (Figure 11.1).

The second belief held in common by neobehaviorists was that learning was central to an understanding of behavior. In simple terms, neobehaviorists leaned heavily toward the nurture end of the nature-nurture continuum, arguing that knowing why people do what they do requires a thorough analysis of the basic principles of how things are learned. This, of course, was one of Watson's guiding principles and the motivation for the Little Albert experiment. The emphasis on learning also provided a bridge between behaviorism and British empiricist thought. When John Locke resurrected the Aristotelian concept of the mind as a blank slate and proclaimed that "experience" was the writer, he was arguing the same point made by Watson when he claimed that fears were the result of learning. For the neobehaviorists, the world in which we live, that is, the environment, shapes our characteristic ways of behaving.

An emphasis on learning was also consistent with American psychology's fixation on practical applications. Watson's appeal with the general public was a result of his genius in showing how the principles of learning could be applied to improve education, child rearing, and sales figures. If we are what we learn, and if learning is the result of specific experiences in certain environments, then by arranging environments in certain ways, behavior can be shaped in any number of productive directions.

It is one thing to herald the importance of learning; it is quite another to know precisely how such learning comes about. Thus, during the era of neobehaviorism, the focus of research and theory was on the manner in which learning occurred. This fundamental issue produced the sharpest divisions among the neobehaviorists, but eventually yielded important knowledge about a variety of learning phenomena. We will examine the ideas of the three most important neobehaviorists: Edward Tolman, Clark Hull, and B. F. Skinner.

EDWARD C. TOLMAN (1886–1959): A PURPOSIVE BEHAVIORISM

Edward Chace Tolman was born into an upper-middle class environment in Newton, Massachusetts, a suburb of Boston. As a youth, he learned the virtues of perseverance and hard work from his father, a successful business executive, and the need for a reflective life with a strong moral foundation from his mother, who had a Quaker background. Although under some pressure to enter the family business, Tolman enrolled at the Massachusetts Institute of Technology (MIT) and graduated in 1911 with a degree in electrochemistry. He did not pursue a career in this field, however, partly because he did not wish to compete with his talented brother, Richard, who had preceded him by five years at MIT (Crutchfield, 1961). Richard Tolman became a well-known physicist who contributed to the development of the atomic bomb during World War II. A second reason for Edward's shift away from physics and chemistry was his discovery of William James during his senior year. *The Principles* gave Tolman's life a new direction.

Immediately following graduation from MIT in 1911, Tolman enrolled in two summer classes at Harvard, a philosophy course and an introductory psychology course, the latter taught by Robert

Yerkes. Yerkes sold him for good on psychology, and he entered graduate school at Harvard, earning his doctorate in 1915. While taking a second course from Yerkes, he worked his way through Watson's *Behavior: An Introduction to Comparative Psychology* (1914), and although he did not become immediately converted to the behaviorist point of view, Tolman saw behaviorism as an attractive alternative to the traditional introspective psychology he was encountering in Hugo Münsterberg's laboratory. As he later put it, he was troubled by the problems with introspection, and the "introduction in Yerkes' course to Watson's behaviorism came as a tremendous stimulus and relief" (Tolman, 1952, p. 326). During his graduate school years, while visiting Germany to prepare for his foreign language competency examination, Tolman met Kurt Koffka and was introduced to gestalt psychology (Chapter 9). The gestalt concept of "wholes" later played an important role in his theorizing about behavior. (Figure 11.2 shows Tolman with Lewin and Koffka at a 1935 meeting of Lewin's Topology Group.) A final important influence on Tolman during his Harvard years was another of his teachers, psychologist Edwin Holt (1873–1946), whose leanings toward behaviorism were infused with the notions of goals and purpose.

FIGURE 11.2   Tolman at a meeting of the Topology group in 1935, with Lewin and Koffka, from Marrow (1969).

Holt believed that Watsonian behaviorism was too reductionistic, that behavior could not be meaningfully reduced to simple physical stimuli and muscular or glandular responses. He argued instead that behavior should be defined more broadly as actions that serve some purpose. That is, behavior is purposive and goal-directed. These ideas would become the core of Tolman's theory of learning.

Tolman taught for three years at Northwestern University during the World War I years. He was dismissed in 1918, allegedly for a lack of teaching skills, but more likely because of his visible antiwar stance (Tolman, 1952). It would not be the first time that his moral convictions, reflecting his mother's Quaker influence, would affect his career.

Tolman joined the faculty at Berkeley in 1918 and remained there for the rest of his academic career. When given an opportunity to develop a new course shortly after his arrival, he remembered "Yerkes' course and Watson's textbook [and] proposed 'comparative psychology.' And it was this that finally launched [him] down the behavioristic slope" (Tolman, 1952, p. 329). The course led to some research in animal maze learning, and Tolman was soon attracting talented graduate students to his laboratory. He began developing his unique form of behaviorism in the early 1920s, publishing articles with titles like "A New Formula for Behaviorism" (Tolman, 1922). His major work, *Purposive Behavior in Animals and Men*, was published in 1932. For the remainder of his career at Berkeley, he continued to develop and revise his system and to generate research support for it.

Tolman's System

Tolman's writings illustrate the complex interplay between empirical research and theorizing in the tradition of logical positivism. A theory makes testable predictions that lead to research, the outcome of which supports or reshapes the theory, which leads to more research, and so on. Because such theories evolve as a consequence of research outcomes, Tolman's theory of learning in 1932, when he produced *Purposive Behavior in Animals and Men*, was different from his theory in 1959, when he con-tributed a chapter ("Principles of Purposive Behavior") to Sigmund Koch's seven-volume series, *Psychology: A Study of a Science*. Nevertheless, there are some constant themes in Tolman's writings. His theories emphasized (a) molar over molecular behavior, (b) the purposiveness or goal-directedness of behavior, and (c) the use of intervening variables.

Molar Versus Molecular Behavior

Taking cues from his gestalt friends and one of his Harvard mentors, Holt, Tolman argued that the unit of study had to be larger than the "molecular" muscle movements, glandular responses, or neurological responses emphasized by Watson. One of Tolman's students, for example, showed that rats taught to swim through a maze were later able to run through it accurately (Macfarlane, 1930). Hence, what was learned could not be simply a series of individual kinesthetic responses. Rather, the animal must come to some general understanding of the pattern of the maze and the behavior needed to be understood in terms of whole response patterns that had meaning beyond the component movements. As a gestaltist would say, the whole behavior is more than the sum of its parts. **Molar behavior**, then, referred to broad patterns of behavior that, as will be seen shortly, were directed at some goal. Tolman provided several examples:

> A rat running a maze; a cat getting out of a puzzle box; a man driving home to dinner; a child hiding from a stranger ...—*these are behaviors* (qua *molar*). And it must be noted that in mentioning no one of them have we referred to, or, we blush to confess it, for the most part have known, what were the exact muscles and glands, sensory nerves, and motor nerves involved. (Tolman, 1932, p. 8, italics in the original)

Tolman called his theory a **field theory** to distinguish it from the more molecular approach of the stimulus-response model, which he likened to a telephone switchboard. Learning did not involve the mere strengthening and weakening of connections between incoming calls (stimulus information) and outgoing ones (motor responses). Instead, he proposed that the brain is more like a "map control room than it is like an old-fashioned telephone exchange" and that during learning, the animal develops a "field map of the environment" (Tolman, 1948, p. 192).

Goal-Directedness

The preceding examples of molar behavior all have another feature: they are directed toward some goal. For Tolman, goal-directedness or **purposiveness** was a universal feature of the behavior that we learn. Although the term "purpose" seems like a return to a subjective, even introspective psychology, Tolman merely meant that behavior "always seems to have the character of getting-to or getting-from a specific goal-object" (1932, p. 10). Tolman was obviously influenced by evolutionary thinking here; goal-directed behavior is adaptive and therefore has survival value for the species. As a term, Tolman used "purposiveness" as descriptive, not causal. That is, it is merely a label for that which can be inferred from an observation of behavior, as when a hungry rat consistently works its way through a maze until food is reached. The causes of such behavior are to be found elsewhere, in the animal's specific learning history and its instinctive behaviors.

Intervening Variables

Tolman deserves credit for introducing a concept that has been widely used in psychology—the intervening variable. Stimulus conditions, or independent variables, are under the direct control of the experimenter; behaviors, or dependent variables, can be measured with precision by the experimenter. **Intervening variables** are hypothetical factors that are not seen directly but are inferred from the manner in which independent and dependent variables are defined. They are assumed to "intervene" between stimulus and behavior, in such a way as to influence learning. For instance, "thirst" is an intervening variable. It is never seen directly, but can be inferred to exist as a consequence of (a) creating some stimulus condition, such as not allowing an animal to drink water for 12 hours, or (b) measuring the completion of some behavior that leads to water, which is consumed by the animal. As you might guess from the earlier discussion, Tolman's intervening variables clearly reflect the influence of logical positivism, with its insistence that abstract, theoreti-

cal terms (i.e., intervening variables) be closely tied to observable events (i.e., stimuli and responses).

Tolman's intervening variables were usually cognitive in nature and followed from his field theory. For example, when exploring a maze, Tolman believed that the rat gradually learned a set of "expectancies" about how the maze was organized. As it would encounter various parts of the maze, it would learn that certain environmental cues (visual, olfactory, tactile, etc.) were associated with certain outcomes. Tolman used the term **sign-gestalt** to refer to learned relationships between these cues and the animal's expectations about what would happen if it chose path A instead of path B. Eventually, the rat developed an overall field map or "cognitive map" of the maze that directed its future goal-oriented behavior. Sign-gestalts, expectancies, and maps are all examples of cognitive intervening variables that decorate Tolman's theory.

Just as the term "purposiveness" strongly implies a subjectivity that seems foreign to behaviorist thinking, so do terms like "expectancy" and "cognitive map." Tolman, however, again reflecting the dictates of logical positivism, carefully tied these cognitive intervening variables to operationally defined stimulus situations and behaviors. That is, he did not believe nor was he interested in whether a rat somehow had a map in its brain. Rather, he inferred the existence of this hypothetical map from the specific stimulus conditions he created and the subsequent behaviors that he observed and measured.

As an example, consider the cognitive intervening variable of expectancy. Tolman believed that one result of learning was that certain expectations were created. Rats finding food at the end of a maze expect to find food there in the future. Furthermore, it is reasonable to assume that they come to expect a particular type of food, an assumption tested in a clever study in Tolman's lab by Elliott (1928). Using the 14-unit T-maze shown in Figure 11.3a, Elliott taught two groups of rats the maze. The experimental group found bran mash in the goal box, whereas the control group found sunflower seeds there. Over the first nine days of the study (i.e., nine trials, one per day), both groups improved, although performance was better for the group fed with bran mash. On the tenth day, Elliott changed the reward for rats in the experi-

FIGURE 11.3 (a) Fourteen-unit multiple T-maze, used by Elliott to study latent learning; (b) Results of Elliott's latent learning study, from Tolman (1932).

(a)

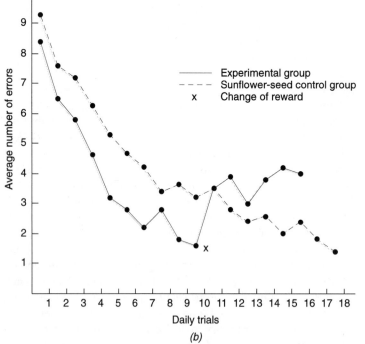

(b)

mental group—they now found sunflower seeds at the goal instead of bran mash. As Figure 11.3b shows, their behavior was disrupted. In Tolman's terms, they had come to expect bran mash; when that expectancy was violated, their behavior changed. In short, expectancy is a process intervening between stimulus and response, but is closely tied to the clearly defined stimulus features of the experiment and the observed and easily measured behaviors.

Tolman's Research Program

Tolman and his students completed dozens of important studies of rats learning mazes. These were reported in a series of *University of California Publications in Psychology* during the 1920s and 1930s, in the *Purposive Behavior* book (1932), and in a famous *Psychological Review* paper entitled "Cognitive Maps in Rats and Men" (1948). The bulk of the research was theory-related, but Tolman also spent considerable time and effort standardizing maze-learning procedures.

In the early 1920s, psychologists were beginning to question the **reliability** of the maze as a research tool. Any measurement is reliable to the extent that repeated measures yield approximately the same results, and the issue was a vital one. Mazes had evolved into a wide variety of shapes and sizes since the days of Willard Small and his adaptation of the Hampton Court design (Chapter 6 Close-Up). Different mazes often produced different outcomes, however, and sometimes even the same maze would yield inconsistent data. In a long series of studies, Tolman and his students (e.g., Tolman & Nyswander, 1927) set out to examine the issue, identify the factors that reduced reliability, and develop a standardized procedure for maze learning that would ensure optimal reliability. On the basis of their research, they recommended that error scores be used rather than time-to-completion scores, that mazes have uniform choice points (e.g., a left-right choice at a "T"), numerous choice points (e.g., a 14-unit T-maze), and gates that closed once an animal had made a correct choice, to prevent retracing. They even developed an automated system for delivering animals from their home cages to the start points of mazes and removing them from the

end points, so as to eliminate the element of human handling of the rats (Tolman, Tryon, & Jeffress, 1929).

Having established procedures for improving the reliability of maze learning data, Tolman and his students focused their attention on the meatier issues related to the evolving learning theory. What follows are descriptions of several of his better known experiments.

Latent Learning

In his studies on latent learning, Tolman attacked the notion that reinforcement was necessary for learning to occur. He believed that food discovered by the rat at the end of the maze did not affect learning directly; it merely influenced the animal's motivation to complete the maze as quickly and accurately as possible. That is, learning needed to be distinguished from performance, and reinforcement affected the latter but not the former. Learning the overall layout of the maze occurred more or less automatically whenever the animal was experiencing the maze, even if no food was to be found in the goal box. Tolman termed the phenomenon **latent learning** because it occurred "below the surface," that is, without being immediately apparent in the animal's performance.

Testing for latent learning required showing that learning occurred even if reinforcement didn't, and Tolman and Honzik (1930) accomplished this by testing three groups of rats (one trial per day) in the same 14-unit T-maze shown in Figure 11.3.a. The first group of rats (no reward or "NR") was never given food reward after completing the maze. The second group ("R") was always rewarded with food. As you can see from Figure 11.4, the error scores for these two groups during the course of just over two weeks was about what you would expect—lots of errors for NR and steady improvement in performance for R. The third group was the key one, however. As suggested by their label—"NR-R"—rats in this group were not rewarded initially (i.e., during the first 10 days), but starting on day 11, they found food in the goal box. Tolman reasoned that if reinforcement was necessary for learning, then no learning would occur on days 1 to 10. Learning would not start until day 11, presumably, and only then would performance gradually begin to improve. That pattern did not happen, though, as is clear from the

FIGURE 11.4 Results of Tolman and Honzik's study of latent learning, from Tolman (1932).

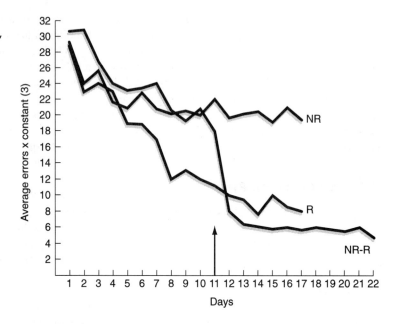

graph. Instead, performance improved *immediately* after day 11. For Tolman, the evidence was clear—the maze was being learned during those first 10 days, even though the learning was not reflected in performance. That is, the learning was "latent," and reinforcement was not needed in order for the learning to occur. As Tolman (1948) put it:

> Interpreting these results anthropomorphically, we would say that as long as the animals were not getting any food at the end of the maze they continued to take their time in going through it—they continued to enter many blinds. Once, however, they knew they were to get food, they demonstrated that during these preceding non-rewarded trials they had learned where many of the blinds were. They had been building up a 'map,' and could utilize the latter as soon as they were motivated to do so. (pp. 194–195)

Which brings us to Tolman's attempts to demonstrate the existence of cognitive maps directly.

Cognitive Maps

As mentioned earlier, Tolman did not believe that rats learned stimulus-response connections when learning a maze. Rather, he argued that they created a **cognitive map** of the maze—an overall knowledge

of the maze's structure and spatial pattern that gave them a general sense of where to go in the maze. A clever pair of studies demonstrated the operation of these maps.[1] In one study (Tolman, Ritchie, & Kalish, 1946a), rats encountered the maze found in Figure 11.5 and were started at either S1 or S2. Some rats, the "response learning" group, always found food by turning to the right. Others, the "place learning" group, always found food in the same place, F1. Tolman, Ritchie, and Kalish (1946a) found that rats in the place learning group learned faster, a result that is of course congenial with Tolman's theory that the rats learn a cognitive map rather than a series of responses to specific stimuli.[2]

---

[1] Tolman's ideas about cognitive maps were similar to those of Karl Lashley (see Chapter 3), and in his "Cognitive Maps in Rats and Men" paper, Tolman specifically referred to Lashley's observation about "a couple of his rats who, after having learned an alley maze, pushed back the cover near the starting box, climbed out and ran directly across the top to the goal-box where they climbed down in again and ate" (Tolman, 1948, p. 203).

[2] "Place" versus "response" learning became a contentious issue, with Tolman's outcome not always replicated, especially by those supportive of Clark Hull's learning theory. Restle (1957) eventually concluded that both types of learning are possible, the outcome depending on whether place or response cues are more dominant in a particular situation.

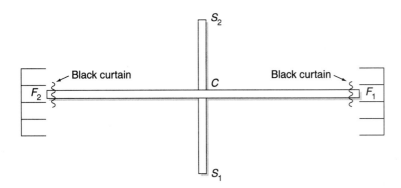

FIGURE 11.5   Maze used in place learning experiment by Tolman, Ritchie, and Kalish (1946a).

In the second study (Tolman, Ritchie, & Kalish 1946b), rats first learned to run the simple maze in Figure 11.6a. Starting at A, they ran across an open circular table to C, the only part of the maze with sidewalls, then eventually to the goal box, G. A light was on at H. There were no errors to be made, so the rats soon learned to move quickly from A to G. After 12 trials, the simple maze was replaced with the one in Figure 11.6b. Now the path down C was blocked and the rats had to choose another route to the food. An S-R behaviorist might expect the rats to choose either 9 or 10, the routes most similar to the original path at C, but Tolman, Ritchie, and Kalish reported that path 6, the best choice to get to the general location of the food, was the most frequently chosen. Tolman (1948) argued that "the rats had ... acquired not merely a strip-map to the effect that the original specifically trained-on path led to food but, rather, a wider comprehensive map to the effect that food was

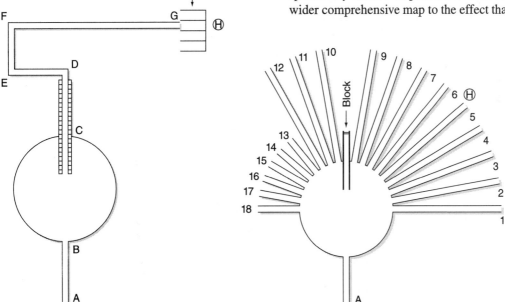

(a) Apparatus used in preliminary training

(b) Apparatus used in the test trial

FIGURE 11.6   (a) Apparatus used in the first phase of Tolman, Ritchie, and Kalish's experiment on the spatial abilities of rats; (b) "Sunburst" apparatus for studying spatial learning, from Tolman (1948).

located in such and such a direction in the room" (p. 204).

Tolman elaborated on this distinction between narrow "strip-maps" and wider "comprehensive maps" in the last section of his 1948 "Cognitive Maps in Rats and Men" paper and tried to show how all of this had relevance for human behavior. According to Tolman, narrow strip-maps, which are maladaptive in the long run, result from too much mindless repetition on the original path, an environment too limited to see the whole picture, and levels of motivation or frustration that are too high. Comprehensive maps are to be preferred. Revealing the idealism and moral sensitivity that were never far from his thoughts, as well as his penchant for viewing the world as a large maze, Tolman (1948) closed his paper with an appeal to the

> ... child-trainers and world-planners [to] see to it that nobody's children are too over-motivated or too frustrated. Only then can these children learn to look before and after, learn to see that there are often round-about and safer paths to their quite proper goals—learn, that is, to realize that the well-beings of White and of Negro, of Catholic and of Protestant, of Christian and of Jew, of American and of Russian (and even of males and females) are mutually interdependent. ...
>
> We must, in short, subject our children and ourselves (as the kindly experimenter would his rats) to the optimal conditions of moderate motivation and of an absence of unnecessary frustrations, whenever we put them and ourselves before that great God-given maze which is our human world. ... (p. 208)

Evaluating Tolman

During the heyday of neobehaviorism, Tolman's research and his theorizing commanded attention, especially from the followers of Clark Hull (soon to come), with whom Tolman disagreed on practically everything except the usefulness of intervening variables and the general precepts of logical positivism. The complexity of his theory contributed to its lack of lasting influence, but Tolman's research program was creative and helped to institutionalize the maze as stan-

dard research apparatus. His students were intensely loyal to him and he in turn treated them as equals. On the other hand, despite their loyalty and devotion, few of Tolman's students continued doing research in "the Tolman tradition" when they left Berkeley. While academia became crowded in the 1940s, 1950s, and 1960s with Hullians and Skinnerians, the "Tolmanian" was a rare creature indeed. Furthermore, Tolman's research with rats in mazes did not produce much in the way of practical application. His plea for training children to have broad cognitive maps, for instance, gave little explicit guidance to parents. Instead of demonstrating the applicability of Tolman's work for everyday problems, the example seemed more like a good illustration of the dangers inherent in extrapolating too far beyond one's data.

Tolman's emphasis on purposiveness and his heavy use of mentalistic variables were both criticized by his contemporaries. Tolman was careful to tie these terms operationally to stimulus conditions and responses, but some critics saw his use of such subjective terms as a step backward. One learning theorist, Edwin Guthrie, complained that Tolman's theory proposed so many intervening cognitive factors that a rat faced with a choice in a maze would be overwhelmed: "In his concern with what goes on in the rat's mind, Tolman has neglected to predict what the rat will do. So far as the theory is concerned the rat is left *buried in thought*" (Guthrie, 1935, p. 172, italics added). The criticism is unfair—Tolman's writings are full of data showing rats doing quite a bit of behaving—but it illustrates the preference of many neobehaviorists for observable action over hypothesized internal states. On the other hand, Tolman's willingness to propose cognitive intervening variables makes him an important link between behaviorism and cognitive psychology (Chapter 14). More specifically, among those studying animal behavior, Tolman's cognitive theory resonates with today's widespread interest in animal cognition. Olton's research on spatial behavior and short-term memory in rats (e.g., Olton, 1979), using a radial maze reminiscent of Tolman's sunburst maze, is an example.

Perhaps Tolman's lasting importance results not from his specific theory of learning but from a set of attitudes and values that he displayed. As a researcher, he was serious about his work and careful in executing it. He was persistent and passionate about developing and supporting his theory. Yet he also had a remarkable sense of perspective that enabled him to be fully absorbed in his research while not taking himself too seriously. He knew that better theories than his were bound to come along and that newer research would supersede his. As he said in one of the last pieces he wrote, published the year he died,

> The system may well not stand up ... But I do not much care. I have liked to think about psychology in ways that have proved congenial to me. Since ... psychology [is] still immersed in such tremendous realms of the uncertain and the unknown, the best that any individual scientist ... can do seems to be to follow his own gleam and his own bent, however inadequate they may be. In fact, I suppose that actually this is what we all do. In the end, the only sure criterion is to have fun. And I have had fun. (Tolman, 1959, p. 152)

In addition to his healthy sense of perspective, Tolman had one other enduring trait—his strong sense of morality. It led him to protest the U.S. involvement in World War I, apparently contributing to his dismissal from Northwestern in 1918. In the midst of World War II, his strong feelings about war resurfaced, this time motivating him to write *Drives Toward War* (1942), in which he combined some of his ideas with those of Freud to explain what leads to warfare and to make some recommendations to eliminate the problem. One of his suggestions, which he granted was unlikely to occur, was the creation of a "World-Federation" that would replace nationalist boundaries and encourage cooperation among the peoples of the world rather than competition. The histories of the League of Nations and of the United Nations have made it clear just how difficult it is to overcome nationalist sentiment.

Near the end of his active career, Tolman's convictions faced a final test. In the early 1950s, America was at the beginning of the so-called cold war, its long ideological struggle with the Soviet Union. The Soviets' expressed desire to spread the gospel of Marxist/Leninist doctrine created images of one country after another being subverted and falling

(like dominoes) into Communist hands. Holding the line against Communism meant defending South Korea in the 1950s and South Vietnam in the 1960s.

It was also feared that Communists would infiltrate the United States, corrupt its youth, and eventually take over the country. These fears were fueled by an obscure Wisconsin senator, Joseph McCarthy, who claimed to know of Communists who had infiltrated the government. Senate hearings, laced with rumor and innuendo, ruined the careers of anyone who was merely accused of being a "Red." McCarthy also hinted that Communists were infiltrating the film industry (dangerous because movies influence attitudes) and higher education (even greater influence).

In this climate, professors at California universities were told by those running the university system to sign oaths of loyalty to the United States and to declare that they were not members of the Communist Party. Professors were told to sign the pledge or resign. As a senior faculty member at Berkeley and by then one of America's leading experimental psychologists, Tolman could easily have left Berkeley and been welcomed anywhere. He courageously refused to sign the oath, however, on the general principle that it violated the First Amendment's right of free speech. And out of concern for younger, more vulnerable (i.e., not tenured) faculty members, he also refused to leave Berkeley. Rather, he led a fight that successfully repealed the oath in California and preserved the concept of academic freedom. In 1957, Tolman received the Distinguished Scientific Contribution Award from the APA, and just before his death in 1959, the Board of Regents of the University of California recognized the significance of his fight for academic freedom by awarding him an honorary degree (Crutchfield, 1961).

CLARK HULL (1884–1952): A HYPOTHETICO-DEDUCTIVE SYSTEM

The life and career of Clark Leonard Hull is a case study in how perseverance and hard work can overcome seemingly insurmountable odds. Born into poverty in a log cabin on a farm in New York, raised on a "good but unimproved" farm in Michigan, and educated in a one-room schoolhouse, Hull grew up under "pioneer conditions" (Hull, 1952, p. 143). In addition to these trying circumstances, he almost died from typhoid fever just before starting college, and after his second year at Alma College, a small Presbyterian school in Michigan, he contracted polio, which left him partially paralyzed at age 24. At the time, he was aiming for a life as a mining engineer, but the polio made it impossible for him to meet the physical demands of that career.

After spending a year at home, during which he regained some degree of health, he decided on a career in psychology. Why psychology? In his words, he was searching for a field related to philosophy that would involve theoretical work, and "one which was new enough to permit rapid growth so that a young man would not need to wait for his predecessors to die before his work could find recognition, and ... would provide an opportunity to design and work with automatic apparatus" (Hull, 1952b, p. 145). The quote reveals two of Hull's enduring features: his strong ambition and his talent with the design and construction of experimental apparatus. The latter first manifested itself during the polio episode, when Hull designed his own leg brace.

Following two years of high school teaching and a marriage, Hull entered the University of Michigan. His most memorable experience was a yearlong course in experimental psychology, taught jointly by John Shepard, who had studied briefly with Watson, and Walter Pillsbury, a doctoral student of Titchener's. More teaching followed graduation, this time at a Normal School in Kentucky. Hull then applied to graduate school and was rejected at Cornell and Yale, but taken in at the University of Wisconsin, where he earned a Ph.D. under the tutelage of Joseph Jastrow, a former Johns Hopkins student of G. Stanley Hall's.

Doctoral dissertations often find their way into the far reaches of filing cabinets, but Hull's (1920) eventually became a well-known study of the processes involved in learning new concepts.[3] For stimuli, Hull used Chinese characters, including the ones in Figure 11.7. Notice that the characters in each row have a common feature, called a "radical." Hull's subjects had to learn to associate a nonsense sound with each radical (e.g., "oo" for the radical that looks like a large check mark). Over the course of several sets ("packs") of stimuli, subjects learned to look at a character and give the correct nonsense sound; eventually they could identify stimuli they had not seen before. There were a number of findings in the study, but the one that impressed Hull the most was the shape of the learning curve—performance improved gradually but steadily. The idea of learning being the result of a gradual increase in "habit strength" eventually became a salient feature of Hull's learning theory.

Hull completed the doctorate in 1918 at age 34, and remained at Wisconsin for another decade. While there he developed two very different interests, both resulting from courses that he taught. Early in his career, he was asked to teach a course in psychological testing. Although he knew little about testing, the subject interested him, especially the mathematics involved in test validation. He immersed himself in the literature of testing, especially that aspect of it concerning tests for vocational guidance, and within a few years produced an authoritative text called *Aptitude Testing* (Hull, 1928). Displaying his mechanical aptitude again, he built a machine to automatically calculate correlations. This saved him the tedium of calculating by hand the numerous correlations (e.g., between test scores and some measure of performance) needed to validate tests. The machine was delicate, however, a problem that prevented widespread use.[4]

Shortly after Hull began teaching the testing course, he was assigned a section of introductory psychology being taught to premedical students. Because he believed that suggestion and physician authority influenced the outcome of many medical treatments, he decided to incorporate the topic into

---

[3] The study was initially ignored by other researchers, which discouraged Hull greatly. However, a brief description of it appeared in a popular general psychology text in the late 1920s, and due to the tendencies of textbook authors to borrow from each other, it became increasingly cited thereafter (Hilgard, 1987).

[4] In a diary entry after traveling by train with Hull to a conference in 1928, Walter Miles of Stanford reported that Hull had built three of the machines but "they are hard to keep in shape and [he] will not send one far away." Consequently, an order that Miles had placed for one had to be canceled (Miles, 1928).

Six of the Chinese radicals that Hull used are shown here. First, the subject was shown a Chinese character and guessed its "name" (for example, oo), then the experimenter gave the correct name, and so on. Characters with the same radicals always were given the same name so that after going through several packs of characters, the subjects improved their performances and were eventually able to correctly name characters they had never seen before.

From Hull (1920)

FIGURE 11.7 Chinese characters used as stimulus materials in Hull's doctoral dissertation on concepts learning, from Hull (1920).

his lectures. This led him to his second interest, hypnosis, and to the understatement that "the subject has largely tended to attract experimenters with a peculiarly unscientific type of approach" (Hull, 1952b, p. 152). Determined to correct the problem, Hull spent about 10 years examining the phenomenon systematically, eventually producing *Hypnosis and Suggestibility: An Experimental Approach* (Hull, 1933). He concluded that hypnosis was a state of hypersuggestibility and a reduction in analytical thought, brought on by hypnotically induced relaxation. He believed that hypnosis was not qualitatively different from normal consciousness, but only differed in degree. Thus, given the proper instructions,

the various hypnotic phenomena (e.g., pain reduction) could be demonstrated in nonhypnotized subjects. Hull also believed that the medical community overestimated the therapeutic value of hypnosis. For example, he found that, contrary to the medical community's widely held belief, memory was not notably improved by hypnosis.

Although working primarily on aptitude testing and hypnosis in the 1920s, Hull did not lose sight of his dissertation topic of learning. Indeed, while Hull's interests in aptitude testing, hypnosis, and learning are often portrayed as three distinct periods in his life, they were intertwined and all three reflected Hull's systematic, analytic approach to research (Triplett, 1982). During the 1920s, Hull was well aware of Watson's writings and was familiar with the research being done by Tolman. Learning became the primary focus of his life, however, after he read the translations of Pavlov's research in the late 1920s. The topic captured his full attention soon after 1929, the year he left Wisconsin to undertake (at age 45) a major new challenge at Yale University.

When he arrived as president of Yale University in 1921, James Angell, one of the leaders of the original Chicago functionalist group (Chapter 7), found that psychology at Yale could only be described as moribund. The psychologists were still part of the philosophy department, virtually no research was being done, and only eight psychology doctorates had been awarded between 1903 and 1921, compared with 46 at Columbia and 51 at Chicago (Morawski, 1986). With the aid of Robert Yerkes, Angell established the Institute of Psychology in 1924. Generous funding from the Laura Spelman Rockefeller Memorial, headed by a psychologist with close ties to both Yerkes and Angell, enabled the Institute to recruit first-class researchers and equip laboratories. In 1929, the Institute expanded into the multidisciplinary Institute of Human Relations (IHR), which had as its lofty goal "to correlate knowledge and coordinate technique in related fields that greater progress may be made in the understanding of human life" (Angell, 1929, cited in Morawski, 1986, p. 219). It was composed of Yale professors taken from a range of disciplines, including psychology, law, sociology, anthropology, and economics; their teaching duties at Yale were reduced to a minimum in order for them to devote the bulk of their time to the Institute. One of the Yale psychologists assigned to IHR was Clark Hull, who had just been recruited from Wisconsin for the now-defunct Institute of Psychology. Hull spent the rest of his career at Yale, dying of a second heart attack just three weeks from retirement. While there, he developed his theory of learning, tested it extensively in the laboratory, and created a small army of "Hullians," students (and their students) and colleagues who extended the research program far beyond New Haven. The best known was Kenneth Spence (1907–1967), who got to know Hull while

studying at Yale with Yerkes. Spence made contributions significant enough for Hull's theory to become known as the Hull-Spence theory among devotees. At the University of Iowa, Spence perpetuated the Hullian legacy by producing no fewer than 73 Ph.D. students between 1940 and 1963 (Hilgard, 1967).

Hull's System

One of Hull's heroes was Sir Isaac Newton. He kept a copy of Newton's *Principia* on his desk, and he urged graduate students to read it so they would understand that Hull's approach to psychological research mirrored Newton's approach to physics. Newton viewed the universe as a giant machine controlled by precise mathematical laws; Hull thought of humans in the same mechanical fashion. Indeed, he believed that an ultimate understanding of human behavior could only occur if a machine could be built that would be indistinguishable from a human. The attitude was undoubtedly influenced by Hull's own highly developed skill as a machine builder.

Newton also affected Hull's beliefs about progress in science and the importance of theory. For Hull, science proceeded by developing sophisticated theories, then testing them, modifying them, testing the revisions, and so on. This system, also used by Tolman and consistent with the dictates of logical positivism, is called a **hypothetico-deductive system**. At the core of this type of theory of human behavior is a set of postulates: These are statements about behavior based on accumulated knowledge from research and logic that are assumed to be true, but cannot be tested directly. From these postulates specific theorems can be logically deduced, however, and these lead directly to experiments. The results of these experiments support or fail to support the theorems, which in turn strengthen or weaken the basic theory and eventually modify its postulates. Consequently, the theory evolves over time on the basis of empirical support or nonsupport.

In addition to emulating Newton, Hull was also motivated to develop his theory by what he saw as a relative absence of systematic theory building among American psychologists, compared to the extensive work on theory compiled by the gestaltists

(Mills, 1988). It was time for American psychology to catch up. As Hull put it,

> ... these Gestalt people are so terrifyingly articulate. Practically every one of them writes several books. The result is that whereas they constitute a rather small proportion of the psychological population of this country, they have written ten times as much in the field of theory as Americans have. (Hull, 1942, quoted in Mills, 1988, p. 393)

Hull worked on the theory right up to his death, and the final account of it, *A Behavior System* (1952a), appeared posthumously. The best-known version of the system, however, can be found in *Principles of Behavior* (1943); it includes a set of 16 postulates, presented both verbally and mathematically, along with descriptions of research supporting the theory. A complete description of Hull's theory is well beyond the scope of this chapter segment, but some insight can be gained from an examination of his most famous postulate, number 4.

Postulate 4: Habit Strength

Postulate 4 reveals the core of Hull's belief about the conditions necessary for learning to occur. It also illustrates the extent to which Hull aimed for theoretical precision and formality—*Principles of Behavior* was not meant to be light reading. Here is how Hull stated the first part of the fourth postulate:

> Whenever an effector activity ($r \rightarrow R$) and a receptor activity ($S \rightarrow s$) occur in close temporal contiguity ($_sC_r$), and this $_sC_r$ is closely associated with the diminution of a need (G) or with a stimulus which has been closely and consistently associated with the diminution of a need (G), there will result an increment to a tendency (Δ_sH_R) for that afferent impulse on later occasions to evoke that reaction. The increments from successive reinforcements summate in a manner which yields a combined habit strength ($_sH_R$) which is a simple positive growth function of the number of reinforcements (N). ... (Hull, 1943, p. 178)

The key elements here are contiguity and reinforcement. According to Hull, learning occurs when there is a close contiguity between stimulus and response. A rat learns to associate a location X in a maze, for instance, with the response "turn right." Contiguity is necessary, but it is not sufficient, however. In addition, reinforcement must be present for learning to occur. Reinforcers for Hull were stimuli that reduce drives; food reduces hunger, for example. Together, S-R contiguity and reinforcement gradually increase $_sH_R$, or **habit strength**. Thus, by repeatedly reaching X, turning right, and finding food, the rat accumulates habit strength with each reinforced trial. To learn is to increase $_sH_R$. That learning is incremental rather than sudden echoes the results of Hull's dissertation on concept learning. The importance to Hull of the ideas in postulate 4 may be inferred from Figure 11.8, a portrait completed late in Hull's career. The graph in the background is an idealized learning curve in which habit strength increases as a function of the number of reinforced trials.

For Hull, then, reinforcement was defined in terms of drive reduction ("diminution of a need"), and his theory is sometimes known as a **drive reduction** theory. Primary drives are those connected directly with survival, and they can be reduced with **primary reinforcers** like food and water. But Hull also described **secondary reinforcers**, stimuli he described in postulate 4 as those that have been associated with primary reinforcers. A tone that has been paired with the primary reinforcer of food can itself become a reinforcer, for instance.

FIGURE 11.8 Portrait of Clark Hull, from Popplestone and McPherson (1994).

Reaction Potential

Although Hull rejected the type of intervening variables used by Tolman, he acknowledged that he borrowed the concept from his fellow neobehaviorist (Hull, 1943, p. 31). An important intervening variable for Hull was what he called **reaction potential**, or $_SE_R$. Introduced in postulate 7, $_SE_R$ refers to the probability ("potential") that a response ("reaction") will occur at a given time, and can be inferred from several kinds of measurable behaviors (e.g., response latency, how long it takes an animal to respond in a particular situation—when reaction potential was high, latency was brief). Hull believed that $_SE_R$ was influenced by several factors, with drive and habit strength being the most important. That is, a response will be most likely to occur if both habit strength and drive are high. And Hull argued that the relationship was multiplicative ($_SE_R = D \times {_SH_R}$) rather than additive. Thus, if either drive or habit strength is zero, the response won't occur. Rats will run a maze correctly only if they are motivated (e.g., hungry) and if they have a sufficient number of reinforced trials under their belts. Figure 11.9a shows how Hull envisioned the theoretical effects of drive and habit strength (i.e., number of reinforced trials) on reaction potential. For empirical support, Hull included data from two studies (Perin, 1942; Williams, 1938) and combined them to form Figure 11.9b.

Evaluating Hull

Throughout the 1940s and into the early 1950s, Clark Hull was arguably the dominant research psychologist in America. His work was cited more often than that of any other psychologist (far more frequently than Tolman's work), and his students (and their students) spread the Hullian gospel far and wide. Between 1941 and 1950, for example, approximately 70% of all research articles published in the areas of learning and motivation referred to and referenced Hull's work (Spence, 1952). For the psychologists of Hull's era, his theory met the need for a clear direction into the future. Introspective psychology had met its demise in the 1920s, but there was nothing to replace it. Watsonian behaviorism appeared, but so did gestalt psychology, Freudianism, mental testing, and a host of other variants. Searching for maturity and respectability as a science, psychologists seized on what appeared to be just the kind of formalized theory that characterized the older sciences, especially physics.

Paradoxically, today's college students not only fail to appreciate Hull's stature, they seldom even recognize his name. Hull's rise and fall is illustrated by an analysis done by Guttman (1977). He examined the reference sections of all of the articles published in the *Journal of Experimental Psychology* in 1940, 1950, 1960, and 1970, counting up the number of references to the work of Hull or his best-known collaborator, Spence. For those four years, respectively, the percentages of articles citing Hull and/or Spence were 4%, 39%, 24%, and 4%.

There are several reasons for the collapse of Hull's theory. For one thing, it was overambitious, attempting to build a theory of extraordinary complexity and mathematical precision on what turned out to be a very narrow empirical base—the behavior of simple organisms in artificial, highly controlled, simple environments. Hullians countered that other sciences do the same thing; biologists, for instance, use isolated tissue cultures to study cellular processes, even though those cultures are "artificial" relative to real-life biological environments. Also, Hull was planning a major work that extended his system to complex human behavior, but was never able to get very far with it before his death. On the other hand, several of his students, along with other members of Yale's IHR, did manage to combine Hullian and Freudian ideas into a testable theory of aggression. In *Frustration and Aggression* (Dollard, Doob, Miller, Mowrer, & Sears, 1939), Hull's students developed the well-known frustration-aggression hypothesis and tested it with both animal subjects and children. The same group later produced *Social Learning and Imitation* (Miller & Dollard, 1941), which launched modern social learning theory.

Another criticism of Hull's theory was that it overlooked the very human nature of research. Consistent with his underlying assumption of human as machine and developed in the context of logical positivism, Hull took it for granted that disputes over the empirical support for the theory would be

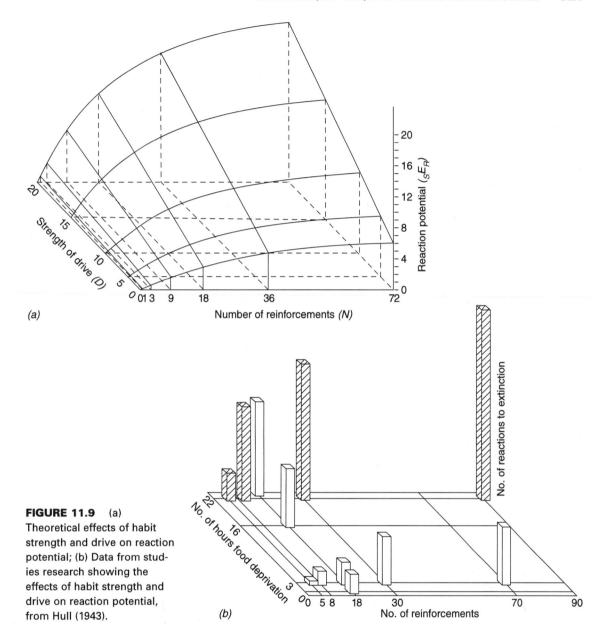

FIGURE 11.9 (a) Theoretical effects of habit strength and drive on reaction potential; (b) Data from studies research showing the effects of habit strength and drive on reaction potential, from Hull (1943).

resolved by dispassionate and completely objective scientists listening to their data. There was faith that "crucial experiments" would decide the "truth" of some issue, but contentious issues never seemed to go away. For example, during the 1930s and 1940s Hull and Tolman engaged in a series of skirmishes over the nature of learning. Tolman's group would produce a study that seemed to refute some aspect of Hull's theory; Hull's group would then rush to the barricades and produce some data that seemed to explain away Tolman's results while simultaneously maintaining the Hullian model. Followers of each theorist felt they had the data on their side; to those outside both camps, it appeared that little was resolved. Furthermore, the failure to settle these disputes about learning contributed to the growing suspicion that behaviorism was flawed as a system, and questions about the adequacy of behaviorism contributed to the development of cognitive psychology in the 1960s (Segal & Lachman, 1972), as will be seen in Chapter 13.

Although Hull's theory might not have survived, his positivist approach to research remains. There might not be many Hullians out there trying to prop up postulate 4 anymore; nonetheless there is a legacy of programmatic research being maintained by Hull's intellectual descendants. In graduate schools of experimental psychology, they are taught to do research systematically; that is, they learn to derive testable hypotheses from working theories, to define terms operationally, to collect data bearing on the hypotheses, and to adjust the theory based on the empirical outcome. The theories are no longer as formal or as mathematical as Hull's, but the same kind of thinking occurs.

One final problem for Hull was also shared by Tolman and was perhaps the most important reason why all three men faded into relative obscurity in the latter half of the twentieth century. The problem was the rising star of B. F. Skinner, who combined the brashness and entrepreneurial spirit of John Watson with the scientific creativity, work ethic, and ability to attract talented students to match Tolman or Hull.

B. F. SKINNER (1904–1990): A RADICAL BEHAVIORISM

Burrhus Frederick Skinner was a product of small-town America (Susquehanna, Pennsylvania) during the Progressive era. He grew up at a time when optimism within the emerging white middle class was high in America—the country had just emerged from difficult economic times in the 1890s, and it had just beaten the overmatched Spanish in the Spanish-American War. The president, Theodore Roosevelt, was the dashing hero of the war and the youngest man ever to hold the office at that time. Parents,

unless poor and/or nonwhite, had every reason to expect great opportunities for their children. Skinner's father was a moderately successful lawyer; his mother stayed at home and cultivated in young Fred the Protestant values of hard work and a constant concern about "what other people might think."

Hard work indeed characterized Skinner's life, but concern about what others thought of his behavior did not become one of his enduring features. On the contrary, independent thinking and an unwillingness to accept the "wisdom of elders" unless accompanied by sound evidence was more his style. It emerged early: his high school principal wrote him a strong recommendation to New York's Hamilton College, but cautioned that young Fred was "passionately fond of arguing with his teachers. He is quite a reader and although I do not think he actually supposes himself wiser than his teachers, I have found him [to give] that impression." (cited in Bjork, 1993, p. 28).

Skinner was initially unhappy in the fraternity/sorority-dominated atmosphere of Hamilton, but he soon found his niche and developed a passion for creative writing. He even sent some short stories to the poet Robert Frost, whom he had met at a writers' conference. Frost's high praise led to a career decision. Determined to be a famous writer, Skinner informed his parents that he wished to take a year off after his 1926 graduation and simply write. This of course created problems for Skinner's parents, who were naturally concerned about what people would think of the new college graduate who was living at home but did not seem to have an actual job. It's not hard to imagine the pressure he felt from his parents to be productive ("And what did you write today, Fred?"), and as the year passed he also had a growing sense that he would never match the achievements of the famous writers whose works he was reading. Although Skinner later referred to this time as his "Dark Year," some of what he read started a sequence of events that eventually led to graduate studies in psychology at Harvard. For instance, during this time he read a number of popular articles on behaviorism, and this led him to Watson and Pavlov. He became intrigued by behaviorism and in the fall of 1928, he was off to Cambridge, Massachusetts.

Figure 11.10 shows Skinner working in the Harvard laboratory two years later.

Skinner developed his system of behaviorism while at Harvard, first as a graduate student, then as a prestigious University Fellow. There was no noticeable change in his general attitude toward authority. He was not impressed by the work of E. G. Boring, the head of the laboratory and as we have seen, Titchener's best-known student and psychology's most famous historian. He referred to Boring's perception course as "simply painful" (Skinner, 1979, p. 47) and lamented that Boring spent three entire lectures explaining a single visual illusion. Boring, in turn, was not inclined toward behaviorism and removed himself from Skinner's doctoral committee. During the defense of his doctoral dissertation, when the noted personality theorist Gordon Allport asked him to describe what he thought to be the shortcomings of behaviorism, Skinner replied that he could think of none (p. 75).

Skinner's first book, *The Behavior of Organisms* (1938), summarized his eight years of research at Harvard. After nine years at the University of Minnesota and another three chairing the psychology department at Indiana University, Skinner returned to Harvard in 1948, where he remained active, even after his retirement in 1974. Just eight days before his death from leukemia in 1990, he addressed the opening session of the APA's annual meeting in Boston. I was in the audience that evening and recall that he needed assistance (from his daughter) getting on stage and walking to the

FIGURE 11.10   B. F. Skinner as a graduate student at Harvard in 1930, from Malone (1991).

podium, but once there he barely glanced at his notes while delivering an articulate and impassioned plea for his brand of behaviorism and an attack on what he viewed as the misguided efforts of cognitive psychologists. The talk was published shortly after Skinner's death as "Can Psychology Be a Science of the Mind?" (Skinner, 1990).

ORIGINAL SOURCE EXCERPT
Skinner and Operant Conditioning:
An Experimental Analysis of Behavior

Skinner believed that psychology should have but two goals—the prediction and control of behavior, both nonhuman and human. This could be accomplished through an "experimental analysis of behavior," that is, a full description of behaviors (e.g., key pecking by a pigeon), the environments in which these behaviors occurred (e.g., a small lighted chamber, a key to be pecked, and a retractable food tray—an apparatus that has come to be called the Skinner box—see Figure 11.11), and the immediate consequences of the behaviors (e.g., food reinforcement for key pecking). The analysis applied equally well to humans, he believed (e.g., tantrum behavior occurring in a toy store environment resulting in the consequence of getting a toy). While recognizing that behaviors are influenced by an individual's innate behavioral tendencies and capabilities, Skinner focused on how behaviors were shaped by the environment. In that sense, then, he made contact with the environmentalism of Watson and illustrated neobehaviorism's emphasis on the centrality of learning.

The best summary of operant conditioning in Skinner's words is to be found in a text he wrote in 1953 called *Science and Human Behavior*. The following excerpt includes material from Chapters 5 (Operant Behavior), 6 (Shaping and Maintaining Operant Behavior), and 7 (Operant Discrimination). In Chapter 4,

FIGURE 11.11   Skinner box for pigeons (there is also a smaller version for rats, featuring a bar to be pressed instead of a key to be pecked).

Skinner described Pavlovian conditioning, the conditioning of reflexes. In Chapter 5, he opened by distinguishing these conditioned reflexes from "operant" behavior:

> Reflexes, conditioned or otherwise, are mainly concerned with the internal physiology of the organism. We are most often interested, however, in behavior which has some effect upon the surrounding world. Such behavior raises most of the practical problems in human affairs and is also of particular theoretical interest because of its special characteristics. The consequences of behavior may 'feed back' into the organism. When they do so, they may change the probability that the behavior which produced them will occur again. The English language contains many words, such as 'reward' and 'punishment,' which refer to this effect, but we can get a clear picture of it only through experimental analysis. (p. 59)

Skinner then credited Thorndike with being among the first "to study changes brought about by the consequences of behavior" (p. 59), and went on to describe a simple **operant conditioning** situation for a pigeon isolated in an experimental chamber:

> To study the process which Thorndike called stamping in, we must have a 'consequence.' Giving food to a hungry organism will do. ...
>
> We select a relatively simple bit of behavior which may be freely and rapidly repeated, and which is easily observed and recorded. If our experimental subject is a pigeon, for example, the behavior of raising the head above a given height is convenient. This may be observed by sighting across the pigeon's head at a scale pinned on the far wall of the box. We first study the height at which the head is normally held and select some line on the scale which is reached only infrequently. Keeping our eye on the scale we then begin to open the food tray very quickly whenever the head rises above the line. If the experiment is conducted according to specifications, the result is inevitable: we observe an immediate change in the frequency with which the

head crosses the line... . We may advance almost immediately to a higher line in determining when food is to be presented. In a minute or two, the bird's posture has changed so that the top of the head seldom falls below the line which we first chose. ...

A response which has already occurred cannot, of course, be predicted or controlled. We can only predict that *similar* responses will occur in the future. The unit of a predictive science is, therefore, not a response but a class of responses. The word 'operant' will be used to describe this class. The term emphasizes the fact that the behavior operates upon the environment to generate consequences. ... The term will be used both as an adjective (operant behavior) and as a noun to designate the behavior defined by a given consequence.

A single instance in which a pigeon raises its head is a *response*. It is a bit of history which may be reported in any frame of reference we wish to use. The behavior called 'raising the head,' regardless of when specific instances occur, is an *operant*. (pp. 63–65, italics in the original)

In this simple case, then, an animal is observed and when it raises its head above a certain height, it receives food immediately. As a result, head-raising behavior increases in frequency. Skinner chose the term **operant** to describe this head-raising activity because the behavior "operates" on the environment—when it happens, it produces a predictable outcome for the pigeon (i.e., food arrives). The behavior has been changed by the reinforcing consequences. The head-raising behavior can also be made to disappear through **extinction**:

When reinforcement is no longer forthcoming, a response becomes less and less frequent in what is called 'operant extinction.' If food is withheld, the pigeon will eventually stop lifting its head. In general when we engage in behavior which no longer 'pays off,' we find ourselves less inclined to behave in that way again. If we lose a fountain pen, we reach less and less often into the pocket which formerly held it. (p. 71)

So a behavior can be conditioned to occur more frequently if it is reinforced, and its frequency will decline if reinforcement is withheld. But what defines a **reinforcer**? Answer—it depends, and it is also necessary to distinguish between *positive* reinforcers and *negative* reinforcers.

The only way to tell whether or not a given event is reinforcing to a given organism is to make a direct test. We observe the frequency of a selected response, then make an event contingent upon it and observe any change in frequency. If there is a change, we classify the event as reinforcing to the organism under the existing conditions. ...

Events which are found to be reinforcing are of two sorts. Some reinforcements consist in *presenting* stimuli, of adding something—for example, food, water, or sexual contact—to the situation. These we call *positive* reinforcers. Others consist of removing something—for example, a loud noise, a very bright light, extreme cold or heat, or electric shock—from the situation. These we call *negative* reinforcers. In both cases the effect is the same—the probability of response is increased. (p. 73, italics in the original)

In the example of a pigeon being conditioned to raise its head more frequently, the operant behavior (head raising) was a fairly typical behavior for pigeons. All that the researcher had to do was wait for a head raise and reinforce it. But what about the creation of a new behavior, one that seldom occurs? Here the researcher would have a long wait before the desired operant would occur. The answer is in the concept of **shaping**, described by Skinner in Chapter 6:

> Operant conditioning shapes behavior as a sculptor shapes a lump of clay. Although at some point the sculptor seems to have produced an entirely novel object, we can always follow the process back to the original undifferentiated lump, and we can make the successive stages by which we return to this condition as small as we wish. At no point does anything emerge which is very different from what preceded it. The final product seems to have a special unity or integrity of design, but we cannot find a point at which this suddenly appears. In the same sense, an operant is not something which appears full grown in the behavior of the organism. It is the result of a continuous shaping process.
>
> ... In the pigeon, the response of pecking at a spot on the wall of the experimental box seems to differ from stretching the neck because no other behavior of the pigeon resembles it. ... To get the pigeon to peck the spot as quickly as possible we proceed as follows: We first give the bird food when it turns slightly in the direction of the spot from any part of the cage. This increases the frequency of such behavior. We then withhold reinforcement until a slight movement is made toward the spot. This again alters the general distribution of behavior without producing a new unit. We continue by reinforcing positions closer to the spot, then by reinforcing only when the head is moved slightly forward, and finally only when the beak actually makes contact with the spot. ... The original probability of the response in its final form is very low; in some cases it may even be zero. In this way we can build complicated operants which would never appear in the repertoire of the organism otherwise. By reinforcing a series of successive approximations, we bring a rare response to a very high probability in a short time. This [shaping] is an effective procedure because it recognizes and utilizes the continuous nature of a complex act. The total act of turning toward the spot from any point in the box, walking toward it, raising the head, and striking the spot may seem to be a functionally coherent unit of behavior; but it is constructed by a continual process of differential reinforcement from undifferentiated behavior, just as the sculptor shapes his figure from a lump of clay. (pp. 91–93)

Skinner called his Chapter 6 "Shaping and Maintaining Behavior." After a behavior has been shaped through operant conditioning procedures, is it necessary to keep reinforcing the behavior all the time in order to maintain it? For Skinner, the answer was no, and his work on what he called **schedules of reinforcement** was perhaps his greatest research contribution, culminating in the massive 739-page *Schedules of Reinforcement* (Ferster & Skinner, 1957). The book is essentially an atlas of dozens of different kinds of reinforcement schedules, each accompanied by graphs ("cumulative records") portraying behavior—921 of them (!). In *Science and Human Behavior*, Skinner introduced the topic of schedules and described two basic ones:

> It is important to distinguish between schedules which are arranged by a system outside the organism and those which are controlled by the behavior itself. An example of the first is a schedule of reinforcement which is determined by a clock—as when we reinforce a pigeon every five minutes, allowing all intervening responses to go unreinforced. An example of the second is a schedule in which a response is reinforced after a certain number of responses have been emitted—as when we reinforce every fiftieth response the pigeon makes. The cases are similar in the sense that we reinforce intermittently in both, but subtle differences in the contingencies lead to very different results, often of great practical significance. (p. 99)

These two varieties of reinforcement schedules are known as interval and ratio schedules, respectively, and both types can be "fixed" or "variable." This produces four varieties of reinforcement schedule—fixed interval, variable interval, fixed ratio, and variable ratio—and each variety produces a different pattern of behavior. As you might recall from general psychology, in the chapter on learning:

Fixed Interval:
- behavior reinforced after fixed periods of time
- produces high rate of behavior just prior to the end of the interval and a low rate at the start of an interval

Variable Interval:
- behavior reinforced after periods of time that vary from trial to trial
- produces a relatively slow but steady rate of behavior

Fixed Ratio:
- behavior reinforced after a fixed number of responses
- produces a high rate of behavior

Variable Ratio:
- behavior reinforced after a number of responses that varies from trial to trial
- produces a very high rate of behavior

Operant behavior is shaped and maintained through the reinforcement, often administered intermittently on a schedule, but behavior also comes under the control of the environment. **Stimulus control** is a key operant concept, elaborated in Chapter 6 of *Science and Human Behavior*. Skinner started with an important distinction between elicited and emitted behavior, referring back to the original head-raising experiment with pigeons:

> Operant conditioning may be described without mentioning any stimulus which acts before the response is made. In reinforcing neck-stretching in the pigeon it was necessary to wait for the stretching to occur; we did not elicit it. ... Stimuli are always acting on an organism, but their functional connection with operant behavior is not like that in a reflex. Operant behavior, in short, is *emitted*, rather than *elicited*. ...
>
> Most operant behavior, however, acquires important connections with the surrounding world. We may show how it does so in our pigeon experiment by

reinforcing neck-stretching when a signal light is on and allowing it to be extinguished when the light is off. Eventually stretching occurs only when the light is on. We can then demonstrate a stimulus-response connection which is roughly comparable to a conditioned or unconditioned reflex: the appearance of the light will be quickly followed by an upward movement of the head. But the relation is fundamentally different. It has a different history and different current properties. We describe the contingency by saying that a *stimulus* (the light) is the occasion upon which a *response* (stretching the neck) is followed by *reinforcement* (with food). We must specify all three terms. The effect upon the pigeon is that eventually the response is more likely to occur when the light is on. The process through which this comes about is called *discrimination*. Its importance in a theoretical analysis, as well as in the practical control of behavior, is obvious: when a discrimination has been established, we may alter the probability of a response instantly by presenting or removing the discriminative stimulus. (pp. 107–108, italics in the original)

At the beginning of this excerpt, I mentioned that Skinner believed psychology should have just two goals—the prediction and control of behavior. From his own words, you can get a sense of what he meant. If we can understand the contingencies of behavior—the environment in which a behavior has resulted in predictable consequences, then we are in a position to predict and control. If a pigeon has been reinforced for head-raising whenever the light is on, we can (a) predict head-raising with the light and no movement without the lights and (b) control the behavior by turning the light on or off.

This is but a small sample of Skinner's writing from a fairly large book (449 pages). I have chosen to excerpt passages describing some of Skinner's fundamental ideas, but the book also ranges far and wide, as is evident from some of the other chapter titles: "Aversion, Avoidance, Anxiety," "The Self," "Religion," and "Designing a Culture." This last example is part of a three chapter closing section collectively labeled "The Control of Human Behavior" by Skinner, and it shows that fairly early in his career, he was thinking far beyond the Skinner box into the realm of how his ideas applied to life. More on this issue shortly.

Skinner and the Problem of Explanation

We have learned that both Tolman and Hull felt it necessary to propose the existence of intervening variables to account for learned behavior, and these variables were carefully tied to stimuli and responses via operational definitions. Skinner rejected the concept, however, mainly because it opened the door to what he called **explanatory fictions**. These refer to a tendency to propose some hypothetical internal factor mediating between observable stimuli and measurable behaviors and then to use the factor as a pseudo-

explanation for the behavior. It is something that we do all the time, at least informally. For example, suppose you discover that your new roommate stays up late at night studying and seems to spend more time in the library than anyone else you know. You ask his friends about him. They say that he has a high need for achievement. According to Skinner, at this point we might make the mistake of thinking that we have explained the studying behavior by attributing it to the high need for achievement. In fact, however, this "need for achievement" is merely a label that summarizes the studying and library-going behaviors and adds nothing to the explanation of them. The explanation, Skinner would contend, lies in the person's overall learning history and the specific reinforcement contingencies in evidence at the time the achievement-related behaviors occur.

The problem with explanatory fictions led Skinner to be critical of physiological psychologists, who sought to explain behavior by reducing it, in his view, to nervous system activity. Although Skinner recognized the importance of studying brain function and nervous system activity, he was certain that a full description of behavior, together with the ability to predict and control it, was possible without reference to the nervous system. In this regard, Skinner mirrored the attitude of the Harvard physiologist W. J. Crozier.[5] Similarly, he rejected most of contemporary cognitive psychology, on the grounds that it also resorted to explanatory fictions (e.g., attributing memory failures to short-term memory limitations). In his final address to the APA in 1990, he sarcastically referred to cognitive psychology as the equivalent of scientific creationism in biology, mainly on the grounds of this explanatory fiction problem.

This is not to say that he denied the obvious fact that thinking, memory, and language occur. However, he rejected the idea that there was a qualitative distinction between public and private events and, as some behaviorists argued, that private events could not be studied scientifically. He argued instead that both public and private events are essentially the same and can be understood through an experimental analysis of them (Skinner, 1953). Running is a public event and problem solving is a private event, but they are both things that humans do, and are therefore subject to the contingencies of reinforcement and stimulus control. A Skinnerian analysis of problem solving, for instance, would focus on how different problem-solving behaviors occur in different environments and how these behaviors have been reinforced in the individual's learning history. Skinner first outlined his views about public and private events in a 1945 paper called "The Operational Analysis of Psychological Terms." In that paper he explicitly labeled his approach a "radical behaviorism," a label that continues to be associated with his system.

A Technology of Behavior

Skinner's approach to a philosophy of science was very different from both Tolman's and Hull's. Rather

---

KEY DATE *1953*

This year marked the publication date of Skinner's influential *Science and Human Behavior*.

These events also occurred:

- General Dwight Eisenhower, American hero of World War II, began first of two terms as President
- The reign of Marshall Tito of Yugoslavia began
- Queen Elizabeth II crowned queen of England
- The Rosenbergs, having been found guilty of spying for the Soviets, were executed
- Sir Edmund Hillary became the first to climb Mt. Everest
- Research reports suggested a link between lung cancer and smoking
- The Boston Braves moved to Milwaukee, becoming the Milwaukee Braves, while the St. Louis Browns moved east and became the Baltimore Orioles (the Yankees won their fifth World Series in a row)
- These people were born:

  Tony Blair, Prime Minister of England

  Pierce Brosnan, American actor

  Ken Burns, American filmmaker
- These people died:

  E. P. Hubble, American astronomer

  Jim Thorpe, Native-American athlete

  Eugene O'Neill, American playwright

---

[5] W. J. Crozier (1892–1955) was a professor of physiology at Harvard and former student of Loeb (Chapter 10, p. 291) who held the strong belief that behavior could be interpreted in mechanical terms and without reference to the nervous system. Skinner (1956) once wrote that it "had been said of Loeb, and might have been said of Crozier, that he 'resented the nervous system.' Whether this was true or not, the fact was that both these men talked about animal behavior without mentioning the nervous system and with surprising success" (pp. 222–223).

than deducing hypotheses from theoretical statements, then designing studies to test the hypotheses, Skinner preferred a less structured (but nonetheless rigorous) inductive approach to research. That is, his modus operandi was to study behavior intensively under a variety of circumstances, then draw general conclusions. The schedules of reinforcement book (Ferster & Skinner, 1957) was the classic example of this strategy—trying out various combinations of reinforcement contingencies, then looking for regularities in behavior (e.g., the pause in responding after reinforcement in a fixed interval schedule). The inductive strategy is in the tradition of Sir Francis Bacon, and Skinner often referred specifically to Bacon as his model (Smith, 1996a). As you recall from Chapter 2 (p. 27), Bacon argued that understanding nature required making systematic observations of it without a preconceived theoretical framework. General principles would emerge out of these systematic observations. Bacon also believed that the control of nature was an important goal for science.

Bacon provided the prototype of what Smith (1992) has referred to as the technological ideal—a scientist who desires not merely to understand nature but to control it. In fact, Bacon argued that true understanding only occurred if one could demonstrate control over some phenomenon, either by manipulating some aspect of the environment and observing a predicted outcome, or by creating some technology that worked reliably. Thus, a thorough understanding of physics can be demonstrated by creating machines that rely on various physical laws. For Skinner, the extrapolation to psychology was easy. He would show that behavior could be predicted, and he would create a technology of behavior, based on reinforcement principles, to show how behavior could be controlled.

Skinner's first full-scale attempt to develop a behavioral technology was known as Project Pigeon (Skinner, 1960). During World War II, he obtained modest funding from government and private sources to pursue the development of a guidance system using pigeons to direct missiles toward targets. Along with a dedicated team of students, he was able to train pigeons to key peck at a target screen. As they pecked at the target, the missile would change

direction until the target remained in the crosshairs of the screen. As a backup measure, each nose cone was fitted with three pigeons, each with its own target. The pigeons, of course, would make just one trip. Skinner was able to build a sophisticated prototype and to demonstrate its effectiveness, but the military eventually killed the project.[6] Nonetheless, the experience convinced Skinner that his brand of behaviorism was applicable far beyond the laboratory. At a 1947 symposium on current trends in psychology, he pointedly argued for "extending the practices of an experimental science to the world at large. We can do this as soon as we wish to do it" (quoted in Capshew, 1996, p. 144).

Despite the setback suffered as a result of Project Pigeon, Skinner was encouraged by the experience, and as the preceding quote makes clear, was more determined than ever to show that operant technology could bring about useful results. In subsequent decades he would (a) follow Watson's lead and delve into the areas of child development and parenting, (b) challenge educational practice and develop a programmed teaching machine to facilitate learning, long before the development of personal computers, and (c) satisfy his long-held desire to write fiction with *Walden Two* (Skinner 1948), the account of a utopian community based on operant principles. It is described more fully in this Chapter's Close-Up. His ideas would also be extended by others into the areas of psychotherapy and business.

Finally, although Skinner was not directly involved, operant technology did manage to find its way into a missile program. On at least two of the early flights that were part of the NASA space program, chimpanzees spent their time in space learning various operant tasks. One psychologist involved in the project wrote that "[e]very technique, schedule, and programming and recording device we used then and subsequently can be traced to [Skinner] or his students" (Rohles, 1992, p. 1533).

---

[6] One of the persons responsible for killing Project Pigeon was Tolman's physicist brother, who was involved with the National Defense Research Committee. Skinner apparently believed that Richard Tolman's "lack of respect ... for his brother's behavioral psychology" (Bjork, 1993, p. 123) contributed to the demise of the project.

CLOSE-UP:
A Skinnerian Utopia

If behavior is inexorably controlled by the contingencies of reinforcement, then why not manipulate those contingencies to create happy, useful, and productive people? Skinner certainly found no good reason not to do so, and he was not shy about calling for the redesign of society according to operant principles. His first attempt at proposing a behavioral technology to improve the world came in 1948, with the publication of *Walden Two*, a story about a community built on operant conditioning ideas.

Like all utopian novels, the story line is thin, merely a device allowing the author to describe the brave new world. In *Walden Two*, a professor named Burris visits the rural community of a thousand or so members in the company of two former students, their girlfriends, and a philosopher colleague. They spend some time at Walden Two, mostly in the company of Frazier, the community's founder and designated tour guide. The philosopher (of course) is skeptical throughout the novel, convinced that Walden's inhabitants have been brainwashed and are under the diabolical control of Frazier. Burris is initially skeptical, but becomes convinced and at the end of the novel, he decides to give up academia and stay at Walden Two

Life in Walden Two seemed idyllic. Members could choose the kinds of work they would do, within the limits of their ability. To receive all the community's benefits (e.g., free health care, education, cultural opportunities), each member had to earn a certain number of labor credits per year; less attractive jobs like collecting the trash earned more credits than more enjoyable ones like tending the gardens. Most members could earn all their credits by working no more than four hours per day. A rotating board of six "Planners" managed the community, along with a larger group of "Managers," who were experts in areas like nutrition or child care, and "Scientists," whose research fed into community decision-making. Everyone, regardless of his or her position in the community, performed some physical labor each day.

Child rearing at Walden Two was not entrusted to individual parents but was shared by the community—echoing Watson, Frazier declared that "[h]ome is not the place to raise children" (p. 132). Children's productive behaviors were shaped through positive reinforcement—aversive conditioning was not used. For example, children learned frustration tolerance by being exposed to a very minor frustrating experience that they could handle and be praised for handling. They then experienced a series of slightly more frustrating events, gradually developing their skills at frustration management (i.e., shaping).

Two other aspects of the community show that Skinner, like all good utopian authors, anticipated movements that were years from developing. First, at Walden there was a strict equality of the sexes, maintained by always having three male and three female Planners, and reflected in the community concept of child rearing. Women could pursue anything that interested them. Second, great care was taken to protect the natural resources of the environment around Walden. The values of living the simple life and protecting the earth pervade the book, and are the reasons why Skinner believed his book had a connection with Thoreau's original *Walden*.

Sales of *Walden Two* were initially sluggish. At a time when they were just emerging from World War II and were entering the cold war, Americans apparently weren't interested in an idea that sounded vaguely communistic and seemed to deny the importance of the competitive spirit and individual initiative. Sales increased during the 1960s and 1970s, however, a time of protest against war and the "establishment," when America's youth embraced countercultural alternatives to conventional behavior. Yet at the same time, the book was controversial and condemned in some quarters, especially concerning the inseparable issues of freedom and the control of behavior (Rutherford, 2003). Skinner makes his position clear through the voice of Frazier, who takes up the issue with the philosopher:

> ... If man is free, then a technology of behavior is impossible. But I'm asking you to consider the other case. ... I deny that freedom exists at all. I must deny it—or my program would be absurd. You can't have a science about a subject matter which hops capriciously about. Perhaps we can never prove that man isn't free; it's an assumption. But the increasing success of a science of behavior makes it more and more plausible. (Skinner, 1948, pp. 241–242)

Skinner repeated this message for the rest of his life. Freedom of choice is illusory and contrary to the assumption that behavior follows predictable laws and is under the control of reinforcement contingencies. If behavior is going to be controlled anyway, why not do it for the general good? Skinner never seemed to grasp the importance of the question "Who controls?" though, which was seized on by critics who blasted *Walden Two* as a totalitarian treatise that treated people like rats in Skinner boxes. Skinner argued that behavioral scientists should naturally play a leading role in the design of society, given their expertise, but it was never very clear just how this was to be accomplished in a democracy.

Evaluating Skinner

Unlike Tolman and Hull, Skinner was never elected president of the American Psychological Association. His research is seldom referenced in mainstream APA journals like the *Journal of Experimental Psychology*. He attracted many enthusiastic graduate students, a few remained devoted operant researchers, and scattered across a number of universities there still exist pockets of true believers, but Skinner's radical behaviorism was (and remains) away from the mainstream of American psychology. Today, few psychology departments have more than one or two "operant" people (Robinson & Woodward, 1996). Skinner himself was concerned about the longevity of his brand of behaviorism, fearing that it would fade after his death. As early as 1974, he wrote about what he perceived to be "the lack of young operant conditioners" (cited in Bjork, 1993, p. 224) and the difficulty they had in finding jobs during a time when cognitive psychology was "in." Yet it is clear that his impact on psychology surpasses that of Tolman and Hull, as well as most of the psychologists encountered in this text. In a survey by Korn, Davis, and Davis (1991), for example, department chairpersons and historians were asked to rank order psychologists in terms of eminence. Two sets of rankings were obtained: one for the top 10 "contemporary" psychologists and another for an "all-time" top 10. Among contemporary psychologists, both chairpersons and historians ranked Skinner no. 1; on the "all-time" list, Skinner again ranked no. 1 among chairpersons, but dropped to no. 8 among historians. Although Skinner's rating might have been inflated by the proximity of the survey to his death in 1990, it is nonetheless clear that psychologists and historians alike consider him to be one of the discipline's premier figures. Incidentally, neither Tolman nor Hull made any of the final top 10 lists.

Throughout this history of modern psychology, we have seen that American psychologists have felt pressured to show that their systems could be applied to improve the general welfare. This is one reason for the failure of Titchenerian psychology and the general success of functional and behavioral psychologies. In this regard, Skinner's contributions are unmatched in the history of psychology. His early research at Harvard, leading to *The Behavior of Organisms*, and his work in the 1950s, which produced *Schedules of Reinforcement*, fall into the category of basic laboratory research, but the bulk of his writing was directed at convincing the world that an experimental analysis of behavior is the only hope for the future welfare of the human species. This, of course, makes Skinner the true heir to Watson, who also labored long and hard to spread the "good word" of behaviorism. The strong and consistent advocacy made Skinner a controversial figure,[7] but it also resulted in his ideas being applied in more ways than ever imagined by either Tolman or Hull.

BEHAVIORISM IN PERSPECTIVE

Behaviorism has been a powerful force in American psychology. It produced some of psychology's most famous persons (e.g., Watson, Skinner), it dominated the research scene for several decades in the middle of the twentieth century, and its applications continue to have widespread use in business, education, psychotherapy, and even daily life. Yet it is important to make two qualifications. First, behaviorism has largely been an American phenomenon. Behaviorist thinking was not widely influential in Europe, for example. Despite the heritage of British empiricism, there was not much of a British community of committed behaviorists, and in Europe, the movement had little impact. We have already seen, in the discussion of Thorndike and his argument with Mills over laboratory methods (pp. 202–203) for example, that European animal psychologists (e.g., Lorenz, Tinbergen) were much more inclined than Americans to study animal behavior in its natural environments than in the lab, and they were much more interested in instinct than learning. A key reason for behaviorism being more American-centered has to do with its applicability. We have seen over and over again that American pragmatism has played a strong role in shaping American psychology.

The second caveat is that although it is true that behaviorism dominated American experimental psychology in the 1930s, 40s, and into the 50s, there was nonetheless a great deal of research being done in American laboratories that had little to do with behaviorism. During these years, the pages of the leading journals still contained numerous articles describing research on such cognitive topics as memory, perception, attention, language, and thinking. Among others, they included, in 1935, one of psychology's most famous papers, a summary of three experiments by an obscure graduate student at George Peabody College in Tennessee, J. Ridley Stroop (1935/1992). The "Stroop effect," a problem in which color naming is hindered by interference from automatic reading processes (e.g., the word RED is printed in green ink and the correct response is "green" not "red"), has been called psychology's most replicated finding (MacLeod, 1992). So not all the research during the heyday of behaviorism involved rats in mazes or pigeons in Skinner boxes.

In the opening paragraph of his book on the alleged mid-twentieth century cognitive revolution in psychology, Bernard Baars (1986) made the observation that behaviorism "is often referred to in the past tense" (p. 1) and that not too many psychologists refer to themselves as behaviorists anymore. There is a grain of truth to this assertion—as we will learn in Chapter 14, behaviorism with a capital "B" has been on the wane for decades and cognitive psychology, which returned the study of mental processes to scientific respectability, has to a certain extent replaced behaviorism as American psycholo-

---

[7] Skinner never wavered in his beliefs and his strong advocacy led many to consider him to be arrogant, condescending, and out of touch with core American values. Yet Rutherford (2003) has argued convincingly that Skinner's ideas for improving society occasionally meshed with contemporary cultural values and were applauded. His post-World War II attempt to build a market for an improvement on a baby's crib, for instance, was viewed favorably by many, in the context of a time when technological improvements to aid life at home were valued. Also, those who knew Skinner consistently described him as a warm, considerate, unassuming, and gentle man. He was also far from the narrow-minded scientist whose work occupied his every waking hour—he was widely read, a published poet, a big opera fan, and part of a Cambridge play-reading group (Smith, 1996b).

gy's predominant conceptual framework. Yet Baars's assertion overstates the case. It overlooks the fact that research on learning and conditioning continues to occur at virtually every major university in America, and that behavioral principles continue to form the basis for many successful applications (e.g., behavior therapy). More important, and an indication of just how influential behaviorism has been, the central message of behaviorism is now taken for granted by every research psychologist. That is, regardless of whether researchers consider them-selves "behaviorists," they all are careful to define psychological concepts in behavioral terms, and even if they are interested in internal, unobservable processes (e.g., insight in problem solving), they limit their evidence to behavioral phenomena (e.g., solutions to problems). Furthermore, I know of no introductory textbook that fails to include the term "behavior" in its definition of psychology. Baars recognized this himself in the preface to his book, writing that in the sense just described, "we are all behaviorists" (p. ix).

SUMMARY

POST-WATSONIAN BEHAVIORISM

- Contrary to traditional historical accounts, American psychology did not become predominantly behaviorist as the immediate result of Watson's program. Behaviorism did begin to take hold in the 1930s, however, partly because of Watson's continued propagandizing but also because full translations of Pavlov's research became available for the first time.

- Logical positivism, which allowed for theories to include abstract concepts but insisted that these concepts be tied to observable events, created a fertile climate for the evolution of behaviorism. Operationism, originating in physics in the late 1920s, also helped to create an environment conducive to objective, behaviorist thinking. Operational definitions define concepts in terms of a set of operations, under the control of the researcher, that are assumed to bring about the term in question (e.g., 24 hours without food brings on hunger). Confidence in the generality of some research outcome increases when various studies, each using a slightly different operational definition, nonetheless converge on the same outcome.

- Neobehaviorists disagreed on a number of issues, but agreed that (a) continuity among species allowed for general rules of behavior to be derived from nonhuman species, (b) understanding behavior required a thorough knowledge of how the organism learns, and (c) research results should have practical applications.

EDWARD C. TOLMAN (1886–1959):
A PURPOSIVE BEHAVIORISM

- Much of Tolman's research used maze learning, and he investigated both the general reliability of the maze as an apparatus and the manner in which rats learn mazes. According to Tolman, rats in a maze do not learn a series of S-R connections; rather, they learn an overall cognitive map of the maze. This spatial ability can be shown in latent learning studies, in which animals can be shown to be learning a maze even though the learning is not reflected in their performance until reinforcement is made available, and in place learning, in which animals learn to go to a location more quickly than they learn to make a specific response.

- Tolman believed that behavior was goal-directed or purposive and that molar rather than molecular behavior should be the unit of study. He did not think that reinforcement was necessary for learning to occur. He developed the concept of the intervening variable, a hypothetical factor internal to the organism that intervenes between stimulus and response and is defined operationally. Many of the intervening variables in Tolman's system (e.g., expectancy) were cognitive.

CLARK HULL (1884–1952):
A HYPOTHETICO-DEDUCTIVE BEHAVIORISM

- Although he is known primarily for his theory of learning based on animal studies, Hull also studied the development of concept learning in humans, aptitude testing, and experimental hypnosis, producing a doctoral dissertation on the first and books on the latter two topics.

- Modeled on Newtonian physics and consistent with the dictates of logical positivism, Hull's hypothetico-deductive system of behavior involved the development of a theory in which specific experiments were created to test hypotheses that were derived from highly formalized postulates. Research outcomes would then strengthen faith in the postulates or bring about their revision.

- Hull's learning theory is a drive-reduction theory. Postulate 4 proposes that learning (i.e., an increase in habit strength) involves stimulus-response contiguity accompanied by reinforcement. Reinforcers are stimuli that reduce drives. They can be primary or biologically based (e.g., food), or secondary (i.e., learned through association with primary reinforcers).

- Hull used a large number of intervening variables. The most important one was reaction potential, $_sE_R$, the probability that a response will occur at a given time. It was said to be influenced by a number of factors, including drive (D) and habit strength ($_sH_R$), both of which Hull believed were necessary for behavior to occur.

B. F. SKINNER (1904–1990): A RADICAL BEHAVIORISM

- Skinner rejected the more formal theories of both Tolman and Hull and argued for a more inductive, descriptive behaviorism that simply looked for evidence of behavior that could be predicted and controlled. He is best known for developing the distinction between classical and operant conditioning and for investigating the latter. To do so, he created the Skinner box, an experimental chamber in which the rate of some response (e.g., bar pressing, key pecking) is recorded continuously by a cumulative recorder. Operant conditioning occurs when behavior is shaped by its immediate consequences. If the consequences are positive, the behavior occurring in a specific environment is more likely to occur in that environment in the future; if they are negative, the behavior becomes less likely to occur.

- Skinner rejected the use of what he called explanatory fictions, hypothetical factors that appear to explain a phenomenon but actually do nothing more than relabel it. Hence, he was critical of nervous system explanations of behavior, and he never accepted the idea that explanations for behavior would be found by cognitive psychologists.

- Skinner called for a technology of behavior to improve child rearing, education, and society as a whole through the use of behavioral techniques. In *Walden Two*, he outlined how an entire community could function according to operant principles.

BEHAVIORISM IN PERSPECTIVE

- Behaviorism was a dominant force in psychology in the 1930s, 40s, and into the 50s. Yet it was influential mainly in the United States, and even in the United States, many experimental psychologists devoted their careers to studying phenomena far removed from conditioning. One lasting legacy of behavior is a recognition among researchers that psychological phenomena, to be studied with any degree of objectivity, must be defined in behavioral terms.

STUDY QUESTIONS

1. Describe the "myth" of the behaviorist revolution.

2. Describe the events of the 1920s that paved the way for neobehaviorism to become dominant in the 1930s.

3. Explain how logical positivism, combined with operationism, dealt with the issue of how to study abstract nonobservable phenomena (e.g., hunger) objectively.

4. Give an example to show that you know what is meant by an operational definition, and explain the importance of using operational definitions in psychological research.

5. There was a degree of consensus among neobehaviorists on several issues. Describe them.

6. Describe the influence of (a) gestalt psychology and (b) Edwin Holt on Tolman's theory of learning.

7. Define intervening variable and give examples to show how the concept was used by (a) Tolman and (b) Hull.

8. Describe Tolman's latent learning study and explain what Tolman thought it demonstrated about the role of reinforcement in maze learning.

9. Describe Tolman's research on cognitive maps and show how it fits into his theory of learning.

10. Describe Tolman's place learning experiment and explain its significance.

11. Describe Hull's doctoral dissertation on concept learning and show how it connected to his subsequent theory of learning.

12. Describe how research is conducted using a hypothetico-deductive approach.

13. Describe Hull's postulate 4.

14. What was the importance of reaction potential to Hull's theory and what was the significance of the relationship between drive and habit strength being multiplicative rather then additive?

15. Explain why Hull was a dominant figure in American psychology in the 1940s and 50s and is virtually forgotten today.

16. Describe the influence of Sir Francis Bacon on B. F. Skinner's ideas.

17. Describe the danger that Skinner saw with explanatory fictions. Use an example.

18. Describe how Skinner applied operant thinking to his utopian novel, *Walden Two*.

19. Write a brief essay that connects these concepts: technological ideal, Project Pigeon.

20. In his book on the history of cognitive psychology, Baars concluded "we are all behaviorists." Explain.

QUESTIONS FROM THE ORIGINAL SOURCE EXCERPT

1. Use the example of the pigeon raising its head to illustrate Skinner's operant conditioning model.

2. Use an example to illustrate Skinner's concept of shaping.

3. Distinguish between (a) interval and ratio schedules of reinforcement and (b) fixed and variable schedules.

4. Summarize the necessary ingredients of an experimental analysis of behavior.

FOR FURTHER READING

Boring, E. G., Langfeld, H. S., Werner, H., & Yerkes, R.M. (Eds.), *A history of psychology in autobiography Vol. 4*. Worcester, MA: Clark University Press.

Part of a series of autobiographies. Volume 4 includes interesting autobiographical chapters written by Hull (pp. 143–162) and Tolman (pp. 323–339).

Bjork, D. W. (1993). *B. F. Skinner: A life*. New York: Basic Books.

A brief and readable biography of Skinner. Not very detailed in treating Skinner's research or that of other operant scientists, but an excellent treatment of Skinner's early development as an operant scientist and his crusade for behavioral engineering.

Delprato, D. J., & Midgley, B. D. (1992). Some fundamentals of B. F. Skinner's behaviorism. *American Psychologist, 47*, 1507–1520.

A solid introduction to the essentials of Skinnerian psychology, designed to counter some of the misconceptions of his work. This is just one of 25 articles on Skinner to be found in the November 1992, special issue of American Psychologist.

Malone, J. C. (1991). *Theories of learning: A historical approach*. Belmont, CA: Wadsworth Publishing Company.

Provides thorough descriptions of the major theories of learning, written from a historical standpoint. In addition to Tolman, Hull, and Skinner, the book covers other important learning theories (i.e., Thorndike, Pavlov, Watson, Guthrie).

Smith, L. D., & Woodward, W. R. (1996). *B. F. Skinner and behaviorism in American culture*. Bethlehem, PA: Lehigh University Press.

A volume edited by two noted historians of psychology that contains 14 different chapters, arranged under the topics of "Skinner as social philosopher," "Skinner as scientist," "Skinner's personal world," and "The diversification and extension of behaviorism."

CHAPTER 12

MENTAL ILLNESS AND ITS TREATMENT

... I should like to formulate what we have learned so far as follows: Our hysterical patients suffer from reminiscences. Their symptoms are residues and mnemic symbols of particular (traumatic) experiences.

—Sigmund Freud, 1909

PREVIEW AND CHAPTER OBJECTIVES

When students first begin to explore psychology, they typically identify the field with the diagnosis and treatment of "mental illness." Of course, they quickly discover that psychology is a much broader subject—in a normal introductory course, they must wade through a dozen or so chapters on such topics as the brain and behavior, perception, learning, and cognition, before they get to the chapters on psychopathology and its treatment. Similarly, most histories of psychology, including this one, focus on how the discipline began applying scientific methods to age-old philosophical questions and how it developed as a "science" in the academic environment. Nonetheless, no history of psychology can be complete without describing, if briefly, the various ways that psychopathology has been conceived of and treated over the years. Most of this chapter is devoted to Sigmund Freud's creation and promotion of psychoanalysis, the name he gave both to his theory of personality and to his method for treating disordered personalities. We will explore the origins and evolution of some of his well-known concepts. Moreover, the Original Source Excerpt in this chapter is from a famous series of lectures that Freud gave during his only visit to the United States in 1909. Preceding the discussion of Freud, however, the chapter examines some early conceptions of mental illness and various attempts at the reform of mental institutions, and briefly discusses the intriguing history of hypnosis.

The final portion of the chapter traces the early history of clinical psychology in the United States from its modest origins to the years just before World War II. Its postwar development, when it emerged as a major force in psychology, will be examined in Chapter 13. Unlike psychoanalysis, which developed in a medical context, an early form of clinical psychology emerged from the laboratory environment that characterized the new psychology of the late nineteenth century. Pioneers such as Lightner Witmer adapted existing laboratory procedures and created new ones to diagnose and treat children with various problems that were hindering their school performance. Modern clinical psychology has roots in these early clinics, and in the mental hygiene and mental testing movements of the early twentieth century. After you finish this chapter, you should be able to:

■ Show how Enlightenment thinking influenced reforms in Pinel's treatment of the mentally ill

■ Describe the features of the "moral treatment" approach used by Pinel and Tuke

■ Describe a medical approach to treatment, as pioneered by Rush

■ Describe the reform efforts of Dix and Beers, and the outcomes of their work

■ Describe Kraepelin's early efforts at classification and diagnosis of mental illness

■ Describe Mesmer's approach to treating hysteria and explain why it was occasionally successful

■ Contrast the theories of hypnosis posed by Liebeault and Bernheim and by Charcot

■ Describe the Freudian myth and show how it was promoted

■ Show how Freud's ideas were influenced by materialist and evolutionary thinking

■ Describe and criticize traditional analysis of the Anna O. case and explain what Freud believed he had learned from it

■ Describe the essential features of Freud's theory of personality and how it evolved over the years

■ Describe the alternatives to psychoanalytic theory proposed by Adler and Jung

■ Critically analyze Freud's contributions to psychology

■ Summarize Witmer's contribution to clinical psychology and explain why he is also considered a pioneer of school psychology

■ Describe the state of clinical psychology in the years prior to World War II

EARLY TREATMENT OF THE MENTALLY ILL

Every society has had to confront the need to deal with people whose thought processes, emotions, and behavior mark them as deviant from the norm. For much of recorded history, such persons, so different from the rest of "us," have sometimes been a source of fear and loathing, their treatment less than humane. They have been regarded as evil or possessed by the devil, to be punished by being tortured and put to death, perhaps by being burned at the stake or drowned as a "witch." Alternatively, they have been considered either morally deficient and dangerous to society because of their transgressions, or incurable nuisances, and in need of being locked away from decent folks, perhaps chained to a wall, with no hope of being freed. Out of sight, out of mind. On the other hand, the picture is not as uniformly bleak as is normally portrayed in standard histories of mental illness (e.g., Zilboorg, 1941). Treatises proposing reasonable biological causes for

mental illness existed in medieval times, at the same time that demonology was a competing hypothesis, and there is accumulating evidence that the insane were frequently treated with compassion in their communities and through organized governmental intervention (Neugebauer, 1978; Kroll, 1973). As is true today, however, community size and socioeconomic status were important predictors of care. The poor, especially those living in the larger population areas, received the worst treatment, if they received any help at all.

"Enlightened" Reform: Pinel, Tuke, and Rush

Several efforts at improving treatment of the mentally ill occurred in the late eighteenth and early nineteenth centuries, a product of the closing years of the Enlightenment, a time of "spreading light into the dark corners of the human mind" (Appleby, Hunt, & Jacob, 1994, p. 36). As you recall from Chapter 3, the hallmark of Enlightenment thinking was a belief in the ideas of progress and reform and a strong faith in the ability of science to improve society. It was the kind of thinking that helped produce political revolutions both in the United States and France, and it elevated "science," the engine of progress, to the status of religion. In that context, mental illness came to be viewed in naturalistic terms as being biologically based and amenable to treatment.

The best-known reformer during this era was the French physician Phillipe Pinel (1745–1826), who instituted humane reforms in Paris, first at the Bicêtre asylum for men (1793), then at the Salpêtrière asylum for women (1795). Pinel's most dramatic action was to remove the chains from patients who had been restrained, in some instances, for years. Although it has been shown (e.g., Weiner, 1979, cited in Micale, 1985) that the number of liberated patients was relatively small (about 15% of the total asylum populations), and that for many patients, the chains were simply replaced by more modern forms of restraint (e.g., an early version of the straitjacket), Pinel nonetheless deserves credit for bringing the concept of reform to mental institutions. He called his overall program *traitement moral* ("moral treatment"), and it featured improvements in patient nutrition, hygiene, and general living conditions, and an early form of behavior modification using rewards and punishments to bring some order into the lives of patients. Pinel's efforts, occurring in the context of the French Revolution, provide a clear example of the combined effects of an "enlightened" approach to insanity and an assault on institutions perceived to be repressing freedom. His reforms united the Enlightenment faith in progress and the revolutionary desire to liberate the oppressed.

While Pinel was effecting change in France, similar reforms were occurring in England, led by the work of William Tuke (1732–1822). A Quaker tea merchant, Tuke was predisposed toward providing relief for subjugated groups (the Society of Friends also became leaders in the antislavery movement), and especially for those Quakers suffering from mental illness. In 1792, a year before Pinel was named director of the Bicêtre, Tuke founded the York Retreat in the north of England, which was dedicated to the benevolent treatment of the insane. Set in a rural environment and designed to resemble a working farm more than a prison, the Retreat established a program of treatment similar in spirit to the one used by Pinel. Patients who behaved well were given greater freedom of movement, allowed more visitors, and given more opportunities for recreation and work; on the other hand, those behaving badly or out of control were punished, usually through isolation from other patients, but sometimes by being tied to their beds (Bell, 1980). Its religious origins in the Society of Friends meant that the York Retreat and its philosophy of treatment would be known to Quakers in other parts of the world who had similar reform motives. According to Grob (1994), Tuke's York Retreat became the model for at least half of the private mental hospitals created in the United States in the first quarter of the nineteenth century.

The person credited with being the first in America to bring a scientific approach to the treatment of the mentally ill was Benjamin Rush (1745–1813), a prominent signer of the Declaration of Independence and surgeon general to the Continental Army of the American Revolution. He has been called the "father" of modern psychiatry, largely because of his *Medical Inquiries and Observations upon the Diseases of the Mind*, which went through five editions between 1812 and 1835. One of the few "doctors" of this era with actual university training in medicine,[1] Rush became a strong advocate of a contemporary belief that many illnesses derived from problems with the blood and circulatory system. Accordingly, a common remedy was to remove diseased or excess blood, and Rush became a promoter of **bloodletting** as a cure for a wide range of illnesses. These included mental ones, which Rush believed stemmed from "hypertension in the brain's blood vessels" (Bell, 1980, p. 9). Reducing the tension, then, involved opening veins and removing blood until the person reached a more tranquil state. This often worked rather well as a temporary means of calming violent patients, probably because these unfortunate individuals, minus a few pints, were too weak to be hyperactive. Rush

[1] His medical training included a stop at the university in Edinburgh, Scotland. As was mentioned in Chapter 5, Edinburgh was Great Britain's foremost center for medical education, the locus of Darwin's unsuccessful attempt to become a doctor.

reported one case in which a violent patient was given 47 different bleedings, involving a total loss of between 400 and 500 ounces of blood. He was eventually pronounced cured and was returned to the community. He wrote a glowing testimonial thanking Rush for the therapy, but then relapsed and hung himself not long after his release (Bell, 1980).

In addition to bloodletting, Rush also created two devices for calming the blood. The *gyrator* was a revolving board on which a patient would be spun rapidly, the idea being to redistribute blood toward the head. The *tranquilizer*, shown in Figure 12.1, was a chair with straps for restraining arms and legs, and a boxlike device that fit tightly over the head. By eliminating movement, the goal was to reduce the pulse rate. Both devices became standard forms of treatment in post-revolutionary asylums, and while they might seem cruel and unusual to us today, they

FIGURE 12.1 The tranquilizer chair, devised by Benjamin Rush for restraining and "calming" agitated mental patients, from Bell (1980).

reflected an important new idea at the time—a belief that the mentally ill could benefit from therapy.

Reforming Asylums: Dix and Beers

During the first third of the nineteenth century, a number of private mental asylums were founded in the United States, influenced by the reforms of men such as Pinel, Tuke, and Rush. Because they were private, however, their patients tended to be relatively affluent and the asylums were seldom overcrowded. For example, the McLean Asylum in Belmont (just outside of Boston), one of the first, housed a yearly average of about 50 patients during its first dozen years of existence and had a staff to patient ratio of approximately 2:1 (Beam, 2001). It developed a progressive moral treatment program based on the York model, and placed emphasis on outdoor therapeutic activities (e.g., gardening). McLean resembled a college campus more than a mental institution, with separate buildings set in a park-like environment that had been laid out by Frederick Law Olmsted (known for his design of Central Park in New York). The mentally insane poor, on the other hand, usually wound up in jails or "almshouses" (poorhouses) or were left to wander the countryside. As the population of the United States expanded, however, and urban areas in particular began to grow, the number of mentally ill patients increased proportionally, and the need for public support for them became increasingly evident. The response was the creation of large, state-funded asylums, designed for both the affluent and the poor, but eventually housing mostly the latter. Some idea of size can be seen from Figure 12.2a, a post card of the asylum opened in 1877 in Worcester, Massachusetts. The Worcester asylum is a classic example of the "Kirkbride design"—a central administration building with long wings on either side, one for females and one for males (Grob, 1983). Better behaved patients tended to be closer to the center and the more "excitable" patients tended to be placed further away. Figure 12.2.b shows a typical floor plan. Asylums tended to be located in rural areas, and/or in the geographical centers of states (i.e., equally accessible to all citizens, but also "out of sight"), and

(a)

(b)   Linear Plan

FIGURE 12.2 (a) Old post card of the asylum opened in 1877 in Worcester, Massachusetts. The asylum became Worcester State Hospital, was the scene of a major fire in 1991, and is abandoned. (b) Floor plan showing the Kirkbride design for asylums. The Worcester asylum had the typical Kirkbride design.

FIGURE 12.3 Dorothea Dix, crusader for mental health reform, from Viney (1996).

because they tended to house the powerless, they quickly became under-funded, overcrowded, filthy beyond imagining, and custodial rather than therapeutic.

Improving the care given in these asylums became the focus of a spirited crusade by Dorothea Dix (1802–1887). Dix (Figure 12.3) was a New England educator whose general concern for the less fortunate led her to examine the conditions for treating those housed in public institutions. In Massachusetts in 1841, she began an 18-month tour of the state's jails, hospitals, and almshouses, and any other location that might house the mentally ill poor. What she encountered was an alarming level of abuse and neglect, with the mentally ill being treated no better than animals. They were often chained to the walls of unheated closet-sized rooms filled with their excrement, poorly fed and clothed, often beat-

en into submission, and generally abandoned. On her return home, she wrote a scathing indictment of the system and did not mince words when describing the details of what she had seen. Her case was presented to the Massachusetts legislature and led to a series of reforms, including an increase of funds to improve the state's public asylum in Worcester. This success prompted her to repeat her modus operandi in other states—a systematic tour of institutions followed by a lengthy and detailed exposé. By 1848, the Dix crusade had found its way to every state except North Carolina, Texas, and Florida, and Dix had logged some 60,000 miles of travel, observing in the process "more than nine thousand idiots, epileptics, and insane ... destitute of appropriate care and protection" (Dix, 1848, quoted in Viney, 1996, p. 22). Her efforts played a role in the creation of 47 mental hospitals and schools for the feebleminded (Viney & Zorich, 1982). Although many of these institutions over the years grew to sizes that prevented effective care and led in the twentieth century to a renewal of problems with overcrowding and abuse, her efforts on behalf of the mentally ill poor dramatically improved the living conditions of those powerless to help themselves. That she was able to accomplish what she did in the face of her own poor health (probably tuberculosis), difficult traveling conditions, and the generally accepted belief that women were not worth listening to, is nothing less than extraordinary.

Dorothea Dix and other nineteenth-century reformers focused their efforts on the treatment of those already mentally ill and living in institutions. Often, even in the best of circumstances, the improvement in care amounted to better living conditions for those doomed to spend most or all of their lives in these places. Shortly after the turn of the century, however, another reform movement began that was based on the related ideas that (a) mental illness could be cured, and (b) with proper care, it might even be prevented. It was called the Mental Hygiene movement and it was launched by Clifford Beers (1876–1943). As a former mental patient himself, he was uniquely qualified to discuss the issue. Beers was a graduate of Yale and apparently had settled into a job in New York with an insurance company when a suicide attempt, followed by a year of depression, landed him in the first of three mental institutions that he would inhabit for just over three years. After being released from the third one in 1903, he compiled his notes into a book describing what life was like for a hospitalized mental patient. *A Mind That Found Itself* appeared in 1908, complete with a prefatory letter from William James, who had read the manuscript and wished to support Beers's cause. Other contemporary exposés of life in mental institutions existed, but Beers's book had special impact because it was written by someone who had lived through the ordeal. Beers was critical of the psychiatrists he had encountered, believing them to be generally incompetent and too willing to use punitive measures, but he saved his heaviest invective for the attendants in charge of the day-to-day operation of the wards. He documented the constant verbal and occasional physical abuse suffered at the hands of the staff, and called for improved conditions and professional training for attendants.

Because Beers had experienced mental institutions and lived to write about them, a second message of his book was that mental illness was curable. This was an important idea at a time when the medical community generally believed that there was little hope for the institutionalized mentally ill. In 1909, Beers founded the National Committee for Mental Hygiene to further the cause of prevention, and he spent his remaining years informing the public of his beliefs about mental illness, promoting programs to enhance mental health, and lobbying for the creation of mental hygiene clinics (Williams, Bellis, & Wellington, 1980).

Progress in the treatment of mental illness necessarily implies improvements in the diagnosis of mental illness. You might know about the modern version of this, the DSM-IV, but this chapter's Close-Up provides some background, and even yields a connection to Wundt.

CLOSE-UP:
Diagnosing Mental Illness

As you might recall from your general psychology course, or a course in abnormal psychology, one of the most valuable tools for psychiatrists and clinical psychologists is DSM-IV, short for *Diagnostic and Statistical Manual of Mental Disorders*, now in its fourth edition (1994). It includes detailed descriptions of symptoms for the various disorders, based on the accumulated research of decades. It is encyclopedic, including more than 400 psychiatric diagnostic categories, arranged in 17 broad categories, and filling close to 900 pages. DSM-IV is just the most recent of a long line of attempts to categorize mental illness. A major advance in diagnosis was made by the German physician Emil Kraepelin (1856–1926), who appears to have used some of what he learned in

Wundt's laboratory to provide the first clear insight into a disorder that he named dementia praecox, and that we now call schizophrenia.

Kraepelin earned a medical degree from the university at Würzburg in 1878, specializing in psychiatry. While working as a resident in psychiatry in Munich, he learned of the new laboratory psychology being developed at Leipzig, and traveled there in 1882 to discover Wundt's laboratory firsthand. He was involved in several research projects during the two years he was in Leipzig, but he did not complete a doctoral degree with Wundt. After several brief appointments at asylums and universities in the 1880s, his big break arrived in 1890—a position as professor of psychiatry in the clinic at Heidelberg University. The prestigious clinic afforded Kraepelin a large patient base, enabling him to begin a process of sorting patients into discrete categories, based partly on symptoms, but primarily on the kinds of outcomes (prognoses) that could be expected. He became known for his massive collections of individual note cards, one per patient, on which he recorded the details of each case, from the information collected at intake to the final outcome. Kraepelin remained at Heidelberg for 13 years, and then finished his psychiatric career in Munich as director of the university clinic there.

Kraepelin began his efforts at building a classification scheme for mental illness in 1883 and his "textbook" went through nine editions, the last one appearing the year after his death. His first effort, published when he was only 27, was apparently completed for the main purpose of providing him money to get married. It has been described as a "slim *Compendium* of no particular merit" (Shorter, 1997, p. 102), but in fact it ran to 400 pages and began to establish Kraepelin's name. By the time he died, the ninth edition had expanded to two volumes and 2,425 pages (Menninger, 1963).

Kraepelin's sixth edition, appearing in 1899, is the best known. In it he identified thirteen categories of mental disease, ranging from those that were relatively mild and had a promising prognosis (e.g., "fright neurosis") to the more serious disorders. Among the most serious were two that he labeled manic-depressive psychosis and dementia praecox (Havens, 1965). Mania and depression had been known for some time and "circular states" had been described as well, but Kraepelin provided the first comprehensive description of the disorder that today is known as a bipolar disorder. But it was his description of **dementia praecox** that made Kraepelin's reputation. He used the name, which translates roughly as "premature dementia," to reflect the fact that this debilitating mental disorder tended to appear relatively early in life, often during late adolescence. The symptoms included "disturbances in apprehension, ... in orientation, ... of attention, ... of memory, of the train of thought, ... of judgment, ... of the emotional field, ... in the volitional field," and "hallucination" (Kraepelin, quoted in Sahakian, 1968, p. 323). Note that several of these symptoms reflect the kinds of cognitive processes that Kraepelin learned about as a student in Wundt's laboratory. Kraepelin believed that one of the clear attributes of dementia praecox was an inability to focus attention, and his theory is similar to modern attentional theories of the disorder. He argued that the thought processes of those with dementia praecox lack the normal apperceptive ability and their attentional capacity is severely limited. While normal people can focus their attention and direct their mental activity along meaningful paths (i.e., they can *apperceive*, to use Wundt's term), those with dementia cannot. Hence, their mental activity resembles random associations. This accounts for one of the common symptoms: the meaningless strings of phrases ("word salad") often emitted by those suffering from the disorder.

Kraepelin also believed that the prognosis was so poor for this form of dementia that any hope for recovery was virtually hopeless. It wasn't long before this fatalistic prognosis was challenged by psychiatrists who pointed to cases where improvement did occur and/or onset occurred later than adolescence. One such researcher was Eugene Blueler (1857–1939), who renamed the disorder *schizophrenia*, the name used today.

Dementia praecox was not the only form of mental deterioration that interested Kraepelin. He also investigated a form of dementia that mysteriously appeared in adults of middle age that was similar in form to that shown by the very elderly. This premature dementia was later studied in greater depth by a close friend and research colleague of Kraepelin's at Heidelberg, Aloys Alzheimer (1864–1915), for whom this terrifying disease is named.

MESMERISM AND HYPNOSIS

At the same time that the various reforms in the treatment of mental illness were occurring, philosophers, psychologists, and medical doctors were developing theories about the causes and defining features of mental illness, and evolving methods for treating the afflicted. We have seen that bloodletting was a popular medical practice in the late eighteenth and early nineteenth centuries and that in several private asylums, various forms of "moral treatment" were instituted to manage behavior through rewards and punishments. And as will be seen shortly, a new approach to psychological treatment became popular when Freud developed psychoanalysis. First, though, it is necessary to set the stage for Freud by briefly describing the history of hypnosis, a technique that Freud learned about in Paris and tried briefly before abandoning it for other procedures. The origins of hypnosis lie with an eccentric Viennese physician who created an occasionally effective therapy based on the idea that illness, mental or otherwise, was the consequence of misaligned magnetic forces within the distressed person.

Mesmerism and Animal Magnetism

The start of Franz Anton Mesmer's (1734–1815) professional career was conventional enough. He earned a medical degree at the prestigious University of Vienna in 1766 and quickly established a thriving practice. Through a fortunate marriage, he entered into Vienna's highest social circles, counting the young composer Wolfgang Amadeus Mozart among his friends. As a scientist, Mesmer was aware of current developments and was especially intrigued by the recent discoveries of forces such as electricity and magnetism. He became convinced that magnetic powers affected humans directly, with good health being the consequence of properly aligned internal magnetic forces. Were these forces to become misaligned, however, ill health (either physical or mental) would result. If you can imagine the effects of trying to push together the plus poles of two magnets, you can get an idea of Mesmer's disease concept. Illness resulted from the disharmony of forces opposing each other. The cure, then, involved straightening out these forces within the body. Mesmer found that he could help many of his patients, especially those suffering from disorders with psychological roots, by giving them medicine containing heavy doses of iron, then passing magnets over their bodies. Patients would fall into a "crisis state," a type of trance, and when they emerged, would find their health improved. He called his theory of illness and cure **animal magnetism**. He did not know it, of course, but he had inadvertently demonstrated the power of suggestion on human behavior, and he had discovered what would later be renamed hypnosis.

Mesmer soon discovered that he could produce cures without the magnets. Convinced that he had special magnetic powers himself, he discarded the magnets and began treating patients directly by passing his hands over them. He would also massage parts of a patient's body that were causing distress (e.g., an apparently paralyzed arm), following the path of the nerves and suggesting that things would improve (Winters, 1950). Mesmer had some success, became convinced that he was quite special, and as a result aroused the ire of the generally conservative medical community in Vienna. After becoming embroiled in several heated controversies over the effectiveness of his magnetic cures, he found himself no longer welcome in Vienna. In May of 1777, he was expelled from the medical faculty of the University of Vienna and ordered to stop practicing medicine in the city (Hoffeld, 1980). It was time to move on.

Hoping to find a more open-minded environment, Mesmer moved his magnetic therapy to Paris in 1778, the same year that Pinel first arrived there (Zilboorg, 1941). Aided by his promotional skills and his "magnetic" personality, he soon began attracting more patients than he could easily handle. His solution to the overcrowding was to create a form of group therapy. In an expensively decorated clinic in one of the most fashionable neighborhoods in Paris, small groups of patients would congregate around Mesmer's famous *baquet*. This was a type of wooden chest or tub that contained various chemicals and had iron rods protruding from it in all directions. Patients would join hands and encircle the baquet, while Mesmer, often dressed in a flowing lilac-colored robe, would pass among them and encourage them to enter the crisis state. There was much swooning and moaning, with many individuals undoubtedly influenced by a kind of group contagion effect. Once the mass crisis passed, patients recovered their composure, pronounced themselves much better, and then left the clinic to spread the good word of its effectiveness. Indeed, many patients seemed to be cured, especially those suffering from a variety of what we would today call psychosomatic complaints (e.g., headaches, fainting spells, digestive problems).

As in Vienna, however, the medical community was not impressed with Mesmer. Paris in the prerevolutionary years was a place of much uncertainty and flux, and it was full of faith healers and others promising simple answers to the anxieties of the day (Hoffeld, 1980). In this context, Mesmer seemed to be just another quack. The question of the validity of **mesmerism**, as Mesmer's technique was now called, was taken up by a distinguished commission of the French Royal Academy of Sciences, appointed by the king. At its head was the renowned Benjamin Franklin, the American ambassador to France and a distinguished scientist in his own right, a pioneer in the study of electricity and the inventor of a remarkable new device, the lightning rod (Cohen, 1995). The commission also included the eminent chemist Lavoisier, the discoverer of oxygen, and the physician Joseph Guillotin. The latter would soon give his name to an execution device that creatively applied Newtonian gravitational principles concerning the accelerated motion of a falling blade of steel.

As might be expected from Mesmer's experience in Vienna, the Franklin commission's 1784 report concluded that his form of therapy had no foundation in science. It recognized that some patients indeed had been helped by Mesmer, but shrewdly attributed any cures to the patients' beliefs rather than to Mesmer's "magnetizing" powers. As Benjamin Franklin put it in a letter to a sick friend contemplating a visit to a mesmerist, if hypochondriacs who overuse medication "can be persuaded to forbear their drugs in expectation of being cured by only the physician's finger or an iron rod pointing at them, they may possibly find good effects tho' they mistake the cause" (quoted in Hoffeld, 1980, p. 380). Mesmer ignored the commission report and continued to practice for a time, but left Paris in 1792 and lived briefly both in London and Germany, practicing mesmerism until his death in 1815.

From Mesmerism to Hypnosis

Mesmer gradually faded from the scene after the Franklin commission's report, but mesmerism itself continued to spread throughout Europe, although mainly at the level of entertainment. Much like today's stage hypnotists, mesmerists toured the countryside giving dramatic demonstrations that awed the locals. Few scientists paid attention, but one who did was John Elliotson (1791–1868), a professor of medicine at University College, London, and senior physician at the teaching hospital affiliated with the college. He was intrigued by the demonstrations of apparent anesthesia, during which mesmerized people would show no signs of pain, even while being poked with sharp needles. Elliotson was one of those open-minded scientists who often antagonizes the establishment—he was already under suspicion for promoting a new contraption that other doctors refused to use, the stethoscope (Boring, 1950). Thus, eyebrows were raised when he began mesmerizing patients, and when he proposed a systematic study of the anesthetic effects of mesmerism in the late 1830s, the storm broke. He was denied permission by his hospital board, which also outlawed any use of mesmerism at the hospital. Elliotson resigned in protest and spent his remaining years promoting mesmerism.

Meanwhile other physicians were starting to use mesmerism to reduce the pain of surgery. In the 1840s, for example, there were numerous reported cases of amputations being done while the patient was in a trance. The largest study was completed by James Esdaile (1808–1859), a Scottish surgeon working in India. In 1845, he summarized the results of several hundred surgeries using mesmerism-induced anesthesia. He reported a mortality rate of less than 5% as a result of the surgery, at a time when mortality was normally 40% (Gravitz, 1988). Keep in mind that these were the days before the existence of chemical anesthetics such as ether, and surgery was a brutal business that prized speed over precision, with screaming patients firmly secured to the operating table. Thus, any procedure for pain reduction was a welcome development. Nonetheless, the medical community was slow to change, and the prevailing medical wisdom was that pain, because it was a naturally occurring phenomenon, was good and even necessary for surgery to succeed.

Mesmerism finally began to gain respectability in the late 1840s, in part by changing its name. The Scottish physician James Braid (1795–1860), a respected member of the conservative medical establishment, initially set out to demolish mesmerism, but was led by the studies he conducted to recognize the validity of some of its effects. Because he thought of the trance state as being similar to a state of sleep, he coined a new term for the phenomenon.

Neurypnology, a contraction of "neuro-hypnology," combined Greek terms for nervous (neuro) and sleep (hypnos) and was defined by Braid as a "nervous sleep." Soon the initial part of the term began to be dropped, and the phenomenon came to be called hypnology or **hypnotism**. Braid discovered that the hypnotic trance could be induced by having patients stare fixedly at an object just above their line of vision, and he came to believe that a general fixation of attention was behind the phenomenon. He also emphasized the importance of suggestion in producing hypnotic effects, and he seemed to recognize the importance of unconscious processing when he reported that memories could persist from one hypnotic session to the next, even though the person had no recollection during the intervening periods of normal consciousness (Boring, 1950). By 1860, when the discovery of ether and chloroform rendered surgical use of hypnosis unnecessary, the phenomenon was recognized in the scientific community as legitimate and worthy of study. Further developments, and controversy, occurred in France.

The Hypnotism Controversies

Hypnotism achieved a degree of legitimacy with Braid, but little consensus existed over its explanation. Two opposing views about the nature of hypnotism developed in France, with a pair of physicians working in the provincial city of Nancy (180 miles east of Paris) on one side of the sometimes acrimonious debate, and the powerful director of the famous Salpêtrière Hospital in Paris on the other.

The so-called Nancy School of hypnosis originated from the curiosity of Auguste Liebeault (1823–1904), an unassuming country doctor practicing just outside of Nancy, who decided to give hypnosis a try after being intrigued by an old book on animal magnetism. He recruited patients for hypnotic treatment by charging no fees for it, and his success produced a legendary local reputation. He soon attracted the attention of a nationally known physician living nearby in Nancy, Hippolyte Bernheim (1840–1919), who traveled to Liebeault's clinic expecting to discover and expose fakery. Instead, he became a convert and the leading voice of the Nancy school.

The central feature of the Liebeault-Bernheim theory of hypnosis was the concept of **suggestion**, which they defined as the ability to uncritically accept an idea or a command suggested by a hypnotist, and transform it into an action (Ellenberger, 1970). They considered suggestibility to be a personality trait like any other, with every person having it to some degree. Hypnotic susceptibility was therefore considered to be a normal phenomenon, experienced by different people with varying degrees of strength. In their medical practices, Liebeault and Bernheim induced hypnosis by having the patient stare into the doctor's eyes while being told to deeply relax. Once in a sleeplike trance, the doctor would suggest to the patient that the symptoms (e.g., headache) would go away. The symptoms often did just that.

Meanwhile, the sprawling Salpêtrière Hospital in Paris had become the European center for the study of hypnosis. Its director, Jean-Martin Charcot (1825–1893), was known throughout Europe for his pioneering work on epilepsy; he was the first to identify the features of grand mal seizures and to distinguish them from petit mal seizures. Charcot was also an expert in the study of **hysteria**, a disorder characterized by a wide range of symptoms that appeared to indicate neurological malfunction, but without apparent physical damage to the nervous system. Some patients experienced epilepsy-like seizures, others developed paralyses that were neurologically impossible (e.g., only the hand), and still others had nervous tics, severe headaches, sensory loss (e.g., deafness), or memory lapses.[2] The term "hysteria" derives from the Greek word for uterus, and for a time it was thought that the disorder was experienced only by females. By Charcot's time, however, numerous cases of male hysteria had been demonstrated (Sulloway, 1979). Charcot's contribution was to take hysteria seriously as a disorder and search for its cause. Contemporary medical opinion, grounded in the materialistic belief that true disorders had a physical basis, was that hysterics were simply malingerers, making up their symptoms. Charcot's willingness to tackle the problem head-on eventually earned him the title of "Napoleon of the Neuroses" (Ellenberger, 1970, p. 95).

Because Charcot observed that many of the symptoms of hysteria were the same as the phenomena demonstrated under hypnosis, he came to believe that hysteria and the ability to be hypnotized shared the same underlying pathology. Thus, although the hypnotists at Nancy considered suggestibility a normal trait and therefore generally useful as a therapy tool, Charcot declared that hypnotism was dangerous if it was used indiscriminately. Furthermore, he argued, susceptibility to hypnosis was an indication of underlying hysteric tendencies, which Charcot believed were the result of an inherited nervous system disorder. Hypnotism, then, was an "innately predisposed reaction on the part of [hysterics] to stroking, fixations of the sensory apparatus, and various other means of hypnotic induction" (Sulloway, 1979, p. 46). Hypnotism could be useful, Charcot proclaimed, primarily as a means of investigating and influencing the symptoms of those suffering from hysteria. Furthermore, because some patients were indeed malingerers, hypnosis was the means of separating the true hysterics from the fakes. Only true hysterics could be hypnotized, Charcot believed.

At the Salpêtrière, Charcot was famous for his elaborate and spectacular clinical demonstrations of hysteria. He would pick his "best" hysteric patients, hypnotize them, and suggest various symptoms to them. Charcot's patients apparently competed with each other for the privilege of being "on stage." Predictably, they performed as expected. Figure 12.4 portrays Charcot giving a clinical demonstration of hypnosis on Blanche Wittman, whose dramatic performances earned her the title among her peers of "Queen of the Hysterics" (Fancher, 1990). Charcot also used hypnosis to suggest the removal of hysteric symptoms in his patients, and claimed some success.

The doctors from Nancy disagreed sharply with Charcot's beliefs about hypnosis, arguing that his dramatic clinical demonstrations merely showed the effects of suggestion. Charcot's patients knew exactly what was expected of them, it was argued, and they delivered. A fierce debate erupted in the mid-1880s and between 1888 and 1893, one bibliographic source

[2] Today, most of these symptoms would earn the patient a diagnosis of conversion disorder.

FIGURE 12.4 Painting of Charcot lecturing on hysteria at the Salpêtrière, with Blanche Wittman as the hypnotized patient, from Gay (1988). Freud bought an engraving of the piece and hung it in his consulting room.

listed 801 publications in journals and magazines on the nature of hypnosis (Sulloway, 1979)! By the mid-1890s, most observers had rejected Charcot's ideas about hypnosis in favor of the Nancy model.[3]

During the height of his fame, young physicians from all over Europe came to the Salpêtrière to experience Charcot and learn from his brilliant lectures and demonstrations. One such man was a young doctor from Vienna whose ideas reverberated through the twentieth century.

SIGMUND FREUD (1856–1939): FOUNDING PSYCHOANALYSIS

That Freud has had a profound influence on Western culture is widely recognized. What is less known is the manner in which his ideas evolved and the sources of influence on him. Indeed, students in

introductory and personality courses often encounter a distorted description of Freud that perpetuates what science historian Frank Sulloway (1979) has called the "myth of the hero." The Freudian myth encompasses two components, according to Sulloway. First, it includes the image of Freud as a solitary heroic figure fighting for his ideas against all odds, in a uniformly hostile environment. Second, it maintains the illusion that the hero's theories were absolutely original to him, without serious precedent. Both aspects of this Freudian myth have been brought into question by recent historical scholarship. As will be seen: (a) Freud was indeed controversial but his ideas were not nearly as revolutionary as is normally portrayed, and (b) *all* of his major concepts have traceable origins to related or identical ideas in existence in the late nineteenth century. Freud's genius was not in creation but in synthesis and advocacy—in weaving ideas together into a unified theory of human behavior and in vigorously promoting this theory in the medical community and beyond.

Interestingly enough, Freud played a role in creating his own myth, in part by hand-picking his first biographer, Ernest Jones, but also by destroying his papers and correspondence on at least two occasions

---

[3] Chapter 8 briefly described some research on hypnosis that embarrassed a young Alfred Binet, in which his apparent success in producing effects with magnets was shown to be the result of suggestion. This study was conducted under Charcot's direction at the Salpêtrière, and the patient was none other than Blanche Wittman (Fancher, 1990).

(1885 and 1907), thereby making it difficult to trace the roots of his ideas. After the first of these events, which occurred long before he began to make a name for himself, Freud wrote to his fiancée that her letters were safe and to make his purpose clear:

> One intention ... I have almost finished carrying out, an intention which a number of as yet unborn and unfortunate people will one day resent ... my biographers. I have destroyed all my notes of the past fourteen years, as well as letters, scientific excerpts, and the manuscripts of my papers. As for letters, only those from the family have been spared. Yours, my darling, were never in danger. ... As for the biographers, let them worry, we have no desire to make it too easy for them. Each one of them will be right in his opinion of "The Development of the Hero," and I am already looking forward to seeing them go astray. (quoted in Sulloway, 1979, p. 7)

This is a remarkable letter. Who was this young man, not yet 30 years old, who was certain that he would someday have biographies written about him?

Early Life and Education

Freud spent most of his life in Vienna, Austria. His father moved a growing family there in 1860, when young Sigmund was four, and Freud left only when the Nazi threat to his personal safety took him to London in 1938, a year before his death. Freud's intellectual promise appeared early. He was a precocious young child in a large household of moderate means, the only one of his siblings given a room of his own for study. He was also given a generous book-buying allowance, and legend has it that when he once complained about the distractions of a younger sister's noisy piano lessons, they ended and the piano was banished from the house.

Freud was the first of eight children produced by the marriage of Jacob and Amalia Freud. Amalia was Jacob's third wife and half his age (20 versus 40). Freud developed a strong emotional attachment to his young mother, while his father was more distant and appeared more grandfatherly than fatherly—the family dynamics undoubtedly played a role in Freud's later thinking about parent-child relationships. Although the Freud family was Jewish, religious practice was not at the center of family life, and Freud would later recall that his father "allowed [him] to grow up in complete ignorance of everything that concerned Judaism" (quoted in Gay, 1988, p. 6). One aspect of Judaism that Freud did manage to experience, however, was Vienna's pervasive anti-Semitism. The period of Freud's youth saw a steady rise in the Jewish population in Vienna, from 2% of the population in 1857, to 10% by 1880 (Gay, 1988). Although liberal reforms made life easier for Jews in the 1860s, a serious economic depression in 1873 led to an all too familiar scapegoating scenario—Jews were blamed for Vienna's problems and became the objects of political (and physical) attack and discrimination. In that same year, Freud entered the University of Vienna's famed medical school after graduating with high honors from the gymnasium (high school). He quickly became aware of his status as a Jew in a setting dominated by non-Jews, but he refused to feel inferior to his peers. In fact, as might be expected from his early promise, he quickly became an academic star.

When he began medical school, Freud had no intention of eventually practicing medicine—his passion was for research. His mentor, one of the most important influences in his life, was Ernst Brücke, director of the university's Physiological Institute. Through Brücke, Freud became immersed in the nineteenth century materialist-mechanist-determinist zeitgeist in physiology (see Chapter 3). Brücke had been a student of the great Johannes Müller, and together with Helmholtz and other students of Müller, he was a leader in the movement that sought to explain all living action by reducing it to physical, mechanical forces. Although Freud's interest in searching for the physiological mechanisms underlying psychological processes diminished over the years, he never wavered in his belief that all events have causes that can be identified through science. His later idea that dreams were not random events, but had deep underlying meanings, is just one example of his strong faith in the essential orderliness and predictability of psychological events.

Freud's immersion in research was the main reason why it took him eight years instead of the typical five to earn his medical degree. Working in Brücke's laboratory from 1876 to 1882, he published articles on the nervous systems of various species and the gonadal structure of eels; he also developed an important research technique for staining nerve fibers. Much of his comparative neurological research carried with it strong evolutionary implications, for Darwin's monumental text was less than 20 years old and its ideas affected the thinking of all physiologists during the era. Indeed, Darwin's thinking would eventually influence Freud profoundly. First, Darwin's basic insight that human nature is rooted in its animal past provided support for Freud's beliefs about the importance of biological instincts in motivating behavior and the fact that behavior is not always "rational." Second, Freud's belief in the central importance of sexual motivation follows logically from the rather obvious point that sex and the resulting perpetuation of the species provides the very foundation for evolution.

Freud had every intention of continuing as a researcher when he completed his medical degree in 1883, but by then he was also deeply in love and faced with a financially uncertain future as a laboratory researcher. And as a Jew, few academic positions would be open to him. If he wished to marry, establishing a medical practice would be necessary. Hence, on Brücke's advice, he reluctantly began to prepare for life as a practitioner by taking three years of instruction at Vienna's General Hospital. For five months of this time, he came under the tutelage of Theodor Meynert (1833–1893), a famous brain anatomist and professor of psychiatry. Freud's earlier research with Brücke led him to be especially interested in disorders of the nervous system, and the time spent with Meynert confirmed in him the decision to specialize in that area. Patients with neurological problems also included hysterics, of course, and it was through his experience with Meynert that Freud first began to encounter the type of patient who would soon become the focus of his life's work. In 1885, he broadened his knowledge of hysteria, and began to learn something about hypnosis, when he earned a six-month travel grant to study with Charcot at the Salpêtrière. He later used hypnosis in the early years of his practice, but eventually abandoned it as an ineffective technique for exploring the unconscious mind.

Breuer and the Catharsis Method

Another important contact that Freud made while in medical school was with the eminent physician/neurologist Joseph Breuer (1842–1925), known for his research on the self-regulatory processes in breathing and his discovery of the role played by the semicircular canals of the inner ear in maintaining balance and equilibrium. From 1880 to 1882, while Freud was still finishing medical school, Breuer had treated a perplexing case of hysteria that was destined to become one of the defining events in the history of psychoanalysis: the **Anna O. case**. It is also just one example of how the story of psychoanalysis has become distorted over the years.

Anna O. (Figure 12.5) was the pseudonym that Breuer created for Bertha Pappenheim, an intelligent woman in her early twenties with a bewildering array of hysteric symptoms.[4] At various times her right (then her left) side appeared to be paralyzed and anesthetic, she had a persistent nervous cough, experienced both visual and auditory deficits, developed bizarre eating habits (e.g., living solely on oranges for a period of several weeks), lost the ability to speak German for a time (while retaining the ability to speak English), and experienced dissociative states that she called "absences" (Sulloway, 1979). The problems appeared to be precipitated by the long-term nursing care she had given to her dying father, although Anna's general frustrations about her situation in life contributed as well. An intelligent young woman, Anna was raised in a family and cultural context that consistently stifled her intellect and ambitions.

---

[4] The family of Bertha Pappenheim (1859–1936) was not pleased when Ernest Jones revealed her true identity in the first volume of his biography of Freud (Jones, 1953). After recovering her health, Bertha became a leader in the women's movement in Germany and once wrote: "if there is any justice in the next world, women will make the laws and men will bear the children" (quoted in Sulloway, 1979, p. 57). The West German government issued a stamp in her honor in 1954.

FIGURE 12.5 Bertha Pappenheim (Anna O.) at the time of her therapy with Breuer, from Sulloway (1979).

According to the traditional description of the case, Breuer found success with what he called the method of **catharsis**. He discovered that if Anna could be made to trace a particular symptom back to the occasion of its first appearance, she would experience an emotional release, which Breuer referred to as a "catharsis," and she would gain relief from the symptom. Anna referred to it as her "talking cure." For example, for a time she was unable to drink water from a glass and thought the practice disgusting. Breuer got her to trace her hydrophobia

back to a situation in which Anna had witnessed a woman who shared the same glass of water with her dog. Once the initial memory had been retrieved, she achieved a catharsis and the hydrophobia disappeared. In like manner, so the story goes, Breuer worked his way laboriously through Anna's remaining symptoms, seeing her every evening for more than a year.

The Anna O. case is a compelling story, but clever detective work by Ellenberger (1972) showed that the case was not as straightforward as it appears in most descriptions. Although the cathartic method had some success, relief of Anna's symptoms was often just temporary; the initial diagnosis of hysteria was only a small part of her problem (she also had psychotic symptoms and possibly a multiple personality disorder). She began to recover only after spending several lengthy confinements in a sanatorium after Breuer ended her treatment. Also, several of the events reported in traditional descriptions were factually wrong. For example, according to the account in the Jones biography of Freud, Breuer's wife was not happy about the amount of time he was spending with this attractive young woman, and when Anna developed a false pregnancy and named Breuer as the father, he did his catharsis magic to relieve the symptom and then terminated the therapy in a mild panic. The very next day he whisked his wife off to a second honeymoon to Venice where they conceived a daughter (and they all lived happily ever after). Ellenberger, however, showed that none of Breuer's case notes mentioned a false pregnancy, and the birth date of his daughter conflicts with the second honeymoon story.

Breuer told his younger colleague Freud about the case, and it eventually became featured as the first of several cases described in their coauthored *Studies on Hysteria* (1895/1955). This book is often considered the founding event for psychoanalysis. For Freud, the case demonstrated that (a) memory of a traumatic event might be actively repressed into the unconscious, but it will continue to influence the person's behavior as a hysteric symptom; (b) the form of a hysterical symptom bears a symbolic relationship to the traumatic event that caused it, as in the hydrophobia example; and (c) a symptom can be alleviated if the person gains insight into the originating event. As Freud would later say in the first of a series of lectures given at Clark University, "[o]ur hysterical patients suffer from reminiscences. Their symptoms are residues and mnemic symbols of particular (traumatic) events" (1909/1992, p. 16).

Freud also believed he detected a strong undercurrent of sexuality in the case. Anna seemed to be unusually attached to her father and near the end of therapy, developed a strong attachment to Breuer as well. Freud would eventually refer to this attachment for the therapist as **transference**, and would consider it an important step on the road to recovery. Breuer, while recognizing that sexuality was involved in the case, rejected Freud's argument that *all* neuroses had sexual origins, and split with Freud over the issue, thus ending a long friendship. It would not be the first time that Freud's insistence on the importance of sexual motivation would cost him a colleague.

Creating Psychoanalysis

From the mid-1880s to the mid-1890s, Freud developed his neurology practice, specializing in the treatment of hysteria. He was not at a loss for patients. Vienna was like other European cities in the Victorian era—sex in marriage was considered a necessary evil, good only for producing heirs, whereas sex for pleasure was confined to males visiting prostitutes. The results included frustrated sexual needs for the faithful wife, lingering guilt for the wandering husband, and good incomes for therapists like Freud. The picture was more complicated, of course—historians continue to debate whether the Victorian female was sexually inhibited (e.g., Sterns, 1985). Nonetheless, neurotic symptoms seemed plentiful at a time when Freud was trying to establish his practice. He tried everything with his patients, from conventional treatments such as hydrotherapy (i.e., similar to a modern whirlpool bath, presumably designed to soothe the nerves) to hypnosis to a procedure in which he pressed on a patient's forehead while insisting that they retrieve repressed memories. He eventually discovered a technique that became the centerpiece of psychoanalytic practice—

free association. Patients were placed in a relaxed position (hence, the famous couch) and encouraged to say whatever came into their minds, without censoring anything. This often proved difficult for patients, who would display what Freud called **resistance**—they would be unable or unwilling to mention something that had occurred to them. Freud welcomed resistances, believing they were sure signs that he was getting to the root of the patient's problem. For example, if a depressed female patient resisted telling the therapist that she was attracted to her brother-in-law, who looked a bit like her father and shared some of Dad's mannerisms, Freud would immediately begin thinking about how her problems might stem from unresolved feelings toward her father.

In addition to free association, Freud also used **dream analysis** as a means to explore the unconscious. He first hit upon the idea while searching for a way to perform psychoanalysis on himself, a task he undertook in the late 1890s. He could recall his dreams in great detail, and he discovered that they provided a rich source of information, both on their own and as a starting point for further free association. He published what is widely considered his most important book, *The Interpretation of Dreams*, in 1900. Freud's dream theory will be elaborated later in the excerpt from his Clark lectures.

The Importance of Sex

As Freud's experience with hysteria grew, he became convinced that unresolved sexual problems were at the heart of the matter. Patients working their way into their pasts by means of free associations and dream reports often seemed to have experienced some type of sexual trauma at a young age. By the mid-1890s, Freud had heard enough of this theme to propose what became known as his **seduction hypothesis**. Hysteria, he argued, was the result of childhood sexual abuse by a parent or other adult. Because the young child had no understanding of what was happening, Freud believed, the experience was forgotten, buried deep in the unconscious mind. Sometime after puberty occurred and the person began to understand about and experience mature sexuality, the long-buried memory would resurface

This year marked the official publication date of Freud's *Interpretation of Dreams*. It appeared a year earlier, but Freud wanted the millennium publication date on his book.

These events also occurred:

• Physicist Max Planck formulated quantum theory

• F. E. Dorn discovered radon

• The Commonwealth of Australia was created

• D. F. Davis was presented an international lawn tennis cup bearing his name

• Puccini's opera, *Tosca*, made its debut in Rome

• These people were born:

Spencer Tracy, American actor

Aaron Copeland, American composer

• These people died:

Oscar Wilde, English author

Friedrich Nietzsche, German philosopher

in the form of one or more hysterical symptoms (Gleaves & Hernandez, 1999).

Freud first presented his seduction theory in public at an 1896 meeting of the Vienna Society for Psychiatry and Neurology, which was presided over by Richard von Krafft-Ebbing, the era's leading authority on sexual pathology. The talk was not well received by the medical community, and Krafft-Ebbing even called Freud's theory a "scientific fairy tale" (Gay, 1988, p. 93). Freud himself soon began to doubt the strength of the abuse-hysteria connection, partly because some of his patients' stories didn't seem to stand up to other evidence. Also, Freud was bothered by the idea that it was only sexual traumas in childhood that led to later problems. What about all the other, nonsexual traumas (e.g., severe illness, bad falls) that children experience? Why didn't they lead to later psychopathologies? It seemed impossible, Freud later wrote, "to suppose that distressing sexual affects so greatly exceed all other unpleasurable affects in intensity. It must be another characteristic of sexual ideas that can explain how it is that

sexual ideas are alone subjected to [pathological] repression" (quoted in Sulloway, 1979, p. 111).

Tradition has it that Freud's great intellectual breakthrough was to abandon his seduction theory and replace it with the idea that sexual events in childhood were not real but imagined and that sexuality did not begin in adolescence but existed in some form from infancy. This insight about universal childhood sexuality supposedly emerged from Freud's self-analysis in the late 1890s. There is probably some truth to Freud's "heroic" account of how, entirely on his own and without the influence of contemporary ideas, he came to abandon his seduction hypothesis and develop his famous Oedipal complex. However, this is an area where the Freudian myth has also been at work. Freud was not operating in an intellectual vacuum here, creating ideas that were unique. For instance, several other noted "sexologists" (e.g., Havelock Ellis) were also proposing that sexual strivings extended into infancy and that repressed sexuality was connected with later psychopathology. Indeed, the 1890s witnessed an outpouring of books on sex, childhood and otherwise, and Freud was fully knowledgeable about them (Sulloway, 1979). Hence, the origins of the concept of infantile sexuality include Freud's self-analysis, but go much deeper to include the intellectual context of late nineteenth-century Europe.

Psychoanalysis Enters the Twentieth Century

By the turn of the twentieth century, Freud was launched on his career as a psychoanalyst specializing in the treatment of hysteria. With *The Interpretation of Dreams*, he also began developing his general theory of behavior, which continued to evolve for the rest of his life. A year after the dream book, in 1901, he published *The Psychopathology of Everyday Life*, and in 1905 two books appeared: *Three Contributions to the Theory of Sex* and *Wit and Its Relation to the Unconscious*. With these publications, Freud's reputation grew, slowly but steadily, throughout the first decade of the twentieth century. In America, his theories caught the enthusiastic attention of G. Stanley Hall of Clark University. As you recall from Chapter 6, Hall's enormous range of interests included the study of children and adolescents, including their sexual development. He described Breuer and Freud's work on hysteria in his two-volume book on adolescence, and he was offering courses on sexuality as early as 1904 (Rosenzweig, 1992). In 1909, to celebrate the twentieth anniversary of Clark University's founding, Hall invited Freud to Worcester to receive an honorary degree and lecture on psychoanalysis. Several other prominent "behavioral scientists" also gave talks and were awarded degrees at the celebration, including Titchener, the noted anthropologist Franz Boas, and Carl Jung, who accompanied Freud on the trans-Atlantic voyage. Still other psychologists came to hear the talks, including James, Cattell, and Goddard. It was Freud's only visit to the United States and he returned with a healthy dislike of the country, especially its food. Nonetheless, he was forever grateful to Hall, crediting him with enhancing the international reputation of psychoanalysis and providing "the first official recognition of our endeavors" (quoted in Gay, 1988, p. 207).

ORIGINAL SOURCE EXCERPT
Freud's Lectures on Psychoanalysis at Clark University

From Tuesday, September 7, 1909 through Saturday, the 11th, Freud gave five improvised lectures, in German, to the assembled audience of educators, scientists, and press. In the opener, he paid homage to Breuer and described the origins of psychoanalysis in the Anna O. case. The lecture included the quote about hysterics suffering from their memories that begins this chapter. Lecture 2 focused on the related processes of resistance and repression and described how Freud shifted from hypnosis to free association as a method for searching the unconscious. The following excerpt comes from lectures 3 and 4, and is taken from a 1977 translation by James Strachey.

Lecture 3 included Freud's dream theory, with its distinction between the manifest and latent content of dreams, and his ideas about slips of the tongue and other so-called accidents. After opening the talk with some further discussion of free association and Jung's related word association procedure, Freud began to discuss dreams, starting with an acknowledgment of American pragmatism:

> I must admit, Ladies and Gentlemen, that I hesitated for a long time whether, instead of giving you this condensed general survey of the whole field of psycho-analysis, it might not be better to present you with a detailed account of dream-interpretation. I was held back by a purely subjective and seemingly secondary motive. It seemed to me almost indecent in a country which is devoted to practical aims to make my appearance as a "dream interpreter," before you could possibly know the importance that can attach to that antiquated and derided art. The interpretation of dreams is in fact the royal road to a knowledge of the unconscious; it is the securest foundation of psychoanalysis and the field in which every worker must acquire his convictions and seek his training. If I am asked how one can become a psycho-analyst, I reply, "By studying one's own dreams." Every opponent of psycho-analysis hitherto has, with a nice discrimination, either evaded any consideration of *The Interpretation of Dreams*, or has sought to skirt over it with the most superficial objections. If, on the contrary, you can accept the solutions of the problems of dream-life, the novelties with which psycho-analysis confronts your minds will offer you no further difficulties. (p. 33)

Freud's comment about critics "evading any evaluation" of the dream book or super-ficially dismissing it, combined with his complaints at other times that nobody would read the book, helped further the Freudian myth. Sales were indeed slow at first—it took six years to sell the first printing of 600 copies (Jones, 1953)—but the book was neither ignored nor condemned. In fact, it was widely reviewed and generally praised as "epoch-making" (Decker, 1975).

After proclaiming the importance of dreams, Freud introduced the central idea that dreams serve the function of wish fulfillment. This is easy to see in children's dreams, but disguised in adult dreams:

> In the first place, not all dreams are alien to the dreamer, incomprehensible and confused. If you inspect the dreams of very young children, from eighteen months upwards, you will find them perfectly simple and easy to explain. Small children always dream of the fulfillment of wishes that were aroused in them the day before but not satisfied. You will need no interpretative art in order to find this simple solution; all you need do is to enquire into the child's experiences on the previous day (the "dream day"). Certainly the most satisfactory solution of the riddle of dreams would be to find that adults' dreams too were like those of children—fulfillments of wishful impulses that had come to them on the dream-day. And such in fact is the case. The difficulties in the way of this solution can be overcome step by step if dreams are analyzed more closely.
>
> The first and most serious objection is that the content of adults' dreams is as a rule unintelligible and could not look more unlike the fulfillment of a wish. And here is the answer. Such dreams have been subjected to distor-tion; the psychical process underlying them might originally have been expressed in words quite differently. You must distinguish the *manifest con-tent of the dream*, as you vaguely recollect it in the morning and laboriously (and, as it seems, arbitrarily) clothe it in words, and the *latent dream-thoughts*, which you must suppose were present in the unconscious. This distortion in dreams is the same process that you have already come to know in investigating the formation of hysterical symptoms. It indicates, too, that the same interplay of mental forces is at work in the formation of dreams as in that of symptoms. The manifest content of the dream is the dis-torted substitute for the unconscious dream-thoughts and this distortion is the work of the ego's forces of defense—of resistances. In waking life these resistances altogether prevent the repressed wishes of the unconscious from entering consciousness; and during the lowered state of sleep they are at least strong enough to oblige them to adopt a veil of disguise. Thereafter, the dreamer can no more understand the meaning of his dreams than the hys-teric can understand the connection and significance of his symptoms.
>
> ... The manifest dream, which you know from your memory when you wake up, can therefore only be described as a *disguised* fulfillment of *repressed* wishes.
>
> You can also obtain a view, by a kind of synthetic work, of the process which has brought about the distortion of the unconscious dream-thoughts

into the manifest content of the dream. We call this process the "dream-work." It deserves our closest theoretical interest, since we are able to study in it, as nowhere else, what unsuspected psychical processes can occur in the unconscious, or rather, to put it more accurately, *between* two separate psychical systems like the conscious and the unconscious. Among these freshly discovered psychical processes those of *condensation* and *displacement* are especially noticeable. The dream-work is a special case of the effects produced by two different mental groupings on each other—that is, of the consequences of mental splitting; and it seems identical in all essentials with the process of distortion which transforms the repressed complexes into symptoms where there is unsuccessful repression. ...

I should like you to notice, too, that the analysis of dreams has shown us that the unconscious makes use of a particular symbolism, especially for representing sexual complexes. This symbolism varies partly from individual to individual; but partly it is laid down in a typical form and seems to coincide with the symbolism which, as we suspect, underlies our myths and fairy tales. It seems not impossible that these creations of the popular mind might find an explanation through the help of dreams. (pp. 34–36, italics in the original translation)

Hence, the manifest content of the dream includes images that serve as symbols for the deeper, more meaningful latent content. For Freud, as you might guess, many of the symbols had sexual content. Elongated objects symbolized male sexuality, while anything symbolizing containers represented females. (A Freudian would have no difficulty interpreting a dream about a train going into a tunnel, as in the final scene of Alfred Hitchcock's *North by Northwest*.) Both condensation and displacement involve symbolism. In **condensation**, two or more latent or unconscious thoughts combine to form a single thought that is symbolized in an image reported in the manifest dream. For example, a dream in which a person hesitates about going into a church with a large (i.e., elongated) steeple might symbolize the conflict between sexuality and morality. In **displacement**, a minor part of the manifest content might be the major part of the latent content, and vice versa. Thus, a long dream about a golf match might include a single moment of indecision about which club to choose. That small part of the manifest content, for a Freudian, might in fact symbolize a deeper problem about the lack of direction in one's life (and because a "club" is involved, sex would surely find a way into the interpretation).

At the end of the third lecture, Freud discussed events that appear to be trivial, yet provide another glimpse of the unconscious mind. He also made his determinist beliefs clear—even the simplest accident points to some predictable unconscious motive:

The phenomena in question are the small faulty actions performed by both normal and neurotic people, to which as a rule no importance is attached: forgetting things that might be known and sometimes in fact *are* known (e.g., the occasional difficulty in recalling proper names), slips of the tongue in talking, by which we ourselves are so often affected, analogous slips of the pen and misreadings, bungling the performance of actions, losing objects or breaking them. All of these are things for which as a rule no psychological determinants are sought and which are allowed to pass without criticism as consequences of distraction or inattention or similar causes. Besides these there are the actions and gestures which people carry out without noticing them at all, to say nothing of attributing any psychological importance to them; playing about and fiddling with things, humming tunes, fingering parts of one's own body or one's clothing and so on. These small things, faulty actions and symptomatic or haphazard actions alike, are not so insignificant as people, by sort of conspiracy of silence, are ready to suppose. They always have a meaning, which can usually be interpreted with ease and certainty from the situation in which they occur. And it turns out that once again they give expression to impulses and intentions which have to be kept back and hidden from one's own consciousness, or that they are actually derived from the same repressed wishful impulses and complexes which we have already come to know as the creators of symptoms and the constructors of dreams. They therefore deserve to be rated as symptoms, and if they are examined they may lead, just as dreams do, to the uncovering of the hidden part of the mind. ...

As you already see, psycho-analysts are marked by a particularly strict belief in the determination of mental life. For them there is nothing trivial, nothing arbitrary or haphazard. They expect in every case to find sufficient motives where, as a rule, no such expectation is raised. Indeed, they are prepared to find *several* motives for one and the same mental occurrence, whereas what seems to be our innate craving for causality declares itself satisfied with a *single* psychical cause. (pp. 37–38, italics in the original translation)

Freud did not give any examples of these Freudian slips in the Clark lecture, but *The Psychopathology of Everyday Life* is full of them. For instance, when a lecturer referred to the "Freuer-Breudian" theory of hysteria instead of "Breuer-Freudian," when referring to their jointly authored hysteria book, Freud suggested that a hostile motive was behind the mistake. In another case, a patient who couldn't recall (i.e., had repressed) where a man had touched her, quickly changed the subject to her summer home. When asked where it was located, she said "near the mountain loin" instead of "mountain lane."

Freud's fourth Clark lecture was a summary of his *Three Contributions on the Theory of Sexuality*, and it included a discussion of childhood sexuality and the Oedipal complex. He began by asserting that:

First and foremost we have found out one thing. Psycho-analytic research traces back the symptoms of patient's illnesses with really surprising regularity to impressions from their *erotic life*. It shows us that the pathogenic wishful impulses are in the nature of erotic instinctual components; and it forces us to suppose that among the influences leading to the illness the predominant significance must be assigned to erotic disturbances, and that this is the case in both sexes. (p. 40, italics in the original translation)

Freud next tried to convince his audience of his assertion that sexual motivation reached back into childhood and defined this sexuality broadly as any pleasurable activity related to the "erogenous" zones:

Put away your doubts, then, and join me in a consideration of infantile sexuality from the earliest age. A child's sexual instinct turns out to be put together out of a number of factors; it is capable of being divided up into numerous components which originate from various sources. Above all, it is still independent of the reproductive function, into the service of which it will be later brought. It serves for the acquisition of different kinds of pleasurable feeling, which, basing ourselves on analogies and connections, we bring together under the idea of sexual pleasure. The chief source of infantile sexual pleasure is the appropriate excitation of certain parts of the body that are especially susceptible to stimulus: apart from the genitals, these are the oral, anal and urethral orifices, as well as the skin and other sensory surfaces. Since at this first phase of infantile sexual life satisfaction is obtained from the subject's own body and extraneous objects are disregarded, we term this phase (from a word coined by Havelock Ellis) that of *auto-erotism*. We call the parts of the body that are important in the acquisition of sexual pleasure "erotogenic zones." (pp. 43–44, italics in the original translation)

As examples of autoerotic behaviors, Freud mentioned such things as thumb-sucking and innocent genital manipulation. He then turned to the question of object-choice, which led him to the Oedipal complex:

... Children's relations to their parents, as we learn alike from direct observations of children and from later analytic examination of adults, are by no means free from elements of accompanying sexual excitation. The child takes both of its parents, and more particularly one of them, as the object of its erotic wishes. In so doing, it usually follows some indication from its parents, whose affection bears the clearest characteristics of a sexual activity, even though of one that is inhibited in its aims. As a rule a father prefers his daughter and a mother her son; the child reacts to this by wishing, if he is a son, to take his father's place, and, if she is a daughter, her mother's. The feelings which are aroused in these relations between parents and children and in the resulting ones between brothers and sisters are not only of a positive or affectionate kind but also of a negative or hostile one. The complex which is thus formed is doomed to early repression; but it continues to exercise a great and lasting influence from the unconscious. It is to be suspected that, together with its extensions, it constitutes the *nuclear complex* of every neurosis, and we may expect to find it no less actively at work in other regions of mental life. The myth of King Oedipus, who killed his father and took his mother to wife, reveals, with little modification, the infantile wish, which is later opposed and repudiated by the *barrier against incest*. Shakespeare's *Hamlet* is equally rooted in the soil of the incest-complex, but under a better disguise. ...

It is inevitable and perfectly normal that a child should take his parents as the first objects of his love. But his libido should not remain fixated to these first objects; later on, it should merely take them as a model, and should make a gradual transition from them on to extraneous people when the time for the final choice of an object arrives. The detachment of the child from his parents is thus a task that cannot be evaded if the young individual's social fitness is not to be endangered. During the time at which repression is making its selection among the component instincts, and later, when there should be a slackening of the parent's influence, which is essentially responsible for the expenditure of energy on these repressions, the task of education meets with great problems, which at the present time are certainly not always dealt with in an understanding and unobjectionable manner.

You must not suppose, Ladies and Gentlemen, that these discussions on sexual life and psychosexual development of children have led us too far from psycho-analysis and the problem of curing nervous disorders. You can, if you like, regard psycho-analytic treatment as no more than a prolongation of education for the purpose of overcoming the residues of childhood. (pp. 47–48, italics in the original translation)

Freud's fifth and final lecture described the importance of transference for the successful outcome of psychoanalysis and held out the hope that the individual's **libido**, the psychic energy associated with the sex drive, could be directed toward socially useful activities, a process he referred to as **sublimation**.

The Evolution of Psychoanalytic Theory

Freud was already 54 years old when he delivered his lectures at Clark, but he was just beginning to develop what he referred to as his **metapsychology**—his general theory of human behavior and mental processes. Over the next 20 years, this metatheory evolved considerably; indeed, many of the concepts most frequently associated with Freud did not appear until after World War I, when he was in his late sixties (for a more thorough description of the content of the theory, refer to any theories of personality textbook). One major postwar change in Freud's metapsychology was his conviction that destructive tendencies were just as powerful as sexual ones in motivating behavior.

Freud did not ignore aggression in the years prior to World War I. Male feelings of hostility toward the father were an integral part of the Oedipal complex and the sex act itself contains elements of male aggression, he believed. Yet the war, with its seemingly unending brutality and appalling loss of life, had a profound impact on Freud's thinking (Gay, 1988). In 1920, he produced *Beyond the Pleasure Principle*, in which he proposed a distinction between **eros**, the life instinct, manifested in sexual motivation, and **thanatos**, a death instinct, which showed itself in the form of aggression and

self-destruction. Hence, he came to believe that human behavior was jointly motivated by life-enhancing (sexual) and life-destroying (aggressive) instincts.

Although his reflections on the world war were the immediate stimulus for his proposal that we all have instinctive destructive tendencies, the concept of a death instinct was also rooted in a lifelong preoccupation that Freud had with death, and his conviction of its reality was strengthened by events in his life during the 1920s. Shortly after he wrote *Beyond the Pleasure Principle*, one of his three daughters died during an influenza outbreak. Soon after that, a favorite grandson died and a niece committed suicide. Then in 1923, Freud, who smoked up to 20 cigars a day, was diagnosed with cancer of the mouth and saw his own demise on the horizon. Over the next 16 years, he endured 33 painful surgeries and had to live with a series of increasingly bulky denture-like prostheses to replace parts of his palate and jaw. Freud saw all of these events as confirmation that death instincts go hand in hand with life instincts.

Other well-known Freudian concepts also developed in his later years. These include his structural analysis of personality into id, ego, and superego components, and his description of the relationship between anxiety and ego defense mechanisms. Freud first wrote about his familiar tripartite structure of personality—id, ego, and superego—in *The Ego and the Id*, a short book that appeared in 1923. The **ego**, partly conscious and partly unconscious, lies at the center of personality, Freud wrote, trying to maintain a balance between three conflicting forces: the id, the superego, and reality. The **id**, repository of the instinctive drives of sex and aggression, constantly demands that its needs be satisfied. On the other hand, the **superego**, the person's learned moral values, works to inhibit the free expression of the instincts. The ego must also take into account the environmental factors operating in the real world, which enter the system through what Freud called the "perception-consciousness" system. The properly functioning ego, according to Freud, serves as a mediator, channeling id-based needs in directions that are realistic and consistent with moral values.

The demands made on the ego necessarily produce some tension. Freud's approach to anxiety was to distinguish three forms of it, one for each of the forces pressuring the ego. **Objective anxiety** (or "realistic" anxiety) is a normal reaction to a perceived threat from the external world, based on the person's memories of past situations of danger. Thus, sailors observing a "red sky in the morning" know they must "take warning" because it means a storm is on the horizon. This perception, combined with memory, would create an understandable level of objective anxiety. More interesting to the psychoanalyst, however, were the other two forms of anxiety, neurotic and moral. In **neurotic anxiety**, the person fears that id-based impulses will get out of control. Memories of being punished for acting out impulsively in the past lead to the feeling of anxiety. In the closely related **moral anxiety**, feelings of guilt and shame arise from a sense that one is about to violate the strict moral code of the superego.

The feeling of anxiety serves as a signal to the ego that it is under attack, Freud reasoned, and it responds through defense. The response to objective anxiety is to deal with the situation realistically (e.g., the sailors prepare the ship for a storm) or to use the fight/flight reflex if true danger is at hand. Because neurotic and moral anxieties are generated internally, however, the responses must also come from within, and they do so in the form of ego **defense mechanisms**. The most common form of defense is **repression**, accomplished by that portion of the ego that is unconscious. In repression, unwanted impulses are actively forced from awareness and into the unconscious. Repression is also an element in the other defenses. In **projection**, for example, personal faults cannot be accepted, so they are attributed to some other person. People who cannot accept the hostility within them, for example, might convince themselves that those around them are the hostile ones. That is, they repress their own hostility and project it onto others. Another common defense is **reaction formation**, in which unacceptable impulses are repressed and replaced with the opposite ones. For instance, feelings of hatred toward an unwanted child, unacceptable to the superego, are transformed into an exaggerated level of attention and an unwillingness to allow any negative feelings about the child to surface (Hall, 1954).

Freud's thinking about defense mechanisms was aided significantly by his daughter and fellow analyst, Anna Freud (1895–1982) (Figure 12.6). Apparently oblivious to the risks, Freud psychoanalyzed Anna as part of her preparation for a career as analyst. Anna survived the analysis and went on to a distinguished career. She was a pioneer in extending psychoanalytic practice to children through the use of play therapy.

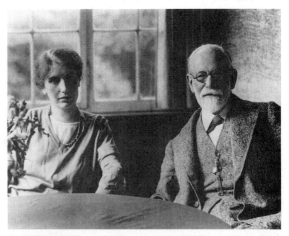

FIGURE 12.6 Freud and his daughter Anna, in 1928, the year of Anna's book on child psychoanalysis, from Gay (1988).

Children lack the verbal fluency for normal analysis, of course, so Anna probed children's psyches by giving them various materials (e.g., Mommy and Daddy dolls) and asking them to just play. She also helped her father develop his own theory, especially the relationship between anxiety and defense. In fact, the lists of defense mechanisms (projection, reaction formation, etc.) normally found in introductory texts are more the outcome of her work than her father's. She articulated them in *The Ego and Mechanisms of Defense* (A. Freud, 1937). After Freud's death, Anna became a fierce protector of her father's reputation, and a collaborator in the "Freudian myth" (Sulloway, 1979).

Freud's Followers: Loyalty and Dissent

By the turn of the twentieth century, Freud had begun attracting the interest of other physicians in Vienna. In 1902, he asked four of them to join him on Wednesday evenings to discuss issues related to psychoanalysis. The group expanded to about 20 by 1908 and began calling itself the Vienna Psychoanalytic Society. Discussions were spirited, but the authoritarian and dogmatic Freud dominated the meetings and made it clear that his word was to be law. As might be expected, while some members remained intensely loyal to Freud for years, others were not so compliant. The first major defector was one of the original five who met in 1902.

Alfred Adler (1870–1937) was trained in ophthalmology and general practice at the University of Vienna medical school, graduating in 1895. He was apparently attracted to Freud's ideas on reading *The Interpretation of Dreams*, and he became an enthusiastic charter member of the Wednesday evening group. Soon, however, he began to question Freud's seeming obsession with the universality of sexual motivation. Instead, he drew on his own troubled childhood, which included illness and feelings of inferiority when compared to an older brother, and proposed the **inferiority complex** as the basis for an alternative theory. All infants are inherently inferior in their abilities, he argued, and life could be viewed as an attempt to compensate for this inferiority. He also pointed out that as we grow, the social environment places obstacles in our paths that also create

feelings of inferiority to be overcome. Adler's emphasis on the importance of social factors over biological ones, along with his writings on inferiority and his belief that behavior was determined as much by conscious planning for the future as by the repressed events of one's past, alienated him from Freud. The official break came in 1911, when he was tossed out of the Vienna Psychoanalytic Society, taking several followers with him. He went on to create a rival school of psychoanalysis that he called **individual psychology.** Adler and Freud never reconciled; indeed Gay (1988) described their subsequent relationship as one of mutual hate, and when Adler died suddenly in 1937, Freud was delighted to learn that he had outlived his rival.

An equally bitter split occurred between Freud and the Swiss psychiatrist Carl Jung (1875–1961), known for his pioneering work with schizophrenia. The two met in Vienna in 1907 after exchanging some earlier correspondence in which Jung's praise for Freud's dream theory was matched by Freud's enthusiasm for a **word association** task that had been developed by Jung (1919). The procedure involved giving patients a prepared list of words and asking them to respond to each with the first word that came to mind. Also, their reactions were timed and some physiological measures were recorded (Watson & Evans, 1991). Jung assumed that longer reaction times and arousal (e.g., increased breathing) would indicate that a particular word had important emotional implications, a rationale similar to the one later used to justify the polygraph's validity as a lie detector.

Jung accompanied Freud to America and the Clark conference of 1909, where he lectured on his word association procedure. In 1911, Freud arranged to have Jung named the first president of the newly formed International Psychoanalytic Society, in part because Freud believed that naming Jung, who was neither Viennese nor Jewish, would make the association appear to be more international and broad-based than it really was. Meanwhile, Freud began thinking of Jung in father-son terms, even writing to him as his "successor and crown prince" (quoted in McGuire, 1974, p. 218). But trouble was looming on the horizon and by 1913, Jung went the way of Adler, expelled from the inner circle.

Like Adler, Jung questioned Freud's emphasis on sex and had some ideas of his own. Over the rest of his career, he developed what came to be called **analytical psychology**, to be distinguished from Freud's psychoanalysis. He went beyond Freud in some ways. For example, to the concept of a "personal" unconscious, similar to Freud's use of the term, he added the evolutionary concept of the **collective unconscious**, said to include the collective experiences of our ancestors. He believed that the common themes found in mythology reflected a shared human legacy. Jung also contributed to personality theory with his distinction between what he saw as two major personality types: introverts and extroverts.

After the defection of Adler, Jung, and another analyst named Stekel, Freud closed ranks. At the suggestion of Ernest Jones, destined to be Freud's hand-picked biographer, Freud formed a secret group of eight called the "Committee." He even gave each member of his new inner sanctum a gold ring. Their task was to safeguard orthodox Freudianism, respond to critics, control the various psychoanalytic organizations, and as it turned out, perpetuate the Freud myth. (Sulloway, 1979).

Psychoanalysis in America

The Clark lectures put Freud on the intellectual map in America, but not all of those in attendance were impressed. An ailing William James, within a year of his death from heart disease, traveled to Worcester to hear Freud's fourth lecture and the two men spent some time together in private. James later wrote to a colleague expressing the hope that Freud would push his interesting ideas to the limit because they "can't fail to throw light on human nature." On the other hand, James had to "confess that [Freud] made on me personally the impression of a man obsessed with fixed ideas. I can make nothing in my own case with his dream theories, and obviously 'symbolism' is a most dangerous method" (quoted in Rosenzweig, 1992, p. 174).

Over the next few years, American psychologists had the opportunity to learn more about Freud. Reviews of Freud's work and articles on psychoanalysis appeared in the *Journal of Abnormal Psychology* with some regularity, but many academic psychologists found psychoanalysis either tangential to their research interests, or annoyingly "unscientific." Robert Woodworth of Columbia (Chapter 7), who might have been congenial to the Freudians because of his own interest in motivation and his general eclecticism, attacked psychoanalysis as being more religion than science (Woodworth, 1917). He was especially annoyed at a clever strategy used by analysts; whenever attacked, they would attribute the criticism to an unconscious resistance on the part of the attacker, thereby providing pseudo-support for a key Freudian concept. It was a perfect Catch-22: analysts could claim support for Freud's ideas regardless of whether critics praised or condemned them. For Woodworth, this attitude was unconscionable. Equally galling to American psychologists was the analysts' claim that to truly understand psychoanalysis and to criticize it, one had to undergo a complete psychoanalysis oneself (Hornstein, 1992).

As mentioned in the previous chapter, some behaviorally inclined psychologists (i.e., John Dollard and Neal Miller) in the late 1930s tried to assimilate psychoanalysis by reinterpreting it in terms understandable to them. Repression, for instance, rather than being some mysterious force that wrestled with unacceptable ideas and shoved them into the deep void of the unconscious, could be considered "more rationally" as a response of non-thinking about certain events that were associated in one's learning history with negative emotions. It was simply a matter of avoidance conditioning—non-thinking about some event was reinforced by the elimination of anxiety associated with that event. Other psychologists tried to bring Freudian concepts into the laboratory and subject them to operational definitions. Repression, for example, could be defined in terms of whether or not people recognized "dirty words" that were flashed at threshold level (e.g., McGinnies, 1949). This research on perceptual defense was interesting in its own right, but whether it adequately tested Freud's ideas was another question.

Freudian psychoanalysis might not have played well within academia, but it had a strong impact on the medical practice of psychiatry, and it caught the imagination of the general public. Between 1912 and 1918, some 170 articles relating to psychoanalysis appeared in medical journals, and about 50 articles appeared in popular magazines ranging from *Ladies' Home Journal* to *The New Republic* (Green & Reiber, 1980). By the 1920s, psychoanalysis was popular enough to be the subject of light satire. In "A Manual of the New Mentality," for example, Stephan Leacock (1924) noted that "[i]n every direction one sees references to psychoanalysis, auto-suggestion, hypnosis, hopnoosis, psychiatry, inebriety, and things never thought of a little while ago" (p. 471). A more sarcastic tone was taken by Grace Adams, a former student of Titchener, in an *Atlantic Monthly* article. Referring to the Clark conference, she noted that the psychologists in the audience didn't realize they were listening to the wave of the future; rather, they thought "they were merely listening to a bearded foreigner make some altogether preposterous remarks" (1934, p. 85). Adams went on to lament the intrusion of psychoanalysis into everyday life, with "its majestic verbiage and high-minded meddlesomeness" (p. 88). Analysts might know nothing about the details of housekeeping, acting, or banking, for instance, "yet from the mastery of their own special subject they were accepted as being able to tell a housewife, an actress, or a banker just how to perform his (sic) tasks" (pp. 86–87).

Despite the criticism and the satire, psychoanalysis persevered. It made significant inroads in the medical community and by the 1930s, training in psychiatry and neurology typically included a strong dose of Freud (Hale, 1971). In addition, psychoanalytic institutes were created in urban areas, especially in the eastern United States, and catered to M.D.s who wished further certification as professional psychoanalysts. Over the years, reflecting differences in institutional contexts and the focus of their interests, academic psychologists and psychoanalysts have tended to go their separate ways.

Freud in Perspective

Near the end of his life, Freud was once again reminded of his Jewish heritage. Ominous signs occurred soon after the Nazis rose to power in 1933.

As you recall from the gestalt chapter, Jewish professors were routinely dismissed from their positions. In addition, psychoanalysis was branded "Jewish science" and outlawed within Germany. Soon, Freud's writings were publicly burned, along with other books by Jews (e.g., Einstein). Freud wryly noted that the world seemed to be making progress: "In the Middle Ages they would have burnt me; nowadays they are content with burning my books" (quoted in Gay, 1988, pp. 592–593). Then in March of 1938, the Nazis occupied Austria. Vienna, that great city of culture and the arts, became a scene of beatings and even of cold-blooded murders of Jews on its streets. Freud was reluctant to leave Vienna, but became convinced that it was time to go, after Nazi sympathizers searched his home and the Gestapo briefly detained his daughter Anna. He left Vienna with his family in June of 1938 and resettled in London, where his cancer finally claimed him on September 23, 1939.[5]

The value of Freud's contributions to psychology has been a matter of considerable debate in recent years. One critic went so far as to refer to psychoanalysis as "the most stupendous intellectual confidence trick of the twentieth century ... [and] a vast structure of radically unsound design and with no posterity" (Medawar, quoted in Sulloway, 1979, p. 499). Scholars dissecting Freud's published case histories have found scant evidence of the effectiveness of psychoanalysis as therapy; he has been chastised for missing the opportunity to expose widespread childhood sexual abuse when he abandoned his original seduction theory, and he has even been accused of plagiarism (Gay, 1988). Defenders, on the other hand, argue that Freud is responsible for some of the most important ideas of the twentieth century and that his influence spreads beyond psychology and deeply into Western culture. This issue will not be resolved here, of course, or at any time in the near future. What can be enumerated are some aspects of Freud's influence and some of the typical criticisms that are made of his work.

[5] Freud never seemed to grasp the precariousness of his situation and like most people living during that era, he had no idea of the extent of the evil to come. Included among the six million killed in the Nazi death camps were four of his sisters (Fancher, 1990).

Contributions

Modern scholars have uncovered many of the sources and antecedents of Freud's ideas. As a result, his ideas are recognized as considerably less than original. Nonetheless, any attempt to understand human nature must include serious consideration of his work. First, although Freud did not discover the unconscious, he popularized the concept, and components of unconscious thinking such as repression, defense, and the "Freudian slip" have become part of the psychological lexicon. Freud's emphasis on unconscious motives also raised awareness of the general need to study motivational processes. Second, we now take it for granted that the events of early childhood can significantly affect later development. We might take issue with the Freudian model of early development, especially the Oedipal complex and its ramifications, but there is no question that he made us more aware of the malleability of the young mind. Third, at a time when the medical community favored biological explanations of mental disorders and their treatment, Freud showed that some problems were psychological in origin and, therefore, could be treated with psychological means (i.e., through psychotherapy).

Criticisms

Many of Freud's conflicts with peers concerned the degree of emphasis he placed on sexual motivation. Breuer, Jung, and Adler all disagreed with him over the issue, and we now recognize that human behavior is too complex to be reduced to single broad motives. Psychoanalysts in the post-Freudian era have paid increasing attention to the roles of interpersonal relationships ("object relations") and the social environment in shaping personality (Pervin, 1991). The criticism of Freud's overemphasis on sex is part of a broader problem—he often overstated the case. Thus, while childhood is clearly an important determiner of later personality, it is an exaggeration to say, as Freud did, that the personality structure is essentially determined during the first five or six years of life. A third frequent criticism of Freud, often delivered by those accustomed to laboratory control over variables, concerns the "scientific status" of his work. Freud has been criticized for relying on a limited sample of case studies, for excessive bias in bending the data from his patients into shapes that suited him, and for defining terms too loosely for his theory to be adequately tested. Freud's dogmatic insistence on his point of view and his demands of loyalty from his followers have also been said to be at odds with the "objectivity" expected of scientists in the positivist tradition. Finally, Freud has been widely criticized for his theoretical views about female psychology, although one must be careful to recognize that few people can step away from the social context in which they live. Thus, Freud was a typical Victorian male with a typical Victorian attitude about the second-class status of most women, and it showed in his work. He believed, for example, that superego development was never complete in women, that they envied the status of men, and that a woman's best hope for fulfillment was to produce male children. Anatomy, Freud declared, was destiny. In fairness, Freud never hindered and even encouraged the development of competent female analysts, most obviously his daughter Anna. And he occasionally acknowledged his meager understanding of the female psyche, once asking plaintively "What does a woman want?" (quoted in Gay, 1988, p. 501).

Freud's grand theory, his metapsychology, may not have held together over the years, but many of his insights have stood the test of time. As early as 1910, this conclusion about Freud was recognized by his contemporary, Havelock Ellis, and is a fitting way to close this section of the chapter: "But if ... Freud sometimes selects a very thin thread [in tying together his theoretical arguments], he seldom fails to string pearls on it, and these have value whether the thread snaps or not" (Ellis, 1910, quoted in Sulloway, 1979, p. 500).

CLINICAL PSYCHOLOGY IN AMERICA

Today, clinical psychologists specialize in the diagnosis and treatment of all types of mental disorders, and they are at the forefront of research concerning these problems. In contrast with psychiatrists, clinical psychologists train in graduate school rather than medical school and earn Ph.D.s or Psy.D.s rather than M.D.s. Many have their own private practice, while others work in Veterans Administration (VA) hospitals or in private clinical settings. Some combine their practice with academic positions at colleges and universities. Some incorporate Freudian concepts into their practice, but most do not. Today, they comprise a highly influential group among those providing mental health services. This type of clinical psychologist began to emerge at the end of World War II, when the number of psychological casualties created a need that the medical community, in particular psychiatry, could not meet. In one sense, then, **clinical psychology** as we know it today is about 50 years old.

On the other hand, a portion of the APA's 1996 annual meeting was devoted to a celebration of clinical psychology's *centennial*. Much was made of a clinic created on the campus of the University of Pennsylvania in 1896 by the director of the psychology laboratory there, Lightner Witmer. The event was undoubtedly important, as will be elaborated shortly, and it set in motion circumstances that eventually produced modern clinical psychology. Yet the clinical psychology that existed prior to World War II was quite different from the discipline that emerged in the postwar era. The APA's centennial celebration is an interesting example of how the historical significance of some event can be created long after the event has occurred, through the decisions of historians and others (e.g., convention planners) who may be motivated by more than just a desire for historical truth. Thus, although the centennial of Witmer's clinic deserved a celebration on its own merits, it is probably no coincidence that it came at a time when clinicians are struggling to maintain their status in the face of cost-conscious health care providers who sometimes question the value of paying for adequate clinical services. One hundred years as a profession looks more substantial than 50.

Lightner Witmer (1867–1956): Creating Psychology's First Clinic

Like a number of other American psychologists, Lightner Witmer (Figure 12.7) was trained in basic laboratory research, but made his reputation by

FIGURE 12.7 Lightner Witmer as a young faculty member at the University of Pennsylvania.

applying psychology to solve real-world problems. A native Philadelphian, Witmer stayed close to home for most of his life, earning a bachelor's degree at nearby University of Pennsylvania in 1888, then taking graduate courses there while teaching at a local college preparatory school. His shifting interests eventually settled on psychology, and for a time he served as the laboratory assistant for Penn's new psychology professor, James McKeen Cattell (Chapter 8). He then followed Cattell's example and went to Leipzig, completing a doctorate in Wundt's laboratory in 1892. On his return to the United States, he was named laboratory director at the University of Pennsylvania, Cattell having moved to Columbia the year before, and he became a vigorous advocate of the new laboratory psychology. Witmer revealed his passion for research in an amusing letter to Hugo Münsterberg in 1893 (quoted in the Chapter 7 Close-Up), in which he described a study on the psychology of memory and pain that he had undertaken on a very personal level by deliberately letting a horse throw him (Witmer, 1893). The episode apparently was in character—one friend later recalled that when on holiday in New York's Adirondacks, Witmer liked to ride his brakeless bicycle "down steep hills ... with [his] legs on the handlebar" (Collins, 1931, p. 9).

Although fiercely committed to a scientific psychology, Witmer, like most American psychologists, believed that psychology should be able to improve people's lives. Thus, he was intrigued when a local schoolteacher, who knew Witmer from taking a summer course with him, came into the laboratory in March of 1896. She brought along one of her students, a 14-year-old who couldn't seem to learn how to spell, even though he was reasonably competent otherwise. Witmer, always willing to try something new, agreed to help and quickly discovered that part of the problem was poor eyesight; once corrected, the boy was able to undertake a training program and his spelling improved somewhat. This episode, and a second one involving a child with a speech disorder, turned a portion of Witmer's laboratory into a clinic and launched clinical psychology, the eventual outcome being several days of symposia and celebrations at the 1996 APA convention.

Word of the new clinic spread, and soon Witmer began seeing other cases of children with physiological, cognitive, and behavioral problems related to school performance, about two dozen during the remainder of 1896 (McReynolds, 1987). In December of that year, he read a paper at the APA's annual meeting in Boston, in which he called for increased research on the kinds of problems he was encountering and the development of training programs to increase the number of experts able to solve such problems. In 1907 he founded the journal, *The Psychological Clinic*, which included descriptions of case studies, research reports, and theoretical articles. The first issue contained a lead essay penned by Witmer; its title, "Clinical Psychology," gave a name to the emerging new specialty (Witmer, 1907/1931). In the article, he described the first 10 years of the

clinic's development and called once more for increased research and training. He urged the creation of "a new profession—that of the psychological expert, who should find his career in connection with the school system, through the examination and treatment of mentally and morally retarded children" (p. 346). Thus, clinical psychology began with a relatively narrow focus—diagnosing and treating children with school-related problems. Today, that area of expertise is associated with **school psychology**. In fact, school psychologists also consider Witmer one of their pioneers, and the APA's Division for School Psychology still gives an annual "Lightner Witmer Award" to a promising young school psychologist (Baker, 1988).

By 1909, Witmer's clinic had expanded and had developed a team approach. A child entering the program would be given a thorough medical examination by a consulting physician, a social worker would compile a family and school history, and Witmer or one of his assistants would do the mental testing, using a battery of tests for such things as memory, attention, and motor coordination (Fernberger, 1931). Witmer disliked paper-and-pencil tests of intelligence, and although he believed that assessments like the Binet tests could yield interesting information about various abilities, he thought they were overused and he saw little value in the IQ scores themselves (McReynolds, 1996). After compiling all the information, the children would be classified as (a) experiencing some correctable medical condition (e.g., defective vision) but not needing special training, (b) possibly experiencing some medical problem but more clearly requiring some special program or other environmental intervention (e.g., improved nutrition), or (c) being severely retarded, untreatable, and requiring custodial care (Baker, 1988).

Unlike most of his contemporaries, Witmer was skeptical of the claims being made for the heritability of traits like mental defectiveness. He clearly recognized individual differences in ability in the students he saw, and he conceded that some degree of deficiency was inherent and unalterable. Severely retarded children, he believed, should be segregated from society in special institutions and prevented from having children. Yet the very existence of his clinic demonstrated his firm belief that some deficiencies could be corrected through proper training and/or control of the environment. Hence, Witmer shared with behaviorists the belief that the environment could shape behavior. He believed that if past environmental influences produced the problem behavior observed in the clinic, then future environmental intervention could alter behavior and make the child more productive as a student. He considered his approach to be an optimistic one, arguing that to emphasize heredity is to give up hope of change: "To ascribe a condition to the environment, is a challenge to do something for its ameliorization or cure; to ascribe it to heredity often means that we fold our hands and do nothing" (Witmer, 1911, p. 232). Witmer introduced the term **orthogenics** to refer to this strategy of "investigat[ing] retardation and deviation and the *methods of restoring to normal condition* those who are found for one reason or another to be retarded or deviate" (Witmer, 1909, p. 122, italics added).

Witmer's clinic grew rapidly in the early decades of the twentieth century, its total case files numbering just under 10,000 by 1931 (Fernberger, 1931). It also added several specialized functions to its general role of diagnosing and treating problems in school-aged children. One was a clinic for speech disorders, developed by E. B. Twitmyer in 1914.[6] Another was a vocational clinic where adolescents and adults could go for testing and advice about careers. It was created by Morris Viteles, who could be added to the Chapter 8 list of pioneers in industrial psychology. Witmer's clinics also spawned numerous copies and variants, about two dozen by the start of World War I (Sexton, 1965). Meanwhile

other forces were at work that would eventually yield modern clinical psychology.

Clinical Psychology Prior to World War II

Chapter 8 chronicled the evolution of the mental testing movement, and this chapter briefly described the drive for mental hygiene that originated with the efforts of Clifford Beers. Both developments contributed to clinical psychology's history. In addition, starting in the post-World War I era, there were several organizational efforts within the APA to professionalize the work of the clinician. It was a difficult struggle. One problem was that psychology's increasing popularity and the apparent success of the war's testing program prompted many unqualified people to claim that they could deliver psychological services. An illustration of the dilemma was the effect of a resolution the APA passed in 1915 requiring that testing be done only by those trained to do so. Most people administering the tests did not belong to APA, however, so the resolution had little effect (Napoli, 1981). A second problem was that clinicians did not always feel welcome in an APA that was centered in the academic environment and maintained strict scholarly requirements for membership. A final problem for clinicians was that unless they worked in clinics like Witmer's, they generally had low status in their work environments, which were often hospitals or private clinics. They were usually limited to administering basic mental tests, while psychiatrists completed the major diagnostic and therapy work. And the medical community had no wish to yield its authority or status.

The first serious effort toward forming an identity for clinicians within the APA was taken at the 1917 annual convention, when J. E. Wallace Wallin organized a meeting "to consider the advisability of establishing a new association to 'encourage and advance professional service in the field of clinical psychology'" (Wallin, 1966, p. 107). The seven people (including Leta Hollingworth—see Chapter 8's Close-Up) who met that winter in Pittsburgh formed the American Association of Clinical Psychologists (AACP). The leadership of the APA was not amused,

[6] Twitmyer's dissertation, under Witmer's direction, was an examination of the knee-jerk reflex (Twitmyer, 1905). During the course of his investigation, he discovered that knee jerks could be elicited by stimuli associated with stimulation of the patellar tendon. That is, shortly after Pavlov discovered classical conditioning in Russia, Twitmyer was making the same discovery in the United States. Pavlov justifiably gets the credit, however, because of the massive research program that he undertook. Twitmyer, on the other hand, after being ignored when presenting his research at the 1904 APA meeting, abandoned conditioning and became involved in Witmer's clinic.

however, fearing the eventual disintegration of the APA. A compromise was reached in 1919 when the APA created a "section" for clinical psychology within the Association and the AACP members abandoned their new organization and joined it. During the 1920s, the Clinical section pursued a number of professional issues, including proper training, certification, and ethics, but little came of their efforts. The only major effect of their growing presence was that the APA relaxed its membership requirements in the mid-1920s, creating two categories: full member and associate member. By the end of the decade, associates outnumbered full members (Napoli, 1981).

During the 1930s, clinical psychologists (and other psychologists with applied interests) kept pushing for recognition in an APA that continued to be dominated by academic interests. Even the most firmly entrenched academician had to face the reality of the Great Depression, however. As you recall from the discussion of Lewin's experiences in the 1930s (Chapter 9, p. 269), academic positions became increasingly difficult to find during the Depression years, making nonacademic employment a growing necessity for young psychologists. The APA created such committees as the Committee on the Social Utilization of Unemployed Psychologists and the Committee on Psychology and the Public Service. Despite these efforts, however, applied psychologists still felt the need for their own organization, and they created one in 1937—the American Association for Applied Psychology (AAAP). By 1940 it claimed more than 600 members, compared to approximately 4000 in APA, and it included sections in clinical, educational, consulting, and industrial psychology (Hilgard, 1987).

The AAAP remained in existence until the end of World War II, independent of the APA, but not in deliberate competition with it—in fact, around 90% of AAAP members also belonged to the APA (Capshew, 1999). The organization made some progress on the issues of training and standards, but the advent of a second world war within a generation once more transformed psychology. The national spirit of unity and interdependence fostered a degree of cooperation between academicians and practitioners that had not existed before (and has not existed since). The outcome was a complete reorganization of the APA to incorporate both scientific and applied interests. It emerged from an "intersociety" convention held in New York in 1943, chaired by E. G. Boring, that brought together 25 delegates from several different organizations, but mainly the APA and AAAP. They approved a new structure for the APA, one that continues today. The new structure was an umbrella organization that included special interest "Divisions," and a revised purpose. Whereas the original APA described its primary goal as the advancement of psychology as a "science," the expanded vision added advancement as a "profession" and as a "means of promoting human welfare" to its list of purposes (Napoli, 1981, p. 127). As we shall see in the next chapter, (a) the war-induced sense of unity in the APA did not last long, and (b) the war brought about a significant transformation in the very nature of clinical psychology.

SUMMARY

EARLY TREATMENT OF THE MENTALLY ILL

• Near the end of the eighteenth century, Enlightenment thinkers pressed for reform in the ways of treating the mentally ill. In France, Phillipe Pinel introduced the concept of "moral treatment," in which institutional living conditions were improved, the tendency to rely exclusively on physical restraint of patients was reduced, and direct efforts were made to improve the behavior of patients. Similar reforms were undertaken at the York Retreat in England by William Tuke. His model was copied extensively in the United States in the nineteenth century. Benjamin Rush, considered to be the founder of modern psychiatry, introduced a medical model as a way of explaining mental illness and developed an approach to treatment that emphasized "improving" the condition of patients' blood and circulatory systems.

• In the middle of the nineteenth century, Dorothea Dix successfully urged the reform of large public asylums and better treatment for the mentally ill poor. At the turn of the twentieth century, Clifford Beers, a former mental patient, agitated for similar reforms; he was also a pioneer in the Mental Hygiene movement, which emphasized prevention.

- The classification of mental illnesses took a major leap forward with the work of Emil Kraepelin, a psychiatrist who also studied with Wundt. Among other things, Kraepelin is known for his description of dementia praecox (later renamed schizophrenia), and his description of it in attentional terms.

MESMERISM AND HYPNOSIS

- In the mid-1700s, Franz Anton Mesmer developed a procedure for treating hysteria (apparent nervous system disorders with no true organic damage), based on his belief that the disorder was the result of disturbed magnetic forces within the body. Believing that he had magnetic powers, he treated patients and effected some cures by "mesmerizing" them. Although he didn't know it, his successes were the result of the power of suggestion, and Mesmer had discovered a procedure that would eventually be known as hypnotism.

- Before the discovery of such drugs as ether in the nineteenth century, mesmerism was championed by the British doctor John Elliotson as an anesthetic for surgery and used extensively in India by another British doctor, James Esdaile. It gained further scientific credibility in the hands of James Braid, who renamed the procedure "neurypnology," which soon came to be called hypnology or hypnotism.

- In France in the mid-nineteenth century, two schools of thought developed about the nature of hypnotism. According to Liebeault and Bernheim of the "Nancy" school, hypnotism was a normal phenomenon that had its effects through the power of suggestion; people differed in their levels of suggestibility. According to Charcot in Paris, however, hypnotic effects mirrored the symptoms of hypnosis and suggestibility was a sign of hysterical neurosis.

SIGMUND FREUD (1856–1939): FOUNDING PSYCHOANALYSIS

- Freud is one of psychology's best-known figures. Over the years, a Freudian myth has developed, a false belief that Freud was the solitary hero fighting for his ideas against overwhelming opposition, and that his ideas were original to him, without important antecedent. Recent scholarship has questioned both aspects of the myth.

- Freud was trained in neurology and influenced, through his contact with Ernst Brücke, by the prevailing materialism and determinism of nineteenth-century physiology. Financial problems led him to the private practice of neurology, where he became interested in the treatment of hysteria. In the 1880s, he studied with two of the leading experts of the problem, Meynert and Charcot. He was also greatly influenced by Darwin's work.

- Through his association with Josef Breuer, Freud learned of the Anna O. case, in which hysteric symptoms were shown to be related to repressed memories and successful treatment occurred (apparently) if the patient would retrieve memories of the events surrounding the first appearance of a symptom. The recall produced an emotional release or catharsis. With Breuer, Freud published *Studies on Hysteria* in 1895, normally considered the founding event for psychoanalysis.

- Freud believed that hysteria resulted from the repression of trauma, real or imagined, into the unconscious, and the purpose of psychoanalysis was to bring repressed memories back to the surface so that insight into the causes of the patient's problem could be gained. To explore the unconscious, Freud developed the procedures of free association, in which a person said whatever came to mind, and dream analysis, in which the surface or "manifest" content of a dream was examined to discover the underlying or "latent" content of the dream. All dreams reflected some disguised wish fulfillment, Freud argued. He also believed that all events have causes; even accidents or slips of the tongue (Freudian slips) can be traced to unconscious purposes.

- Freud believed that sexual problems were a critical determinant of hysteria. He initially believed that hysteria resulted from the effects of childhood sexual abuse, but he later abandoned this "seduction" hypothesis, arguing that the memories of abuse were actually the results of imagined sexual feelings originating in childhood. This led to his theory of infantile sexuality and the Oedipal complex.

- International recognition for psychoanalysis came when Freud was invited to deliver a series of five lectures at Clark University in 1909. His lectures included descriptions of Anna O., his dream theory, Freudian slips, and infantile sexuality.

- Freud cultivated an inner circle of followers loyal to psychoanalysis. Two early converts, Alfred Adler and Carl Jung, both broke with Freud over the issue of sex and established their own schools of thought, individual psychology (Adler) and analytical psychology (Jung). One of Freud's most loyal followers was his daughter Anna, known for extending psychoanalysis to the treatment of children.

• After World War I, Freud's theory evolved to include the proposals (a) that both life (sex) and death (aggression) instincts are a part of human nature; (b) that personality structure centers on the ego, which mediates between the instinctive demands of the id, the moral restrictions of the superego, and the constraints placed on behavior by reality; and (c) that each of the three sources of pressure on the ego can create anxiety, and the ego reacts through defense mechanisms such as repression, projection, and reaction formation.

• Freud's ideas were treated with some skepticism by academic psychologists, and were more influential, at first, in the medical community and in the general public. His contributions include the concepts of the unconscious and repression, his emphasis on the importance of early childhood, and his insistence on the psychological nature of mental disorders. Critics have cited his overemphasis on sex, problems with the scientific status of psychoanalysis, and his description of female psychology.

CLINICAL PSYCHOLOGY IN AMERICA

• Lightner Witmer is usually credited with establishing, in 1896, the first clinic for the treatment of psychological disorders in the United States. His clinic focused on "psycho-educational" problems similar to those encountered by modern school psychologists—physiological, cognitive, and behavioral problems related to school performance. He believed that the problems he studied could be cured and he called his treatment program orthogenics.

• Prior to World War II, clinical psychologists for the most part provided mental testing services and did not have high status, either in clinical settings, which were dominated by psychiatrists, or in the APA, which was controlled by academics. The American Association for Applied Psychology was formed in 1937 as a way of professionalizing the practice of psychology. The APA reorganized at the close of World War II, and expanded its mission, beyond science, to include the professional practice of psychology.

STUDY QUESTIONS

1. Explain how Pinel was influenced by the general ideals of the Enlightenment.

2. Describe the practice of "moral treatment," as used by Pinel and Tuke.

3. Describe what it might be like to be a patient of Benjamin Rush.

4. As crusaders for mental health reform, describe the work of (a) Dorothea Dix and (b) Clifford Beers.

5. Describe the contribution of Emil Kraepelin to the classification of mental disorders.

6. What was the theory behind mesmerism? Why did the treatment sometimes work?

7. Describe the origins of the term hypnotism.

8. What was the theory of hypnotism developed by the Nancy school, and why did Charcot consider the theory dangerous? Which approach prevailed?

9. Describe the two main components of the so-called Freudian myth. What role did Freud play in perpetuating the myth?

10. How were Freud's ideas influenced by (a) 19th century materialist thought and (b) Darwinian theory?

11. Describe the traditional version of the Anna O. case, what really happened, and what Freud learned from the case (or thought he learned).

12. Describe the methods used by Freud to probe the unconscious.

13. Describe Freud's seduction hypothesis and what happened to it.

14. Describe the evolution of Freud's theory after World War I.

15. What were Anna Freud's contributions to her father's theories?

16. What were the alternatives to Freudian psychoanalysis proposed by (a) Alfred Adler and (b) Carl Jung?

17. What was the effect of Freudian psychoanalysis on America, both in the general public and in academic circles?

18. Write an analysis of the contributions of Freud to twentieth century psychology, and the ways in which he has been criticized.

19. Lightner Witmer is sometimes considered the founder of clinical psychology in America. What is the basis for the claim? Why could he be considered the founder of school psychology instead?

20. Describe the typical work done by a clinician in the period prior to World War II.

QUESTIONS FROM THE ORIGINAL SOURCE EXCERPT

1. Describe Freud's theory of dreaming. Be sure to distinguish between manifest and latent content, and give examples of what he called the "dream work."

2. Freud's determinist beliefs are evident in his description of "Freudian slips." Explain.

3. Describe Freud's ideas about childhood sexuality.

FOR FURTHER READING

Hornstein, G. A. (1992). The return of the repressed: Psychology's problematic relations with psychoanalysis, 1909–1960. *American Psychologist, 47,* 254–263.

An excellent analysis (and for a scholarly article, witty) of how American psychologists reacted to psychoanalysis over the years; shows how the Americans first rejected analysis outright and then tried to incorporate it into mainstream experimental psychology.

McReynolds, P. (1994). *Lightner Witmer: His life and times.* Washington, DC: American Psychological Association.

The definitive biography of Witmer; includes detailed descriptions of the work of his clinic and the early cases that he treated, and covers the expansion of the clinic in later years.

Rosenzweig, S. (1992). *The historic expedition to America (1909): Freud, Jung, and Hall the king-maker.* St. Louis: Rana House.

An authoritative source for information about Freud's trip to America; although it lacks contextual analysis, its extensive footnoting provides a wealth of detail; a translation of Freud's lectures gives the reader a chance to read Freud in the original and provides a good summary of Freud's thinking, circa 1909.

Sexton, V. S. (1965). Clinical psychology: An historical survey. *Genetic Psychology Monographs, 72,* 401–434.

A bit dated, but a good summary of clinical psychology in America; includes information on mental testing, mental hygiene, and clinical psychology's efforts at achieving professional status; also useful is a similar, but even older, article by Watson (1953).

Sulloway, F. J. (1979). *Freud: Biologist of the mind.* New York: Basic Books.

One of several biographies of Freud, and an excellent one, focusing on an analysis of the Freudian myth; includes extensive treatment of the contemporary sources of ideas often thought to be original to Freud (e.g., infantile sexuality); more critical than another first-rate biography by Gay (1988).

CHAPTER 13

PSYCHOLOGY'S PRACTITIONERS

One brief way of describing the change which has taken place in me is to say that in my early professional years I was asking the question, How can I treat, cure, or change this person? Now I would phrase the question this way: How can I provide a relationship which this person may use for his own personal growth?

—Carl Rogers, 1961

PREVIEW AND CHAPTER OBJECTIVES

After an introductory discussion of a fundamental but somewhat artificial division in psychology between scientists and practitioners, this chapter continues where the last one ended—with the practice of clinical psychology. As you will learn, World War II transformed clinical psychologists from psychiatric assistants, engaged mainly in administering psychological tests, into highly trained professionals who diagnose and treat the full range of mental and behavioral disorders. Also after the war, traditional psychotherapy based on a Freudian model came under fire for its questionable effectiveness, spawning alternative approaches. The alternatives to be considered here will be behavior therapy, derived from behaviorist conditioning principles, and therapies that evolved out of an approach that called itself the Third Force. This "Humanistic Psychology" created its distinct identity by contrasting itself with psychology's other two forces, psychoanalysis and behaviorism. Its most visible advocates were Abraham Maslow and Carl Rogers, creator of client-centered therapy. This chapter's Original Source Excerpt is an essay by Rogers that sums up the essence of his therapeutic approach.

The professional practice of psychology extended beyond clinical psychology and its cousin, counseling psychology, however. One major focus of application, as you know from Chapter 8, was in the general area of business and industry. Modern industrial/organizational psychology continues the tradition begun by such pioneers as Scott, Münsterberg, and Bingham. The chapter will continue Chapter 8's discussion of psychology as it applied to business and industry, highlighted by an examination of a famous series of studies at a plant that manufactured components for telephone systems in Hawthorne, Illinois. After you finish this chapter, you should be able to:

- Understand the reasons for the historical divide between psychological scientists and those who focus on the professional practice of psychology
- Describe the effect of World War II on the development of clinical psychology
- Compare the Boulder and Vail models of graduate training for clinical psychologists and describe the status of both approaches
- Describe the Eysenck studies of psychotherapy effectiveness and their impact on clinical psychology

- Describe the history of the lobotomy as a medical tool for "treating" severe mental illness
- Describe behavior therapy, especially the history of systematic desensitization, and show its connection to behaviorist principles
- Explain why humanistic psychology is sometimes called the "third force" in psychology
- Describe the development of the concept of self-actualization and how it fits into the philosophy of humanistic psychology
- Describe the essence of Rogers' client-centered therapy, showing how the therapeutic atmosphere is crucial for personal growth of the client
- Describe important developments in industrial psychology in the 1920s, 1930s, and in the postwar era
- Describe the Hawthorne experiments and critically analyze them

RESEARCHERS AND PRACTITIONERS

At the close of the last chapter, you learned about the first hints of a professional identity for clinical psychologists. They formed the short-lived American Association of Clinical Psychologists in 1917, then had a "section" created for them in the APA, and then joined other applied psychologists in forming a vigorous association, the American Association for Applied Psychology (AAAP), in 1937. Near the end of World War II, they played a major role in the reorganization of the APA. The new APA would no longer be devoted only to the pursuit of science; it would now also have the additional stated goals of advancing psychology as a profession and promoting human welfare (Hilgard, 1987). Prior to World War II, academic psychology had dominated the APA, but after the war, the power began to shift, and a turning point occurred in 1962, when psychologists working in nonacademic jobs outnumbered those working in colleges and universities for the first time (Tryon, 1963).

For psychologists working in the academic environment, the shift was not a welcome one. Of course, this was not the first time that academic/research psychologists had been unhappy with the APA. As early as 1898, none other than Lightner Witmer, at that time more interested in

experimental research than in his fledgling clinic, had proposed that researchers split from APA to form their own organization. G. Stanley Hall described the idea to Titchener this way:

> A line from Witmer says that he wants to join you, me, and others in forming a new Psychological organization which shall put the lab on a proper basis and exclude half-breeds and extremists. Do you want to consider it? (quoted in Goodwin, 1985, p. 386)

Witmer's revolt went nowhere, but as you know from Chapter 7 (pp. 181–183), Titchener formed his "Experimentalists" group soon thereafter (in 1904). It evolved into the Society of Experimental Psychologists after Titchener's death in 1927, and continues to this day as an honorary society for distinguished researchers.

Even before practitioners outnumbered academician/researchers in 1962, the latter group had become distressed about the direction the reorganized APA was taking. They were especially concerned about the structure of the annual meeting, which, after the war, seemed to be more and more devoted to practice issues, and was structured in a way that made presentation of research difficult. As one small example, the APA in 1959 decided not to allow slides to be shown during any of the presentations, a move that infuriated experimentalists, who were accustomed to using slides to present their data (Dewsbury & Bolles, 1995). The incident helped bring about a major defection of experimental psychologists, who formed the Psychonomic Society near the end of the 1950s. It held its first meeting in 1960, devoted to the presentation of research (including slides), and it continues today as an important organization for experimental psychologists.

Most members of the Psychonomic Society remained members of APA as well, and continued to agitate for conditions favorable to the researcher/academician. APA, however, kept shifting its resources toward the practice of psychology, and focused much of its energy to issues of relevance to practitioners (e.g., whether clinical psychologists should gain the legal right to prescribe medication). Researchers agitated for a new reorganization of APA in the mid-1980s that would restore some of their status, and when the effort failed, a group of prominent experimental psychologists banded together and formed the American Psychological Society (APS). Membership reached more than 5,000 within the first six months, indicating that the group had struck a chord, and APS quickly became a strong advocate for psychological research, created a group of high quality journals (e.g., *Psychological Science*), and developed an annual convention entirely devoted to research. When it celebrated its 15th anniversary in 2003, it had reached a membership of just over 13,500.

This researcher-practitioner split, reflected in the histories of APA and APS, can easily be overstated. Most APS members also belong to APA, APA has an energetic "Science Directorate," most of the APA journals are devoted to research, and in 2001, APS launched a new journal, *Psychological Science in the Public Interest*, that includes research-based articles on topics of relevance for the practice of psychology, as you can see from the following sample article titles:

> *Psychological Science Can Improve Diagnostic Decisions*
> *Treatment and Prevention of Depression*
> *Does High Self-Esteem Cause Better Performance, Interpersonal Success, Happiness, or Healthier Lifestyles?*

Yet the division between researcher/academicians and practitioners is a real one, representing different value systems and different interests. The next two chapters will be organized with reference to these two ways of looking at the world of psychology. This chapter will pick up where Chapter 12 finished, and focus on the professional practice of psychology, especially clinical and industrial psychology; Chapter 14 will examine post-World War II developments on the research side of psychology.

THE EMERGENCE OF MODERN CLINICAL PSYCHOLOGY

As you recall from the close of the last chapter, prior to World War II, clinical psychologists struggled to establish their status as independent professionals. In the 1930s, for example, they tended to be employed in mental hospitals or clinics, under the supervision of psychiatrists; their "practice" was limited primarily to administering mental and other forms of tests; and, because there was virtually nothing in the way of formal clinical training available to them, they developed their skills on the job or in internship-like arrangements (Capshew, 1999). The cruel circumstances of the war, however, created a permanent place for clinicians, who were among those providing professional services to the mentally wounded. Organized psychiatry, which had controlled the delivery of therapeutic services to the mentally ill prior to the war, was overwhelmed by the need for therapy. As in the first world conflict, applied psychologists continued to contribute their services through various testing programs, but in the second war they also gained experience treating those who were damaged psychologically by their war experiences. And the need was great. During the vicious Pacific battle for Guadalcanal in 1942, for example, 40% of the casualties that were serious enough to require evacuation were psychological breakdowns (Herman, 1995). Furthermore, of the first 1.5 million soldiers given medical discharges, about 675,000 (45%) were for psychiatric reasons (Vandenbos, Cummings, & DeLeon, 1992). When the war ended, there were approximately 44,000 veterans who were in Veterans Administration hospitals suffering from various mental disorders resulting from the war, compared with 30,000 hospitalized with physical wounds (Sexton, 1965). Psychiatry simply could not cope with the caseload and was forced to abandon its therapeutic monopoly. In addition, the federal government, perceiving the increased need, launched an aggressive program to support the training of graduate students in clinical psychology. In the academic year 1946–1947, for instance, the VA funded training programs in 22 universities that enrolled 200 students (Capshew, 1999).

Out of these circumstances the modern clinical psychologist emerged—no longer limited to testing, but gradually recognized as an expert diagnostician and therapist; no longer limited to children and juveniles in school settings, but now capable of delivering services to anyone in need of them; no longer restricted to a clinic setting, but now more likely to develop a private practice; no longer under the supervision of psychiatrists, but increasingly on a par with them. As this new clinician emerged, however, it quickly became clear that standardized training and some form of accreditation were needed.

The Boulder Model

In 1947, with the financial support of the federal government, through the Veterans Administration and the U. S. Public Health Service, the APA formed a Committee on Training in Clinical Psychology (CTCP). It was chaired by David Shakow (1901–1981), who already had been quite active in promoting his ideas about the training of clinical psychologists. As chief psychologist at Worcester State Hospital (refer back to Figure 12.2), Shakow had been an active member of the original American Association of Applied Psychologists, and, just before World War II, had served on their committee for the training of clinicians. Shakow's influence on the CTCP is evident from the fact that the committee report is usually referred to as the "Shakow Report" (Baker & Benjamin, 2000). It formed the backbone for deliberations about clinical training held during a 15-day intensive conference that attracted 73 clinical psychologists and other professionals to the University of Colorado in Boulder in the late summer of 1949.

Out of the Boulder conference came a blueprint for clinical training that was ideally designed to balance what Shakow saw as the three primary forms of expertise that any clinical psychologist should have—they should be experts in the diagnosis of mental disorders, they should be skilled psychotherapists, and they should be able to complete high quality empirical research. The "Boulder model," because it ideally combined training in the science and in the practice of psychology, came to be known as the **scientist-practitioner model** of clinical training. The

KEY DATE *1949*

This was the year of the Boulder conference that established the scientist-practitioner model for the training of clinical psychologists.

These events also occurred:

- In China, the Communist People's Republic proclaimed, under the leadership of Mao Tse-tung
- The North Atlantic Treaty Organization (NATO) created
- British House of Commons recognized the independence of the Republic of Ireland, with Dublin as capital, but confirmed the status of Northern Ireland within the United Kingdom
- Program of apartheid officially established in South Africa
- Arthur Miller's *Death of a Salesman* won a Tony award and a Pulitzer Prize
- Rogers and Hammerstein launched the first production of *South Pacific*
- Soviet Union tested its first atomic weapon
- "Silly Putty" invented

These people were born:

> George Foreman, world heavyweight champion from 1973 to 1974
>
> John Belushi, comedian and actor

- These people died:

> Margaret Mitchell, author of *Gone with the Wind*
>
> Solomon Guggenheim, U.S. art collector

training was to include a thorough grounding in basic knowledge of the principles of psychology and in the research methods for generating these principles; a thorough understanding of psychometrics (psychological testing), psychopathology, and psychotherapy; a doctoral dissertation that involved empirical research; and a year-long internship at a professional clinic, VA hospital, or similar setting. Total preparation would take four to five years and lead to a Ph.D. in clinical psychology. With a training model in place and a strong need for their services, clinical psychologists rapidly increased their numbers and, as mentioned earlier, their influence in the APA.

The Eysenck Study: Problems for Traditional Psychotherapy

The conference at Boulder provided a new ideal for the training of clinical psychologists. At about the same time, the ability of clinicians to deliver effective therapy was enhanced by the development of new forms of psychotherapy. Two of these approaches, behavior therapy and client-centered therapy, will be featured in this chapter. They developed and prospered in the context of a time when traditional psychoanalytic and related "insight" therapies were being questioned as to whether they really worked. The doubts were magnified by a brief (six pages) article that appeared in 1952, written by a British psychologist Hans Eysenck with the title: "The Effects of Psychotherapy: An Evaluation." In the article, Eysenck examined the efficacy of traditional insight approaches to psychotherapy by combining the results reported in nineteen other studies—five of them evaluating psychoanalytic therapy and the remaining fourteen evaluating what was called "eclectic" therapy. In the absence of a control group not receiving therapy, Eysenck combined the results of two other studies that examined improvement among "neurotics" in the absence of formal psychotherapy (e.g., from insurance claims of disability). While recognizing problems with this comparison group, Eysenck claimed an improvement rate of about 72% in the absence of therapy (over the course of two years). When he looked at the recovery rates for patients undergoing psychotherapy, however, he found that the reported percentage improved in Freudian psychoanalysis was a paltry 44%. A recovery rate of 64% for the eclectic therapy was better, but still less than the rate for those receiving no therapy at all. Eysenck concluded that no evidence existed to support the effectiveness of psychotherapy, as it was then being practiced. He even went as far as to suggest that training in psychotherapy was a waste of time. Later research uncovered a number of methodological problems that made Eysenck's conclusions questionable, but the damage was done. Throughout the 1950s and 1960s, psychologists proposing alternatives to traditional psychoanalysis often pointed to Eysenck's work as evidence that new strategies were needed. Two of those new approaches were therapies deriving from behaviorism and those coming from what was called "humanistic" psychology. Before examining these therapeutic strategies, however, consider this chapter's Close-Up, which describes an unfortunate chapter in the history of medical procedures for the treatment of mental illness.

CLOSE-UP:
The Medical Strategy—Lobotomies, Transorbital and Otherwise

In the late nineteenth century, the practice of psychiatry was centered on the asylum and the treatment of patients who were seriously mentally ill. Little could be done for them beyond custodial care, and "treatment" often amounted to restraint and sedation. With the advent of Freudian psychoanalysis, psychiatrists began to start private practices and to treat patients with less serious disorders (Shorter, 1997), shifting from medical treatment to a psychological analysis. Yet the seriously disturbed, their numbers steadily increasing in the twentieth century, remained in asylums and hospitals, with little hope for improvement. In the 1920s and 1930s, however, several new medical treatments appeared on the scene, with the promise of providing some help for the desperate. As another lesson in the dangers of presentism, it is easy to dismiss some of these therapies as the misguided ideas of quack doctors. It is important to keep in mind that the psychiatric community was honestly attempting to provide some relief to patients at a time when nothing else seemed to work and patients were clearly suffering. Also, especially during the Depression era of the 1930s, psychiatrists felt some pressure to justify their fees by showing that their procedures had some measurable effect (Grob, 1983). Nonetheless, some techniques seemed to come into fairly widespread practice even though there was a surprising lack of scientific basis for their implementation, and little if any evidence for their effectiveness. Consider, for example, the **lobotomy**.

The story begins with a paper presented at the Second International Congress on Neurology, held in London in 1935. It reported some interesting research by two American scientists, Carlyle Jacobsen and John Fulton. They reported that surgical damage to the frontal lobes of chimpanzees could have a beneficial effect. Prior to the surgery, the animals had been quite aggressive, but the aggression diminished after the surgery and the animals' mental functions seemed otherwise unimpaired. By severing the connections between frontal lobes and lower brain centers involved with emotional behaviors, the researchers seemed to have found a way to calm the easily agitated chimps. In the audience that day was a Portuguese neuropsychiatrist, Egas Moniz. He was already well known and highly respected, having been nominated for a Nobel Prize for his discovery of methods to create images of cerebral blood flow. It occurred to Moniz that the Jacobsen/Fulton procedure could be applied to seriously disturbed (and agitated) psychotic patients (Grob, 1983).

With no science other than the Jacobsen and Fulton primate study for support, Moniz developed a procedure that he called a *prefrontal leucotomy* (roughly means cutting white matter in the prefrontal area of the cortex), carried out with a device he created called a leucotone. After a series of small holes were drilled in both sides of the skull, just above and in front of the temples, the thin leucotone would be inserted successively into each hole to a fixed depth and moved side to side, thereby severing brain tissue that connected the frontal and prefrontal lobes with lower brain centers. By early 1936, Moniz had tried the procedure on 20 patients, primarily with manic-depression or obsessive-compulsive disorders that were severe enough that they were suicidal or showed signs of being dangerous. Moniz reported (without any substantial supporting data), that the procedure was mostly successful (14 of 20 "improved") (Shorter, 1997). Although many of the patients later became surprisingly listless, apathetic, and emotionally passive after recovering from the surgery, Moniz believed it was small price to pay for the relief from their severe, even life-threatening symptoms. To his credit, Moniz urged that the procedure not be used except in extreme cases and only after all alternative methods of helping a patient had failed. For this work he was awarded the Nobel Prize in 1949.

If Moniz was careful about the use of his new procedure, two American neurologists were not. Walter Freeman and James Watt thought that the Moniz procedure was a major breakthrough in the treatment of a wide range of psychiatric disorders, and they set about to spread the good news far and wide, while at the same time completing as many of these surgeries as they could. They renamed the procedure a lobotomy, and in 1946 Freeman invented a new technique called a *transorbital lobotomy*. It involved inserting a device similar in design to an ice pick through the eye sockets and into the prefrontal and frontal lobes. The new technique enabled a greater number of fibers to be cut than the Moniz technique, but it also increased the risk of severing a major artery. Freeman was undeterred by the occasional death (about 2.5% of patients), however, and vigorously promoted the new procedure, partly because it could be completed more quickly than the old Moniz technique, and it could be completed on an outpatient basis (i.e., more lobotomy income per unit of time). Freeman's enthusiasm caused a split with Watt, who appeared increasingly nervous about Freeman's crusading zeal for the procedure. Freeman soldiered on, even traveling around the country doing "demonstrations" like the one pictured in Figure 13.1, in which he can be seen tapping his transorbital leucotone into the eye of a patient, while nurses hold on and onlookers carefully observe (and don't sneeze, one hopes).

FIGURE 13.1 A demonstration of a prefrontal transorbital lobotomy by Walter Freeman in 1949.

By 1951, more than 18,000 patients had undergone lobotomies, according to one estimate (Grob, 1991), despite growing uneasiness about the procedure. A lobotomy was certainly effective in calming agitated patients, but it often resulted in permanent changes in personality, sometimes creating virtual zombies. Also, the procedure was occasionally used simply to manage unruly or disagreeable patients, a situation portrayed disturbingly well in *One Flew Over the Cuckoo's Nest*, a 1962 novel by Ken Kesey that was made into a movie in 1975 and swept the Oscars the following year. Lobotomies quickly went out of fashion in the mid-1950s, with the advent of a number of effective antipsychotic drugs.

Behavior Therapy

We learned in Chapter 10 that one reason for the popularity of the behaviorist ideas of promoters like Watson was the promise of application to daily life, through such things as the improvement of child-rearing practices. If behaviors are primarily the result of learning, then presumably dysfunctional behaviors could be unlearned and replaced with more adaptive ones. This rationale was part of Watson's thinking as he formulated the Little Albert study. As you recall from Chapter 10, although he and Rayner made no attempt to remove Albert's fear of rats, they had several proposals about how to do so, based on their beliefs about conditioning. Furthermore, some of these ideas were tested in the 1920s, especially by Mary Cover Jones, who is often credited with pioneering behavior therapy. She tried all of Watson's suggestions and several of her own ideas on a number of different children, and is remembered for one particular case in which she removed a young boy's fear of rabbits by gradually moving the rabbit closer to the child while he was eating, using a procedure that she called "direct conditioning."

During the 1920s and 1930s, there were several other demonstrations of how conditioning principles could be applied to alter behavior in a clinical setting. In Russia, for example, researchers applied Pavlovian principles to treat alcoholism by pairing alcohol (CS) with electric shock (UCS), and hysteria by conditioning movement in limbs that appeared initially to be paralyzed (Kazdin, 1978). In the United States, O. Hobart and Willie M. Mowrer developed a treatment program for bed-wetting based on conditioning principles by creating a crib pad that rang a bell as soon as it became wet. The Mowrers used the success of their procedure to attack psychoanalytic concepts of bed-wetting, which relied on the usual deep-seated conflicts to explain the problem. Instead, the Mowrers argued, it is much simpler to assume that the problem results from a failure to recognize the cues connected with bladder tension. If conditioning is the problem, they believed, then it is also the solution (Mowrer & Mowrer, 1938).

Behavior therapy gained impetus in the 1950s through (a) the work of Eysenck and his colleagues in London and (b) the development of an effective therapy technique descended from the work of Mary Cover Jones. At Maudsley Hospital in London, Eysenck followed his 1952 critique of traditional psychotherapy by assembling a team of colleagues to examine the possibility of developing a new therapy approach, one based on the conditioning principles of Pavlov and Hull. By 1960, he and his group had assembled a sufficient number of applications of conditioning principles to justify producing a book (Eysenck, 1960) that was the first to include the term "behavior therapy" in the title (Glass & Arnkoff, 1992). Three years later Eysenck launched behavior therapy's first journal, *Behaviour Research and Therapy*, with a title that made clear Eysenck's belief that therapies should not be used unless they can be shown effective through research evidence.

Joseph Wolpe, a South African at the University of Witwatersrand, created a procedure based on Jones's work and called it **systematic desensitization** (Wolpe, 1958). It remains one of the best known and most effective behavior therapy techniques. Wolpe, a medical doctor, was trained in traditional psychoanalytic procedures but became dissatisfied with them. He began studying learning theory, especially Hull's, and benefited from the presence in South Africa of an American psychologist who had studied with Kenneth Spence, Hull's alter ego.

Wolpe began exploring behavioral techniques by studying the phobic reactions of cats. After creating fears by shocking the animals whenever they reached for food, he tried to eliminate the fear. Like Jones, he assumed that fear and eating were incompatible responses, so he tried to replace the fear responses by substituting eating responses. Wolpe accomplished this by feeding the animal first in a room that vaguely resembled the original room where the shock occurred, then in a room that more closely resembled the original room, and so on. That is, the fear response was gradually weakened, replaced by the approach to food (Kazdin, 1978).

Wolpe discovered a way to apply this procedure to phobic humans after reading a book by the Chicago physiologist Edmund Jacobson, which described a technique called **progressive relaxation** (Jacobson, 1929). Jacobson had been using relaxation to treat patients with nervous disorders; Wolpe viewed the procedure as a substitute for the eating response he had used with cats. In essence, Wolpe's systematic desensitization procedure involved relaxation training, then the creation of an "anxiety hierarchy," a list of situations that created increasingly greater levels of anxiety. Patients would become relaxed and imagine the situation of least anxiety, then gradually ascend the hierarchy. Wolpe found that after just a few sessions, patients could remain relaxed in the presence of their most feared objects.

With additional modifications over the years, Wolpe's procedure has been shown to be highly effective with certain types of anxiety problems (Paul, 1966). A number of other behavior therapy techniques have evolved over the years, ranging from token economy/reinforcement systems based on a Skinnerian model, to cognitive-behavior therapy, which synthesizes learning theory and the insights from cognitive psychology. A good summary can be found in Kazdin (1978).

The Humanistic Approach to Psychotherapy

Humanistic psychology started as a revolt. It came to be known as psychology's "Third Force," rejecting what it believed to be the "mechanistic, impersonal, hierarchical, elitist psychoanalytic establishment and [the] overly scientistic, cold, removed behaviorism" (Cushman, 1992, p. 55). Humanistic psychologists criticized the ideas that human behavior could be reduced to repressed biological instincts or simple conditioning processes, rejected the idea that individuals' past histories placed limits on what their futures could be, and denied the deterministic assumptions of the other two "forces" in psychology, psychoanalysis and behaviorism. Instead, they proposed that the qualities best characterizing humans are free will and a sense of responsibility and purpose, a forward-looking lifelong search for meaning in one's life, and an innate tendency to grow toward what was called **self-actualization**. To become self-actualized meant to reach one's full potential in life.

The two American psychologists most closely associated with humanistic psychology were Abraham Maslow and Carl Rogers. Maslow (1908–1970; Figure 13.2) was trained as an experimental psychologist and researched dominance behavior in primates, but later exchanged what he saw as a sterile and reductionist scientific approach for the more wholistic humanistic strategy. After completing a doctorate in 1934, he came to New York and eventually settled into a faculty position at Brooklyn College, where he stayed until 1951, when he moved to Brandeis University (near Boston) and completed his career.[1] Maslow is known to all students in general psychology for his hierarchy of needs, a model that proposed a series of need systems, arranged in a pyramid, with lower level and more primitive needs at the bottom and self-actualization at the top. Achieving self-actualization

FIGURE 13.2 Humanistic psychologist Abraham Maslow.

required satisfying all the needs below it—physiological needs, safety needs, the need for love and belonging, and the need for self-esteem, in that order. Maslow argued that studying self-actualization, in contrast with a strategy that examines psychological disorders (e.g., as Freud did), would produce a healthier psychology. As he put it in a famous quote, "the study of crippled, stunted, immature, and unhealthy specimens can yield only a cripple psychology. ... The study of self-actualizing people must be the basis for a more universal science of psychology" (Maslow, 1954, p. 234). Maslow followed his own advice and examined the concept of self-actualization more closely, identifying real historical individuals who seemed to be actualized, then looking for commonalities among them. The work began informally, with his reflections about two people he had come to know in New York—the anthropologist Ruth Benedict and the gestalt psychologist Max Wertheimer. He later reported that when studying Benedict and Wertheimer, he realized "their two patterns could be generalized. I was talking about a kind of person, not about two incomparable individuals ... I tried to see whether this pattern could be found elsewhere" (Maslow, 1971, pp. 41–42). It could. Through a variety of techniques, Maslow identified a number of people who seemed to share some of the attributes of Benedict and Wertheimer. Maslow found that self-actualizers perceived reality accurately, were highly independent and creative, were

---

[1] Maslow surely influenced a number of students. One whose career he definitely affected was Elliot Aronson, a prominent social psychologist who was a doctoral student of Leon Festinger (featured in the next chapter). As an undergraduate at Brandeis University, Aronson wandered into an introductory psychology lecture on prejudice being given by Maslow. The topic caught the attention of Aronson, who had been on the receiving end of the behavioral products of prejudice while growing up as a Jewish child in the tough working class town of Revere, Massachusetts. Aronson immediately changed his major to psychology and developed a close and lasting friendship with Maslow. Aronson earned the APA's Award for Distinguished Scientific Contribution to psychology in 1999.

spontaneous and natural around others, thought of their work as a career or a calling rather than a job, had a strong moral code, and would occasionally have moments of intense enjoyment or satisfaction that Maslow called **peak experiences**.

Carl Rogers and Client-Centered Therapy

Humanistic psychology's second major figure was Carl Rogers (1902–1987), the creator of client-centered therapy, an approach that appealed to a large number of clinicians in the 1960s and 1970s. Rogers (Figure 13.3) was the product of a highly controlled home environment, but managed to build a career of his own design despite his early experiences. The fourth of six children, he was raised in a Chicago suburb in an extremely conservative Protestant family that valued hard work and considered all pleasures sinful. As Rogers (1961) later recalled: "[E]ven carbonated beverages had a faintly sinful aroma, and I remember my slight feeling of wickedness when I had my first bottle of 'pop'" (p. 5). When Rogers was 12, his father moved the family to a large farm in Wisconsin, partly to remove his children from the evils of suburbia. He was determined to run the farm according to the principles of "scientific agriculture," and Carl developed a keen appreciation for science out of the experience. It led him to enroll in the college of agriculture at the University of Wisconsin, but the enthusiasm soon faded as the sheltered young man discovered a bright new world of people and ideas. He switched to studying history and, determined to be a minister, entered New York's Union Theological Seminary after graduating from Wisconsin in 1924. The theology students at Union were encouraged to think for themselves in this liberal environment, and Rogers (1961) "thought [himself] right out of religious work" (p. 8) and into psychology.

Rogers began taking courses across the street from Union at Columbia's Teachers College, where he came under the influence of Leta Hollingworth (Chapter 8). She sparked his interest in doing child guidance work, and he began for the first time to think that he might like to be a clinical psychologist. He completed an internship at the Freudian-based Institute for Child Guidance in New York, where he

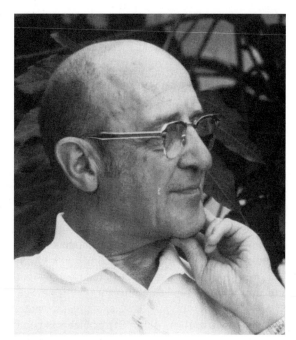

FIGURE 13.3 Carl Rogers, creator of client-centered therapy.

gained some insights about unconscious processes but developed a distaste for psychoanalysis, and earned a doctorate from Columbia in 1931. Rogers then took a position as a staff psychologist at a child guidance clinic in Rochester, New York, where he remained for a dozen years. It was there that he began developing his unique brand of therapy. Professionally, he attended APA meetings, but found them "full of papers on the learning processes of rats and laboratory experiments which seemed ... to have no relation to what [he] was doing" (Rogers, 1961, p. 12). When the American Association for Applied Psychology (AAAP) formed in 1937, however, he became an active member, and in 1939 he advocated a training model for clinicians that reduced the heavy emphasis on research and enhanced the opportunities for supervised practice in the craft of diagnosis and therapy. Academia ignored his proposal, but the idea was in essence identical to the one that emerged 30 years later at the University of Illinois in the form of the Psy.D. degree (Napoli, 1981).

Rogers entered academia himself in 1940, accepting a position at Ohio State University. There the stimulus provided by critically thinking, assertive graduate students sharpened his ideas about therapy and the nature of personality, and resulted in his first book, *Counseling and Psychotherapy*, in 1942. Three years later he went to the University of Chicago as a professor of psychology and director of the counseling center. In 1946 he was elected president of the APA, the second president following the big postwar reorganization, and a clear sign to research-oriented academicians that the APA had begun to shift in the practitioner direction. Rogers spent twelve years at Chicago, and then four back at Wisconsin, where he had a joint appointment in psychology and psychiatry. The Wisconsin years were not happy ones—his client-centered therapy had come under attack as being relevant only for articulate people with mild problems, and Rogers wanted to show that more seriously disturbed clients could benefit as well. He launched an ambitious project to apply the therapy to schizophrenic patients at a local hospital, but the results were at best "equivocal"

(Lakin, 1996). That outcome, combined with a generally cool reception from the experimentally oriented psychology department at Wisconsin, led Rogers to look for greener pastures. He found them in California in 1961, where he accepted the invitation of a former student to join the staff at the Western Behavioral Sciences Institute at La Jolla. Several years later, he founded the Center for the Study of the Person in La Jolla, where he extended his client-centered therapy to a group setting.

The essence of Rogers' client-centered therapy is quite simple. First, consistent with one of humanistic psychology's cornerstone ideals, Rogers rejected the idea that it was important to delve into the client's past history in order for therapy to be effective. Second, Rogers believed that if the therapist succeeded in creating the right kind of therapeutic environment, then the client would be able to take control of his or her life and begin to grow in the direction of being self-actualized. The ideal therapeutic atmosphere included several components, as you will discover in the following excerpt from a talk that Rogers gave in 1954.

ORIGINAL SOURCE EXCERPT
Rogers on Creating a Therapeutic Environment

In 1961, Rogers published a series of essays and lectures under the general title, *On Becoming a Person*. It including an autobiographical essay, from which I have taken much of the story of his life. It also included an essay entitled "Some hypotheses regarding the facilitation of personal growth" (Rogers, 1961a), based on a talk that he gave at Oberlin College. He opened by describing the challenge of therapy, and some of the influences on him as he developed his client-centered therapy:

> To be faced by a troubled, conflicted person who is seeking and expecting help, has always constituted a great challenge to me. Do I have the knowledge, the resources, the psychological strength, the skill—do I have whatever it takes to be of help to such an individual?
>
> For more than twenty-five years I have been trying to meet this kind of challenge. It has caused me to draw upon every element of my professional background: the rigorous methods of personality measurement at Teacher's College, Columbia; the Freudian psychoanalytic insights and methods of the Institute for Child Guidance where I worked as an intern; the continuing developments in the field of clinical psychology, with which I have been closely associated; ... and other resources too numerous to mention. But most of all it has meant a continual learning from my own experience and that of my col-

leagues at the Counseling Center as we have endeavored to discover for ourselves effective means of working with people in distress. ... (pp. 31–32)

Rogers described his fundamental philosophy of therapy, one that shows how he gradually distanced himself from the psychiatric model of the expert physician directing the course of treatment for a patient:

One brief way of describing the change which has taken place in me is to say that in my early professional years I was asking the question, How can I treat, or cure, or change this person? Now I would phrase the question this way: How can I provide a relationship which this person may use for his own personal growth?

It is as I have come to put the question in this second way that I realize that whatever I have learned is applicable to all of my human relationships, not just to working with clients with problems. It is for this reason that I feel it is possible that the learnings which have had meaning for me in my experience may have some meaning for you in your experience, since all of us are involved in human relationships. ... (p. 32)

This last paragraph gets at a theme that runs through much of Rogers' writings. Although he developed his therapy approach in the context of a therapist trying to help a client, he believed that his process was equally useful for any type of human relationship. As you will see, he expands on this theme later in the essay. He now gets to the main point, stated first as a general hypothesis. He then elaborated on each of the three components of the hypothesis:

I can state the overall hypothesis in one sentence, as follows. If I can provide a certain type of relationship, the other person will discover within himself the capacity to use that relationship for growth, and change and personal development will occur.

The Relationship

But what meaning do these terms have? Let me take separately the three major phrases in this sentence and indicate something of the meaning they have for me. What is this certain type of relationship I would like to provide?

I have found that the more that I can be genuine in the relationship, the more helpful it will be. This means that I need to be aware of my own feelings ... rather than presenting an outward facade of one attitude, while actually holding another attitude at a deeper ... level. Being genuine also involves the willingness to be and to express, in my words and my behavior, the various feelings and attitudes which exist in me. It is only in this way that the relationship can have reality, and reality seems deeply important as a first condition. It is only by providing the genuine reality which is in me, that the other person can successfully seek for the reality in him. ...

As a second condition, I find that the more acceptance and liking I feel toward this individual, the more I will be creating a relationship which he can use. By acceptance I mean a warm regard for him as a person of unconditional self-worth—of value no matter what his condition, his behavior, or his feelings. ... It means an acceptance of and regard for his attitudes of the moment, no matter how negative or positive, no matter how much they may contradict other attitudes he has held in the past. This acceptance of each fluctuating aspect of this other person makes it for him a relationship of warmth and safety, and the safety of being liked and prized as a person seems a highly important element in a helping relationship.

I also find that the relationship is significant to the extent that I feel a continuing desire to understand—a sensitive empathy with each of the client's feelings and communications as they seem to him at that moment. Acceptance does not mean much until it involves understanding. It is only as I *understand* the feelings and thoughts which seem so horrible to you, or so weak, or so sentimental, or so bizarre—it is only as I see them as you see them, and accept them and you, that you feel really free to explore all the hidden nooks and frightening crannies of your inner and often buried experience. ... (pp. 33–34, italics in the original)

These three attributes are the essence of client-centered therapy. The therapist's job is not to diagnose and treat, it is to create a healthy atmosphere in which the client can begin to change. First, therapists must be genuine, which implies that therapists must be emotionally healthy themselves. Although Rogers doesn't say it, this genuineness also enables the therapist to act as a model for the kind of emotional health being sought in the client. Second, therapists must show what Rogers elsewhere called **unconditional positive regard**. This means accepting a person as having value by virtue of simply being a human being. In practical terms, it can mean avoiding labels. For example, I once heard a tape of Rogers talking with a teenager who had been in various kinds of trouble. The boy, very defensively, opened the conversation by saying that he imagined Rogers must have had a lot of experience dealing with delinquents. Rogers, very calmly, simply responded that he would prefer to think of the boy as "Mike." The message—the boy was a person, not the label "delinquent." The third component of an effective therapist-client relationship, **empathy**, follows from the humanistic philosophy proposing that reality is the reality as perceived and experienced by a person. Hence, understanding someone else requires trying to understand how that person views things. Rogers recognized that a complete understanding of another person was impossible, but it was the effort that counted. This effort included the major therapeutic technique used by Rogers, called **reflection**. This meant taking something said by the client and rephrasing it in a way that leads the client to think "this therapist understands what I'm saying." To illustrate, consider this exchange from a transcript of a therapy session with Rogers:

C: I suppose from the practical point of view it could be said that what I ought to be doing is solving some ... day-to-day problems. And yet, ... what I'm trying to do is solve ... something else that's a great ... deal more important than little day-to-day problems.

T: I wonder if this will distort your meaning, that from a hard headed point of view you ought to be spending time thinking through some specific problems. But you wonder if perhaps maybe you aren't on a quest for this whole you and perhaps that's more important than a solution to the day-to-day problems.

C: I think that's it. I think that's it. That's probably what I mean. (Rogers, 1961b, p. 90)

If the therapist succeeds in establishing the proper therapeutic environment, good things will happen, according to Rogers, and he did not mince words about the certainty of a good outcome:

... I would say that when I hold in myself the kind of attitudes I have described, and when the other person can to some degree experience these attitudes, then I believe that change and constructive personal development will *invariably* occur—and I include the word "invariably" only after long and careful consideration.

The Motivation for Change

So much for the relationship. The second phrase in my overall hypothesis was that the individual will discover within himself the capacity to use this relationship for growth. ... [M]y experience has forced me to conclude that the individual has within himself the capacity and the tendency, latent if not evident, to move forward toward maturity. In a suitable psychological climate this tendency is released, and becomes actual rather than potential. ... Whether one calls it a growth tendency, a drive towards self-actualization, or a forward-moving directional tendency, it is the mainspring of life, and is, in the last analysis, the tendency upon which all psychotherapy depends. ... This tendency may become deeply buried under layer after layer of encrusted psychological defenses; it may be hidden behind elaborate facades which deny its existence; but it is my belief that it exists in every individual, and awaits only the proper conditions to be released and expressed. (p. 35, italics in the original)

This passage illustrates another central component of the humanistic message—everyone has the potential for growth and the opportunity to move in the direction of self-actualization. The third part of Rogers' hypothesis concerns the outcome of successful therapy (keep in mind that Rogers was writing at a time when the phrase "gender-neutral language" did not yet exist):

In such a relationship the individual becomes more integrated, more effective. He shows fewer of the characteristics which are usually termed neurotic or psychotic, and more of the characteristics of a healthy, well-functioning person. He changes the perception of himself, becoming more realistic in his views of self. He becomes more like the person he wishes to be. He values himself more highly, He is more self-confident and self-directing. He has a better understanding of himself, becomes more open to his experience, denies or represses less of his experience. ...

In his behavior he shows similar changes. He is less frustrated by stress, and recovers from stress more quickly. He becomes more mature in his everyday behavior as this is observed by friends. He is less defensive, more adaptive, more able to meet situations creatively. (p. 36)

Rogers concluded his essay by returning to a point he mentioned briefly at the outset—what he had to say about a therapeutic relationship applied to *all* human relationships:

... There seems every reason to suppose that the therapeutic relationship is only one instance of interpersonal relations, and that the same lawfulness governs all such relationships. Thus it seems reasonable to hypothesize that if the parent creates with his child a psychological climate such as we have described, then the child will become more self-directing, socialized, and mature. To the extent that the teacher creates such a relationship with his class, the student will become a self-initiated learner, more original, more self-disciplined, less anxious and other-directed. If the administrator, or military or industrial leader, creates such a climate within his organization, then his staff will become more self-responsible, more creative, better able to adapt to new problems, more ... cooperative. It appears possible to me that we are seeing the emergence of a new field of human relationships, in which we may specify that if certain attitudinal conditions exist, then certain definable changes will occur. (p. 37)

As an alternative to Freudian-based insight therapies, in which the therapist played the controlling role, client-centered therapy (first called nondirective therapy) and a number of similar humanistic therapies, quickly became popular among clinical psychologists. In contrast with analytic approaches, it was easier to grasp conceptually and it actually seemed to help people. It was also based on a more optimistic assessment of human potential for change, reflecting Rogers's own ability to take control of his life and a general Midwestern faith that things can be improved if one works hard enough. Also, Rogers was able demonstrate the therapy's effectiveness on the basis of a program of research that he and his students developed. Perhaps stemming from his earlier experiences with scientific agriculture, Rogers took great pleasure in completing empirical research on therapy outcomes, complete with comparisons between those in treatment and those in waiting list control groups. He was able to show that his approach brought about measurable positive changes in people's lives (e.g., Rogers, 1954). The next to last segment of the excerpt, when he described the positive changes that could occur, derived from the outcome research he completed.

Humanistic psychology enjoyed a period of great popularity in the 1960s and 1970s. A *Journal of Humanistic Psychology* was started in 1961, largely through Maslow's efforts, the American Association of Humanistic Psychologists was created a year later, Maslow was elected APA President in 1968, and the APA created a division for humanistic psychology (Division 32) in 1972. That it was popular during this period of American history is no surprise. As a rebellion against the forces of psychoanalysis and behaviorism, it fit well into the context of a time marked by numerous challenges to existing authority. And as a philosophy centered on the individual person (e.g., SELF-actualization), it was consistent with some of the values of the 1970s, a decade sometimes referred to as the "Me Decade" (Schulman, 2001). Despite its popularity, however,

the humanistic movement has been on the fringe of psychology. It has been faulted for overemphasizing the self at the expense of the importance of the community and for being clearer about what it was against than what it proposed as an alternative (e.g., Farson, 1978; Wertheimer, 1978). Nonetheless, it has had an important impact on the clinical practice of psychology, especially through the work of Rogers.

The Vail Conference and the Psy.D. Degree

Before leaving this section of the chapter on clinical psychology, it is worth noting how the Boulder model fared over the years and how a significant alternative to it developed. As you recall, the Boulder model was designed to provide the ideal synthesis of scientist and practitioner, someone able to conduct high quality research and also able to provide effective clinical services. Although the model continues to be the dominant approach to the training of clinicians, it is not clear that it often reached the ideal. In their analysis of Boulder's first fifty years, for example, Benjamin and Baker (2000) reported that it "is a model that has been much praised, much maligned, and according to some, rarely if ever tried" (p. 233). What were the problems?

First, because academic departments of psychology controlled the clinical training programs, in many cases the scientist side of the training received much greater emphasis than the practitioner side. By the late 1950s, many Ph.D. clinicians were complaining that they were unprepared for the practice of psychology and, because they were working in clinical settings for the most part, and not in academia, they were not getting much use out of their research skills. A second and related problem was that professors of clinical psychology, according to the Boulder recommendations, were expected to "maintain their clinical skills by continuing some clinical practice" (Raimy, 1950, p. 130). Most did so, but only to a limited extent. In the academic environment, professors of clinical psychology were under the usual pressure to publish extensively, and that made it very difficult for them to maintain their clinical skills. As a result, graduate students did not always get the best training in how to do clinical work. Many departments took the attitude that students would develop all the needed clinical skills when they did their year-long internship, but the original Boulder model made it clear that training in clinical practice should occur throughout the four to five year program and that the internship should not be seen as a "repair shop" for a prior lack of experience (Stricker & Cummings, 1992).

Criticisms of the Boulder model led to considerations of an alternative, one that emphasized the practice of clinical psychology more than research. It was an idea that actually preceded Boulder. For example, in the mid-1920s, Crane (1925) wrote an article called "A Plea for the Training of Psychologists." Written at a time when there were *no* doctoral training programs for clinical psychologists (Capshew, 1999), he argued that the typical Ph.D. training in psychology, with its emphasis on basic research in traditional topic areas (e.g., perception, learning), was inappropriate. Instead, aspiring clinicians ought to be given much more instruction in the actual practice of psychology and he suggested the creation of a new kind of degree that he called a "Doctor of Psychology" degree (Peterson, 1992). At a time when clinical psychologists had little status, however, the proposal went nowhere. The same was true for a similar idea floated by Carl Rogers in 1939 (Napoli, 1981).

By the 1960s, however, dissatisfaction with the Boulder model was beginning to produce new proposals for the way in which clinicians ought to learn their craft. And the general climate of dissent that permeated the 1960s led to several attempts to create a new direction for training. First, an APA committee on training recommended that alternatives to the scientist-practitioner model be explored, including one that would accentuate clinical practice and lead to a new degree, a Doctorate of Psychology, or **Psy.D.** degree (American Psychological Association, 1967). Second, in an academic context, the University of Illinois decided to implement the recommendation, thereby creating, in 1968, the first university-based Psy.D. program in the United States. The prestige of the University of Illinois immediately gave the Psy.D. some respectability, and other universities soon began developing similar programs. Third, Psy.D. programs began developing as free-standing schools of professional psychology, not affiliated with universities. The first one was created in California—the California School of Professional Psychology or CSPP. It opened with two campuses (San Francisco and Los Angeles) in 1970, and added two more (San Diego and Fresno) two years later.

Just as the strong need for clear training guidelines for the new post-war clinical psychologist led to the Boulder conference in 1949, the need for some degree of standardization in the training of the new Psy.D. clinician led to its own conference, held at Vail, Colorado, in 1973. The goal of the Vail conference was to legitimize the Psy.D. degree and provide a clear distinction between it and programs yielding a Ph.D. in psychology. In essence, the Ph.D. was designed to produce the traditional scientist-practitioner, while the Psy.D. would produce a practitioner-scientist, knowledgeable about research, but primarily trained to deliver psychological services. Although it took some time for Psy.D. programs to attain perceived legitimacy, the APA now provides accreditation for both Ph.D. Boulder model programs and Psy.D. Vail model programs.

A major part of the postwar story of clinical psychology has been its increased status in the community of mental health care providers. As you recall from Chapter 12, clinical psychologists prior to World War II had relatively low standing among health care professionals and were often under the direct supervision of psychiatrists. Since the war, however, organized psychiatry's hegemony has gradually diminished. Over the past half century, sometimes after intense legal battles, clinical psychologists have gained the rights to (a) admit and release patients from mental hospitals, (b) serve as expert witnesses in court (e.g., in insanity cases), and (c) receive third-party payments from insurance companies. At present, organized psychology and psychiatry are skirmishing over prescription privileges, and there is every indication that before too long, psychiatrists will not be the only ones writing psychopharmacological prescriptions (Wiggins, 1994).

PSYCHOLOGY AND THE WORLD OF BUSINESS AND INDUSTRY

We have already seen (in Chapter 8) that it did not take psychology long to become involved in the world of business and industry. Soon after the turn of the twentieth century, Walter Dill Scott was writing on the application of psychology to advertising and how business could be made more efficient (Scott, 1903; 1910); Hugo Münsterberg was doing the consulting work that would produce *Psychology and Industrial Efficiency* (1913), some of which you read in the Original Source Excerpt for Chapter 8; Walter Bingham was creating his Division of Applied Psychology at the Carnegie Institute in Pittsburgh and consulting with local businesses; the Gilbreths were establishing their successful industrial consulting business; and the Hollingworths were doing their caffeine research for Coca-Cola.

During the 1920s, a period of growth and prosperity in America (after a period of recession in 1921–1922), these kinds of activities increased. Following the highly visible Army testing program in

World War I (Chapter 8), psychologists began developing tests as fast as they could be printed, for applications in education as well as business, and many businesses and industries hired psychologists to revamp their personnel departments, primarily by developing tests for the selection and evaluation of workers. Many of these efforts produced tests of questionable quality, prompting Anne Anastasi, author of a legendary textbook on psychological testing, to conclude that the "testing boom of the 1920s probably did more to retard than to advance the progress of testing" (1993, p. 17).[2] Problems with the reliability and validity didn't slow the momentum of the testing "boom" until the late 1920s, and the apparent success of the enterprise spawned a new development in the 1920s—companies designed to provide psychological consulting services.

The first one, The Scott Company, was created by Walter Dill Scott shortly after the end of World War I (see the notice in Figure 13.4), but it only lasted for a few years, partly because Scott's leadership disappeared when he was named president of Northwestern University in 1920. A second attempt, although it floundered initially, was the Psychological Corporation, which still exists and is highly successful today. It was the brainchild of James McKeen Cattell, who, as you recall from earlier chapters (4 and 8), was a doctoral student of Wundt, the promoter of the failed Galtonian approach to mental testing, and chair of the psychology department at Columbia during a time when it became a leading graduate school in psychology (as you recall, two of his students were Thorndike and Woodworth). In the early 1920s, Cattell was out of academia, having been fired from Columbia for his anti-war views. He continued as editor-in-chief of the journal *Science*, but he was looking for a way to return to prominence among fellow psychologists. He was also concerned about the growing number of people fraudulently claiming expertise in psychology and cashing in on the widespread interest in psychological testing (Sokal, 1981). His idea for the company was to create a nationwide network of

---

[2] The first edition of this remarkable text appeared in 1954, and it went through seven editions in Anastasi's lifetime (1908–2001). The 7th edition, which appeared in 1997, is still in print and widely used as a text.

FIGURE 13.4 Announcement of the formation of The Scott Company, the first consulting company for business organized by psychologists.

Ph.D. psychologists with recognized expertise in testing and experimental methodology. The Corporation would be a central clearinghouse—a business in St. Louis, for instance, in need of psychological assessment in its personnel department, would contact the Psychological Corporation in New York (or one of its planned branch offices), and would be referred to local expert psychologists who had signed on with the Corporation. The psychologists would perform the service and collect their fee, half of which went back to the Corporation.

The Psychological Corporation began in 1921, with Cattell as its first president. It was a fine idea in principle, but almost immediately it ran into difficulty, primarily because of Cattell's leadership style. He was never very clear about precisely what services would be offered, making businesses hesitant to sign contracts, and he did not have a good head for business. As late as 1925, for instance, the Corporation's net income was $51.75, while renting offices in prime New York real estate and paying $2,500 to the person

in charge of day-to-day operations; to keep the operation afloat, Cattell had to contribute $5,000 of his own money (Sokal, 1981). This wouldn't do, and by 1926 Cattell was ousted by his Board of Directors. Walter Van Dyke Bingham, with better connections in the business world because of his experiences running the applied psychology operation at the Carnegie Institute in Pittsburgh (Chapter 8, pp. 242–243) replaced him. Although the Psychological Corporation suffered during the Great depression of the 1930s, as most businesses did, it survived, and then flourished, especially after World War II. In the year that a publishing house purchased the corporation, 1969, it was worth $2.5 million in total assets and was selling about $5 million in psychological tests per year (Sokal, 1981).

The field of industrial psychology achieved an increase in perceived legitimacy with the publication of a large and important textbook in 1932 with the simple title of *Industrial Psychology*. It was written by Morris Viteles, Lightner Witmer's best-known doctoral student. Viteles completed his degree with Witmer at the University of Pennsylvania in 1921, a study on competency testing for streetcar employees (McReynolds, 1997). Two years later, Witmer named Viteles director of a new branch of the Psychological Clinic, named the Vocational Guidance Clinic. It offered testing and consulting services to businesses, but it was primarily for the purpose of helping high school and college students prepare for and enter the world of work. Viteles spent the rest of his career at the Clinic, while also working as a consultant to various businesses and industries in the Philadelphia area. His consulting work went far beyond the typical employee selection realm—Viteles conducted valuable studies on safety and accident prevention for the Yellow Cab Company and, for the Bell Telephone Company, he developed a program to help managers develop leadership skills and participate more effectively in corporate decision making (Hilgard, 1987).

The Hawthorne Studies

A major event in the 1920s was the start of a series of applied research experiments that stretched into the 1930s. The research led to the naming of an effect that was supposedly demonstrated over and over in the studies, and today appears regularly in textbooks in industrial psychology, social psychology, and research methodology—the so-called Hawthorne effect. The name derives from the city in Illinois where the research took place, the home of the Western Electric Plant. The plant manufactured equipment for the American Telephone and Telegraph company (AT&T).

The experiments at Hawthorne began in 1924 with a series of studies, extending over three years, to examine the effects of lighting on worker productivity. Although they appeared to be well-designed and objective, they were in fact sponsored in part by the electrical industry, which hoped to find evidence for its belief that there was a simple correlation between lighting and productivity—the more light in the work space, the higher the productivity (Gillespie, 1991). Evidence for this, of course, would help sell light bulbs. Unfortunately for the industry, however, the research failed to show any consistent relationship between lighting and work output. Productivity remained about the same, regardless of lighting level, and even when lighting was poor. We now know that productivity is highly complex, influenced by a variety of factors. But at Hawthorne the outcome of the lighting study was the conclusion that the physical environment was not as important for productivity as the "human factor." Workers knew they were in a study and that the results were important, so their productivity remained high

because they felt valued. At least that is the standard interpretation. What was not mentioned was that several other factors surely contributed to the high level of productivity—for instance, supervision was increased during the lighting experiments (Gillespie, 1991).

The findings of the illumination experiments were confirmed and then some, or at least that is the standard line, in the most famous of the Hawthorne studies, the Relay Assembly Test Room (RATR) study. In this experiment, six female workers were selected from a larger group in the plant. Their job was to assemble electrical relays for telephones. Five workers did the actual assembly, and the sixth kept them supplied with parts. Figure 13.5 shows the work room from two angles. The assembly was a time-consuming, labor-intensive, repetitive job requiring the assembly of some 35 parts per relay. Western Electric produced about 7 million relays a year (Gillespie, 1988), so naturally they were interested in making workers as productive as possible.

The first series of relay studies extended from May 1927 through September 1928. During that time, several workplace variables were studied (and confounded with each other, actually). At various times there were changes in the scheduling of rest periods, total hours of work, and bonuses paid for certain levels of production. The typical account, similar to the outcome for the lighting studies, has it that productiv-

FIGURE 13.5 The working arrangements in the Relay Assembly Test Room experiment at the Hawthorne plant. On the left can be seen the chutes that took the completed relays and counted them. On the right is the room as the workers saw it.

ity for this small group quickly reached high levels and stayed there even when working conditions were worsened. The example always mentioned concerned the infamous "12th test period" when workers were informed that the work week would increase from 42 to 48 hours per week, and that rest periods and free lunches would be discontinued (Gillespie, 1988). Virtually all research methodology textbooks describe the results somewhat like this:

> With few exceptions, no matter what changes were made—whether there were many or few rest periods, whether the workday was made longer or shorter, and so on—the women tended to produce more and more telephone relays. (Elmes, Kantowitz, & Roediger, 2003, p. 138)

Supposedly, the workers remained productive because they believed they were a special group and the focus of attention—they were part of an experiment. This, along with the similar outcome of the lighting studies, is the origin of the concept called the **Hawthorne Effect**, the tendency for performance to be affected because people know they are being studied. The effect may be genuine in a research context, but whether it truly happened at Western Electric is uncertain.

A close look at what actually happened in the RATR study reveals some interesting alternative explanations. First, although accounts of the study typically emphasize how delighted the women were to be in this special testing room, the fact is that of the five original assemblers, two had to be removed from the room for insubordination and low output. One was said to have "gone Bolshevik" (Bramel & Friend, 1981). Remember, the Soviet Union was brand new in the 1920s and the "red menace" was a threat to industrial America, resulting in things like a fear of labor unions. Of the two replacements, one was especially talented and enthusiastic and quickly became the group leader. She apparently was selected because she "held the record as the fastest relay-assembler in the regular department" (Gillespie, 1988, p. 122). Her efforts contributed greatly to the high level of productivity.

A second problem with interpreting the relay data is a simple statistical problem. In the famous 12th period, productivity was recorded as output per week rather than output per hour, yet workers were putting in an extra 6 hours per week compared to the previous test period. If the more appropriate output per hour is used, productivity actually *declined* slightly (Bramel & Friend, 1981). Also, the women were apparently angry about the change, but afraid to complain lest they be removed from the test room, thereby losing bonus money (there were not so subtle hints to them that such an outcome could occur if they messed up). Last, it could have been that in the RATR, as well as in some of the other Hawthorne experiments, increased worker productivity could have been simply the result of feedback about performance, along with concrete rewards for productivity (Parsons, 1974).

As you know by now, historical events must be understood within their entire political, economic, and institutional context, and the Hawthorne studies are no exception. Painting a glossy picture of workers unaffected by specific working conditions and more concerned with being considered special ushered in the human relations movement in industry and led corporations to emphasize the humane management of employees in order to create the impression of one big happy family of labor and management. Paying attention to the well being of workers was a significant advance, in the context of the long history of workers' needs being ignored by management. However, such a picture also helps to maintain power at the level of management and impede efforts at unionization, which some historians (e.g., Bramel & Friend, 1981) believe were among the true motives behind the studies completed at Western Electric.

THE PRACTICE OF PSYCHOLOGY IN PERSPECTIVE

We have seen that World War II was responsible for the creation of modern clinical psychology. The war provided an impetus to other areas of applied psychology as well. As was the case during the first world conflict, psychologists were heavily involved in developing tests for such tasks as the selection of officers and the placement of soldiers into military jobs that suited them. The first war produced Army Alpha and Beta; the second war produced a much more sophisticated test, the Army General Classification Test (AGCT). It graded soldiers into five ability levels, had adequate reliability as a test, and had a degree of validity in that it correlated reasonably well with educational level (Capshew, 1999). The war also gave a boost to applied psychologists whose work examined the relationship between humans and machines, and the war produced a new subdiscipline in psychology—**engineering psychology**. This field had as its goals the creation of machines that were designed for efficient human use. A well-engineered airplane cockpit, for example, would have seats that reduced fatigue and instruments that avoided perceptual errors. As you recall from Chapter 8, an important pioneer in this area, also known as ergonomics, was Lillian Gilbreth.

The focus of this chapter has been on the application of psychology to the diagnosis and treatment of those with mental and behavioral disorders (clinical psychology) and the use of psychological principles to improve business (industrial psychology). It is important to note that applied psychology extends to other areas that have not been a part of this chapter. These include counseling, school, forensic, and educational psychology.

The reorganization of the APA ushered in a period of tremendous growth for psychology in America. Applied psychology was the beneficiary of APA's new charter, which added advancing psychology as a profession to its original goal of advancing the science of psychology. As we saw at the outset of this chapter, one outcome was a growing feeling of alienation among the scientists in APA. But the scientific side of psychology also prospered in the years after World War II, especially in the form of a major postwar movement called cognitive psychology. The story of cognitive psychology's post-war ascendance, along with discussion of other important historical landmarks in scientific psychology during this time, will be told in the next chapter.

SUMMARY

RESEARCHERS AND PRACTITIONERS

- One result of the reorganization of the APA in 1945 was increased visibility for professional practitioners of psychology. This did not sit well with academic psychologists, whose primary activities were teaching and research, and who had controlled the APA in the years between the world wars.

- Believing the APA was becoming too focused on professional practice, psychological scientists formed the Psychonomic Society in 1960 and the American Psychological Society (APS) in 1988.

THE EMERGENCE OF MODERN CLINICAL PSYCHOLOGY

- Modern clinical psychology emerged from the terrible necessity of World War II. Psychiatry, up to then in control of treatment for mental illness, could not keep up with the caseload. Shortly after the war, a conference on the training of clinical psychologists was held at Boulder, under the leadership of David Shakow. The outcome was a training model featuring a combination of scientific expertise along with expertise in the diagnosis and treatment of mental disorders. The clinical psychol-

ogist earned a Ph.D. degree and had to complete a research-based doctoral dissertation.

- A study by Eysenck in 1952 questioning the effectiveness of traditional insight forms of psychotherapy (e.g., Freudian psychoanalysis), focused attention on the need for high quality research on therapy effectiveness, and led to the development of several new approaches to therapy, most notably behavior therapy and a variety of humanistic therapies.

- A controversial medical strategy for treating mental illness, the leucotomy or lobotomy, was created in the 1930s by Egas Moniz, who won the Nobel Prize for his work, but was cautious in using the procedure. The procedure was based on the idea that by severing the connections between the frontal lobe and lower brain centers, the person would be better able to control emotions. Less cautious was Walter Freeman, who developed by more efficient procedure, the transorbital lobotomy, by entering through the eye socket. The procedure fell out of favor in the 1950s—it was of questionable effectiveness, it was sometimes used for dubious reasons, and better forms of treatment (drugs) appeared.

- Behavior therapy is based on the idea that many of life's

problems are the result of learning and that experiences influence the disorders that develop. Therapies based on behaviorist principles existed well before World War II, but after the war it came into its own, especially with the work of Joseph Wolpe, who developed a form of therapy called systematic desensitization.

- Humanistic psychology is sometimes called psychology's "third force," because it rejected the determinism of psychoanalysis and behaviorism and proposed that humans are free to develop and control their own lives, rather than being tied to their past. Humanistic psychologists believe that all humans have the potential for personal growth and self-actualization, a concept investigated by Abraham Maslow, who studied real life exemplars of self-actualized people (e.g., Max Wertheimer). Self-actualizers perceive reality accurately; are independent, creative, spontaneous, moral, and natural; are devoted to a career; and have occasional peak experiences.

- Carl Rogers rejected traditional psychotherapy and developed a humanistic approach to treatment. The emphasis in client-centered therapy is on positive growth in a client, said to occur if the therapeutic atmosphere is healthy. The job of the therapist is to create this atmosphere, which includes being a model of the self-actualized person ("genuine"), showing unconditional positive regard for the client, and displaying empathy. The therapeutic technique of reflection is designed to aid the process.

- In 1973, the Vail conference produced a new training model for clinicians, one that focused more on practice than on research and did not necessarily require a research-based dissertation. It results in a Psy.D. degree (doctorate of psychology), rather than the traditional

Ph.D. Today, APA accredits programs based on both the Boulder and the Vail model.

PSYCHOLOGY AND THE WORLD OF BUSINESS AND INDUSTRY

- During the 1920s, many psychologists worked as consultants to business and industry, a development fueled in part by the great interest in testing in the 1920s. Psychologists also joined together to form consulting businesses that would provide a range of services. The Scott Company was the first, but did not survive the 1920s. The Psychological Corporation, under the wayward leadership of James McKeen Cattell, did survive, and eventually prospered, but not until Cattell was ousted.

- The Hawthorne studies, extending from 1924 to 1933, have traditionally been seen as providing evidence that productivity will be high if workers are cared for and given healthy work conditions. Productivity did not seem to be affected by such things as lighting conditions and changes in work breaks; what seemed to matter was that workers felt important because they were part of an experiment (i.e., the traditional Hawthorne effect). Historians have shown that the traditional version of what happened at Hawthorne is questionable, however, and that the Hawthorne studies had the effect of maintaining management control over the workplace.

- World War II contributed to the creation and growth of engineering psychology—a form of applied experimental psychology that examines the relationship between humans and machines, the goal being the development of machines that humans can use efficiently, comfortably, and safely.

STUDY QUESTIONS

1. What is the nature of the division between academician/researchers and practitioners? What effect did the reorganization of APA have?

2. Describe the essential problem that led to the creation of the Psychonomic Society and the APS.

3. How did the activities of clinical psychologists after World War II differ from their activities prior to the war? What brought about the change?

4. Compare the two major training models for clinicians—the Boulder model and the Vail model. What were the problems with the former that led to the creation of the latter?

5. What was the scientific basis for the development of the

lobotomy and how did Freeman alter the procedure invented by Moniz? Why did lobotomies more or less disappear after the mid-1950s?

6. What did Hans Eysenck find in his analysis of studies that evaluated psychotherapy? What was the impact of the Eysenck study?

7. Describe Wolpe's systematic desensitization and show how it relates to behaviorist principles.

8. Why is humanistic psychology sometimes referred to as psychology's "third force"?

9. Briefly summarize the basic beliefs of humanistic psychologists.

10. Describe Maslow's work with self-actualization. What did he conclude were the attributes of a self-actualized person?

11. In addition to creating client-centered therapy, Rogers is also known for being interested in research on therapy effectiveness. Explain how his personal history might have contributed to that interest.

12. Humanistic psychology was popular in the 1960s and 1970s, but then it faded. Explain.

13. Describe the origins of the Psychological Corporation, how it was designed to operate, and what happened to it.

14. What did Morris Viteles contribute to industrial psychology in the 1920s and 1930s?

15. How do most texts describe the Hawthorne effect?

16. What was the original purpose of the lighting studies at Hawthorne, what was the outcome, and what is the traditional interpretation of the results?

17. What was the original purpose of the relay assembly test room at Hawthorne, what was the outcome, and what is the traditional interpretation of the results? What really happened in the relay assembly test room?

18. The Hawthorne studies were said to show that relationships with workers were the key to productivity, but historians have interpreted the Hawthorne studies differently. Explain.

QUESTIONS FROM THE ORIGINAL SOURCE EXCERPT

1. Describe the three necessary conditions for therapy to be effective, according to Rogers.

2. Describe the therapy technique of reflection and explain its purpose.

3. Rogers believed that what worked in client-centered therapy could also work for all relationships. Explain.

FOR FURTHER READING

Gillespie, R. (1991). *Manufacturing knowledge: A history of the Hawthorne experiments.* New York: Cambridge University Press.

A comprehensive description and analysis of all the Hawthorne studies, which extended from 1924 to 1933; shows how the results have been interpreted in ways congenial to the human relations movement in business, but that a close analysis questions the traditional interpretation of the so-called Hawthorne effect; a briefer analysis can be found in Gillespie (1988).

History of psychology: The Boulder conference. (2000). *American Psychologist, 55,* 233–254.

A set of articles commemorating the fiftieth anniversary of the creation of the Boulder scientist-practitioner model for the training of clinical psychologists; includes articles on clinical training prior to Boulder, the impact of the Boulder conference, and a series of brief reflections on Boulder.

Rogers, C. R. (1961). *On becoming a person.* Boston: Houghton Mifflin.

A set of articles written by and compiled by Rogers; includes an opening autobiographical essay, several essays on his basic philosophy, articles on therapy outcome research, and articles on client-centered therapy, including the one in this chapter's excerpt.

Sokal, M. M. (1981). The origins of the Psychological Corporation. *Journal of the History of the Behavioral Sciences, 17,* 54–67.

Describes the uneasy beginnings of one of psychology's most successful applied ventures; shows how Cattell's nineteenth-century vision of psychology made it impossible for him to lead effectively, and fits the story nicely into the context of America in the 1920s and 1930s.

CHAPTER 14

PSYCHOLOGICAL SCIENCE
IN THE POST-WAR ERA

The basic reason for studying cognitive processes has become as clear as the reason for studying anything else: because they are there. ... Cognitive processes surely exist, so it can hardly be unscientific to study them.

—Ulric Neisser, 1967

PREVIEW AND CHAPTER OBJECTIVES

The most important development in academic psychology since World War II has been the advent and development of modern cognitive psychology. During the 1950s and especially the 1960s, American psychologists began to shift their research and theoretical interests. Whereas in the 1930s and 1940s behaviorism and the search for basic laws of conditioning occupied the attention of most laboratory researchers, the postwar period saw a reemergence of interest in studying cognitive processes such as perception, memory, attention, imagery, and thinking. The shift was evolutionary rather than revolutionary—many psychologists were interested in cognition during the heyday of behaviorism, and behaviorists, especially Skinnerians, remained active and productive in the face of the shift toward cognitive psychology. Nonetheless, academic psychology in 1970 was quite different from the 1950 version. Most of this chapter will examine the rise of cognitive psychology and its influence on other subdisciplines of psychology. The Original Source Excerpt is from a series of studies of human memory by Sir Frederick Bartlett of England. Its importance to cognitive psychology was not immediately recognized when it was published in 1932, because it appeared during the heyday of neobehaviorism. It has since been recognized as a classic, but Mark Twain might have been right when he said that a classic is a book everyone can name but nobody has read. After reading the excerpt, Twain's comment won't be true, for you at least.

After examining the rise of cognitive psychology, the last third of the chapter examines four other prominent areas of research in psychology, physiological or neuropsychology, social psychology, personality psychology, and developmental psychology. For each of these areas, the influence of one historically prominent researcher will be highlighted—Donald Hebb, Leon Festinger, Gordon Allport, and Jean Piaget, respectively. After you finish this chapter, you should be able to:

▪ Describe examples of cognitive research that occurred during the era of neobehaviorism, especially the work of Sir Frederick Bartlett

▪ Describe the factors within psychology and in fields external to psychology that influenced the development of cognitive psychology

▧ Critically examine the issue of whether a "cognitive revolution" occurred in psychology

▧ Describe the landmark research (e.g., STM capacity) that established cognitive psychology as a force in psychology

▧ Describe the influence of Neisser's first book on cognitive psychology and compare its emphasis with that of his second cognitive book

▧ Distinguish between cognitive psychology and cognitive science and describe the contribution of the latter to the field of artificial intelligence

▧ Critically examine the impact of cognitive psychology on psychology as a whole

▧ Describe the contributions of Donald Hebb to the study of the relationship between brain and behavior

▧ Describe the contributions of Leon Festinger to the study of social psychology

▧ Describe the contributions of Gordon Allport to the study of personality

▧ Describe the contributions of Jean Piaget to the study of developmental psychology

COGNITIVE PSYCHOLOGY ARRIVES (AGAIN)

When psychology began to identify itself as a separate discipline in the latter half of the nineteenth century, it aimed at a scientific understanding of human conscious experience, and Ebbinghaus, Wundt, Külpe, Wertheimer, Titchener, and other pioneers studied such mental phenomena as memory, attention, perception, and thinking. Psychologists in America also took up these same topics, gave them a functional twist, and investigated them vigorously in the early years of the twentieth century. Then Watson appeared and said that the study of mental life was unscientific and that everyone should be a behaviorist, studying the relationships between environmental stimuli and the individual's responses. Not everyone listened, of course, and as we learned in Chapter 10, Watson's message took a long time to produce significant effects. By the mid-1930s, however, behaviorism had become a force in American psychology, and the most typical image of the psychology laboratory in those days included rats and mazes. After World War II, however, interests began to shift again, and the study of cognitive processes came once more to the forefront. This time the methods were different and more rigorous, and the models were based on a new technological break-

through—the computer. But the topics of interest remained the same. Some psychologists began calling themselves cognitive psychologists, and a new movement, which was in a sense a return to an old one, was born. In the latter half of the twentieth century, cognitive psychology has been the dominant conceptual framework in American psychology.

The Roots of Modern Cognitive Psychology

Despite Watson's best efforts at promotion, American psychology did not become behaviorist overnight, and even when behaviorism was "in" among American psychologists, not everyone joined the party. In the 1920s, '30s, and '40s, the pages of the leading journals still contained numerous articles describing research on such cognitive topics as memory, perception, attention, language, and thinking. Among others, they included the famous "Stroop effect" study (Stroop, 1935) mentioned in Chapter 11 (p. 339), and a study by Jenkins and Dallenbach (1924) that still appears regularly in general psychology books. The experiment examined the effect of cognitive interference on memory, showing that after studying verbal materials, recall could be improved if a period of sleep (i.e., minimal interference) intervened between study and recall.

Books dealing with cognitive topics also appeared during behaviorism's heyday, even including one with the title *Cognitive Psychology* (Moore, 1939). Although its treatment of cognition was more of a look back to the earlier years of the century than a call for a new approach to cognition (Knapp, 1985), it dealt with many of the same topics that would concern cognitive psychologists two decades later. And on the theoretical front, the gestaltists (Chapter 9) promoted the study of cognition and argued with behaviorists throughout the 1930s and 1940s.

Behaviorism was a distinctly American phenomenon, and hence it is not surprising to learn that (a) there were several important European psychologists doing cognitive work during behaviorism's glory years, and (b) most American experimental psychologists, focused intently on whether their rat was going to turn left or right at a choice point in a maze, paid little attention to this ongoing cognitive research. These Europeans included the famous Swiss developmental psychologist, Jean Piaget, whose ideas about cognitive development first appeared in the 1920s (Piaget, 1923/1959), but weren't influential in the United States until the 1960s. Piaget and his work will be profiled later in the chapter, in a section on research in developmental psychology. The second famous name was England's Sir Frederick Bartlett, who took memory research in a distinctly non-Ebbinghaus direction in the 1930s (Bartlett, 1932/1967).

Frederick C. Bartlett (1886–1969): Constructing Memory

In 1932, a brief book with the simple title of *Remembering: A Study in Experimental and Social Psychology* appeared, authored by a psychologist from England's Cambridge University, Frederick Bartlett. In the United States, the book was ignored, and an American reviewer of the book, writing three years after its publication, concluded his generally dismissive review by saying that the book would "find a place upon the shelves of those who study remembering, but it will not be in the special section reserved for those investigators whose writings have become landmarks in the advance towards the comprehension of this important problem" (Jenkins, 1935, p. 715). The reviewer probably had Ebbinghaus in mind as a "landmark." Today, Bartlett's book is recognized as being equal to Ebbinghaus's in importance. We will get to it shortly.

Frederick Bartlett was born and raised in the rural Cotswolds region of England, northwest of London and near Oxford and Stratford-upon-Avon. Much of his early education was at home, and his first formal higher degree was by correspondence course from London University. He then completed a more traditional undergraduate program at Saint John's College of Cambridge University in 1914. He remained at Cambridge for graduate studies and completed the research on memory as his doctoral thesis, shortly after World War I. Thus, the studies in *Remembering* were completed about 15 years before they were published (Oldfield, 1972). During the 1920s, Bartlett became head of the Psychology Laboratory at Cambridge, and set about establishing one of the few centers of experimental psychology in Great Britain. He directed the laboratory until his retirement in 1952, producing, with his students, research on topics ranging from pilot fatigue to animal learning. He also adapted some of the methods used in his memory book to the study of thinking, the result being *Thinking: An Experimental and Social Study*, which appeared in 1958. It was the memory book that made his reputation, however. The following excerpt is from a 1967 reprinting of the book.

ORIGINAL SOURCE EXCERPT
Bartlett on Memory

Bartlett opened his memory book by raising questions about the usefulness of research in the Ebbinghaus tradition, with its emphasis on the effects of rote repetition on the memorization of highly artificial stimuli, the famous nonsense syllables, and its theoretical basis in associationism. Instead, Bartlett argued that research on memory should focus more on the attributes of the memorizer and less on the nature of the stimulus materials, and that memory must be understood in the context of realistic situations using everyday materials, rather than artificial nonsense syllables. He also believed that the memorizer, rather than passively accumulating associative strength as the result of practice and repetition, *actively* organizes the material into meaningful wholes that he referred to as **schemata** (plural form of "schema"). Bartlett defined these schemata as "active organisation[s] of past reactions, or of past experiences, which must always be supposed to be operating in any well-adapted organic response" (1932/1967, p. 201). For example, as a result of our experiences, we will develop a schema relating to the concept of death. This schema will in turn influence our current and future perceptions of death and dying and affect our memory of these experiences. People with different experiences and from different cultures will have different schemata about death.

To provide empirical support for his arguments, Bartlett developed a series of tasks on perception, imagination, and memory. The memory experiments are the best known and two of them will be excerpted here. Bartlett called the first the Method of Description.

> I endeavored, in this series of experiments, to avoid as far as possible the artificiality which hangs over laboratory experiments in psychology. I therefore discarded the use of nonsense syllables and throughout employed material a part of which, at least, might fairly be regarded as interesting and sufficiently normal. ...
>
> A series of five picture post-cards was used [Figure 14.1]. On each card was a representation of the face of a navy, or military, officer or [enlisted] man. The experiments were carried out during the early days of the Great War [WWI], when there was a very widespread interest in the fighting services. The particular cards were chosen because the faces ... were sufficiently

FIGURE 14.1 Post card stimuli used by Bartlett (1932) for his "Method of Description."

alike to render their grouping easy, while at the same time each face had definite individual peculiarities. (pp. 47–48)

Bartlett placed the five cards face down in front of each of 20 participants, always arranged in the same sequence. The volunteers were given ten seconds to examine each of the five cards, and when studying a particular card, the other four were face down. Bartlett then let 30 minutes pass, during which he engaged participants in conversation unrelated to the experiment. After the interval, participants were asked to describe the contents of the pictures in the same order they studied them, and they were asked a series of questions about the pictures. You will note in Bartlett's description that except for an occasional frequency count, his results are described in narrative form, not as summary statistics, and his descriptions of methodology are often vague. As one reviewer pointed out, Bartlett's studies are better conceived of as "controlled demonstrations, rather than true experiments" (Roediger, 1997, p. 489). Bartlett's rather casual attitude toward experimental control is evident as he described the questions asked of participants:

It is not necessary to give the questions in detail, particularly as I did not hesitate to adapt them or to supplement them in accordance with what I judged to be the psychological needs of the moment. They could all be grouped very well under the following four headings:

(a) those dealing with position or with direction of regard;
(b) those dealing straightforwardly with particular detail;
(c) those suggesting detail not present in the case in question, but found elsewhere in the series;
(d) those suggesting detail not present anywhere in the series. (p. 49)

What did Bartlett find? First with regard to "position," by which he meant the ability to recall accurately in sequence, he found something similar to a modern serial position effect. Perfect recall of the first face, and better recall for the beginning and end than the middle. By "direction of regard," he meant whether the faces were turned to the left or right; here he found little accuracy—the wrong choice was made more than half the time. As for accuracy of detail, transposing detail ("transferring") from one picture to another, and reporting detail not in the cards ("importation"), Bartlett found numerous mistakes:

All but six of the twenty subjects transferred detail, and in nearly every case this was done at the very outset. ...

Four cases concerned the pipe, four the mustache and four the badge. That is to say, the detail most frequently transferred was generally of an outstanding character, for at that time military cap badges were matters of considerable interest among my subjects. ...

In the first free description of the faces, nineteen cases occurred of details being introduced into the series from outside, and thirteen of the subjects were involved. The influence of questions—even of straightforward questions of fact—in inducing this kind of importation of detail may be very strong. ...

It is perhaps most curious that importation seemed definitely most liable to occur in relation to salient detail. However, when we consider that salience of detail in the main is determined by specialized interest, we can see that this is after all just what might be expected. For example, one subject, an Army officer, was especially interested in military cap badges. In his descriptions he changed these into badges of regiments with which he was most familiar on active service. (pp. 57–58)

Bartlett's results with his method of description, although not described in very great detail, sound remarkably like modern studies of eyewitness memory—the lack of accuracy, the addition of detail not originally seen, and the damaging effects of leading questions. The study also illustrates one of the main themes of his book, an emphasis on the interests and attitudes of the memorizer (e.g., the officer interested in badges) rather than the nature of the stimulus material itself. Earlier in the book, Bartlett had made the point clear in a passage that is reminiscent of the gestaltists' distinction between geographical (the stimulus) and behavioral environments (the stimulus as perceived):

The psychologist ... must not stand in awe of the stimulus. Uniformity and simplicity of structure of stimuli are no guarantee whatever of uniformity and simplicity of structure inorganic response, particularly at the human level. We may consider the old and familiar illustration of the landscape artist, the naturalist, and the geologist who walk in the country together. The one is said to notice and recall the beauty of the scenery, the other details of flora and fauna, and the third the formation of soils and rock. In this case, no doubt, the stimuli, being selected in each instance from what is present, are different for each observer, and obviously the records made in recall are different also. (pp. 3–4)

The most famous of Bartlett's memory studies used what he called the "method of repeated reproduction." Participants were given a 328-word story to read through twice at their own speed. The story was a Native American folk tale called "The War of the Ghosts." Thus, the story reflected a culture quite different from that of early twentieth century England, and the story had certain elements that would not seem to "make sense" from the standpoint of a typical Britisher. Here is the story in its entirety:

One night two young men from Egulac went down to the river to hunt seals, and while they were there it became foggy and calm. Then they heard warcries, and they thought: "Maybe this is a war-party." They escaped to the shore, and hid behind a log. Now canoes came up, and they heard the noise of paddles, and saw one canoe coming up to them. There were five men in the canoe, and they said:

"What do you think? We wish to take you along. We are going up the river to make war on the people."

One of the young men said: "I have no arrows."

"Arrows are in the canoe," they said.

"I will not go along. I might be killed. My relatives do not know where I have gone. But you," he said, turning to the other, "may go with them.

So one of the young men went, but the other returned home.

And the warriors went on up the river to a town on the other side of Kalama. The people came down to the water, and they began to fight, and many were killed. But presently the young man heard one of the warriors say: "Quick, let us go home: that Indian has been hit." Now he thought: "Oh, they are ghosts." He did not feel sick, but they said he had been shot.

So the canoes went back to Egulac, and the young man went ashore to his house, and made a fire. And he told everybody and said: "Behold I accompanied the ghosts, and we went to fight. Many of our fellows were killed, and many of those who attacked us were killed. They said I was hit, and I did not feel sick."

He told it all, and then he became quiet. When the sun rose he fell down. Something black came out of his mouth. His face became contorted. The people jumped up and cried.

He was dead. (p. 65)

Unless you are a member of this particular culture, I suspect that you found the passage to be a bit odd. So did Bartlett's twenty participants (seven women, thirteen men). Fifteen minutes after reading the story, they were asked to reproduce as much of it as they could. Additional reproductions were elicited at later intervals ranging from hours to months. Bartlett even found one former participant six *years* later and asked him to recall the story. Bartlett reported the results by reproducing dozens of the actual recalled stories, then summarizing the kinds of errors found. Total recall declined with the passage of time, of course, but what was more intriguing to Bartlett was the quality of the reproductions. Participants did not just recall less; what they recalled was shaped by their need to form a coherent, understandable story within the context of their own knowledge systems. Thus, "something black coming out of his mouth," was transformed to "foaming at the mouth" for one participant and the soul leaving the body for another. Also, the ambiguity about the ghosts (if they are already ghosts, how come they can be killed?) led one participant to decide that "Ghosts" was just a label for a particular tribe; that transformation (or "rationalisation," as Bartlett called it) "made the whole thing more comprehensible" (p. 68). Others recalled erroneously but logically, that the "ghosts" appeared only after some Indians were killed in the battle. In all, then, participants recalled the story within the framework of their own cultural ideas and understanding about battle and death. On the basis of the Ghosts study and other studies reported in the book, Bartlett drew some general conclusions about memory. First, he made the point about the need to make the story meaningful:

In these experiments rationalisation was applied sometimes to the stories as a whole and sometimes to particular details. In the first case, the process expressed the need, felt by practically every educated observer, that a story should have a general [meaning]. Hardly ever, at the outset, was there an attitude of simple acceptance. Every story presented had to be connected, certainly as a whole, and, if possible, as regards its details also, with something else. This is ... the factor which I have ... called "effort after meaning" coming ... into play. It could be said that there is a constant effort to get the maximum possible of meaning into the material presented. ...

The rationalisation which gives to material as a whole its appropriate [meaning] is only part of the total process. Details must also be dealt with, and every chain of reproductions illustrated how the rationalising process was applied to particular items. ... [R]ationalisation in regard to form found its main expression in the linking together of events within the stories; rationalisation as concerned with details of material was usually carried out by connecting the given items with something outside the story and supplied by the observer himself. This is analogous to what I have called "importation" [and] it was of three main types:

First, there was the process, in all instances witting during its early stages, but later producing unwitting transformations, by which presented material was connected with other matter outside the story, but having the same general nature. For example, in *The War of the Ghosts* the "something black" was frequently interpreted as a materialisation of the dying man's breath.

The second process of rationalisation ... was unwitting from start to finish. The transformation of "something black" into "foamed at the mouth" was a case in point. So was the introduction of an "island" into *The War of the Ghosts* by several subjects.

The third type of rationalisation is very closely related to the second. It is the case in which some particular, and maybe isolated detail, is transformed immediately into a more familiar character. Thus "canoe" became "boat;" "paddling" became "rowing;" ... and so on in a very large number of cases.

The general function of rationalisation is in all instances the same. It is to render material acceptable, understandable, comfortable, straightforward; to rob it of its puzzling elements. As such it is a powerful factor in all perceptual and [memory] processes. (pp. 84–89)

In Chapter 10 of his book, Bartlett outlined a theory of memory. As implied by the description of "effort after meaning," memory was not merely an act of reproducing intact memory traces; rather, it was an active process of construction:

We must, then, consider what does actually happen more often than not when we say that we remember. The first notion to get rid of is that memory is primarily or literally reduplicative, or reproductive. In a world of constantly changing environment, literal recall is extraordinarily unimportant. ...

In the many thousands of cases of remembering which I collected, ... literal recall was very rare. With few exceptions, ... re-excitement of individual traces did not look to be in the least what was happening. ... In fact, if we consider the evidence rather than presupposition, remembering appears to be far more decisively an affair of construction rather than one of mere reproduction. ... [C]ondensation, elaboration and invention are common features of ordinary remembering, and these all very often involve the mingling of materials belonging originally to different "schemata." (pp. 204–205)

Bartlett borrowed the term schema from a British neurologist, Henry Head. After saying that he did not like the term ("It is at once too definite and too sketchy"—p. 201), Bartlett proceeded to rely on it for his theory. As described earlier, schemata (plural of schema) can be thought of as general concepts that make up our understanding of the world, and memories are constructed with reference to them. So, for instance, when Bartlett's participant recalled "foaming at the mouth" instead of the more obscure "something black came out of his mouth," that person's schemata about illness and death contributed to the construction of the memory. Bartlett's ideas about memory did not make much of a stir in the United States, appearing during the height of neobehaviorism. It was only in the 1960s, after cognitive psychology had emerged from multiple sources, that the significance of the work began to be appreciated. His notion of memory as constructive is now widely accepted and central to the understanding of such phenomena as false memory (e.g., Roediger & McDermott, 1995) and eyewitness memory (e.g., Loftus, 1979).

A Convergence of Influences

The influences that produced modern cognitive psychology came both from within psychology, in the form of a growing suspicion about the applicability of conditioning and associationist principles, and outside of psychology, through several disciplines that received their initial impetus in the context of World War II or developed after the end of the conflict (Segal & Lachman, 1972).

Influences Within Psychology

Among psychologists during the 1940s and 1950s, there was growing concern that conditioning and associationist principles could not adequately account for all human behavior, especially language behavior. Although the radical behaviorists had either reduced mental events to subtle muscular responses to stimuli (Watson), or viewed them merely as other types of behavior under the control of reinforcement contingencies (Skinner), Tolman and Hull had attempted to address the problem of "representation." That is, both recognized that individuals acted as if they were influenced by representations or conceptions of the external world (e.g., memories). Hull dealt with the issue by avoiding mentalistic concepts and proposing internal sequences of stimuli and responses that became chained together through reinforced experiences. Tolman went further and proposed that such internal constructs as cognitive maps and expectancies served to guide behavior. Both approaches fell short when it came to explaining distinctly human behavior such as language, however, and attempts to force language into conditioning terms failed.

The adequacy of associationism's principles was also called into question, most notably by the neuropsychologist Karl Lashley (Chapter 3, pp. 77–80), a former research colleague of Watson's at Johns Hopkins, but a longtime critic of simple Watsonian S-R formulations. In 1948, Lashley participated in the Hixon Symposium, an interdisciplinary meeting that brought together psychologists,

KEY DATE *1932*

This year marked the publication of Bartlett's classic study on memory, *Remembering: A Study in Experimental and Social Psychology.*

These events also occurred:

- Amelia Earhart became the first woman to fly solo across the Atlantic, traveling from Newfoundland to Ireland in 13.5 hours
- Work began on the Golden Gate Bridge in San Francisco
- Jack Sharkey (U.S.) defeated Max Schmeling (Germany) to capture the world heavyweight boxing crown
- Austrian-born Adolph Hitler was granted German citizenship
- Aldous Huxley published *Brave New World*
- Johnny Weissmuller made his first Tarzan movie and 4-year-old Shirley Temple made her movie debut
- These people were born:
    John Updike, American author
    Andrew Young, U.S. civil rights leader, politician, and diplomat
    Sylvia Plath, American author
- These people died:
    George Eastman, American inventor of photographic materials
    John Philip Souza, American composer of marches
    William Wrigley, American founder of chewing gum empire

mathematicians, neurologists, and psychiatrists to consider the general topic of the relationship between the cerebral cortex and behavior. Lashley's talk, published three years later in the collected symposium papers, dealt with the problem of serial order and the general failure of association theory to account for it (Lashley, 1951). Simply stated, the **serial order problem** concerns the question of how to explain, in terms of cerebral mechanisms, linear sequences of behavior, ranging from the series of finger movements while playing the violin to the memorization of a list of words to the production of language in sentences. A basic tenet of association theory was that adjacent elements in a sequence become associated or "chained" together because they are experienced together (i.e., contiguously). Lashley argued that such a formulation was inadequate. In complex motor skills such as playing the violin, for example, the sequence of behaviors occurs much too rapidly for one element to depend on the neurological analysis of the preceding element and be the stimulus for the next element. Also, the oral production of a sentence is more complex than a simple sequencing of words, as illustrated by the rules of syntax and slips of the tongue. Thus, two sentences, one in the active voice and the other in the passive, have completely different syntactical orders yet convey the same meaning. And certain errors of speech, called Spoonerisms, involve anticipations of words or word segments that were meant to occur later in the sentence.[1] Instead of a cortical model based on the concept of linear associative chains, Lashley argued that the brain was a system that exercised organizational control over complex patterns of behavior.

Lashley's paper was well received, but like Bartlett's work, its significance for the development of cognitive psychology was not immediately recognized, as shown in a careful citation analysis by psychologist/historian Darryl Bruce (1994). References to the article accumulated at a leisurely pace throughout the 1950s and then increased dramatically in the mid-1960s, the decade in which cognitive psychology achieved its greatest momentum. Thus, the serial order paper was a bit ahead of its time. Nonetheless, it contributed to the critical mass that was developing in the postwar years that eventually led to cognitive psychology's appearance.

Influences External to Psychology

Other events relevant for the cognitive movement took place in disciplines far removed from psychology. One of the most critical was the development of computer science, which was accelerated in the 1940s by the military needs of World War II, with its demands for such things as automated radar-tracking systems (Baars, 1986). Of course, philosophers and psychologists have a long history of using contemporary technology as metaphors relating to human behavior. Examples range from Descartes' use of hydraulic garden figures in his model of the nervous system to Watson's belief that the telephone switchboard paralleled the S-R connections underlying the relationship between stimulus and action. In the postwar era, it wasn't long before scientists began to see parallels between the computer and the brain.

The computer is essentially a device for taking in information from the environment, processing it internally, and producing some output. By analogy, the brain could be seen as doing the same thing. The mathematician John von Neuman explicitly developed this metaphor in the opening address given at the Hixon Symposium in 1948. The analogy reappeared on occasion in the 1950s, and by the 1960s it was commonplace to hear cognitive phenomena described in computer language and its models portrayed as computer flowcharts. The best-known example, soon to be a regular feature in the memory chapters of introductory psychology books, was the model proposed by Atkinson and Shiffrin (1968). Some form of the flowchart in Figure 14.2, a simplified version of theirs, is probably familiar to you. It introduced the well-known distinctions between the limited capacity short-term memory (STM), analogous to a computer's RAM, and long-term memory (LTM), likened to a computer's permanent memory stores, and it freely used computer jargon. Thus, humans don't just memorize things, they "transfer

[1] An example of a Spoonerism might be saying "Let me sew you to your sheets" instead of the intended "Let me show you to your seats."

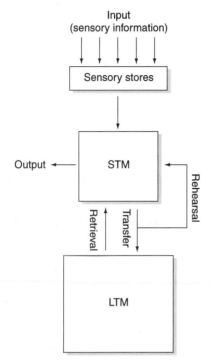

Input
(sensory information)

Sensory stores

Output ← STM

Rehearsal

Retrieval   Transfer

LTM

FIGURE 14.2 A typical example of the use of a flow chart to illustrate the two-stage model of memory like the Atkinson and Shiffrin (1968) model.

information from STM to LTM," and they don't just recall things, they "retrieve information from LTM."

One advantage of the computer metaphor was that it provided a scientifically respectable way to discuss complex internal mental processes, thus muting behaviorism's criticisms that psychological scientists shouldn't be dealing with mysterious unobservable entities that intervene between stimulus and response, and avoiding the old problems with introspection. As George Miller put it, "[c]omputers give us an existence-proof of the complexity that is possible in information-processing systems. This made us all feel a lot freer" (quoted in Baars, 1986, p. 212). Further respectability came from a refinement in the way of describing the flow of information through the system. This occurred in 1949 with the publication of *The Mathematical Theory of Communication* by Shannon and Weaver, which introduced **information theory** and the concept of

the **bit**, an abbreviation of "binary digit." An electrical engineer, Shannon recognized a connection between the logical operators of "true" and "false" and the two states, "on" and "off," of any electromagnetic relay. Working with Weaver, he defined the bit as the amount of information that would enable a decision between two equally likely alternatives. Thus, information reduces uncertainty. A coin toss, for instance, contains one bit of information because it tells us which of two possible outcomes is true. Each time the number of alternatives doubles, one additional bit of information is added: with four alternatives, it takes two bits of information to reduce uncertainty, with eight alternatives, it takes three bits, and so on. The significance of the concept was that it provided a way of standardizing units of information, regardless of the form that the information took (e.g., coin toss, dice throw, numbers, letters, etc.). The bit wound up being more important for computer science than for cognitive psychology, but in the 1950s it added further legitimacy to the scientific study of the mind.

A third area of development outside of psychology, but relating to the assault on behaviorism within psychology, was linguistics. Led by Noam Chomsky (b. 1928) of the Massachusetts Institute of Technology (MIT), theories of language structure and language production began to proliferate in the 1950s, and they went beyond anything conceivable to behaviorists. Chomsky came to the attention of psychologists in 1959, when he wrote a highly critical review of *Verbal Behavior*, B. F. Skinner's (1957) creative attempt to put language into operant terms (Chomsky, 1959). Language development occurs too rapidly for conditioning to be relevant, he argued. Even if we could learn a sentence per second, there are not enough seconds in a lifetime to learn all the sentences that we are capable of producing. Furthermore, people routinely create and/or understand sentences they have never experienced before. Language was simply too complex for what Chomsky took to be an overly simplistic behaviorist explanation.

As the result of the work of Chomsky and other linguists, language came to be viewed not as verbal behavior that was the outcome of conditioning and associative learning, but as the result of the application of a hierarchical set of rules called a **grammar**. These rules allow the individual to generate a virtually infinite number of grammatical sentences, while also enabling the person to immediately identify nongrammatical sentences. For instance, to use one of Chomsky's favorite examples (Gardner, 1985), we easily recognize "Colorless green ideas sleep furiously" as perfectly grammatical, if silly, while we have no difficulty rejecting these same words in a different order, "Sleep ideas green colorless furiously," as ungrammatical. The sentences we use cannot be the result of simple learning, Chomsky argued, but must follow from the systematic application of a grammar. Furthermore, this ability to use a grammar is instinctively human—Chomsky believed that language was the attribute that most clearly distinguished humans from other species. He believed that all languages shared common principles which he called **linguistic universals** and that the human brain is structured to be able to understand these uni-

versals automatically (Chomsky, 1966). Chomsky and other linguists supported their nativist arguments about language by pointing out that (a) as with other species-specific behaviors, there appears to be a critical period for language development, and (b) attempts to teach language skills to other species (e.g., through the use of sign language) have failed.[2]

Questions about behaviorism/associationism, along with developments in computer science, information theory, and linguistics, helped to change the intellectual climate among experimental psychologists. Then during the 1950s and early 1960s, several landmark publications led to the recognition that experimental psychology was somehow different than it had been before. Some have referred to the events at this time as a "revolution" in psychology, an issue that is examined in this chapter's Close-Up. Whether revolutionary or evolutionary, however, it is clear that several events reflected a change in direction of experimental psychology.

CLOSE-UP:
What Revolution?

There is little doubt that more experimental psychologists in America were interested in studying cognitive processes in the 1960s than in the prior two decades, and that except for dedicated diehard Skinnerian holdouts, behaviorism began to decline as a force at the same time. Some have referred to the change as a "revolution" in psychology (e.g., Segal & Lachman, 1972; Sperry, 1993), and at least two books chronicling the shift to cognition include "cognitive revolution" in their titles (Baars, 1986; Gardner, 1985). On the other hand, psychologist/historian Thomas Leahey (1992) has argued that the development of cognitive psychology does not meet any of the accepted criteria of a scientific revolution. Clearly, resolving the issue requires some understanding of what is meant by a "revolution" in science.

In 1962, a brief (172 pages) but momentous book entitled *The Structure of Scientific Revolutions* appeared on the academic scene, proposing a new way to look at progress in science. Its author, physicist-turned-historian Thomas Kuhn, argued against the traditional Enlightenment-based notion that scientific progress involves a gradual accumulation of objective knowledge over time. Rather, in Kuhn's version, science proceeds through history by establishing agreed-upon "paradigms" that guide scientists, and then shifts from one paradigm to another. When such a shift occurs, a revolution has happened.

---

[2] Chimpanzees and other primates have been quite successful at learning to use sign language and communicating their needs symbolically, but the general consensus among both linguists and experimental psychologists is that their learning is imitative and does not show evidence of the use of a true rule-bound grammar (see Anderson, 1990, for a review).

According to Kuhn, all sciences begin in a "preparadigmatic stage." During this time there are competing schools of thought within a discipline, and they argue over fundamental conceptual and definitional issues. Eventually, one of those schools gains a majority of adherents and becomes established as a **paradigm**. A Kuhnian paradigm is an all-embracing worldview within the scientific community that organizes what is known into a grand theory, determines how terms are defined and what problems are to be solved by scientists, and dictates appropriate research methods. Newtonian physics is the typical example. Once a paradigm has been established, there exists a period of **normal science**, during which the paradigm guides research designed to provide empirical evidence for it. Because all paradigms have some truth to them, much of this research indeed supports the paradigm, but not all of it does. Anomalous findings can usually be ignored or explained away, but sometimes predictions keep failing and the science enters a "crisis" period, during which confidence in the paradigm starts to wane. Eventually, a creative scientist or two will come up with a new idea that explains the anomalies along with everything else explained by the paradigm-in-crisis. If this new idea is sufficiently powerful and well promoted, it can become a new paradigm, replacing the old one. If so, a revolution is said to have occurred. The replacement of Newtonian physics with Einsteinian physics is the typical example.

Kuhn's ideas have been applied to the history of psychology. Kirsch (1977), for example, claimed that psychology's first paradigm could be called "mentalism," and it encompassed Wundtian, structuralist, and functionalist thinking. Its guiding interest was the scientific study of human conscious experience. Problems with introspection led to a paradigm crisis, however, leading to the behaviorist revolution. Similar arguments were made by Palermo (1971), who believed that psychology in the 1960s and 1970s was in the midst of a second revolution, from behaviorism to cognitive psychology. The shifts from mentalism to behaviorism and then to cognitive psychology have a certain intuitive appeal and there is a degree of truth to the broad overview.

According to Leahey (1992), however, clothing psychology's history in Kuhnian garb can oversimplify complex events and perpetuate myths. Concerning the so-called cognitive revolution, for instance, he argued that (a) behaviorists disagreed on too many basic issues (e.g., S-R or S-O-R?) for behaviorism to be anything close to a Kuhnian paradigm, (b) any shift from behaviorism to cognition was too gradual for the term "revolutionary" to have any meaning, (c) the early research in cognition was not motivated by the perception of a "crisis" in behaviorism, but by a variety of other factors, and (d) cognitive psychologists themselves disagreed on too many fundamentals for cognitive psychology to resemble a Kuhnian paradigm.

Leahey (1992) also made the interesting suggestion that the 1962 appearance of Kuhn's book *by itself* helped to create the "myth" that a cognitive *revolution* was in progress. Reflecting on that era, researcher James Jenkins recalled it as a "tremendously exciting time. The basic assumption was that things were boiling over, and ... a new day was coming. And of course, everyone toted around their little copy of Kuhn's [book]" (quoted in Baars, 1986, p. 249). Although not denying that changes were indeed occurring, Leahey concluded *"there was no awareness of revolution until Kuhn's book suggested it"* (p. 315, italics in the original). It is worth noting that all of this was going on during a particularly turbulent time in American history. In the 1960s, protests against the war in Vietnam and the civil rights movement produced a climate in which talk of overthrowing the existing order, not trusting anyone over 30, and rejecting institutional authority was commonplace on university campuses. As a graduate student in cognitive psychology myself at that time, I can recall how Kuhn's message of revolutionary change seemed to resonate with my professors and peers. For instance, the book was the first one we had to read in a seminar on "higher mental processes," and it colored the discussion for a whole semester. By formulating a new way of looking at the history of science, then, in a culture awash with calls for change, Kuhn's book might have helped to create the idea of a "cognitive revolution."

Magical Numbers, Selective Filters, and TOTE Units

Perhaps the first psychologist to recognize the relevance of information theory to psychology was George A. Miller (b. 1920). As a research fellow in Harvard's Psycho-Acoustic Laboratory from 1944 to 1948, Miller (Figure 14.3) investigated speech perception, a problem that derived from a military context—the difficulty in hearing spoken messages while sitting in loud airplanes (Hilgard, 1987). Out of this research came a course offered to Harvard undergraduates called "The Psychology of Speech and Communication," and from the course came Miller's first book, *Language and Communication* (1951). Shortly after Shannon and Weaver produced their groundbreaking work (discussed previously), Miller introduced information theory to psychologists in a *Psychological Review* article (Miller & Frick, 1949). Then, seven years later, he published an article with a title more whimsical than normally found in stuffy academic journals—"The Magical Number Seven, Plus or Minus Two: Some Limits on Our Capacity for Processing Information" (Miller, 1956/1994). The conclusions of the paper were destined to become a standard feature in the memory chapters of introductory textbooks, and the article itself has become the most frequently cited paper in the 100-year history of the journal *Psychological Review* (Kintsch & Cacioppo, 1994).

In the article, which was a printed version of an address given at the Eastern Psychological Association the year before, Miller showed how information theory concepts such as bits and channel capacity could be used to describe limits on our ability to process information in several kinds of tasks. The last portion of the paper contains the most fre-quently cited information, Miller's analysis of the limited capacity of immediate memory. Depending on the type of information being memorized, he argued that people could only process between five (for monosyllabic words) and nine (for binary digits) items at a time. Recognizing that the amount of information in bits varies dramatically, depending on the type of material being studied, Miller introduced a new term, the **chunk**, to refer to the information being held in immediate memory. Hence, the capac-

FIGURE 14.3 George Miller.

ity limit on short-term memory was identified as seven, plus or minus two, chunks of information, the chunk being a small, meaningful unit of information. Further, Miller applied the information theory concept of **recoding** to take into account the fact that humans have the ability to reorganize data, thereby squeezing in more information per chunk. In his words, because "the memory span is a fixed number of chunks, we can increase the number of bits of information that it contains simply by building larger and larger chunks, each chunk containing more information than before" (Miller, 1956/1994, p. 349). Miller used the example of learning Morse code to drive home the point. The learner first hears each dot and dash as individual units. With experience, however, combinations of these sounds are recoded ("chunked") as whole letters, then words, then phrases, so that the experienced operator can, in effect, keep many more dots and dashes in immediate memory than the novice.

The mid-1950s also saw the publication of several works from England that applied information theory ideas to attention, a cognitive phenomenon largely neglected since Wundtian times. The prime mover was a student of Bartlett's at Cambridge, Donald Broadbent (1926–1993), who first became interested in psychology during World War II, while being trained as a pilot in the Royal Air Force. Although impressed by the technical complexity of the aircraft he was flying, he was frustrated by the failure of engineers to take the human pilot into account when designing the cockpit instrumentation and controls. The similarity of gauges often induced perceptual and attentional errors—for instance, Broadbent recalled that while landing on one occasion, he thought he was flying at 2,000 feet, only to discover that he was attending to the wrong gauge and that he was actually flying at 2,000 rpm (Broadbent, 1980).

After the war, Broadbent went to Cambridge, studied with Bartlett, and was eventually named director of Bartlett's laboratory there, the Applied Psychology Unit. During the 1950s, he and Colin Cherry, a professor of telecommunications, pioneered modern research on attention by using a **dichotic listening** procedure, in which research par-

ticipants would experience two channels of information at the same time, one sent to each ear via headphones. They were able to document limits on the ability to use multiple communication channels, showing, for instance, that while attending to one message, very little of a second message could be recalled (e.g., Cherry, 1953). Broadbent summarized this research in *Perception and Communication* (1958) and proposed a simple **selective filter** model of attention. When confronted with two streams of information, he suggested, our limited capacity system separates the information on the basis of physical characteristics, enabling us to filter out one message and select the other for attention and further processing. The problem of selective attention, which introductory textbooks soon began labeling the "cocktail party phenomenon" because the task resembled that of trying to listen to two conversations at once, remains an important and vigorous area of research in cognitive psychology.

A third example of the shift toward cognitive psychology in the 1950s took the form of a book. Entitled *Plans and the Structure of Behavior*, it appeared in 1960, the outcome of a collaboration between George Miller, of 7±2 fame; Eugene Galanter, a Harvard experimental psychologist with expertise in math and computers; and Karl Pribram, a well-known neuroscientist. The book centered on the idea of a "Plan," defined as "any hierarchical process in the organism that can control the order in which a sequence of operations is to be performed" (Miller, Galanter, & Pribram, 1960, p. 16). In keeping with the computer metaphor that was rapidly coming into vogue, the authors explicitly likened these Plans to the program written for a computer. The second main concept was that of the "Image," which the authors defined broadly as "all the accumulated, organized knowledge that the organism has about itself and its world" (p. 17). The main problem for the book was said to be to "explore the relationship between the Image and the Plan" (Miller, Galanter, & Pribram, 1960, p. 18).

The book is perhaps best remembered for borrowing the concept of feedback from the field of **cybernetics** (i.e., the study of the principles involved in controlling any living or nonliving system). In a radical departure from behaviorist/associationist tradition, they proposed that a feedback system could be substituted for the reflex arc as the basic unit of behavioral control. In a feedback system, the operation of one part of the system produces results that are fed back and monitored by the system, thereby affecting its future operation. The thermostat and furnace, for instance, operate together as a simple feedback system. On a cold day, the thermostat sends a signal to the furnace to start, which increases the air temperature, which is read by the thermostat, which eventually tells the furnace to stop. The temperature then drops, triggers another signal from the thermostat to restart the furnace, and so on. In the long run, the feedback system produces a "steady state," a temperature that does not vary much from the thermostat setting. For human feedback systems, Miller and his colleagues created the basic concept of the **TOTE unit**, TOTE being an acronym for Test-Operate-Test-Exit. It is shown in Figure 14.4. It begins with a Test phase that looks for incongruities in the system (e.g., in the thermostat example, a difference between the desired temperature and the actual temperature). If there are no incongruities, nothing happens, but if there are, an operation occurs to reduce the incongruity. Another Test then occurs, and so on until no incongruity exists. For humans, these TOTE units are organized hierarchically, as in the example shown in Figure 14.5, which represents the authors' example of a two-level system for ham-

mering a nail. The first Test is to see if the nail is sticking up; if not, no hammering is needed; if so, the second level TOTE units engage to alter the state of the nail.

Neisser and the "Naming" of Cognitive Psychology

Miller's 7±2 paper, the British work on attention, and *Plans* were just three prominent examples of events that marked an important shift in experimental psychology during the 1950s, legitimizing the study of heretofore frowned-on mentalistic topics. The momentum continued to build in the 1960s, a tumultuous decade in which change from the existing order became a familiar theme (refer again to this chapter's Close-Up). In addition, experimental psychology benefited from increased government funding of all scientific research, part of the attempt during the cold war to reestablish American scientific supremacy in the wake of Soviet successes in space (e.g., launching the first satellite—"Sputnik"—into orbit in 1957). By the mid-1960s, sufficient research existed to warrant book-length summaries, and texts in cognitive psychology began to appear, most notably Ulric Neisser's *Cognitive Psychology* in 1967, which gave a specific name to the converging

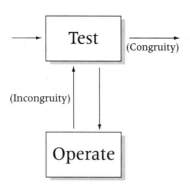

FIGURE 14.4 The basic TOTE (Test-Operate-Test-Exit) unit proposed by Miller, Galanter, and Pribram's *Plans and the Structure of Behavior* (1960).

FIGURE 14.5 TOTE units arranged to illustrate a hierarchical plan for hammering nails, from Miller, Galanter, and Pribram (1960).

FIGURE 14.6   Ulric Neisser.

In his opening chapter, Neisser (1967) began by pointing out that the times had changed in psychology:

> A generation ago, a book like this one would have needed at least a chapter of self-defense against the behaviorist position. Today, happily, the climate of opinion has changed, and little or no defense is necessary. Indeed, stimulus-response theorists themselves are inventing hypothetical mechanisms with vigor and enthusiasm and only faint twinges of conscience. The basic reason for studying cognitive processes has become as clear as the reason for studying anything else: because they are there. ... Cognitive processes surely exist, so it can hardly be unscientific to study them. (p. 5)

As for the question of what cognitive psychology actually meant, Neisser considered it to be the experimental study of all cognitive process, and by cognition, he meant

> ... *all the processes by which the sensory input is transformed, reduced, elaborated, stored, recovered, and used.* It is concerned with these processes even when they operate in the absence of relevant stimulation, as in images and hallucinations. Such terms as sensation, perception, imagery, retention, recall, problem-solving, and thinking, among many others, refer to hypothetical stages or aspects of cognition. (p. 4, italics in the original)

The content chapters of Neisser's *Cognitive Psychology* are full of rich experimental detail about some of the ways that the human information processor can transform information. Reflecting the newness of cognitive psychology, about 60% of the book's 321 references are to research published in the decade of the 1960s (Weaver, 1998). The bulk of the book concerns the initial processing of visual and auditory information, but there are also chapters on memory, language, and a brief concluding chapter on the relationship between memory and thought.

ideas of such people as Miller, Broadbent, and Bruner. Neisser (Figure 14.6) would later recall getting "letters from people saying that they were glad that I had given [the movement] a name, because they were interested in all the topics I considered, but the area had not had a theoretical identity" (quoted in Baars, 1986, p. 278). After Neisser, it did.

As an undergraduate at Harvard, Ulric Neisser (b. 1928) studied with George Miller, later recalling that Miller's course on speech and communication "covered some pretty unusual topics ... [such as] linguistics, acoustics, articulatory physiology, and engineering mathematics" (Neisser, 1988, p. 82). Neisser's interest in cognition was aroused by the experience, and he followed his undergraduate degree with a master's degree from Swarthmore, adopted home of the gestaltist Köhler, and further graduate study at MIT before earning a doctorate in psychoacoustics at Harvard in 1956. He subsequently taught at Brandeis, Cornell, and Emory, before returning to Cornell, where he now teaches.

The Evolution of Cognitive Psychology

Interest in cognitive psychology continued to grow rapidly after the publication of Neisser's 1967 book. Psychology departments rushed to create cognitive laboratories and to hire cognitive psychologists, conferences on cognition were held, their contents later published in edited books (e.g., the Loyola Symposium, in Solso, 1973), and informal networks such as S.W.I.M. (Southeastern Workers in Memory) were formed. Traditional journals such as the *Journal of Experimental Psychology* featured more cognitive research, and new journals appeared— *Cognitive Psychology* in 1970, *Cognition* in 1972, *Cognitive Science* in 1977, and *Memory and Cognition* in 1983. In addition, cognitive psychology spread to psychology's other subdisciplines, such as developmental, social, personality, and abnormal psychology. Even animal psychology was not immune—researchers began investigating "animal cognition" (e.g., Flaherty, 1985).

Within cognitive psychology itself, changes occurred in the 1970s, once again led by Neisser. In *Cognition and Reality* (1976), he argued that the laboratory tradition in cognitive psychology, while producing important results, nonetheless had failed to yield enough useful information about information processing in real-world contexts. He was even critical of his own 1967 text for being top heavy with pure laboratory research. Instead, explicitly recognizing the influence of Bartlett, he called for more research concerning what he referred to as **ecological validity**—research with relevance for the everyday cognitive activities of people trying to adapt to their environment. Experimental psychologists, Neisser (1976) urged, "must make a greater effort to understand cognition as it occurs in the ordinary environment and in the context of natural purposeful activity. This would not mean an end to laboratory experiments, but a commitment to the study of variables that are ecologically important rather than those that are easily manageable" (p. 7).

Neisser's call to arms was embraced by many (but not all, of course) cognitive researchers, and the 1980s and 1990s saw increased research in such topics as eyewitness memory (e.g., Loftus, 1979) and the long-term recall of topics learned in school, such as Spanish (e.g., Bahrick, 1984). Although these events are too close to the present for detached historical analysis, the turn to everyday cognition should not be surprising, given what we know about

the history of functionalist thinking in American psychology. Research that helps us to understand how the individual adapts to the environment and has practical applications is the type of research that has always resonated with American psychology's functional/pragmatic spirit.

In addition to the interest in ecological validity, another aspect of the evolution of interests among research psychologists has been the creation of **cognitive science**, an interdisciplinary field that includes cognitive psychology, linguistics, computer science, cultural anthropology, and even epistemology. Gardner (1985) defined the field broadly as an "empirically based effort to answer long-standing epistemological questions—particularly those concerned with the nature of knowledge, its components, its sources, its development, and its deployment" (p. 6). The term "cognitive science" began to appear in the mid-1970s and became institutionalized with the naming of a journal devoted to it in 1977. In the opening editorial for *Cognitive Science*, Collins (1977) pointed out that the discipline could have been called "applied epistemology or intelligence theory, but someone on high declared it should be cognitive science and so it shall" (p. 1).

It is worth noting, of course, that while the label is relatively new, cognitive science is not. The initial stirrings of the new discipline can be seen in the postwar era, when the above-mentioned "influences external to psychology" (information theory, computer science, linguistics) contributed to the emergence of what psychologists began calling "cognitive psychology." From a broader perspective, however, it is clear that something more than a new psychology was developing and that some of the key players were aware of it. George Miller, for instance, traced the origins of cognitive science to a 1956 symposium on information theory, held at MIT (Baars, 1986), and in 1960, Miller and Jerome Bruner cofounded the Center for Cognitive Studies at Harvard, designed explicitly to foster the interdisciplinary study of cognition. Bruner later recalled that he and Miller decided "that psychology was too complicated a field to leave to the psychologists, [so] what we needed was an alliance with colleagues from other disciplines who were, each in his or her own context, concerned about how humans acquired and used knowledge" (Bruner, 1988, p. 92).

Artificial Intelligence

One important focus of interest among cognitive scientists has been in the applied computer science area of **artificial intelligence** (AI), which may be defined simply as the field that attempts to examine whether machines can act with some degree of intelligence. Workers in AI are interested in a variety of topics, but they generally fall into two broad categories. Some researchers are mainly interested in understanding human intelligence, studying it by attempting to write computer programs that simulate human cognitive processing. Consider human problem solving, for example. The idea is that if a computer can be made to solve problems in the same way that humans solve problems, then the problem-solving strategies built into the computer program can be seen as analogous to human strategies. This was the approach taken by two nonpsychologist pioneers in AI, Herbert Simon (b. 1916) and Alan Newell (1927–1992). Simon, whose work on decision making produced a Nobel Prize in economics in 1978, and Newell, a physicist, collaborated on computer simulations of thinking and problem solving in the 1950s and 1960s. Their first effort, the Logic Theorist (LT), was designed to solve problems in formal logic, while their later and more ambitious project, the General Problem Solver (GPS), was aimed at a broader range of problems (Newell & Simon, 1972).

Both LT and GPS illustrate an important distinction in computer science between algorithms and heuristics. An **algorithm** is a set of rules guaranteed to produce a solution by working systematically through all possible steps. A **heuristic**, on the other hand, is a more creative strategy or "rule of thumb" that, while not guaranteeing a solution, is more efficient than an algorithm. A common anagram problem can illustrate the difference. When asked to rearrange the letters "LTEAGST" so that a real word is formed, an algorithmic approach would try every possible combination of letters until a solution was reached. This would not present a problem for a computer, which performs operations very quickly and does not get bored in the process. Humans, how-

ever, would probably attempt to solve the anagram by using heuristics, such as "do not consider uncommon combinations of pairs of letters." Thus, the solver would try the combination "ST" but not "GT", on the way toward solving the anagram (hint: it's a word found throughout Chapter 9).

The primary heuristic built into Simon and Newell's GPS was called a **means-ends analysis**. A feedback system, it involved assessing the current state with the goal state, identifying a difference between the two, identifying and applying an operator (some behavior) to reduce the difference, reassessing the new state with the goal, and so on, until the current state became the goal state. Newell and Simon (1972) developed the program by giving problems (e.g., algebra problems) to people and asking them to externalize their thinking by describing their thought processes as they occurred, a procedure bearing an interesting similarity to introspection. They then wrote the GPS program in a way that attempted to simulate what their human subjects were doing. Hence, the goal was to understand human thinking, on the assumption that if they could simulate it, with the computer producing solutions just like human solutions, then they would increase their understanding of it. This simulation strategy was used in attempts to study cognitive processes ranging from pattern recognition to memory to thinking, although interest in such simulations reached its peak in the 1970s, in part because of the abandonment of GPS when it failed to be as "general" a problem solver as originally hoped (Gardner, 1985).

The second approach to AI, and the more dominant one since the 1980s, is to create a computer program that will perform some task in the most efficient way possible, regardless of how humans might approach the task. That is, the goal is to create expert systems that deal with problems intelligently. The outcome has been such things as computerized chess programs that can beat world-class human players, robots, and interactive tutoring systems. This second usage of AI has raised the question of whether computers can be said to think, which in turn has led to debates on the nature of thinking and what it is to be human. That is, AI has perpetuated some of the issues that have always been of interest to psychologists.

The question of whether true intelligence can be found in computers was posed as early as 1950, in an article entitled "Computing Machinery and Intelligence," by Alan Turing (1912–1954), a brilliant English mathematician. Turing was instrumental in ensuring the allied victory in World War II by helping to break the supposedly unassailable "Enigma" code of the Germans, thereby informing allied strategists of German troop movements, strategies, and the like. In his 1950 article, Turing described an "imitation game" that provided a set of criteria to determine whether computers could be said to think. This has since been called the **Turing test**. Imagine, wrote Turing, a situation in which a person in one room can ask a series of any questions to a human and a computer, both located in a second room. On the basis of the two sets of answers, the questioner must try to distinguish between the human and the machine. The human tries to convince the questioner that he or she is human, as does the computer. If the questioner cannot discriminate human from machine on the basis of the answers, according to Turing, then it must be concluded that no significant differences exist between computer intelligence and human intelligence—that is, computers can think just like humans.

The idea of the computer as thinker equivalent to the human as thinker, sometimes referred to as strong AI, has been sharply criticized, most cogently by John Searle. Proponents of **strong AI** believe that thinking is essentially rule-bound symbol manipulation, a skill possessed by both humans and computers. Searle, while accepting the validity of what is called **weak AI**, the idea that computers can yield important insights about the nature of human thinking, argued that strong AI was not justified. To illustrate the point, Searle described a thought problem that has come to be called the **Chinese Room problem** (1990). Imagine that you are isolated in a room with a massive rule book that specified all of the combinations of markings that comprise Chinese writing. This book enables you to examine a sequence of such markings presented to you in the form of a written question from a native Chinese speaker and accurately produce a written response using other Chinese symbols. That is, a Chinese speaker could write a question to you in Chinese symbols and you could use your rule book to

generate a response that would be acceptable to the questioner. Indeed, your responses might be indistinguishable from those given by a native speaker of Chinese, which means that you would pass the Turing test. The question is whether this means that you understand Chinese, and for Searle the answer is no. Thinking involves more than just symbol manipulation according to fixed rules, he has argued; it also includes semantics—a deeper level of understanding that goes beyond the rules for organizing the symbols. Computers can manipulate symbols in remarkably complex ways, but they have no understanding of what they are doing for the same reason that you would have no understanding of Chinese while in the Chinese room.

Your growing knowledge of psychology's history can help put the AI debates about thinking in some perspective, for the problem is not new, but merely an extension of the age-old mind-body (or mind-brain) problem. One of psychology's recurring issues has concerned whether purely mechanical explanations are sufficient for an understanding of human behavior and mental processes. From the time of Descartes' fascination with the hydraulically driven figures in the gardens of French royalty, to the nineteenth-century physiologists who believed that all living function could be reduced to the movements of material objects, to Watson's mechanistic S-R model that likened human functioning to a telephone switchboard, mechanical metaphors for human functioning have been commonplace. It is not likely that the AI debates will resolve the issue.

Evaluating Cognitive Psychology

Although some have considered cognitive psychology to be an all-encompassing framework, even a "paradigm," for modern psychology, the movement has also been sharply criticized. Understandably, the most vocal critic was B. F. Skinner (Chapter 11), the leading behaviorist of the second half of the twentieth century. Skinner objected to the creation of hypothetical mental mechanisms (e.g., short-term memory), which all too easily could become reified, he believed, into "explanatory fictions" (refer back to Chapter 11, pp. 334–335). That is, instead of looking for the causes of behavior in the environment and one's learning history, where they belonged (in Skinner's view), the cognitive psychologist turned these hypothetical mechanisms into real, causal entities. Attributing failures of recall to limited short-term memory capacity hardly explains the phenomenon, he argued. Skinner deplored the spread of cognitive ideas throughout the field of psychology, sarcastically observing that a graph showing the use of the term "cognitive" in psychology's literature would show exponential growth after 1960—"Is there any field of psychology today in which something does not seem to be gained by adding that charming adjective to the occasional noun?" (Skinner, 1987, p. 783).

A second general criticism of cognitive psychology derives from the computer metaphor, with its human-as-machine implication. Such a view ignores significant aspects of human behavior, critics charge, such as emotion and motivation (e.g., Zajonc, 1980), or intentionality (Searle, 1980). Hilgard (1980), referring back to the eighteenth-century tripartite division of mental activities—the cognitive, the affective (emotional), and the conative (motivational/behavioral)—made a similar argument that cognitive psychology addresses only a portion of the whole. A related criticism has been that cognitive psychologists sometimes ignore neurological reality, building models of mental processing that contradict what is known about how the nervous system operates.

Despite the problems, the study of cognitive processes has worked its way into virtually every area of modern psychological investigation. The pervasiveness of cognitive factors is perhaps an indication of how important such processes have always been to psychology, even when their importance may have been questioned by prominent behaviorists, and how central they are to the very definition of what it means to be human.

OTHER RESEARCH AREAS

In Descartes' time, the first half of the seventeenth century, serious scholars believed that it was possible to gain a complete understanding of all scientific knowledge. Descartes himself made that his goal with the writing of his *The World* (completed in 1633 but not published until after his death), which included topics ranging from anatomy to meteorology. Today, of course, in an age of information explosion and specialization, nobody could hope to have a thorough knowledge of a single science, never mind all science. Even within a particular science such as psychology, comprehensive knowledge is virtually impossible. The cognitive psychologist who studies eyewitness memory, for example, probably knows very little about developmental psychology's research on children's attachment behavior. In fact, the cognitive psychologist studying eyewitness memory almost certainly finds it impossible to keep up with the literature in other areas of cognitive psychology.

We have just seen that cognitive psychology came to dominate the interests of the typical academician/research in the second half of the twentieth century. Concepts from cognitive psychology also had important influences on a variety of other subdisciplines in psychology. In social psychology, for example, a great deal of research on "social cognition" began appearing in the 1980s (e.g., Fiske & Taylor, 1984). But these specialties have their own histories, and while a comprehensive analysis of them is way beyond the scope of this book, let us briefly examine some of the history of four research areas outside of cognitive psychology. Instead of attempting to string together a sentence or two about the long list of contributors to each of these areas (and the list is long for each), I will focus on one well-known person from each subdiscipline and look closely at that person's influence. The four areas to be considered involve the (a) study of the relationship between brain and behavior, which used to be called physiological psychology and is now usually referred to as neuroscience; (b) social psychology, the study of how behavior is influenced by social factors; (c) personality psychology, the study of individual differences in various personal traits; and (d) developmental psychology, the study of how behavior changes as we age.

The Brain and Behavior

One of psychology's enduring mysteries concerns the relationship between stimulus events that produce physical changes in the body, especially in the nervous system, and the psychological experience of those events. Research psychologists long ago gave up on the idea of solving the mind-body problem through science—it is a philosophical question. Thus, although researchers might be able to specify in extraordinary detail how the operation of certain combinations of neurons in the striate cortex is correlated with the perception of a line presented at a certain angle, they cannot answer the question: But how does the firing of these neurons actually result in the psychological experience of the tilted line? Recognizing this fundamental limitation, physiological psychologists have concentrated their attention on the search for relationships between physical and mental events by examining the functioning of the brain and nervous system and how the activity of these structures corresponds to experience and behavior.

Chapter 3 sketched the history of attempts to understand the brain, focusing on the past 200 years and ending with Karl Lashley. Lashley, you recall, investigated the localization of function question in the early years of the twentieth century, agreeing with Pierre Flourens, the great French neurologist of a century before, that the brain operates more like an integrated system than a set of structures with different functions. Ironically, Lashley's 1929 conclusions about mass action and equipotentiality had a dampening effect on brain research and encouraged behaviorists to think that the detailed study of conditioning could proceed without concern for the nervous system. Skinner (1938) reinforced the argument, explicitly rejecting the need for physiological explanations of behavior (Hilgard, 1987).

Donald O. Hebb (1904–1985)

Interest in the brain and behavior was rekindled by a student of Lashley's, Donald Hebb, the only Canadian psychologist ever elected to the presidency (in 1960) of the American Psychological Association (Hilgard, 1987). Hebb started slowly, barely graduating from college and being accepted into the graduate program at Montreal's McGill University because of personal connections. At McGill, he encountered two former students of Pavlov and learned the

Pavlovian conditioning techniques.[3] Like Pavlov, Hebb wondered about the relationship between brain and behavior, but became skeptical of Pavlov's model of the cortex. After earning his master's degree in 1934, Hebb was encouraged to apply to Chicago and study with Lashley, who was at the height of his reputation. Lashley accepted the young Canadian, and when the mentor moved to Harvard the following year, he took Hebb with him. Hebb completed his doctorate there in 1938. Job prospects were bleak, however, a combination of the lingering effects of the Great Depression and the fact that "[p]hysiological psychology was in its long period of decline, between 1930 and 1950" (Hebb, 1980, p. 287).

Hebb was fortunate enough to land a job as research assistant to McGill's Wilder Penfield, who was looking for someone to study the behavioral effects of brain surgery. Penfield was just beginning his famous research on the surgical treatment of epilepsy, in which some patients reported what appeared to be intact memories during electrical stimulation of the temporal lobe (Penfield & Perot, 1963). This research was also consistent with Lashley's equipotentiality idea—patients' mental capacities did not seem to deteriorate even after the loss of substantial portions of their frontal lobes. Hebb was right in the center of this research and it had a profound effect on him—it "set the main course for all my subsequent work, and I would not have met it anywhere else" (Hebb, 1980, p. 290). From this experience and his earlier research, Hebb came to the general conclusion that human intelligence develops during early childhood and that "[i]njury to the infant brain interferes with that process, but the same injury at maturity does not reverse it" (p. 292). Thus, early childhood experiences were crucial for the kind of cortical development related to intelligence, Hebb believed.

Two fruitful years with Penfield were followed by three years of teaching at Ontario's Queen's University. In 1942, Hebb returned to Lashley, who had just been appointed director of the Yerkes

---

[3] One was Boris Babkin, whose 1949 biography of Pavlov included the description of Pavlov's lab that was featured in Chapter 10, pp. 282–283.

Laboratory of Primate Biology in Florida, and studied primate behavior for five years. In 1947, his career came full circle when he was appointed to a professorship at McGill. Within a year, Hebb was named department chair, and he finished his distinguished career at McGill.

Hebb is best known for his 1949 book, *The Organization of Behavior*, which revived interest among American psychologists in the relationship between brain and behavior (Glickman, 1996). From the title, it is clear that the book is more than just a description of nervous system functioning. Rather, Hebb was aiming at a theory that would fully integrate physiology and psychology, not simply reduce the psychological to the physiological. As he later wrote, in criticism of such reductionist thinking, it was "not possible to substitute neurophysiological conceptions for psychological ones, either now or in the future, but it is possible to maintain liaison (translatability of terms) between the two universes of discourse" (Hebb, 1960, p. 744).

Hebb proposed that cortical organization occurs through the development of what he called "cell assemblies" and "phase sequences." A **cell assembly** is the basic unit, referring to a set of neurons that become associated with each other because they have been activated together by repeated sensory experiences. Hebb (1949) recognized the associationist roots of his construct, writing that the "general idea is an old one, that any two cells or systems of cells that are repeatedly active at the same time will tend to become 'associated,' so that activity in one facilitates activity in the other" (p. 70). Cell assemblies can be triggered by sensory events or by other cell assemblies. **Phase sequences** are higher levels of organization involving the incorporation of several cell assemblies, and for Hebb, they were the physiological equivalent of thinking. Taken together, cell assemblies and phase sequences accounted for the fact that stimuli do not simply produce responses, but are mediated by the brain. You will recognize this as similar to the "O" in the S-O-R formulation of Robert Woodworth (Chapter 7) and the neobehaviorists Tolman and Hull (Chapter 11), but more explicitly physiological.

To account for the effects of experience and hence to provide a physiological account of learning,

Hebb proposed that cell assemblies and phase sequences are formed because the repeated stimulation of adjacent cells produces structural changes at the synaptic level. Thus, according to Hebb (1949), "[w]hen an axon of cell A is near enough to excite cell B and repeatedly ... takes part in firing it, some growth process or metabolic change takes place in one or both cells such that A's efficiency, as one of the cells firing B, is increased" (p. 62). This idea has come to be called "Hebb's rule," and synapses that change as the result of experience are often called **Hebb synapses**.

Hebb applied his theory to topics ranging from attention to emotion to mental illness, and his small book, combined with such technological advances as the electroencephalograph (EEG) for measuring brain waves, triggered a renewal of interest in the relationship between brain and behavior. The story is much too complex to be described here, but some of the more important developments in the 1950s and 1960s included (a) discovery of reinforcement centers in the brain, by Hebb's students James Olds and Peter Milner (1954); (b) the use of EEG to identify stages of sleep and the discovery of REM sleep by Eugene Aserinsky and Nathaniel Kleitman (1953); (c) the development of the split brain operation as a way to control epilepsy and to examine left and right hemisphere functions by Roger Sperry (1961); and (d) the identification of cortical cells ("feature detectors") that respond to specific events in the visual field by David Hubel and Torsten Wiesel (1963). Sperry, Hubel, and Wiesel all earned Nobel Prizes for their efforts.

In more recent years, the study of the brain-behavior interface has become increasingly interdisciplinary. Thus, just as cognitive science combines several disciplines, "biopsychology," "neuropsychology," "behavioral neuroscience," "cognitive neuroscience," and even "social cognitive neuroscience" all refer to evolving specialties that cross disciplinary boundaries and involve graduate training in psychology, biology, and computer science departments.

Social Psychology

Social psychology began to develop as an identifiable subdiscipline of psychology through the efforts of Floyd Allport (1890–1978), whose brother Gordon will be highlighted in this chapter's section on personality psychology. Floyd studied with Hugo Münsterberg at Harvard, earning a doctorate in 1919. His dissertation research was on social facilitation, the influence of others on the behavior of an individual, and this research set the tone for Allport's approach to social psychology. It was behaviorist in spirit, and Allport deliberately contrasted his social psychology, with its emphasis on the behavior of the individual, and its influence by the social environment, and a different version that evolved into modern sociology, which has more of an emphasis on group processes (Parkovnick, 2000). For example, when studying group problem solving, Allport insisted that the eventual explanation for the behavior that ensued was to be found in the actions of the individual persons making up the group. From a more group-oriented standpoint, emphasis might be on some "group process" that would influence the solution to the problem at hand. Allport criticized the tendency to explain behavior by referring to group processes as the "group fallacy" (Danziger, 2000). Allport promoted his view in his 1924 text, *Social Psychology* (F. Allport, 1924), a text said to have created social psychology as a course routinely found in department of psychology course listings (Hilgard, 1987).

Leon Festinger (1919–1989)

Allport's emphasis on the individual in social psychology was challenged by the work of Kurt Lewin. We have already seen that in addition to his many other contributions, Lewin (Chapter 9, pp. 271–273) was an important pioneer in social psychology, through his studies of leadership and much of his action research. The gestalt influence was evident in Lewin's concepts of group processes—to relate the gestalt anthem to social psychology, one could say that group behavior is more than the sum of the behaviors of the group's individual members. Lewin's influence was widespread, and he had a direct effect on his most famous student, Leon Festinger (Figure 14.7), although Festinger's approach to methodology emphasized tighter experimental controls than Lewin's (Danziger, 2000).

Leon Festinger was born and raised in New York City, the son of Jewish immigrants from Eastern

FIGURE 14.7   Leon Festinger.

Europe. When he graduated from City College of New York in 1939, he already had a publication (with one of his college teachers, Max Hertzman) in the prestigious *Journal of Experimental Psychology* (Hertzman & Festinger, 1940). Hertzman was also responsible for introducing Festinger to Lewin's ideas, prompting Festinger to apply to graduate school at the University of Iowa to study with Lewin. Festinger earned a Ph.D. under Lewin's direction after just three years, in 1942, and remained connected with Lewin until the latter's early death in 1947. During World War II, Festinger served as a statistician for the Committee on Selection and Training of Aircraft Pilots; then after the war, he rejoined Lewin at MIT in Boston, where Lewin had just inaugurated the Research Center for Group Dynamics. After Lewin's death, Festinger was part of the group that moved the Center to the University of Michigan. Festinger went from Michigan to the University of Minnesota in 1951, then Stanford in 1955, and then returned home to New York in 1968, where he held the Staudinger Professorship at the

New School for Social Research until his death (Zajonc, 1990). It was during his Stanford tenure that Festinger made his reputation and attracted students who became prominent social psychologists themselves (e.g., Elliot Aronson). Over the years, his students remained fiercely loyal to him, even though he could be a hard taskmaster and was not tolerant of imprecise thinking (Brehm, 1998).

Festinger completed important research in several social psychology topics, but he is remembered for developing what could be the most important theory that social psychology has yet seen, the theory of cognitive dissonance. Festinger drafted a version of it in 1954, and then produced the first thorough description in book form in 1957 (Festinger, 1957). The theory's influence has been substantial. A social psychology text will give you a better description of the theory and its famous studies, but in general, the theory of cognitive dissonance can be summarized as follows:

- people are motivated to be consistent in their thoughts, feelings, and actions;

- whenever people hold two or more thoughts that are inconsistent with each other, a state of **cognitive dissonance** will occur; cognitive dissonance is a state of emotional and cognitive discomfort; and

- whenever people experience dissonance, they are motivated to reduce it and return to a state of internal consistency

To illustrate the theory, consider an example that Festinger frequently used, the intelligent person who smokes. Like everyone, the smoker desires to be consistent. Yet there are two thoughts that are inconsistent—"I am smoking" and "there is research indicating that smoking will kill me." Assuming the person is not suicidal, these thoughts create dissonance, which the person is motivated to reduce. This can be accomplished in several ways: the person can stop smoking, might question the validity of the evidence, or might add other elements to the situation, saying, for instance, that everyone has to die, and while the smoking might not be ideal, it helps with weight control. One of the criteria of good theories is that they produce research and by that measure,

Festinger's dissonance theory has been exceptionally productive, generating literally hundreds of experiments and applied to situations ranging from the consequences of decision making to the effects of hypocrisy (Harmon-Jones & Mills, 1999).

From a historical standpoint, Festinger's research is important because it created an experimental tradition in social psychology that was distinctive in its use of elaborately staged and deceptive research settings (Korn, 1997). These research environments were designed to involve research participants in the experiment so that their "true" reactions to dissonance-arousing situations could be measured and the theory given a strong test. Probably the most famous example was a study by Festinger and a Stanford undergraduate, Merrill Carlsmith (Festinger & Carlsmith, 1959). Students who signed up for the study first spent an hour completing a series of incredibly boring tasks, then, through an elaborate deception, they were induced to tell the person who seemed to be the next participant that the study was really interesting. Thus, Carlsmith (who ran the study) convinced participants to lie, a situation producing dissonance ("I am an honest person" is dissonant with "I just told someone that a very boring experiment was actually interesting"). As an incentive, participants were to be paid either $1 or $20 for their lie. Afterwards, apparently as part of a survey being run by the psychology department (another deception), participants were asked what they really thought of the experiment. The results? Those paid $20 still thought the experiment was boring, but those paid just $1 shifted their attitude and decided the study was fairly interesting after all. Festinger and Carlsmith concluded that when faced with the dissonance about lying, participants in the $20 justified it by saying it was a small lie and worth the money. Those paid $1, however, did not have sufficient justification for the lie, so they convinced themselves that they had not actually lied—the study really was kind of interesting after all. One effect of dissonance reduction, then, can be a change in attitude or belief.

The Festinger and Carlsmith (1959) study was typical of the research that emerged from Festinger's laboratory. They were intricately staged productions, often requiring many hours of rehearsal. Of

Carlsmith's performance, for example, Aronson (1991) later wrote:

> One of the most vivid memories of my years as a graduate student in Leon's lab involves the exciting and tedious hours Leon and I spent prior to that experiment, coaching and directing the performance of a very precocious undergraduate named Merrill Carlsmith until he got it right. Initially, Merrill ... persisted in delivering his lines in a very stiff and wooden way; we kept walking him through the procedure, over and over again, until he eventually became extremely convincing. (p. 216)

The care with which these productions were choreographed resulted in what social psychologists call *experimental reality* (Aronson, 1999)—research participants were completely taken in by the research situations and reacted as if they were really involved in the situations being created. Of course, that meant participants in Festinger's studies were routinely deceived about the true purpose of the studies, which made Festinger's research the object of numerous discussions about the ethics of deception in research (e.g., Korn, 1997). Festinger later indicated that he stopped doing research in social psychology in 1964, mainly because he was looking for a new challenge (he found it in the study of archeology), but also because he found the increased concern about research ethics annoying. Festinger was not insensitive to the problem, harshly criticizing Army research that gave unwitting soldiers LSD to see their reactions (see Thomas, 1995 for more on this unfortunate episode). Compared to that, however, he saw little danger "in temporarily deceiving persons in order to study some important question" (Festinger, 1980, p. 249). Nonetheless, Festinger's procedures set the tone, and social psychological research in the 1960s and 1970s became known for its high level of deception.

Another legacy of the Festinger research program concerned research design. Festinger was clearly influenced by Lewin in terms of the topics he studied, but Festinger thought Lewin's approach to research design was rather casual and in need of more precise control. Also, it was during the early 1950s that the analysis of variance (ANOVA), developed by British statistician Sir Ronald Fisher in the 1920s,

became widely used as the way to analyze data (Rucci & Tweney, 1980).[4] The ANOVA fit perfectly into Festinger's research designs, allowing for precise analyses of the main effects of manipulated independent variables (e.g., $1 vs. $20), as well as interactions among variables. Also, as Danziger (2000) observed, ANOVA was becoming widely used in the more traditional areas of experimental psychology in the 1950s, and by applying ANOVA logic to his research, Festinger helped enhance the scientific reputation of social psychology, which was not held in high esteem by experimentalists at that time.

Festinger might have left social psychology in 1964, but his influence has continued. For example, the longevity of dissonance is evident from the publication of an edited volume in 1999 with the title: *Cognitive Dissonance: Progress on a Pivotal Theory in Social Psychology* (Harmon-Jones & Mills, 1999). It included chapters by former students of Festinger, and students of those former students. Rather than just being a summary designed to wrap up a half century of dissonance theory, it also looked ahead, its editors believing "that the future of dissonance research promises to be as exciting as the past 40 years of work on the theory" (pp. 18–19).

Festinger, a heavy smoker, died of liver cancer in 1989. Perhaps thinking of his often quoted dissonance example of the smoker, and perhaps reducing dissonance to the end, he is said to have announced during his illness, "Make sure everyone knows it wasn't lung cancer!" (quoted in Zajonc, 1990, p. 662).

Personality Psychology

For most of the research encountered in this chapter, the goal has been to understand some general principles about behavior or cognitive processes. Thus,

---

[4] Fisher developed the ANOVA in the context of agricultural research, in which he would examine, for instance, the effects of some type or some amount of fertilizer on corn production. He published his work on ANOVA in a general text in statistics in the 1920s (Fisher, 1925), but his most elaborate description of the technique appeared a decade later (Fisher, 1935). If you are familiar with the technique from a statistics class, and remember calculating an "*F* ratio," or reading one from an SPSS printout, you have probably already guessed that the "*F*" stands for the test's inventor.

when Miller declared a limit to the capacity of short-term memory, when Hebb detailed the actions of cell assemblies, and when Festinger discussed dissonance reduction processes, they were describing principles that presumably affect humans in general. This is an approach to science that is known as a **nomothetic** one. On the other hand, there is an approach to science that focuses on a detailed analysis of the unique individual and examines ways of determining how one individual differs from another. A scientific strategy that concentrates on the unique individual takes an **idiographic** approach. The nomothetic-idiographic distinction is sometimes attributed to Gordon Allport, the featured psychologist in this section of the chapter, but Hugo Münsterberg (one of Allport's teachers) also used the terms, and the distinction was proposed originally by the German philosopher Windelband, in the nineteenth century (Hilgard, 1987).

The psychology of personality has both nomothetic and idiographic elements to it. Personality researchers look for general principles (e.g., factors influencing shyness behavior) and they also examine individuals carefully, measure them with reference to their traits, and determine how one person's traits differ from another's (Fred's shyness level, compared with Ted's). The concept of "personality" is largely a twentieth century invention and the inventor, as you are about to learn, was Gordon Allport.

Gordon Allport (1897–1967)

Social psychology and personality psychology have important historical connections, including a family link. Gordon Allport (Figure 14.8) was born in Indiana and raised in Cleveland, Ohio, the last of his parents' four boys. He and his brothers were raised to value hard work, self-sacrifice, a strong moral code, and the kind of idealism that manifested itself in a duty to serve others (Bruner, 1968). You read about one of Gordon's older brothers in this chapter—Floyd's 1924 social psychology text was an important step in the creation of social psychology as an identifiable subdiscipline of psychology. Gordon had the exact same effect on personality psychology when he published a text in 1937 called *Personality: A Psychological Interpretation* (G.

FIGURE 14.8   Gordon Allport.

Allport, 1937). The Allports both appeared at Harvard's 1919 Commencement, with Gordon completing his undergraduate years and Floyd becoming a Ph.D.

Following his graduation from Harvard, Allport was unsure of his future, but spent a year reflecting on it while teaching English and sociology at an American-based men's school in Istanbul, Turkey. Following the urging of his brother, who was now an instructor at Harvard, Allport applied to graduate school there and was accepted, with financing assured by a fellowship. Following Floyd's suggestion, he chose the emerging topic of personality as his dissertation topic. That his topic was away from mainstream experimental psychology became evident to him in 1921, when he presented his work on personality to a meeting of Titchener's Experimentalists at Clark University, invited by Herbert Langfeld of Harvard, who was a regular at the meetings. As Boring (1967) later reported in his history of the group:

> There was a long discussion of David Katz's modes of appearance of colors, and after that Langfeld was asked for a report and he put up Gordon Allport to tell about his analysis of personality. Allport's communication was followed by a long silence, and then Titchener said: "As we were saying, the modes of appearance of colors are. ..." Social psychology and personality were as much taboo at the Experimentalists as animal psychology. "What did you let him work on that for?" Titchener later asked Langfeld. (p. 323)

Undeterred, Allport completed his doctorate on personality traits in a mere two years, in 1922. He then toured Europe for two more years on a study grant before returning to Harvard as an instructor in the new department of Social Ethics. There he developed a course in personality that eventually led to his famous text of 1937 (Allport, 1937). Many years later, his mature views on personality appeared in *Pattern and Growth in Personality* (Allport, 1961). He stayed at Harvard for two years, then went to Dartmouth for four years, and then was enticed to return to Harvard in 1930, where he finished his distinguished career.

Although he contributed research in the nomothetic tradition, Allport was a champion of the idiographic ideal that everyone was a unique personality and that much could be learned by the careful study of individuals. In Allport's conception of personality, the basic unit of the individual personality was the **trait**, which for him meant a particular pattern of thinking, feeling, and behaving that was characteristic of a person and a means of distinguishing that person from others. A trait was "a kind of higher order habit, although it was much more generalized" (Nicholson, 2003, p. 154). Allport identified three varieties of traits that differed in level of generality and importance—cardinal, central, and secondary. *Cardinal traits*, not possessed by everyone, were attributes that were dominant in a person, to the point where describing a person's cardinal trait would identify that person to others, and most of what that person would do was related to the trait.

Napoleon, for instance, might be described by a cardinal trait of a need for power. *Central traits* are those dozen or so attributes that provide a reasonable accurate summary description of an individual. For example, they are the kinds the terms typically described in letters of recommendation (Hilgard, 1987). *Secondary traits* are less obvious characteristics, manifested in relatively few behaviors, and perhaps known only to close friends of an individual.

In line with his idiographic sentiments, Allport advocated the **case study**, an in-depth analysis of a person, as a way to study personality. As editor or associate editor of the *Journal of Abnormal and Social Psychology* from 1937 until his death in 1967, he was responsible for accepting many case study articles for inclusion in the journal (Pettigrew, 1969). Although he completed just one detailed case study himself, it was a famous one: *Letters from Jenny* (1965). The book-length study described the personality of "Jenny Masterson" (a fictitious name), based on a close analysis of a series of 301 letters written over a 12-year period by a middle-aged woman to a young married couple (Hall & Lindzey, 1970). But Allport also completed research in nomothetic tradition, in part to gain "scientific" legitimacy for his chosen field of personality, at a time (the 1930s) when psychology in general was dominated by nomothetic neobehaviorist experimental research, and psychology at Harvard was dominated by the presence of the prototype experimentalist, E. G. Boring (Nicholson, 2003). So, for instance, with Philip Vernon, a visiting professor from England who had been a student of Bartlett, Allport developed *A Study of Values* (Allport & Vernon, 1931), a test that measured the strength of a person's value systems, based on a theory of six "ideal types" developed by the German psychologist Eduard Spranger. The six types were theoretic, aesthetic, social, political, economic, and religious, and Allport and Vernon developed a popular self-report survey to measure the strength of each of them.

Allport came to prominence at a time when Freud's psychoanalytic theories were becoming very popular in America, and it is worth noting that Allport was no fan of psychoanalytic theory. He did not reject the concept of the unconscious, but did not think it was essential for understanding someone's personality. He also thought Freud's emphasis on sex was excessive, and he rejected the idea that our past history had an overwhelming effect on our present and future. He also was not impressed with the psychoanalytic strategy for measuring personality that came on the scene, the best example being the inkblot test developed by Hermann Rorschach in 1921, which was popular enough to have 38 articles written about it in the 1920s, and about 230 more in the 1930s (Klopfer, 1973). Such "projective" tests assumed that people were not capable of giving an accurate description of their personality on a self-report, because much of the personality was said to be buried in the unconscious. After giving responses to ambiguous stimuli (inkblots), the "true" personality could be inferred through a process of interpretation, so the argument went. Allport did not buy it. Instead, perhaps because of his own calm rationality, he firmly believed people capable of knowing themselves and therefore able to respond accurately to self-report personality inventories. The psychoanalytic strategy, Allport (1953, quoted in Hall & Lindzey, 1970) argued:

> ... seems to mark the culmination of a century-long era of irrationalism, and therefore of distrust. Has the subject no right to be believed? ... The individual's conscious report is rejected as untrustworthy, and the contemporary thrust of his motives is disregarded in favor of a backward tracing of his conduct to earlier formative stages. The individual loses his right to be believed. And while he is busy leading his life in the present with a forward thrust into the future, most [psychoanalysts] have become busy tracing it backward into the past. (p. 280)

Allport's criticism of Freudian psychoanalysis was genuine and intellectually legitimate. However, his distaste might also have been influenced to a degree by a meeting that he had with Freud in Vienna, while on his way back from the year in Turkey, just before he started graduate studies. After brashly making an appointment to see Freud, and being ushered into the famous office (with couch), Allport found himself at a loss for a way to open the conversation in a way that might impress the great man. Hoping to get a quick Freudian interpretation, he described an incident he witnessed on a tram in which a small boy seemed to be overly concerned about dirt: "He kept saying to his mother, 'I don't want to sit there ... don't let that dirty man sit beside me'" (Allport, 1967, quoted in Nicholson, 2003, p. 69). Allport apparently expected Freud to give an analysis of the relationship between mother and son, but instead, he "fixed his kindly therapeutic eyes upon me and said, 'And was that little boy you?'" (p. 69).

Allport is accurately considered the father of modern personality theory and the title of a recent biography, *Inventing Personality*, (Nicholson, 2003) is right on target. It was Allport who was primarily responsible for taking the nineteenth century study of "character" and turning it into the twentieth century study of "personality." It is also worth noting that he made important contributions to his brother's area of social psychology (*The Nature of Prejudice*, 1954) and his deep spirituality led him to write on the psychology of religion (*The Individual and His Religion*, 1950).

For his contributions to personality psychology and his advocacy of an idiographic psychology, Gordon Allport earned numerous honors and awards during his career, but his prized possession was a two-volume set of papers published by 55 of his former Ph.D. students and presented to him near the end of his career. In his autobiography, Allport (1967) wrote that his students had "presented me with two handsomely bound volumes of their own writings with the following inscription: 'From his students—in appreciation of his respect for their individuality.' This is an intimate honor, and one I prize above all others" (p. 24).

Developmental Psychology

Interest in development has a long history that predates the creation of psychology. We have already seen that the nature-nurture issue is timeless. Since the creation of psychology as a discipline, interest in development among psychologists has been high, from the child study movement initiated by G. Stanley Hall at the turn of the twentieth century, to the emphasis on the importance of the early years shown by both Freudians and behaviorists (but for different reasons of course). During neobehaviorism's prominent years, a Swiss psychologist, soon to be among the twentieth century's most famous psychologists, was carefully examining the cognitive development of young children, including his own.

Jean Piaget (1896–1980)

All students who have taken a course in developmental psychology will recognize the name Jean Piaget and will probably recall seeing a photo in their text of a 6- or 7-year-old schoolchild staring at the water levels in two different-sized containers. Piaget was a master at creating simple demonstrations of complex cognitive phenomena, and his conservation of volume task, in which "preoperational" children typically fail to recognize that the volume of a liquid remains constant when it is transferred to a taller or shorter container, is among the better known of them.

Jean Piaget (Figure 14.9) was a native of Switzerland, and except for a few brief interludes, spent most of his life there. Much like John Stuart Mill and Francis Galton before him, he was a precocious child. He developed a strong interest in the biological sciences as a schoolboy, and at the age of 10, he managed to publish a one-page description of an albino sparrow in a local natural history journal. He spent most of his adolescence collecting and classifying mollusks, publishing several articles and even being offered a job as curator of mollusks at a reputable museum in Geneva, which he had to decline on the grounds that he still had two years of high school remaining (Piaget, 1952). He completed his college degree at age 18. Within another three years, in 1918, he had earned a Ph.D. in biology and an international reputation as an expert on mollusks.

During his school years, Piaget also became interested in the philosophical problems of epistemology, especially the question of how we obtain our knowledge of the world. He read widely in philosophy and psychology (including William James and Sigmund Freud) and after finishing his biology doctorate, decided to examine the problem more closely. An opportunity arose in 1919 when he met Théodore Simon, of Binet-Simon fame, who asked

FIGURE 14.9 Jean Piaget, with two of his favorite research subjects, from Popplestone and McPherson (1994).

the young biologist to work on an intelligence testing project in the Binet laboratory in Paris. Consequently, Piaget spent the next few years studying verbal intelligence in school-aged children. His initial task was to standardize a reasoning test developed by British psychologist Cyril Burt, but while doing so, he discovered that he was less interested in whether the children answered questions correctly than in the thinking processes they used to answer the questions. Especially revealing were the cognitive processes involved when children got the wrong answers. To explore these strategies, Piaget began interviewing the children about how they solved the problems. From this experience, he concluded that children's cognition differs from adult cognition not just quantitatively, but qualitatively. That is, children do not just know less than adults, they think in an entirely different manner. Eventually, this insight led to Piaget's well-known stage theory of cognitive development.

Following the experience in the Binet lab and on the basis of the resulting publications, Piaget was offered a position as director at a research institute for the study of children in Geneva in 1921. During the 1920s, he also taught at the Universities of Geneva and Neuchâtel (his hometown) and published numerous articles and five books. The first of the five, *The Language and Thought of the Child* (1923/1959), gave Piaget an international reputation while he was still in his late twenties (Brainerd, 1996).

Piaget and his wife also had three children during this time, daughters in 1925 and 1927, and a son in 1931. Piaget was not about to miss an opportunity, so he and his wife made systematic observations of their three children as they grew. One important lesson for Piaget was that the verbal interviews he used in the Binet laboratory were useless for preverbal infants—other observational procedures had to be used. For instance, he inferred that infants were learning about cause and effect by observing their tendency to systematically repeat their actions, and he developed his famous concept of "object permanence" by noting whether or not infants would search for objects that were out of sight. It was during these years, the decade of the 1930s, that Piaget developed some of his most famous demonstrations of children's cognition and formulated his stage theory of cognitive development (Brainerd, 1996).[5] He referred to his approach as a **genetic epistemology**, using the term "genetic" to refer to developmental processes, not heredity (i.e., in the same way that G. Stanley Hall had used the term a generation earlier). That is, Piaget's focus was on determining precisely how knowledge, as represented by hypothetical mental structures that he called **schemata** devel-

oped within the individual.[6] He believed that children were active formulators of their knowledge rather than passive recipients of their experiences, and he believed that knowledge structures formed "wholes" that could not be reduced to their elements. This latter point connects with gestalt psychology (Chapter 9), of course, and Piaget was well aware of and generally appreciative of the gestaltists for showing him that he was not alone in formulating a theory based on "structures-of-the-whole." As he put it, "contact with the work of Köhler and Wertheimer made [an] ... impression on me. ... I had the distinct pleasure of concluding that my previous research was not sheer folly, since one could design on such a central hypothesis of the subordination of the parts to the organizing whole not only a consistent theory, but also a splendid series of experiments" (Piaget 1952, p. 248).

In the early 1950s, Piaget established a research institute of his own at the University of Geneva, the International Center for Genetic Epistemology, and remained its director for all of his remaining years (Voyat, 1981). Despite his reputation in Europe, however, he was still relatively unknown in the United States, partly because not all of his work was being translated into English, but also because of the American preoccupation with behaviorism. He was not completely unknown in America—he had been among the group of young international psychologists participating in the 1929 International Congress at Yale (others: Pavlov and Lewin), and Harvard had given him an honorary degree at a conference celebrating its three-hundredth birthday in 1936 (Kessen, 1996). Also, as you might have noticed from the citation in the last paragraph, the editors of the prestigious *History of Psychology in Autobiography* series (including E. G. Boring) saw fit to include Piaget in their fourth edition, which appeared in 1952. Nonetheless, his work was not widely known in the United States until the 1960s, just when cognitive psychology was coming to the forefront of American experimental psychology. Following a 1960 confer-

---

[5] As you may recall, the stages are sensorimotor (0–2), preoperational (2–7), concrete operational (7–11), and formal operational (11–adult). For details, refer to any textbook of developmental psychology.

[6] Thus, independently of Bartlett, Piaget arrived at a similar conclusion about cognitive structures and used the same term—the schema.

ence devoted to his work in Dedham, Massachusetts, sponsored by the Social Science Research Council (Kessen & Kuhlman, 1962) and the publication of John Flavell's *The Developmental Psychology of Jean Piaget* (1963), Piaget's ideas exploded onto the scene, and he began accumulating the status he retains today as one of the century's most influential psychologists (Kessen, 1996).

RESEARCH PSYCHOLOGY IN PERSPECTIVE

Chapter 13 opened with a description of a split in modern psychology between those who study the principles of psychology, the researcher/academicians, and those who apply these principles, the practitioners. Chapter 13 focused on the latter and this chapter has concerned the former. For both chapters, it is important to note that the surface has barely been scratched. Chapter 13 concentrated on clinical and industrial psychology and left out other majors areas of application, school psychology, community psychology, rehabilitation psychology, and forensic psychology, just to name a few. Similarly, this chapter concentrated on cognitive psychology, then sampled from physiological, social, personality, and developmental psychology. A glimpse at any modern introductory text will tell you that much was omitted. But my goal was never to be comprehensive in my descriptions of psychology during the latter two-thirds of the twentieth century. Rather my purpose was partly to give you a glimpse of the tremendous diversity of interests among psychologists, partly to show some of the interconnections among them, and partly to entice you to become interested in these topics and study them in more depth. The final chapter elaborates on the theme of diversity and ends with a brief discussion of whether there is one psychology or many.

SUMMARY

COGNITIVE PSYCHOLOGY ARRIVES (AGAIN)

- After World War II, psychologists became increasingly involved in studying mental processes, a topic that had been a central interest for psychology's earliest pioneers. This cognitive psychology movement in America developed gradually during the 1950s, 1960s, and 1970s, while behaviorism became a less powerful force. The change was more evolutionary than revolutionary.

- During the period when behaviorism dominated American psychology (1930s and 1940s), some American researchers (e.g., Stroop) still investigated cognitive topics and European psychologists, who never became as enamored of behaviorism as the Americans did, made important contributions to the understanding of mental processes. The British psychologist Frederick Bartlett is a prime example. He was critical of the laboratory-based, nonsense-syllable type of memory research being done, and proposed instead that research on memory should emphasize real-life situations. He believed that memory was constructive and was influenced by schemata, that is, one's basic concepts about the phenomenal world. His "War of the Ghosts" research showed that memory is influenced by schemata unique to one's culture.

- Within psychology, the cognitive movement gained momentum from problems that developed within the behaviorist/associationist tradition. At the Hixon Symposium in 1948, Lashley showed that associationist principles could not explain the problem of serial order, and behaviorism seemed incapable of explaining language behavior.

- Outside of psychology, developments in computer science, information theory, and linguistics contributed to the evolution of cognitive psychology. Researchers began to create models of cognitive processes that used the computer program as a metaphor and emphasized the concept of the individual as an information processor rather than as a responder to stimuli. Chomsky argued that Skinnerian behaviorism was not relevant for the study of language and proposed a nativist account of language development.

- During the decade of the 1950s, several landmark papers and books appeared. These included Miller's paper on the limited capacity of information processing in immediate memory (7±2), Broadbent's research on selective attention, and the book by Miller, Galanter, and Pribram on "plans," which featured the idea of information feedback in the form of TOTE units as a replacement for the reflex arc concept.

- The first major summary of laboratory research in cognitive psychology appeared in 1967 with Neisser's book; the book also produced a self-identification of the field as "cognitive psychology." About a decade later, Neisser questioned cognitive psychology's emphasis on basic laboratory research and in the spirit of Bartlett, called for an increase in research on cognitive processes as they operate in the everyday world to help individuals adapt to their environments (i.e., research having ecological validity).

- Cognitive psychology has spread to other specialty areas within psychology. In addition, the interdisciplinary field of cognitive science evolved in parallel with cognitive psychology. Cognitive science includes psychology, computer science (e.g., artificial intelligence), linguistics, anthropology, and epistemology. The field of artificial intelligence includes the study of computer simulations of human cognitive processes and the development of expert systems in which the computer acts intelligently. Researchers disagree on the extent to which machine thinking resembles human thinking.

OTHER RESEARCH AREAS

- In addition to the area of cognitive psychology, there were important developments in other research topics of interest to psychologists. Important advances were made in understanding (a) the relationship between the brain and behavior, (b) the effect of the social environment on individual behavior, (c) the nature of human personality, and (d) the process of human development.

- During the second half of the twentieth century, there was an acceleration of interest in studying the brain-behavior relationship. Interest was sparked by technological breakthroughs (e.g., EEG), but especially by the research and theorizing of Donald Hebb. Hebb's model of the brain centered on the cell assembly, an interrelated combination of associated neurons, and the phase sequence, an organization of cell assemblies and the neurological equivalent of thinking. Hebb synapses are synapses that have undergone structural change as a result of some learning process.

- Floyd Allport and Kurt Lewin are important pioneers in social psychology, but Leon Festinger (a student of Lewin) developed the most important social psychological theory of the twentieth century, the theory of cognitive dissonance. Festinger's experiments were known for the precision and elegance of their design, and their extensive use of deception.

- Gordon Allport was a champion of the idiographic tradition, which emphasizes the in-depth study of individuals, as opposed to the nomothetic tradition, the study of general principles. More then anyone, Allport is responsible for making personality psychology a topic of study in psychology. He believed that people could be characterized with reference to their cardinal, central, and secondary traits.

- In development psychology, the most important figure in the twentieth century was the Swiss psychologist Jean Piaget, whose genetic epistemology (i.e., an interest in understanding the growth and development of knowledge within an individual) and stage theory of cognitive development eventually became influential in America, after American psychologists turned from behavior to an interest in cognitive processes.

STUDY QUESTIONS

1. Describe an example of research that demonstrates an interest in cognitive psychology even during the heyday of behaviorism.

2. What was the serial order problem and why did it create a problem for behaviorism?

3. Describe how the development of cognitive psychology was influenced by computer science and information theory.

4. Chomsky argued that behaviorism failed to explain language. What were his arguments?

5. Describe how scientific revolutions occur, according to Thomas Kuhn's model.

6. The Close-Up argues that a cognitive "revolution" did not really occur. Explain.

7. What did George Miller discover about the nature of STM?

8. Describe how Broadbent studied selective attention and what he concluded about it.

9. What was the influence of the "Plans" book on cognitive psychology?

10. Consider the two books by Neisser that are described in the chapter. What was the influence of each?

11. What is the difference between cognitive psychology and cognitive science?

12. Use an anagram problem to distinguish between an algorithm and a heuristic.

13. What is artificial intelligence and how does it relate to the Turing test?

14. Distinguish strong from weak AI, and show how the Chinese Room problem leads one to favor one over the other.

15. Donald Hebb is said to have revived interest in studying the relationship between brain and behavior. Explain.

16. Describe Hebb's ideas about cortical organization and the effects of experience on the brain.

17. Floyd Allport and Kurt Lewin had different ways of conceptualizing social psychology. How did they differ?

18. Describe Festinger's theory of cognitive dissonance.

19. Describe Festinger's impact on the nature of research in social psychology.

20. Distinguish between nomothetic and idiographic approaches to psychology.

21. Describe Gordon Allport's influence on personality psychology. Why is he said to have "invented" personality?

22. Why did Piaget call himself a genetic epistemologist. Why was the importance of his work late in achieving recognition in the United States?

QUESTIONS FROM THE ORIGINAL SOURCE EXCERPT

1. Describe Bartlett's criticism of the Ebbinghaus approach to memory. How did his methodology differ?

2. From Bartlett's method of "description," what did he discover about the visual memory for a series of postcards?

3. Describe the "War of the Ghosts" study and use it to explain why Bartlett believed memory to be constructive. Be sure to work the term "schema" into your answer.

FOR FURTHER READING

Baars, B. J. (1986). *The cognitive revolution in psychology.* New York: Guilford Press.

A detailed description of the cognitive movement, taken from the standpoint that cognitive psychology represents a revolutionary shift away from behaviorism; noteworthy for containing extensive interviews with key figures, including B. F. Skinner, George Miller, Ulric Neisser, and Noam Chomsky.

Bruce, D. (1994). Lashley and the problem of serial order. *American Psychologist, 49,* 93–103.

A highly readable description of Lashley's paper on serial order given at the Hixon Symposium, its impact at the time and later on different audiences; shows that Lashley's paper was not immediately recognized as a breakthrough for cognitive psychology, but its importance was eventually recognized, once cognitive psychology had become more established.

Korn, J. H. (1997). *Illusions of reality: A history of deception in social psychology.* Albany, NY: SUNY Press.

A thorough and balanced analysis of the use of deception in social psychological research, and the ethical implica-tions of its use; includes whole chapters on the work of Lewin, Festinger, and Stanley Milgram, whose obedience studies in the 1960s and '70s always seem to be included in the ethics chapters of research methods textbooks.

Leahey, T. H. (1992). The mythical revolutions of American psychology. *American Psychologist, 47,* 308–318.

A careful description of several models of the criteria necessary for there to be a "revolution" in science, followed by an analysis of why both behaviorism and cognitive psychology, while important developments in psychology's history, cannot be considered revolutionary.

Nicholson, I. A. M. (2003). *Inventing personality: Gordon Allport and the science of selfhood.* Washington, DC: American Psychological Association.

An intellectual biography of Allport, focusing on the first half of his career, showing how he took the nineteenth century study of "character" and transformed it into the twentieth century study of personality; emphasizes Allport's advocacy of an idiographic approach to psychology, and places his work and his life into the contemporary social, political, and institutional context.

CHAPTER 15

LINKING PSYCHOLOGY'S PAST AND PRESENT

But there is a sense in which we are nothing if not our history. Our history is our binding force.

—Sigmund Koch, 1992

PREVIEW AND CHAPTER OBJECTIVES

This chapter will of necessity be incomplete—the growth of psychology has been exponential in the last 30 to 40 years and would require its own book just to tell the story in broad outline (800-page introductory psychology texts barely scratch the surface). The more modest goal for the chapter will be to examine some of the important trends that have developed in recent years. One way in which psychology has changed in the recent years is in the area of diversity. Women and minority group members have found it difficult to make inroads into a field dominated historically by white males, but some improvements occurred in the postwar years, especially during the past 20 years and especially for women. Other recent trends in psychology will be sketched in the second part of the chapter and doing so will highlight one of the book's themes—to understand the present requires understanding the past. The chapter closes with a discussion of whether psychology can be considered a unified discipline. After you finish this final chapter, you should be able to:

- Describe the indicators of increased diversity in psychology
- Describe the barriers to advancement in psychology faced by women and minorities
- Describe the career and contributions of Eleanor Gibson
- Describe the career and contributions of Kenneth and Mamie Clark, especially the effect of their work on the 1954 *Brown v. Board of Education* decision
- Summarize five current trends in psychology and show how their understanding requires knowing history
- Understand why it can be argued that psychology is many disciplines, not just one
- Understand the role of history as a unifying force in psychology

THE GROWTH AND DIVERSITY OF PSYCHOLOGY

One indication of organized psychology's growth over the past 100 years lies in the membership data for its largest professional organization, the American Psychological Association. From its origins in G. Stanley Hall's study in 1892 until the mid-1920s, the APA showed steady but unspectacular expansion. The initial 31 charter members rose to about 125 by the turn of the century and to about 375 by the end of World War I (Fernberger, 1932, p. 5). With the creation of the associate member status in 1925, however, the growth curve changed direction, as can be seen in Figure 15.1. After World War II, the total membership stood at approximately 5,000 and, as Figure 15.2 shows, it has climbed steadily since that time, reaching the 70,000 mark by 1990 (Bulatao, Fulcher, & Evans, 1992). As the twenty-first century begins, full APA membership is rapidly approaching 100,000.[1] And the future promises continued growth—psychology is among the most popular majors on campus, new graduate programs appear each year, and applications to graduate school far outnumber available places.

Along with the expansion reflected in APA membership rolls, psychology has also become more diverse over the years. One form of this diversity has been specialization. As you know from the last two chapters, psychologists are no longer just psychologists, they are developmental psychologists, social psychologists, industrial psychologists, clinical psychologists, cognitive psychologists and personality psychologists, among many others. Even these labels are far too broad. Developmental psychologists, to take just one example, cannot hope to be knowledgeable about their entire subfield, but must specialize further within it, perhaps by establishing expertise in infant memory, adolescent peer relations, or reasoning processes in the elderly. A second form of psychology's increased diversity is in various types of persons who enter the field. After the 1990s, psychologists were more likely than ever to be female and/or nonwhite.

[1] In August of 2003, there were 90,000 full members of APA, according to the APA membership office.

Women in Psychology's History

The problems for women in psychology have been examined several times in the book. From Chapter 6, you recall the difficulties experienced by such pioneering women as Mary Calkins, Margaret Washburn, and Christine Ladd-Franklin, who were either unable to secure full-time academic positions (Ladd-Franklin) or were limited to teaching at small women's colleges without graduate programs (Calkins and Washburn). This latter problem actually got worse in the 1920s, when many of these small colleges began replacing female professors with males to "enhance" their prestige (Diehl, 1992). Another long-standing barrier to advancement was that women were excluded from the all-important informal communication network of scientific psychologists, as described in Chapter 7. Although allowing some women into his graduate program at Cornell, in part because of a university requirement, E. B. Titchener kept them out of his Experimentalist "club." After Titchener's death in 1927, the group reorganized as the Society of Experimental Psychologists (SEP) and voted to include women, but the de facto obstacles remained. Two women, Washburn and June Downey of Wyoming (who died before attending any meetings), were made charter members of the new group, and Washburn even hosted an SEP meeting at Vassar in 1931.[2] Yet photos of the group in the 1940s and early 1950s simply don't include female faces, and no other woman was elected until 1958 (Furumoto, 1988). Although relatively small in number, the SEP constituted a closed network that influenced academic hiring and advancement (Goodwin, 1985).[3] Hence, for

[2] Walter Miles of Stanford attended the 1931 Vassar meeting and recorded an interesting comment made by Washburn about Titchener. Miles's diary for April 1, 1931, includes this entry: "Washburn's attitude toward T. He never discovered anything, he did not create any apparatus, or methods, he was simply not an experimenter. ... His great points were his learning and his ability to give a lecture." Washburn apparently also believed that part of the reason why Titchener "gave her but little" was that "they were too near the same age" (Miles, 1931).

[3] The SEP exists today, primarily as an honor society for esteemed experimental psychologists. There are about 200 members, about 30 of them women. Most of the women members were elected in the decade of the 1990s (Goodwin, 2001).

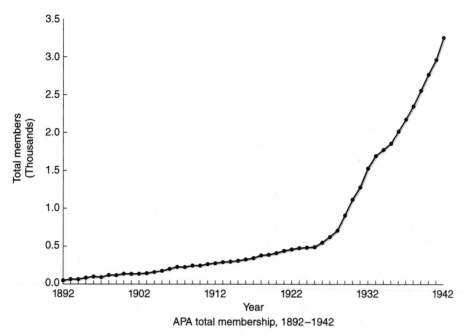

APA total membership, 1892–1942

FIGURE 15.1 The growth of APA membership, 1892–1942, from Bulatao, Fulcher, & Evans (1992).

APA total membership, 1942–1990

FIGURE 15.2 The growth of APA membership since 1942, from Bulatao, Fulcher, & Evans (1992).

many years, the exclusion of women from the group made it virtually impossible for them to fashion successful scientific careers. Some did, despite the odds, and a good postwar example is one of developmental psychology's most celebrated scientists.

Eleanor Gibson (1910–2002)

In a Rose Garden ceremony in June of 1992, George Bush awarded the National Medal of Science, the highest honor a president can confer on a scientist, to Eleanor Gibson (Figure 15.3). The award was for a lifetime of research on topics ranging from the development of depth perception to the basic processes involved in reading. Only nine other psychologists had earned this award up to that time (Kent, 1992). Gibson is also the person referred to previously as the first woman since Downey and Washburn to be elected to the SEP. Today, students are most likely to recall Gibson as the creator of the "visual cliff," used to study depth perception in infants. Her career is a case study in perseverance.

Gibson first became interested in psychology at Smith College, a liberal arts college for women in western Massachusetts, where she learned to run rats in mazes from a student of Harvey Carr and studied psychology's history with a student of E. G. Boring. In her senior year, she took a course from Smith's new German professor, Kurt Koffka, but found the experi-

ence less than enthralling—the gestaltist did little more than read notes from his forthcoming book on gestalt psychology (Koffka, 1935). She had better luck in a laboratory course taught by a newly minted experimental psychologist from Princeton, James Gibson, later to become one of the best-known twentieth-century researchers in perception. Eleanor fell in love with both the lab course and the professor. She remained at Smith for a year after graduation, earned a master's degree, and married her favorite teacher.

Full of enthusiasm for research in psychology, Gibson went to Yale in 1935, eager to work in the primate lab of the famous Robert Yerkes. There, however, she quickly encountered a world very different from the sheltered one of Smith. She managed with some difficulty to get an appointment to see Yerkes, who seemed curious about why she was there. When she said that she wished to work for him, "[h]e stood up, walked to the door, held it open, and said, 'I have no women in my laboratory'" (Gibson, 1980, p. 246). Although angered and somewhat disillusioned, Gibson stubbornly refused to leave Yale, and eventually managed to convince the neobehaviorist Clark Hull of her abilities and earned a doctorate under his direction in 1938. After a brief return to Smith, she moved to Ithaca, New York, when her husband was hired by Cornell University. Antinepotism rules, a major problem for many

FIGURE 15.3 Eleanor Gibson receiving the National Medal of Science in 1992.

women psychologists married to professors, kept her from employment at Cornell, yet she persevered once again. For 16 years, she labored as an unpaid "research associate," earning her keep by winning a series of competitive and prestigious research grants. It was during these years that she created the visual cliff and completed the pioneering studies on depth perception with Richard Walk (e.g., Gibson & Walk, 1960). When Cornell removed its nepotism rules in 1966, Gibson was immediately made a full professor. In 1974, she was named the Susan Linn Sage Endowed Professor of Psychology and while she never actually retired, she was named Professor Emeritus in 1980 (Pick, 1994). She continued to be an active scholar and as late as 1994, addressed the question of psychology's future by vigorously arguing for a theory of organism-environmental interaction that was grounded in a developmental approach (Gibson, 1994). Shortly after her death in 2002, a former student wrote about her skills as a teacher:

> She was a very special mentor for her students. She excited our curiosity and engaged us as her collaborators in seeking knowledge about development right from the start. She was always available to talk, and eager to discuss one's ideas. She had an amazing knack for taking a student's most ill-formed idea, pondering it for a while, and then returning it—and the credit for it—barely recognizable, as it had been turned into a really good idea, elaborated, clarified, and often made precise as an elegant plan for a study. Her standards were very high and she taught us by example while generously sharing the credit. Her science was characterized by rigorous and clever experimental design, attention to detail in experimental procedures, and a profound concern for the conceptual and theoretical bases of the problem being investigated. (Pick, 2003, p. 26)

Eleanor Gibson is just one example of a highly talented scientist who faced barriers to advancement simply because she was a woman. The situation improved somewhat in the 1960s and 1970s, when the women's movement emerged as part of the drive for civil rights. The Civil Rights Act of 1964 prohibited discrimination against women as well as minorities and in 1972, Title IX specifically prohibited gender discrimination in higher education (Russo, 1988). Within the APA, committees on the status of women were formed in the 1960s and 1970s, and in 1973 the APA created a division for the psychology of women (Division 35—The Society for the Psychology of Women). Today, women undergraduate majors in psychology outnumber men by about two to one, and about 60% of doctorates in psychology are awarded to women. Although most faculty continue to be male, changes are beginning to occur—the proportion of women faculty in graduate departments of psychology shifted from one-fifth in the mid-1980s to one-third a decade later ("Sex, Race/Ethnicity Data," 1995).

Minorities in Psychology's History

Like women, members of minority groups have been on the outside looking in for most of psychology's history. Unlike the case for women, however, significant gains for blacks and most other minorities were not made in the years following World War II, and minorities continue to be underrepresented in psychology. In 1991, for example, only 14% of all bachelor's degrees, 11% of master's degrees, and 9% of doctoral degrees were granted to minorities ("Sex, Race/Ethnicity Data," 1995). Of these, about one-half went to African American students, a quarter to Hispanic students, and the remainder to Asian Americans and Native Americans. The APA is currently addressing the issue with a Commission on Ethnic Minority Recruitment, Retention, and Training, and the APA's Board of Educational Affairs has a Task Force on Diversity.

Despite barriers at least as high as those confronting women, minority psychologists have made contributions to psychology's history. We have already seen that displaced European Jewish psychologists such as Wertheimer and Lewin became major figures in American psychology. They did so in the face of an anti-Semitism that, though less virulent than the version found in Nazi Germany, occurred in subtle ways nonetheless. The gestaltists were already enough well known to secure positions, but job searches were not quite so easy for other Jewish psychologists, especially during the Great Depression when all jobs were scarce. As historian Andrew

Winston (1996) has shown, for example, letters of recommendation during the 1930s frequently reinforced the stereotype of Jewish persons as being shrewd and calculating, oversensitive to perceived slights, argumentative, clannish, and defensively aggressive. Candidates for academic positions could be doomed by a letter indicating that they possessed these attributes, and their chances were hardly improved if they were praised by saying, in effect, that while they might be Jewish, they were not like a "typical" Jew. In recommending one of his students, for example, Robert Woodworth wrote that "as his name indicates, [he is] a Jew, but I am sure you would find him a very satisfactory colleague ... cooperative and eager to fit into the group" (quoted in Winston, 1996, p. 30).

The difficulties faced by Jews paled in comparison to those encountered by African Americans, however. At least nobody accused Jews of lacking intellectual ability. Blacks, on the other hand, have often had their basic abilities questioned, and this was especially true during psychology's formative years. As you recall from Chapter 6 (pp. 147–148), scholars such as Francis Sumner faced enormous obstacles when trying to obtain graduate education and then employment in academia. Sumner eventually found his way to Howard University in Washington, D.C., where he established the most prominent psychology program at a historically black university. Two of his most prominent students were Kenneth and Mamie Phipps Clark.

Kenneth B. (b. 1914) and Mamie Phipps (1917–1983) Clark

On May 17, 1954, the United States Supreme Court issued a ruling that has come to be recognized as one of the most important court decisions of the twentieth century. Concerning a suit brought against the Board of Education in Topeka, Kansas, the Court declared, by a unanimous 7-0 vote, that "in the field of public education the doctrine of 'separate but equal' has no place. Separate educational facilities are inherently unequal" (quoted in Morison, 1965, p. 1086). The *Brown v. Board of Education* ruling reversed an earlier decision from another time; in 1896, the Court, in *Plessy v. Ferguson,* had ruled that it was legal for there to be separate public facilities (e.g., schools,

restrooms) for whites and blacks, as long as the facilities reserved for blacks were of equal quality to those reserved for whites. By declaring the doctrine of "separate but equal" unconstitutional, the Brown decision helped pave the way for the civil rights movement of the 1960s and 1970s. Of importance for psychology's history, the Brown decision was notable because the Court's decision was influenced by, and made specific reference to, research by psychologists demonstrating the adverse effects of segregation on young African Americans. Although it was not the only research that contributed to the decision, studies on the self-esteem of black children, completed by Kenneth and Mamie Phipps Clark (Figure 15.4), have come to symbolize the contribution of psychology to a watershed moment in American history.[4]

Kenneth B. Clark was born in the Panama Canal Zone, educated in the public school system of New York City, and went to college at Howard University in Washington, D.C. Mamie Phipps was a rarity—an African American raised in a comparatively affluent environment. Her father was a physician in Hot Springs, Arkansas, and although she "learned the things not to do" when growing up (quoted in Lal, 2002, p. 21), she was insulated from many of the daily indignities of being black and growing up in the South. Mamie also found her way to Howard University, where she planned to study math. That plan changed, however, when she met her future husband, who convinced her to join him as a psychology major. Together, they came under Sumner's influence. Kenneth and Mamie both completed bachelor's and master's degrees at Howard (1935 and 1936 for Kenneth; 1938 and 1939 for Mamie), and both went on to earn doctorates from Columbia (1940 and 1943). They eloped a few months before Mamie's 1938 graduation from Howard.

The research for which the Clarks are best known originated in and grew out of Mamie's master's thesis in the late 1930s (Lal, 2002) and was summarized later as "Racial identification and preference in Negro children" (Clark & Clark, 1947). Eventually known as

---

[4] In its decision, the Supreme Court did not specifically cite the research completed by the Clarks, but did cite Kenneth Clark's general summary of all the social scientific research relating to the issue of the effects of segregation on development (Keppel, 2002).

FIGURE 15.4 Kenneth and Mamie Phipps Clark.

the "doll studies," the procedure involved early school age black and white children from both the North and the South. They were shown four dolls, a female and a male with light-colored skin and a female and a male with dark skin, and asked a series of questions, including, "Show me the doll that you would like to play with," "Show me the doll that looks bad," and "Show me the doll that looks like you" (quoted in Phillips, 2000, p. 147). What they found was that black children showed a preference for the white dolls and tended to consider the black dolls "bad." In some cases, the children even thought they looked more like the white dolls. In a slightly different procedure, children were given dolls and crayons and told to color in the dolls. Black children consistently colored the skins of the dolls lighter than their own (Herman, 1995). The Clarks concluded that one insidious effect of segregation was that the self-esteem of black children suffered. And if childhood shapes the adult, these effects would have lasting deleterious effects.

The legal strategy in *Brown v. Board of Education* evolved out of four different state court fights over the same basic issue—reversing the separate but equal doctrine. An architect of the legal strategy was Thurgood Marshall, who later became the first African American named to the Supreme Court. He explained it this way:

> If your car ran over my client, you'd have to pay up, and my function as an attorney would be to put experts on the stand to testify to how

much damage was done. We needed exactly that kind of evidence in the school cases. When Bob Carter came to me with Ken Clark's doll test, I thought it was a promising way of showing injury to these segregated youngsters. (quoted in Kluger, 1987, p. 316)

Kenneth Clark testified in three of the four cases leading up to the Supreme Court case, even bringing the dolls with him to show jurors (Benjamin & Crouse, 2002). These cases culminated in the Brown decision, and although the "doll studies" were not cited in the text of the decision, Chief Justice Earl Warren's decision made specific reference to the importance of the expert testimony of social scientists that testified to the effects of segregation on black children (Jackson, 2000).

After earning her doctorate in 1943, Mamie Clark took a position at the Riverdale Home for Children, providing psychological services for homeless black children. In 1946, with her husband's support and some funds from her father, she established and became the executive director for the Northside Center for Child Development in Harlem. The center provided counseling and therapy for the youth of Harlem and their families and was a model of an interdisciplinary team approach to treatment—Clark's staff included "psychiatrists, psychologists, social workers, case workers, teachers, and consulting pediatricians" (Lal, 2002, p. 25). During this same time, Kenneth joined the faculty of City College of New York and began a distinguished academic career that culminated in his election to the presidency of the American Psychological Association in 1970. He was the first, and so far the only, African American to hold the office.

As noted earlier, minority group members are not well represented in psychology today. Nonetheless, the APA has made a few organizational efforts over the years to create a climate of inclusiveness. In 1950, for example, the APA Council passed a resolution that it would only hold its annual meeting in cities free from overt discriminatory practices. The 1957 meeting, for instance, was moved from Miami to New York, after it was learned that some hotels would not register blacks (Smith, 1992). Mainly through the efforts of Kenneth Clark during his APA presidency, the APA also created the Board of Social and Ethical Responsibility for Psychology in 1972 (Pickren & Tomes, 2002); it in turn spawned today's Board of Ethnic Minority Affairs. The APA's Minority Fellows Program began awarding financial aid for graduate study in 1974, and in 1987, Division 45, the Society for the Psychological Study of Ethnic Minority Issues, was created.

TRENDS IN CONTEMPORARY PSYCHOLOGY

Chapter 1 included the argument that understanding psychology's present requires knowing something of its past, a point made eloquently by E. G. Boring in the quote that opened that first chapter. I hope that what you have learned from your history of psychology course and from this book have combined with the knowledge accumulated in other psychology courses to enhance your understanding of psychology's present. This next-to-last segment of the book briefly identifies five contemporary trends in psychology, none of which can be properly understood without knowing something about psychology's history. As I see them, these trends are:

1. *The accelerated study of the relationship between the brain and behavior*, with the term neuroscience being added to an increasing number of subdisciplinary labels (e.g., cognitive

neuroscience). Dramatic technological innovations have fueled this development, but our current understanding rests on a long history of studying the brain (Chapter 3), and the basic issues involved (e.g., the mind-body question; localization of function) remain deeply rooted in the histories of philosophy and physiology (Chapters 2 and 3).

2. *The vigorous return of evolutionary thinking*, accompanied by a shift toward the nature end of the nature-nurture issue. Chapter 5 told the story of Darwin and his influence during psychology's formative years. One aspect of that influence was the tendency to explain some behaviors with reference to evolutionary mechanisms and, consequently, to take the nature side of the nature-nurture issue. Evolutionary explanations went out of vogue in American psychology during the era of behaviorism, which produced a shift to the nurture side of the debate. In recent years, however, the balance seems to be shifting back again. Much attention is being given to behavior genetics, the study of genetic influences on behavior and mental processes, and evolutionary psychology has reached the status of a course in the psychology curriculum, with several textbooks now available (e.g., Buss, 1999).

3. *Significant changes in research brought about by the capacities of modern computers*. The history of research methodology is a topic worthy of its own text, but you have encountered some elements of it—Woodworth's text (the "Columbia bible"—Chapter 8), and the influence of ANOVA on research designs in social psychology (Chapter 14). One effect of both the Woodworth text and ANOVA has been a relative neglect of correlational research designs, but they have become increasingly commonplace (and more sophisticated) in recent years with the development of statistical software capable of performing highly complex multivariate analyses (e.g., multiple regression) quickly.

4. *The increased professionalization of psychological practitioners*. As you know from the opening section of Chapter 13, there is a long history of

uneasiness between academician/researchers and those who practice psychology professionally. Knowing something of that history helps understand tensions between these groups and puts into perspective any attempts to bridge the gap between them.

5. *The increased fragmentation of psychology.* This requires a section of the chapter all its own, one that will close the book.

THE FUTURE: PSYCHOLOGY OR PSYCHOLOGIES?

Clearly, psychology has shown enormous growth and increased specialization during the last half of the twentieth century; it is therefore worth considering whether the field can be said to be unified in any way. At the beginning of the twenty-first century, is there a field of psychology or are there multiple psychologies?

First, the question implies that psychology was once unified, yet it is unclear if psychology has ever been a coherent discipline. It may have approached unity in its early years, when it was trying to forge an identity separate from physiology and philosophy, but it is evident that strong disagreements existed even then. The conflicts between Titchener and others over psychology's very definition illustrate the point, as do the long-standing squabbles within the APA among various constituencies. As was discussed in Chapters 12 and 13, psychologist-practitioners were dissatisfied with the APA in the two decades prior to World War II, but the 1945 reorganization made the APA more attractive to them. The wartime spirit of cooperation that reshaped the APA soon dissipated, however, and conflicts developed between those who wanted the APA to retain its traditional role as the promoter of scientific psychology and those who thought of the organization as a means to promote the practice of psychology. Frustration among scientific psychologists produced the Psychonomic Society in 1960 and attempts to further reorganize the APA, including a failed one in the mid-1980s that led directly to the creation of the American Psychological Society (APS). Organizationally, at least, psychology at the opening of the twenty-first century seems to be characterized more by disunity than unity.

As for modern psychology as an intellectual discipline, few commentators seem willing to consider it a unified field, other than in the institutional sense that despite the new interdisciplinary fields that are developing, most psychologists continued to be trained in "departments of psychology" (Hilgard, 1987), and in the fairly consistent definition—the science of behavior and mental processes—that appears in most modern introductory textbooks. When addressing the issue of fragmentation at an APA symposium celebrating the centennial of Wundt's laboratory in 1979, George Miller, trained in the traditional experimental psychology of E. G. Boring, "discovered several other psychologies, all claiming proprietary rights to the label, all competing for disciples, and each contemptuous of the others. In short, I discovered that psychology is an intellectual zoo" (Miller, 1992, p. 40). Some understanding of the range of species in this zoo can be achieved by examining the specialties of just a few of the 53 divisions of the APA:

3	Experimental Psychology
7	Developmental Psychology
14	Industrial/Organization Psychology
12	Clinical Psychology
16	School Psychology
22	Rehabilitation Psychology
25	Behavior Analysis
26	History of Psychology
28	Psychopharmacology and Substance Abuse
30	Psychological Hypnosis
36	Psychology of Religion
38	Health Psychology
52	International Psychology

Many psychologists belong to more than one division, but it is clear that widely divergent interests are represented under the APA's broad umbrella. Also, some of the experimental psychology areas represented by the APS extend the range of specialties even further. It is difficult to imagine a neuropsychologist studying the effects of neurotransmitter X on memory, a developmental psychologist studying parallel play in children, an industrial psychologist developing a performance evaluation procedure, and a counselor in a rape crisis center having much in common.

Perhaps it is most reasonable to assume that psychology is not a single discipline but a collection of them. One of psychology's major theoreticians, Sigmund Koch, argued this point for years, recommending that the term "psychology" be replaced with the more pluralistic label of "psychological studies" (Koch, 1993). He viewed this as a historical process similar to that found in other sciences—biology, for instance, encompasses a wide range of "biological studies" (e.g., botany, zoology). Similarly, memory researcher and former APS president Gordon Bower, in an APA symposium on "The Fragmentation of Psychology," suggested that a more positive connotation results from labeling the phenomenon "specialization" rather than "fragmentation" (Bower, 1993). Although the term "psychology" has not been replaced with "psychological studies," most psychologists would agree with Koch's and Bower's general point

that psychology today is really a plurality of subdisciplines, each a specialty in its own right. Bower used the metaphor of a growing tree to make his point, likening the growth and diversity of psychology to the growth process of a tree, with age producing increased branching. He compared the individual psychological scientist to a "small bug feeding on a succulent leaf at one end of a very tiny branch and perhaps talking to the other bugs feeding on the same leaf" (p. 905).

If there is any sense of a unifying force in modern psychology, other than the institutional one deriving from the academic category of "psychology department," and the definitional one found in general psychology texts, one could argue that it derives from psychology's history. As Koch (1992) put it, "there is a sense in which we are nothing if not our history. Our history is our binding force" (p. 966). Regardless of one's modern specialty, there are common origins (to follow the tree metaphor, one trunk and one root system) and familiar themes, many of which have been discussed in this book. I hope that what you have read in those pages will entice you to learn more about what connects psychologists and will deepen your understanding of psychology's rich heritage.

SUMMARY

THE GROWTH AND DIVERSITY OF PSYCHOLOGY

- Psychology has shown vigorous growth during its 100-plus years of existence as an independent discipline and, as it has grown, the interests of psychologists have become more specialized. Throughout most of its history, leading psychologists were white and male, a situation that is now changing, especially as more women enter the field. Although women were excluded from psychology's inner circles throughout most of the twentieth century, some made important contributions. Eleanor Gibson is a prime postwar example. She overcame negative stereotypes of "woman-as-scientist" and became a leading developmental psychologist, known for her research on depth perception (visual cliff research) and reading.

- Minority groups, including Jews and African Americans, also have faced discrimination throughout psychology's history. Blacks in particular had to confront the prejudices deriving from the early twentieth-century belief in the inherited racial superiority of white males and the

social policy of separate but (not really) equal schools. Research on the self-esteem of black children, completed by Kenneth and Mamie Phipps Clark, was instrumental in helping to strike down the concept of separate but equal education for blacks and whites in the *Brown v. the Board of Education* decision of 1954.

TRENDS IN MODERN PSYCHOLOGY

- There are five major trends evident in modern psychology—increased interest in neuroscience, the development of evolutionary psychology, the expanding impact of computers, an increased level of professionalization, and increased specialization. Each cannot be thoroughly understood without knowing something about history.

PSYCHOLOGY OR PSYCHOLOGIES?

- Psychology in the late twentieth century is not a unified discipline, and with its recurring debates over fundamental issues, it may never have been one. Modern psychology is marked by increased specialization, and it might be more appropriate to replace the idea of a single field

of psychology with Koch's concept of there being a set of psychological studies. One unifying force in psychology lies in the discipline's history, however.

STUDY QUESTIONS

1. Describe the effects of Titchener's experimentalists and the SEP on the opportunities for women in experimental psychology.

2. What were the barriers faced by Eleanor Gibson on her way to a career as a prominent developmental psychologist?

3. Why was it difficult for some Jewish professors to find academic positions in the United States, especially in the 1930s?

4. What was the essence of the *Brown v. Board of*

Education decision, what prior decision did it overcome, and what role did psychology play?

5. Describe the Clark's doll studies and how they contributed to *Brown v. Board of Education.*

6. Describe five trends that are evident in modern psychology.

7. Explain why it might be better to use the term "psychologies" instead of "psychology."

8. For which reasons can psychology be considered a unified discipline?

FOR FURTHER READING

Guthrie, R. V. (1976). *Even the rat was white: A historical view of psychology.* New York: Harper & Row.

A brief volume that documents the nineteenth- and early twentieth-century research on psychology and race, including chapters on early research comparing the performance of blacks and whites on numerous measuring scales and the effects of eugenic-based legislation; includes chapter-length biographical information on Sumner, and briefer sketches of the contributions of several other African American psychologists (e.g., Herman Canady, the Clarks).

History of psychology: The contributions of Kenneth B. and Mamie Phipps Clark. (2002). *American Psychologist, 57,* 19–59.

A series of four articles (by Lal, Keppel, Benjamin & Crouse, and Pickren & Tomes) describing the life, work, and impact of the Clarks, from the Northside Center to the Brown *decision to the formation of the Board of Social and Ethical Responsibility.*

Koch, S. (1992). Postscript: The second century of psychology at age 12 and the American Psychological

Association at age 100. In S. Koch & D. E. Leary (Eds.), *A century of psychology as science* (pp. 951–968). Washington, DC: American Psychological Association.

The final section of a large set of chapters on developments in psychology over 100 years (plus 12); a reissuing and updating of a book first appearing in 1985 and based on a 1979 symposium celebrating 100 years since Wundt's lab; an eloquent description of Koch's beliefs about the disciplinary status of psychology.

Winston, A. S. (1996). "As his name indicates": R. S. Woodworth's letters of reference and employment for Jewish psychologists in the 1930s. *Journal of the History of the Behavioral Sciences, 32,* 30–43.

A close analysis of Robert Woodworth's letters of recommendation on behalf of Jewish psychologists, set in the context of exclusionary hiring practices in academia and elsewhere, especially during the 1930s; avoids the simplistic presentism of condemning Woodworth for anti-Semitism, using the letters to illustrate what was taken for granted in non-Jewish society at the time.

REFERENCES

Adams, G. (1934, January). The rise and fall of psychology. *The Atlantic Monthly*, 82–92.

Allport, F. H. (1924). *Social psychology*. Boston: Houghton Mifflin.

Allport, G. W. (1937). *Personality; A psychological interpretation*. New York: Holt.

Allport, G. W. (1950). *The individual and his religion*. New York: Macmillan.

Allport, G. W. (1954). *The nature of prejudice*. Cambridge, MA: Addison-Wesley.

Allport, G. W. (1961). *Pattern and growth in personality*. New York: Holt, Rinehart, & Winston.

Allport, G. W. (1965). *Letters from Jenny*. New York: Harcourt, Brace, & World.

Allport, G. W. (1967). Gordon Allport. In E. G. Boring & G. Lindzey (Eds.), *A history of psychology in autobiography. Vol. 5* (pp. 3–25). New York: Appleton-Century.

Allport, G. W., & Vernon, P. E. (1931). *A study of values*. Boston: Houghton.

Anastasi, A. (1954). *Psychological testing*. New York: Macmillan.

Anastasi, A. (1993). A century of psychological testing: Origins, problems, and progress. In T. K. Fagan & G. R. VandenBos (Eds.), *Exploring applied psychology: Origins and critical analyses* (pp. 13–36). Washington, DC: American Psychological Association.

Anderson, J. R. (1990). *Cognitive psychology and its implications* (3rd ed.). New York: Freeman.

Angell, J. R. (1904). *Psychology*. New York: Holt.

Angell, J. R. (1948). The province of functional psychology. In W. Dennis (Ed.), *Readings in the history of psychology* (pp. 439–456). New York: Appleton-Century-Crofts. (Original article published 1907)

Appleby, J., Hunt, L., & Jacob, M. (1994). *Telling the truth about history*. New York: W. W. Norton.

Aronson, E. (1991). Leon Festinger and the art of audacity. *Psychological Science, 2*, 213–217.

Aronson, E. (1999). *The social animal* (8th ed.). New York: W. H. Freeman.

Asch, S. E. (1968). Wolfgang Köhler: 1887–1967. *American Journal of Psychology, 81*, 110–119.

Aserinsky, E., & Kleitman, N. (1953). Regularly occurring periods of eye motility and concomitant phenomena during sleep. *Science, 118*, 273–274.

Ash, M. G. (1985). Gestalt psychology: Origins in Germany and reception in the United States. In C. E. Buxton (Ed.), *Points of view in the modern history of psychology* (pp. 295–344). New York: Academic Press.

Ash, M. G. (1992). Cultural contexts and scientific change in psychology: Kurt Lewin in Iowa. *American Psychologist, 47*, 198–207.

Atkinson, R. C., & Shiffrin, R. M. (1968). Human memory: A proposed system and its control processes. In K. W. Spence & J. T. Spence (Eds.), *The psychology of learning and motivation: Advances in research and theory* (pp. 89–195). New York: Academic Press.

Averill, L. A. (1982). Recollections of Clark's G. Stanley Hall. *Journal of the History of the Behavioral Sciences, 18*, 341–346.

Baars, B. J. (1986). *The cognitive revolution in psychology*. New York: Guilford Press.

Babkin, B. P. (1949). *Pavlov: A biography*. Chicago: University of Chicago Press.

Bache, R. M. (1895). Reaction time with reference to race. *Psychological Review, 2*, 475–486.

Baddeley, A. (1990). *Human memory: Theory and practice*. Boston: Allyn & Bacon.

Bahrick, H. P. (1984). Semantic memory content in permastore: 50 years of memory for Spanish learned in school. *Journal of Experimental Psychology: General, 113*, 1–29.

Bakan, D. (1966). The influence of phrenology on American psychology. *Journal of the History of the Behavioral Sciences, 2*, 200–220.

Baker, D. B. (1988). The psychology of Lightner Witmer. *Professional School Psychology, 3*, 109–121.

Baker, D. B., & Benjamin, L. T., Jr. (2000). The affirmation of the scientist-practitioner: A look back at Boulder. *American Psychologist, 55*, 241–247.

Balance, W. D. G., & Bringmann, W. G. (1987). Fechner's mysterious malady. *History of Psychology Newsletter, 19 (1,2)*, 36–47.

Baldwin, J. M. (1913). *History of psychology: A sketch and an interpretation*. New York: Putnam.

Barker, R., Dembo, T., & Lewin, K. (1941). Frustration and regression: An experiment with young children. *University of Iowa Studies in Child Welfare, 18*, No. 1.

Barone, D. F. (1996). John Dewey: Psychologist, philosopher, and reformer. In G. A. Kimble, C. A. Bonneau, and M. Wertheimer (Eds.), *Portraits of pioneers in psychology, Volume II* (pp.

47–61). Washington, DC: American Psychological Association.

Bartlett, F. C. (1958). *Thinking: An experimental and social study.* London: Allen & Unwin.

Bartlett, F. C. (1967). *Remembering: A study in experimental and social psychology.* Cambridge, UK: Cambridge University Press. (Original work published 1932)

Bayton, J. A. (1975). Francis Sumner, Max Meenes, and the training of black psychologists. *American Psychologist, 30,* 185–186.

Beam, A. (2001). *Gracefully insane: The rise and fall of America's premier mental hospital.* NY: Perseus Books.

Beers, C. W. (1908). *A mind that found itself.* New York: Longmans Green.

Bell, C. (1965). Bell on the specificity of sensory nerves, 1811. In R. J. Herrnstein & E. G. Boring (Eds.), *A sourcebook in the history of psychology* (pp. 23–26). Cambridge, MA: Harvard University Press. (Original work published 1811)

Bell, L. V. (1980). *Treating the mentally ill: From colonial times to the present.* New York: Praeger Publishers.

Benjamin, L. T., Jr. (1993). *A history of psychology in letters.* Dubuque, IA: Brown & Benchmark.

Benjamin, L. T., Jr. (1996). Harry Hollingworth: Portrait of a generalist. In G. A. Kimble, C. A. Bonneau, & M. Wertheimer (Eds.), *Portraits of pioneers in psychology, Volume II* (pp. 119–135). Washington, DC: American Psychological Association.

Benjamin, L. T., Jr. (2000). Hugo Münsterberg: Portrait of an applied psychologist. In G. A. Kimble & M. Wertheimer (Eds.), *Portraits of pioneers in psychology. Volume IV* (pp. 112–129). Washington, DC: American Psychological Association.

Benjamin, L. T., Jr., & Baker, D. B. (2000). Boulder at 50: Introduction to the section. *American Psychologist, 55,* 233–236.

Benjamin, L. T., Jr., & Crouse, E. M. (2002). The American Psychological Association's response to Brown v. Board of Education. *American Psychologist, 57,* 38–50.

Benjamin, L. T., Jr., Durkin, M., Link, M., Vestal, M., & Accord, J. (1992). Wundt's American doctoral students. *American Psychologist, 47,* 123–131.

Benjamin, L. T., Jr., Rogers, A. M., & Rosenbaum, A. (1991). Coca-Cola, caffeine, and mental deficiency: Harry Hollingworth and the Chattanooga trial. *Journal of the History of the Behavioral Sciences, 27,* 42–55.

Bergin, A. E. (1971). The evaluation of therapeutic outcomes. In A. E. Bergin & S. L. Garfield (Eds.), *Handbook of psychotherapy and behavior change: An empirical analysis.* New York: John Wiley & Sons.

Berkeley, G. (1948). An essay towards a new theory of vision. In A. A. Luce & T. E. Jessup (Eds.), *The works of George Berkeley, Bishop of Cloyne. Vol. 1.* London: Thomas Nelson & Sons. (Original work published 1709)

Berkeley, G. (1957). *Treatise concerning the principles of human knowledge.* Indianapolis: Bobbs-Merrill. (Original work published 1710)

Binet, A., & Henri, V. (1965). Alfred Binet (1857–1911) and Victor Henri (1872–1940) on the psychology of individual differences. In R. J. Herrnstein & E. G. Boring (Eds.), *A sourcebook in the history of psychology* (pp. 428–433). Cambridge, MA: Harvard University Press. (Original work published 1895)

Bingham, W. V. (1952). Walter Van Dyke Bingham. In E. G. Boring, H. S. Langfeld, H. Werner, & R. M. Yerkes (Eds.), *A history of psychology in autobiography. Vol. 4* (pp. 1–26). Worcester, MA: Clark University Press.

Bjork, D. W. (1983). *The compromised scientist: William James in the development of American psychology.* New York: Columbia University Press.

Bjork, D. W. (1993). *B. F. Skinner: A life.* New York: Basic Books.

Blodgett, H. C. (1929). The effect of the introduction of reward upon the maze performance of rats. *University of California Publications in Psychology, 4,* 113–134.

Blumenthal, A. L. (1975). A reappraisal of Wilhelm Wundt. *American Psychologist, 30,* 1081–1088.

Blumenthal, A. L. (1980). Wilhelm Wundt and early American psychology: A clash of cultures. In R. W. Reiber & K. Salzinger (Eds.), *Psychology: Theoretical-historical perspectives* (pp. 25–42). New York: Academic Press.

Boakes, R. (1984). *From Darwin to behaviourism: Psychology and the minds of animals.* New York: Cambridge University Press.

Boorstin, D. J. (1971). *Democracy and its discontents: Reflections on everyday America.* New York: Random House.

Boorstin, D. J. (1983). *The discoverers.* New York: Vintage Books.

Boring, E. G. (1929). *A history of experimental psychology.* New York: Century.

Boring, E. G. (1942). *Sensation and perception in the history of experimental psychology.* New York: Appleton-Century-Crofts.

Boring, E. G. (1950). *A history of experimental psychology* (2nd ed.). Englewood Cliffs, NJ: Prentice-Hall.

Boring, E. G. (1950). The influence of evolutionary theory upon American psychological thought. In R. I. Watson & D. T. Campbell (Eds.), *History, psychology, and science: Selected papers by Edwin G. Boring, Harvard University* (pp. 159–184). New York: John Wiley.

Boring, E. G. (1961). *Psychologist at large: An autobiography and selected essays.* New York: Basic Books.

Boring, E. G. (1961). Edward Bradford Titchener, 1867–1927. In E. G. Boring (Ed.), *Psychologist at large: An autobiography and selected essays* (pp. 246–265). New York: Basic Books. (Original work published 1927)

Boring, E. G. (1963a). Eponym as placebo. In R. I. Watson & D. T. Campbell (Eds.), *History, psychology, and science: Selected papers by Edwin G. Boring, Harvard University* (pp. 5–25). New York: John Wiley.

Boring, E. G. (1963b). Fechner: Inadvertent founder of psychophysics. In R. I. Watson & D. T. Campbell (Eds.), *History, psychology, and science: Selected papers by Edwin G. Boring, Harvard University* (pp. 126–131). New York: John Wiley.

Boring, E. G. (1967). Titchener's Experimentalists. *Journal of the History of the Behavioral Sciences, 3*, 315–325.

Boring, E. G., Langfeld, H. S., & Weld, H. P. (1939). *Introduction to psychology.* New York: John Wiley.

Bouchard, T. J., Jr., & McGue, M. (1981). Familial studies of intelligence. *Science, 212,* 1055–1059.

Bower, G. H. (1993). The fragmentation of psychology? *American Psychologist, 48*, 905–907.

Brainerd, C. J. (1996). Piaget: A centennial celebration. *Psychological Science, 7*, 191–195.

Bramel, D., & Friend, R. (1981). Hawthorne, the myth of the docile worker, and class bias in psychology. *American Psychologist, 36*, 867–878.

Bregman, E. O. (1934). An attempt to modify the emotional attitudes of infants by the conditioned response technique. *Journal of Genetic Psychology, 45*, 169–198.

Brehm, J. W. (1998). Leon Festinger: Beyond the obvious. In G. A. Kimble & M. Wertheimer (Eds.), *Portraits of pioneers in psychology. Volume III* (pp. 329–344). Washington, DC: American Psychological Association.

Breuer, J., & Freud, S. (1955). *Studies on hysteria.* New York: Basic Books. (Original work published 1895)

Bridgman, P. W. (1927). *The logic of modern physics.* New York: Macmillan.

Brigham, C. C. (1923). *A study of American intelligence.* Princeton, NJ: Princeton University Press.

Bringmann, W. G., Balance, W. D. G., & Evans, R. B. (1975). Wilhelm Wundt 1832–1920: A brief biographical sketch. *Journal of the History of the Behavioral Sciences, 11*, 287–297.

Bringmann, W. G., Bringmann, N. J., & Balance, W. D. G. (1980). Wilhelm Maximilian Wundt 1832–1920: The formative years. In W. G. Bringmann & R. D. Tweney (Eds.), *Wundt studies: A centennial collection* (pp. 13–32). Toronto: C. J. Hogrefe.

Bringmann, W. G., Bringmann, N. J., & Ungerer, G. A. (1980). The establishment of Wundt's laboratory: An archival and documentary study. In W. G. Bringmann & R. D. Tweney (Eds.), *Wundt studies: A centennial collection* (pp. 123–157). Toronto: C. J. Hogrefe.

Broadbent, D. E. (1980). Donald E. Broadbent. In G. Lindsey (Ed.), *A history of psychology in autobiography. Vol. 7* (pp. 39–73). San Francisco: Freeman.

Broadbent, D. E. (1958). *Perception and communication.* London: Pergamon Press.

Broca, P. (1965). Paul Broca (1824–1880) on the speech center, 1861. In R. J. Herrnstein & E. G. Boring (Eds.), *A sourcebook in the history of psychology* (pp. 223–229). Cambridge, MA: Harvard University Press. (Original work published 1861)

Brown, R., & McNeill, D. (1966). The tip of the tongue phenomenon. *Journal of Verbal Learning and Verbal Behavior, 5*, 325–327.

Browne, J. (1995). *Charles Darwin: A biography. Vol. 1. Voyaging.* New York: Knopf.

Brozek, J., Watson, R. I., & Ross, B. (1970). A summer institute on the history of psychology: Part II. *Journal of the History of the Behavioral Sciences, 6*, 25–35.

Brubacher, J. S., & Rudy, W. (1976). *Higher education in transition: A history of American colleges and universities, 1636–1976* (3rd ed.). New York: Harper and Row.

Bruce, D. B. (1986). Lashley's shift from bacteriology to neuropsychology, 1910–1917, and the influence of Jennings, Watson, and Franz. *Journal of the History of the Behavioral Sciences, 22,* 27–44.

Bruce, D. B. (1991). Integrations of Lashley. In G. A. Kimble, M. Wertheimer, & C. L. White (Eds.), *Portraits of pioneers in psychology* (pp. 306–323). Washington, DC: American Psychological Association.

Bruce, D. B. (1994). Lashley and the problem of serial order. *American Psychologist, 49*, 93–103.

Bruner, J. S. (1968). Gordon Willard Allport: 1897–1967. *American Journal of Psychology, 81,* 279–284.

Bruner, J. S. (1988). Founding the Center for Cognitive Studies. In W. Hirst (Ed.), *The making of cognitive science: Essays in honor of George A. Miller* (pp. 90–99). New York: Cambridge University Press.

Buckley, K. W. (1989). *Mechanical man: John Broadus Watson and the beginnings of behaviorism.* New York: Guilford Press.

Bulatao, E. Q., Fulcher, R., & Evans, R. B. (1992). Appendix: Statistical data on the American Psychological Association. In R. B. Evans, V. S. Sexton, & T. C. Cadwallader (Eds.), *The American Psychological Association: A historical perspective* (pp. 391–394). Washington, DC: American Psychological Association.

Burnham, J. C. (1972). Thorndike's puzzle boxes. *Journal of the History of the Behavioral Sciences, 8*, 159–167.

Buss, D. M. (1999). *Evolutionary psychology: The new science of the mind.* Boston: Allyn & Bacon.

Calkins, M. C. (1894). Association I. *Psychological Review, 1,* 476–483.

Calkins, M. C. (1896). Association II. *Psychological Review, 3,* 32–49.

Calkins, M. C. (1930). Mary Whiton Calkins. In C. Murchison (Ed.), *A history of psychology in autobiography, Vol. 1* (pp. 31–62). Worcester, MA: Clark University Press.

Calkins, M. W. (1906). A reconciliation between structural and functional psychology. *Psychological Review, 13*, 61–81.

Calkins, M. W. (1907). *The persistent problems of philosophy.* New York: Macmillan.

Calkins, M. W. (1913). Psychology and the behaviorist. *Psychological Bulletin, 10*, 288–291.

Camfield, T. M. (1973). The professionalization of American psychology, 1870–1917. *Journal of the History of the Behavioral Sciences, 9*, 66–75.

Capshew, J. H. (1996). Engineering behavior: Project Pigeon, World War II, and the conditioning of B. F. Skinner. In L. D. Smith & W. R. Woodward (Eds.), *B. F. Skinner and behaviorism in American culture* (pp. 128–150). Bethlehem, PA: Lehigh University Press.

Capshew, J. H. (1999). *Psychologists on the march: Science, practice, and professional identity in America, 1929–1969.* New York: Cambridge University Press.

Capshew, J. H., & Hearst, E. (1980). Psychology at Indiana University: From Bryan to Skinner. *Psychological Record, 30,* 319–342.

Carmichael, L. (1957). Robert Mearns Yerkes, 1876–1956. *Psychological Review, 64,* 1–7.

Carr, E. H. (1961). *What is history?* New York: Vintage Books.

Carr, H. A. (1925). *Psychology: A study of mental activity.* New York: Longmans, Green.

Carr, H. A. (1935). *An introduction to space perception.* New York: Longmans, Green.

Carr, H. A., & Watson, J. B. (1908). Orientation in the white rat. *Journal of Comparative Neurology and Psychology, 18,* 27–44.

Cashman, S. D. (1993). *America in the gilded age* (3rd ed.). New York: New York University Press.

Cattell, J. M. (1885). The influence of the intensity of the stimulus on the length of the reaction time. *Brain, 8,* 512–515.

Cattell, J. M. (1886). The time it takes to see and name objects. *Mind, 11,* 63–65.

Cattell, J. M. (1895). Report of the Secretary and Treasurer for 1894. *Psychological Review, 2,* 149–152.

Cattell, J. M. (1948). Mental tests and measurements. In W. Dennis (Ed.), *Readings in the history of psychology* (pp. 347–354). New York: Appleton-Century-Crofts. (Original work published 1890)

Cherry, E. C. (1953). Some experiments on the recognition of speech with one and with two ears. *Journal of the Acoustical Society of America, 25,* 975–979.

Chomsky, N. (1959). Review of Skinner's Verbal Behavior. *Language, 35,* 26–58.

Chomsky, N. (1966). *Cartesian linguistics.* New York: Harper & Row.

Clark, K., & Clark, M. (1947). Racial identification and racial preferences in Negro children. In T. M. Newcomb & E. L. Hartley (Eds.), *Readings in social psychology* (pp. 169–178). New York: Holt.

Cohen, E. (1991, Fall). Psychology's attic. *Akron, 6(1),* 12–19.

Cohen, I. B. (1995). *Science and the founding fathers.* New York: W. W. Norton.

Coleman, S. R. (1996). Skinner's progress during the 1930s: Reflexes, operants, and apparatuses. In L. D. Smith & W. R. Woodward (Eds.), *B. F. Skinner and behaviorism in American culture* (pp. 109–127). Bethlehem, PA: Lehigh University Press.

Collins, A. (1977). Why cognitive science? *Cognitive Science, 1,* 1–2.

Collins, J. (1931). Lightner Witmer: A biographical sketch. In R. A. Brotemarkle (Ed.), *Clinical psychology: Studies in honor of Lightner Witmer* (pp. 3–9). Philadelphia, University of Pennsylvania Press.

Colp, R., Jr. (1986). "Confessing a murder:" Darwin's first revelations about transmutation. *Isis, 77,* 9–32.

Conley, J. J. (1984). Not Galton, but Shakespeare: A note on the origin of the term "nature and nurture." *Journal of the History of the Behavioral Sciences, 20,* 184–185.

Coon, D. J. (1992). Testing the limits of sense and science: American experimental psychologists combat spiritualism, 1880–1920. *American Psychologist, 47,* 143–151.

Coon, D. J. (1994). "Not a creature of reason": The alleged impact of Watsonian behaviorism on advertising in the 1920s. In J. T. Todd & E. K. Morris (Eds.), *Modern perspectives on John B. Watson and classical behaviorism* (pp. 37–63). Westport, CT: Greenwood Press.

Costall, A. (1993). How Lloyd Morgan's Canon backfired. *Journal of the History of the Behavioral Sciences, 29,* 113–122.

Cottingham, J. (1986). *Descartes.* New York: Basil Blackwell.

Crane, L. (1925). A plea for the training of psychologists. *Journal of Abnormal and Social Psychology, 20,* 228–233.

Cravens, H. (1992). A scientific project locked in time: The Terman genetic studies of genius, 1920s–1950s. *American Psychologist, 47,* 183–189.

Croce, P. J. (1995). *Science and religion in the era of William James: Eclipse of certainty, 1820–1880.* Chapel Hill: University of North Carolina Press.

Cronbach, L. J. (1957). The two disciplines of scientific psychology. *American Psychologist, 12,* 671–684.

Cronbach, L. J., Hastorf, A. H., Hilgard, E. R., & Maccoby, E. E. (1990). Robert R. Sears (1908–1989). *American Psychologist, 45,* 663–664.

Crutchfield, R. S. (1961). Edward Chace Tolman: 1886–1959. *American Journal of Psychology, 74,* 135–141.

Cushman, P. (1992). Psychotherapy to 1992: A historically situated interpretation. In D. K. Freedheim (Ed.), *History of psychotherapy: A century of change* (pp. 21–64). Washington, DC: American Psychological Association.

Dallenbach, K. M. (1913). The measurement of attention. *American Journal of Psychology, 24,* 465–507.

Danziger, K. (1980). The history of introspection reconsidered. *Journal of the History of the Behavioral Sciences, 16,* 241–262.

Danziger, K. (2000). Making social psychology experimental: A conceptual history, 1920–1970. *Journal of the History of the Behavioral Sciences, 36,* 329–347.

Darwin, C. (1839). *Journal of researches into the geology and natural history of the various countries visited by the H.M.S. Beagle.* London: Henry Colburn.

Darwin, C. (1871). *The descent of man, and selection in relation to sex.* London: Murray.

Darwin, C. (1872). *The expression of the emotions in man and animals.* London: Murray.

Darwin, C. (1877) A biographical sketch of an infant. *Mind, 2,* 285–294.

Darwin, C. (1958). Autobiography. In F. Darwin (Ed.), *The autobiography of Charles Darwin and selected letters* (pp. 5–58). New York: Dover.

Darwin, C. (1958). *On the origin of species by means of natural selection, or the preservation of favoured races in the struggle for life.* New York: Mentor Books. (Original work published 1859)

Davidson, J. W., & Lytle, M. H. (1982). *After the fact: The art of historical detection.* New York: Knopf.

Decker, H. S. (1975). "The Interpretation of Dreams": Early reception by the educated German public. *Journal of the History of the Behavioral Sciences, 11*, 129–141.

Degler, C. N. (1991). *In search of human nature: The decline and revival of Darwinism in American social thought.* New York: Oxford University Press.

Dennett, D. C. (1995). *Darwin's dangerous idea: Evolution and the meanings of life.* New York: Simon & Schuster.

Dennis, P. M. (1984). The Edison questionnaire. *Journal of the History of the Behavioral Sciences, 20*, 23–37.

Dennis, W. (Ed.). (1948). *Readings in the history of psychology.* New York: Appleton-Century-Crofts.

Denny-Brown, D. (1952). Charles Scott Sherrington: 1857–1952. *American Journal of Psychology, 65*, 474–477.

Descartes, R. (1960). *Discourse on method* (L. J. Lafleur, Trans.). Indianapolis: Bobbs-Merrill. (Original work published 1637)

Descartes, R. (1969). Passions of the soul. In E. S. Haldane & G. R. T. Ross (Trans.) *The philosophical works of Descartes, Volume I* (pp. 329–427). New York: Cambridge University Press. (Original work published 1649)

Desmond, A., & Moore, J. (1991). *Darwin: The life of a tormented evolutionist.* New York: W. W. Norton.

Dewey, J. (1886). *Psychology.* New York: Harper.

Dewey, J. (1899). *The school and society.* Chicago: University of Chicago Press.

Dewey, J. (1900). Psychology and social practice. *Psychological Review, 7*, 105–124.

Dewey, J. (1948). The reflex arc concept in psychology. In W. Dennis (Ed.), *Readings in the history of psychology* (pp. 355–365). New York: Appleton-Century-Crofts. (Original work published 1896)

Dewsbury, D. A. (1984). *Comparative psychology in the twentieth century.* Stroudsburg, PA: Hutchinson Ross.

Dewsbury, D. A. (1990). Early interactions between animal psychologists and animal activists and the founding of the APA committee on precautions in animal experimentation. *American Psychologist, 45*, 315–327.

Dewsbury, D. A. (1990). Whither the introductory course in the history of psychology? *Journal of the History of the Behavioral Sciences, 26*, 371–377.

Dewsbury, D. A. (1992). Triumph and tribulation in the history of comparative psychology. *Journal of Comparative Psychology, 106*, 3–19.

Dewsbury, D. A. (1994). John B. Watson: Profile of a comparative psychologist and proto-ethologist. In J. T. Todd & E. K. Morris (Eds.), *Modern perspectives on John B. Watson and classical behaviorism* (pp. 141–144). Westport, CT: Greenwood Press.

Dewsbury, D. A. (1996). Robert M. Yerkes: A psychobiologist with a plan. In G. A. Kimble, C. A. Bonneau, & M. Wertheimer (Eds.), *Portraits of pioneers in psychology. Vol. II* (pp. 87–105). Washington, DC: American Psychological Association.

Dewsbury, D. A., & Bolles, R. C. (1995). The founding of the Psychonomic Society. *Psychonomic Bulletin and Review, 2*, 216–233.

Diagnostic and statistical manual of mental disorders (4th ed.)(1994). Washington, DC: American Psychiatric Association.

Diamond, I. T. (1985). A history of the study of the cortex: Changes in the concept of the sensory pathway. In G. A. Kimble & K. Schlesinger (Eds.), *Topics in the history of psychology. Vol. 1* (pp. 305–387). Hillsdale, NJ: Lawrence Erlbaum Associates.

Diehl, L. A. (1992). The discovering of Iva Lowther Peters: Transcending male bias in the history of psychology. In J. C. Christer & D. Howard (Eds.), *New directions in feminist psychology: Practice, theory, and research* (pp. 101–115). New York: Springer.

Dollard, J., Doob, L. W., Miller, N. E., Mowrer, O. H., & Sears, R. R. (1939). *Frustration and aggression.* New Haven: Yale University Press.

Donnelly, M. E. (Ed.). (1992). *Reinterpreting the legacy of William James.* Washington, DC: The American Psychological Association.

Dorn, H. (1972). Ernst Heinrich Weber. In C. C. Gillespie (Ed.), *Dictionary of scientific biography. Vol. XIV.* New York: Charles Scribner's Sons.

Duncan, C. P. (1980). A note on the 1929 International Congress of Psychology. *Journal of the History of the Behavioral Sciences, 16*, 1–5.

Duncker, K. (1945). On problem solving. *Psychological Monographs, 58, Whole No. 270.* (Original work published 1935)

Ebbinghaus, H. (1908). *Psychology: An elementary textbook* (M. Meyer, Trans.). Boston: D. C. Heath.

Ebbinghaus, H. (1964). *Memory: A contribution to experimental psychology* (H. A. Ruger & C. A. Bussenius, Trans.). New York: Dover. (Original work published 1885)

Ebbinghaus, H. (1965). Hermann Ebbinghaus (1850–1909) on the completion test. In R. J. Herrnstein & E. G. Boring (Eds.), *A sourcebook in the history of psychology* (pp. 433–437). Cambridge, MA: Harvard University Press. (Original work published 1897)

Eiseley, L. (1958). *Darwin's century: Evolution and the men who discovered it.* New York: Doubleday.

Ellenberger, H. F. (1970). *The discovery of the unconsciousness.* New York: Basic Books.

Ellenberger, H. F. (1972). The story of "Anna O": A critical review with new data. *Journal of the History of the Behavioral Sciences, 8*, 267–279.

Elliott, M. H. (1928). The effect of change of reward on the maze performance of rats. *University of California Publications in Psychology, 4*, 19–30.

Elmes, D. G., Kantowitz, B. H., & Roediger, H. L., III. (2003). *Research methods in psychology* (7th ed.). St. Paul, MN: West.

Emde, R. N., Plomin, R., Robinson, J., Corley, R., DeFries, J., Fulker, D. W., Resnick, J. S., Campos, J., Kagan, J., & Zahn-

Waxler, C. (1992). Temperament, emotion, and cognition at fourteen months: The MacArthur longitudinal twin study. *Child Development, 63*, 1437–1455.

English, H. B. (1929). Three cases of "conditioned fear response." *Journal of Abnormal and Social Psychology, 24*, 221–225.

Estes, W. K. (1981). The bible is out. *Contemporary Psychology, 26*, 327–330.

Evans, R. B. (1972). E. B. Titchener and his lost system. *Journal of the History of the Behavioral Sciences, 8*, 168–180.

Evans, R. B. (1984). The origins of American academic psychology. In J. Brozek (Ed.), *Explorations in the history of psychology in the United States* (pp. 17–60). Lewisburg, PA: Bucknell University Press.

Evans, R. B., & Cohen, J. B. (1987). "The American Journal of Psychology": A retrospective. *American Journal of Psychology, 100*, 321–362.

Evans, R. B., Sexton, V. S., & Cadwallader, T. C. (1992). *The American Psychological Association: A historical perspective*. Washington, DC: American Psychological Association.

Eysenck, H. J. (1952). The effects of psychotherapy: An evaluation. *Journal of Consulting Psychology, 16*, 319–324.

Eysenck, H. J. (Ed.). (1960). *Behaviour therapy and the neuroses*. London: Pergamon.

Fancher, R. E. (1985). *The intelligence men: Makers of the IQ controversy*. New York: W. W. Norton.

Fancher, R. E. (1990). *Pioneers of psychology* (2nd ed.). New York: W. W. Norton.

Farr, R. M. (1983). Wilhelm Wundt (1832–1920) and the origins of psychology as an experimental and social science. *British Journal of Social Psychology, 22*, 289–301.

Farson, R. (1978). The technology of humanism. *Journal of Humanistic Psychology, 18*, 5–35.

Fearing, F. (1930). *Reflex action: A study in the history of physiological psychology*. New York: Hafner.

Fernberger, S. W. (1931). The history of the psychological clinic. In R. A. Brotemarkle (Ed.), *Clinical psychology: Studies in honor of Lightner Witmer* (pp. 10–36). Philadelphia: University of Pennsylvania Press.

Fernberger, S. W. (1932). The American Psychological Association: A historical summary, 1892–1930. *Psychological Bulletin, 29*, 1–89.

Ferrier, D. (1876). *The functions of the brain*. New York: Putnam.

Ferster, C. B., & Skinner, B. F. (1957). *Schedules of reinforcement*. New York: Appleton-Century-Crofts.

Festinger, L. (1957). *A theory of cognitive dissonance*. Evanston, IL: Row, Peterson, & Co.

Festinger, L. (1980). Looking backward. In L. Festinger (Ed.), *Retrospections on social psychology* (pp. 236–254). New York: Oxford University Press.

Festinger, L., & Carlsmith, J. M. (1959). Cognitive consequences of forced compliance. *Journal of Abnormal and Social Psychology, 58*, 203–211.

Finger, S. (2000). *Minds behind the brain: A history of the pioneers and their discoveries*. New York: Oxford University Press.

Fisher, R. A. (1925). *Statistical methods for research workers*. London: Oliver & Boyd.

Fisher, R. A. (1935). *The design of experiments*. London: Oliver & Boyd.

Fiske, S. T., & Taylor, S. E. (1984). *Social cognition*. Reading, MA: Addison-Wesley.

Flaherty, F. C. (1985). *Animal learning and cognition*. New York: McGraw-Hill.

Flavell, J. H. (1963). *The developmental psychology of Jean Piaget*. Princeton, NJ: Van Nostrand Reinhold.

Flourens, P. (1978). Phrenology examined (C. D. Meigs, Trans.). In D. N. Robinson (Ed.), *Significant contributions to the history of psychology. Series E. Volume II*. Washington, DC: University Publications of America. (Original work published 1846)

Forrest, D. W. (1974). *Francis Galton: The life and work of a Victorian genius*. New York: Taplinger.

Frank, J. D. (1978). Kurt Lewin in retrospect—A psychiatrist's view. *Journal of the History of the Behavioral Sciences, 14*, 223–227.

Freeman, F. N. (1922). The mental age of adults. *Journal of Educational Research, 6*, 441–444.

Freeman, F. S. (1977). The beginnings of Gestalt psychology in the United States. *Journal of the History of the Behavioral Sciences, 13*, 352–353.

Freud, A. (1928). *Introduction to the technique of child analysis*. New York: Nervous and Mental Disease Publishing Co.

Freud, A. (1937). *The ego and mechanisms of defense*. New York: International Universities Press.

Freud, S. (1938). *The interpretation of dreams*. In A. A. Brill (Ed. & Trans.), *The basic writings of Sigmund Freud* (pp. 179–549). New York: Random House. (Original work published 1900)

Freud, S. (1938). *The psychopathology of everyday life*. In A. A. Brill (Ed. & Trans.), *The basic writings of Sigmund Freud* (pp. 33–178). New York: Random House. (Original work published 1901)

Freud, S. (1938). *Three contributions to the theory of sex*. In A. A. Brill (Ed. & Trans.), *The basic writings of Sigmund Freud* (pp. 551–629). New York: Random House. (Original work published 1905)

Freud, S. (1938). *Wit and its relation to the unconscious*. In A. A. Brill (Ed. & Trans.), *The basic writings of Sigmund Freud* (pp. 631–803). New York: Random House. (Original work published 1905)

Freud, S. (1959). *Beyond the pleasure principle* (J. Strachey, Trans.). New York: Bantam Books. (Original work published 1920)

Freud, S. (1959). *The ego and the id* (J. Strachey, Trans.). New York: Bantam Books. (Original work published 1923)

Freud, S. (1977). *Five lectures on psycho-analysis* (J. Strachey, Trans.). New York: W. W. Norton. (Original work published 1909)

Fritsch, G., & Hitzig, E. (1965). Gustav Fritsch (1838–1927) and Eduard Hitzig (1838–1907) on cerebral motor centers, 1870.

In R. J. Herrnstein & E. G. Boring (Eds.), *A sourcebook in the history of psychology* (pp. 229–233). Cambridge, MA: Harvard University Press. (Original work published 1870)

Fuchs, A. H. (2000). Contributions of American mental philosophers to psychology in the United States. *History of Psychology, 3*, 3–19.

Fuchs, A. H., & Viney, W. (2002). The course in the history of psychology: Present status and future concerns. *Journal of the History of the Behavioral Sciences, 5*, 3–15.

Furumoto, L. (1979). Mary Whiton Calkins (1863–1930): Fourteenth president of the American Psychological Association. *Journal of the History of the Behavioral Sciences, 15*, 346–356.

Furumoto, L. (1988). Shared knowledge: The Experimentalists, 1904–1929. In J. G. Morawski (Ed.), *The rise of experimentation in American psychology* (pp. 94–113). New Haven, CT: Yale University Press.

Furumoto, L. (1989). The new history of psychology. In I. S. Cohen (Ed.), *The G. Stanley Hall lecture series. Vol. 9* (pp. 9–34). Washington, DC: American Psychological Association.

Furumoto, L. (1991). From "paired associates" to a psychology of self: The intellectual odyssey of Mary Whiton Calkins. In G. A. Kimble, M. Wertheimer, & C. L. White (Eds.), *Portraits of pioneers in psychology* (pp. 56–72). Washington, DC: American Psychological Association.

Furumoto, L. (1992). Joining separate spheres—Christine Ladd-Franklin, woman-scientist (1847–1930). *American Psychologist, 47*, 175–182.

Galef, B. G., Jr. (1998). Edward Thorndike: revolutionary psychologist, ambiguous biologist. *American Psychologist, 53*, 1128–1134.

Gall, F. J. (1965). Franz Joseph Gall (1758–1828) on phrenology, the localization of the functions of the brain, 1825. In R. J. Herrnstein & E. G. Boring (Eds.), *A sourcebook in the history of psychology* (pp. 211–220). Cambridge, MA: Harvard University Press. (Original work published 1825)

Gallistel, C. R. (1981). Bell, Magendie, and the proposals to restrict the use of animals in neurobehavioral research. *American Psychologist, 36*, 357–360.

Galton, F. (1874). *English men of science: Their nature and nurture.* London: Macmillan.

Galton, F. (1883). *An inquiry into human faculty and its development.* London: Macmillan.

Galton, F. (1891). *Hereditary genius.* New York: D. Appleton. (Original work published 1869)

Galton, F. (1908). *Memories of my life.* London: Methuen.

Galton, F. (1965). Galton on mental capacity, 1883. In R. J. Herrnstein & E. G. Boring (Eds.), *A sourcebook in the history of psychology* (pp. 421–423). Cambridge, MA: Harvard University Press. (Original work published 1883)

Gantt, W. H. (1973). Reminiscences of Pavlov. *Journal of the Experimental Analysis of Behavior, 20*, 131–136.

Gardner, H. (1985). *The mind's new science: A history of the cognitive revolution.* New York: Basic Books.

Garrett, H. E. (1951). *Great experiments in psychology* (3rd ed.). New York: Appleton-Century-Crofts.

Gay, P. (1988). *Freud: A life for our time.* New York: W. W. Norton.

Gibson, E. J. (1980). Eleanor Gibson. In G. Lindsey (Ed.), *A history of psychology in autobiography. Vol. 7* (pp. 239–271). San Francisco: Freeman and Company.

Gibson, E. J. (1994). Has psychology a future? *Psychological Science, 5*, 69–76.

Gibson, E. J., & Walk, R. D. (1960). The "visual cliff." *Scientific American, 202*, 64–71.

Gilbreath, F. B., & Gilbreath, L. M. (1916). *Fatigue study: The elimination of humanity's greatest unnecessary waste.* New York: Sturgis & Walton.

Gilbreath, F. B., & Gilbreath, L. M. (1917). *Applied motion study.* New York: Sturgis & Walton.

Gilbreth, F. B., Jr., & Carey, E. G. (1949). *Cheaper by the dozen.* New York: Bantam.

Gilderhus, M. T. (2000). *History and historians: A historiographic introduction* (4th ed.). Upper Saddle River, NJ: Prentice-Hall.

Gillespie, R. (1988). The Hawthorne experiments and the politics of experimentation. In J. G. Morawski (Ed.), *The rise of experimentation in American psychology* (pp. 114–137).

Gillespie, R. (1991). *Manufacturing knowledge: A history of the Hawthorne experiments.* New York: Cambridge University Press.

Gillies, D. (1993). *Philosophy of science in the twentieth century: Four central themes.* Oxford, UK: Blackwell Press.

Glass, C. R., & Arnkoff, D. B. (1992). Behavior therapy. In D. K. Freedheim (Ed.), *History of psychotherapy: A century of change* (pp. 587–628). Washington, DC: American Psychological Association.

Gleaves, D. H., & Hernandez, E. (1999). Recent formulations of Freud's development and abandonment of his seduction theory: Historical/scientific clarification or a continued assault on truth? *History of Psychology, 2*, 324–354.

Glickman, S. E. (1996). Donald Olding Hebb: Returning the nervous system to psychology. In G. A. Kimble, C. A. Bonneau, & M. Wertheimer (Eds.) *Portraits of pioneers in psychology. Vol. II* (pp. 227–244). Washington, DC: American Psychological Association.

Goddard, H. H. (1910). Four hundred feeble-minded children classified by the Binet method. *Journal of Genetic Psychology, 17*, 387–397.

Goddard, H. H. (1912). *The Kallikak family: A study in the heredity of feeble-mindedness.* New York: Macmillan.

Goddard, H. H. (1913). The Binet tests in relation to immigration. *Journal of Psycho-Asthenics, 18*, 105–107.

Goddard, H. H. (1917). Mental tests and the immigrant. *Journal of Delinquency, 2*, 243–277.

Goddard, H. H. (1928). Feeblemindedness: A question of definition. *Journal of Psycho-Asthenics, 33*, 219–227.

Goldstein, E. B. (1996). *Sensation and perception* (4th edition). Pacific Grove, CA: Brooks/Cole.

Goodenough, F. L. (1950). Edward Lee Thorndike: 1874–1949. *American Journal of Psychology, 63,* 291–301.

Goodwin, C. J. (1985). On the origins of Titchener's Experimentalists. *Journal of the History of the Behavioral Sciences, 21,* 383–389.

Goodwin, C. J. (1987). In Hall's shadow: Edmund Clark Sanford (1859–1924). *Journal of the History of the Behavioral Sciences, 23,* 153–168.

Goodwin, C. J. (1991). Misportraying Pavlov's apparatus. *American Journal of Psychology, 104,* 135–141.

Goodwin, C. J. (1991). Using psychologists' letters to teach about introspection. *Teaching of Psychology, 18,* 237–238.

Goodwin, C. J. (1993, August). *Experimental psychology first-hand: The diaries of Walter Miles.* American Psychological Association, Toronto, Canada.

Goodwin, C. J. (2001, August). *Reorganizing Titchener's experimentalists.* American Psychological Association, San Francisco, CA.

Gould, S. J. (1981). *The mismeasure of man.* New York: W. W. Norton.

Gravitz, M. A. (1988). Early uses of hypnosis as surgical anesthesia. *American Journal of Clinical Hypnosis, 30,* 201–208.

Gray, J. A. (1979). *Ivan Pavlov.* New York: Viking.

Gray, P. H. (1962). Douglas Alexander Spalding: The first experimental behaviorist. *Journal of General Psychology, 67,* 299–307.

Green, M., & Rieber, R. W. (1980). The assimilation of psychoanalysis in America. In R. W. Rieber & K. Salzinger (Eds.), *Psychology: Theoretical-historical perspectives* (pp. 263–304). New York: Academic Press.

Greenwood, J. D. (2003). Wundt, Volkerpsychologie, and experimental social psychology. *History of Psychology, 6,* 70–88.

Grmek, M. D. (1972). François Magendie. In C. C. Gillespie (Ed.), *Dictionary of scientific biography. Vol. IX.* New York: Scribner.

Grob, G. N. (1983). *Mental illness and American society, 1875–1940.* Princeton, NJ: Princeton University Press.

Grob, G. N. (1991). *From asylum to community: Mental health policy in modern America.* Princeton, NJ: Princeton University Press.

Grob, G. N. (1994). *The mad among us: A history of the care of America's mentally ill.* New York: Free Press.

Gundlach, H. U. K. (1986). Ebbinghaus, nonsense syllables, and three-letter words. *Contemporary Psychology, 31,* 469–470.

Guthrie, E. R. (1935). *The psychology of learning.* New York: Harper and Brothers.

Guthrie, R. V. (1976). *Even the rat was white: A historical view of psychology.* New York: Harper & Row.

Guttman, N. (1977). On Skinner and Hull: A reminiscence and projection. *American Psychologist, 32,* 321–328.

Haldane, J. B. S. (1954). Introducing Douglas Spalding. *British Journal of Animal Behavior, 2,* 1–11.

Hale, N. G., Jr. (1971). *Freud and the Americans: The beginnings of psychoanalysis in the United States, 1876–1917.* New York: Oxford University Press.

Hall, C. S. (1954). *A primer of Freudian psychology.* New York: World Publishing Company.

Hall, C. S., & Lindzey, G. (1970). *Theories of personality* (2nd ed.). New York: John Wiley & Sons.

Hall, G. S. (1887). Editorial. *American Journal of Psychology, 1,* 3–4.

Hall, G. S. (1890–1891). Review of "The Principles of Psychology." *American Journal of Psychology, 3,* 578–591.

Hall, G. S. (1904). *Adolescence.* New York: Appleton.

Hall, G. S. (1922). *Senescence: The last half of life.* New York: Appleton.

Hall, G. S. (1923). *Life and confessions of a psychologist.* New York: Appleton.

Hall, G. S. (1948). The contents of children's minds. In W. Dennis (Ed.), *Readings in the history of psychology* (pp. 255–276). New York: Appleton-Century-Crofts. (Original work published 1883)

Hannush, M. J. (1987). John B. Watson remembered: An interview with James B. Watson. *Journal of the History of the Behavioral Sciences, 23,* 137–152.

Harlow, J. M. (1869). *Recovery from the passage of an iron bar through the head.* Boston: Clapp.

Harmon-Jones, E., & Mills, J. (Eds.). (1999). *Cognitive dissonance: Progress on a pivotal theory in social psychology.* Washington, DC: American Psychological Association.

Harris, B. (1979). Whatever happened to Little Albert? *American Psychologist, 34,* 151–160.

Harrower-Erickson, M. R. (1942). Kurt Koffka: 1886–1941. *American Journal of Psychology, 55,* 278–281.

Hartley, D. (1971). *Observations on man, his frame, his duty, and his expectations. Volume I.* New York: Garland. (Original work published 1749)

Havens, L. L. (1965). Emil Kraepelin. *Journal of Nervouse and Mental Disease, 141,* 16–28.

Hawkins, H. (1960). *Pioneer: A history of the Johns Hopkins University, 1874–1899.* Ithaca, NY: Cornell University Press.

Hebb, D. O. (1949). *The organization of behavior.* New York: John Wiley.

Hebb, D. O. (1959). Karl Spencer Lashley (1890–1958). *American Journal of Psychology, 72,* 142–150.

Hebb, D. O. (1960). The American revolution. *American Psychologist, 15,* 735–745.

Hebb, D. O. (1980). D. O. Hebb. In G. Lindsey (Ed.), *A history of psychology in autobiography. Vol. 7* (pp. 273–303). San Francisco: Freeman and Company.

Heidbreder, E. (1933). *Seven psychologies.* New York: Appleton-Century-Crofts.

Heims, S. (1978). Kurt Lewin and social change. *Journal of the History of the Behavioral Sciences, 14,* 238–241.

Helmholtz, H. (1965). Hermann Ludwig Ferdinand von Helmholtz (1821–1894) on the three-color theory of vision and visual specific nerve energies, 1860. In R. J. Herrnstein & E. G. Boring (Eds.), *A sourcebook in the history of psychology* (pp. 223–229). Cambridge, MA: Harvard University Press. (Original work published 1860)

Henle, M. (1974). E. B. Titchener and the case of the missing element. *Journal of the History of the Behavioral Sciences, 10,* 227–237.

Henle, M. (1980). The influence of Gestalt psychology in America. In R. W. Rieber & K. Salzinger (Eds.), *Psychology: Theoretical-historical perspectives* (pp. 177–190). New York: Academic Press.

Henle, M. (1986). One man against the Nazis—Wolfgang Köhler. In M. Henle (Ed.), *1879 and all that: Essays in the theory and history of psychology* (pp. 225–237). New York: Columbia University Press.

Herman, E. (1995). *The romance of American psychology: Political culture in the age of experts.* Berkeley, CA: University of California Press.

Hertzman, M., & Festinger, L. (1940). Shifts in explicit goals in a level of aspiration experiment. *Journal of Experimental Psychology, 27,* 439–452.

Hicks, L. H., & Ridley, S. E. (1979). Black studies in psychology. *American Psychologist, 34,* 597–602.

Hilgard, E. R. (1948). *Theories of learning.* New York: Appleton-Century-Crofts.

Hilgard, E. R. (1957). Lewis Madison Terman: 1877–1956. *American Journal of Psychology, 70,* 472–479.

Hilgard, E. R. (1964). *Introduction to Dover Edition of "Memory: A contribution to experimental psychology."* New York: Dover.

Hilgard, E. R. (1967). Kenneth Wartinbee Spence: 1907–1967. *American Journal of Psychology, 80,* 314–318.

Hilgard, E. R. (1980). The trilogy of mind: Cognition, affection, and conation. *Journal of the History of the Behavioral Sciences, 16,* 107–117.

Hilgard, E. R. (1982). Robert I. Watson and the founding of Division 26 of the American Psychological Association. *Journal of the History of the Behavioral Sciences, 18,* 308–311.

Hilgard, E. R. (1987). *Psychology in America: A historical survey.* San Diego: Harcourt Brace Jovanovich.

Hindeland, M. J. (1971). Edward Bradford Titchener: A pioneer in perception. *Journal of the History of the Behavioral Sciences, 7,* 23–28.

Hoffeld, D. R. (1980). Mesmer's failure: Sex, politics, personality, and the zeitgeist. *Journal of the History of the Behavioral Sciences, 16,* 377–386.

Hofstadter, R., & Hardy, C. D. (1952). *The development and scope of higher education in the United States.* New York: Columbia University Press.

Hollingworth, H. L. (1916). *Vocational psychology: Its problems and methods.* New York: D. Appleton and Company.

Hollingworth, H. L. (1990). *Leta Stetter Hollingworth: A biography.* Bolton, MA: Anker Publishing. (Original work published 1943)

Hornstein, G. A. (1992). The return of the repressed: Psychology's problematic relations with psychoanalysis, 1909–1960. *American Psychologist, 47,* 254–263.

Hothersall, D. (1995). *History of psychology* (3rd ed.). New York: McGraw-Hill.

Hubel, D. H., & Wiesel, T. N. (1963). Receptive fields of cells in the striate cortex of very young, visually inexperienced kittens. *Journal of Neurophysiology, 26,* 994–1002.

Hull, C. L. (1920). Quantitative aspects of the evolution of concepts. *Psychological Monographs, 28,* No. 123.

Hull, C. L. (1928). *Aptitude testing.* Yonkers-on-Hudson, NY: Word Book.

Hull, C. L. (1933). *Hypnosis and suggestibility: An experimental approach.* New York: Appleton-Century.

Hull, C. L. (1943). *Principles of behavior.* New York: Appleton-Century-Crofts.

Hull, C. L. (1952a). *A behavior system.* New Haven, CT: Yale University Press.

Hull, C. L. (1952b). Clark L. Hull. In E. G. Boring, H. S. Langfeld, H. Werner, & R. M. Yerkes (Eds.), *A history of psychology in autobiography. Vol. 4* (143–162). Worcester, MA: Clark University Press.

Hume, D. (1969). *A treatise of human nature* (E. C. Mossner, Ed.). Baltimore: Penguin. (Original work published 1739–1740)

Hunter, W. S. (1919). *General psychology.* Chicago: University of Chicago Press.

Hunter, W. S. (1949). James Rowland Angell, 1869–1949. *American Journal of Psychology, 62,* 439–450.

Izard, C. E. (1977). *Human emotions.* New York: Plenum.

Jackson, J. P., Jr. (2000). The triumph of the segregationalists? A historiographic inquiry into psychology and the Brown litigation. *History of Psychology, 3,* 239–261.

Jacobson, E. (1929). *Progressive relaxation.* Chicago: University of Chicago Press.

James, W. (1891, December 20). *Letter to M. W. Calkins.* Calkins Papers, Wellesley College, Wellesley, MA.

James, W. (1950). *Principles of psychology. Vol. 1.* New York: Dover. (Original work published 1890)

James, W. (1950). *Principles of psychology. Vol. 2.* New York: Dover. (Original work published 1890)

James, W. (1961). *Psychology: The briefer course.* New York: Harper & Row. (Original work published 1892)

Jaynes, J. (1969). The historical origins of "ethology" and "comparative psychology." *Animal Behaviour, 17,* 601–606.

Jaynes, J. (1969). Edwin Garrigues Boring: 1886–1968. *Journal of the History of the Behavioral Sciences, 5,* 99–112.

Jeffreys, M. V. C. (1967). *John Locke: Prophet of common sense.* London: Methuen.

Jenkins, J. G. (1935). Review of Remembering by F. C. Bartlett. *American Journal of Psychology, 47,* 712–715.

Jenkins, J. G., & Dallenbach, K. M. (1924). Minor studies from the psychological laboratory of Cornell University: Oblivescence during sleep and waking. *American Journal of Psychology, 35,* 605–612.

Johnson, M. G., & Henley, T. B. (Eds.). (1990). *Reflections on "The Principles of Psychology."* Hillsdale, NJ: Lawrence Erlbaum.

Johnston, T. D. (2003). Three pioneers of comparative psychology in America, 1843–1890. *History of Psychology, 6,* 14–51.

Jonçich, G. (1968). *The sane positivist: A biography of Edward L. Thorndike.* Middletown, CT: Wesleyan University Press.

Jones, E. (1953, 1955, 1957). *The life and work of Sigmund Freud (Vols. 1–3).* New York: Basic Books.

Jones, M. C. (1924a). The elimination of children's fear. *Journal of Experimental Psychology, 7,* 382–390.

Jones, M. C. (1924b). A laboratory study of fear: The case of Peter. *Pedagogical Seminary, 31,* 308–315.

Joynt, R. J. (1973, October). Phrenology in New York State. *New York State Journal of Medicine,* 2382–2384.

Jung, C. G. (1919). *Studies in word association.* New York: Moffat-Yard.

Kant, I. (1952). *Critique of judgment* (J. C. Meredith, Trans.). Oxford: Oxford University Press. (Original work published 1788)

Kant, I. (1959). *Critique of practical reason.* (T. K. Abbott, Trans.). New York: Longmans, Green. (Original work published 1790)

Kant, I. (1965). *Critique of pure reason.* (N. K. Smith, Trans.). New York: St. Martin's. (Original work published 1781)

Katona, G. (1940). *Organizing and memorizing.* New York: Columbia University Press.

Kazdin, A. E. (1978). *History of behavior modification: Experimental foundations of contemporary research.* Baltimore: University Park Press.

Kent, D. (1992, September). E. Gibson, A. Newell receive National Medal of Science. *APS Observer, 5(1),* 14–15.

Keppel, B. (2002). Kenneth B. Clark in the patterns of American culture. *American Psychologist, 57,* 29–37.

Kessen, W. (1996). American psychology just before Piaget. *Psychological Science, 7,* 196–199.

Kessen, W., & Kuhlman, C. (Eds.). (1962). Thought in the young child: Report of a conference on intellective development with particular attention to the work of Jean Piaget. *Monographs of the Society for Research in Child Development, 27* (Serial No. 83).

Kevles, D. J. (1968). Testing the Army's intelligence: Psychologists and the military in World War I. *Journal of American History, 55,* 565–581.

Kimble, G. A. (1991). Psychology from the standpoint of a mechanist: An appreciation of Clark L. Hull. In G. A. Kimble, M. Wertheimer, & C. L. White (Eds.), *Portraits of pioneers in psychology.* Washington, DC: American Psychological Association.

King, D. B. (1992). Evolution and revision of the Principles. In M. E. Donnelly (Ed.), *Reinterpreting the legacy of William James* (pp. 67–75). Washington, DC: The American Psychological Association.

King, H. (1955). *The history of the telescope.* London: Griffin.

Kinnaman, A. J. (1902). Mental life of two Macacus rhesus monkeys in captivity. II. *American Journal of Psychology, 13,* 173–218.

Kintsch, W. (1985). Reflections on Ebbinghaus. *Journal of Experimental Psychology: Learning, Memory, and Cognition, 11,* 461–463.

Kintsch, W., & Cacioppo, J. T. (1994). Introduction to the 100th anniversary issue of the *Psychological Review. Psychological Review, 101,* 195–199.

Kirsch, I. (1977). Psychology's first paradigm. *Journal of the History of the Behavioral Sciences, 13,* 317–325.

Klein, A. G. (2002). *Forgotten voice: A biography of Leta Stetter Hollingworth.* Scottsdale, AZ: Great Potential Press.

Klein, D. B. (1970). *A history of scientific psychology: Its origins and philosophical background.* New York: Basic Books.

Kline, L. W. (1899). Suggestions toward a laboratory course in comparative psychology. *American Journal of Psychology, 10,* 399–430.

Klopfer, W. G. (1973). The short history of projective techniques. *Journal of the History of the Behavioral Sciences, 9,* 60–65.

Kluger, R. (1987). *Simple justice: The history of* Brown v. Board of Education *and black America's struggle for equality.* New York: Knopf.

Knapp, T. J. (1985). Contributions to the history of psychology: XXXIX. T. V. Moore and his Cognitive Psychology of 1939. *Psychological Reports, 57,* 1311–1316.

Koch, S. (1992). Postscript: The second century of psychology at age 12 and the American Psychological Association at age 100. In S. Koch & D. E. Leary (Eds.), *A century of psychology as science* (pp. 951–968). Washington, DC: American Psychological Association.

Koch, S. (1992). Wundt's creature at age zero—and as centenarian: Some aspects of the institutionalization of the "new psychology." In S. Koch & D. E. Leary (Eds.), *A century of psychology as science* (pp. 7–35). Washington, DC: American Psychological Association. (Original work published 1985)

Koch, S. (1993). "Psychology" or "the psychological studies"? *American Psychologist, 48,* 902–904.

Koffka, K. (1922). Perception: An introduction to Gestalt-theorie. *Psychological Bulletin, 19,* 531–585.

Koffka, K. (1924). *The growth of the mind: An introduction to child psychology* (R. M. Ogden, Trans.). New York: Harcourt, Brace. (Original work published 1921)

Koffka, K. (1935). *Principles of Gestalt psychology.* New York: Harcourt, Brace.

Köhler, W. (1926). *The mentality of apes* (E. Winter, Trans.). New York: Harcourt, Brace. (Original work published 1917)

Köhler, W. (1947). *Gestalt psychology.* New York: Liveright. (Original work published 1929)

Köhler, W. (1969). *Gestalt psychology.* In D. L. Krantz (Ed.), Schools of psychology: A symposium (pp. 69–85). New York: Appleton-Century-Crofts. (Original work published 1967)

Korn, J. H. (1997). *Illusions of reality: A history of deception in social psychology.* Albany, NY: SUNY Press.

Korn, J. H., Davis, R., & Davis, S. F. (1991). Historians' and chairpersons' judgments of eminence among psychologists. *American Psychologist, 46,* 789–792.

Krantz, D. L. (1969). The Baldwin-Titchener controversy. In D. L. Krantz (Ed.), *Schools of psychology: A symposium* (pp. 1–19). New York: Appleton-Century-Crofts.

Kroll, J. (1973). A reappraisal of psychiatry in the Middle Ages. *Archives of General Psychiatry, 29,* 276–283.

Kuhn, T. S. (1962). *The structure of scientific revolutions.* Chicago: University of Chicago Press.

Lakin, M. (1996). Carl Rogers and the culture of psychotherapy. *The General Psychologist, 32,* 62–68.

Lal, S. (2002). Giving children security: Mamie Phipps Clark and the racialization of child psychology. *American Psychologist, 57,* 20–28.

Landy, F. J. (1992). Hugo Münsterberg: Victim or visionary? *Journal of Applied Psychology, 77,* 787–802.

Landy, F. J. (1993). Early influences on the development of industrial/organizational psychology. In T. K. Fagan & G. R. VandenBos (Eds.), *Exploring applied psychology: Origins and critical analyses* (pp. 83–118). Washington, DC: American Psychological Association.

Larson, C., & Sullivan, J. J. (1965). Watson's relation to Titchener. *Journal of the History of the Behavioral Sciences, 1,* 338–354.

Lashley, K. S. (1929). *Brain mechanisms and intelligence.* Chicago: University of Chicago Press.

Lashley, K. S. (1951). The problem of serial order in behavior. In L. A. Jeffress (Ed.), *Cerebral mechanisms in behavior: The Hixon symposium* (pp. 112–146). New York: John Wiley.

Lathem, E. C. (1994). *Bernard Bailyn on the teaching and writing of history: Responses to a series of questions.* Hanover, NH: University Press of New England.

Leacock, S. (1924, March). A manual of the new mentality. *Harper's Monthly Magazine, 47,* 480.

Leahey, T. H. (1979). Something old, something new: Attention in Wundt and modern cognitive psychology. *Journal of the History of the Behavioral Sciences, 15,* 242–252.

Leahey, T. H. (1981). The mistaken mirror: On Wundt's and Titchener's psychologies. *Journal of the History of the Behavioral Sciences, 17,* 273–282.

Leahey, T. H. (1992). The mythical revolutions of American psychology. *American Psychologist, 47,* 308–318.

Leary, D. E. (1992). William James and the art of human understanding. *American Psychologist, 47,* 152–160.

Leibnitz, G. W. (1982). *New essays on human understanding* (P. Remnant & J. Bennett, Trans.). New York: Cambridge University Press. (Original work published 1765)

Lesch, J. E. (1972). George John Romanes. In C. C. Gillespie (Ed.), *Dictionary of scientific biography. Vol. XI.* New York: Scribner.

Lewin, K. (1931). Environmental forces in child behavior and development. In C. Murchison (Ed.), *Handbook of child psychology* (pp. 94–127). Worcester, MA: Clark University Press.

Lewin, K. (1935). *A dynamic theory of personality* (D. K. Adams & K. E. Zener, Trans.). New York: McGraw-Hill.

Lewin, K. (1936). *Principles of topological psychology* (F. Heider & G. M. Heider, Trans.). New York: McGraw-Hill.

Lewin, K. (1937). Cark Stumpf. *Psychological Review, 44,* 189–194.

Lewin, K., Lippitt, R., & White, R. (1939). Patterns of aggressive behavior in experimentally created "social climates." *Journal of Social Psychology, 10,* 271–299.

Lewis, R. W. B. (1991). *The Jameses: A family narrative.* New York: Farrar, Straus, & Giroux.

Ley, R. (1990). *A whisper of espionage.* Garden Park, NY: Avery Publishing Group.

Leys, R., & Evans, R. B. (1990). *Defining American psychology: The correspondence between Adolf Meyer and Edward Bradford Titchener.* Baltimore, MD: The Johns Hopkins University Press.

Lippit, R., & White, R. K. (1943). The "social climate" of children's groups. In R. G. Barker, J. S. Kounin, & H. F. Wright (Eds.), *Child behavior and development* (pp. 485–508). New York: McGraw-Hill.

Lippmann, W. (1922a). A future for tests. *New Republic, 33,* 9–10.

Lippmann, W. (1922b). The abuse of tests. *New Republic, 32,* 297–298.

Lloyd, M. A., & Brewer, C. B. (1992). National conferences on undergraduate education. In A. E. Puente, J. R. Matthews, & C. B. Brewer (Eds.), *Teaching psychology in America: A history* (pp. 263–284). Washington, DC: American Psychological Association.

Locke, J. (1960). *Two treatises on government.* New York: Cambridge University Press. (Original work published 1690)

Locke, J. (1963). *Some thoughts concerning education.* Germany: Scientia Verlag Aalen. (Original work published 1693)

Locke, J. (1963). *An essay concerning human understanding.* Germany: Scientia Verlag Aalen. (Original work published 1690)

Loftus, E. F. (1979). *Eyewitness testimony.* Cambridge, MA: Harvard University Press.

Logan, C. A. (2002). When scientific knowledge becomes scientific discovery: The disappearance of classical conditioning before Pavlov. *Journal of the History of the Behavioral Sciences, 38,* 393–403.

Macfarlane, D. A. (1930). The role of kinesthesis in maze learning. *University of California Publications in Psychology, 4,* 277–305.

Mach, E. (1914). *Analysis of sensations.* La Salle, IL: Open Court. (Original work published 1886)

MacLeod, C. M. (1992). The Stroop task: The "gold standard" of attention measures. *Journal of Experimental Psychology: General, 121,* 12–14.

MacMillan, M. B. (1986). A wonderful journey through skull and brain: The travels of Mr. Gage's tamping iron. *Brain and Cognition, 5,* 67–107.

Madigan, S., & O'Hara, R. (1992). Short-term memory at the turn of the century: Mary Whiton Calkins's memory research. *American Psychologist, 47,* 170–174.

Magendie, F. (1965). François Magendie (1783–1855) on spinal nerve roots, 1822. In R. J. Herrnstein & E. G. Boring (Eds.), *A sourcebook in the history of psychology* (pp. 19–22). Cambridge, MA: Harvard University Press. (Original work published 1822)

Malone, J. C. (1991). *Theories of learning: A historical approach.* Belmont, CA: Wadsworth.

Marrow, A. J. (1969). *The practical theorist: The life and work of Kurt Lewin.* New York: Basic Books.

Maslow, A. H. (1954). *Motivation and personality.* New York: Harper.

Maslow, A. H. (1971). *The farther reaches of human nature.* New York: Viking.

Mayer, R. E. (1992). *Thinking, problem solving, cognition* (2nd ed.). New York: Freeman.

Mazlish, B. (1975). *James and John Stuart Mill: Father and son in the nineteenth century.* New York: Basic Books.

McCullough, D. (1992). *Brave companions: Portraits in history.* New York: Simon & Schuster.

McDougall, W. (1908). *Introduction to social psychology.* London: Methuen.

McGinnies, E. (1949). Emotionality and perceptual defense. *Psychological Review, 56,* 244–251.

McGuire, W. (Ed.). (1974). *The Freud/Jung letters.* Princeton, NJ: Princeton University Press.

McReynolds, P. (1987). Lightner Witmer: Little-known founder of clinical psychology. *American Psychologist, 42,* 849–858.

McReynolds, P. (1996). Lightner Witmer: The father of clinical psychology. In G. A. Kimble, C. A. Bonneau, & M. Wertheimer (Eds.), *Portraits of pioneers in psychology. Vol. II* (pp. 63–71). Washington, DC: American Psychological Association.

McReynolds, P. (1997). *Lightner Witmer: His life and times.* Washington, DC: American Psychological Association.

Menninger, K. (1963). *The vital balance: The life process in mental health and illness.* New York: Viking Press.

Merton, R. K. (1961). Singletons and multiples in scientific discovery: A chapter in the sociology of science. *Proceedings of the American Philosophical Society, 105,* 470–486.

Micale, M. S. (1985). The Salpêtrière in the age of Charcot: An institutional perspective on medical history in the late nineteenth century. *Journal of Contemporary History, 20,* 703–731.

Miles, W. R. (1928, March 29). *Diary entry.* Walter Miles papers, Archives of the History of American Psychology, University of Akron, Akron, Ohio.

Miles, W. R. (1929). *Diary insertion* (Box 1165, Folder 4). From the Walter R. Miles papers, Archives of the History of American Psychology, Akron, Ohio.

Miles, W. R. (1930). On the history of research with rats and mazes: A collection of notes. *Journal of General Psychology, 3,* 324–337.

Miles, W. R. (1931, April 1). *Diary entry.* Walter Miles papers, Archives of the History of American Psychology, University of Akron, Akron, Ohio.

Mill, J. S. (1869). *The subjection of women.* London: Longmans, Green, Reader, and Dyer.

Mill, J. (1948). Analysis of the phenomena of the human mind. Excerpt in W. Dennis (Ed.), *Readings in the history of psychology* (pp. 140–154). New York: Appleton-Century-Crofts. (Original work published 1829)

Mill, J. S. (1987). *The logic of the moral sciences.* LaSalle, IL:

Open Court Classics. (A reprinting of the sixth book of Mill's *A system of logic, ratiocinative and inductive, being a connected view of the principles of evidence, and the methods of scientific investigation;* Original work published 1843)

Mill, J. S. (1989). *Autobiography.* London: Penguin. (Original work published 1873)

Miller, G. A. (1951). *Language and communication.* New York: McGraw-Hill.

Miller, G. A. (1956/1994). The magic number seven plus or minus two: Some limits on our capacity for processing information. *Psychological Review, 63,* 81–97.

Miller, G. A. (1992). The constitutive problem of psychology. In S. Koch & D. E. Leary (Eds.) *A century of psychology as science* (pp. 40–45). Washington, DC: American Psychological Association.

Miller, G. A., & Frick, F. C. (1949). Statistical behavioristics and sequences of responses. *Psychological Review, 56,* 311–324.

Miller, G. A., Galanter, E., & Pribram, K. H. (1960). *Plans and the structure of behavior.* New York: Holt.

Miller, N. E., & Dollard, J. (1941). *Social learning and imitation.* New Haven, CT: Yale University Press.

Mills, J. A. (1988). The genesis of Hull's Principles of Behavior. *Journal of the History of the Behavioral Sciences, 24,* 392–401.

Mills, W. (1899). The nature of animal intelligence and the methods of investigating it. *Psychological Review, 6,* 262–274.

Minton, H. L. (1987). Lewis M. Terman and mental testing: In search of the democratic ideal. In M. M. Sokal (Ed.), *Psychological testing and American society, 1890–1930* (pp. 95–112). New Brunswick, NJ: Rutgers University Press.

Minton, H. L. (1988). *Lewis M. Terman: Pioneer in psychological testing.* New York: New York University Press.

Monastersky, R. (1997, March 1). The call of catastrophes. *Science News, 151,* 20.

Montague, H., & Hollingworth, L. S. (1914). The comparative variability of the sexes at birth. *American Journal of Sociology, 20,* 342.

Moore, T. V. (1939). *Cognitive psychology.* Philadelphia: Lippincott.

Moorehead, A. (1969). *Darwin and the Beagle.* New York: Harper & Row.

Morawski, J. G. (1986). Organizing knowledge and behavior at Yale's Institute of Human Relations. *Isis, 77,* 219–242.

Morgan, C. L. (1903). *An introduction to comparative psychology.* London: Walter Scott. (Original work published 1895)

Morgan, M. J. (1977). *Molyneux's question.* New York: Cambridge University Press.

Morison, S. E. (1965). *The Oxford history of the American people.* New York: Oxford University Press.

Moskowitz, M. J. (1977). Hugo Münsterberg: A study in the history of applied psychology. *American Psychologist, 32,* 824–842.

Mowrer, O. H., & Mowrer, W. M. (1938). Enuresis—a method for its study and treatment. *American Journal of Orthopsychiatry, 8,* 436–459.

Münsterberg, H. (1908). *On the witness stand.* New York: The McClure Company.

Münsterberg, H. (1909). *Psychotherapy.* New York: Moffat, Yard.

Münsterberg, H. (1913). *Psychology and industrial efficiency.* New York: Houghton Mifflin.

Murchison, C. (Ed.). (1926). *Psychologies of 1925.* Worcester, MA: Clark University Press.

Murchison, C. (Ed.). (1930). *Psychologies of 1930.* Worcester, MA: Clark University Press.

Murphy, G., & Ballou, R. O. (Eds.). (1960). *William James on psychical research.* New York: Viking.

Napoli, D. S. (1981). *Architects of adjustment: The history of the psychological profession in the United States.* Port Washington, NY: Kennikat Press.

Neisser, U. (1967). *Cognitive psychology.* New York: Appleton-Century-Crofts.

Neisser, U. (1976). *Cognition and reality.* San Francisco: Freeman and Company.

Neisser, U. (1988). Cognitive reflections. In W. Hirst (Ed.), *The making of cognitive science: Essays in honor of George A. Miller* (pp. 81–88). New York: Cambridge University Press.

Neugebauer, R. (1978). Treatment of the mentally ill in medieval and early modern England: A reappraisal. *Journal of the History of the Behavioral Sciences, 14,* 158–169.

Newell, A., & Simon, H. A. (1972). *Human problem solving.* Englewood Cliffs, NJ: Prentice-Hall.

Newman, E. B. (1944). Max Wertheimer: 1880–1943. *American Journal of Psychology, 57,* 428–435.

Nicholson, I. A. M. (2003). *Inventing personality: Gordon Allport and the science of selfhood.* Washington, DC: American Psychological Association.

Nicolai, G. F. (1907). Die physiologische methodik zur erforschung der tierpsyche, ihre möglichkeit und ihre anwendung [The physiological method for research in animal psychology, its method and application]. *Journal für Psychologie und Neurologie, 10,* 1–27.

Ogden, R. M. (1951). Oswald Külpe and the Würzburg school. *American Journal of Psychology, 64,* 4–19.

Oldfield, R. C. (1972). Frederick Charles Bartlett: 1886–1969. *American Journal of Psychology, 85,* 133–140.

Olds, J., & Milner, P. (1954). Positive reinforcement produced by electrical stimulation of septal area and other regions of rat brain. *Journal of Comparative and Physiological Psychology, 47,* 419–427.

Olton, D. S. (1979). Mazes, maps, and memory. *American Psychologist, 34,* 583–596.

O'Donnell, J. M. (1979). The crisis of experimentalism in the 1920s: E. G. Boring and his uses of history. *American Psychologist, 34,* 289–295.

O'Donnell, J. M. (1979). The clinical psychology of Lightner Witmer: A case study of institutional innovation and intellectual change. *Journal of the History of the Behavioral Sciences, 15,* 3–17.

O'Donnell, J. M. (1985). *The origins of behaviorism: American psychology, 1870–1920.* New York: New York University Press.

O'Sullivan, J. J., & Quevillon, R. P. (1992). 40 years later: Is the Boulder model still alive? *American Psychologist, 47,* 67–70.

Palermo, D. (1971). Is a scientific revolution taking place in psychology? *Science Studies, 1,* 135–155.

Palmer, R. R. (1964). *A history of the modern world* (2nd ed.). New York: Alfred A. Knopf.

Parkovnick, S. (2000). Contextualizing Floyd Allport's Social Psychology. *Journal of the History of the Behavioral Sciences, 36,* 429–441.

Parsons, H. M. (1974). What happened at Hawthorne? *Science, 183,* 922–932.

Pastore, N. (1990). Espionage. *Journal of the History of the Behavioral Sciences, 26,* 366–371.

Paul, G. L. (1966). *Insight vs. desensitization in psychotherapy.* Palo Alto, CA: Stanford University Press.

Pavlov, I. P. (1906, November). The scientific investigation of the psychical faculties or processes in the higher animals. *Science, 24,* 613–619.

Pavlov, I. P. (1928). *Lectures on conditioned reflexes* (W. H. Gantt, Trans.). New York: International Publications.

Pavlov, I. P. (1960). *Conditioned reflexes: An investigation of the physiological activity of the cerebral cortex* (G. V. Anrep, Trans.). New York: Dover. (Original work published by Oxford University Press in 1927)

Penfield, W., & Perot, P. (1963). The brain's record of auditory and visual experience. *Brain, 86,* 595–696.

Perin, C. T. (1942). Behavior potentiality as a joint function of the amount of training and the degree of hunger at the time of extinction. *Journal of Experimental Psychology, 30,* 93–113.

Perloff, R., & Naman, J. L. (1996). Lillian Gilbreth: Tireless advocate for a general psychology. In G. A. Kimble, C. A. Bonneau, & M. Wertheimer (Eds.), *Portraits of pioneers in psychology. Vol. II* (pp. 107–116). Washington, DC: American Psychological Association.

Pervin, E. J. (1991). *Introduction to personality* (5th ed.). New York: HarperCollins.

Peterson, D. R. (1992). The doctor of psychology degree in professional psychology. In D. K. Freedheim (Ed.), *History of psychotherapy: A century of change* (pp. 829–849). Washington, DC: American Psychological Association.

Pettigrew, T. F. (1969). Gordon Willard Allport, 1897–1967. *Journal of Personality and Social Psychology, 12,* 1–5.

Phillips, L. (2000). Recontextualizing Kenneth B. Clark: An Afrocentric perspective on the paradoxical legacy of a model psychologist-activist. *History of Psychology, 3,* 142–167.

Piaget, J. (1952). Jean Piaget. In E. G. Boring, H. S. Langfeld, H. Werner, & R. M. Yerkes (Eds.), *A history of psychology in autobiography. Vol. 4* (pp. 237–256). New York: Russell & Russell.

Piaget, J. (1959). *The language and thought of the child.* London: Routledge and Kegan Paul. (Original work published 1923)

Pick, A. (2003). A role model for generations. *APS Observer, 16(4),* 26.

Pick, H. L., Jr. (1994). Eleanor J. Gibson: Learning to perceive and perceiving to learn. In R. D. Parke, P. A. Ornstein,

J. J. Rieser, & C. Zahn-Waxler (Eds.), *A century of developmental psychology* (pp. 527–544). Washington, DC: American Psychological Association.

Pickren, W. E., & Tomes, H. (2002). The legacy of Kenneth B. Clark to the APA: The Board of Social and Ethical Responsibility for Psychology. *American Psychologist, 57,* 51–59.

Pillsbury, W. B. (1955). Harvey A. Carr: 1873–1954. *American Journal of Psychology, 67,* 149–151.

Poffenberger, A. T. (1940). Leta Stetter Hollingworth: 1886–1939. *American Journal of Psychology, 53,* 299–301.

Poffenberger, A. T. (1957). Harry Levi Hollingworth: 1880–1956. *American Journal of Psychology, 70,* 136–140.

Poffenberger, A. T. (1962). Robert Sessions Woodworth: 1869–1962. *American Journal of Psychology, 75,* 677–689.

Popplestone, J. A. (1975). Retrieval of primary sources. *Journal of the History of the Behavioral Sciences, 11,* 20–22.

Popplestone, J. A. (1987). The legacy of memory in apparatus and methodology. In W. Traxel (Ed.), *Ebbinghaus-Studien 2* (pp. 203–215). Passau: Passavia Universitätsverlag.

Popplestone, J. A., & McPherson, M. W. (1984). Pioneer psychology laboratories in clinical settings. In J. Brozek (Ed.) *Explorations in the history of psychology in the United States* (pp. 196–272). Lewisburg, PA: Bucknell University Press.

Popplestone, J. A., & McPherson, M. W. (1994). *An illustrated history of American psychology.* DuBuque, IA: Brown & Benchmark.

Porter, J. P. (1904). A preliminary study of the psychology of the English sparrow, *American Journal of Psychology, 15,* 313–346.

Prentice, W. C. H. (1951). Edgar John Rubin: 1886–1951. *American Journal of Psychology, 64,* 608–609.

Prytula, R. E., Oster, G. D., & Davis, S. F. (1977). The "rat rabbit" problem: What did John B. Watson really do? *Teaching of Psychology, 4,* 44–46.

Radbill, S. X. (1972). Robert Whytt. In C. C. Gillespie (Ed.), *Dictionary of scientific biography. Vol. XIV.* New York: Scribner.

Raimy, V. C. (Ed.). (1950). *Training in clinical psychology.* Englewood Cliffs, NJ: Prentice-Hall.

Ramón y Cajal, S. (1999). *Advice for a young investigator.* (Trans. N. Swanson & L. W. Swanson). Cambridge, MA: MIT Press.

Raphelson, A. C. (1973). The pre-Chicago association of the early functionalists. *Journal of the History of the Behavioral Sciences, 9,* 115–122.

Reed, J. (1987). Robert M. Yerkes and the mental testing movement. In M. M. Sokal (Ed.), *Psychological testing and American society, 1890–1930* (pp. 75–94). New Brunswick, NJ: Rutgers University Press.

Restak, R. (1984). *The brain.* Toronto: Bantam Books.

Restle, F. (1957). Discrimination of cues in mazes: A resolution of the "place-vs.-response" question. *Psychological Review, 64,* 217–228.

Richards, R. J. (1983). Why Darwin delayed, or interesting problems and models in the history of science. *Journal of the History of the Behavioral Sciences, 19,* 45–53.

Richardson, J. T. E. (2003). Howard Andrew Know and the origins of performance testing on Ellis Island, 1912–1916. *History of Psychology, 6,* 143–170.

Rilling, M. (2000). How the challenge of explaining learning influenced the origins and development of John B. Watson's behaviorism. *American Journal of Psychology, 113,* 275–301.

Robinson, D. N. (1981). *An intellectual history of psychology* (2nd ed.). New York: Macmillan.

Robinson, J. K., & Woodward, W. R. (1996). Experimental analysis of behavior at Harvard: From cumulative records to mathematical models. In L. D. Smith & W. R. Woodward (Eds.), *B. F. Skinner and behaviorism in American culture* (pp. 254–272). Bethlehem, PA: Lehigh University Press.

Roediger, H. L., III. (1985). Remembering Ebbinghaus. *Contemporary Psychology, 30,* 519–523.

Roediger, H. L. III. (1997). Remembering. *Contemporary Psychology, 42,* 488–492.

Roediger, H. L. III, & McDermott, K. B. (1995). Creating false memories: Remembering words not presented in lists. *Journal of Experimental Psychology: Learning Memory, and Cognition, 21,* 803–814.

Rogers, C. R. (1942). *Counseling and psychotherapy.* Boston: Houghton Mifflin Company.

Rogers, C. R. (1954). Changes in the maturity of behavior as related to therapy. In C. R. Rogers & J. A. Precker (Eds.), *Psychotherapy and personality change* (pp. 215–237). Chicago: University of Chicago Press.

Rogers, C. R. (1961a). Some hypotheses regarding the facilitation of personal growth. In C. R. Rogers (Ed.), *On becoming a person* (pp. 31–38). Boston: Houghton Mifflin.

Rogers, C. R. (1961b). Some directions evident in therapy. In C. R. Rogers (Ed.), *On becoming a person* (pp. 73–106). Boston: Houghton Mifflin.

Rohles, F. H., Jr. (1992). Orbital bar pressing: A historical note on Skinner and the chimpanzees in space. *American Psychologist, 47,* 1531–1533.

Romanes, G. J. (1886). *Animal Intelligence.* New York: D. Appleton. (Original work published 1882)

Rosenzweig, S. (1992). *The historic expedition to America (1909): Freud, Jung, and Hall the king-maker.* St. Louis: Rana House.

Rosnow, R. L., & Rosenthal, R. (1993). *Beginning behavioral research.* New York: Macmillan.

Ross, D. (1969). The "zeitgeist" and American psychology. *Journal of the History of the Behavioral Sciences, 5,* 256–262.

Ross, D. (1972). *G. Stanley Hall: The psychologist as prophet.* Chicago: University of Chicago Press.

Rubin, E. (1958). Figure and ground. In D. C. Beardslee & M. Wertheimer (Eds.), *Readings in perception* (pp. 194–203). Princeton, NJ: Van Nostrand. (Original work published 1915)

Rucci, A. J., & Tweney, R. D. (1980). Analysis of variance and the "second discipline" of scientific psychology: A historical account. *Psychological Bulletin, 87,* 166–184.

Ruse, M. (1979). *The Darwinian revolution: Science red in tooth and claw.* Chicago: University of Chicago Press.

Russo, N. F. (1988). Women's participation in psychology: Reflecting and shaping the social context. In A. N. O'Connell & N. F. Russo (Eds.), *Models of achievement: Reflections of eminent women in psychology. Vol. 2* (pp. 9–27). Hillsdale, NJ: Lawrence Erlbaum.

Rutherford, A. (2003). B. F. Skinner's technology of behavior in American life: From consumer culture to counterculture. *Journal of the History of the Behavioral Sciences, 39,* 1–23.

Ryalls, J. (1984). Where does the term "aphasia" come from? *Brain and Language, 21,* 358–363.

Ryan, W. C. (1939). *Studies in early graduate education.* New York: Carnegie Foundation.

Sahakian, W. S. (Ed.). (1968). *History of psychology: A source book in systematic psychology.* Itasca, IL: F. E. Peacock.

Sahakian, W. S. (1975). *History and systems of psychology.* New York: John Wiley.

Samelson, F. (1981). Struggle for scientific authority: The reception of Watson's behaviorism in 1913. *Journal of the History of the Behavioral Sciences, 17,* 399–425.

Samelson, F. (1985). Organizing for the kingdom of behavior: Academic battles and organizational policies in the twenties. *Journal of the History of the Behavioral Sciences, 21,* 33–47.

Sanford, E. C. (1910, August 8). *Letter to E. B. Titchener.* Titchener papers, Cornell University Archives, Ithaca, NY.

Satariano, W. A. (1979). Immigration and the popularization of social science, 1920 to 1930. *Journal of the History of the Behavioral Sciences, 15,* 310–320.

Scarborough, E., & Furumoto, L. (1987). *Untold lives: The first generation of American women psychologists.* New York: Columbia University Press.

Schlereth, T. J. (1991). *Victorian America: Transformations in everyday life.* New York: HarperCollins.

Schulman, B. J. (2001). *The seventies: The great shift in American culture, society, and politics.* Cambridge, MA: Perseus.

Schultz, D. P. (1981). *A history of modern psychology* (3rd ed.). New York: Academic Press.

Schultz, D. P., & Schultz, S. E. (1987). *A history of modern psychology* (4th ed.). San Diego: Harcourt, Brace, Jovanovich.

Scott, W. D. (1903). *The theory and practice of advertising.* Boston: Small & Maynard.

Scott, W. D. (1910). *Human efficiency in business.* New York: Macmillan.

Scott-Kakures, D., Castagnetto, S., Benson, H., Taschek, W., & Hurley, P. (1993). *History of philosophy.* New York: HarperCollins.

Scripture, E. W. (1895). *Thinking, feeling, doing.* New York: Chautauqua-Century Press.

Searle, J. R. (1980). Minds, brains, and programs. *Behavioral and Brain Sciences, 3,* 417–424.

Sechenov, I. M. (1965). *Reflexes of the brain.* Cambridge, MA: MIT Press. (Original work published 1863)

Sechzer, J. A., (1983). The ethical dilemma of some classical animal experiments. *Annals of the New York Academy of Sciences, 406,* 5–12.

Segal, E. M., & Lachman, R. (1972). Complex behavior or higher mental processes: Is there a paradigm shift? *American Psychologist, 27,* 46–55.

Sex, race/ethnicity data available. (1995, Winter). *Trends in Education: APA Education Directorate News, 2(1),* 2–3.

Sexton, V. S. (1965). Clinical psychology: An historical survey. *Genetic Psychology Monographs, 72,* 401–434.

Shakow, D. (1930). Hermann Ebbinghaus. *American Journal of Psychology, 42,* 505–518.

Shannon, C. E., & Weaver, W. (1949). *The mathematical theory of communication.* Urbana: University of Illinois Press.

Sherrington, C. S. (1906). *The integrative action of the nervous system.* New Haven, CT: Yale University Press.

Shorter, E. (1997). *A history of psychiatry: From the era of the asylum to the age of Prozac.* New York: Wiley.

Simon, L. (1998). *Genuine reality: A life of William James.* Chicago: University of Chicago Press.

Simonton, D. K. (1994). *Greatness: Who makes history and why.* New York: Guilford Press.

Singer, C. A. (1957). *A short history of anatomy and physiology from the Greeks to Harvey.* New York: Dover.

Skinner, B. F. (1938). *The behavior of organisms: An experimental analysis.* New York: Appleton-Century-Crofts.

Skinner, B. F. (1945). An operational analysis of psychological terms. *Psychological Review, 52,* 270–277.

Skinner, B. F. (1948). *Walden two.* New York: Macmillan.

Skinner, B. F. (1953). *Science and human behavior.* New York: Macmillan.

Skinner, B. F. (1956). A case history in scientific method. *American Psychologist, 12,* 221–223.

Skinner, B. F. (1957). *Verbal behavior.* New York: Appleton-Century-Crofts.

Skinner, B. F. (1960). Pigeons in a pelican. *American Psychologist, 15,* 28–37.

Skinner, B. F. (1979). *The shaping of a behaviorist.* New York: Knopf.

Skinner, B. F. (1981). Pavlov's influence on psychology in America. *Journal of the History of the Behavioral Sciences, 17,* 242–245.

Skinner, B. F. (1987). Whatever happened to psychology as the science of behavior? *American Psychologist, 42,* 780–786.

Skinner, B. F. (1990). Can psychology be a science of the mind? *American Psychologist, 45,* 1206–1210.

Small, W. S. (1901). Experimental study of the mental processes of the rat. II. *American Journal of Psychology, 12,* 206–239.

Smith, L. D. (1992). On prediction and control: B. F. Skinner and the technological ideal of science. *American Psychologist, 47,* 216–223.

Smith, L. D. (1996a). Knowledge as power: The Baconian roots of Skinner's social meliorism. In L. D. Smith & W. R. Woodward (Eds.), *B. F. Skinner and behaviorism in American culture* (pp. 56–82). Bethlehem, PA: Lehigh University Press.

Smith, L. D. (1996b). Conclusion: Situating B. F. Skinner and behaviorism in American culture. In L. D. Smith & W. R. Woodward (Eds.), *B. F. Skinner and behaviorism in American culture* (pp. 294–315). Bethlehem, PA: Lehigh University Press.

Smith, L. D., Best, L. A., Cylke, V. A., Stubbs, D. A. (2000). Psychology without p values: Dadat analysis at the turn of the century. *American Psychologist, 55,* 260–263.

Smith, M. B. (1992). The American Psychological Association and social responsibility. In R. B. Evans, V. S. Sexton, & T. C. Cadwallader (Eds.), *The American Psychological Association: A historical perspective* (pp. 327–345). Washington, DC: American Psychological Association.

Sobel, D. (1995). *Longitude: The true story of a lone genius who solved the greatest scientific problem of his time.* New York: Walker.

Sobel, D. (2000). *Galileo's daughter: A historical memoir of science, faith, and love.* New York: Penguin.

Sokal, M. M. (1971). The unpublished autobiography of James McKeen Cattell. *American Psychologist, 26,* 626–635.

Sokal, M. M. (1981a). The origins of the Psychological Corporation. *Journal of the History of the Behavioral Sciences, 17,* 54–67.

Sokal, M. M. (Ed.). (1981b). *An education in psychology: James McKeen Cattell's journal and letters from Germany and England, 1880–1888.* Cambridge, MA: The MIT Press.

Sokal, M. M. (1984). The Gestalt psychologists in behaviorist America. *American Historical Review, 89,* 1240–1263.

Sokal, M. M. (1987). James McKeen Cattell and mental anthropometry: Nineteenth-century science and reform and the origins of psychological testing. In M. M. Sokal (Ed.), *Psychological testing and American society* (pp. 21–45). New Brunswick, NJ: Rutgers University Press.

Sokal, M. M. (1992). Origins and early years of the American Psychological Association, 1890–1906. *American Psychologist, 47,* 111–122.

Sokal, M. M., & Rafail, P. A. (1982). *Guide to manuscript collections in the history of psychology and related areas.* Millwood, NY: Kraus International.

Solso, R. L. (Ed.). (1973). *Contemporary issues in cognitive psychology: The Loyola symposium.* Washington, DC: V. H. Winston.

Spalding, D. A. (1873). Instinct, with original observations on young animals. *Macmillan's Magazine, 27,* 282–293.

Spence, K. W. (1952). Clark Leonard Hull: 1884–1952. *American Journal of Psychology, 65,* 639–646.

Sperry, R. W. (1961). Cerebral organization and behavior. *Science, 133,* 1749–1757.

Sperry, R. W. (1993). The impact and promise of the cognitive revolution. *American Psychologist, 48,* 878–885.

Spillman, J., & Spillman, L. (1993). The rise and fall of Hugo Münsterberg. *Journal of the History of the Behavioral Sciences, 29,* 322–338.

Spurzheim, J. G. (1978). Outlines of phrenology. In D. N. Robinson (Ed.), *Significant contributions to the history of psychology. Series E. Volume II.* Washington, DC: University Publications of America. (Original work published 1832)

A stash in the stacks. (1996, August/September). *Civilization, 3(4),* 15.

Sterns, C. Z. (1985). Victorian sexuality: Can historians do it better? *Journal of Social History, 18,* 625–634.

Stetson, G. R. (1897). Some memory tests of whites and blacks. *Psychological Review, 4,* 285–289.

Steudel, J. (1972). Johannes Peter Müller. In C. C. Gillespie (Ed.), *Dictionary of scientific biography. Vol. IX.* New York: Scribner.

Stevens, S. S. (1935). The operational definition of concepts. *Psychological Review, 42,* 517–527.

Stocking, G. W., Jr. (1965). On the limits of "presentism" and "historicism" in the historiography of the behavioral sciences. *Journal of the History of the Behavioral Sciences, 1,* 211–217.

Stricker, G., & Cummings, N. A. (1992). The professional school movement. In D. K. Freedheim (Ed.), *History of psychotherapy: A century of change* (pp. 801–828). Washington, DC: American Psychological Association.

Stroop, J. R. (1992). Studies of interference in serial verbal reactions. *Journal of Experimental Psychology: General, 121,* 15–23. (Original work published 1935)

Strunk, O., Jr. (1972). The self-psychology of Mary Whiton Calkins. *Journal of the History of the Behavioral Sciences, 8,* 196–203.

Sulloway, F. J. (1979). *Freud: Biologist of the mind.* New York: Basic Books.

Sulloway, F. J. (1982). Darwin and his finches: The evolution of a legend. *Journal of the History of Biology, 15,* 1–53.

Swazey, J. P. (1972). Charles Scott Sherrington. In C. C. Gillespie (Ed.), *Dictionary of scientific biography. Vol. XII.* New York: Scribner.

Taylor, D. W. (1972). Santiago Ramón y Cajal. In C. C. Gillespie (Ed.), *Dictionary of scientific biography. Vol. XI.* New York: Scribner.

Temkin, O. (1947). Gall and the phrenological movement. *Bulletin of the History of Medicine, 21,* 275–321.

Terman, L. M. (1906). Genius and stupidity: A study of some of the intellectual processes of seven "bright" and seven "stupid" boys. *Pedagogical Seminary, 13,* 307–373.

Terman, L. M. (1924). The mental test as a psychological method. *Psychological Review, 31,* 93–117.

Terman, L. M. (1925). *Genetic studies of genius. Vol. 1. Mental and physical traits of a thousand gifted children.* Stanford, CA: Stanford University Press.

Terman, L. M. (1932). Trails to psychology. In C. Murchison (Ed.), *A history of psychology in autobiography. Vol. II* (pp. 297–332). Worcester, MA: Clark University Press.

Terman, L. M., & Oden, M. H. (1947). *Genetic studies of genius. Vol. 4. The gifted child grows up: Twenty-five years' follow-up of a superior group.* Stanford, CA: Stanford University Press.

Terman, L. M., & Oden, M. H. (1959). *Genetic studies of genius. Vol. 5. The gifted group at mid-life: Thirty-five years' follow-up of the superior child.* Stanford, CA: Stanford University Press.

Thomas, E. (1995). *The very best men.* New York: Simon & Schuster.

Thomson, K. S. (1975). HMS Beagle, 1820–1870. *American Scientist, 63,* 664–672.

Thorndike, E. L. (1899). A reply to "The nature of animal intelligence and the methods of investigating it." *Psychological Review, 6,* 412–420.

Thorndike, E. L. (1900). Comparative psychology. *Psychological Review, 7,* 424–426.

Thorndike, E. L. (1936). Edward Lee Thorndike. In C. Murchison (Ed.), *A history of psychology in autobiography. Vol. 3* (pp. 263–270). Worcester, MA: Clark University Press.

Thorndike, E. L. (1948). Animal intelligence. In W. Dennis (Ed.), *Readings in the history of psychology* (pp. 377–387). New York: Appleton-Century-Crofts. (Original work published 1898)

Thorndike, E. L., & Woodworth, R. S. (1901). The influence of improvement in one mental function upon the efficiency of other functions. I. *Psychological Review, 8,* 247–261.

Thorndike, E. L. (2000). *Animal intelligence: Experimental studies.* New Brunswick, NJ: Transaction Publishers. (Original work published 1911)

Thorndike, R. L. (1991). Edward L. Thorndike: A professional and personal appreciation. In G. A. Kimble, M. Wertheimer, and C. L. White (Eds.), *Portraits of pioneers in psychology* (pp. 139–151). Washington, DC: American Psychological Association.

Titchener, E. B. (1895). Note. *American Journal of Psychology, 7,* 448–449.

Titchener, E. B. (1898). Postulates of a structural psychology. *Psychological Review, 7,* 449–465.

Titchener, E. B. (1899). *An outline of psychology.* New York: Macmillan. (Original work published 1896)

Titchener, E. B. (1901). *Experimental psychology: A manual of laboratory practice. Vol. 1: Qualitative experiments. Part 1: Student's manual; part 2: Instructor's manual.* New York: Macmillan.

Titchener, E. B. (1905). *Experimental psychology: A manual of laboratory practice. Vol. 2: Quantitative experiments. Part 1: Student's manual; part 2: Instructor's manual.* New York: Macmillan.

Titchener, E. B. (1905). Review [of Thorndike's *Elements of Psychology*]. *Mind, 56,* 552–554.

Titchener, E. B. (1906, June 6). *Letter to L. N. Wilson.* Wilson Papers, Clark University, Worcester, MA.

Titchener, E. B. (1909). *A text-book of psychology.* New York: Macmillan.

Titchener, E. B. (1914). On "Psychology as the behaviorist views it." *Proceedings of the American Philosophical Society, 53,* 1–17.

Titchener, E. B. (1921). Wilhelm Wundt. *American Journal of Psychology, 32,* 161–178.

Todd, J. T. (1994). What psychology has to say about John B. Watson: Classical behaviorism in psychology textbooks, 1920–1989. In J. T. Todd & E. K. Morris (Eds.), *Modern per-spectives on John B. Watson and classical behaviorism* (pp. 75–107). Westport, CT: Greenwood Press.

Todd, J. T., & Morris, E. K. (1986). The early research of John B. Watson: Before the behavioral revolution. *The Behavior Analyst, 9,* 71–88.

Todes, D. P. (1997). From the machine to the ghost within: Pavlov's transition from digestive physiology to conditional reflexes. *American Psychologist, 52,* 947–955.

Tolman, E. C. (1922). A new formula for behaviorism. *Psychological Review, 29,* 44–53.

Tolman, E. C. (1932). *Purposive behavior in animals and men.* New York: Appleton-Century-Crofts.

Tolman, E. C. (1938). The determiners of behavior at a choice point. *Psychological Review, 45,* 1–41.

Tolman, E. C. (1942). *Drives toward war.* New York: D. Appleton-Century Company.

Tolman, E. C. (1948). Cognitive maps in rats and men. *Psychological Review, 55,* 189–208.

Tolman, E. C. (1952). Edward Chace Tolman. In E. G. Boring, H. S. Langfeld, H. Werner, & R. M. Yerkes (Eds.), *A history of psychology in autobiography, Vol. 4* (pp. 323–339). Worcester, MA: Clark University Press.

Tolman, E. C. (1959). Principles of purposive behavior. In S. Koch (Ed.), *Psychology: A study of a science. Study 1. Volume 2* (pp. 92–157). New York: McGraw-Hill.

Tolman, E. C., & Honzik, C. H. (1930). Introduction and removal of reward, and maze performance in rats. *University of California Publications in Psychology, 4,* 257–275.

Tolman, E. C., & Nyswander, D. B. (1927). The reliability and validity of maze-measures for rats. *Journal of Comparative Psychology, 7,* 425–460.

Tolman, E. C., Ritchie, B. F., & Kalish, D. (1946a). Studies in spatial learning. II. Place learning versus response learning. *Journal of Experimental Psychology, 36,* 221–229.

Tolman, E. C., Ritchie, B. F., & Kalish, D. (1946b). Studies in spatial learning. I. Orientation and the short-cut. *Journal of Experimental Psychology, 36,* 13–24.

Tolman, E. C., Tryon, R. C., & Jeffress, L. A. (1929). A self-recording maze with an automatic delivery table. *University of California Publications in Psychology, 4,* 99–112.

Tolstoy, L. (1942). *War and peace* (L. Maude and A. Maude, Trans.). New York: Simon and Schuster.

Triplett, R. G. (1982). The relationship of Clark L. Hull's hypnosis research to his later learning theory: The continuity of a life's work. *Journal of the History of the Behavioral Sciences, 18,* 22–31.

Tryon, R. C. (1963). Psychology in flux: The academic-professional polarity. *American Psychologist, 18,* 134–143.

Turing, A. M. (1950). Computing machinery and intelligence. *Mind, 59,* 433–460.

Turner, R. S. (1972). Hermann von Helmholtz. In C. C. Gillespie (Ed.), *Dictionary of scientific biography. Vol. VI.* New York: Scribner.

Turner, R. S. (1982). Helmholtz, sensory physiology, and the disciplinary development of German psychology. In W. R.

Woodward & M. G. Ash (Eds.), *The problematic science: Psychology in nineteenth-century thought* (pp. 147–166). New York: Praeger.

Twitmyer, E. B. (1905). Knee-jerks without stimulation of the patellar tendon. *Psychological Bulletin, 2,* 43–44.

Valentine, C. W. (1930). The innate bases of fear. *Journal of Genetic Psychology, 37,* 394–420.

Vandenbos, G. R., Cummings, N. A., & DeLeon, P. H. (1992). A century of psychotherapy: Economic and environmental influences. In D. K. Freedheim (Ed.), *History of psychotherapy: A century of change* (pp. 65–102). Washington, DC: American Psychological Association.

Veysey, L. R. (1965). *The emergence of the American university.* Chicago: University of Chicago Press.

Viney, W. (1996). Dorothea Dix: An intellectual conscience for psychology. In G. A. Kimble, C. A. Bonneau, & M. Wertheimer (Eds.), *Portraits of pioneers in psychology. Vol. II* (pp. 15–31). Washington, DC: American Psychological Association.

Viney, W., & Zorich, S. (1982). Contributions to the history of psychology: XXIX. Dorothea Dix and the history of psychology. *Psychological Reports, 50,* 211–218.

Voyat, G. (1981). Jean Piaget: 1896–1980. *American Journal of Psychology, 94,* 645–648.

Vrooman, J. R. (1970). *René Descartes: A biography.* New York: Putnam.

Wade, N. J. (1994). Hermann von Helmholtz. *Perception, 23,* 981–989.

Wallin, J. E. W. (1966). A red-letter day in APA history. *Journal of General Psychology, 75,* 107–114.

Warner, L. H., & Warden, C. J. (1927). The development of a standardized animal maze. *Archives of Psychology, 15* (No. 92).

Warren, R. M. (1984). Helmholtz and his continuing influence. *Music Perception, 1,* 253–275.

Washburn, M. F. (1908). *The animal mind.* New York: Macmillan.

Washburn, M. F. (1932). Margaret Floy Washburn. In C. Murchison (Ed.), *A history of psychology in autobiography. Vol. 2* (pp. 333–358). Worcester, MA: Clark University Press.

Watson, J. B. (1903). *Animal education: An experimental study of the psychical development of the white rat, correlated with the growth of its nervous system.* Chicago: University of Chicago Press.

Watson, J. B. (1907). Kinesthetic and organic sensations: Their role in the reactions of the white rat to the maze. *Psychological Review Monograph Supplements, 8 (#33).*

Watson, J. B. (1909). Some experiments bearing upon color vision in monkeys. *Journal of Comparative Neurology and Psychology, 19,* 1–28.

Watson, J. B. (1910, February). The new science of animal behavior. *Harper's Monthly Magazine, 120,* 346–353.

Watson, J. B. (1913). Psychology as the behaviorist views it. *Psychological Review, 20,* 158–177.

Watson, J. B. (1914). *Behavior: An introduction to comparative psychology.* New York: Holt.

Watson, J. B. (1916). The place of the conditioned reflex in psychology. *Psychological Review, 23,* 89–116.

Watson, J. B. (1926, June). How we think: A behaviorist's view. *Harper's Monthly Magazine, 153,* 40–45.

Watson, J. B. (1928). *Psychological care of infant and child.* New York: W. W. Norton.

Watson, J. B. (1930). *Behaviorism* (2nd ed.). New York: W. W. Norton. (Original work published 1924)

Watson, J. B. (1936). Autobiography. In C. Murchison (Ed.), *A history of psychology in autobiography. Vol. 3* (pp. 271–281). Worcester, MA: Clark University Press.

Watson, J. B., & Morgan, J. J. B. (1917). Emotional reactions and psychological experimentation. *American Journal of Psychology, 28,* 163–174.

Watson, J. B., & Rayner, R. (1920). Conditioned emotional reactions. *Journal of Experimental Psychology, 3,* 1–14.

Watson, R. I. (1953). A brief history of clinical psychology. *Psychological Bulletin, 50,* 321–346.

Watson, R. I. (1960). The history of psychology: A neglected area. *American Psychologist, 15,* 251–255.

Watson, R. I., & Evans, R. B. (1991). *The great psychologists: A history of psychological thought* (5th ed.). New York: HarperCollins.

Weaver, K. A. (1998). Capturing the fervor of cognitive psychology's emergence. *Teaching of Psychology, 25,* 136–138.

Webb, M. E. (1988). A new history of Hartley's "Observations on Man." *Journal of the History of the Behavioral Sciences, 24,* 202–211.

Weiner, J. (1994). *The beak of the finch.* New York: Vintage Books.

Wertheimer, M. (1967). Gestalt theory. In W. D. Ellis (Ed.), *A source book of Gestalt psychology* (pp. 1–11). London: Routledge and Kegan Paul. (Original talk delivered 1924)

Wertheimer, M. (1967). Laws of organization in perceptual forms. In W. D. Ellis (Ed.), *A source book of Gestalt psychology* (pp. 71–88). London: Routledge and Kegan Paul. (Original work published 1923)

Wertheimer, M. (1982). *Productive thinking.* Chicago: University of Chicago Press. (Original work published 1945)

Wertheimer, M. (1978). Humanistic psychology and the humane but tough-minded psychologist. *American Psychologist, 33,* 739–745.

White, M. (1997). *Isaac Newton: The last sorcerer.* Reading, MA: Perseus Books.

White, R. K. (1978). Has "field theory" been "tried and found wanting"? *Journal of the History of the Behavioral Sciences, 14,* 242–246.

Wiggins, J. G., Jr. (1994). Would you want your child to be a psychologist? *American Psychologist, 49,* 485–492.

Williams, D. H., Bellis, E. C., & Wellington, S. W. (1980). Deinstitutionalization and social policy: Historical perspectives and present dilemmas. *American Journal of Orthopsychiatry, 50,* 54–64.

Williams, S. B. (1938). Resistance to extinction as a function of the number of reinforcements. *Journal of Experimental Psychology, 23,* 506–521.

Windholz, G. (1986). A comparative analysis of the conditional reflex discoveries of Pavlov and Twitmyer, and the birth of a paradigm. *Pavlovian Journal of Biological Science, 21*, 141–147.

Windholz, G. (1997). Ivan P. Pavlov: An overview of his life and psychological work. *American Psychologist, 52*, 941–946.

Windholz, G., & Lamal, P. A. (1985). Köhler's insight revisited. *Teaching of Psychology, 12*, 165–167.

Winston, A. S. (1990). Robert Sessions Woodworth and the "Columbia Bible": How the psychological experiment was redefined. *American Journal of Psychology, 103*, 391–401.

Winston, A. S. (1996). "As his name indicates": R. S. Woodworth's letters of reference and employment for Jewish psychologists in the 1930s. *Journal of the History of the Behavioral Sciences, 32*, 30–43.

Winters, B. (1950). Franz Anton Mesmer: An inquiry into the antecedents of hypnosis. *Journal of General Psychology, 43*, 63–75.

Wissler, C. (1965). Clark Wissler (1870–1947) on the inadequacy of mental tests. In R. J. Herrnstein & E. G. Boring (Eds.), *A sourcebook in the history of psychology* (pp. 442–445). Cambridge, MA: Harvard University Press. (Original work published 1901)

Witmer, L. (1893, July 14). *Letter to Hugo Münsterberg.* Münsterberg papers, Boston Public Library, Boston, MA.

Witmer, L. (1909). The study and treatment of retardation: A field of applied psychology. *Psychological Bulletin, 6*, 121–127.

Witmer, L. (1911). Criminals in the making. *The Psychological Clinic, 4*, 221–238.

Witmer, L. (1931). Clinical psychology. In R. A. Brotemarkle (Ed.), *Clinical psychology: Studies in honor of Lightner Witmer* (pp. 341–352). Philadelphia: University of Pennsylvania Press. (Original work published 1907)

Wolpe, J. (1958). *Psychotherapy by reciprocal inhibition.* Palo Alto, CA: Stanford University Press.

Woodworth, R. S. (1917). Some criticisms of the Freudian psychology. *American Journal of Psychology, 12*, 174–194.

Woodworth, R. S. (1918). *Dynamic psychology.* New York: Columbia University Press.

Woodworth, R. S. (1921). *Psychology.* New York: Holt.

Woodworth, R. S. (1931). *Contemporary schools of psychology.* New York: Ronald Press.

Woodworth, R. S. (1938). *Experimental psychology.* New York: Holt.

Woodworth, R. S. (1958). *Dynamics of behavior.* New York: Holt.

Woodworth, R. S., & Schlosberg, H. (1954). *Experimental psychology* (2nd ed.) New York: Holt.

Wright, R. (1994). *The moral animal.* New York: Vintage Books.

Wundt, W. (1904). *Principles of physiological psychology* (5th ed.)(E. B. Titchener, Trans.). New York: Macmillan. (Original work published 1873–1874)

Yerkes, R. M. (1911). *Introduction to psychology.* New York: Holt.

Yerkes, R. M. (Ed.). (1921). Psychological examining in the United States Army. *Memoirs of the National Academy of Sciences, 15*, 1–890.

Yerkes, R. M., & Morgulis, S. (1909). The method of Pawlow in animal psychology. *Psychological Bulletin, 6*, 257–273.

Yoakum, C. S., & Yerkes, R. M. (1920). *Army mental tests.* New York: Holt.

Young, R. M. (1972). Franz Joseph Gall. In C. C. Gillespie (Ed.), *Dictionary of scientific biography. Vol. V.* New York: Scribner.

Zajonc, B. F. (1980). Feeling and thinking: Preferences need no inferences. *American Psychologist, 35*, 151–175.

Zeigarnik, B. (1967). On finished and unfinished tasks. In W. D. Ellis (Ed.), *A source book of Gestalt psychology* (pp. 300–314). London: Routledge and Kegan Paul. (Original work published 1927)

Zilboorg, G. (1941). *A history of medical psychology.* New York: W. W. Norton.

GLOSSARY

A

Ablation Method of studying the brain, pioneered by Flourens, in which the function of some brain area is assessed after that portion of the brain has been destroyed.

Absolute Threshold Point on the continuum of a physical dimension where an increase in physical stimulation results in the initial perception of a stimulus.

Accommodation Visual phenomenon described by Berkeley; the tendency of the lens of the eye to change shape as objects move toward and away from the person.

Algorithm In math and computer science, a set of rules guaranteed to produce an eventual solution to a problem by exhaustively working through all possible solutions.

Analytical Psychology Jung's theory of psychology, which differed from Freud's in a number of ways, including a decreased emphasis on sex.

Anecdotal Method Research method in which evidence takes the form of an accumulation of examples supporting some principle or theory; associated with Romanes and the origins of comparative psychology; also used by phrenologists; heavy reliance on such evidence leads one to ignore counter-instances that might disprove a hypothesis.

Animal Magnetism Belief held by Mesmer and contemporaries that living organisms were influenced by magnetic forces and that cures for illness could result from the proper use of magnets.

Animal Spirits Hypothetical essence once believed (e.g., by Descartes) to inhabit the nervous system and to be the driving force behind muscle movement.

Anna O. Case Famous case of hysteria treated by Breuer and reported by Breuer and Freud in *Studies on Hysteria*; gave Freud the insight that hysterics suffer from their memories of traumatic events; details distorted over the years.

Anthropomorphism Tendency to attribute human characteristics to nonhuman entities; associated with Romanes and the origins of comparative psychology.

Apparent Motion Phenomenon studied by Wertheimer in which stationary stimuli appear to move under certain circumstances.

Apperception A high level of awareness, in which we focus our full attention on some object and apprehend it fully; associated with Leibniz originally; central concept for Wundt's psychology.

Approach-Approach Conflict For Lewin, a situation in which a conflict exists within a person, resulting from having to make a choice between two goals with a positive valence.

Approach-Avoidance Conflict For Lewin, a situation in which a conflict exists within a person, occurring when a goal elicits both approach and avoidance tendencies.

Archive A repository of unpublished data of use to historians.

Argument From Design Explained the great complexity in nature by arguing that it required a superior being (i.e., God) to produce it; associated with Reverend Paley.

Army Alpha Group intelligence test developed by Yerkes for testing the abilities of literate soldiers in World War I.

Army Beta Group intelligence test developed by Yerkes for testing the abilities of illiterate soldiers in World War I.

Artificial Intelligence The study of whether machines can be said to act with some degree of intelligence.

Association For Locke, analogous to Newtonian gravity; a force that attracts ideas.

Associationism Philosophical school of thought, related to empiricism, which emphasizes the rules by which relationships between ideas and experiences are formed.

Atomism Belief that nature can be understood best by reducing complexity to its smallest, most fundamental elements (opposed to holism).

Attributes In Titchener's system, these were the ways of classifying the various elements of conscious experience; for example, the element of sensation had the attributes of quality, intensity, duration, and clarity.

Attrition Methodological problem in longitudinal research, when participants drop out of the study; notably low in Terman's longitudinal study of giftedness.

Avoidance-Avoidance Conflict For Lewin, a situation in

which a conflict exists within a person, resulting from having to make a choice between two goals with a negative valence.

B

Behavioral Environment For the gestaltists, this referred to the environment as perceived, as contrasted with the physical environment (the geographical environment).

Behaviorist Manifesto Watson's 1913 paper that argued for a behaviorist approach to psychology.

Bell-Magendie Law A statement that the posterior roots of the spinal cord controlled sensation, while the anterior roots controlled motor movement; sometimes considered an example of a "multiple."

Binocular Vision Vision involving the use of two eyes; aids in depth perception.

Bit Abbreviation of "binary digit"; the amount of information that enables a choice between two alternatives.

Bloodletting Medical technique promoted by Benjamin Rush; drawing blood was believed to relieve, among other things, mental disorders brought about by excessive tension in the circulatory system.

Boulder Model Another name for the scientist-practitioner model for the training of clinical psychologists.

Brass Instrument Psychology Term used (sarcastically) by William James to describe the German reaction time and psychophysics research, which relied heavily on apparatus made of brass.

C

Cartesian Dichotomy From Descartes, the distinction between humans (mind + body) and animals (only a mechanical body).

Case Study Research method involving an in-depth analysis of a single individual; advocated by Allport as a way to investigate personality.

Catastrophism Theory in geology that geological change occurred infrequently and as a consequence of such catastrophic events as the Biblical flood.

Catharsis In Freudian psychoanalysis, an emotional release that occurs when one gains insight into the unconscious origins of some problem; key part of the Anna O. case.

Cause and Effect One of Hume's laws of association; Hume argued that we cannot be certain of the fundamental causes of events, only that events occur together regularly.

Cell Assembly For Hebb, a basic unit in the nervous system, a set of neurons that become associated with each other because they have been repeatedly activated together.

Chain of Being Belief that all species on earth could be placed on a linear scale with reference to their level of complexity.

Chinese Room Problem Thought problem by Serle that illustrates a problem that would pass the Turing test but would still not support strong AI.

Chunk For Miller, a meaningful unit of information; short-term memory capacity said to be 7±2 chunks of information.

Client-Centered Therapy Humanistic approach to psychotherapy created by Rogers; it assumed that responsibility for therapeutic change ultimately belonged to the client, while the therapist's responsibility was to create an atmosphere conducive to such change.

Clinical Method Method of studying the brain, pioneered by Broca, in which existing behavioral or cognitive deficits are correlated with brain damage upon autopsy.

Clinical Psychology Field of psychology concerned with the diagnosis and treatment of mental and behavioral disorders; named by Witmer.

Closure Gestalt organizing principle, a tendency to fill in missing gaps in our perception in order to perceive whole figures.

Cognitive Dissonance In a theory proposed by Festinger, a state of cognitive discomfort resulting from the experience of holding two inconsistent thoughts simultaneously or behaving in a way that is inconsistent with one's beliefs.

Cognitive Map For Tolman, a hypothetical spatial memory of a maze, acquired simply as a result of experiencing the maze (i.e., reinforcement not needed).

Cognitive Science An interdisciplinary field that includes cognitive psychology, linguistics, computer science, cultural anthropology, and epistemology.

Collective Unconscious Jung's concept that the unconscious included the collective experiences of our ancestors; reflected in the common themes that occur in the mythology of various cultures.

Comparative Psychology Study of the similarities and differences among species; originated from the implication of Darwin's theory of evolution that continuity existed among species.

Completion Test Mental test designed by Ebbinghaus to measure mental fatigue in school children; because it focused on higher mental activity, it anticipated the approach later taken by Binet.

Complex Idea For Locke, ideas that were combinations of simple ideas.

Complication Experiment A nineteenth-century reaction time experiment, typically using the Donders subtractive method, in which reaction times for simple tasks were subtracted from reaction times for more "complicated" tasks.

Concomitant Variation From Mill's Logic, method that examines whether changes in event X are associated with changes in event Y.

Condensation In Freudian dream analysis, said to occur in dreams when two or more unconscious thoughts combine into one symbol.

Conditional Stimulus Any stimulus in Pavlovian conditioning that will be paired with an unconditioned stimulus to produce a conditioned response (e.g., tone).

Conditioned Reflex The outcome of Pavlovian conditioning; by pairing a conditioned (conditional) stimulus (e.g., tone) with an unconditioned stimulus (e.g., food), the conditioned stimulus eventually elicits a conditioned response or reflex.

Connectionism Thorndike's model of learning, emphasizing the development and strengthening of connections between stimulus situations and responses that became stronger with trial and error learning.

Conscious Attitudes In the Würzburg school, referred to such mental processes as hesitation and doubt; occurred during the imageless thought studies.

Consciousness Sense of awareness; how to study it became a contentious issue in the late nineteenth and early twentieth centuries.

Conservation of Energy Associated with Helmholtz and used by him to combat vitalism; proposed that the total energy within a system remains constant, even if changes occur within the system.

Contiguity One of Hume's laws of association and Hartley's fundamental law; events experienced together, either simultaneously (spatial contiguity) or successively (temporal contiguity), become associated with each other.

Convergence Visual phenomenon described by Berkeley; the tendency of the eye muscles to make the eyes move in the direction of "crossing" as objects move closer to the person.

Converging Operations Refers to a series of studies, each with different operational definitions of the main constructs that nonetheless lead to the same general conclusion.

Correlation Statistical tool that assesses the degree of relationship between two variables; concept originated with Galton and his studies of intelligence.

Critical Period Certain instinctive behaviors (e.g., imprinting) must develop within a limited time frame, if they are to develop at all; associated with Lorenz and other European ethologists, but also proposed by Spalding.

Cybernetics Study of principles (e.g., feedback) involved in controlling and maintaining any living or nonliving system; feedback loop borrowed by Miller, Galanter, and Pribram for their TOTE unit.

D

Darwin's Finches Key data for his theory of evolution came from different species of finch on the Galápagos islands; birds on islands with different ecosystems evolved different adaptive mechanisms (e.g., beak shape).

Dedifferentiation For Lewin, a process that occurs under stress, in which a person reverses the normal differentiation process and reverts to an earlier, more primitive way of behaving; similar to Freudian regression.

Defense Mechanisms In Freudian theory, ways of behaving or thinking that serve to defend the ego against anxiety.

Dementia Praecox Term used by Kraepelin that literally means a premature dementia, a disorder later named schizophrenia.

Dependent Variable Any variable in research that is measured as an outcome of an experimental study; this usage introduced by Woodworth.

Derived Ideas For Descartes, ideas that result from one's experiences in the world.

Determinism Philosophical position that all events in the universe have prior causes.

Dichotic Listening A procedure in research on selective attention in which a person wearing headphones hears one message in one ear and a second message in the other ear.

Difference Threshold Point on the continuum of a physical dimension where a difference between two stimuli is first detected.

Differentiation For Lewin, a developmental process in which a child's life space becomes more complex; for Pavlov, refers to discrimination, the ability to distinguish between two stimuli.

Direct Action of the Nervous System Darwin's principle of emotional expression, stating that some expressions (e.g., blushing) are the side effects of the physiological arousal accompanying strongly felt emotions.

Displacement In Freudian dream analysis, a minor part of the manifest content might be the major part of the latent content, and vice versa.

Doctrine of the Skull The phrenological belief that skull contour reflected brain shape; enabled measurement of faculties by measuring contour of the skull.

Dream Analysis A cornerstone of Freudian psychoanalysis; for Freud, dreams were the "royal road" to the unconscious; surface or manifest content of dreams needed to be analyzed for their deeper, or latent, content.

Drill Courses Instructional courses in basic laboratory techniques, predominant in American universities in the late nineteenth century.

Drive Term referring to motivational processes (e.g., the hunger drive), introduced to psychology by Woodworth as an example of a factor that intervenes between stimulus and response; important intervening variable for Hull.

Drive Reduction Central to Hull's theory of learning; learning required reinforcers, which were any stimuli (e.g., food) that reduced a strong drive (e.g., hunger).

Dualist On the mind-body problem, someone (e.g., Descartes) who believes that mind and body are two separate and distinguishable essences.

E

Ecological Memory Study of memory as it occurs in everyday situations.

Ecological Validity In cognitive psychology, research that is relevant for understanding everyday cognitive activities is said to have ecological validity.

Ego In Freudian theory, the center of personality, the mediator between the demands of the id and superego, and the constraints of reality.

Empathy Ability to understand, both cognitively and emotionally, what another person is experiencing; important prerequisite for therapy success, according to Rogers.

Empiricist Someone who believes that our knowledge of the world is constructed from our experiences in it; school of thought associated with such British philosophers as Locke, Berkeley, and Mill.

Engineering Psychology That branch of psychology concerned with the design of objects to improve their use by humans (e.g., by reducing perceptual errors, by reducing fatigue).

Enlightenment Historical period from mid-eighteenth century to late nineteenth century, characterized by a belief that true knowledge could be found through the use of science and reason and that progress was inevitable and good.

Epistemology Branch of philosophy concerned with studying the nature of and the origins of human knowledge.

Eponyms Historical periods or movements named with reference to some important historical person (e.g., Darwinian biology).

Equilibrium For Lewin, a steady state in which all needs have been satisfied for the moment.

Equipotentiality Principle associated with Lashley, proposing that if some portion of the brain is destroyed, other areas will be able to serve the same function (to a degree).

Ergonomics Study of how systems and equipment can be best designed to avoid human error; pioneered by Gilbreth.

Eros In Freudian theory, the name given to the life instinct and manifested in the sex drive.

Ethology The study of animal behavior in its natural surroundings; associated with Lorenz, but with roots in Spalding's work.

Eugenics Term created by Galton, referring to a variety of methods (e.g., selective breeding) for enhancing the quality of a species, especially humans.

Evolutionary Psychology Late twentieth century development in psychology, with roots in Darwinian thinking; proposes that virtually all human behavior, especially social behavior, must be understood in an evolutionary context, as the product of natural selection.

Experimental Neurosis In Pavlovian conditioning, an emotional response that occurs after training a discrimination between two stimuli, then making the stimuli too similar to be discriminated.

Explanatory Fictions For Skinner, hypothetical constructs proposed as mediators between stimuli and responses that erroneously become used as explanations for behavioral phenomena (e.g., recalling only a few words because of limited short-term memory).

External History A history that examines factors external to a discipline (e.g., social, political, institutional, economic) that influence the history of that discipline.

Extinction In Pavlovian conditioning, the gradual elimination of a conditioned response following the repeated presentation of a conditioned stimulus in the absence of an unconditioned stimulus.

F

Faculty Psychology Prevalent early and mid-nineteenth-century approach to psychology, derived from Scottish Realism; emphasized real existence of mind, which they believed held a number of innate attributes ("faculties"), such as intelligence and judgment.

Field Theory Associated with Lewin and Tolman; for Lewin, derived from his belief that to understand behavior requires knowing about all of the forces acting on a person at a particular time; for Tolman, reflected the extent to which his neobehaviorism was influenced by the gestaltists.

Figure-Ground Gestalt organizing principle stating that

a fundamental perceptual tendency is to separate whole figures from their backgrounds.

Foreign Hull For Lewin, all events outside of the person's life space, and therefore having no effect on the individual at a given moment.

Forensic Psychology The application of psychology to the law, pioneered by Münsterberg.

Form-Quality As described by von Ehrenfels, the overall quality of some entity (e.g., a melody, a square) that exists over and above its individual components (e.g., notes, lines).

Fractionation Procedure developed in Külpe's laboratory in Würzburg, in which complicated events were broken down into sections ("fractionated"); then separate introspections were accomplished for each section.

Free Association In Freudian psychoanalysis, a procedure to probe the unconscious, in which patients describe whatever occurs to them without internal censorship.

Freudian Slip An apparent accident, error, or slip of the tongue that Freud considered a reflection of some unconscious motive.

Functional Fixedness Failure to solve a problem because of an inability to think of using some object in a manner different from its normal function.

Functionalism School of psychology favored by most early American psychologists; focused on the study of human conscious experience from an evolutionary perspective, concerned with studying the adaptive value of various mental and behavioral processes.

G

Generalization The tendency for a response learned to one stimulus to occur after the presentation of a second stimulus similar to the first.

Genetic Epistemology Piagetian psychology, which examined the manner in which knowledge developed within the individual.

Genetic Psychology Approach that emphasizes the evolution and development of the mind, including developmental psychology, comparative psychology, and abnormal psychology; associated with Hall.

Geocentric Ancient astronomical viewpoint that placed earth at the center of the known universe.

Geographical Environment For the gestaltists, this referred to the physical environment, as contrasted with the environment as perceived (the behavioral environment).

Gestalt Organizing Principles Perceptual principles described by the gestaltists that summarize the ways in which sensory phenomena become organized into a whole, meaningful figure.

Good Continuation Gestalt organizing principle, a tendency to organize perceptions in a smoothly flowing direction.

Grammar Set of rules allowing for (a) the production of all possible sentences in a language and (b) the recognition and rejection of nonsentences.

H

Habit Strength For Hull, an intervening variable influencing behavior that was a direct function of the number of reinforced trials ($_SH_R$).

Hawthorne effect In experimental psychology, refers to the effect on an experiment's outcome when the participants know they are in an experiment; named for the studies completed at the Hawthorne, Illinois plant of Western Electric.

Hebb Synapses For Hebb, synapses that change their structure as a result of learning.

Heliocentric Astronomical viewpoint proposed by Copernicus and elaborated by Galileo that placed the sun at the center of the known universe.

Heuristic In math and computer science, a creative rule of thumb that, while not guaranteeing to produce a problem solution, is likely to produce one, and will be more efficient than an algorithm (e.g., means-ends analysis).

Historicist An interpretation of historical events made from the vantage point of the knowledge and values in place at the time of the events.

Historiography The writing of history; historical methodology and theory.

Holism The philosophical assumption underlying gestalt psychology; argues that wholes (e.g., complex ideas) are more than the sum of their constituent elements (e.g., sensations, simple ideas); opposed to atomism.

Humanistic Psychology Movement pioneered by Rogers, Maslow, and others as a reaction to the deterministic assumptions of behaviorism and psychoanalysis; assumed that humans are characterized by free will, a search for meaning, and the potential for self-actualization.

Hypnotism State of heightened suggestibility, pioneered by Mesmer, Elliotson, and named by Braid.

Hypothetico-Deductive System General approach taken by Hull in which hypotheses for research are deduced from the formal postulates of the theory, and the outcomes of research support the theory or lead to its modification.

Hysteria Disorder in which a number of symptoms (e.g., paralysis) indicate neurological damage, but no such damage exists.

I

Id In Freudian theory, that part of personality that reflects the basic biological instincts of sex and aggression.

Ideas For Hume, ideas were "faint copies" of sensory impressions.

Idiographic A research strategy that focuses on an in depth analysis of individual cases; also examines differences from one individual to another; contrasted with a nomothetic strategy.

Imageless Thought Any thought process that could not be further reduced to mental images; considered nonexistent by Titchener, who believed that all thought included images.

Impressions For Hume, these were basic sensations, the raw data of experience.

Imprinting Instinctive tendency for newly hatched ducklings (and other related species) to follow the first moving object they encounter; associated with Lorenz, but also observed by Spalding and Watson.

Independent Variable Any variable in research that can be directly manipulated by an experimenter; this usage introduced by Woodworth.

Individual Differences Originally referring to the individual variation among members of a particular species, became for psychology the more general study of the characteristics that differentiated one person from another (e.g., intelligence).

Individual Psychology Label used by both Binet and Adler; for Binet, psychology should focus on ways of identifying and measuring individual differences (e.g., mental testing) rather than on general laws; for Adler, individual psychology was his version of psychoanalysis, which emphasized social factors in the development of the individual.

Inductive An approach to knowledge that emphasizes that general scientific principles are generalizations made after the collection of large amounts of data; associated with Sir Francis Bacon.

Inferiority Complex Concept associated with Adler, who believed that much of human behavior could be viewed as an attempt to compensate for feelings of inferiority.

Information Theory An influence external to psychology that helped develop cognitive psychology; concerns the manner in which information is structured (bits) and processed.

Inheritance of Acquired Characteristics Theory that characteristics developed as a result of experience during one's lifetime could be passed on biologically to offspring; associated with Lamarck.

Innate Idea Idea that exists or can be deduced in the absence of direct experience, through reasoning (the idea of a material object's "extension" in space was used by Descartes as an example).

Insight For the gestaltists, a sudden problem solution that occurred when the individual reorganized the elements of the problem situation into a new configuration.

Instinct Behavior is said to be instinctive when alternative explanations in terms of learning or experience can be ruled out; pioneering work done by early comparative psychologists, especially Spalding.

Intelligence Quotient Term invented by Stern and used by Terman in the Stanford-Binet tests; "IQ" equaled mental age divided by chronological age, the result multiplied by 100.

Interactionist A dualist who believes that body and mind directly influence each other.

Internal History A history of the ideas, theories, and findings of a discipline, without regard for the influence of external, contextual factors.

Internal Perception Wundt's version of introspection, in which "observers" would give brief verbal responses to controlled stimuli (e.g., in reaction time or psychophysics experiments).

Intervening Variables Used by Tolman and Hull; referred to hypothetical internal factors (e.g., cognitive map for Tolman; habit strength for Hull) that intervened between stimulus and response.

Introspection Method of experiencing some phenomenon, then giving a description of the conscious experience of the phenomenon.

Introspective Habit The result of extensive practice with introspection, this was a dissociative ability to make mental notes about an experience while the experience was occurring.

Isomorphism For the gestaltists, the idea that perceptual experience and underlying physiological events are functionally equivalent.

J

James-Lange Theory of Emotion Theory that held that strong emotions were in essence the physiological reaction that followed the perception of some emotion-eliciting event.

jnd Or just noticeable difference; point where the difference (in weight, color, pitch, etc.) between two stimuli becomes just barely detectable.

Jost's Law If two associations have equal strength, additional practice strengthens the older of the associations more than the younger.

L

Latent Learning For Tolman, learning that occurred but was not reflected in an animal's performance.

Law of Effect Thorndike's principle that behaviors that were effective in problem solving would be strengthened (stamped in), while behaviors that were not effective would be weakened (stamped out).

Law of Exercise Thorndike's principle that learned connections between stimuli and responses were strengthened with additional practice.

Libido For Freud, psychic energy associated with the sex drive.

Life Space For Lewin, a field within which a person operates; includes all the factors that influence a person's behavior at a certain moment.

Linguistic Universals For Chomsky, common principles shared by all languages, the existence of which supports the notion that language is innate to the human species.

Lloyd Morgan's Canon Principle of parsimony, stating that the best explanation for some phenomenon was the one with the fewest assumptions; Morgan argued that there was no need to propose mental capabilities beyond the level needed for survival in a given species.

Lobotomy Surgical procedure pioneered by Moniz in the 1930s that involves severing connections between the cortex and lower brain centers; originally designed to treat severe mental illness but abandoned when found to be of marginal effectiveness and often abused.

Localization of Function Concerns the issue of whether specific parts of the brain have specific functions.

Logical Positivism Philosophical movement associated with the Vienna Circle that extended positivist thinking; distinguished between theoretical and observable events and described ways of connecting the two through operational definitions.

M

Mass Action Principle associated with Lashley, proposing a limit on equipotentiality; the greater the amount of brain destroyed, the greater the difficulty for remaining areas of the brain to take over brain function.

Materialism Philosophical position that the only reality is physical reality and that living matter can be reduced to physical and chemical properties; held by most physiologists of the nineteenth century; opposed to vitalism.

Means-End Analysis Primary heuristic used in GPS (General Problem Solver), a computer simulation of logic by Newell and Simon; involves a feedback system of recognizing a difference between present state and goal state, then applying a series of operations to reduce the difference until it disappears.

Mechanist Someone who explains bodily actions in mechanical terms.

Memory Drum Device for presenting verbal stimuli in a memory experiment; invented by G. E. Müller.

Mental Age Mistranslation of Binet's mental level; indicated a child's level of mental ability, reported in terms of years.

Mental Chronometry Name given to nineteenth-century reaction time research, in which the goal was to measure the time taken for various mental events.

Mental Level Term used by Binet to indicate a child's level of mental functioning; those in need of remediation scored two levels below the norm for their chronological age.

Mental Set In the Würzburg laboratory, referred to the effect of giving observers some instructions that predispose them to think in certain ways; for the gestaltists, a fixed, habitual way of thinking.

Mental Test Any test designed to measure mental activity or ability; term introduced in 1890 by Cattell.

Meritocracy A model of society based on the idea that the most mentally competent should be the leaders; championed by most American mental testers, especially Terman.

Mesmerism Early version of hypnotism, associated with Mesmer; held that hysteria and other disorders could be cured through the use of magnets.

Metapsychology For Freud, a general theory about the causes of human behavior and mental processes.

Method of Adjustment Method of psychophysics, described by Fechner, in which the subject directly controls a physical stimulus, adjusting it until it is just barely detected.

Method of Agreement From Mill's Logic, a method in which a proposed cause is present whenever the effect is also present.

Method of Constant Stimuli Method of psychophysics, described by Fechner, in which stimuli of varying physical intensities are presented in random order.

Method of Difference From Mill's Logic, a method in which the absence of a proposed effect is always accompanied by the absence of a proposed cause.

Method of Limits Method of psychophysics, described by Fechner, which alternates ascending trials (stimulus is first below threshold, then increased until detected) and descending trials (stimulus is first well above threshold, then decreased until no longer detected).

Molar Behavior For Tolman, broad patterns of behavior that were goal-directed, in contrast with the molecular behavior that was the result of a reductionist model of behavior.

Monads For Leibniz, the fundamental elements of both physical and mental reality.

Moral Anxiety In Freudian theory, feelings of guilt or shame that result from fear of violating one's moral code.

Moron Term invented by Goddard as a label for adolescents or adults scoring at a mental age of 8 through 12.

Motor Aphasia Found in Broca's patient Tan; speech apparatus normal, intelligence normal, but a serious inability to express ideas verbally.

Multiple The simultaneous or near simultaneous discovery of some phenomenon, used to support the importance of the zeitgeist and a naturalistic approach to history.

N

Nativism An extreme nationalist tendency, in which outsiders are considered inferior and dangerous; characterized by the United States in 1920s, contributing to restrictions placed on immigration.

Nativist Someone who argues for the existence of innate ideas or, more generally, believes that some knowledge, faculties, or abilities are innate.

Natural Selection Central idea in Darwin's theory of evolution; held that in the struggle for existence, those organisms with adaptive variations would be most likely to survive (i.e., be selected by nature) and pass their attributes on to the next generation.

Naturalistic An approach to history that emphasizes the importance of environmental and situational forces in shaping history.

Neobehaviorism Behaviorist movement that emerged in the 1930s, associated with Tolman, Hull, and others.

Neurotic Anxiety In Freudian theory, anxiety that results from a fear that id-based impulses will get out of control.

Neurypnology Term created by Braid to reflect his belief that hypnotism was related to the state of sleep.

Nomothetic A research strategy that focuses on discovering general principles that apply, to a calibrated degree to all individuals; contrasted with an idiographic strategy.

Nonsense Syllables Consonant-vowel-consonant combinations, invented by Ebbinghaus as stimulus materials in his studies on the formation and retention of associations.

Normal Science In Kuhn's approach to the history of science, this is a period during which a paradigm is in control and a scientist's activities are shaped by the constraints of the paradigm.

O

Objective Anxiety In Freudian theory, the anxiety that results from a genuine threat from reality.

Observer Name used for someone participating in a psychological experiment in the late nineteenth and early twentieth centuries, so-called because the primary activity was observing one's mental activities through introspection.

Operant Any behavior emitted by an organism and controlled by the immediate consequences of the behavior.

Operant Conditioning Skinnerian conditioning in which a behavior occurs, and the immediate consequences of the behavior determine its future probability of occurrence.

Operational Definition A definition in terms of a specific, observable set of operations (e.g., hunger = 24 hours without food); more generally, defining scientific terms with precision.

Operationism Philosophical position that scientific concepts were to be defined in terms of a set of operations used to measure those concepts.

Ophthalmoscope Device for examining the retina, invented by Helmholtz.

Opponent Process Theory Theory of color vision associated with Hering, which proposed that color-sensitive cells are arranged in opponent pairs (e.g., red-green, blue-yellow).

Orthogenics Witmer's term for his therapeutic strategy of helping those with school-related problems (e.g., learning disabilities) to recover.

P

Paired-Associate Learning Popular learning procedure in which pairs of stimuli are presented; after a study time, stimuli are presented and the associated response must be given; invented by Calkins.

Paradigm In Kuhn's approach to the history of science, an all-encompassing theory that determines which problems are to be solved and the methods used to solve them.

Parallelism Dualistic position on the mind-body problem, associated with Leibniz and others; asserts that mind and body are separate and noninteracting, but in perfect harmony.

Peak Experience In humanistic psychology, a rare experience of extreme joy, pleasure, or accomplishment.

Periodic Function Concept used in the early twentieth century to refer to a woman's alleged incapacity during the time of menstruation.

Personal Equation Calibrating the reaction of one astronomer against another astronomer; needed because different reaction times among astronomers yielded different astronomical measurements.

Personalistic An approach to history that emphasizes persons and their roles in shaping historical events.

Petites Perceptions For Leibniz, perceptions below the level of awareness, but essential for higher levels of perception.

Phase Sequences For Hebb, a higher level of cortical organization than the cell assembly, in which combinations of assemblies are formed.

Phi Phenomenon Wertheimer's term for apparent motion, chosen to avoid the connotation that "apparent" motion was not really perceived, but was illusory.

Pineal Gland Portion of the brain selected by Descartes as the locus for mind-body interactions.

Positivism Philosophical position associated with Comte who argued that the only certain knowledge is obtained through objective, publicly observable events.

Pragmatism Position taken by several late nineteenth-century American philosophers, most notably William James; judged the value of ideas by their usefulness in helping someone adapt to the environment.

Pragnänz Gestalt organizing principle of perception (translation—"good figure"), a tendency for our perceptions to mirror reality as closely as possible.

Presentist An interpretation of historical events made from the vantage point of present-day knowledge and values.

Primary Qualities For Locke, attributes of some object that are inherent to that object that exist regardless of perception (e.g., extension in space).

Primary Reinforcers For Hull, unlearned reinforcers (e.g., food).

Primary Source Materials written or created at or near the time of some historical event, such as correspondence, diaries, speeches, minutes of meetings, university records.

Principle of Antithesis Darwin's principle of emotional expression, stating that some emotions that were the opposite of each other were reflected in expressions that were likewise opposed.

Principle of Serviceable Associated Habits Darwin's belief that emotional expressions were the product of evolutionary forces; certain expressions (e.g., sneer) originally had some survival function.

Problem of Perception For Helmholtz, it was the dilemma posed by the fact that human perception is extraordinary, while the mechanisms (e.g., eye, ear) appeared to have design flaws.

Progressive Education Associated with Dewey, an approach to education that emphasized making the student an active learner (learning by doing).

Progressive Relaxation Technique of gradually and systematically relaxing major muscle groups; pioneered by Jacobson and used by Wolpe in systematic desensitization.

Projection A Freudian defense mechanism in which unwanted personal characteristics are attributed to others.

Proximity Gestalt organizing principle of perception, a tendency to perceive that objects in close proximity "belong" together.

Psychophysics Study of the relationship between physical stimuli and the perception of those stimuli; pioneered by Weber and (especially) Fechner.

Psy.D. Degree given to clinical psychologists trained with reference to the Vail model, which places a heavier emphasis on practice and a lighter emphasis on research expertise than does the Boulder scientist-practitioner model.

Purposiveness For Tolman, this referred to goal-directedness and was believed by him to be a universal feature of learned behavior.

R

Rationalist Philosophical tradition emphasizing the use of reason and logic to arrive at truth; associated with Descartes.

Reaction Formation A Freudian defense mechanism in which unacceptable impulses are repressed and replaced with their opposites.

Reaction Potential For Hull, the probability that a response will occur at a given time, depending on such factors as drive and habit strength (SER).

Recapitulation Hall's theory, taken from a similar idea in biology, that the development of the individual mirrors the evolution of that individual's species.

Recoding For Miller, a process of reorganizing information to increase the amount of information per chunk.

Reflection Therapy technique used by Rogers to show that the therapist could empathize; involved rephrasing a client's comment in a way to show understanding.

Reflex Arc Basic unit of behavior, reduced by physiologists into the stimulus producing sensation, the central processing producing an idea, and the motor response; analysis rejected by Dewey, who argued that the arc should be seen instead as a coordinated unit that adapted the individual to the environment.

Reinforcer When following as an immediate consequence of some behavior, any stimulus that has the effect of strengthening the behavior.

Reliability The extent to which repeated measures yield the same outcome; some of Tolman's research on mazes concerned the factors influencing the reliability of mazes.

Remote Associations Indirect associations between list items separated by more than a single item; studied by Ebbinghaus.

Repetition For Hartley and other British philosophers, the factor that most directly influences the strength of an association.

Replication Process of repeating an experiment to judge its validity and generality.

Repression A Freudian defense mechanism in which unwanted impulses or traumatic memories are forced out of awareness and into the unconscious.

Resemblance One of Hume's laws of association; objects similar to each other become associated with each other.

Resistance In Freudian psychoanalysis, occurs when a person is unable to free associate, and indicates (to a Freudian) the presence of repressed material.

Resonance Theory Theory of hearing associated with Helmholtz, which proposed that different frequencies of sound stimulated receptors located in different places along the basilar membrane of the cochlear (found in the inner ear).

Respondent Conditioning Term sometimes used in place of Pavlovian or what Skinner called Type S conditioning.

Retroactive Inhibition Interference from some activity that intervenes between the learning of a list of stimulus items and its recall.

S

S-O-R Model Proposed by Woodworth to recognize the importance of the organism intervening between stimulus and response.

Savings Method Measure of memory used by Ebbinghaus, based on the difference between the amount of time to learn a list of nonsense syllables during original learning and the amount of time to relearn the list some time later.

Schedules of Reinforcement Specification of the relationship between the number or pattern of responses and the delivery of reinforcers, whenever reinforcement does not follow each behavior.

Schemata Term used both by Piaget and Bartlett to refer to hypothetical mental structures that represent knowledge.

Scholasticism Educational tradition combining the careful use of reason with the received wisdom of the Church and Aristotelian authority.

School Psychology Field of psychology concerned with the development of programs for treating children and adolescents with school-related problems (e.g., learning disabilities); pioneered by Witmer, although he did not use the term.

Scientist-Practitioner Model Training model for Ph.D. in clinical psychology that emphasizes a research dissertation; also called the Boulder model.

Secondary Qualities For Locke, attributes of some object that depend on perception for their existence (e.g., color).

Secondary Reinforcers For Hull, reinforcers that are learned through association with primary reinforcers (e.g., money).

Secondary Source Materials written or created some time after a historical event that serve to summarize or analyze that event.

Seduction Hypothesis Freud's original belief that hysteria originated from actual childhood sexual abuse.

Selective Filter For Broadbent, a model of selective attention emphasizing our tendency to separate information on the basis of physical characteristics (e.g., pitch), then focus on one message, while filtering out other ones.

Self-actualization For humanistic psychologists, a state in which people have reached their full potential.

Self Psychology Theoretical approach to psychology taken by Calkins, influenced by James; held that all consciousness is ultimately self-consciousness.

Sensory Aphasia A disorder characterized by the inability to comprehend speech and while there is no difficulty producing speech, the speech product is incoherent and/or illogical.

Serial Learning Procedure used by Ebbinghaus that involved memorizing a list of verbal stimuli (e.g., nonsense syllables), then recalling them in the exact order of presentation.

Serial Order Problem The problem of explaining sequences of behavioral events in neurological terms; posed by Lashley as a problem not solvable by traditional S-R behaviorist models.

Shaping Operant procedure for developing a complex behavior by reinforcing successive approximations to the final behavior.

Sign-Gestalt For Tolman, intervening variable referring to learned relationships between stimuli and an animal's expectation about the consequences of choosing path A over path B.

Similarity Gestalt organizing principle of perception, a tendency to perceive that objects resembling each other "belong" together.

Simple Ideas For Locke, ideas resulting from sensory experience or simple reflection.

Social Contract Proposal that an implied contract exists between government, which provides for the common good, and the governed, which agrees to follow laws, pay taxes, etc.

Social Darwinism The belief that evolutionary forces were natural and inevitable and that any attempt to disrupt them (e.g., by creating programs for the poor) was misguided and doomed to failure; associated with Spencer.

Spatial Contiguity When experiencing two events simultaneously, they become associated, according to Hartley.

Spatial Summation Process described by Sherrington; individual stimuli fail to elicit a response, but several stimuli simultaneously in close spatial proximity to each other will produce one; supported Sherrington's proposal of the synapse.

Species Problem Problem of the origin of species, addressed by Enlightenment thinkers faced with increasing uncertainty over Biblical accounts.

Specific Energy of Nerves Doctrine proposed by Bell and Müller that different sensory nerves convey different qualities; pointed out that we perceive the world indirectly through the action of our nervous systems.

Spiritualism Popular nineteenth-century belief in the afterlife and in the ability to communicate with the dead; William James was a strong believer that spiritualist claims needed to be evaluated seriously.

Stimulus Control In a stimulus environment in which a behavior is reinforced regularly, the stimulus is said to gain stimulus control over the behavior.

Stimulus Error To be avoided for proper introspection, according to Titchener, this was a tendency to report the products of conscious experience instead of the conscious experience itself.

Strong AI Approach to artificial intelligence; argues that machine intelligence is ultimately the equivalent of human intelligence (see also Weak AI).

Structuralism School of psychology, associated with Titchener, that focused on identifying the structural elements of human conscious experience, primarily through basic laboratory and introspective methods.

Struggle for Existence Key idea in Darwin's theory; derived from Malthus, who argued that population growth would eventually surpass food supplies, creating competition for limited resources.

Subjective Idealism For Berkeley, the philosophical position that the reality of the material world cannot be determined with certainty; we can be certain of the reality of our own perceptions, however.

Sublimation For Freud, a process in which psychic energy associated with sex or aggression would be channeled into socially acceptable activities.

Subtractive Method Method of measuring the duration of mental events, pioneered by Donders; reaction times for simple tasks were subtracted from reaction times for more "complicated" tasks.

Subvocal Speech Watson's definition of thinking.

Suggestion The ability to uncritically accept an idea or command from another; underlies hypnosis and was central to the view of hypnosis held by Liebeault and Bernheim of the Nancy school.

Superego In Freudian theory, that part of personality that reflects the person's moral values.

Survey Method Research method that originated with Darwin's questionnaires on emotion and Galton's questionnaires on a variety of topics; Galton normally credited with their creation.

Synapse Physical space between neurons, first proposed by Sherrington.

Systematic Desensitization Behavior therapy procedure in which fear response is replaced by an incompatible response (e.g., relaxation); pioneered by Jones and Wolpe, who named it.

Systematic Experimental Introspection Form of introspection associated with Külpe and Titchener, in which the experience of complex mental events was followed by detailed introspective descriptions; a more elaborate form of introspection than Wundt's.

T

Temporal Contiguity When experiencing two events in immediate succession, they become associated, according to Hartley.

Temporal Summation Process described by Sherrington; individual stimuli fail to elicit a response, but several stimuli in close temporal contiguity will produce one; supported Sherrington's proposal of the synapse.

Thanatos In Freudian theory, the name given to the death instinct and manifested in aggression.

Thresholds Points on a continuum of awareness where one passes from no conscious awareness to some awareness (absolute threshold) or from an awareness that one stimulus is noticeably different from another stimulus (difference threshold); associated with Leibniz and begun as a topic in experimental psychology by Weber and Fechner.

Topology Mathematical field of nonquantitative spatial geometry, used by Lewin as a basis for his field theory.

TOTE Unit Feedback unit (Test-Operate-Test-Exit) to replace reflex arc; proposed by Miller, Galanter, and Pribram, and influenced by developments in cybernetics.

Transfer The effect of learning in one situation on learning in a second situation; could be positive or negative; pioneer studies by Woodworth and Thorndike.

Transference In Freudian psychoanalysis, occurs when the patient develops a strong emotional attachment to the therapist.

Trial and Error Learning Thorndike's explanation for the behavior of his cats in puzzle boxes—they escaped by trying various behaviors until hitting on one that worked; also used by Morgan to provide a parsimonious explanation for the behavior of dogs escaping from yards.

Trichromatic Theory The Young-Helmholtz theory of color vision, which proposed the existence of three different color-sensitive cells in the eye, one for each of the primary colors (red, green, blue); color vision believed to result from various combinations of firings of these cells.

Tropisms Forced movements, automatic responses to specific stimuli, as studied by Loeb.

Turing Test In artificial intelligence, a thought problem posed by Turing to distinguish humans from computers.

Twin Studies First suggested by Galton as a means of demonstrating the heritability of intelligence.

Two-Point Threshold Point where the perception of two points touching the skin changes from "one point perceived" to "two points perceived;" studied extensively by Weber.

U

Unconditional Positive Regard For Rogers, refers to a regard for the client that is not conditional on specific behaviors; the client is valued simply by virtue of being human.

Unconditioned Reflex For Pavlov, any stimulus-response connection (e.g., food-salivate) that does not have to be learned.

Unconditioned Stimulus Any stimulus that will produce a specific reflex response (e.g., food elicits saliva).

Unconscious Inference For Helmholtz, a process, outside of our awareness, by which our perceptions are influenced by past experiences.

Uniformitarianism Theory in geology, championed by Lyell, that geological change occurred gradually, over a long period of time, and as a consequence of such regular phenomena as erosion.

V

Valence For Lewin, term used to describe whether an object is valued by the person (positive valence) or not valued (negative valence).

Variability Hypothesis The idea that men had a greater degree of variability in most traits, compared to women, and were therefore at a selective advantage in evolutionary terms.

Vector For Lewin, refers to the direction of a desired goal.

Vitalism Belief that a "life force" or vital force existed that went beyond the physical and chemical components of living organisms; opposed to materialism.

Voluntarism Wundt's system of psychology, so-called because of his emphasis on the idea that the mind actively organizes information.

Von Restorff Effect Increased recall of information that stands out in some manner from other to-be-learned information.

W

Weak AI Approach to artificial intelligence; argues that machine intelligence can provide unique insights into the nature of human intelligence, but does not argue that machine intelligence is ultimately the equivalent of human intelligence (see also Strong AI).

Weber's Law As stimulus A increases in intensity, it takes progressively larger differences between stimulus A and stimulus B for a person to detect a difference between the two; the jnd divided by the size of the standard stimulus is a constant.

White Paper Locke's term, borrowed from Aristotle, for the nature of the mind at birth; knowledge acquired through experience is analogous to writing on this white paper.

Word Association Test Procedure associated with both Galton and Jung to investigate the nature of associations in the mind; involves responding to a stimulus word with the first response word that comes to mind.

Z

Zeigarnik Effect Named for student of Lewin, refers to a tendency to be more likely to recall unfinished tasks than finished tasks.

Zeitgeist The overall intellectual, political, and cultural climate of a particular historical era.

PHOTO, TEXT, AND ILLUSTRATION CREDITS

PHOTO CREDITS

Chapter 1 Figure 1.1: Courtesy of Harvard Alumni Bulletin. Figure 1.2: Rick Zaidan/Zaidan Photography.

Chapter 2 Figure 2.1: Courtesy The New York Public Library. Figure 2.2: From Rene Descartes, L'homme et un Traitsé de la Formation du Foetus. Figure 2.4: The Granger Collection.

Chapter 3 Figure 3.2: The Granger Collection. Figure 3.3: From M.B. MacMillan: Brain and Cognition, 1986, pg. 85. Reproduced with permission of Academic Press. Figure 3.4: Rues des Archives//Granger Collection. Figure 3.7: Science Photo Library/Photo Researchers.

Chapter 4 Figure 4.4: Courtesy Archives of the History of American Psychology, University of Akron. Figure 4.5: Clark University Archives.

Chapter 5 Figure 5.1: The Granger Collection. Figure 5.2: Reproduced with permission of Syndics of Cambridge University Library. Figure 5.3: From Darwin: The Expression of the Emotions in Man and Animals, 1872. Murray Publishers, Ltd. Figure 5.5: Corbis.

Chapter 6 Figure 6.1: Clark University Archives. Figure 6.2 and Figure 6.3: Courtesy The Houghton Library, Harvard University. Figure 6.4: Courtesy Archives of the History of American Psychology, University of Akron. Figure 6.5a and Figure 6.5b: Clark University Archives. Figure 6.7: Photo by Partridge, Courtesy Wellesley College Archives.

Chapter 7 Figure 7.1: Courtesy Archives of the History of American Psychology, University of Akron. Figure 7.3a: From Titchener: Experimental Psychology, Volume II, 1905. MacMillan Publishing. Figure 7.3b: From Titchener: Experimental Psychology, Volume II, 1905. MacMillan Publishing. Figure 7.4: Courtesy Archives of the History of American Psychology, University of Akron. Figure 7.7: Courtesy University Press of New England. Reproduced with permission. Figure 7.8a and Figure 7.8b: Robert Mearns Yerkes Papers, Manuscripts and Archives, Yale University Library.

Chapter 8 Figure 8.1: From Scripture, E.E. (1895), Thinking, Feeling, Doing. Meadville, PA: Chautauga-Century Press.

Figure 8.2, Figure 8.3, Figure 8.4, Figure 8.6 and Figure 8.10: Courtesy Archives of the History of American Psychology, University of Akron. Figure 8.8: Courtesy National Research Council. Reprinted with permission of National Academy Press. Figure 8.11: UPI/Corbis-Bettmann.

Chapter 9 Figure 9.1: UPI/Corbis-Bettmann. Figure 9.2: Courtesy Archives of the History of American Psychology, University of Akron. Figure 9.3: Image drawn by Thelka. From W. Kohler, The Mentality of Apes, 1926. Routeledge, Ltd. Reproduced with permission. Figure 9.4c: Courtesy of The Pittsburgh Zoo & PPG Aquarium. Figure 9.7: From The Mentality of Apes by W. Kohler, 1926. Routeledge, Ltd. Reproduced with permission.

Chapter 10 Figure 10.2: Courtesy International Publishers, Co. Reproduced with permission. Figure 10.3a: ©1991 by the Board of Trustees of the University of Illinois. Reproduced with permission. Figure 10.3b: From G.F. Nicolai, Die physiologische methodik zur erforschung der tierpsyche, ihre meglichkeit und ihre anwendung, 1907. Journal für Psychologie und Neurologie, 10:1-27. Figure 10.5: Courtesy Archives of the History of American Psychology, University of Akron. Figure 10.6a, Figure 10.6b and Figure 10.6c: From PSYCHOLOGICAL CARE OF INFANT & CHILD by John B. Watson. Copyright 1928 by W.W. Norton & Company, Inc. Used by permission of W.W. Norton & Company, Inc. Figure 10.7 and Figure 10.8: Courtesy Archives of the History of American Psychology, University of Akron.

Chapter 11 Figure 11.2 and Figure 11.8: Courtesy Archives of the History of American Psychology, University of Akron. Figure 11.10: UPI/Corbis-Bettmann. Figure 11.11: Courtesy of Robert W. Allan, Department of Psychology, Lafayette College.

Chapter 12 Figure 12.1: Courtesy National Library of Medicine. Figure 12.3: Corbis. Figure 12.2a: From the collection of Robert Foster. Figure 12.4: Courtesy National Library of Medicine. Figure 12.5: Courtesy Frank J. Sulloway. Figure 12.6: Mary Evans/Sigmund Freud Copyrights. Figure 12.7: University of Pennsylvania Archives.

Chapter 13 Figure 13.1: Bettmann/Corbis Images. Figure 13.2: ©Ted Polumbaum/LIFE. Figure 13.3: Bettmann/Corbis Images. Figure 13.5 (left) and Figure 13.5 (right): Property of AT&T Archives. Reprinted with permission of AT&T.

Chapter 14 Figure 14.3: ©1998 J. T. Miller. Figure 14.6: Courtesy Emory University. Figure 14.7: ©Estate of Francis Bello/Photo Researchers. Figure 14.8: Bettmann/Corbis Images. Figure 14.9: Courtesy Archives of the History of American Psychology, University of Akron.

Chapter 15 Figure 15.3: Courtesy George Bush Presidential Library and Museum. Figure 15.4 (left) and Figure 15.4 (right): Archives of the History of American Psychology, Robert V. Guthrie Papers-The University of Akron.

TEXT AND ILLUSTRATION CREDITS

Chapter 1 Pages 13–14: From "The 'zeitgeist' and American Psychology," by D. Ross, 1969, *Journal of the History of the Behavioral Sciences, 5*, p. 257. Copyright 1969. Reprinted by permission of John Wiley & Sons, Inc.

Chapter 2 Pages 29–33: "Passions of the Soul" from *The Philosophical Works of Descartes,* Vol. 1, by Rene Descartes, translated by Elizabeth S. Haldane and G. R. T. Ross, New York: Cambridge University Press. (Original work published 1649.) Copyright 1969. Reprinted with permission. Pages 45–48: From *Autobiography* by J. S. Mills, New York: Penguin Books Ltd. (Original work published 1873.) Copyright 1989.

Chapter 3 Page 63: From "Helmholtz and his continuing influence," by R. M. Warren, *Music Perception, 1*, p. 257. Copyright 1984. Reprinted by permission of University of California Press and Dr. Warren. Pages 70–73: From Broca cited in *A Source Book in the History of Psychology*, by Herrnstein and Boring, 1965, Cambridge, MA: Harvard University Press. (Original publication 1861.) Figure 3.5: From Fritsch & Hitzig cited in *A Source Book in the History of Psychology*, by Herrnstein and Boring, 1965, Cambridge, MA: Harvard University Press. (Original publication 1870.) Figure 3.6: From *A History of Experimental Psychology*, by E. G. Boring, 1950, Englewood Cliffs, NJ: Prentice Hall. Copyright 1950. Reprinted by permission of Frank Boring. Figures 3.8 and 3.9: From *Brain Mechanisms and Intelligence*, by K. S. Lashley, 1963, (Original work published 1929.) Copyright 1963. Reprinted by permission of Simon & Schuster.

Chapter 4 Figure 4.2 and 4.3: From *Sensation and Perception in the History of Experimental Psychology*, by E. G. Boring, 1942. Copyright 1942. Reprinted with permission of Frank Boring. Pages 97–99: From *An education in Psychology: James McKeen Cattell's Journal and Letters from Germany and England*, by M. M. Sokal (Ed.), 1981, Cambridge, MA: MIT Press. Copyright 1981. Reprinted by permission of MIT Press. Pages 102–107: From *Memory: A Contribution to experimental psychology*, by H. Ebbinghaus, 1964, New York: Dover Publications. (Original work published 1885.) Copyright 1964. Page 110: From "Oswald Kulpe and the Wurzburg school," by R. M. Ogden, 1951, *American Journal of Psychology, 64*, p. 9. Copyright 1951. Considered public domain by University of Illinois Press.

Chapter 5 Figure 5.4: From *From Darwin to Behaviorism*, by Robert Boakes, 1984, Cambridge, MA: Cambridge University Press. Copyright 1984.

Chapter 6 Pages 151–154: From *The Principles of Psychology, Vol. 1*, by W. James, 1950, New York: Dover Publications. (Original Publication 1890.) Copyright 1950. Pages 154–157: From *Psychology: The Briefer Course*, by W. James, 1961, New York: Harper Collins. (Original Publication 1892.) Copyright 1961. Pages 159–160: From "letter of 6 June 1906 to L. N. Wilson" by E. B. Titchener. Reprinted from the Wilson papers found in the Clark University Archives. Page 162: From "Recollections of Clark's G. Stanley Hall" by L. A. Averill, 1982, *Journal of the History of the Behavioral Sciences, 18,* p. 342. Copyright 1982. Reprinted by Permission of John Wiley & Sons, Inc. Page 164: From "On the history of research with rats and mazes," by R. W. Miles, 1930, *Journal of General Psychology, 3,* p. 331. Copyright 1930. Reprinted with Permission of The Helen Dwight Reid Educational Foundation. Published by Heldref Publications, Washington D.C.

Chapter 7 Page 177: From "Edward Bradford Titchener, 1867-1927" by E. G. Boring, 1927, *American Journal of Psychology, 38*, p. 489. Copyright 1927. Considered public domain by University of Illinois Press. Pages 185–186: From "letter of 8 August 1910 to E. B. Titchener" by E. C. Sanford. Reprinted from the Titchener papers by permission of the Division of Rare and Manuscript Collections, Cornell University Library. Page 186: From "The letter of 14 July 1983 to Hugo Münsterberg" by Lightner Witmer. Reprinted from the Münsterberg papers by courtesy of the Trustees of the Boston Public Library. Page 188: From "Psychology as the Behaviorist views it," by J. B. Watson, 1913, *Psychological Review, 20*, p. 164. Copyright 1913. In the public domain by the American Psychological Association. Pages 197–202: From *Animal Intelligence: Experimental Studies*, by E.L. Thorndike, Copyright 2000 by Transaction Publishers. Reprinted by permission of the publisher. Further reproduction or dissemination without permission from the publisher is expressly prohibited.

Chapter 8 Figures 8.6 and 8.7: From *Army Mental Tests*, by Yoakum and Yerkes, 1920, New York: Henry Holt & Company. Copyright 1920. Figure 8.8: From *The Mismeasure of Man* (p. 178) by J. S. Gould, 1981, New York: W. W. Norton. Copyright 1981. Pages 236–242: From *Psychology and Industrial Efficiency*, by H. Münsterberg, 1913, Boston, MA: Houghton Mifflin Co. Copyright 1913.

Chapter 9 Pages 258–262: From *The Mentality of Apes* by W. Kohler, 1926, UK: Routledge Ltd. Copyright 1926. Reprinted by permission of Routledge. Figures 9.8 and 9.9: Four Figures as specified from *Productive Thinking* by Max Wertheimer, 1982, New York: Harper Collins Publishers. (Original work published 1945.) Copyright 1959 by Valentin Wertheimer. Copyright Renewed 1987 by Michael Wertheimer. Reprinted by Permission of

NAME INDEX

Accord, J., 85, 97, 161
Ach, Narziss, 110
Adams, Grace, 369
Adler, Alfred, 367, 368, 370, 375
Agassiz, Louis, 150
Allin, Arthur, 194
Allport, Floyd, 423, 424, 427, 433
Allport, Gordon, 329, 401, 423, 424,
    427–429, 433
Alzheimer, Aloys, 350
Amberly, Lady, 127, 129
Amberly, Lord, 127, 129
Anastasi, Anne, 233, 394
Anderson, J. R., 412–413
Angell, Frank, 167, 178, 192
Angell, James Rowland, 176, 191–194,
    203, 206, 212, 232, 291, 324
Anna O., 356–357, 360, 375
Anrep, G. V., 284
Appleby, Joyce, 20, 21, 55, 344
Aristotle, 25, 26
Arnkoff, D. B., 385
Aronson, Elliot, 386, 425, 426
Aserinsky, Eugene, 423
Ash, M. G., 250, 267, 269, 274
Atkinson, R. C., 410–411
Averill, L. A., 162

Baars, Bernard J., 339–340, 410–413,
    417, 418
Babkin, Boris P., 281, 282, 287, 288, 422
Bache, R. M., 147
Bacon, Francis, 27, 34, 38, 51, 55, 280,
    336
Baddeley, A., 264
Bahrick, H. P., 418
Bailyn, Bernard, 9
Bakan, D., 66
Baker, D. B., 372, 381, 393
Balance, W. D. G., 88, 90
Baldwin, James Mark, 2, 188, 293
Ballou, R. O., 158, 159
Barker, R., 270–271
Barone, D. F., 190
Bartholow, Roberts, 69

Bartlett, Frederick C., 401, 403–409, 415,
    418, 428, 431–433
Bascom, John, 132
Bayton, J. A., 148
Beam, A., 346
Beers, Clifford, 348, 373, 375
Bekhterev, Vladimir, 77, 290, 293
Bell, Charles, 57–59, 80, 190
Bell, L. V., 345, 346
Bellis, E. C., 348
Benedict, Ruth, 386
Benjamin, L. T., Jr., 85, 97, 158, 159,
    161, 235, 244, 381, 393, 441
Benson, H., 115
Berger, Gustav, 95, 98
Bergström, John, 223
Berkeley, George, 52, 54, 143
Bernheim, Hippolyte, 352–353, 375
Binet, Alfred, 108, 135, 209, 214,
    216–218, 224, 354
Bingham, Walter Van Dyke, 242–243,
    246, 378, 394, 395
Bischoff, Theodor, 56
Bjork, D. W., 150, 336, 338
Blueler, Eugene, 350
Blumenthal, Arthur L., 18–19, 84, 94,
    99–101
Boakes, R., 129, 130, 189
Boas, Franz, 234, 360
Bolles, R. C., 380
Bolton, T. L., 244
Boorstin, Daniel J., 5, 26, 28, 35
Boring, E. G., 1, 2, 4, 11–12, 17–19, 57,
    59, 75, 86, 88–95, 99, 108, 124, 143,
    145, 177, 179, 182, 195, 209, 228,
    236, 311, 329, 352, 374, 428, 431,
    438, 442, 443
Bowditch, H. P., 161
Bower, Gordon, 444
Boyle, Robert, 38
Braid, James, 352, 375
Brainerd, C. J., 431
Bramel, D., 397
Bregman, E. O., 302
Brehm, J. W., 425

Breuer, Joseph, 356–357, 360, 370
Brewer, C. B., 3
Bridgman, Percy, 310–311
Brigham, Carl, 233
Bringmann, N. J., 90
Bringmann, W. G., 88, 90, 92
Broadbent, Donald, 415, 417, 432–433
Broadus, John, 290
Broca, Paul, 54, 69–73, 81
Brown, R., 153
Brown, Thomas, 144, 148
Browne, J., 118
Brozek, Joseph, 3
Brubacher, J. S., 147
Bruce, Darryl B., 77, 410
Brücke, Ernst, 60, 355, 356, 375
Bruner, J. S., 417, 419, 427
Bryan, William, 223
Buckley, K. W., 17, 298, 302, 303, 305
Bulatao, E. Q., 436, 437
Bunsen, Robert, 90, 92
Burdon-Sanderson, John, 178
Burnham, John C., 198, 199
Burnham, William, 162
Burt, Cyril, 430
Bush, George H. W., 438
Buss, D. M., 442

Cacioppo, J. T., 414
Cadwallader, T. C., 2
Calkins, Mary Whiton, 16, 17, 142, 152,
    167–171, 173, 182, 236, 298, 436
Camfield, T. M., 165
Canady, Herman, 147
Cannon, Walter B., 203
Capshew, J. H., 223, 336, 374, 380, 381,
    393, 398
Carey, E. G., 243
Carlsmith, Merrill, 425–426
Carlyle, Thomas, 11
Carmichael, L., 227–229
Carnegie, Andrew, 188
Carr, E. H., 4
Carr, Harvey, 176, 194–195, 206,
    291–293, 438

Cashman, S. D., 189, 191, 211, 221
Castagnetto, S., 115
Cattell, James McKeen, 13–14, 95–99, 149, 159, 161, 165, 171, 176, 195, 196, 204, 206, 209, 212–215, 217, 219, 242–244, 280, 290, 294, 360, 371, 394–395, 399
Charcot, Jean-Martin, 353–354, 356, 375
Cherry, Colin, 415
Chomsky, Noam, 94, 411–412, 432
Christina, Queen of Sweden, 33–34
Churchill, Winston, 18
Clark, Kenneth, 440–442, 444
Clark, Mamie Phipps, 440–442, 444
Cohen, E., 15, 16
Cohen, I. B., 55, 351
Collins, A., 418
Collins, J., 372
Colp, R., Jr., 122
Comte, Auguste, 279–280
Conley, J. J., 134
Coon, Deborah J., 158, 159, 303
Copernicus, Nicolas, 26
Costall, A., 131
Cottingham, J., 33
Crane, L., 393
Cravens, H., 225
Croce, P. J., 149, 151
Cronbach, Lee J., 205, 225
Crouse, E. M., 441
Crozier, W. J., 335
Crutchfield, R. S., 321
Cummings, N. A., 380, 393
Cushman, P., 386

Dallenbach, Karl M., 185, 402
Danziger, K., 93, 99, 424, 426
Darwin, Charles Robert, 11, 13–14, 114–127, 129, 130, 132, 138–140, 142, 143, 153, 157, 172, 176, 189, 284, 375, 442
Darwin, Erasmus, 13, 115, 139
Darwin, Robert, 116
Darwin, Susannah, 116
Darwin, William, 124, 125
Davis, R., 149, 338
Davis, S. F., 149, 302, 338
Decker, H. S., 361
Degler, C. N., 233, 234
DeLeon, P. H., 380
Dembo, T., 270–271
Dennett, D. C., 124
Dennis, W., 136, 218, 232
Denny-Brown, D., 76
Descartes, René, 24–36, 39, 41, 43, 49, 51, 52, 55, 56, 66, 80, 410, 420, 421

Desmond, A., 116, 118–120, 122, 125, 129
Deutsch, Morton, 273
Dewey, John, 13–14, 176, 190–192, 209, 211, 213
Dewsbury, D. A., 14, 164, 172, 228, 233, 293, 294, 380
Diamond, I. T., 75
Dickens, Charles, 5
Diehl, L. A., 436
Dix, Dorothea, 347–348, 374–375
Doll, Edgar, 16
Dollard, John, 326, 368
Donaldson, Henry, 291
Donders, F. C., 95
Donnelly, M. E., 149
Doob, L. W., 326
Dorn, H., 85
Downey, June, 436, 438
du Bois Reymond, Emil, 60, 61, 151
Duncan, C. P., 290
Duncker, Karl, 264, 265, 276
Durkin, M., 85, 97

Ebbinghaus, Hermann, 25, 51, 83, 101–109, 136, 167–169, 192, 215, 216, 402, 403
Einstein, Albert, 252, 369
Eiseley, L., 124
Eliot, Charles W., 150, 151, 161, 236
Ellenberger, H. F., 353, 357
Elliotson, John, 351–352, 375
Elliott, M. H., 315–317
Ellis, Havelock, 359, 364, 370
Elmes, D. G., 397
English, H. B., 301–302
Esdaile, James, 352, 375
Estes, W. K., 205
Evans, R. B., 2, 90, 144, 178, 183, 187, 219, 367, 436, 437
Eysenck, Hans J., 382, 385, 398

Fancher, R. E., 66, 216, 218, 353, 354, 369
Farr, R. M., 178
Farson, R., 392
Fearing, F., 31, 56, 57
Fechner, Gustav, 83, 85, 87–90, 101, 108, 111
Fernberger, S. W., 372, 373, 436
Ferrier, David, 74–75, 81
Ferster, C. B., 332, 336
Festinger, Leon, 273, 386, 401, 424–427, 433
Finger, S., 31–33

Fisher, Ronald, 426
Fiske, S. T., 421
FitzRoy, Robert, 117, 121
Flaherty, F. C., 418
Flavell, John, 432
Flourens, Pierre, 54, 64, 68–69, 73, 78, 81, 129, 422
Ford, Henry, 3
Forrest, D. W., 132, 134, 135, 138
Fowler, Charlotte, 67
Fowler, Lorenzo, 67
Fowler, Orson, 67
Frank, J. D., 268
Frank, Jerome, 273
Franklin, Benjamin, 55, 88, 351
Franklin, Fabian, 171
Franz, S. I., 77
Freeman, F. N., 234
Freeman, F. S., 267
Freeman, Walter, 383–384, 398
Freud, Amalia, 355
Freud, Anna, 366–367, 369, 370
Freud, Jacob, 355
Freud, Sigmund, 11, 17, 50, 139, 173, 321, 343, 350, 354–371, 375–376, 386, 429, 430
Frick, F. C., 414
Friend, R., 397
Frisch, Karl von, 203
Fritsch, Eduard, 74, 81
Frost, Robert, 328
Fuchs, A. H., 3, 143, 144
Fulcher, R., 436, 437
Fulton, John, 383
Furumoto, Laurel, 7, 14, 17, 146, 167, 168, 170, 171, 183, 436

Gage, Phineas, 69–70, 81
Galanter, Eugene, 415–416, 433
Galef, B. G., Jr., 197
Galileo Galilei, 26–29, 36, 38, 51, 55
Gall, Franz Josef, 64, 65, 74, 81, 144
Gallistel, C. R., 58
Galton, Francis, 6, 13, 114, 124, 132–138, 140, 153, 209, 212–216, 430
Gamble, Eleanor, 109, 170
Gantt, W. H., 287
Gardner, H., 412, 418, 419
Garrett, H. E., 95
Gay, P., 354, 355, 359, 360, 365–367, 369, 370
Gesell, Arnold, 16
Gibbens, Alice Howe, 151
Gibson, Eleanor, 253, 438–439, 444
Gibson, James, 438

Gilbreth, Frank, 243, 394
Gilbreth, Lillian Moller, 243–244, 246, 394, 398
Gilderhus, M. T., 3
Gilles, D., 310
Gillespie, R., 395, 397
Gilman, Daniel Coit, 145, 161
Glass, C. R., 385
Gleaves, D. H., 359
Glickman, S. E., 183, 423
Goddard, Henry, 8, 16, 218–223, 233, 234, 245, 360
Goldstein, E. B., 62, 89, 251, 255
Golgi, Camillo, 75–77, 81
González y García, Manuel, 253, 254, 260
Goodenough, F. L., 203, 232
Goodwin, C. J., 16–18, 164, 180, 182, 185, 288, 290, 436
Gould, John, 121
Gould, S. J., 132, 232
Gratiolet, Louis Pierre, 75
Gravitz, M. A., 352
Gray, J. A., 281
Gray, P. H., 129
Green, M., 369
Greenwood, J. D., 84, 92
Grmek, M. D., 58, 59
Grob, G. N., 345, 346, 383, 384
Guillotin, Joseph Ignace, 56, 351
Gundlach, H. U. K., 103
Gutenberg, Johannes, 26
Guthrie, Edwin, 320
Guthrie, R. V., 147, 148
Guttman, N., 326

Haldane, J. B. S., 128
Hale, N. G., Jr., 369
Hall, C. S., 366, 428, 429
Hall, G. Stanley, 2, 7, 13–14, 16, 142, 152, 159–163, 165–167, 172, 173, 179, 181, 189, 190, 194, 223, 322, 359–360, 379, 429–431, 436
Hannush, M. J., 291
Hardy, C. D., 145
Harlow, J. M., 69, 70
Harmon-Jones, E., 425, 426
Harper, William Rainey, 189–190, 291
Harris, B., 300, 301
Harrower-Erickson, M. R., 252
Hartley, David, 41, 42–44, 46, 48, 49, 52, 57, 143
Harvey, William, 28, 30, 38, 55
Hastorf, A. H., 225
Havens, L. L., 349
Hawkins, H., 145, 162

Head, Henry, 408
Hearst, E., 223
Hebb, Donald O., 77, 183, 401, 422–423, 427, 433
Hegel, G. W. F., 3, 10
Heidbreder, Edna, 2, 87, 186
Heider, Fritz, 273
Heims, S., 272
Helmholtz, Hermann von, 59–63, 81, 85, 88, 91, 94, 108, 151, 171, 251, 355
Henle, M., 187, 251, 252, 255
Henley, T. B., 149
Henri, Victor, 217
Henslow, John, 117, 139
Hering, Ewald, 62, 108
Herman, E., 380, 441
Hernandez, E., 359
Hertzman, Max, 424
Hicks, L. H., 148
Hilgard, Ernest R., 2, 13, 102, 103, 144, 172, 191, 223, 225, 234, 236, 243, 265, 290, 311–312, 322, 324, 374, 379, 395, 414, 421, 422, 424, 427, 428, 443
Hindeland, M. J., 186, 187
Hitchcock, Alfred, 362
Hitler, Adolph, 248, 252, 255
Hitzig, Edward, 74, 81
Hobart, O., 385
Hoffeld, D. R., 351
Hofstadter, R., 145
Hollingworth, Harry, 212, 244–246, 394
Hollingworth, Leta Stetter, 225–227, 244, 245, 373, 387, 394
Holt, Edwin, 313–314
Honzik, C. H., 317–318
Hooker, Joseph, 122
Hopkins, Johns, 145
Hornstein, G. A., 368
Hothersall, D., 69, 149
Hubel, David, 423
Hull, Clark, 163, 308, 318, 320–328, 338–341, 385, 409, 423, 438
Hume, David, 41–43, 48–50, 52, 143, 186
Hunt, Lynn, 20, 21, 55, 344
Hunt, William Morris, 150
Hunter, Walter S., 193, 289
Hurley, P., 115
Husserl, Edmund, 249, 275
Huxley, Thomas, 130

Ickes, Mary, 302
Izard, C. E., 157

Jackson, J. P., Jr., 441
Jacob, Margaret, 20, 21, 55, 344

Jacobsen, Carlyle, 383
Jacobson, Edmund, 385
James, Alice, 149
James, Henry, Jr., 149, 150
James, Henry, Sr., 149
James, William, 10, 13–14, 17, 128, 142, 143, 148, 148–150, 152–155, 161, 167, 168, 170, 173, 189, 190, 192, 195–196, 203, 235, 242, 313, 348, 360, 368, 430
Jastrow, Joseph, 322
Jaynes, J., 11, 129, 195
Jeffress, L. A., 317
Jeffreys, M. V. C., 34
Jenkins, J. G., 402, 403
Jenkins, James, 413
Jennings, H. S., 77
Johnson, M. G., 149
Johnston, T. D., 129, 132
Jončich, G., 195, 196, 202, 203
Jones, Ernest, 354, 356, 357, 361, 368
Jones, Mary Cover, 301, 303, 306, 384, 385
Joynt, R. J., 67
Jung, Carl, 167, 360, 367–368, 370, 375

Kalish, D., 318–319
Kant, Immanuel, 49, 50, 52, 249, 275
Kantowitz, B. H., 397
Katona, George, 264, 265, 276
Katz, David, 428
Kaufmann, Edgar, 243
Kazdin, A. E., 385
Kelley, Harold, 273
Kent, D., 438
Keppel, B., 440
Kesey, Ken, 384
Kessen, W., 431, 432
Kevles, D. J., 229
King, D. B., 149
King, H., 26, 152
Kinnaman, A. J., 165
Kintsch, W., 108, 414
Kirsch, I., 413
Klein, A. G., 226, 227
Klein, D. B., 26, 39, 41, 44, 49
Kleitman, Nathaniel, 423
Kline, Linus, 132, 164
Klopfer, W. G., 429
Kluger, R., 441
Knapp, T. J., 403
Koch, Sigmund, 6, 314, 435, 444
Koffka, Kurt, 242, 244, 248, 251–253, 257–258, 266, 270, 275, 276, 313, 438
Köhler, Thekla, 254

Köhler, Wolfgang, 242, 248, 251–255, 258–263, 274–276, 417, 431
Koller, Carl, 16
Korn, J. H., 149, 338, 425, 426
Kraepelin, Emil, 100, 348–350, 375
Krafft-Ebbing, Richard von, 359
Krantz, D. L., 188
Kreidl, Alois, 287
Kroll, J., 344
Kuhn, Thomas, 412–413
Kulman, C., 432
Külpe, Oswald, 83, 93, 95, 101, 109–111, 178, 184, 187, 250, 402

Lachman, R., 328, 409, 412
Ladd-Franklin, Christine, 109, 170, 171, 173, 182, 436
Lakin, M., 388
Lal, S., 440, 441
Lamal, P. A., 263
Lamarck, Jean Baptiste de, 116, 139
Landy, F. J., 236
Lange, Carl, 154
Langfeld, Herbert, 427–428
Larson, C., 178, 298
Lashley, Karl Spencer, 54, 69, 77–81, 258, 274, 318, 409, 410, 422, 432
Lathem, E. C., 9
Lavoisier, Antoine-Laurent, 351
Lazarus, Emma, 221
Leacock, Stephan, 369
Leahey, Thomas H., 19, 99, 100, 412–414
Leary, David, 150
Leborgne, 70–73
Leeuwenhoek, Antonie van, 27, 31
Leibniz, Gottfried Wilhelm, 49–50, 52
Lenin, Vladimir I., 287
Leonardo DaVinci, 26
Lesch, J. E., 129
Lewin, Kurt, 248, 255, 258, 265–274, 313, 424, 426, 431, 433, 439
Lewis, R. W. B., 149, 151, 152, 158
Ley, Ronald, 253, 254
Leys, R., 178, 183
Liebeault, Auguste, 352–353, 375
Lincoln, Abraham, 3
Lindley, Ernest, 223
Lindzey, G., 428, 429
Link, M., 85, 97, 161
Lipperhey, Hans, 26
Lippitt, Ronald, 271, 272
Lippmann, Walter, 234
Lloyd, M. A., 3
Lloyd Morgan, Conway, 127, 130–132, 140, 165, 195

Locke, John, 24, 34–38, 40, 48, 49, 51–52, 143, 312
Loeb, Jacques, 291, 335
Loftus, E. F., 409, 418
Logan, C. A., 287
Lorenz, Konrad, 128, 203, 294, 339
Lubbock, John, 163
Ludwig, Karl, 60
Lyell, Charles, 118–119, 122, 124, 139

McCarthy, Joseph, 321
Maccoby, E. E., 225
McCullough, David, 4, 5
McDermott, K. B., 409
McDougall, William, 236
Macfarlane, D. A., 314
McGinnes, E., 368
McGuire, W., 367
Mach, Ernst, 249, 275
MacLeod, C. M., 339
MacMillan, M. B., 70
McNeill, D., 153
McPherson, Marion White, 2–3, 15, 160, 179, 182, 212, 217, 219, 251, 325
McReynolds, P., 372, 395
Madigan, S., 169
Magendie, François, 57–59, 80, 190
Malone, J. C., 329
Malthus, Thomas, 121, 123, 139
Marbe, Karl, 111
Marrow, A. J., 265–268, 270–273, 313
Marsh, Francis, 213
Marshall, Thurgood, 441
Martin, Lillien, 109
Maslow, Abraham, 15, 378, 386–387, 392, 399
Maudsley, H., 227
May, Lucy, 11
Mayer, R. E., 265
Mazlish, B., 46
Mead, Margaret, 272
Medawar, P., 369
Mellon, Andrew, 188
Melville, Herman, 119
Mendel, G., 219
Menninger, Karl, 349
Merton, Robert, 13
Mesmer, Franz Anton, 350–351, 375
Meyer, Adolf, 298
Meynert, Theodor, 356, 375
Micale, M. S., 345
Miles, Walter R., 16, 17, 164, 288, 322, 436
Mill, James, 44–45, 47, 48, 52

Mill, John Stuart, 24, 34, 44–49, 51, 52, 56, 83, 127, 132, 143, 430
Miller, George A., 105, 411, 414–418, 432, 433, 443
Miller, Neal E., 326, 368
Mills, J., 425, 426
Mills, J. A., 325
Mills, Wesley, 202–203, 339
Milner, Peter, 423
Minton, H. L., 223–225, 232, 234, 244
Mitchell, Maria, 170
Molyneux, William, 37
Monastersky, R., 118
Moniz, Egas, 383, 398
Montague, Helen, 227
Moore, J., 116, 118–120, 122, 125, 129
Moore, T. V., 403
Moorehead, A., 119
Morawski, J. G., 324
Morgan, J. J. B., 299, 300
Morgan, J. P., 188
Morgan, M. J., 37
Morgulis, Sergius, 288, 289
Morison, S. E., 440
Morris, E. K., 294
Moskowitz, M. J., 235, 236
Moulton, Elizabeth, 196
Mowrer, O. H., 326, 385
Mowrer, Willie M., 385
Mozart, Wolfgang Amadeus, 350
Müller, Adolph Jost, 109
Müller, G. E., 83, 101, 108–109, 171, 251, 252, 255, 266
Müller, Johannes, 59–61, 63, 80, 108, 355
Münsterberg, Hugo, 18, 157, 168, 170, 186, 209, 235–242, 245, 313, 372, 394, 424, 427
Münsterberg, Scott, 378
Murchison, C., 309
Murphy, G., 158, 159

Naman, J. L., 243, 244
Napoleon, Bonaparte, 13
Napoli, D. S., 269, 373, 374, 387, 393
Neisser, Ulric, 401, 416–418, 433
Neugebauer, R., 344
Newell, Alan, 419
Newman, E. B., 250
Newton, Isaac, 9, 11, 27, 35, 38, 55, 80, 324
Nicholson, I. A. M., 428, 429
Nicolai, G. F., 288, 289
Nightingale, Florence, 46
Nyswander, D. B., 317

Oden, M. H., 225

O'Donnell, John M., 10, 19, 149, 172, 192, 211
Ogden, Robert, 110, 267
O'Hara, R., 169
Oldfield, R. C., 403
Olds, James, 423
Olmsted, Frederick Law, 346
Olton, D. S., 320
Oster, G. D., 302

Palermo, D., 413
Paley, William, 115
Palmer, R. R., 84
Pappenheim, Bertha, 356–357
Paracelsus, 9
Parkovnick, S., 424
Parsons, H. M., 397
Pastore, N., 254
Paul, G. L., 385
Pavlov, Ivan Petrovich, 6, 14, 43, 77, 195, 274, 278, 280–290, 300, 305, 310, 312, 324, 328, 340, 373, 385, 422, 431
Pearson, Karl, 135
Peirce, Charles S., 10
Penfield, Wilder, 422
Perin, C. T., 326
Perloff, R., 243, 244
Perot, P., 422
Pervin, C. T., 370
Peterson, D. R., 393
Pettigrew, T. F., 428
Phillips, L., 441
Piaget, Jean, 401, 430–433
Pick, H. L., Jr., 439
Pickren, W. E., 442
Pillsbury, W. B., 194, 296
Pilzecker, Alfons, 109
Pinel, Phillipe, 345, 346, 374
Piper, Leonore, 158
Planck, Max, 249, 275
Plato, 25, 26
Poffenberger, A. T., 203, 212, 226
Popplestone, John. A., 2, 15, 17, 109, 160, 179, 182, 212, 217, 219, 251, 325
Porter, J. P., 165
Pribram, Karl, 415–416, 433
Prytula, R. E., 302

Radbill, S. X., 57
Rafail, P. A., 16
Raimy, V. C., 393
Ramón y Cajal, Santiago, 76, 77, 81
Raphelson, A. C., 190, 192
Rayner, Rosalie, 299–302, 304–306, 384
Reed, J., 228

Reiber, R. W., 369
Reid, Thomas, 143–144
Renouvier, Charles, 151
Restak, R., 76
Restle, F., 318
Richards, R. J., 121
Richardson, J. T. E., 222
Ridley, S. E., 148
Rilling, M., 294
Ritchie, B. F., 318–319
Robinson, Daniel, 40
Robinson, J. K., 338
Rockefeller, John D., 188, 189
Roediger, H. L., III, 108, 397, 405, 409
Rogers, A., 244
Rogers, Carl, 378, 386–393, 399
Rohles, F. H., Jr., 336
Romanes, George, 127, 129–130, 132, 140, 178, 200
Roosevelt, Theodore, 236, 328
Rorschach, Hermann, 429
Rosenbaum, A. M., 244
Rosenthal, R., 48
Rosenzweig, S., 166, 360, 368
Rosnow, R. L., 48
Ross, Barbara, 3
Ross, Dorothy, 13, 159–162, 165–167
Royce, Josiah, 10
Rubin, Edgar, 255–256
Rucci, A. J., 426
Rudy, W., 147
Ruse, M., 115–117
Rush, Benjamin, 345–346, 374
Russell, Bertrand, 127
Russo, N. F., 439
Rutherford, A., 338, 339
Ryalls, J., 73
Ryan, W. C., 146, 189, 190

Sahakian, W. S., 84, 110, 349
Samelson, F., 279, 298, 309
Sanford, Edmund Clark, 16, 17, 132, 161, 162, 164, 170, 173, 179–180, 182–183, 185, 194
Satariano, W. A., 234
Scarborough, Elizabeth, 146, 168, 170, 171
Schlereth, T. J., 222
Schlosberg, H., 205
Schulman, B. J., 392
Schultz, D. P., 19
Schultz, S. E., 19
Schumann, Friedrich, 109, 251, 253
Scott, Walter Dill, 235, 242, 245, 303, 394
Scott-Kakures, D., 115
Scripture, E. W., 210, 211

Searle, John R., 420, 421
Sears, R. R., 326
Sechenov, Ivan M., 281, 284
Sechzer, J. A., 59
Sedgwick, Adam, 117, 118, 139
Segal, E. M., 328, 409, 412
Sexton, V. S., 2, 373, 381
Shakespeare, William, 44, 132, 364
Shakow, David, 108, 381, 398
Shannon, Claude, 411
Shepard, John, 322
Sherrington, Charles, 76–77, 81, 204
Shiffrin, R. M., 410–411
Shorter, E., 349, 382, 383
Simon, Herbert, 419
Simon, L., 149–151
Simon, Theodore, 217, 218, 430
Simonton, D. K., 3
Singer, C. A., 26
Skinner, B. F., 27, 202, 203, 290, 303, 308, 328–339, 341, 409, 411, 420–421
Small, Willard S., 132, 163–165, 194, 291–292, 317
Smith, L. D., 27, 336, 339, 442
Snarksi, Anton, 284
Sobel, D., 26, 94
Sokal, M. M., 16, 95, 97, 213–216, 243, 253, 394
Spalding, Douglas, 127–129, 132, 140, 203
Spearman, Charles, 233
Spence, Kenneth W., 324, 326, 385
Spencer, Herbert, 189
Sperry, R. W., 412
Sperry, Roger, 423
Spillman, J., 236
Spillman, L., 236
Spranger, Eduard, 428
Spurzheim, Johann, 65–66, 68, 74, 81
Stekel, W., 368
Stern, William, 224
Sterns, C. Z., 358
Stetson, G. R., 147
Stetter, Leta, *See* Hollingworth, Leta Stetter
Steudel, J., 59
Stevens, S. S., 311
Stocking, George, 7–8
Stogdill, Emily, 16
Stout, G. F., 44
Strachey, James, 360
Stricker, G., 393
Stroop, J. Ridley, 339, 402, 432
Strunk, O., Jr., 170
Stumpf, Carl, 59, 249, 250, 252, 255,

266, 275, 276
Sullivan, J. J., 178, 298
Sulloway, Frank J., 120, 353–356, 359, 367–370
Sultan (chimpanzee), 259–263
Sumner, Francis, 142, 147–148, 172, 440
Swazey, J. P., 76

Tan (patient), 70–73
Taschek, W., 115
Taylor, D. W., 76
Taylor, Harriet, 45–46
Taylor, Helen, 46
Taylor, John, 46
Taylor, S. E., 421
Temkin, O., 64
Terman, Louis M., 209, 221, 223–225, 228, 232–234, 244, 245
Thomas, E., 426
Thomas, K. S., 117
Thomas Aquinas, 25, 115
Thoreau, Henry David, 337
Thorndike, Edward L., 13, 130, 132, 163, 165, 176, 195–207, 221, 226, 232, 234, 242, 244, 258, 259, 262, 274, 280, 284, 305, 330, 339, 394
Thorndike, R. L., 198
Tinbergen, Niko, 128, 203, 294, 339
Titchener, Edward B., 11, 12, 16–19, 36, 93, 99–100, 108, 109, 111, 159–160, 166, 167, 171, 172, 176–189, 193, 195, 203, 204, 206, 235, 236, 270, 295, 296, 298, 329, 360, 369, 379, 402, 428, 436, 443
Todd, James T., 294, 298, 302, 304
Todes, D. P., 282, 284
Tolman, Edward Chace, 80, 163, 308, 312–321, 326, 327, 338–341, 409, 423
Tolman, Richard, 313, 336
Tolstoy, Leo, 13
Tomes, H., 442
Triplett, R. G., 324
Tryon, R. C., 317, 379
Tuke, William, 345, 346, 374
Turing, Alan, 420
Turner, R. S., 60
Twain, Mark, 401
Tweney, R. D., 426
Twitmyer, E. B., 287, 373

Ungerer, G. A., 92
Upham, Thomas, 144–145, 172

Valentine, C. W., 301–302
Vandenbos, G. R., 380
Vanderbilt, Cornelius, 188
Vassar, Matthew, 146–147
Vernon, Philip, 428
Vesalius, Andreas, 26
Vestal, M., 85, 97, 161
Veysey, L. R., 145
Viney, W., 3, 347
Viteles, Morris, 373, 395
von Ehrenfels, Christian, 249, 250
von Neuman, John, 410
Von Restorff, Hedwig, 264–265, 276
Voyat, G., 431
Vrooman, J. R., 27–29, 33
Vul'fson, S. G., 282

Wade, N. J., 63
Walk, Richard, 439
Wallace, Alfred Russell, 13, 14, 122–123, 139
Wallin, J. E. Wallace, 373–374
Warden, C. J., 194
Warner, L. H., 194
Warren, R. M., 60, 63
Washburn, Margaret Floy, 170–173, 182, 183, 436, 438
Watson, John Broadus, 10, 17, 36, 77, 79, 80, 178, 188, 194, 195, 204, 242, 278–280, 290–306, 309, 310, 312–314, 328, 330, 336, 339, 340, 384, 402, 409, 410, 420
Watson, Mary Ickes, 302
Watson, R. J., 219
Watson, Robert I., 2, 3, 13, 15, 21, 100, 367
Watson, Rosalie Rayner, 299–302, 304–306, 384
Watt, James, 110, 383–384
Weaver, K. A., 417
Weaver, W., 411
Webb, M. E., 42
Weber, Ernst, 85–87, 89, 111
Wedgwood, Emma, 120
Weiner, J., 120, 121, 345
Welles, Samuel, 67–68

Wellington, S. W., 348
Wernicke, Carl, 73
Wertheimer, Max, 248–253, 255–257, 263–265, 275, 276, 386, 392, 399, 402, 431, 439
White, M., 9
White, Ralph, 271–274
Whytt, Robert, 57, 76, 80
Wiesel, Torsten, 423
Wiggins, J. G., Jr., 394
Williams, D. H., 348
Williams, S. B., 326
Willis, Thomas, 31
Wilson, L. N., 159
Windelband, W., 427
Windholz, G., 263, 282, 284
Winston, Andrew, 205, 440
Winters, B., 351
Wissler, Clark, 214, 215
Withington, 290
Witmer, Lightner, 183, 186, 343, 371–373, 376, 379, 395
Wittman, Blanche, 353, 354
Wolpe, Joseph, 385, 399
Woodward, W. R., 338
Woodworth, Robert S., 109, 110, 176, 201, 203–207, 244, 274–275, 280, 303, 309, 310, 368, 394, 423, 440, 442
Wordsworth, William, 45
Wright, R., 139
Wundt, Wihelm, 2, 18, 19, 21, 50, 83, 85, 90–95, 97–101, 109–112, 143, 151, 152, 159, 161, 167, 171, 178, 181, 183, 186, 206, 209, 212, 213, 235, 278, 348–349, 371, 375, 394, 402

Yerkes, Robert M., 10, 14, 209, 221, 227–234, 236, 243, 245, 288–290, 313, 324, 438
Yoakum, C. S., 229–231
Young, R. M., 64
Young, Thomas, 61

Zajonc, B. F., 421, 425, 426
Zeigarnik, Bluma, 268–270, 276
Zilboorg, G., 344, 351
Zorich, S., 347

SUBJECT INDEX

AAAP, *see* American Association for Applied Psychology

AACP, *see* American Association of Clinical Psychologists

Ablation, method of, 68–69, 90

Absolute threshold, 89

Accommodation, 39, 62

Acquired characteristics, inheritance of, 116

Acquisitiveness, 65, 66

Adjustment, method of, 89

Adolescence (G. Stanley Hall), 166

Advertising, 302–303

African Americans, 147–148, 439–441

AGCT, *see* Army General Classification Test

Aging, 166

Agreement, Method of, 47, 48

AHAP, *see* Archives of the History of American Psychology

Aids in the Selection of Salesmen, 242

Alchemy, 6, 9

Algorithms, 419

Alma College, 322

American Association for Applied Psychology (AAAP), 374, 379, 387

American Association for the Advancement of Science, 165

American Association of Clinical Psychologists (AACP), 373–374, 379

American Association of Humanistic Psychologists, 392

American Association of the Feeble-Minded, 219

American Association of University Professors, 191

American Civil Liberties Union, 191

American Journal of Psychology, 161, 162, 166, 171, 179, 181

American Philosophical Association, 157

American Psychological Association (APA), 2–4, 7, 12, 78, 159, 164, 165, 170, 171, 181, 182, 191, 193, 202, 203, 205, 211, 214, 223, 228, 235, 253, 269, 272, 294, 298, 305, 312, 321, 329, 335, 371–374, 379–382, 387, 388, 392–394, 398, 422, 436, 439, 441–444

American Psychological Society (APS), 4, 380, 443, 444

American Psychologist, 2

American universities, 145–147, 172, 179. *See also specific universities*

Amherst College, 67, 203

Analysis, 183

Analysis of the Phenomena of the Human Mind (James Mill), 44, 46

Analysis of variance (ANOVA), 426

Analytical psychology, 368

Anecdotal evidence, 66

Anecdotal method, 129–130

Anesthesia, 352

Anglican Church (Church of England), 116–117, 124

Animal Education (John B. Watson), 291

Animal Intelligence (George Romanes), 129–130

Animal Intelligence: Experimental Studies (Edward L. Thorndike), 196–202

Animal Life and Intelligence (Conway Lloyd Morgan), 130

Animal magnetism, 350

The Animal Mind (Margaret Floy Washburn), 172

Animal spirits, 30

Anna O. case, 356–357

ANOVA (analysis of variance), 426

Anthropometric Laboratory, 135

Anthropomorphism, 130

Antioch College, 160–161

Anti-Semitism, 355, 369, 439–440

Antithesis, principle of, 127

Antivivesectionism, 293

Anxiety:
  moral, 366
  neurotic, 366
  objective, 366

APA, *see* American Psychological Association

Aphasia, 73

Apparent motion, 250–251

Apperception, 50, 100–101, 349

Applied psychology, 209–234, 394–397
  for business, 234–244
  and Hawthorne studies, 395–397
  mental testing movement as example of, 212–234
  origins of, 210–212

Approach-approach conflicts, 268

Approach-avoidance conflicts, 268

A priori knowledge, 50, 249

APS, *see* American Psychological Society

Aptitude Testing, 322

Archives, 15

Archives of the History of American Psychology (AHAP), 3, 15–17

Area, concept of, 264

Argument from design, 115

Army Alpha, 229, 230, 232

Army Beta, 229, 231, 232

Army General Classification Test (AGCT), 243, 398

Artificial intelligence (AI), 419–420

Asian-Americans, 439

Association:
  Mary Whiton Calkin's research on, 169
  Francis Galton's research on, 134–138

Associationism, 36, 40–44, 101–102, 143
  behaviorism and, 279
  definition of, 41
  David Hartley and, 42–44
  David Hume and, 41–42
  John Stuart Mill and, 48

Asylums, 345–348

Atlantic Monthly, 233, 235, 369

Atomism, 36, 38, 43, 252

Attention, selective filter model of, 415

Attributes, 186

Attrition, 226

Authoritarianism, 271, 272

Auto-erotism, 364

Avoidance-avoidance conflicts, 268

Barnard College, 244

Bed-wetting, 385

A Beginner's Psychology (E. G. Titchener), 179

Behavior:
  brain and, 421–423, 442
  molar, 314
Behavior: An Introduction to Comparative Psychology (John B. Watson), 313
Behavioral environment, 257
Behaviorism, 36, 100, 178, 194, 255, 269, 278–305, 308–340
  advertising and, 302–303
  antecedents of, 279–280
  and cognitive psychology, 403, 413, 417, 420–421
  Clark Hull's hypothetico-deductive, 321–328
  influence of, on American psychology, 339–340
  logical positivism and, 310
  and neobehaviorism, 312–313
  operationism and, 310–312
  Ivan Pavlov's contribution to, 280–290
  B. F. Skinner and, 328–339
  Edward C. Tolman's contribution to, 313–321
  John B. Watson and founding of, 279, 290–305
Behaviorism (John B. Watson), 303, 309–310
Behaviorist Manifesto, 279, 294–298, 309
The Behavior of Organisms (B. F. Skinner), 339
A Behavior System (Clark Hull), 325
Behavior therapy, 384–385
Behaviour Research and Therapy, 385
Bell-Magendie Law, 57–59
Berlin Psychological Institute, 252
Beyond the Pleasure Principle (Sigmund Freud), 365
Bible, 115, 118
Binet-Simon scales, 217–219, 222, 224
Binocular vision, 62
Bits, 411
Bloodletting, 345–346
Boston State Hospital, 228
Boulder model, 381, 382, 392–393
Bowdoin College, 144
Brain, 314
  and behavior, 421–423, 442
  as center of consciousness, 56
  as computer, 410–411, 421
  and isomorphism, 258
  mapping of the, 73–75
  methods for hardening the, 75
  Ivan Pavlov and, 281, 282, 285

of rats, 291
Brain function, localization of, 64–75, 79
  ablation studies on, 68–69
  clinical studies on, 69–73
  and mapping the brain, 73–75
  and phrenology, 64–68
Brain Mechanisms and Intelligence (Karl Lashley), 78
Brandeis University, 386
Brasenose College (Oxford University), 178
Brass instrument psychology, 153, 163, 179
Breslau (Germany), 214–215
Broca's area, 73
Brooklyn College, 386
Brown University, 243
Brown v. Board of Education, 440, 441
Business, psychology applied to, 234–244

Caffeine, 244
Cambridge University, 116, 117, 178, 213, 403, 415
"Can Psychology Be a Science of the Mind?" (B. F. Skinner), 329
Cardinal traits, 428
Carnegie Institute (Carnegie Institute of Technology), 242, 394, 395
Carnegie Mellon University, 242
Cartesian dichotomy, 29
Cartesianism, 25–34
  precursors of, 25–27
  and rationalism, 28–29
  and science, 27–28
Case study, 428
Case Western Reserve University, 203
Catharsis, method of, 357–358
Catholic Church, 26–29, 38
Cause and effect, 42, 431
CCI (Commission on Community Interrelations), 273
Cell assemblies, 423
Center for the Study of the Person, 388
Central traits, 428
Cerebellum, 68–69
Cerebral cortex, 68–69, 75
Chain of being, 116
Cheaper by the Dozen (Gilbreth and Carey), 243
Cheiron Society, 3
Children:
  and developmental psychology, 429–432
  Freud on sexuality in, 358–359, 364
  frustration in, 270–271
  giftedness in, 224

play therapy with, 366–367
  and Stanford-Binet IQ test, 223–224
Child Welfare Research Station (University of Iowa), 267, 270
Chinese Room problem, 420
Choice reaction time (CRT), 95, 96
Christ's College (Cambridge), 116
Chunks, 414–415
Church of England, *see* Anglican Church
City College of New York, 424, 441
Civilization, 16
Civil Rights Act of 1964, 439
Clark University, 2, 10, 12, 16, 17, 95, 96, 132, 145, 147, 148, 162–168, 172, 179–181, 190, 194, 218, 223, 244, 291, 359–360, 367, 369, 427
Classical conditioning, 300
Clinical method, 69–70, 73
Clinical psychology, 370–374, 380–394. *See also* Psychoanalysis
Clockmaking, 26, 29
Closure, 257
Coca-Cola Company, 244, 394
Cognition, gestalt approach to, 258–265
Cognition and Reality (Ulric Neisser), 418
Cognitive dissonance, 425
Cognitive Dissonance (Harmon-Jones and Mills), 426
Cognitive maps, 318–320
"Cognitive Maps in Rats and Men" (Edward Tolman), 317, 318*n*.1, 320
Cognitive psychology, 100, 402–421
  and artificial intelligence, 419–420
  Frederick Bartlett's contribution to, 403–409
  evaluation of, 420–421
  evolution of, 417–420
  influences on, 409–412
  and information theory, 410–417
  George Miller's contribution to, 414–416
  Ulric Neisser's contribution to, 416–417
  roots of modern, 402–403
Cognitive Psychology (journal), 418
Cognitive Psychology (T. V. Moore), 403
Cognitive Psychology (Ulric Neisser), 416–417
Cognitive science, 418
Cognitive Science, 418
Collective unconscious, 368
College de la Flèche, 27
Color vision, 61–63, 171
Columbia University, 109, 171, 172, 176, 191, 194–205, 213–214, 226, 242, 244, 279, 294, 301, 324, 368, 387, 440

Commission on Community Interrelations (CCI), 273
Committee on Training in Clinical Psychology (CTCP), 381
Comparative psychology, 9–10, 125
Completion test, 214–215
Complex ideas, 36
Complication experiment, 95–97
Computer science, 410–411, 419–420, 442
"Computing Machinery and Intelligence" (Alan Turing), 420
Concomitant Variation, 48
Condensation, 362
Conditional (conditioned) stimulus (CS), 285–287, 300, 385
Conditioned reflex (CR), 285, 287
Conditioned Reflexes (Ivan Pavlov), 284, 290
Conditioning, 77, 80, 384–385
    classical, 300
    operant, 330
Connectionism, 195–196, 200–202
Conscious attitudes, 111
Consciousness, 93, 125
    James R. Angell's views on, 193
    William James on, 153–154
    structuralist approach to, 186–187
Conservation of energy, 60
Constant stimuli, method of, 89
Contemporary Schools of Psychology (Robert S. Woodworth), 204, 309
Contiguity, 41–43
Contralateral function, 64
Contributions to a Theory of Sensory Perception (Wilhelm Wundt), 91, 92
Control:
    over nature, 279–280
    stimulus, 333
Convergence, 39
Converging operations, 311–312
Cornell University, 11, 19, 99, 170–172, 176–179, 183, 187, 195, 235, 253, 267, 269, 270, 280, 438–439
Correlation, 135
Correlational research, 205
Counseling and Psychotherapy (Carl Rogers), 388
CR, *see* Conditioned reflex
Cranioscopy, 64–65
Critical periods, 128–129
Critique of Practical Reason (Immanuel Kant), 50
Critique of Pure Judgment (Immanuel Kant), 50

Critique of Pure Reason (Immanuel Kant), 50
CRT, *see* Choice reaction time
CS, *see* Conditional (conditioned) stimulus
Ctastrophism, 118
CTCP (Committee on Training in Clinical Psychology), 381
Curve of forgetting, 25
Cybernetics, 415–416

Darwinian evolution, 9
Darwinian thinking, 8
Data selection, problems with, 17–18
Day View, 88, 89
Débiles, 217–219
Declaration of Independence, 34
Dedifferentiation, 271
Defense mechanisms, 366
Dementia praecox, 348, 349
Democracy, 224, 271, 272
Dependent variable, 205
Derived ideas, 29
The Descent of Man (Charles Darwin), 124, 125, 127
Determinism, 38
Developmental psychology, 165–166, 429–432
The Developmental Psychology of Jean Piaget (John Flavell), 432
Diagnostic and Statistical Manual of Mental Disorders (DSM-IV), 348
Diaries (as sources), 18
Dichotic listening, 415
Difference, Method of, 48
Difference thresholds, 89
Differentiation, 270, 285
Direct action of the nervous system, 127
Direct conditioning, 384
Discourse on Method (René Descartes), 28
Discrimination reaction time (DRT), 95, 96, 111
Displacement, 362
Diversity in psychology, 436, 438–442
Doctrine of the skull, 65
Dream analysis, 358
Drill courses, 179, 181
Drive, 204
Drive reduction, 325, 327
Drives Toward War (Edward Tolman), 321
DRT, *see* Discrimination reaction time
DSM-IV *(Diagnostic and Statistical Manual of Mental Disorders),* 348
Dualism, 29

Dynamic Psychology (Robert S. Woodworth), 204
Dynamics of Behavior (Robert S. Woodworth), 204

Ecological memory, 108
Ecological validity, 418
Education, John Locke on, 37–38
Educational Psychology (Edward L. Thorndike), 203
An Education in Psychology (Michael Sokal), 97
EEG (electroencephalograph), 423
Effect, law of, 200
"The Effects of Psychotherapy: An Evaluation" (Hans Eysenck), 382
Ego, 366
The Ego and Mechanisms of Defense (Sigmund Freud), 367
The Ego and the Id (Sigmund Freud), 366
Electrical stimulation (of the brain), 73–75
Electroencephalograph (EEG), 423
Elements of Mental Philosophy (Thomas Upham), 144–145
Elements of Psychophysics (Gustav Fechner), 89–90, 101
Ellis Island, 222
Emotions:
    William James on, 154–157
    structuralist approach to, 186
Emotional expressions, evolution of, 125–127
Empathy, 390
Empiricism, 34–50, 99, 101–102, 143, 310
    of George Berkeley, 38–40
    and British associationism, 40–44
    Locke and origins of, 34–38
    of John Stuart Mill, 45–49
    rationalist responses to, 49–50
Employee selection, 236–242
Energy(-ies):
    conservation of, 60
    specific, 59, 75
Engineering psychology, 398
English Men of Science (Francis Galton), 134
Enlightenment, 55–56, 115, 344–345, 412
Epilepsy, 353
Epistemology, 35, 431
Eponyms, 11
Equilibrium, 268
Equipotentiality, 69, 79
Ergonomics, 244
Erogenous zones, 363

Eros, 365
An Essay Concerning Human Understanding (John Locke), 34–36, 49
An Essay Towards a New Theory of Vision (George Berkeley), 39
Ethology, 127, 203
Eugenics, 134–135, 212, 221
Eugenics Society, 134
Evolution, theory of, 9, 13, 14, 116–127
   Darwin's development of, 120–123
   and Darwin the person, 116–117
   elements of, 123–124
   Lamarck's contribution to, 116
   and psychology, 124–127
   recent renewed interest in, 442
   and voyage of the *Beagle,* 117–120
Evolutionary biology, 178
Evolutionary psychology, 139
Examination of Phrenology (Pierre Flourens), 68
Examination of Sir William Hamilton's Philosophy (John Stuart Mill), 46
Exercises, law of, 200, 201
Experience(s), 39
   immediate vs. mediate, 93
   peak, 387
Experimentalists, 4, 182, 183
Experimental method, 205, 250
Experimental neurosis, 285–286
Experimental psychology, 153
   Oswald Külpe's contribution to, 109–111
   mazes in, 163–165
   G.E. Müller as founder of, 108–109
   and structuralism, 179–183
Experimental Psychology (Robert S. Woodworth), 205
Experimental Psychology: A Manual of Laboratory Practice (E. B. Titchener), 180
Experimental reality, 426
"Experimental Studies on the Perception of Movement" (Wertheimer et al.), 250
Explanation (as goal of psychology), 183
Explanatory fictions, 334–335
Expressions of the Emotions in Man and Animals (Charles Darwin), 124, 125
External history, 9–10
Extinction, 285, 331

Fabric of the Human Body (Andreas Vesalius), 26
Faculties, 144, 212–213

Faculty psychology, 143–144
Feeblemindedness, 223
Feedback, 415–416
Field theory, 249, 267, 314
Figure-ground segregation, 255–256, 265
Fingerprinting, 133
"The First Sure Steps Along the Path of a New Investigation" (Ivan Pavlov), 281
Force fields, 249
Foreign hull, 267
Form-quality *(Gestaltqualität),* 250
Fowler and Wells, Inc., 67, 68
Fractionation, 110
Fragmentation of psychology, 443–444
Free association, 358
Free will, 151
French Revolution, 345
French Royal Academy of Sciences, 351
Freudianism, 236
Frustation and Aggression (Dollard et al.), 326
Frustration, 270–271
Frustration-aggression hypothesis, 326
Functional fixedness, 265
Functionalism, 125, 188–205
   James R. Angell and, 191–194
   Harvey Carr and, 194
   at Columbia University, 194–205
   definition of, 189
   John Dewey and, 190–191
   structuralism vs., 177
   Edward L. Thorndike and, 195–203
   at University of Chicago, 189–194
   Robert S. Woodworth and, 203–205
Functions of the Brain (David Ferrier), 74–75
Furman University (Greenville, SC), 291

G. Stanley Hall Lecture Series, 7
Galapagos Islands, 119–121
Galton whistle, 135–136
Generalization, 285, 301
General Problem Solver (GPS), 419
Genetic epistemology, 431
Genetic mutation, 123
Genetic psychology, 160, 165
Genetic Studies of Genius (Lewis Terman), 225
Geocentric view of the universe, 26
Geographical environment, 257
George Peabody College, 339
German universities, 84–85, 145, 172, 179. *See also specific universities*
Gestalt organizing principles, 255

Gestalt psychology, 191, 244, 248–275, 313, 324–325
   in America, 274–275
   and apperception, 255–258
   cognition and learning as viewed by, 258–265
   Kurt Koffka and, 252–253
   Kurt Lewin and, 265–274
   origins and development of, 249–255
   Max Wertheimer and, 250–252
Gestalt Psychology (Wolfgang Köhler), 255
Gestaltqualität (form-quality), 250
Gifted Children (Leta Hollingworth), 226
Giftedness, 224–225
Gilbreth, Inc., 243
Goal-directedness, 315
God, 35, 40, 42, 115, 118, 120–121, 124, 143, 150
Good continuation, 257
GPS (General Problem Solver), 419
Grammars, 412
"Great Man" theory, 10–11
Greece, ancient, 25
The Growth of the Mind (Kurt Koffka), 252
Guillotine, 56, 351
Gyrator, 346

Habits, 154
Habit strength, 322, 325, 327
Hamilton College, 328
Hampton maze (Hampton Court design), 164, 292, 317
Handbook of Human Physiology (Johannes Müller), 59
Handbook of Physiological Optics (Hermann von Helmholtz), 61, 62
Harper's magazine, 232, 235, 303
Harvard University, 10, 12, 17, 70, 77, 145, 146, 150, 151, 161, 168, 170, 186, 192, 195, 203, 227–228, 232, 235, 236, 311, 313, 328–329, 339, 414, 417, 424, 427–428, 431
Hawthorne studies (Hawthorne Effect), 395–397
Hebb synapses, 423
Hebrew University in Jerusalem, 272
Heliocentric theory, 26
Heliotropism, 291
Hereditary Genius (Francis Galton), 133–134
Heroic science, 55–56
"Heterodoxy Club," 226
Heuristics, 419

Higher mental processes, Wundt's studies of, 93–94
Hispanic Americans, 439
Historical truth, 20–21
Historicism, 7–9
Historiography, 15–21
    definition of, 15
    and historical truth, 20–21
    problems with, 17–20
    and sources of data, 15–17
History, reasons for studying, 3–6
History of British India (James Mill), 44
A History of Experimental Psychology (E. G. Boring), 2, 12, 13, 19, 100
History of psychology, 2–3
    diversity in, 436, 438–442
    internal vs. external, 9–10
    key issues in, 7–11, 13–15
    old vs. new, 7
    personalistic vs. naturalistic, 10–11, 13–14
    presentism vs. historicism in, 7–9
    reasons for studying, 6–7
    and recent trends, 442–444
"The History of Psychology" (Robert Watson), 2
History of Psychology Group, 2
A History of Psychology in Autobiography, 149, 234, 431
History of Science, 3
Hixon Symposium, 409, 410
HMS Beagle, 117–120, 123, 126
Holism, 43–44
"Hot-Air Club," 270, 273
Howard University, 148, 440
Hull-Spence theory, 324
Human Efficiency in Business (Walter Dill Scott), 235
Humanistic psychology, 385–392
Hydrophobia, 357–358
Hydrotherapy, 358
Hypnosis, 358
Hypnosis and Suggestibility: An Experimental Approach (Clark Hull), 323
Hypnosis/hypnotism, 216, 236, 323, 352–354
Hypothetico-deductive systems, 324
Hysteria, 216, 353, 356–359

Id, 366
Ideas:
    complex, 36
    derived, 29
    Hume's concept of, 41

innate, 29
simple, 36
Idealism, subjective, 40
Idiographic approach to science, 427
Idiots, 217
IHR, *see* Institute of Human Relations
Imbeciles, 217
Immediate conscious experience, 93
Immigration, 221–222, 233–234
Impressions, 41
Imprinting, 128, 203
Independent variable, 205
Index of Prohibited Books, 26, 29
Indiana University, 223, 329
The Individual and His Religion (Gordon Allport), 429
Individual differences, 125, 132–135, 138, 187–188
Individual psychology, 217, 367
Inductive approach, 27, 213
Industrial psychology, 236, 394–397. *See also* Applied psychology
Industrial Psychology (Morris Viteles), 395
Industrial Revolution, 56, 116
Inferiority complex, 367
Information theory, 411
Inheritance of acquired characteristics, 116
Innate ideas, 29
An Inquiry into Human Faculty and Its Development (Francis Galton), 135
Inquisition, 26
Insight, 258–259
Instinct, 128, 356
Institute for Child Guidance (New York), 387
Institute of Experimental Medicine (St. Petersburg), 281–283, 288
Institute of Human Relations (IHR), 324, 326
The Integrative Action of the Nervous System (Charles Sherrington), 76
Intelligence:
    controversy over, within testing movement, 233–234
    Francis Galton on nature of, 133–135
Intelligence quotient, *see* IQ/IQ test
Interactionism, 29
Internal history, 9–10
Internal perception, 93, 94, 183
International Center for Genetic Epistemology (Geneva), 431
The Interpretation of Dreams (Sigmund Freud), 358, 359, 367
Intervening variables, 315

An Introduction to Comparative Psychology (Conwy Lloyd Morgan), 130
Introspection, 93, 110, 152, 184, 188, 310, 311
Introspective habit, 184–186
Inventing Personality (I. A. M. Nicholson), 429
"IQ Farming," 244
IQ/IQ test, 6, 7, 68, 218, 223–225, 232, 234, 305, 372
Isomorphism, 258
Ivy League schools, 145, 146

James-Lange theory, 186, 203
Jesuits, 27
jnd (just noticeable difference), 87
Johns Hopkins University, 77, 95, 97, 145–146, 161–163, 165–166, 170–171, 190, 194, 213, 293, 298–299, 302, 322, 409
Joint Method, 48
Jost's law, 109
Journal of Abnormal Psychology, 368
Journal of Experimental Psychology, 299, 326, 338, 418, 424
Journal of Genetic Psychology, 165
A Journal of Humanistic Psychology, 392
Journal of the History of the Behavioral Sciences, 3, 7
Judgments, making, 87
Just noticeable difference (jnd), 87
Juvenile delinquency, 222

The Kallikak Family (Henry Goddard), 220
Kinesthetic sense, 292–293
Knowledge, 40, 50, 279
Kymograph, 109

Laboratory methods, debate about, 202–203
Lafayette College (Easton, PA), 212
Laissez-faire leadership style, 271, 272
Language and Communication (George Miller), 414
Language and linguistics, 411–412, 420
The Language and Thought of the Child (Jean Piaget), 431
Latent learning, 317–318
Latent period, 285
The Later Maturity of the Gifted (Lewis Terman), 225
Laura Spelman Rockefeller Memorial Fund, 303, 324

Law of Effect, 200
Law of Exercise, 200, 201
Law of parsimony, 131–132, 280
Lawrence Scientific School (Harvard University), 150
Leadership styles, 271, 272
Learning:
  behaviorist view of, 314–320, 322–328, 334
  gestalt approach to, 258–263
  latent, 317–318
  neobehaviorist view of, 312–313
  paired-associate, 169
  serial, 103
  Edward L. Thorndike's views of, 105–202
  trial-and-error, 200
Lectures on Human and Animal Psychology (Wilhelm Wundt), 91, 195
Letters (as sources), 18
Libido, 365
Liebeault-Bernhim theory of hypnosis, 353
Life and Confessions of a Psychologist (G. Stanley Hall), 166
Life space, 258, 267
Limits, method of, 89
Lincoln University, 148
Linguistic universals, 412
Linnean Society, 122
Little Albert study, 299–302, 384
Lloyd Morgan's canon, 130
Lobotomy, 383–384
Logical positivism, 310, 324
The Logic of Modern Physics (Percy Bridgman), 310–311
Logic Theorist (LT), 419
London University, 403
Long-term memory (LTM), 410–411
Los Angeles State Normal School, 223
LT (Logic Theorist), 419
LTM, *see* Long-term memory
Lying, 425

McCarthyism, 321
McGill University, 422
McLean Asylum, 346
"The Magical Number Seven, Plus or Minus Two: Some Limits on Our Capacity for Processing Information" (George Miller), 414
"The Manuals" (E. B. Titchener), 180, 183
Massachusetts Institute of Technology (MIT), 267, 273, 313, 411, 417, 418, 424

Mass action, 69, 79
Materialism, 38, 60, 61, 88, 89
The Mathematical Theory of Communication (Shannon and Weaver), 411
Maze studies, 163–165, 194–196, 291–293, 312, 314–320
Means-end analysis, 419
Mechanism, 29, 281
Mediate experience, 93
Medical Inquiries and Observations upon the Diseases of the Mind (Benjamin Rush), 345
Mediums, 157–159
Memory:
  Frederick Bartlett's study of, 403–409
  Mary Whiton Calkin's study of, 169
  and chunks, 414–415
  and computer science, 410–411
  Hermann Ebbinghaus' study of, 102–108
  ecological, 108
  gestalt approach to, 264–265, 268–269
  G.E. Müller's study of, 108–109
Memory and Cognition, 418
Memory drum, 109
Mental age, 218, 219, 223–224
Mental chronometry, 94–97
Mental Hygiene movement, 348
Mental illness:
  and clinical psychology in America, 370–374
  diagnosis of, 348–350
  early treatments for, 344–348
  Freud's psychoanalysis and treatment of, 354–370
  mesmerism and hypnosis as treatments for, 350–354
The Mentality of Apes (Wolfgang Köhler), 253, 254, 258–263
Mental level, 218, 219
Mental set, 110–111
Mental tests, 213
Mental testing movement, 212–234, 309, 373
  Alfred Binet's role in, 215–218
  James McKeen Cattell's role in, 212–215
  and controversy over intelligence, 233–234
  Henry Goddard's role in, 218–223
  Lewis Terman's role in, 223–225
  Robert M. Yerkes' role in, 227–233
Meritocracy, 224, 234, 244
Mesmerism, 351–352

Metapsychology, 365
Method of ablation, 68–69, 90
Method of adjustment, 89
Method of Agreement, 47, 48
Method of catharsis, 357–358
Method of constant stimuli, 89
Method of Difference, 48
Method of limits, 89
Method of repeated reproduction, 406
Microscope, 27–28
Mind, 144
Mind (journal), 124, 213
A Mind That Found Itself (Clifford Beers), 348
Minorities, in history of psychology, 439–442
MIT, *see* Massachusetts Institute of Technology
Molar behavior, 314
Monads, 49–50
Moniz procedure, 383, 384
Moral anxiety, 366
Morons, 219, 222, 223, 233
Morrill Land Grant Act of 1862, 145
Morse code, 415
Motion, apparent, 250–251
Motor aphasia, 73
Multiples, 13
"Myth of the hero," 354–355

Nancy School of hypnosis, 352–354
NASA, 336
National Academy of Sciences, 171, 203
National Committee for Mental Hygiene, 348
National Intelligence Tests, 232
National Origins Act of 1924, 234
National Research Council, 232
National Science Foundation, 3
Native Americans, 439
Nativism, 233, 412
Naturalistic history, 10, 11, 13–14
Natural selection, 114, 121, 123–124, 146
Natural Theology (William Paley), 115
Nature, control over, 279–280
The Nature of Prejudice (Gordon Allport), 429
Nature vs. nurture, 49
Negative reinforcers, 331
Neobehaviorism, 312–313
Nervous system, direct action of the, 127
Neural impulses, speed of, 60–61
Neuron theory, 75–77
Neurophysiological context of psychology, 54–80

brain function, localization of, 64–75
early 20th-century studies, 75–80
and Enlightenment, 55–56
sensory physiology, 56–63
Neurosis, experimental, 285–286
Neurotic anxiety, 366
Neurotransmitters, 77
Neurypnology, 352
New Anatomy of the Brain (Charles Bell), 58
New Essays On Human Understanding (Gottfried Leibniz), 49
"New Psychology," 25, 87, 90–94, 101, 190
New Republic, 234
New School for Social Research, 252, 303, 424–425
Newtonian physics, 36, 413
Night View, 88, 90
Nomothetic approach to science, 427
Nonsense syllables, 102–108
Normal science, 413
Northside Center for Child Development, 441
Northwestern University, 314, 394

Objective anxiety, 366
Objectivity, 56, 279
Observation, 250, 279
Observations on Man, His Frame, His Duty, and His Expectations (David Hume), 42
Observer, 180
Occipital cortex, 75
Occipital lobe, 75
Oedipal complex, 359, 363–365, 370
Ohio State University, 222, 388
Olfactometer, 180
On Becoming a Person (Carl Rogers), 388
One Flew Over the Cuckoo's Nest (Ken Kesey), 384
"On Gestalt Qualities" (Christian von Ehrenfels), 250
On Liberty (John Stuart Mill), 46
On Memory (Hermann Ebbinghaus), 102–108, 136
On the Origin of Species (Charles Darwin), 121, 122, 124, 189*n*.5, 281, 356
On the Witness Stand (Hugo Münsterberg), 236
Operant, 331
Operant conditioning, 330
"The Operational Analysis of

Psychological Terms" (B. F. Skinner), 335
"The Operational Definition of Concepts" (S. S. Stevens), 311
Operationism, 310–312
Ophthalmoscope, 61
Opponent process theory, 62
Optics, 27–28, 39–40
Optic nerve, 75
The Organization of Behavior (Donald O. Hebb), 423
Organizing and Memorizing (George Katona), 265
Orthogenics, 373
An Outline of Psychology (E. B. Titchener), 177
Outline of Psychology (E. G. Titchener), 179
Outlines of Phrenology (Johann Spurzheim), 65, 66
Oxford University, 35, 178

Paired-associate learning, 169
Paradigms, 413
Parsimony, law of, 131–132, 280
The Passions of the Soul (René Descartes), 29–33, 42
Pattern and Growth in Personality (Gordon Allport), 428
Pavlov Institute (St. Petersburg), 288
Pavlov pouch, 281
Peak experiences, 387
Pedagogical Seminary, 165
Perception:
    and Gestalt psychology, 249–252, 255–258
    internal, 93, 94, 183
    problem of, 63
"Perception: An Introduction to Gestalt-Theorie" (Kurt Koffka), 252
Perception and Communication (Donald Broadbent), 415
Periodic function, 146, 226, 227
Permanent Perceiver, 40
The Persistent Problems of Philosophy (Mary Calkins), 170
Personal equation, 95
Personalistic history, 10–11, 13–14
Personality psychology, 426–429
Petites perceptions, 50
Phase sequences, 423
Phenomenology, 249
Philosophical context of psychology, 10, 24–51
    British empiricism, 34–49

Cartesianism, 25–34
    and rationalist responses to empiricism, 49–50
Philosophische Studien, 94, 171
Phi phenomenon, 251
Phrenological Journal, 67
Phrenology, 54, 64–68, 74, 117*n*.2, 144
Physics, 249
Pineal gland, 32–33
Plans and the Structure of Behavior (Miller, Galanter, and Pribram), 415, 416
Play therapy, 366–367
"A Plea for the Training of Psychologists" (L. Crane), 393
Plessy v. Ferguson, 440
Popular Science Monthly, 280
Population growth, 121
Positive knowledge, 279
Positive reinforcers, 331
Positivism, 279, 304, 310, 324
"The Postulates of Structural Psychology" (James R. Angell), 193
Pragmatism, 151, 211. *See also* Applied psychology
Pragmatism (William James), 157
Prägnanz, 257
Prefrontal leucotomy, 383
Presentism, 7–9
Primary qualities, 36–37
Primary reinforcers, 325
Primary sources, 15
Primer of Psychology (E. G. Titchener), 179
Princeton University, 182, 188
Principia Mathematica (Isaac Newton), 35, 55, 324
Principles of Behavior (Clark Hull), 325
Principles of Geology (Charles Lyell), 118
Principles of Gestalt Psychology (Kurt Koffka), 253, 257
Principles of Physiological Psychology (Wilhelm Wundt), 90–92, 161
The Principles of Psychology (William James), 128, 149–154, 157, 159, 168, 169, 190, 192, 195, 203, 235, 313
Printing press, 26
"The Prison of the Present" (Daniel Boorstin), 5
Problem of perception, 63
Problem solving, 265, 335, 419
Proceedings of the British Society for Psychical Research, 158

Productive thinking, 263–264
Productive Thinking (Max Wertheimer), 252, 258
Productivity, 272–273
Professionalization of psychology, 159–160, 442
Progressive education, 191
Progressive relaxation, 385
Projection, 366
Project Pigeon, 336
Property (Acquisitiveness), 65, 66
Proximity, 256
Psychoanalysis, 350, 354–370, 429
  in America, 368–369
  catharsis method as precursor of, 356–358
  development of, 358–360
  Freud's Clark University lectures on, 360–365
  and Freud's contributions to psychology, 369–370
  and Freud's followers, 367–368
  and Freud the person, 354–356
  and psychoanalytic theory, 365–367
Psycholinguistics, 94
Psychological Bulletin, 252, 258, 288
Psychological Care of Infant and Child (John B. Watson), 303, 304
The Psychological Clinic, 372
Psychological Corporation, 214–215, 243, 303, 394–395
Psychological Institute (Berlin), 266, 268
Psychological Monographs, 265
Psychological Review, 177, 202, 214, 298, 317, 414
Psychological Review Monograph, 168
Psychological Science in the Public Interest, 380
Psychologies of 1925 (C. Murchison), 309
Psychologische Forschung, 255
Psychology (John Dewey), 190
Psychology (Robert S. Woodworth), 205
Psychology: A Study of a Science (Sigmund Koch), 314
Psychology: A Study of Mental Activity (Harvey Carr), 194
Psychology: The Briefer Course (William James), 152, 154
Psychology and Industrial Efficiency (Walter Dill Scott), 394
Psychology From the Standpoint of a Behaviorist (John B. Watson), 298
Psychology of Productive Thought (Karl Duncker), 265
Psychonomic Society, 380, 443

The Psychopathology of Everyday Life (Sigmund Freud), 359, 363
Psychophysical parallelism, 43, 49
Psychophysics, 85–91, 111
  definition of, 85
  Gustav Fechner's contribution to, 87–90
  Ernst Weber's contribution to, 85–87
Psychotherapy (Hugo Münsterberg), 236
Psy.D. degree, 387, 393–394
Purposive Behavior in Animals and Men (Edward Tolman), 314, 317
Purposiveness, 315
Puzzle boxes, 130, 132, 197–201, 258, 280

Qualitative experiments, 180
Quantitative experiments, 180

Racism (in education), 147
Radcliffe College, 146, 170
RAM, 410
Rationalism, 28–29
RATR, *see* Relay Assembly Test Room
Reaction formation, 366
Reaction potential, 326, 327
Reaction time, 94–97, 181
Recapitulation, 166
Recoding, 415
Red Scare, 233
Reflection, 390
Reflex(es):
  conditioned, 285, 287
  unconditioned, 285
Reflex action, 56–57, 76–77
Reflex arc, 190–191, 193
Reflexes of the Brain (Ivan Sechenov), 281
Reinforcement, schedules of, 332–333
Reinforcers:
  positive vs. negative, 331
  primary vs. secondary, 325
Relativism, historical, 20
Relay Assembly Test Room (RATR), 396–397
Reliability, 317
Remembering: A Study in Experimental and Social Psychology (Frederick C. Bartlett), 403
Renaissance, 25–26, 29
Repeated reproduction, method of, 406
Repetition, 43
Replication, 282, 311
Repression, 366, 368
Research Bureau for Retail Training, 242–243
Research Center for Group Dynamics (MIT), 267, 273

Resemblance, 41
Resistance, 358
Response, unconditioned, 300
Retroactive inhibition, 109
Rockefeller Institute, 290
Rorschach inkblot test, 429
Royal Air Force, 415
Royal College of Science (London), 130
Royal Geographical Society, 132
Royal Society, 35, 134
Russia, *see* Soviet Union
Russian Academy of Science, 287

St. Louis World's Fair (1904), 280, 290
St. Mary's College, 3
Salpêtrière asylum, 345, 352–354
Savings method, 105–106
Schedules of reinforcement, 332–333
Schedules of Reinforcement (Ferster and Skinner), 332–333, 339
Schemata, 404, 408, 431
Schizophrenia, 100n.5, 348–350
Scholasticism, 27, 38
The School and Society (John Dewey), 191
School of Life Insurance Salesmanship, 243
School psychology, 372
Schools of Contemporary Psychology (Robert Woodworth), 274
Science, 26–28
  heroic, 55–56
  nomothetic vs. idiographic approaches to, 427
  normal, 413
  positivist view of, 279–280
  and pragmatism, 211
Science, 159, 214, 394
Science and Human Behavior (B. F. Skinner), 330–334
Scientist-practitioner model, 381–382
Scotland Yard, 133
The Scott Company, 394
Scottish Realism, 143–144
Secondary qualities, 37
Secondary reinforcers, 325
Secondary sources, 15, 289
Secondary traits, 428
Sectioning, 75
Seduction hypothesis, 358–359
Segregation, 440–441
Selective filter model, 415
Self-actualization, 386
Self-observation, 93, 110, 152
Self psychology, 170

Semantics, 420

Senescence: The Last Half of Life (G. Stanley Hall), 166

Sensory aphasia, 73

Sensory circles, 86

Sensory physiology, 56–63
  and Bell-Magendie Law, 57–59
  Helmholtz' contribution to, 59–63
  reflex studies, 57
  and specific energies of nerves, 59

SEP, *see* Society of Experimental Psychologists

Serial learning, 103

Serial order problem, 410

Serviceable associated habits, 126

Seven Psychologists (Edna Heidbreder), 2

Sexism, 135, 146, 167, 171, 182–183, 438

Sexuality:
  Freud's focus on, 358–360, 362–365
  G. Stanley Hall's attitude toward, 166–167

"Shakow Report," 381

Shaping, 332

Short-term memory (STM), 410–411

Sign-gestalt, 315

Simple ideas, 36

Simple reaction time (SRT), 95, 96, 111

Smith College, 167, 253, 270, 438

Social action, 273

Social contract, 34

Social Darwinism, 189

Social Learning and Imitation (Dollard et al.), 326

Social psychology, 271–273, 423–426

Social Psychology (Floyd Allport), 424

Society for Psychical Research, 158, 159

Society for the Psychological Study of Social Issues (SPSSI), 272

Society of Experimental Psychologists (SEP), 379, 436, 438

Some Thoughts Concerning Education (John Locke), 34, 37–38

Sorbonne, 216–217

S-O-R model, 204

Sources, primary vs. secondary, 15, 289

Soviet Union, 287–288, 321, 397

Spatial contiguity, 43

Spatial summation, 77

Special education, 217

Species problem, 115–116

Specific energies (of nerves), 59, 75

Spinal cord, 57, 58, 76

Spiritualism, 157–159

SPSSI (Society for the Psychological Study of Social Issues), 272

SRT, *see* Simple reaction time

Stanford-Binet IQ test, 223–224

Stanford University, 109, 145, 223, 267, 270, 424, 425

State universities, 145

Stimulus:
  conditional (conditioned), 285–287, 300, 385
  unconditioned, 285, 286, 300, 385

Stimulus control, 333

Stimulus error, 184

STM, *see* Short-term memory

Strong AI, 420

Stroop effect, 339, 402

Structuralism, 36, 99, 100, 177–188
  and experimental psychology, 179–183
  functionalism vs., 177
  and Titchener's concept of introspection, 183–1881
  and Titchener the person, 178–179

The Structure of Scientific Revolutions (Thomas Kuhn), 412–414

Struggle for existence, 123

Studies on Hysteria (Freud and Breuer), 357

A Study of American Intelligence (Carl Brigham), 233

A Study of Values (Gordon Allport), 428

The Subjection of Women (John Stuart Mill), 46

Subjective idealism, 40

Sublimation, 365

Subtractive method, 95

Subvocal speech, 296

Suggestion, 353

Superego, 366, 370

Surgery, 352

Survey method, 134

Swarthmore College, 255, 265

Synapse, 76–77

Synthesis, 183

Systematic desensitization, 301, 385

Systematic experimental introspection, 110, 184

Systematic Psychology (E. B. Titchener), 187

A System of Logic (John Stuart Mill), 46, 47

Technological ideal, 336

Telescope, 27–28

Telling the Truth About History (Appleby, Hunt, and Jacob), 20

Temporal contiguity, 43

Temporal summation, 77

Tenerife, 253–254

"Termites," 226

A Textbook of Psychology (E. G. Titchener), 179, 183

Thanatos, 365

Theories of Learning (Ernest Hilgard), 290

The Theory and Practice of Advertising (Walter Dill Scott), 235

The Theory of the Sensation of Tone as a Physiological Basis for the Theory of Music (Hermann von Helmholtz), 62–63

Thinking: An Experimental and Social Study (Frederick C. Bartlett), 403

Thinking, as subvocal speech, 296

Thinking, Feeling, Doing (E. W. Scripture), 210–211, 235

Three Contributions to the Theory of Sex (Sigmund Freud), 359, 363

Time-and-motion studies, 243

Title IX (Civil Rights Act of 1964), 439

Topology, 267

Topology Group, 270, 313

TOTE units, 416

Tower of Silence, 282–283

Training, clinical, 381–382

Traits, 428

Traitement moral, 345

Tranquilizer chair, 346

Transfer, 204, 300, 301

Transference, 358

Transorbital lobotomy, 383–384

Treatise Concerning the Principles of Human Knowledge (George Berkeley), 39, 40

A Treatise of Human Nature (David Hume), 41

Treatise on Man (René Descartes), 31

Trends in psychology, recent, 442–444

Trial-and-error learning, 200

Trichromatic theory, 61–63

Tropisms, 291

Truth, 20–21, 279

Turing test, 420

Twin studies, 134

Two-point thresholds, 85–87

Two Treatises on Government (John Locke), 34

UCLAS, 223

UCR, *see* Unconditioned reflex; Unconditioned response

UCS, *see* Unconditioned stimulus

Unconditional positive regard, 390

Unconditioned reflex (UCR), 285
Unconditioned response (UCR), 300
Unconditioned stimulus (UCS), 285, 286, 300, 385
Unconscious, collective, 368
Unconscious inference, 63
Uniformitarianism, 118–119
Union Theological Seminary, 160, 387
U.S. Army, 228, 394, 426
U.S. Constitution, 55
U.S. Public Health Service, 381
U.S. Supreme Court, 440, 441
University College, Bristol, 130
University College, London, 351–352
University of Akron, 3, 15
University of Berlin, 60, 63, 84, 85, 90, 109, 151, 161, 192, 252, 255
University of Bonn, 61, 101
University of California, Berkeley, 243, 321
University of California Publications in Psychology, 317
University of Chicago, 77, 145, 162, 165, 172, 176, 189–194, 242, 279, 290, 291, 293, 294, 302, 324, 388
University of Colorado, 194, 381, 382
University of Edinburgh, 116, 252
University of Frankfurt, 251–253
University of Freiburg, 235, 266
University of Giessen, 252
University of Göttingen, 84, 108, 171, 255
University of Halle, 145
University of Heidelberg, 61, 63, 85, 90–92, 94, 151, 349
University of Illinois, 387
University of Iowa, 267, 270, 272, 424
University of Königsberg, 60–61
University of Leipzig, 84, 85, 87, 88, 91, 92, 94, 95, 97–101, 108–110, 161, 176, 178, 183, 192, 235, 349
University of Michigan, 190, 192, 322, 424
University of Minnesota, 77, 192, 228, 232, 329, 424
University of Munich, 266, 349
University of Nebraska, 244
University of New Hampshire, 3

University of Pennsylvania, 183, 186, 213, 371, 395
University of Pittsburgh, 77
University of Prague, 250
University of St. Petersburg, 281
University of Tübingen, 90
University of Vermont, 190, 191
University of Vienna, 350, 351, 355, 367
University of Wisconsin, 253, 322, 387, 388
University of Witwatersrand, 385
University of Würzburg, 109, 187, 252, 280
University of Zurich, 91
Untold Lives (Scarborough and Furumoto), 170

VA hospitals, *see* Veterans Administration hospitals
Valence, 268
Validity, ecological, 418
Van Restorff effect, 265
Variability hypothesis, 146, 226, 227
Variables:
    dependent vs. independent, 205
    intervening, 315
Varieties of Religious Experience (William James), 157
Vassar College, 146–147, 170–172
Vectors, 268
Vestiges of Creation (Charles Darwin), 122
Veterans Administration (VA) hospitals, 371, 380–381
Vienna Psychoanalytic Society, 367
Vineland Training School for the Feeble-Minded (New Jersey), 218–222
Vision, theory of, 39–40, 61–63, 171
Visual cliff, 438
The Vital and Other Involuntary Motions of Animals (Robert Whytt), 57
Vital force, 60
Vitalism, 60, 61
Vocational Psychology (Harry Hollingworth), 227
Völkerpsychologie (Wilhelm Wundt), 93–94, 99, 100

Voluntarism, 100

Walden Two (B. F. Skinner), 280, 336–338
War and Peace (Leo Tolstoy), 13
"The War Landscape" (Kurt Lewin), 266
Weak AI, 420
Weber's Law, 85, 87
Wellesley College, 109, 167, 168, 170
Wesleyan University, 195
Western Electric, 396–397
West Virginia State College, 147, 148
West Virginia University, 77
What is history? (E.H. Carr), 4
A Whisper of Espionage: Wolfgang Köhler and the Apes of Tenerife (Ronald Ley), 254
White paper, mind as, 36, 49
Wilberforce College, 148
Williams College, 160
Wit and Its Relation to the Unconscious (Sigmund Freud), 359
Women:
    educational opportunities for, in 19th century America, 146–147, 167–168
    Freud's attitudes toward, 370
    in history of psychology, 436, 438–439
    and variability hypothesis, 226–227
Women's suffrage, 191
Worcester Asylum, 346, 347
Word association, 137, 250, 367
The World (René Descartes), 28, 421
World War I, 228–229, 236, 266, 397
World War II, 243, 272, 380–381, 397–398

Yale University, 145, 146, 192, 232, 266, 269, 290, 310, 324, 431, 438
Yerkes Laboratories of Primate Biology (Jacksonville, FL), 232–233
York Retreat, 345

Zeigarnik effect, 268–269
Zeitgeist, 10, 13–14, 57, 124
Zeitschrift für Psychologie und Physiologie der Sinnesorgane, 108
Zoonomia (Erasmus Darwin), 115–116

TIMELINE : 1900-1950

	1950	
Boulder model for clinical training		Gilbreth & Carey's *Cheaper by the Dozen*
Lashley's Hixon paper on serial order		
		Transistor invented at Bell Labs
Spock's *Baby and Child Care*		
Wertheimer's *Productive Thinking*	1945	Atom bombs dropped on Japan, war ends
Hull's *Principles of Behavior*		Academy Award to *Casablanca*
		Pearl Harbor attack, U.S. enters war
Hilgard & Marquis' *Conditioning and Learning*	1940	
		Germany invades Poland, W.W.II begins
Woodworth's "Columbia Bible"		
AAAP formed by applied psychologists		Steinbeck's *Of Mice and Men*
		Berlin Olympics, 4 golds for Jesse Owens
Koffka's *Principles of Gestalt Psychology*	1935	Gershwin's *Porgy and Bess* opera
		Hitler appointed German Chancellor
Bartlett's *Remembering*		Al Capone arrested for tax evasion
Lewin introduces B = f (P, E)	1930	
International Conference at Yale		U.S. stock market crashes
Sumner begins tenure at Howard University		
		Ruth hits 60 home runs
Köhler's *Mentality of Apes*	1925	Scopes "monkey trial"
		21 day protest fast by Ghandi
Freud's *The Ego and the Id*		
Watson & Rayner's Little Albert study	1920	Wharton's *The Age of Innocence*
Army Alpha/Army Beta		Rockne named Notre Dame coach
Terman's Stanford-Binet IQ test		
	1915	Einstein proposes theory of relativity
		W.W.I begins/Panama Canal opens
Watson's behaviorist manifesto		
Wertheimer's apparent motion study		S.S. *Titanic* sunk by iceberg
	1910	DuBois founds NAACP
Freud's Clark lectures		
Washburn's *The Animal Mind*		Foster's *A Room with a View*
		Powell founds Boy Scouts
Calkins first female APA president		
	1905	
Nobel Prize to Pavlov		Barrie's *Peter Pan*
		Doyle's *Hounds of the Baskervilles*
First of Titchener's *Manuals*		
Small's maze learning study	1900	Planck formulates quantum theory